LEARNING AND THINKING

LEARNING AND THINKING

A PRIMER FOR TEACHERS

Bryce B. Hudgins
WASHINGTON UNIVERSITY

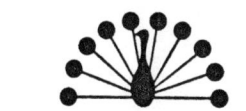

F. E. PEACOCK PUBLISHERS, INC.
ITASCA, ILLINOIS 60143

*Copyright © 1977
F. E. Peacock Publishers, Inc.
All rights reserved
Library of Congress
Catalog Card No. 76-41996*

To My Three Thinkers—

> Robert
> Catherine
> Christine

Contents

Preface		ix

Chapter
1	Learning and Thinking: An Introduction	1
2	How We Learn and What We Remember	23
3	The Improvement of Learning in School Settings	64
4	Conceptual Learning	109
5	The Generality of Learning: Issues in Transfer	142
6	The Pupil As Thinker: Critical Thinking	173
7	The Pupil As Thinker: Problem Solving	210
8	The Pupil As Thinker: Creative Thinking	256

Name Index	295
Subject Index	299

Preface

I have called this book a "primer for teachers" because it introduces some of the basic and, I think, important concepts about how children learn in school. In addition, a considerable effort has been made to provide illustrations for the teacher of how individual concepts might apply to his or her classroom work. It is my hope that readers of this book will find in it a utility and an applicability to the demands of teaching that surpasses what they would derive from an examination of the research literature upon which it is based, or even from a discourse that lacked the numerous attempts that have been made here to point to ways in which what the educational psychologist knows can be helpful to the classroom teacher.

Through the years I have offered a series of courses for teachers at Washington University that have dealt with various aspects of the educational psychology of learning. There is hardly an idea or a piece of research reported in this book that has not been chewed over by classes of teachers who have been interested in finding out more about the processes of learning and thinking, or who were at least willing to listen and judge for themselves the merit of what they heard and read. I have no way to assess how great the contribution of those teachers has been, but I know that it has been extensive. Sometimes they have offered a criticism, or expressed a lack of understanding, or they have suggested an application that had not previously occurred to me and that has stimulated prolonged thought on my part. This has helped me to clarify and express my ideas better and more fully than I could have done without the exchange.

The audience for which this book was written is teachers and students who are preparing to become teachers. Any virtue they may find in the book is largely owing to the impact that my students have had upon my thinking, and their emphasis upon the need to show relationships between the study of learning as the educational psychologist views it and as it appears to the practicing teacher.

The educational psychology of learning and thinking is a fertile and exciting field at the present time. Many research workers and general writers who possess innovative theoretical or applied notions about how children and adolescents learn have virtually transformed the area since the 1950s. Some of the newer research programs are not yet conclusive about how or whether their underlying ideas will offer sound progress for schools, teachers, and their pupils. I have included a variety of research of that sort in the book, but I have always tried to select those ideas, and that evidence in support of them, that seemed to me to have a good chance of proving themselves in the near future. Teachers have a right, and I think most of them have a desire, to know something about newer ideas in research, even though no one can see definite applications to Monday morning's reading group or certify that the idea will ultimately yield knowledge of practical use to the teacher. I look forward to a time, now five or six years in the future, when it will be possible to develop some kind of a box score of the survival value of the ideas and the programs of research around which this book is built. I think the batting average will turn out to be high, because I regard the intellectual quality of new ideas in the educational psychology of learning and thinking to be good. Although there have been exciting and productive ideas in the field, at least since the time of Edward L. Thorndike at the turn of the century, their incidence seems to be greater now than at any time in the past.

Learning and thinking are usually dealt with separately. The position that I have tried to express in the first chapter is that, despite the fact that learning and thinking can be thought of apart from each other, they also have much in common. This may be more true in the everyday classroom (or everyday life as a whole) than it is in the psychology laboratory. The major emphases are on the fact that learning depends upon how meaningful the material is that is to be learned, upon the ability of the learner to comprehend it and fit it into his or her structure of knowledge, and upon the learner's willingness or even need to act upon whatever he or she already knows. The key to this latter point is that the learner must be a highly active agent in his own process of learning. This is true of thinking as well. One cannot think at all, in the productive sense of that term, without the same kind of acting upon the materials of a problem. My view is that learning and thinking have a lot more common ground than is usually recognized.

In the final analysis, the teacher may help students achieve more and better learning if the purposes for that learning, both large and small, can be held before the learner. Let me try to illustrate what I mean. The teacher might have a beautifully worked-out unit that is reduced to 25 lessons, including worksheets, written assignments, readings, illustrations for pupils to draw, and so forth. When these are all laid side by side, they represent to the teacher, or maybe to other adults, an integrated and comprehensive study of the topic. And so they may be. But to the learner they may appear as nothing more than 25 discrete entities, each of which she or he must process and hand in at a given time. The sense of wholeness and unity that is both so important and so gratifying to the teacher as a knowledgeable adult may be almost completely lacking for the student. When that happens, school tasks become closer to isolated bits of learning, quickly forgotten and noncumulative in their overall effect, compared with the high levels of retention associated with meaningful learning.

I think that this is the fundamental idea that Ned Flanders developed years ago when he observed that the teacher's role ought to be to assist students to express and extend their own ideas, and to help them clarify what they are after until such time as the goals or purposes of learning have become clear to them. This may be a useful junction between students of classroom interaction and those of school learning. My guess is that the reason indirect teaching is effective when used as Flanders suggests is because it facilitates the teacher's efforts to render meaningful to the learners what it is the teacher wants them to learn. Once the dimensions of the task are seen as meaningful, the learner can begin the process of attending to new learning, translating it when necessary and storing it for future use with ideas which are already known to him and which are classified and organized in ways that make storage and retrieval of them convenient.

To produce any book, even a simple textbook, requires the work of many people. Ted Peacock and Thomas LaMarre of F. E. Peacock Publishers were unfailingly cheerful, supportive, and helpful under circumstances during the writing of this book that were trying. I wish to thank them for their confidence. Martin V. Covington of the University of California at Berkeley has kindly kept me informed of new evidence bearing upon his delightful and provocative Productive Thinking Program. E. A. Peel, whose outstanding research on adolescent thought is well known in Britain but much less so in the United States, allowed me to visit him at the University of Birmingham. From that exchange ultimately emerged a major section of Chapter 6. I hope that American teachers, especially secondary teachers to whom his work may be new, will find in it the same stimulation I have. John B. Carroll of the University of North Carolina read initial drafts of most of the manuscript. In acting upon his suggestions and in attempting to overcome his many criticisms, I think I have been able to write a much better book than the original version. Professor Carroll is not responsible for any of the remaining shortcomings of the volume, but he deserves credit for much of whatever good there is to be found. I am grateful to him for the detail and incisiveness of his dissection.

Washington University has always made it possible for faculty members to teach courses of interest to them and to pursue knowledge down whatever elusive trail it may appear to traipse. I am grateful for the freedom that comes with being part of a fine university. A sabbatical leave during the spring of 1975 made it possible for the first draft of what became this book to get underway. I wish also to say a word of thanks to the good people at the Institute of Education Library of the University of London who, during the summer of 1975, accorded me a quiet, private place in which to write, access to their outstanding library resources, and unfailingly good-natured assistance.

Barbara Subin, Camille Boyd, and Rose Mary Smith of the Graduate Institute of Education staff, Washington University, all typed parts of one or another draft of the manuscript. The final manuscript was prepared by Patricia Simmons. My thanks to each of them for painstaking, thoughtful work.

Finally, my deepest debt is to my wife, Betty, who has a gift for seeing events in perspective.

Bryce B. Hudgins

St. Louis, Mo.
October 1976

Chapter 1

Learning and Thinking: An Introduction

The events that transpire in classrooms have a deceptively simple appearance. The teacher assigns a lesson, the pupils learn it. The textbook asks questions, the students write their answers. From one day to the next, there may be a sameness, an ordinariness in the learning tasks and the learning activities that involve students and teachers in the process of education. Yet, upon further reflection, it is clear that children learn better from some kinds of activities than they do from others. The thinking of a high school student is stimulated by a question asked by his physics teacher today, but tomorrow he sits passively through one more lesson.

This book has a single purpose: to reflect the educational psychology of learning and thinking in language which teachers may find both familiar and useful in their daily teaching practice. As an aid, numerous examples based upon events in elementary and secondary school classrooms have been included to illustrate how a learning phenomenon might appear to the teacher, or as an explicit example of how some knowledge about learning or thinking might be put into practice by the teacher.

Fundamental Precepts

Three fundamental precepts summarize my beliefs about how learning and thinking occur in the classroom. They can be stated simply here, and their elaboration and delineation continue throughout the book.

Learning and Thinking

First tenet

When we talk about how people learn and how they think, even though our chief focus is upon children and adolescents in schoolrooms, what we say must be derived from some larger view about how all people learn, whether or not they are in schools and whether they are young or old. These perspectives, in turn, evolve from some broader conception we hold about the nature of mankind. A major view that has been popular in psychology for a long time sees the person as an organism that responds to events around him or her. We can more or less prescribe the range of behaviors of the individual if we can control those events and the sequence in which they occur. More especially, by taking pains to ensure that certain consequences attend or follow the individual's responses, we can "shape" his or her behavior to a fine degree. Furthermore, the same basic principles or schedules of reinforcement can be used, with some modifications, to shape the behavior of organisms across vastly disparate phyla; pigeons and man, for example.

While the aptness with which such views capture some aspects of human behavior, and also the undeniable success with which some types of behavior can be modified, should be acknowledged, nonetheless it should be observed that the image of man thus created is incomplete. If the history of the species gives us any hint as to the nature of man, it tells us that he is a fiercely active organism, rather than one who responds passively to his environment. Indeed, since the contest began between man and nature (if we can for the moment see them as distinct and antagonistic), although man has surely learned to adapt to his environment, he has also never ceased struggling to control it.

The next time the occasion presents itself, watch carefully the antics of an infant in her crib, or a nine-month-old who has really developed locomotion skills. Do you have the impression that they are responding to the surrounding world, or that they are bending every effort to find out what is in it? If you are not teaching, visit several classrooms. Preschools and primary-grade classrooms are extremely good laboratories for this purpose, largely because of the uninhibited exuberance their occupants are willing to express toward learning and thinking. The phenomenon has greater physical manifestations among young children than older ones or adults, but the principle of activity in exploration and learning is not unique to them.

Our first tenet, then, is that man is disposed to be active, searching, and inquiring more than he is to be placid, quiescent, and stationary. This disposition applies to man as a learner in and out of the schoolroom. Use of the term *active*, however, does not signify diffuseness or disorganization. Man's survival as a species has depended upon his diversity and his adaptability, but behavior and seeking that at one time are seemingly random or stimulated by motives such as need or curiosity may at another time play a crucial role in answering questions or solving problems.

Learning requires activity that is directed and focused upon what is to be learned. The learner must actively attend to what he is learning. For example, when a student, out of fatigue or sheer boredom, halfway dozes off during a lesson or reading assignment, it is folly to suppose that he learned what was intended. Learning (at least other than learning such things as fear and anxiety) depends upon active attention on the part of the learner and upon his intellectual participation. This occurs when the student, for example, translates the words of the text or lecture into his own language, and when he tries to see how this point fits or does not fit with something else he knows, and so on.

Second tenet

Learning is organized. For content to be effectively learned, the learner must construct a clear and comprehensive framework of it. Of course, it is important that such construction should bear a similarity to the organization of the field of study. When we say that learning is organized, or that processes of organization are fundamental to learning, we mean that the organization resides in the internal representation constructed by the learner. This is not the same thing as saying that each learning stimulus, such as a class discussion or a textbook assignment, must possess an optimal degree of organization, or that each newly encountered stimulus must be perfectly articulated with what the learner already knows.

The organization which occurs in learning comes about as the learner engages in the processing that is necessary to see relationships among facts and principles, and his classification of new learning content according to external representations of knowledge (such as the subject matter domains) that make it possible for him to categorize and subsequently to retrieve what he has learned. In this enterprise the learner can and ought to be aided as much as possible by his or her educational environment. For example, teachers should stress relationships, and they should assist students in differentiating among the more and less important aspects of a study. Textbooks, on the whole, are of more use to learners if their content is organized so that major principles are highlighted in the beginning, and the detailed supporting information is placed in subordinate positions. Nonetheless it is only the learner who can compare and contrast his knowledge, who can juxtapose it and finally array it in a usable cognitive configuration. I recall the image aroused by one of my earliest teachers, who announced her desire to drill a hole in children's heads and pour knowledge into them. She was a large, unsmiling woman, intimidating to a sensitive small boy who imagined himself lined up with the others, a funnel embedded in his head, awaiting his turn to have something akin to his lunchtime bowl of alphabet soup poured into it. No doubt generations of conscientious teachers have had similar wishes in moments of frustration. But it is only the learner who can learn. This point is often ignored, for the teacher is frequently the most active member of a classroom, when it is the students, not the teacher, who need to be stimulated into processing, organizing, and relating new learning.

Although the point should not be overly stressed, there is a degree of similarity between the activity of organizing engaged in by the learner and that of the detective, scholar, or research scientist. The learner understands or comprehends what he is studying when he masters the relationships among the lower and higher order concepts and principles of the content, and when he learns their connections with other more extensive bodies of knowledge. For the most part the learner may be *given* the information he needs in order to comprehend a concept or principle, and in this way he is not like the investigator in a field who must invent or discover clarifying principles. But neither can he perform as a passive vehicle through which knowledge is transmitted. Effort to classify, order, and integrate his knowledge is mandatory to effective learning. It is clear that the first tenet of active participation by the learner applies to this task as well. Students sometimes protest that learning should not be too "structured," by which they mean that it should be less than perfectly organized. Something should remain for the learner to sort out or to organize, rather than assimilating a given task in its original state.

Third tenet

Learning depends upon the learner's stage of development. Both what the child is capable of learning and the way in which learning proceeds are governed by the intellectual schemata or structures that are available to the learner, and these become more numerous and more elaborate with the passage of time. The work of the psychologist and philosopher Jean Piaget has been most illuminating of these points. Piaget's work, at least in outline form, has become increasingly well known to American teachers during the past decade. The final section of this chapter will further consider the relationship of development to learning, using Piaget's system as a means to classify and demarcate the major shifts in children's ability to learn and think.

Learning and Thinking: An Introduction 5

Introductory Examples of Thinking and of Learning in the Classroom

Some concrete episodes of thinking and learning as they occur in day-to-day classroom settings are given in the following two examples, which were chosen to provide contrast. In the first situation, the learners must utilize previous knowledge in order to solve problems and formulate a generalization. In the second, ostensibly at least, the learning task is provided ready-made, and the student needs only to commit it to memory. In fact, as the episodes should show, the two tasks have more in common than might ordinarily be supposed, and both depend heavily upon the learner's involvement in the processes of learning.

The example of Peter

Peter and three of his sixth-grade friends have been given a simple balance beam and a set of weights like those shown in Figure 1.1. They have been told to place a weight on one arm of the balance at the point marked 9 and then to find a way to balance the beam by placing more than one weight on the other arm. The boys are uncertain of how to do this. Peter begins to flip the arm of the balance up and down. Two of the others slide the weights across the table in a miniature shuffleboard game. David says, "Cut it out, you guys. Here comes the teacher."

FIGURE 1.1
Balance beam and weights used by sixth-grade students

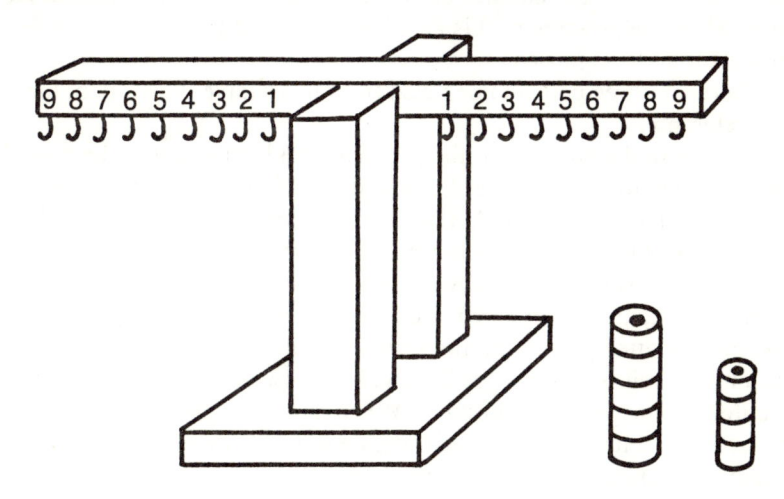

Mrs. Jansen approaches Peter's group, smiling and interested. "All right, Peter. Put one of the weights over here." She points to the 9. He does. The arm tilts.

"Now, where will you put the weights on the other side?"

"I'd put it on the 9, too," says Peter.

"Okay," answers the teacher. "Try it."

Peter places the weight and the beam balances. He looks proud.

"Great, Pete," says David. "Only the book says we have to use *more* than one."

"Oh, yeah," Peter replies, a little subdued. "I forgot."

"Boys, be sure to keep a record of everything you do and the result. Then after a while, see if you can state a rule for balancing the two sides. Remember what we studied about levers last week, and our practice with the seesaws on the playground. Those things should help you to solve this problem."

On the playground a few days before, the class had seen that the weight of one of the heaviest boys in the class could be counterbalanced by one of the smallest girls if she sat at the end of the seesaw on her side, and the boy moved toward the center on his side. Later they had also seen that two lighter children, sitting at different places, could balance the seesaw with the same large boy on the other end.

At first, Peter and his group place the weights here and there, trying to get a balance. David, who is more serious about the activity than the others, keeps a record as the teacher directed. After a series of trials, he is able to tell his friends where to place the weights in order to make the scale balance. He observes that when the combined weight and distance from the center of the balance are equal on both sides, the arm will balance. All the boys agree to this generalization, and they are able to demonstrate it to Mrs. Jansen.

There are three points to be noted from this simple illustration, for future reference.

First, to find a solution to the problem, the learner had to be actively involved in searching for one. Peter and the others did not pay much attention to what was required. They were content to manipulate the beam and the weights without much sense of directed purpose. David, on the other hand, was the prime mover. Because he kept in mind what was to be discovered, and he observed and recorded with care the results of each preliminary attempt to bring the scale into balance, he was able to generate a hypothesis or make a prediction about how the weights could be distributed to answer the question. When he subsequently checked this prediction and found it to be accurate, he was able to compose a generalization that summarized his observations.

Thus we refine our preliminary statement of the role of activity in learning. All four of these boys were "active" in a rudimentary way. But it was only David, whose activity was guided and focused by a sense of purpose and system, who made it possible for the solution to be found.

Second, earlier experiences had paved the way for the solution to the problem. The class had studied levers a week earlier. We can construe this to mean that they were familiar with terms such as *fulcrum* and *mechanical advantage*. Their playground experience with the seesaws constituted a concrete if inexact application of the same principle involved in balancing the beam. By reminding the boys of these previous experiences, Mrs. Jansen clearly believed that they should be able to apply or transfer that learning to the new and somewhat altered circumstance of the balance beam. Her actions stressed an organized and systematic approach to the problem, first by recalling to the children a useful body of knowledge, and also by suggesting that they maintain a record of how they manipulated the weights and what happened each time they did so.

Third, thinking was involved. The boys were confronted with a novel situation for which they did not have a solution. Even by applying what they knew about the shifting of weights on the seesaw, they were still left with the need to induce an exact statement of the relationship between weights and distances. More than just learning was involved. There had to be an extension of effort to fill the gap between what they had to work with and the solution required of them.

The example of Marcie and Donald

A different example of classroom learning comes from the secondary school. Marcie and Donald sit next to each other in Mr. Grant's third-period English class. They spend a great deal of time together, in and out of school, and they share many interests. On one thing they do not agree, and that is Mr. Grant's English class. Today they read some Shakespearean sonnets, and Mr. Grant told them that for Friday's quiz they would be asked to write any one of those sonnets from memory. That announcement was greeted with some moans and groans, the loudest of them from Donald.

Donald is not a poor student; in fact, his grades in science and mathematics courses are consistently good. English, however, he finds to be a bore. But to Marcie the class is exciting. When they studied Hamlet last month, she learned several of the soliloquies, even though Mr. Grant did not require that. Now that she had been introduced to the sonnets, she thought them even more beautiful and moving.

That evening she and Donald work together on the assignment at her house. Their absorption in the task is very different. Donald stops every two or three minutes to tell her a joke, eat a cookie, or just walk around. Marcie tries to ignore him. She reads the first two lines of the sonnet:

> Shall I compare thee to a summer's day?
> Thou art more lovely and more temperate.

Then, looking away from the page, she recites those lines twice. After that she reads and recites the next two lines, and then tries to say all four of them without looking at the text. Marcie recalls the rhyme scheme for the sonnets that Mr. Grant had placed on the board, and she uses it as a check on the proper order of the lines.

When Friday morning comes, Donald's paper has a few gaps in it, and two of the lines he did remember are in the wrong order. Marcie memorized four sonnets during the week, rather than the one that was required. However, on Friday, she has time only to write two of them. Marcie is unaware of it, but even with her devoted study of the lines, although the substance of them is correct, she has intruded some minor variations from the printed text. Mr. Grant gallantly overlooks these and congratulates Marcie for her zeal.

This task was very different from the balance problem described as the first example. Again, there are several points to be abstracted and noted.

First, Marcie paid careful attention to what she was to learn. The exact wording and the flow from line to line were important to her. She monitored her practice to keep both her language and the order of the lines correct. Donald paid much less attention. He was not very concerned that what he learned was an inexact and incomplete copy of the original.

Second, the task to be learned was totally defined by the text of the source. Nothing had to be added or subtracted. No solution had to be sought. The task did not impose a need for thinking on the learner, as the earlier one did.

Third, once more we see that the learner's involvement in the task is important for learning. This is best seen in the outcomes that correspond to the difference between the two students in their willingness to commit themselves to learning the sonnet. Note that the learning product is *not* just a copy or duplicate of the text. For example, Marcie's reproduction departed from the original, even though the deviations were trivial.

Fourth, this task can be approached in alternative ways. One could learn it as a meaningless exercise in memorization, or construe it as a task that has meaning and can therefore be understood. As we shall see, tasks are learned more easily and remembered better if they are meaningful and are learned in a meaningful way.

What Do We Mean by Learning?

Learning always involves a change of some kind in what the learner knows, or in his disposition toward someone or something, or in what he is able to do. Learning occurs through an interaction with the environment. We observe that students in school learn how to add and subtract, how to decode printed messages, and how to read a map. They learn what government means, and the differences among socialism, democracy, and communism. They may commit a sonnet to memory, or learn to recognize a Chopin waltz or a symphony by Beethoven. The students also learn attitudes toward these learnings. They learn that poetry is beautiful, or that it is effeminate; that chemistry is an exciting, orderly way to learn about the world, or that it is a jumble of malodorous test tubes and meaningless formulas.

Let us return briefly to Marcie, the high school student who was memorizing sonnets. When her memorization was completed, what had Marcie learned? How had she changed? We might agree that the change is not of very great magnitude. She was able to write or speak 14 lines of poetry that she didn't know before. Unless she reviews them from time to time, she will soon forget some of the words and lines. In fact, if Marcie learned the sonnets only for the purpose of passing Friday's quiz, she may later on remember little more than that she once learned some Shakespeare in school. In other words, learning is not always permanent. As we shall see, there are ways that teachers can help students to remember important things.

The sonnet is different in some ways from most of what students learn in school. The language and the form must be reproduced as they appear in the text. We could scarcely say that Marcie had "learned" the sonnet if she could relate its substance, but not in its precise poetic form. For most purposes in the classroom, it is just that kind of comprehension of an idea that we do want the student to learn. Rarely do we want him to memorize a lesson. Often, in fact, we strongly prefer that memorization be held to a minimum. It requires excessive time, and it may seriously interfere with the learner's ability to understand what he is doing and what he is to learn.

What Do We Mean by Thinking?

Thinking has several general characteristics. First of all, it is important to distinguish thinking from habitual, reproductive responses by the learner. Thinking always involves restructuring or reorganizing one's knowledge or way of viewing a situation in order to remove a gap or to generate a new response. A second characteristic of thinking is its energizing impact upon the learner. When a student is engaged in thinking, he is not a passive recipient of information to be stored. On the contrary, he is actively searching for possible solutions, trying them out tentatively, seeking to learn whether they will resolve the difficulty, answer the question, or satisfy the creative demand.

The activity may at first seem haphazard or random, but it always has a purpose. The high school student who is writing an essay may search widely for the proper construction of paragraphs or choice of words and phrases to convey his meaning precisely. This activity is not physical in a gross motor sense. It is principally cognitive—mental activity that is directed at the problem to be solved, evidence to be weighed and sifted, solutions to be created and evaluated for their appropriateness or utility.

Development and Learning: Piaget's Stages of Intellectual Growth

One of the fundamental ideas of Piaget's system which is of importance to the teacher's effort to improve classroom learning is that the child, from early infancy onward, is actively engaged in constructing his or her view and understanding of the world in which he or she lives. This is not an easy idea to grasp, yet its validity is evident. How can any external agent—parent, teacher, or sibling—communicate larger conceptions of the world to the baby? He cannot understand their language, and even if he knew the words, their referents would defy his understanding. Given his total lack of experience with the physical environment into which birth has thrust him, his only route to knowledge lies in the personal construction that begins in his crib.

Piaget's view of intellectual development casts the years from birth to midadolescence into three broad stages. Development proceeds within each stage as well as from one stage to the next. The ages associated with the various stages are only rough approximations and conveniences for Piaget's readers. He cares little for the precise age labels. More important to him is the idea that the sequence of developmental events is invariant. It is on that invariance that the validity of his conception of developmental stages rests.

The first stage is called *sensorimotor*. It extends from birth until the onset of language, normally about the age of one and a half or two years. This is followed by a long developmental period that conforms in our society roughly with the years of preschool and elementary school. Its two major subdivisions are a period of *preoperational thought* (from about age 2 until 7) and a period of *concrete operational thought* (7 to 11). From about age 11 or 12 the young adolescent moves into a stage of *formal operational thinking*.

The stage of sensorimotor development

From birth onward the child is moving in the direction of adult logic (formal or propositional reasoning). His early experiences in the prelinguistic first two years permit him to construct some important aspects of the world. Primary among these is the child's construction of the concept of the permanence of objects. We rarely reflect on the fact that the infant must, in an intellectual sense, build the world he lives in. There is no way to communicate to the small child that an object or person who disappears from his view may materialize once more. At first, if an object in which the child shows interest is placed behind a sheet, the baby will not look for it. During the early months of life he learns some basic concepts about objects, movement, space, and time that become building blocks for his ensuing cognitive development. The term *construction* deserves special emphasis. The titles of many of Piaget's monographs contain the phrase, "The child's construction of ... " It signifies what we have already said about building the child's psychological world. The stress in Piaget's system is on active operation by the individual upon objects and events in his environment, and upon the reconstruction or reformulation of them in successive rounds of development. Once the child begins to acquire language, he has to relearn in a new form the things that he achieved earlier in the absence of a symbolic system.

This principle of reconstruction applies throughout the course of cognitive development. There is a regularity of these developments in their sequence (but distinctly *not* in the precise age at which they emerge) that suggests the control exercised by principles of biological development. For Piaget development is inextricably involved with both biological growth and differentiation, and with the child's environment, but environment is construed in the broadest possible sense. The total complexity of the child's environment is the occasion for the emergence of one operation or structure after another, and not minor variations such as programs of specialized and limited training.

The preoperational child

We place a glass of orange juice before a child four or five years of age. Next to it we place a taller glass of narrower diameter. Now we pour the juice into the taller but thinner glass. Then we ask the child whether there is the same amount of juice as before, or more, or less. Since a child of this age focuses his attention on a single dimension (what Piaget calls centering), he will notice the higher level to which the juice rises and tell us that there is more than before. Or, alternatively, we show him a small ball of clay and then roll it out into a sausage shape. Is there now more or less clay, or the same? Again the answer is that there is more clay in the sausage, since it is longer than it was before. These results occur repeatedly with young children, even though they can see that the amount of matter is not altered.

This is an interesting phenomenon to observe. Although you have read about it, there is a certain element of shock the first time a kindergartener or first-grader looks at the sausage lying on a table between the two of you and confidently asserts that there is more clay now than when he had a ball of it. But the proper question to ask about this phenomenon is whether it has any significance for our understanding of how children's intellectual development affects their learning and their ability to think.

At the heart of the Piagetian system of cognitive development lies the concept of an *operation*. Operations possess many attributes. They are interiorized actions; they are reversible. They are always linked to other operations and are never isolated. Intellectual operations are of many types; they develop over time, and they are influenced by the perceptual and experiential events of the child. But they are not the same thing as those perceptions or experiences. They are independent structures which emerge and allow the developing learner to increasingly cognize the world with the logic of an adult, and correspondingly to decrease the frequency of egocentric and unsystematic constructions the young child produces. The various operations the growing human being achieves emerge through the stages that have been elucidated.

Let us return now to the example of the young child and the ball of clay. The preoperational child (that is, one who cannot comprehend the reversibility of an operation) focuses or centers upon one dimension of a phenomenon at a time. If the ball is converted into a sausage, as we noted before, the preoperational child supposes it to contain more substance in its altered stage. Another way to express this is to say that his thought is dominated by perception, and his perceptions are in turn governed by salient dimensions of an object, such as its length. Suppose now, however, that we continue to extend the clay sausage. There comes a point at which the child objects that it is "too thin" and there is less, rather than more, clay. Centering thus shifts from one dimension to another. Through a series of such changes, according to Piaget, a process of equilibration or self-regulation occurs. This is for the child a most important process, since judgments become successively less bound by their empirical attributes or by perceptions.

It is not until the age of seven or eight that most children will conserve substance. When that occurs, the child is positive that alterations in form do not change the amount of clay in the roll. The author made a tape recording of these conservation tasks for use with college classes one month after the seventh birthday of one of his children. When the question was asked whether the sausage contained more or less clay than the ball had, there was a long pause, and then, slowly, "Mmm—that's a hard question!"—as it surely was for a child moving into the stage of concrete questions.

We need to pause here and ask again the question: Does it really matter whether the child can or cannot conserve substance? Or perhaps, What is significant about the child's cognitive development when such a stage occurs? Operations are reversible. If X is added to A, it can be subtracted to produce A once more. Reversibility includes the idea of reciprocity. If $A > B$, $B < A$. Obviously, many tasks that children are to learn at school depend upon the availability of these operations. Otherwise the learning must occur without meaning. However, principles of conservation do not all develop simultaneously. Piaget's experiments reveal that conservation of matter occurs first, and it is one of the primary indicators of the arrival of concrete operational thinking. The conservation of weight develops about two years later, typically at age 9 or 10, and conservation of volume (inferred from the displacement of water) emerges still later, around the age of 11 or 12.

The preoperational child lacks structures that would allow him to perform such operations as classifying objects in a systematic fashion according to some demonstrable principle. When the child at this stage is given problems of classification and explanation, his or her behavior has an ostensible randomness about it, and often the child contradicts himself.

Inhelder and Piaget (1958) have studied the development of the law of floating bodies with children of many ages. The individual to be interviewed is shown a variety of objects—keys, block of wood, needles, wire, candles, and so forth—and asked to classify each of them according to whether they will float on water or sink. He is also asked to explain his classifications. Subsequently he observes the behavior of each object as he immerses it, and he is asked to summarize his observations and try to formulate a law that governs which objects will float. Preoperational children (those of four and five) give contradictory explanations. On one occasion an object is predicted to float; the next time the child anticipates that it will sink. After several opportunities to observe, a four-year old boy is shown two metal needles identical in appearance: " 'This one?' 'It will float.' 'And that one?' 'It will sink.' " We must add that although he generalizes little, his explanations can be reduced to the format: " 'The pebble?' 'It will sink.' 'Why?' 'Because it stays on the bottom.' " (Inhelder and Piaget, 1958, p. 22)

Stage of concrete operations

The child's arrival at the stage of concrete operations is of great consequence. Although his thinking is highly bound by the empirical world, and it depends upon the presence of concrete objects and manipulable materials, there is an increasing systematization to his thinking that was not present in his preoperational years. It is during this period that he becomes capable of operations of seriation, classification, and correspondence, and other cognitive structures emerge. These are not yet sufficient to allow him to think at an abstract level, but they are prerequisites to such formal operations. We cannot begin to review exhaustively the myriad ways in which this is manifested, but two examples will illustrate the broader range.

Piaget and Inhelder (1958) also asked children at a concrete operational level to predict which items would float on water and to explain why. For the child to formulate the appropriate law (that objects float if their specific gravity is less than that of water), he must possess two relational concepts; density, or the relation of weight to volume, and specific gravity, the relation between the weight of the object being judged and an equivalent volume of water. At the age of nine or thereabouts the child develops conservation of weight. He does not, however, achieve conservation of volume at this time. Thus, when he makes judgments about objects, he describes those of high specific gravity as more "full" than others. However, lacking the concept of conservation of volume, the child at this stage relates the weight of the object to that of all the water in the container instead of to that of an equivalent volume.

For example, one subject who had previously classified the objects responded in the following terms when pressed.

Why do these things float?

Child: Because they are quite light.
Investigator: And why do these things sink?
Child: Because they are heavy.

And later this sequence occurs with the same child:

Investigator: Which is heavier, the plate or the wood?
Child: The piece of wood.
Investigator: Then why does the plate stay at the bottom?
Child: Because it's a little lighter than the wood, when there is water on top there is less resistance and it can stay down. (Inhelder and Piaget, 1958, p. 33)

A second illustration is taken from the writings of the British psychologist E. A. Peel, one of whose students had given children of various ages some passages to read about King Alfred. He followed their reading of one passage about the burned cakes with this question: "Could Alfred cook?" The first answer, from a seven-year-old preoperational child, shows centering, first on king's authority, then on his fighting ability, but with no relationship seen between the centerings.

Could Alfred cook?
(7 year old girl): Yes. (Why?) Because he's the king.
(Can every king cook?) No.
(Why could Alfred cook?) Because he can fight. (Peel, 1967, p. 72)

These can be compared with answers to the same question given by several slightly older children who were thinking at a concrete stage.

No! (Why do you think so?) Because he was a king and not a housemaid.
No! (Why not?) He forgot all about the cakes. He was a man and that's why he couldn't cook as well as a woman who does. A woman is a proper cook.
No! Because he forgot all about the cakes.
Yes! Well he ought to be able to. Well most men can cook a bit. (Could he cook?) No because he did not take any notice of the cakes and let them burn. (Peel, 1967, p. 78)

The child who operates at the concrete level is able to think more systematically and with fewer contradictions in his reasoning than the preoperational child. As we have seen, his increasing achievement of conservation, with its implications for extended conceptions of the reversibility of operations, enables him to handle intellectually a broad range of problems as long as they can be solved at an empirical level; that is, in terms of objects and phenomena which are directly available in the learner's environment and which succumb to the application of his personal or immediate experience. He cannot formulate abstract generalizations, such as a principle to predict which bodies will float.

16 Learning and Thinking

Formal operations: The development of adolescent thinking

The great advances that occur in the child's ability to think during the years of middle childhood (that is, from about 7 or 8 until 11 or 12) are marked by the emergence of operations: seriation, one-to-one correspondence, double entry classification, and so on. However, these advances are limited by their dependence upon the presence of objects in the environment and by the child's reliance upon his direct and personal experience. Peel (1967) provides a perfect example of this constrictedness of concrete thinking in the reply of an eight-year-old to an absurdity problem in an intelligence test:

> Question: Tell me what is wrong or silly with the following statement. In an old graveyard in Spain, they have discovered a small skull which they believe to be that of Christopher Columbus, when he was about ten years old.
>
> Answer: *It is wrong because you should not dig up graveyards—they are holy places.* (Peel, 1967, p. 79)

In the preadolescent and adolescent years (between the ages of 12 and 15), formal operations emerge as the student takes on more of the characteristics of adult thinking. Although there are specific new logical operations that occur and classes of reasoning that can be cited, the chief properties of thought at this stage are that it is hypothetical; that is, the individual can think about propositions whose representations are not immediately present, and he can reason about propositions without regard for their truth value or whether he believes in the proposition. His thinking is capable of considering new logical relationships that were previously unknown to him. He can formulate generalizations based upon his intellectual operations and without regard for concrete properties. In this sense his thinking gains broad new qualities of abstraction and flexibility.

At the age of 11 or 12, the child develops the ability to perform many new operations. These schemes include proportion, more complex concepts of probability, the use of double systems of reference, and others. It is also at this stage that what Piaget refers to as "experimental spirit" emerges spontaneously, but its emergence clearly depends upon the availability of the structures and schemes already outlined. Piaget considers that it has seldom been taught in schools (perhaps a dubious assumption, in view of the heavy emphasis upon scientific training in the past generation), but that even if it were, it would still have to be assimilated by the required logical structures, and it is the direct result of propositional (in contrast to concrete) operations. As an example he cites experiments at Geneva in which children are presented with a bundle of metal rods and are asked to account for their differences in flexibility. The rods differ in length, thickness, shape (some are square, some cylindrical, and so forth), and composition (steel or brass). Children who are concrete thinkers fail to dissociate the factors from one another and to assess the effects of one variable at a time. Piaget cites the example of one nine-year-old who showed them a long thin rod and a short thick one "because you can see the difference better!" (Inhelder & Piaget, p. 146)

The student who is capable of formal reasoning at the age of 11 or 12 behaves quite differently. He examines the effects of one variable at a time, holding each of the others constant. For Piaget the ability to reason by means of propositions, with the implications for abstract and generalizable thought, begins about age 11 or 12, and it is impossible for children before that time. At least, the various stages and substages of operations must emerge before the child is capable of the fundamentals of propositional logic. However, Piaget's explicit and comprehensive statements about intellectual development are not universally accepted. Gagné (1968) has argued that learning plays a more pervasive role in the emergence of thinking than Piaget allots to it. Furthermore, Ennis (1975) has disputed the correctness of Piaget's propositional logic and challenges his contention that children younger than 11 or 12 cannot think propositionally. Ennis cites outcomes of his own work and that of others which suggest that the transition to formal thinking may not be as bound to age (or operations) as Piaget's formulation has it. A review and assessment of independent research bearing upon Piaget's conservation concepts led Hilgard and Bower (1975) to the conclusion that Piaget's system is not of "exceptionless validity and that difficulties in measurement procedures allow for some contradictory findings" (p. 331).

There can be no question at all that Piaget's work has had a mighty effect upon how psychologists and educators view the intellectual development of children. He has demonstrated the complexity of the development, and at the same time he has identified the details of that growth and the mechanisms that account for it. His insistence upon the essentially biological and spontaneous nature of development was a healthy counterweight, especially in the United States, to psychology and education, which were extremely behavioristic in outlook. Finally, it must be borne in mind that Piaget's own purposes have virtually nothing to do with education. The stages may serve as valuable guidelines to development, and in that sense may be of help to teachers, but they are not intended to direct curriculum development or teaching practice.

Piaget's view of development and learning

We have already alluded to the fact that for Piaget the continuous emergence of increasingly complex cognitive structures is primarily a matter of the spontaneous development of the growing human organism. Its roots are biological, and although many years are required for the full panoply of intellectual structures to emerge, they do so in an essentially natural way, and, within limits, the course of their emergence is predictable. Thus, as between development and learning, Piaget regards development as the broader and more all-encompassing concept, whereas learning is narrower in scope and is subordinate to development.

We must now try to answer the question of what forces or events are at work in the child which govern his transition from one level of development to another. Piaget has identified four such factors. It is a credit to the comprehensiveness of his system that all the factors are seen to play some role in intellectual development, with no one of them capable of accounting totally for the development. The four factors he identifies are (1) maturation, (2) physical experience, (3) social transmission, and (4) equilibrium.

Maturation. The role of maturation is obvious, especially in the early months of life. There is a natural unfolding of development that defies all but the severest forms of trauma. Piaget acknowledges this role but observes that its contribution is limited, if for no other reason than that little is known about the maturation of the human central nervous system beyond the first two years. In addition, the stages of intellectual development that Piaget has outlined occur at dramatically different ages in different parts of the world. For example, the same investigators who found that children in Montreal develop concepts of conservation at the same age as children in Geneva subsequently discovered that the processes occur four years later in children in Martinique. Obviously if maturation played a very critical role in intellectual development at ages 7 to 11, such wide differences would not be present.

Physical Experience. An important but limited part is played by physical experience in the child's cognitive development—important because the physical environment must provide the substance for the child's thinking. Glasses of milk, juice, and water; rocks; marbles; pieces of string; balls; bathtubs; and all the paraphernalia of childhood, including the language the child has heard from birth, constitute the materials which contribute to his cognitive advancement. But Piaget cites two limitations to the role played by physical experience. His first example is that the child develops the concept of the conservation of substance long before those of weight or volume. To Piaget there is no direct experience or perception from which the child can learn that concept. He might conceivably form concepts of weight and volume conservation through direct experience and external reinforcement, but what experience could lead to the concept of substance conservation? Piaget says:

> This conservation of substance is simply a logical necessity. The child understands that when there is a transformation something must be conserved because by reversing the transformation you can come back to the point of departure and once again have the ball. He knows that something has been conserved, but he doesn't know what. It is not yet the weight, it is not yet the volume; it is simply a logical form—a logical necessity. There, it seems to me, is an example of a progress in knowledge, a logical necessity for something to be conserved even though no experience can have led to this notion. (Piaget, 1964, p. 179)

His second objection to the concept of experience as an explanation for development is to the equivocal nature of the term. There are two types of experience to be distinguished. The first is physical experience, what we might call experience that furnishes the child with empirical knowledge of the world. The second type Piaget calls logical-mathematical experience; in this type, knowledge comes not from the objects in the child's environment but from the actions he takes upon the object. As an example, Piaget describes a childhood recollection by a mathematician friend pertaining to his discovery of the conservation of number. At age four or five the child was playing with an assortment of pebbles. He strung them in a line and counted them. Then he counted them from the other end, and noticed that he had the same number as before. Similarly, when the pebbles were placed in a circle, the number of them did not change. What the child discovered was not a property of pebbles (virtually any substance could have been the vehicle) but a property of the *actions* he performed. Piaget sees this as the beginning of deductive reasoning. It is not experience in the ordinary empirical sense of the term. Piaget also conceives logic to be independent of language and to have its roots in a source that is "much more profound": the coordination of the action of the subjects, an experience that is necessary before the development of operations but upon which later reasoning does not depend once the operations have been attained.

Social Transmission. All those aspects of knowledge which children receive through language and education are encompassed in the third factor. Without minimizing the contribution of these aspects, Piaget reasons that children can benefit from them only to the extent that they can understand the information, and that understanding in turn depends upon the development of appropriate structures.

Equilibration. The fourth factor, which has already been cited, is a self-regulating process in the sense that it provides both feedback and feedforward. Equilibration proceeds through a series of levels, and one does not proceed to a second level before equilibrium has been reached at the first. With the clay sausage as an example once more, the child will probably concentrate on the dimension of length, but at some point, if it is increasingly drawn out, the dimension of width will become salient. Thus a second level is reached. At a third level he oscillates between length and width, and finally discovers that the two are related.

Learning, by contrast, is a much narrower and more limited concept in Piaget's system. In his view the psychology of learning vastly underestimates the complexity of the human organism as a learner. It deals with stimuli, responses, and associations, whereas Piaget believes learning occurs as a result of a process of assimilation. His emphasis is upon the active struggle of the individual to incorporate and to integrate new knowledge into his existing cognitive structures.

A question that repeatedly occurs, given the stages theory, is whether the child's learning (development) can be accelerated through manipulations of the environment. In this connection Piaget cites the work of Smedslund (1961), who tested the conception of the conservation of weight by means of a series of experiments. Through the use of a scale, children were able to see that changes in the shape or form of clay did not result in any change in weight. After a series of trials, they learned that the weight of a substance is conserved even though it is altered in form. Smedslund's studies also included the transitivity of weights (if $A > B$, and $B > C$, $A > C$; or if $A < B$ and $B < C$, $A < C$). His attempts to teach transitivity through reinforcement failed. Piaget regards both of these outcomes as conforming to what his system predicts. The conservation of weight can be learned through direct physical experience (although he would ask a series of questions about that learning: Is it permanent, and will it transfer to other problems?), but conceptions of transitivity are logical-mathematical. They emerge as spontaneous structures which follow the earlier outlined principles of development and which are not susceptible to manipulation through instruction.

Questions for Review and Discussion

1. Great emphasis was placed in the chapter on the role of the learner's activity in learning. What does it mean for the learner to be active? Can you think of counterexamples; that is, of occasions when you learned effectively without active involvement?

2. Organization was also stressed as a principal determinant of learning. Identify two or three different types of learning tasks. How should each of them be organized? What importance does the author attach to the organization of a learning task? To the learner's internal organization of knowledge?

3. How does the learner's intellectual development affect his ability to learn? For example, would it matter whether a first-grade child who is to learn number combinations has entered the stage of concrete operational thinking? Why or why not?

Readings for Further Reflection

The first two books mentioned here are addressed to some of the same topics as this book. Both are systematic in their theoretical orientation, and they are quite different from each other.

Ausubel, David P. *Educational Psychology: A Cognitive View.* New York: Holt, Rinehart, & Winston, 1969.

Ausubel explains his basic theory in Chapters 2–5.

Staats, Arthur W. *Learning, Language, and Cognition.* New York: Holt, Rinehart, & Winston, 1968.

A stimulus-response theorist extends his position to deal with broader topics of language, learning, and thinking. Staats's book represents a theoretical view which is in contrast to that presented by Ausubel.

Pollio, Howard R. *The Psychology of Symbolic Activity.* Reading, Mass.: Addison-Wesley Publishing Co., 1974.

Pollio's book also deals with some topics similar to this one, but his audience is students of psychology rather than education. Pollio adopts an interesting tactic: He divides his book into two major reviews of the psychology of thinking, one from the position of stimulus-response theory, the other that of information processing. Each set of chapters is intended to provide an informative but essentially nonevaluative look at a major body of theory and research.

The volumes that have been written by Piaget or about his system are so numerous that it is difficult to identify only a handful that would repay reading. However, for readers of this book, two books written by Piaget in collaboration with Barbel Inhelder should be of particular interest.

Inhelder, Barbel, and Piaget, Jean. *The Growth of Logical Thinking from Childhood to Adolescence.* New York: Basic Books, 1958.

Piaget, Jean, and Inhelder, Barbel. *The Psychology of the Child.* New York: Basic Books, 1969.

This little book was written by Piaget and Inhelder in 1969 as a brief and simple synthesis of their work in child psychology to that time. Because of the diversity and difficulty of the many volumes upon which this statement is based, and because it was written by Piaget and Inhelder themselves rather than by one of their numerous interpreters, it represents a particularly useful source for the introductory student.

Probably the best known secondary source for Piaget's writings in the United States is:

Flavell, John. *The Developmental Psychology of Jean Piaget.* Princeton, N.J.: D. Van Nostrand, 1963.

A more recent and somewhat briefer secondary source of value is:
Ginsburg, Herbert, and Opper, Sylvia. *Piaget's Theory of Intellectual Development: An Introduction.* Englewood Cliffs, N.J.: Prentice-Hall, 1969.

A valuable source of a somewhat different type is the book of research papers stimulated by various ideas of Piaget.:
Sigel, Irving E., and Hooper, Frank H. (Eds.). *Logical Thinking in Children.* New York: Holt, Rinehart, & Winston, 1968.

References

Ennis, Robert, H. Children's ability to handle Piaget's propositional logic: A conceptual critique. *Review of Educational Research,* 1975, *45,* 1–41.

Gagné, Robert M. Contributions of learning to human development. *Psychological Review,* 1968, *75,* 177–191.

Hilgard, Ernest R., & Bower, Gordon H. *Theories of learning* (4th ed.). Englewood Cliffs, N.J.: Prentice-Hall, 1975.

Inhelder, Barbel, & Piaget, Jean. *The growth of logical thinking: from childhood to adolescence.* New York: Basic Books, 1958.

Peel, E. A. *The pupil's thinking.* London: Oldbourne, 1967.

Piaget, Jean. Development and learning. *Journal of Research in Science Teaching,* 1964, *2,* 176–186.

Smedslund, Jan. The acquisition of conservation of substance and weight in children. *Scandinavian Journal of Psychology,* 1961, *2,* 11–20; 71–87; 153–160; 203–210.

Chapter 2

How We Learn and What We Remember

This chapter, which outlines the processes that are involved in learning and remembering school-type material, begins with a series of statements to lay the groundwork.

1. *School learning is meaningful.* The majority of tasks teachers ask their pupils to learn can be accomplished in a meaningful way. This assertion has several consequences for our examination of the processes of learning and of retention. For one thing, it suggests that the material to be learned can be related to other knowledge and propositions, and therefore it need not be remembered as a separate entity unrelated to other bodies of knowledge and information. This point is of extreme significance for the study of school learning. As we shall see, material that is meaningful can usually be expressed or represented in alternate ways. This permits the learner to integrate the new ideas he encounters with those he already knows. In this way little of the new meaning is lost to the learner, but she or he is freed of the burden of trying to memorize the specific language in which the idea is cast.

2. *Learning and retention are both affected by how the learning task is organized.* Like the filing clerk who has developed an effective system for storing a company's correspondence and can quickly locate any requested item, the learner can retrieve requested knowledge quickly if it has been organized and stored systematically. Some of the research on learning and memory that will be examined in this chapter deals with the fascinating story of how people organize their learning and how material is more easily retrieved and reproduced if it is hierarchically arranged

than if it lacks coherent organization. The possibility for differentiating and organizing school-type learning in hierarchical fashion is enhanced by its meaningful nature. That is, some concepts and propositions are more abstract and encompassing than others. They hold high positions within a knowledge hierarchy, and numerous lower order concepts and specific facts, dates, names, places, and similar types of information can be systematically organized according to these most general ideas. With meaningful, school-type learning, the learner must represent and organize his knowledge in accordance with the demands of the subject matter—be it history, mathematics, or science—and not his own idiosyncratic classification schemes.

3. *What the learner already knows plays a part in subsequent learning.* It is an uncomfortable situation for a learner to enter a class in which other students and the teacher seem to share a set of ideas and information that are unknown to him. It is almost as though they speak a foreign language that he has not learned, and in a sense that is the case. For example, Dan's schedule in the fall semester would not allow him to enter a year-long course in English History, but in January he persuaded the teacher to let him join the class for the second term. By the end of the third day Dan wondered if he had made a mistake. The second semester began with the study of the accession of the House of Hanover to the British throne. At the first three meetings of the class Dan felt completely at sea. The discussions alluded to the Civil War (he knew they didn't mean the American Civil War, but what *were* they talking about?) to Cromwell, Roundheads, and Cavaliers. The students' questions concerned William and Mary, and the Revolution of 1689, and in general the discussions frustrated and bewildered Dan. He could hear everything that was being said, and he knew the words, but little of it made sense to him. He lacked the necessary background of knowledge about the events, people, and historical trends to organize what was occurring into a coherent whole.

When Dan complained to the teacher of the trouble he was having, he was given some background reading to do and a set of questions to help him focus on the central ideas of what he had missed in the first term. By the middle of the semester, Dan was able to participate adequately in the class. Through hard work and active involvement in catching up, he was as ready as the others to understand Victorian England and Britain's emergence into the 20th century.

A learner's possession of concepts and propositions about a field of knowledge enables him to fit new information into an appropriate place within the framework he has. Such differentiated prior learning also has the most important property of enabling the learner to differentiate between the more and the less consequential information he acquires. Thus the knowledgeable learner may attend only peripherally to what he sees and hears at some times but devote his full attention to those aspects he can recognize as both new and important. The beginner in an area, lacking the conceptual or knowledge framework necessary for establishing effective criteria to make such judgments, may wind up trying to notice everything simultaneously and remember it precisely as it appeared. He has no basis for discriminating important elements from trivial ones or for knowing what must be remembered in an unaltered form and what can be substantively recalled.

4. *Learners take an active role rather than a passive one in transforming and storing what they have learned.* Because of the way a learner's previous knowledge and his beliefs and attitudes help to shape what he remembers, rarely is what he remembers an exact duplicate of what he has experienced or tried to learn. As we shall see, people try to make sense out of the stimuli to which they respond. In doing this, they frequently "go beyond the information given," as one eminent psychologist once put it.

5. *How well the learner remembers what he learns may also depend upon interference from other learning.* Psychologists discovered years ago that when materials such as lists of pairs of words or nonsense syllables were learned, the ability to recall them was influenced by the nature of the lists that were learned subsequently. In general, if a second list learned is similar to the first one but not exactly the same, the learner will have trouble recalling the first list. It was thought for a long time that interference was limited to tasks such as the learning of word lists and that it did not occur when the material to be learned was highly meaningful, on the order of pages in a textbook. Recent studies, however, have found such interference even with meaningful, connected material, and some investigators contend that these materials also conform to the findings of interference theory. We shall examine the pros and cons of these arguments and seek their implications for school learning.

An Overview of the Learning Process

What are the basic events that occur in learning and remembering something, and what variables and processes are involved? Figure 2.1 is an outline of the fundamental events, variables, and processes, presented in a simplified manner. The learner in school is constantly confronted by what we have labeled *environmental events.* The term could include all the external stimuli of his environment, but there are certain groups or classes of these to which his attention is particularly directed: such tasks as learning the meanings of new vocabulary or the French equivalents for English words, solving quadratic equations, memorizing the capitals of the United States, learning how to bisect an angle, or gaining comprehension of the phases of simple cell division. The identifiable tasks which the typical student is expected to learn in the dozen or so years that constitute his elementary and secondary school education run into the thousands.

FIGURE 2.1
Schematic representation of the basic events and processes involved in school-type learning

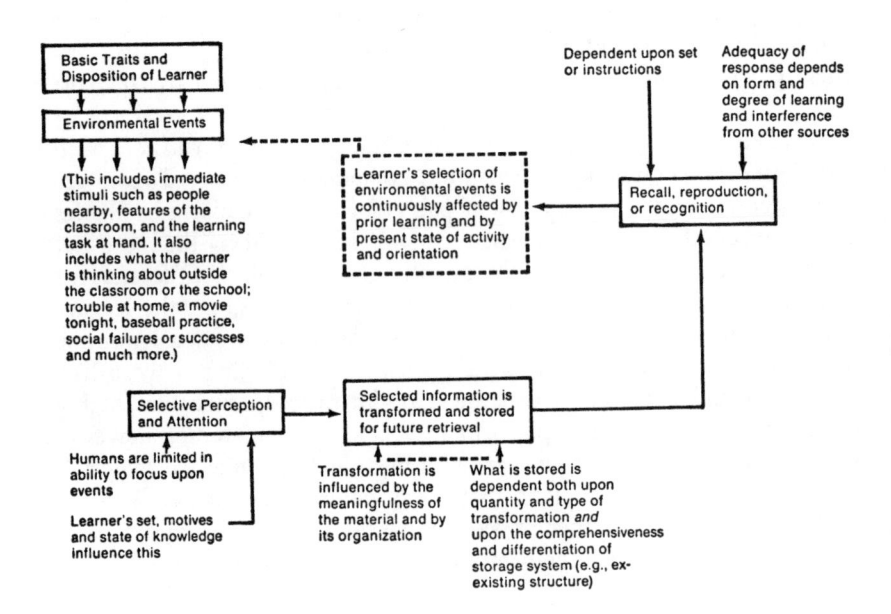

```
┌─────────────────────┐                              Dependent upon set      Adequacy of
│ Basic Traits and    │                              or instructions         response depends
│ Disposition of Learner│                                                    on form and
└─────────────────────┘                                                      degree of learning
      ↓   ↓   ↓                                                              and interference
┌─────────────────────┐                                                      from other sources
│ Environmental Events│ ←─────────────┐
└─────────────────────┘               │
   ↑   ↑   ↑   ↑        ┌──────────────────────────┐   ┌──────────────────────┐
                        │ Learner's selection of   │   │ Recall, reproduction,│
(This includes immediate│ environmental events is  │←──│ or recognition       │
stimuli such as people  │ continuously affected by │   └──────────────────────┘
nearby, features of the │ prior learning and by    │                ↑
classroom, and the learning│ present state of activity│
task at hand. It also   │ and orientation          │
includes what the learner└──────────────────────────┘
is thinking about outside
the classroom or the school;
trouble at home, a movie
tonight, baseball practice,
social failures or successes
and much more.)
                    ┌──────────────────────┐    ┌──────────────────────────┐
                    │ Selective Perception │    │ Selected information is  │
                    │ and Attention        │───→│ transformed and stored   │──┘
                    └──────────────────────┘    │ for future retrieval     │
                            ↑                   └──────────────────────────┘
Humans are limited in                                    ↑
ability to focus upon       Transformation is        What is stored is
events                      influenced by the       dependent both upon
                            meaningfulness of       quantity and type of
Learner's set, motives ─┘   the material and by     transformation and
and state of knowledge      its organization        upon the comprehensiveness
influence this                                      and differentiation of
                                                    storage system (e.g., ex-
                                                    existing structure)
```

One task of a hypothetical junior high school student can be used as a vehicle to gain an overall but not highly detailed first view of the learning process. The class is studying the U.S. Constitution, and the assignment for the next day is to learn definitions for 20 words. The list includes *constitution, confederation, legislature, executive,* and *judiciary,* among others. In this particular case, the assignment demands that students spell each word correctly and provide its definition. Sources for obtaining the definitions include the history textbook in use by the class, as well as a separate pamphlet, *Framers of the Constitution,* but students may also use encyclopedias and other library materials. The teacher has added two other requirements to the assignment that are unusual but useful. The students must prepare definitions in their own language (that is, they cannot satisfy the assignment by memorizing the definition as given by any of the sources), and they must be ready to write their definitions of the terms at noon the next day.

Let us apply the schema of Figure 2.1 to this social studies assignment. It is easy but unwise to overlook the fact that the learner's basic constitution is a fundamental determinant of his learning. That box in the figure labeled "Basic traits and disposition of learner" is shorthand for such characteristics as the learner's physical and intellectual ability, his level of energy, and his temperament; that is, for his personality broadly conceived. Although his success in learning is not totally circumscribed by his personality it does firmly impose limits on what he can achieve. The school is virtually unable to alter these fundamental characteristics of students, but there is sufficient flexibility that it can materially affect what and how much they learn. While a child with intelligence in the low normal range will not ordinarily learn as much or as rapidly as a child with high intelligence, a rich and purposeful educational program will result in better achievement for him than a program of lower quality would.

"Environmental events" is another label representing the idea that, in the present illustration, the learners have multitudinous stimuli impinging upon them besides those to which the school wishes them to respond. A 14-year-old boy who is to carry out this assignment may sit next to a girl whom he finds very attractive; ogling her may be much more gratifying to him than defining 20 words pertaining to the U.S. Constitution. The young lady may be a finalist in the competition for class president, and this holds her thoughts captive. Somehow the teacher must succeed in riveting the students' attention on the task they need to learn. To do this means either expanding the task to command their attention or reducing the attraction of other events in the environment. Every teacher, of course, finds her or his own way to manage this, but it is well to remember that students may require a brief interval in which to disengage their thoughts from a handsome boy, or from the low grade received on last period's mathematics test.

As the word-list assignment is introduced, the teacher wants students to perceive the task and attend to it, to the exclusion of other events. It is futile to prescribe how to do this, but many teachers would probably highlight the assignment by writing it on the chalkboard and drawing students' attention to it visually. If questions can be solicited from students, misunderstandings can be aired. More importantly, this is a good opportunity to focus the students' attention upon the task.

The assignment makes explicit demands upon each student, one of which is that he must arrive at his own definitions of the terms. Attention to this demand is critical, for it keeps the student from simply memorizing definitions as they appear in his textbook or elsewhere. The process described here bridges two steps from the model of Figure 2.1. First the learner must attend to the directions of the assignment: "Selective perception and attention." He must adopt a set, or attitude, which results in the search and integration of existing definitions. Second, he must transform these definitions into broadly paraphrased ones. In general terms, the storage of these definitions in the learner's memory will depend upon the extensiveness of the semantic processing that goes into their generation. The fuller the processing of the words and relationships in the definitions, the better the definition can be integrated with the learner's cognitive structure, that is, his current knowledge and conceptual framework for thinking about these topics.

Suppose a student looks up the word *confederation* as part of this assignment. His dictionary tells him that this is the "(1) act of joining together in a league; state of being united in a league or alliance; (2) group of countries, states, etc., joined together for a special purpose."[1] These definitions are highly meaningful; the learner understands the meaning of "joining together," "group," "countries," and so forth. He may know from his interest in sports that teams are organized into leagues for their mutual benefit. Then in his history textbook he learns that "The states were to be joined in a union known as the Confederation."[2] This does not greatly expand his earlier understanding, but his history book goes on to provide specific information. *This* confederation had a plan called the Articles of Confederation. The government had a single branch, the Congress or legislature, and each state had an equal voice in the law-making process. The text also proceeds to teach him explicit powers and limitations of the government under the Articles of Confederation.

The student must be able to produce definitions on demand the next day, and one who has carried out the assignment as outlined would probably succeed in doing this. However, if he merely memorizes definitions without extending their meanings, his ability to use the terms will be limited. Suppose that on the *second* day after the assignment the teacher were to give the class a quiz containing items of this sort:

---

[1] *Thorndike-Barnhart Advanced Junior Dictionary*, 4th ed. (Glenview, Ill.: Scott-Foresman & Co., 1968), p. 169.

[2] *This Is America's Story*, 3rd ed. (Boston: Houghton Mifflin Co., 1970), pp. 214–215.

Which one of the following people is employed by the executive branch of the government?

(A) Judge Brown   (B) A member of Representative Jones's staff

(C) Agent Smith of the Internal Revenue Service.

If the student has not developed a meaningful definition of the term *executive branch* he is likely to answer the question incorrectly. The teacher and the learner, too, need to consider the range of conditions under which information and concepts are to be recalled. If that range is extensive, then the breadth of the associations in cognitive structure needs to be quite wide.

The concept of cognitive structure

Cognitive structure is the formulation of knowledge that the learner carries in his head. The term can be understood by reference to the discussion in Chapter 1 of the child's construction of the world. There is no way to impose accurate representations in the learner's central nervous system of the nature of the physical, natural, or social world. The learner acquires these only through his own experiences, and largely through his own efforts. Theoretically, at least, the more extensive and intensive his interaction with the materials, concepts, theories, and specific information that constitute a branch of knowledge, the closer will be his cognitive structure to the structure of that content.

Learning Meaningful Material

Let us return now to the basic points outlined at the beginning of the chapter and attend to them in greater depth. The first observation was that, with some exceptions, the learning tasks students encounter in school are meaningful. We need to consider two fundamental questions here:

1. What is *meaningful* material, and with what other kinds of learning material can it be contrasted?

2. What difference does it make for purposes of learning—and retention—whether the material the student is to learn is meaningful?

One prominent characteristic of meaningful material is that it does not ordinarily require the learner to memorize it and to reproduce it verbatim. Indeed if the learner reproduces, word for word, material that is meaningful, we begin to wonder whether he has learned it in a meaningful way; that is, whether he has comprehended the material. Anderson (1972) insists that comprehension can be inferred only when the learner is able to paraphrase the ideas he has studied. That ability seems to be an acid test of comprehension. William James, in his famous *Talks to Teachers and Students* (1900), related a still-timely story.

> A friend of mine, visiting a school, was asked to examine a young class in geography. Glancing at the book, she said: "Suppose you should dig a hole in the ground, hundreds of feet deep, how should you find it at the bottom —warmer or colder than on top?" None of the class replying, the teacher said: "I'm sure they know, but I think you don't ask the question quite rightly. Let me try." So, taking the book, she asked: "In what condition is the interior of the globe?" and received the immediate answer from half the class at once: "The interior of the globe is in a condition of igneous fusion." (p. 150)

Who would believe that those children had an image of the liquid, steaming, molten, bubbling substance at the core of the planet represented by the label "igneous fusion"? Obviously when we learn only the linguistic labels or symbols, even when they represent meaningful and comprehensible ideas, our ability to apply our learning beyond its narrow context (as in the James example) is tremendously abridged.

Thus a new concept begins to emerge about the nature of meaningful material: It represents something or some idea. There is a referent that underlies the language or symbols, diagrams, or other media of expression. Often, particularly in the years of elementary education, the referent may be concrete. For example, as the child is schooled about the causes of day and night, concrete objects are required to render the phenomena comprehensible to the learner. A globe, or some other object to represent the planet, and a source of light for the sun are necessary, at a minimum. But by no means is it always the case that meaningful material possesses a concrete referent. Much of what the student is to learn, especially in the years of secondary or higher education, depends upon comprehending abstract relationships among concepts. But there is no requirement that concrete representations underlie the concepts to be related; they may, in turn, be expressed by means of other abstract relationships.

Furthermore, material that is meaningful will usually bear some relationship to other bodies of content. Figure 2.2 is an illustrative network of concepts and examples associated with the idea of territoriality which might arise in either biology or social studies classes. The concept can be expressed abstractly as a definition, as it appears at the top of the figure. Note that, because the idea is a meaningful one, it can be expressed and referred to in a variety of ways. For example, a teacher might choose to use a *simple and familiar analogy* to introduce the term. He might begin by asking his biology class, "Suppose you came into the laboratory this morning halfway through the term, and found another student sitting at your place and using your instruments. What would you do?" The students' answers would probably range from telling the interloper to go to his own table to an expression of anger. Or if the teacher asked whether a relative, such as a grandmother or an aunt, had ever tried to take charge of their mother's kitchen, the students probably could give a blow-by-blow description of the tension and conflict that resulted. From such homey examples as these it is an easy step to a fuller definition and illustration of the idea.

FIGURE 2.2
Meaningful material as related to other principles, concepts, and facts

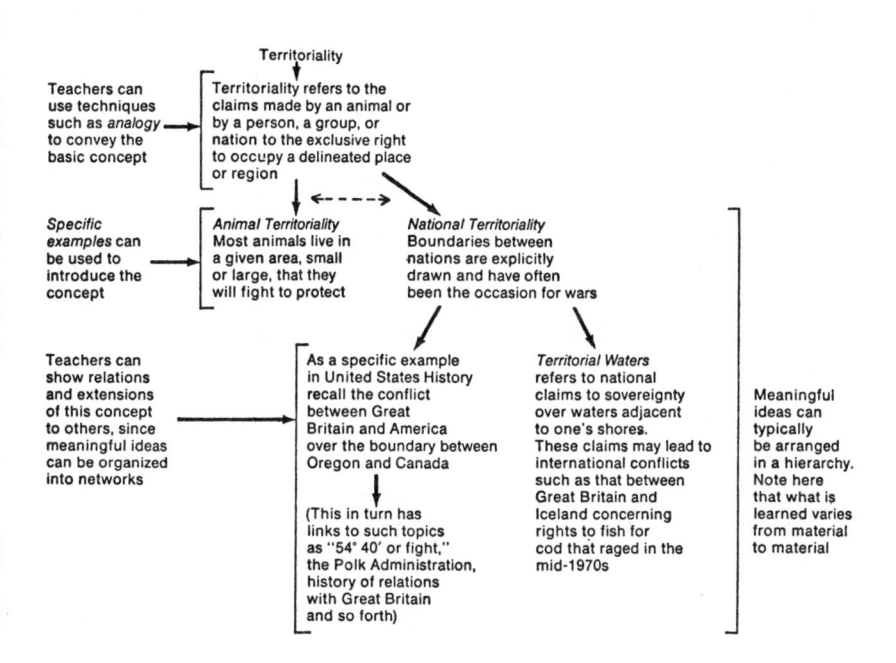

```
                              Territoriality
                                   ↓
Teachers can        ┌ Territoriality refers to the
use techniques      │ claims made by an animal or
such as analogy ──→ │ by a person, a group, or
to convey the       │ nation to the exclusive right
basic concept       │ to occupy a delineated place
                    └ or region
                              ←- - - →
Specific            ┌ Animal Territoriality    National Territoriality
examples can        │ Most animals live in     Boundaries between
be used to          │ a given area, small      nations are explicitly
introduce the  ───→ │ or large, that they      drawn and have often
concept             └ will fight to protect    been the occasion for wars
                              ↙           ↘
Teachers can        ┌ As a specific example    Territorial Waters
show relations      │ in United States History refers to national       ┐
and extensions      │ recall the conflict      claims to sovereignty    │ Meaningful
of this concept ──→ │ between Great            over waters adjacent     │ ideas can
to others, since    │ Britain and America      to one's shores.         │ typically
meaningful ideas    │ over the boundary between These claims may lead to│ be arranged
can be organized    │ Oregon and Canada        international conflicts  │ in a hierarchy.
into networks       │         ↓                such as that between     │ Note here
                    │                          Great Britain and        │ that what is
                    │ (This in turn has        Iceland concerning       │ learned varies
                    │ links to such topics     rights to fish for       │ from material
                    │ as "54° 40' or fight,"   cod that raged in the    │ to material
                    │ the Polk Administration, mid-1970s                │
                    │ history of relations                              │
                    │ with Great Britain                                │
                    └ and so forth)                                     ┘
```

Figure 2.2 also shows the possibility that *specific examples* can be used to help students learn meaningful ideas. Examples from animal territoriality are abundant and interesting. They may be stories of animals of the same species who will fight to the death unless the intruder retreats from the territory of the other to calculations of the varying size of different animals' territories. A network of related concepts can be pointed out in connection with these observations, and students should be encouraged to seek for and suggest their own *extensions and relations*. The territoriality of animals and the territoriality of nations are kindred, and rigid subject matter divisions which discourage the biology student from seeing the political, economic, and psychological manifestations of what is essentially the same idea introduce artificial restraints on his opportunity to learn in a meaningful way. Such devices teach students not to expect relationships among the things they study, especially when the different subjects are also associated with different teachers.

We should notice, too, that several levels of conceptual specificity are included in the figure. These are arbitrary, and different people would work out different hierarchies. The levels descend from the abstract definition to timely instances of disputes over territorial waters, such as the recent "cod war" between Iceland and Great Britain.

Some writers stress the wrong attributes of such hierarchies when they argue that learning must proceed from the most general to the most concrete, or that certain kinds of knowledge (such as a concept or a principle) can only be learned when certain other learning has taken place first. This can lead to the erroneous conclusion that meaningful content can only be learned in an invariant sequence. On the contrary, the teacher can introduce the idea of territoriality at any level she or he chooses, with no loss of learning to the student, as long as it is recognized that what the student will learn is different from level to level. Suppose, for example, a student says in class that the British and Icelandic people are quarreling about the right of Iceland to control cod fishing in waters up to 200 miles off its coast. Such an observation could render an isolated fact which most of the students will quickly forget, unless some effort is made to place the episode in context. If the students begin to see that this particular event can be classified as an example of territorial waters, and the ramifications of that idea are made clear, the chances are improved that the information will be remembered. Even more importantly, the students will have a further elaborated cognitive structure within which to classify further specific facts and examples.

The discussion to this point has concentrated upon the properties of meaningful material. This can be contrasted with nonsense material, which, by definition, does not possess the same properties. Without referents or relationships to bodies of organized knowledge, nonsense materials must of necessity be learned by rote. A good portion of what is known about the learning and retention of verbal material has been acquired through experimental studies of materials which, if not always properly classified as nonsense, fall short of our definition of meaningful material.

The earliest studies of this kind were conducted by the German psychologist Hermann Ebbinghaus, who contributed to the experimental psychology of verbal learning in several important ways. He developed the nonsense syllable (MUV, JAT, XOR) as a way to control for individual differences in previous knowledge, and he supplied the basic data for curves of forgetting based upon his own learning of lists of nonsense syllables (see Figure 2.3 below). It was also Ebbinghaus who devised the savings method for the study of retention. After a period of time one cannot recall any members of lists of nonsense syllables. Ebbinghaus compared the time necessary to learn the list again with that required to learn it in the first place. The amount saved is expressed as a percentage, based upon the comparison between trials or time for relearning and initial learning. If a student requires five trials to relearn a task so he knows it as well as he did after studying it for ten trials two days earlier, we would say that he saved 50 percent of his initial learning over the ensuing two days.

Students sometimes complain that they remember nothing at the end of the school year of what was learned in the early weeks or months. That may be true of such specifics as names of characters in plays or the authors and titles of books. The names of rocks and minerals, and symbols for rarely studied chemical elements are other kinds of specific information that may not be retained at a later time. However, if all these specifics are given to the student in a convenient form before examination time, learning can be refurbished in a fraction of the time required to learn it originally. The ratio of the time for relearning divided by the time for original learning, expressed as a percent and subtracted from 100 percent, represents the savings.

The second question about meaningful material posed above, which concerns the consequences of learning meaningful as opposed to nonsense material, has already been answered in part by showing how meanings are developed from school-type learning tasks. The most important difference in retention between meaningful and nonsense material is that memory for the ideas of a passage, once learned, tends to be good. Measures of retention for the substance of ideational learning show slight decrements over extended periods of time, whereas subjects' ability to retain lists of nonsense materials diminishes sharply in the minutes and hours immediately after acquisition.

Just how sharp the decrement is was first demonstrated by Ebbinghaus (1885), who memorized many lists of nonsense syllables. Each task consisted of learning eight lists, and each list contained 13 syllables.

34 Learning and Thinking

When a group of lists had been memorized to the point where it could be recited on two consecutive trials with no errors, it was put aside. Then, according to a schedule of retention intervals which varied from 20 minutes to 31 days, Ebbinghaus relearned the lists. Retention was expressed as the percent saved. The percent retained, plotted across the several retention intervals, is shown as a graph in Figure 2.3.

FIGURE 2.3
Curve of forgetting for nonsense syllables

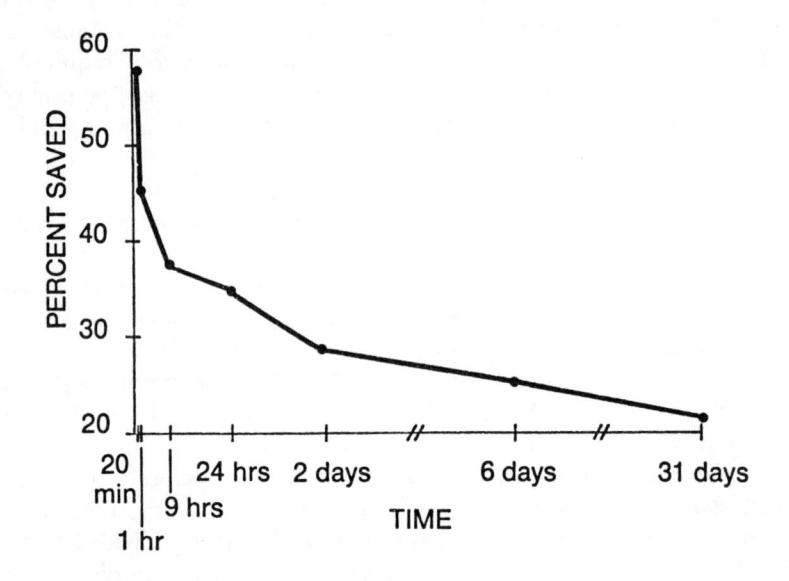

Source: Based on Ebbinghaus (1885).

Although this curve is well known to students of the psychology of learning, it represents a highly specialized case. Of course it is based on data from only a single learner (Ebbinghaus), but perhaps more important is the nature of the learning material on which the tests were made. We do not often encounter situations that are as totally devoid of meaning as this. Especially in school, where we expect an emphasis upon the meaningfulness of what is studied, little nonsense learning should be required. Even so, teachers might expect that when students are learning lists, as of major products, exports and imports, presidents, rulers, or the names of bones and nerves in their study of biology, the course of their retention might be close to what is seen in Figure 2.3. Of course, this does not mean that the material is irrevocably lost, as the figure shows. Practice and review schedules, and overlearning, can be of great help in retaining information.

But let us compare a meaningful task of the kind that pupils learn at school with the nonsense series of the Ebbinghaus experiments. Different things are learned when children pursue meaningful as contrasted with nonsense tasks. As an example of what we would regard as a meaningful task, consider that students are to learn the parts of a flower. This topic often is part of the science curriculum in the intermediate grades and may be learned or reviewed in a secondary school botany class. The task to be learned has several aspects.

First, there is a series of new and largely unfamiliar terms to be learned: *receptacle, calyx, corolla, stamen, pistil*. By themselves, these terms are no more meaningful than the task of learning an unrelated series of words or syllables.

Second, a pronounced difference from nonsense material is that each of these terms refers to a part of the flower which can be identified in diagrams, pictures, and in the flower itself. The student learns that the calyx, which lies at the base of the flower, consists of a series of green leafy sepals, and its principal function is to encapsulate and protect the immature bud of the flower. Later it opens and separates as the petals mature, and its sepals may fall away.

Third, each term possesses meaning which can be developed through learning. Beyond that, as the student learns the various elements or parts of the flower, this knowledge contributes to his ability to comprehend relationships among the various parts. When the student learns that the reproductive system of flowers consists of the stamen and pistils, he is in a position to comprehend such processes as pollination. But unless he also knows that in many flowers the anthers, which contain the pollen, attract insects who carry the pollen to pistils where it is deposited in the ovary, the learner cannot form a clear conception of the process, nor will he have a basis for understanding the variety of subconcepts and variations, such as self-pollination and cross-pollination, or the absence of bright, attractive color in plants which depend only upon the wind for pollination.

Fourth, meaningful learning facilitates subsequent learning, as illustrated above. This does not necessarily require that the elements of a complex task be learned in a particular order, but it does mean that meaningful learning is organized, and its parts are differentiated. The learner who has a clear, accurate, and comprehensive concept of plant pollination can accommodate information about variations on the basic process more easily than the learner whose knowledge of the topic has come about through a process of rote learning. In that case, each new aspect of a topic or variant upon a central theme has to be learned as a separate entity, and its retention depends upon the same rote process. The burden of such learning on human memory is excessive, and most of it may be expected to undergo decay (and hence, forgetting) in a brief period of time. This is why students easily forget information they memorize in cram sessions for examination purposes instead of digging out the meanings of what they are to learn.

On the basis of personal experience, you already know that the substance of material that is meaningful, once it has been learned, is retained for a much longer period of time than nonsense material, but we can briefly identify the difference. Briggs and Reed (1943) had college students read a series of 12 paragraphs and answer true-false questions immediately afterward. Average immediate recall of the material was about 70 percent. Delayed recall intervals ranged from 1 week through 4, 8, and 12 weeks. Students tested a week after learning retained about 68 percent, and there was a gradual decrement subsequently, with average retention scores for the groups being 63 percent after four weeks and about 61 percent for the other two retention intervals. The contrast between retention of *meaningless* material learned by *rote* with that of the *substance* or *idea* of *meaningful* material is thus very sharp. In the former case half or more of what has been learned recedes within a few minutes or in an hour or two. With meaningful material, the basic ideas are well remembered even months after the initial acquisition.

Ausubel (1968) observes that two conditions are required for meaningful learning to take place. One is that the material to be learned must be capable of meaningful development, as we have noted. In addition, the learner must adopt a meaningful set to learn. This would seem to be both a simple and an obvious point, but it is easily violated. The learner who has a set for meaningful learning will attempt to comprehend the ideas he hears or reads; he will expect them to "make sense." He will search for relationships between the new material he is to learn and other similar or related ideas that he already possesses.

To demonstrate what difference it makes whether the learner's learning is meaningful or is accomplished through rote memorization, we can briefly explore Ausubel's conception of cognitive structure and the organization of knowledge within it. We have noted that material which is learned by rote, even though it may be susceptible to meaningful learning, must be stored in the learner's memory in a form similar to that in which it was learned. If parts of the material are forgotten or defy retrieval, it is tantamount to losing the entire message, for, lacking meaning, the learner has no way to regenerate the missing parts. With meaningful learning, the story is different. When the learner encounters new material with which he is unacquainted, it is related to other ideas that are already stored in his cognitive structure. Knowledge is organized in the cognitive structure ranging from the most general and overarching to the most concrete and specific. It is the larger and more abstract principles and generalizations of a topic that are learned initially, and they are at the apex of the hierarchy. Under them are subsumed the less general, more limited concepts and propositions. Over a period of time and with the acquisition of new meanings, the fundamental ideas become progressively differentiated to include more specific and concrete aspects under the most general conceptual rubrics.

Material that is meaningful, therefore, can be integrated into existing elements of the learner's cognitive structure. This leads naturally to a discussion of the relationship between how material is organized and how it is learned, the topic of future discussion. Ausubel has extended his theory about meaningful learning and its integration with cognitive structure to argue that the learning of new and unfamiliar ideas can be facilitated by helping the learner to construct the broad outline or organization of a new topic prior to his exposure to it in detail. This is done through the use of *advance organizers*, which provide a general and abstract framework into which specific learning material can be subsequently fitted. The success of this concept and similar efforts to improve learning and retention will be reviewed in Chapter 3.

The Role of Organization in Learning and Remembering

The central point that the problems of acquiring and retaining information are affected vitally by processes of organization holds true not only for meaningful material but for learning tasks that are less than meaningful or that are conveniently learned without their meaning being fully developed. These are tasks such as learning the capitals of all the states, the major exports of Latin America, one's locker combination, or the telephone number of a girl in one's history class. As we shall see, organization is not simply a property of the material to be learned; it is also the result of the active processes of grouping, classifying, and discriminating that are used by the learner.

Organization of meaningful material

Students often are given assignments which instruct them to read a few pages of a textbook or listen to the teacher's explanation of an event, or something of a similar nature. Unless the teacher identifies points to be repeated or stressed, that single exposure may constitute the students' opportunity to learn the material. How much do pupils learn from a single trial of that sort, or to ask the question differently, what is it that pupils learn under those conditions? There are several studies that bear upon this question, but they have been conducted with adults (college students) and their conclusions may not apply well to the learning of younger children, particularly those who are still at the level of concrete operational thinking. This limitation should be held in mind.

An early investigation along these lines was reported by Katona (1940), who constructed a 600-word passage about the principle of acceleration of production, a concept bearing upon understanding of business cycles. Along with the passage, Katona inserted a table of information to illustrate how the principle might operate in a specific instance. College students read one of two somewhat different versions of the material. In one the passage deliberately lacked sequential, logical organization, and in the other, seen by a different class of students, a table was included which was not well integrated with the text. Four weeks after the study sessions, students were examined about the principle of acceleration. It is not surprising that students who received the less well-organized version could recall less than other students. Katona adds an interesting and apt observation that the specific items that were not recalled tended to be those that did not add anything conceptually to the basic message. Katona suggested that such statements are lost because they are *embedded* in the more general idea of the passage. Some specific information that was not subsumed by the more general principle was also recalled; this information was separate from the general idea but coordinate with it. The point is similar to the one made in the lesson on parts of the flower discussed above. Once the learner has mastered the basic concepts, functions, and relationships, he can learn and retain exceptions to these general ideas, such as that some species have only pistillate flowers on one plant and only staminate flowers on another plant of the same kind.

A recent study by Meyer and McConkie (1973) provides preliminary answers to questions about learning and the organization of tasks. Their basic question was, "What is recalled after hearing a passage?" They adapted and tape-recorded two articles from *Scientific American,* then played the tapes for groups of college students. One important variation in this study is that they examined the effects of repeated hearings of the same lesson. Some students heard the tapes once, some twice, and some heard them three times. This made it possible to evaluate just what a student learns when he has repeated opportunities to hear the same lecture.

Meyer and McConkie were interested, of course, in finding out how much students can remember immediately after they have heard a tape which can be roughly equated with a portion of a college-level lecture. The practical import of that question for teachers in general seems apparent. However, their interest extended to trying to identify which ideas are learned first and determining whether variables that are important for such things as learning lists of words, for example, are also significant in the learning of meaningful material.

The number of ideas in each passage was ascertained, and the ideas were classified by coders according to how many other ideas were superordinate or subordinate to them. Students wrote everything from the passage they could recall immediately after hearing the tape. Those protocols were scored for the total number of ideas recalled, and an estimate was made of the importance of the ideas. With some risk of oversimplifying the results of the study, they can be summarized into the following points.

1. There is an increment in the number of ideas recalled for each repetition of the learning passage. However, the increments are negatively accelerated (that is, the rate of improvement for recall diminishes from one hearing to the next).

2. The ideas which had been independently rated by the coders as most important in the logical structure of the passages were the ones most likely to be recalled.

3. Some evidence for the hierarchical nature of learning emerged in that if an idea were recalled, it was very likely that the idea immediately above it in rated importance was also recalled.

4. Evidence for the occurrence of serial phenomena, such as that found in studies of list learning, was weak. When such a phenomenon did occur, it could be accounted for by the logical organization of ideas in the passage.

5. The ideas recalled are stable. If an idea was recalled on one attempt, it was likely to be recalled on others as well.

6. Since the ideas at the apex of the logical structure tended to be the best recalled, there seems to be evidence for Ausubel's contention that it is the most general and abstract principles that are learned first. The second part of his generalization, that lower order ideas are subsequently learned, did not receive much support.

The work of Meyer and McConkie breaks new ground for the study of school learning, and its contribution is important. However, additional studies that confirm or dispute their interpretations are very much needed. This is especially true for any statement we might wish to make about learning by younger children at the elementary and perhaps even at the secondary school levels. Because of the great developmental differences in language and cognition that exist between children of 7 or 8 to

11 or 12 and adult students of college age, we cannot safely conclude that these findings can be extended downward. However, Paris's (1975) work, to be examined later in this chapter, supports the idea that children draw inferences from discourse according to the same rules followed by adults.

Organization of other verbal materials

Although most learning tasks presented by the school are meaningful in nature, students encounter numerous tasks that are treated as though they were not very meaningful. This happens even though, at some deeper level, the material is related to broader conceptions or structures of knowledge. For example, children are to learn the names of birds which inhabit different regions of North America, or the rulers of England according to lineage, such as the Plantagenets, Lancasters, Yorks, Tudors, Stuarts, and so forth. As with more meaningful and connected material, learners tend to impose organization upon these tasks, and instructions which contain a specified organization of the task contribute to their learning and recall.

One interesting demonstration of the tendency to impose an organizational scheme upon words that are presented at random was published by Bousfield (1953). To study the tendency to recall words in clusters, Bousfield generated 60 words, 15 of which fit into each of four categories (names, animals, professions, and vegetables). He mixed the words together for a random distribution and then read each in turn to samples of college students who, immediately after hearing the entire list, were to write down as many as they could recall. On the average that turned out to be about 25 words, but, as expected, learners tended to recall them in clusters that belong together; that is, a student might write down four or five animals, although he had not heard the words read to him in any order resembling these categories. Bousfield also found that the clustering peaked midway through the recall, and in the latter parts of it words tended to be recalled more at random, presumably because the implicit superordinate labels had been exhausted.

Mandler's (1967) work provided extensive data showing that learners impose their own systems of organization when they are permitted free recall of word lists. The tendency of the learner to strain toward organizing material to enhance its retention seems to be very great, at least for adult human beings. Notice, too, that this tendency is one example of the principle that learning and retention depend heavily upon the active involvement and participation of the learner.

Suppose the task is organized so as to provide the learner with categories, instead of depending upon him to construct or infer suitable ones. Will that improve his ability to recall the words? Several lines of research suggest that the provision of categories facilitates learners' ability to remember larger numbers of items. One of the earlier investigations to demonstrate this was conducted by Mathews (1954), who gave college students 24 names which could be classified into two, three, or six different categories. Her specific interest was in whether the number of categories is related to learning. Students were to read their lists of 24 words and indicate in the margin whether the name was that of an athlete, a poet, or an artist, for example. They were not to make an effort to memorize the names. Ten minutes later, they were asked to write as many of the names on the original list as possible. Students who used six categories to classify names recalled more than those who used three categories, who in turn recalled more than those whose 24 names were in only two categories.

Mathews observes that this relationship is probably strengthened by the fact that all the category names were distinct, and they were easily remembered by the college students who participated in the research. It is well worth considering that children for whom the category labels and the inclusiveness of the categories would represent additional parts of the task to be learned might be hindered rather than helped. For the adult learner, the major task is simply to sort out the classifications. Their appropriateness is familiar to him; that is, he possesses adequate concepts of "poet," "conqueror," and "artist," for example, so that no additional burden of learning is imposed. Children at concrete levels of operational thinking probably need to have an opportunity to learn how inclusive the class is and a chance to associate the appropriate labels with the classes before a set to use such categories can assist their recall effectively.

In an influential paper bearing upon our capacity to process information, Miller (1956) observed that human beings are limited in the number of items they can perceive and retain in mind simultaneously. This number is approximately six or seven, but Miller observed that this capacity is in fact much greater if the learner uses strategies to organize and subsume information under more general rubrics. The number of such rubrics that can be kept in mind is limited, but each of them may, in turn, contain very large amounts of information.

Bower and his associates (1969) provided some graphic demonstrations of the utility of strategies which emphasize categories. One of their experiments examined two variables that are relevant to classroom learning: organization of the task and whole versus part presentation. In all, a list of 112 words were first to be learned and then recalled. The scheme reproduced in Figure 2.4, *one* of four hierarchies used, was part of an array for the group that saw the whole task at one time in a highly organized form. Another group saw the words simultaneously, and also laid out in tree forms comparable to that of Figure 2.4, but with the words *randomly* assigned to the various levels. For example, look at the figure and imagine the 26 words rearranged so that, perhaps, *emerald* replaces *minerals*, which replaces *rare*, and that *stones* and *lead* trade places, and so forth. Still other groups saw only parts of the task at a time.

FIGURE 2.4
The "minerals" conceptual hierarchy

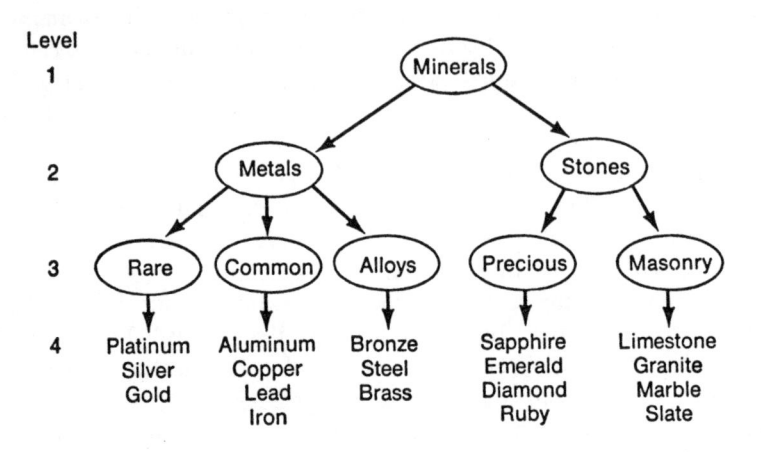

```
Level
  1                                    (Minerals)
                                       /         \
  2                          (Metals)              (Stones)
                            /   |   \              /      \
  3              (Rare)  (Common) (Alloys)   (Precious) (Masonry)
                   |        |       |            |          |
  4            Platinum  Aluminum  Bronze     Sapphire   Limestone
               Silver    Copper    Steel      Emerald    Granite
               Gold      Lead      Brass      Diamond    Marble
                         Iron                 Ruby       Slate
```

Source: Bower, Clark, Lesgold, & Winzenz (1969), p. 324.

The results of this experiment are very clear. After two trials, students who were given the organized task in its entirety made very few errors (on the average they were able to recall 106 of the 112 words), and on the third and fourth trials, there were no errors. Those who also saw the entire task, but randomly arranged, did not do nearly as well. Even after the fourth trial, they still could recall only 70 of the 112 words.

Because teachers might suppose that presenting parts of such a lengthy task at a time would facilitate learning, another result of this study is worth relating. Students who received the part presentation saw Levels 1 and 2 words on Trial 1. The Level 3 words were added on Trial 2, and all the words were exposed on Trials 3 and 4. If the conceptual hierarchy was available, this worked reasonably well. On the third trial, students recalled 93 words on the average, and 108 after the fourth trial. Learning was faster and more accurate when all the words were available from the beginning, and especially if a conceptual framework was used.

The same general outcome as this study can be seen in other investigations that have quite different origins. For example, Bruner, Goodnow, and Austin (1956) used a series of 81 cards, each containing a different combination of geometric forms and colors in their study of concept formation. (This work is discussed in Chapter 4.) When the learner had immediate access to the total array of cards, his learning was much faster than if he had to deal with the instances one at a time. Similarly, Taba (1966) demonstrated that when elementary school teachers placed on the board specific examples given by children, they could more easily group and classify the examples into conceptual categories.

Not only does clustering or categorizing words aid in their free recall, as demonstrated by the studies reviewed above, but the learner can also do a great deal to assist the process. One of the ways that has been studied involves processes of mediation. For example, the learner uses his own associations (which are therefore meaningful to him) to assist him in remembering the material. Bower (1973) had students learn lists of words in groups of four. For example, one group consisted of:

    dog   hat   bicycle   cigar

Subjects were instructed to create vivid mental images to link the groups of words together; "a *dog* wearing a homburg *hat* is smoking a huge *cigar* while pedaling along on a *bicycle*." After learning, subjects were asked to recall all the words they had learned. The total words recalled came in groups of two to four that had been associated in the learning trials. When other subjects studied lists of words that varied in their grouping from trial to trial, the number of words recalled declined.

Learners appear to develop their own strategies for grouping together words they are asked to learn. When subjects had learned a list of words, Bower asked them to identify groups of four into which they had organized the words. Half the subjects were given another learning trial in which quartets of words were exposed in the same grouping as given by the learners. Each of the remaining half of the learners was given quartets designed to interfere with the groupings he had previously used. Free recall showed an increment of about two words for the first half of the learners, but a decrement of about two words for the other half. When learners construct their own mediators, they apparently select words with high association strength, and this leads to the best free recall. However, in school learning, the grouping of words or phrases together must occur in certain orders and predetermined sequences. The idiosyncratic associations of learners may interfere with rather than facilitate the recall of what has been learned.

Remembering

Hunter (1964) tells of an episode at the Cambridge Psychological Society that illustrates some important points about human memory. One evening the discussion that followed the meeting was carefully recorded by two individuals, without the knowledge of the rest of the membership. Two weeks later those who had been present at the meeting were asked to write an account of what had occurred in the discussion. On the average, each statement included only about 8 percent of what had actually transpired, and more than 40 percent of what people included in their reports was inaccurate. Either the event they recounted had not happened, or the person erroneously attributed it to the wrong occasion. A strong impression is left that what people remember about an episode is the product of their own construction of the world, their sets and attitudes, and expectations of what would occur under certain circumstances, at least as much as it is of the events as they might be recorded by an objective and comprehensive observer.

One of the finest and most influential books about memory ever written is Bartlett's *Remembering* (1932). The product of almost 20 years of research and thought about memory, Bartlett's book stresses the active and constructive role of the individual in shaping his memories. According to Bartlett,

> Remembering is not the re-excitation of innumerable fixed, lifeless and fragmentary traces. It is an imaginative reconstruction, or construction, built out of the relation of our attitude towards a whole active mass of organized past reactions or experience, and to a little outstanding detail which commonly appears in image or in language form. It is thus hardly ever really exact, even in the most rudimentary forms of rote recapitulation, and it is not at all important that it should be so. (p. 213)

Bartlett's research emphasized the active nature of the individual in the process of remembering. As his definition indicates, the learner is not a passive repository for inanimate traces and images. Quite to the contrary, past experiences are interpreted and reconstructed with the passage of time to fit cultural norms or expectations, or to make sense of a situation. For example, several of Bartlett's experiments involved what he called the method of serial reproduction. The procedure is simple. A story or a drawing is presented to one person, who studies it with care. He then repeats it either orally or, if a picture, on paper for another individual who did not hear or see the initial presentation. This procedure continues through some 10 or 12 reproductions. One of the most widely known of these experiments is based upon a story called "The War of the Ghosts."

The original version of the story is as follows:

The War of the Ghosts

One night two young men from Egulac went down to the river to hunt seals, and while they were there it became foggy and calm. Then they heard war-cries, and they thought: "Maybe this a war-party." They escaped to the shore, and hid behind a log. Now canoes came up, and they heard the noise of paddles, and saw one canoe coming up to them. There were five men in the canoe, and they said:

"What do you think? We wish to take you along. We are going up the river to make war on the people."

One of the young men said: "I have no arrows."

"Arrows are in the canoe," they said.

"I will not go along. I might be killed. My relatives do not know where I have gone. But you," he said, turning to the other, "may go with them."

So one of the young men went, but the other returned home.

And the warriors went up the river to a town on the other side of Kalama. The people came down to the water, and they began to fight, and many were killed. But presently the young man heard one of the warriors say: "Quick, let us go home: that Indian has been hit." Now he thought: "Oh, they are ghosts." He did not feel sick, but they said he had been shot.

So, the canoes went back to Egulac, and the young man went ashore to his house, and made a fire. And he told everybody and said: "Behold I accompanied the ghosts, and we went to fight. Many of our fellows were killed, and many of those who attacked us were killed. They said I was hit, and I did not feel sick."

He told it all, and then he became quiet. When the sun rose he fell down. Something black came out of his mouth. His face became contorted. The people jumped up and cried.

He was dead. (Bartlett, 1932, p. 65)

As people reproduce the story verbally for others who have not heard it previously, and then ask them to repeat it to still another individual, the story undergoes reliable kinds of alterations. Here, from Bartlett's account, is the tenth reproduction of the same story in one series.

Reproduction 10: The War of the Ghosts

Two Indians were out fishing for seals in the Bay of Manapapan, when along came five other Indians in a war-canoe. They were going fighting.

"Come with us," said the five to the two, "and fight."

"I cannot come," was the answer of the one, "for I have an old mother at home who is dependent upon me." The other also said he could not come, because he had no arms. "That is no difficulty," the others replied, "for we have plenty in the canoe with us"; so he got into the canoe and went with them.

In a fight soon afterwards this Indian received a mortal wound. Finding that his hour was come, he cried out that he was about to die. "Nonsense," said one of the others, "you will not die." But he did. (Bartlett, 1932, p. 124)

Few additional changes, other than minor ones, occur if the reproductions are pursued beyond this point. Essentially the same kinds of changes occur when the stimulus material is a picture. A series of reproductions from an original drawing called Portrait D'Homme appears in Figure 2.5. What happens as the materials are reproduced time after time is that they move in the direction of more concrete and more conventional representations. For English people in the 1930s the folk tale of the North American Indians lacked much attachment to experience. Similarly, after the first or second reproduction of the Portrait D'Homme symbol, subjects needed an organizing principle or theme to enable them to determine what to reproduce.

It is very clear that we do not simply remember the details of what we have heard or seen, especially when that stimulus is unfamiliar or not anchored in our previous experience. Then we strive to impose meaning upon it. Verbal materials, such as the story, are markedly shortened and condensed. Such things as titles and proper names are dropped, transposed, or recalled incorrectly. Bartlett observes, especially in the case of picture reproduction, that isolated details, especially if they are not representative of the picture as a whole, tend to be retained in later reproductions. This point is congruent with Katona's finding, mentioned earlier, that students retained specific information that could not be subsumed under some broader principle in the economics passage. One more point may be mentioned. When the material to be remembered is ambiguous or unattached to one's cognitive structure, a name attached to it has a very strong tendency to determine what will be remembered or reproduced.

A study by Carmichael (cited in Hunter, 1964) further illustrates this point. Two different groups of subjects were shown a series of figural stimuli that are highly ambiguous (these appear in the middle column of Figure 2.6). One group was told one name to go with a stimulus (bee hive, seven, hourglass, pine tree); the other group was given a different name (hat, four, table, trowel). Each group was asked to reproduce the stimuli. The drawings in Figure 2.6 give eloquent support to Bartlett's

FIGURE 2.5
Transformation of unfamiliar representations toward conventional forms

Source: Bartlett (1932), pp. 178–179.

48 Learning and Thinking

observation of the impact of naming upon the interpretation and reproduction of verbal and figural material.

FIGURE 2.6
Effect of naming on the recall of ambiguous figural material.

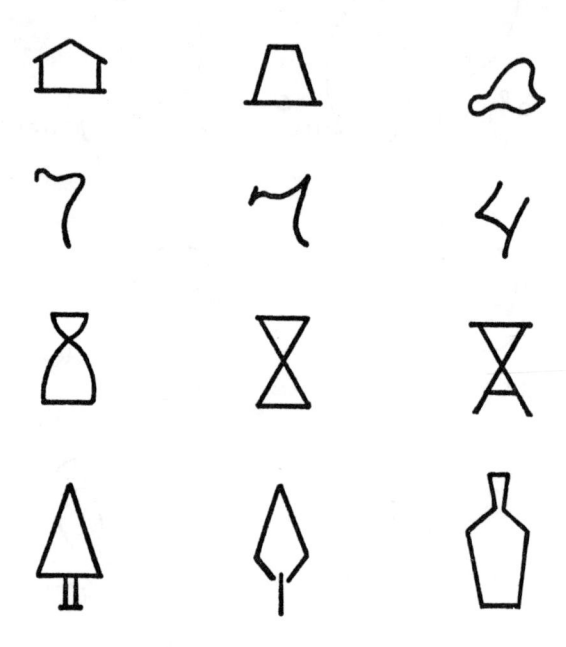

Source: Carmichael (1932), from Hunter (1964), p. 162.

Bartlett's insistence upon "effort after meaning" in memory was not very explicit with regard to materials such as those that students learn in school. However in recent years several programs of research that are more pertinent to school learning have begun to substantiate Bartlett's themes of the previous generation. Psychologists who study verbal learning and memory have been curious about what people learn when they hear or read sentences or longer passages composed of sentences. One view is that a trace or image of the specific sentence is stored in memory. But another, akin to Bartlett's theory, is that people do not store the precise language they hear, but a transformation of it based upon its meaning.

Bransford and Franks (1971) argue that people abstract meaningful ideas from sentences; they do not store precisely what is heard. Their experimental procedure, which has been more or less followed by a series of investigators, is quite ingenious. They presented to college students groups of sentences which contained one, two, three, or four ideas from a total message which contained four ideas. For example, the complete message might be: "The rock which rolled down the mountain crushed the tiny hut at the edge of the woods." The students might hear this as a single sentence, or in a series of two, three, or four sentences. After a brief lapse of time, students were asked to listen to additional sentences and to indicate whether precisely those sentences had been previously heard.

Some of the sentences were new to the learners; they might express part of the idea of the total passage, or they might be incongruent with the ideas. The sentences that were new to the learner but contained new related ideas were frequently "recognized" by the learners as having been heard before. The unrelated sentences were not "recognized." Bransford and Franks also asked learners to indicate how sure they were of their judgment that a sentence had been previously heard. As it turned out, the more ideas a sentence contained, the more certain was the learner that he had heard it before. Sentences that contained all four of the ideas were given higher certainty ratings than those with three of the ideas, which in turn were rated more certain as having been heard before than the sentences with two ideas, and so forth. The sequence was invariant.

Bransford and Franks interpret their experimental findings to mean that human beings' memory for sentences is *semantic* rather than *syntactic*. We abstract the ideas and store them, rather than the specifics of the sentence. It should be noted, however, that the ideas and language used in the Bransford and Franks experiments, and in the others to be reviewed here, were both simple and familiar. They did not deal with issues in which, as is often the case, the elementary or high school student has to decode difficult prose dotted with technical and unknown words. Although the research provides some evidence that people seem to store ideas, this does not rule out the possibility that phonological or syntactic storage may also occur, and in some cases it almost certainly does.

Paris (1975) and his associates have examined similar issues, with children of elementary school age as the targets of their inquiries. I am particularly happy that such studies are available because so much of the theory and research on memory has used only adults as subjects. There is also a certain amount of comfort to be found in Paris's work because the processes do not appear to be markedly different for children than they are for adults. Of course, we cannot extend that generalization beyond the particular issues that Paris and his colleagues have examined.

An initial question was how children remember sentences. This is similar to the question Bransford and Franks used, and it was answered in much the same manner. If sentences are learned by rote, or if their syntactic structure influences recall, then children should be able to discriminate previously heard sentences from new ones. Paris and Carter (Paris, 1975) presented a series of carefully developed stories to second- and fifth-grade children. For example:

1. The bird is in the cage. (premise)
2. The cage is under the table. (premise)
3. The bird is yellow. (filler)

After an interpolated task the children heard four more sentences. The child was to tell whether they were just like the first sentences. These four included two sentences that were semantically true—one a true premise, and the other a true inference. The other two sentences were false—one a false inference and the other a false premise.

4. The bird is in the cage. (true premise)
5. The cage is over the table. (false premise)
6. The bird is under the table. (true inference)
7. The bird is on top of the table. (false inference)

Children in both grades consistently classified the true premises and the true inferences as "old" sentences, that is, as sentences they had heard before. There was no reliable difference between children in the two grades in the frequency with which they made such identifications. A natural objection to this finding is that the children may simply have been confused about the whole thing. However, Paris and Carter were able to show three kinds of evidence that refute that criticism. Only about 20 percent of the children accepted the false premises as "old." In general the children who accepted the true inferences as "old" were the same ones who recognized the true premise. Finally, the children gave high certainty scores to the true inferences. It then appears that even by the second grade, children store inferences from sentences in memory and not just total copies of the sentences.

Although Paris is confident about what his findings mean, he has also been careful to suggest the context within which his interpretation lies.

> The principal finding of this study is that children, like adults, could not discriminate old from new sentences which shared consistent meaning. This conclusion should not be overgeneralized, but when the sentences are not grossly different in length, vocabulary, or construction, when they are not overlearned, and when the sentences are contextually or thematically related, children appear to be unable to discriminate old and new sentences that are congruent with their semantically integrated memory representations. This result is inconsistent with the assertion that comprehension and memory of sentences can be described by word associations or interpreta-

tions of syntactic features. Although lexical and syntactic factors influence understanding, an adequate account of how children remember sentences must attempt to characterize the generation of the semantic context that the sentences describe. (Paris, 1975, pp. 228–229)

How do children comprehend prose?

An important extension of Paris's (1975) work was consideration of children's comprehension of prose. Four linguistic inferences were chosen to study as representatives of inferential behavior. Two of these were called contextual inferences, because the content of several sentences had to be integrated in order for an inference to be drawn. One of these was *presupposition*, the other *inferred consequences*. The other two inferences were lexical inferences, *semantic entailment* and *implied instruments*. Six paragraphs were read to each of 12 children from kindergarten through the fifth grade. After each story the child was asked four questions of a factual nature, to provide base-line data about comprehension, and four others that were inferential. Figure 2.7 reproduces one of the paragraphs

FIGURE 2.7
Illustrative materials used in Paris's investigation of how children comprehend prose

Linda was playing with her new doll in front of her big red house. Suddenly she heard a strange sound coming from under the porch. It was the flapping of wings. Linda wanted to help so much, but she did not know what to do. She ran inside the house and grabbed a shoe box from the closet. Then Linda looked inside her desk until she found eight sheets of yellow paper. She cut up the paper into little pieces and put them in the bottom of the box. Linda gently picked up the helpless creature and took it with her. Her teacher knew what to do.

Question type		Questions	Answer
Adjective	1.	Was Linda's doll new?	Yes
Adjective	2.	Did Linda grab a metal box?	No
Preposition	3.	Was the strange sound coming from under the porch?	Yes
Preposition	4.	Was Linda playing behind the house?	No
Presupposition	5.	Did Linda like to take care of animals?	Yes
Consequence	6.	Did Linda take what she found to the police station?	No
Entailment	7.	Did Linda find a frog?	No
Instrument	8.	Did Linda use a pair of scissors?	Yes

Source: Paris (1975), p. 233.

52   Learning and Thinking

used, and the table in this figure lists the eight questions based upon it, their type, and the answers. The children, of course, were not given the information on question type. As Table 2.1 and Figure 2.8 indicate, they

TABLE 2.1
Mean percentage of correct responses by question categories

	Grade		
Question Category	K	2	4
Adjectives and prepositions	61.7	78.9	76.6
Nouns and verbs	72.7	83.6	80.5
Contextual inferences	60.2	78.1	80.5
Lexical inferences	77.3	89.8	87.5

Source: Paris (1975), p. 238.

were able to answer an increasing percentage of the questions as they grew older. The data shown also reflect the fact that kindergarten and second-grade children draw a much higher percentage of correct inferences from simple stories than has commonly been supposed. Paris sees the increments in retention of explicit and inferential meaning not as a simple growth in memory capacity between ages 5 and 11 but as an improvement in operations necessary for inferential learning, which undergo development during these ages corresponding roughly to the stage of concrete intellectual operations.

Interference as a Source of Forgetting

When we learn something that is rather like something we have learned before, the new learning often makes it difficult for us to recall the old. This common phenomenon is called interference. Hunter (1964) for example, sees interference as the major cause of forgetting.

Let us consider an example of interference that is both concrete and typical of the classroom. Mark's sixth-grade geography teacher gave the class a dittoed sheet of the major exports of Latin America countries, with the instruction to learn the exports as they appeared on the sheet. Mark studied the list for each country and after a while felt that he knew them. Then, in class, Mark's teacher asked him to name the major exports of Argentina. Mark tried to visualize the sheet where the name *Argentina* appeared in capital letters. What were the words under it?

"Corn," said Mark. "And wheat's another one."

"Good," said his teacher. "Go on."

FIGURE 2.8
Mean percentage of correct responses on verbatim and inferential questions, by grades

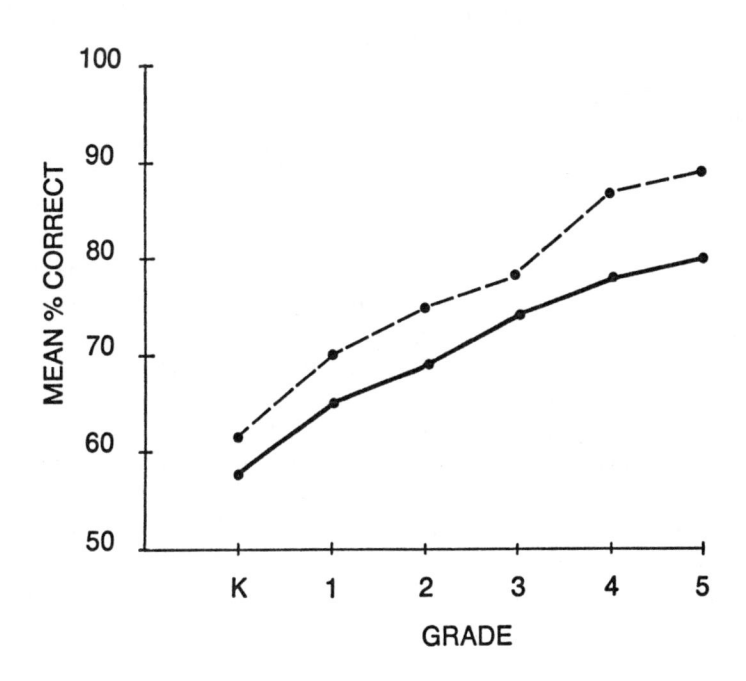

Source: Paris (1975), p. 234.

Mark began to feel pretty tense. He knew there were more, but which ones were from Argentina? He wished he had studied harder. He remembered that oil, coffee, and bananas were on the list, but were they from Argentina?

"Oil?" Mark said tentatively.
"Oil? In Argentina? Come now."
"No, I meant coffee."
"Mark!" The teacher's smile vanished.
"Bananas?"
"It's clear that you didn't learn this, Mark. Who did?"

And so Mark's exchange with the teacher drew to an unsettling conclusion. He did not learn the material thoroughly. Especially when material is not highly meaningful, interference is intensified by inadequate learning. The teacher's assignment did not lack meaning altogether, but Mark would have had considerably less difficulty in remembering the products of Argentina if he had had an integrated conception of Latin American geography and climate, for example. Were his ideas of the relative locations and topography of Argentina, Venezuela, and Brazil clear and sharp, the confusion of Venezuela's oil production and Brazil's rich coffee harvests with the cattle and grain crops of the Argentine might have been avoided.

Mark's approach to the task fits the basic conditions that psychologists have isolated in laboratory studies of interference, often called retroactive inhibition. Suppose you learn a task that can be conveniently separated into stimuli and responses. For instance, a woman visits your school periodically, perhaps to administer tests. You learn that she is Ms. Brown. After you have met her three or four times you find that she has married, and she is now Ms. Jones. Since you do not know her well and you see her infrequently, you may from time to time think of her or even call her Ms. Brown, although you know that her name has changed. In general, when a new response (Ms. Jones) has to be learned for an old stimulus (the person herself), interference is likely to occur.

Laboratory investigations of verbal learning (mostly of lists of nouns and adjectives) revealed regularities in the amount of facilitation and interference in recall as relationships between stimuli and responses are changed along dimensions of similarity. These regularities are of such a dimension that Osgood (1949) was able to summarize the relationships in his transfer and retroaction surface. Osgood hypothesized that maximum facilitation (or positive transfer) results when the new stimuli and responses are identical to the old ones. This, of course, is nothing more than continued practice on the same tasks. Maximum interference occurs when a new and "antagonistic" response is to be learned to an old stimulus, a circumstance illustrated above.

The effects of interpolated activity on people's ability to recall a previously learned task have been systematically investigated in psychology laboratories. Students are required to learn one or more lists of nonsense syllables or words. After learning them, the students study another task. This interpolated activity may not bear any relationship to the first one, or it may be quite similar. Finally, the students attempt to recall the first task. The amount of interference or facilitation generated by a particular type of interpolated activity can be inferred by comparing the recall scores of students who are equal in ability and who learned the same initial task but different interpolated tasks.

Hunter (1964) summarized the results of one early investigation of retroaction which showed that the closer the interpolated activity comes to the original one, short of identity with it, the greater is the amount of interference. Students had learned lists of adjectives. Those who read jokes in the interval were still able to recall 45 percent of the adjectives. Students whose interpolated learning was nonsense syllables or adjectives could recall much less. The poorest recall (only 12 percent) was for students who learned synonyms for the original adjectives. Hunter summarizes three important relationships between interpolated learning and our ability to remember the previous task.

1. The greater the similarity between original and interpolated activities, the greater the interference.
2. Interference is a function of the magnitude of the interpolated learning. When a student is actively involved in learning for an extended period, he or she will experience more interference than if original learning can be followed by rest, a tennis game, or dinner, for example.
3. Interference is diminished if the original task is thoroughly learned.

There has long been a dispute about whether interference only occurs when the learning tasks are such things as nonsense syllables or lists of words, or whether meaningful materials, such as the prose of textbooks or most other materials that are studied in school are also susceptible to it. In recent years there has been vigorous inquiry into this question, and it appears that retroactive inhibition also occurs in the learning of meaningful material when careful control is exercised over relevant variables.

A few studies of interference with meaningful material had appeared in the literature as early as the 1930s and 1940s, but they were scattered and not definitive. In the early 1960s, Slamecka (1959, 1960a, 1960b, 1962; Slamecka & Ceraso, 1960) published several studies in which interference was produced. The material studied was meaningful, but his research procedures precluded his subjects from learning it in a meaningful manner. Words were shown one at a time on a memory drum instead of as complete sentences. Students had to learn the material verbatim, and they were tested on it in that form. We can question whether the procedures used, rather than the meaningful nature of the material, account for the production of interference. Entwistle and Huggins (1964) found retroactive inhibition when engineering students learned topics in circuitry. Experimental students studied voltage principles for 15 minutes, after which they spent another 15 minutes studying current principles. Control students also studied voltage principles for 15 minutes, but they devoted the next 15 minutes to an unrelated task. At the end of that period, all the students took a brief test on voltage. The control group scored significantly higher than the experimental subjects. Since the materials used in this investigation were highly quantitative and involved formulas, it is possible that some subjects learned by rote instead of with meaning. On the other hand, the study was conducted with normal curriculum materials in an ongoing classroom, which argues strongly that retroactive inhibition can be produced in school settings.

Ausubel examined interference and facilitation in school learning in two separate experiments of interest. In the first of these (Ausubel, Robbins, & Blake, 1957), students read a lengthy passage about Buddhism. The next day an interpolated passage was studied; one group read an article that compared Buddhism with Christianity, another read a passage that reviewed Christianity, while still others read the original passage on Buddhism again. The final test, a week later, supported Ausubel's basic hypothesis that, with meaningful or ideational material, retroactive inhibition is a negligible concern. The outcome "suggests that retroactive inhibition is an important determining factor in forgetting only in artificial laboratory situations employing nonsense learning tasks, and is at most a relatively minor variable in the retention of most newly learned school materials" (Ausubel et al., 1957, p. 341).

A later study (Ausubel, Stager, & Gaite, 1968) examined the effects of two variables, interpolated learning and overlearning, on retroaction with school-type learning materials. High school students in this experiment read a passage on Zen Buddhism. Two days later half the students read that passage once more. Two days after that some students studied material on Buddhism in a passage which was different from but related to the original one, while others read a passage about drug use. This latter passage was unrelated to the experimental materials. At the end of a week all the participants answered a multiple-choice test based upon the Zen Buddhism passage. The students who had read that passage twice had the highest scores, thus demonstrating the positive effect of overlearning. The result of major interest, however, is that students who read the related Buddhism passage as an interpolated activity scored better than their control counterparts who studied the unrelated passage about drugs. Thus the effect of reading an interpolated passage of similar but conflicting content with the original learning material was not to produce retroactive inhibition, as interference theory predicts. On the contrary, those students who read the Buddhism article as an interpolated activity experienced retroactive *facilitation*. Ausubel suggests that the facilitative effects may have occurred because students who read the Buddhism passage were able to use it as a vehicle to review and clarify the concepts presented in the Zen passage. Note, though, that in these studies by Ausubel and his associates, facilitation rather than interference was the outcome when the interpolated passage was of similar but conflicting content to the original learning, and when both were ideational, of the type that students encounter daily in the classroom.

Anderson and Myrow (1971) designed a complex experiment using high school students as learners. The investigators' analysis of earlier work (including the papers by Ausubel we have reviewed) led them to suspect that retroactive inhibition may not have been found in those studies because the criterion tests used in them failed to balance and to differentiate items that should facilitate recall from those which should inhibit it or have no particular bearing either way. They wrote two extensive passages concerning two different mythical primitive tribes. For their criterion test, one third of the questions dealt with material that was highly similar between the two passages, another third of the items were based on conflicting material, and the rest of the test inquired into material that was covered by the article on the first primitive tribe, for which there was no counterpart discussion in the second paper. All the students first read the paper about one of the tribes. Some of them subsequently studied the paper that discussed the second tribe. On the criterion test, based upon the first paper, those students retained over 90 percent of what they had learned on the facilitating items, less than 80 percent on the neutral ones, and their retention for the interfering items was about 70 percent. The other students read a neutral passage instead of the paper about the second tribe. These students scored approximately the same on test items of all three types. Anderson and Myrow concluded that their results conformed well with the predictions of interference theory.

In a second study (Myrow & Anderson, 1972) the investigators once again verified the existence of retroactive interference with school-type meaningful materials. Interference occurred when students answered multiple-choice test questions that contained directly competing responses. For example, the two tribes described in the passages both had complex clan systems, one based on occupation and the other on the stars. When students were asked a question about the clan system of one tribe, and the possible answers included the directly competing response about the other tribe, interference occurred. So, in this very explicit case, the paradigm of interference theory was followed, with results consistent with those that are found in the learning laboratory. However, there is also the general expectation that interference occurs in daily life on a nonspecific basis. Hunter suggested the same point when he observed that the more active the individual, the greater the likelihood of interference.

Myrow and Anderson looked explicitly at this issue. One third of their test items and passage content was unrelated from one passage to the other. For example, one tribe lived as foresters, the other as hunters. When students were asked questions about the occupations of the first tribe, after having also read about the second one, there was some decrement in their recall, but the drop was not significant. The point of this study is that, when questions were designed that follow explicitly the demands of interference theory (identical stimuli, competing responses), retroactive interference occurred. But when more ordinary daily life situations were tested (as with the foresters versus hunters) the effects of interference were not significant. It appears, at least from this study, that the constraints necessary to produce retroaction with meaningful school materials are so severe that teachers or textbooks would seldom reproduce them. Myrow and Anderson (1972) conclude that

> Observers of the classroom may wonder how frequently in the "real world" forgetting analogous to retroactive inhibition actually occurs. How often does it happen that preconditions to retroactive interference—similar stimuli paired with different responses—coincidentally appear in ordinary classroom activity? We seldom teach students different answers to the same question. If retroactive interference is generated in prose only when the materials are so closely similar, we must question the efficacy of the interference model as an inclusive explanation of forgetting in the classroom. (p. 308)

The issue of whether school learning suffers interference effects when students learn sequences of related information is not resolved. Ausubel's persistent contention that facilitation rather than interference is to be expected appeals to teachers, for his argument certainly conforms to their daily experience in the classroom. Students know more in June than they did in September. Their scores on standardized achievement tests reflect this, but it is of greater importance to teachers that they can see the progress from their own records. If the increments of improvement are not obvious from day to day, they are surely discriminable between September and Thanksgiving, from January until Easter, and so forth. It is a good deal easier for teachers to feel comfortable with Ausubel's assertion that proactive variables are more significant in school learning than retroactive ones, and that the effects are primarily facilitative rather than inhibitive.

Summary

This chapter has stressed the role of the learner as an active participant in the processes of learning and remembering. The child in school learns principally what he pays attention to, and for that reason teachers want to ensure that they control the learner's attentional process and direct it toward the proper stimuli.

A great advantage accrues to the teacher and to the school because virtually everything students are to learn in the classroom possesses at least a degree of meaning. Most school tasks, of course, are highly meaningful.

The student's cognitive structure provides a framework for the acquisition and incorporation of new meaningful material. Memory is also facilitated by the same active processes as those involved in learning. Information that can be accommodated by the learner's cognitive structure is relatively resistant to forgetting. We have seen that meaningless learning tasks, on the contrary, must be learned by rote, and they are swiftly forgotten. From this it follows that students should avoid treating meaningful material as though it lacked meaning. Even if, in some circumstances, rote learning is faster or easier than meaningful learning, the long-term benefits are minimal. Not only is the material forgotten in large part, but it is of no use to the learner except in the precise form in whch it was learned.

Substantive material, such as that learned in classrooms, is learned better when its organized properties are utilized. Organization includes the hierarchical arrangement of ideas as proposed by Ausubel, among others, and as disclosed in the research of Meyer and McConkie on what people recall from hearing a lecture. The point was also made that learning materials need not always be presented according to such hierarchical arrangements. A variety of approaches is possible as long as account is taken of the underlying structure of the content.

Nothing is less useful than knowledge which the learner has acquired and stored but which he does not know how or when to apply. If meaningful material is learned in a meaningful way, that hazard can be reduced and perhaps eliminated. Meaningful learning implies that the student comprehends relationships between specific learning and broader bodies of content, concepts, and principles. When formulas are learned in the forms and in the contexts of their most likely use by students in mathematics or science, the risk of inert learning is also reduced.

Interference has been portrayed as a principal source of forgetting of school learning. Research has shown that retroactive inhibition can be obtained with classroom tasks when the technical demands of the interference paradigm are adhered to with care. However, the occurrence of the nonspecific interference that we would expect to be the source of most classroom forgetting has turned out to be difficult to demonstrate.

Questions for Review and Discussion

1. The view of learning adopted in this chapter ascribes an important role to attention. What does it mean "to pay attention to" something? Reflect on occasions when you have paid careful attention to an event.

Compare that with what happens when you try to recall something you did not attend to very well.

2. Much was written in Chapter 2 about the meaningful nature of school learning. Identify four or five topics in a field that you teach or that you are studying which are highly meaningful. Why are they meaningful? Make an analysis for one of them similar to the text analysis of "territoriality."

3. We saw that nonsense material is quickly forgotten, and we made the point that meaningful material should not be treated as if it did not possess meaning. Have you ever learned meaningful material by rote? Multiplication facts are a good case in point. Why aren't they easily forgotten?

4. The theory of remembering we have discussed (à la Bartlett) stresses the active construction of the learner in what he recalls. What does such a position do to the idea that what each person remembers about an episode is an accurate "photographic" image of what transpired? Have several friends or colleagues reproduce "The War of the Ghosts" or "Portrait d'Homme." What happens?

5. Recall an event or two from your learning when you have experienced interference. What were the circumstances that surrounded the events? Identify one or two kinds of content in your field that seem to be sources of interference. Devise a way to teach them so as to reduce or avoid interference on the part of the learner.

Readings for Further Reflection

Learning and memory are both fields of such active research and theory development at this time that it is difficult to identify only a small number of books that reflect the scope of either topic. However, the following sources should have something to say to interested teachers.

Introductory level

Almost every introductory textbook in general psychology and educational psychology contains chapters on learning and memory. Two books in educational psychology that propose explicit ways of looking at classroom learning are:

Ausubel, David P. *Educational Psychology: A Cognitive View.* New York: Holt, Rinehart, & Winston, 1968.

Gagné, Robert M. *The Conditions of Learning* (2nd ed.). New York: Holt, Rinehart, & Winston, 1970.

An excellent general review of research and interpretation in the field of memory is to be found in:

Hunter, Ian M.C. *Memory.* Baltimore: Penguin Books, 1964.

Advanced level

For the reader who wishes to obtain a more intensive, critical view of psychological theories of learning, the classic book is:

Hilgard, Ernest R., and Bower, Gordon H. *Theories of Learning* (4th ed.). Englewood Cliffs, N. J.: Prentice-Hall, Inc., 1975.

This book reviews the ideas and experiments of major learning theorists from Ivan Pavlov and Edward L. Thorndike forward. It is helpful to teachers because it selects and organizes studies that are often widely scattered and inaccessible. The authors interpret the research and assess each theory for its power and productivity. The latest edition includes a chapter on the work of Piaget, and there is extensive discussion of the educational implications of theory and research in learning.

Bartlett, Frederick. *Remembering.* Cambridge: Cambridge University Press, 1932.

This book is a classic of a different kind. It is specialized, presenting as it does the numerous and detailed research studies of its author. However, the book is unusually readable, and the accounts are notable for their interest rather than their technicality. Almost half a century after its publication, this book is still frequently cited by investigators of memory for its fundamental ideas about the constructive role of the individual in shaping his memory. Bartlett is well worth reading for his timeliness and not just as an old standard that one ought to know.

Among other more advanced books, you might consult the following:

Adams, J. A. *Human Memory.* New York: McGraw-Hill, 1967.

Paivio, Allan. *Imagery and Verbal Processes.* New York: Holt, Rinehart, & Winston, 1971.

References

Anderson, Richard C. How to construct achievement tests to assess comprehension. *Review of Educational Research,* 1972, *42,* 145–170.

Anderson, Richard C., & Myrow, David L. Retroactive inhibition of meaningful discourse. *Journal of Educational Psychology*, 1971, *62*, 81–94.

Ausubel, David P. *Educational psychology: A cognitive view.* New York: Holt, Rinehart, & Winston, 1968.

Ausubel, David P., Robbins, Lillian C., & Blake, E., Jr. Retroactive inhibition and facilitation in the learning of school materials. *Journal of Educational Psychology*, 1957, *48*, 334–343.

Ausubel, David P., Stager, Mary, & Gaite, A. J. H. Retroactive facilitation in meaningful verbal learning. *Journal of Educational Psychology*, 1968, *59*, 250–255.

Bartlett, Frederick. *Remembering.* Cambridge: Cambridge University Press, 1932.

Bousfield, W. A. The occurrence of clustering in the recall of randomly arranged associates. *Journal of General Psychology*, 1953, *49*, 229–240.

Bower, Gordon H. How to remember. *Psychology Today*, 1973, *7*, 62–70.

Bower, Gordon H., Clark, Michael C., Lesgold, Alan M., & Winzenz, David. Hierarchical retrieval schemes in recall of categorized word lists. *Journal of Verbal Learning and Verbal Behavior*, 1969, *8*, 323–343.

Bransford, John D., & Franks, Jeffrey J. The abstraction of linguistic ideas. *Cognitive Psychology*, 1971, *2*, 331–350.

Briggs, Leslie J., & Reed, Homer B. The curve of retention of substance material. *Journal of Experimental Psychology*, 1943, *32*, 513–517.

Bruner, Jerome S., Goodnow, Jacqueline, & Austin, George A. *A study of thinking.* New York: John Wiley & Sons, 1956.

Carmichael, Leonard, Hogan, H. P., & Walter, A. A. An experimental study of the effect of language on the reproduction of visually perceived form. *Journal of Experimental Psychology*, 1932, *15*, 73–86.

Ebbinghaus, Hermann. *Memory: A contribution to experimental psychology* (Henry A. Roger & Clara E. Bussevius, trans.). New York: Dover Publications, 1964. (Originally published, 1885)

Entwistle, Doris R., & Huggins, W. H. Interference in meaningful learning. *Journal of Educational Psychology*, 1964, *55*, 75–78.

Hunter, Ian M. L. *Memory.* (Rev. Ed.) Baltimore: Penguin Books, 1964.

James, William. *Talks to teachers and students.* New York: Holt, 1900.

Katona, George A. *Organizing and memorizing.* New York: Columbia University Press, 1940.

Mandler, George. Organization and memory. In K. W. Spence & J. T.

Spence (Eds.), *The psychology of learning and motivation* (Vol. I, pp. 327-372). New York: Academic Press, 1967.
Mathews, Ravenna. Recall as a function of number of classificatory categories. *Journal of Experimental Psychology*, 1954, *47*, 241-247.
Meyer, Bonnie J. F., & McConkie, George W. What is recalled after hearing a passage? *Journal of Educational Psychology*, 1973, *65*, 109-117.
Miller, George A. The magical number seven, plus or minus two: Some limits on our capacity for processing information. *Psychological Review*, 1956, *63*, 81-96.
Myrow, David L. & Anderson, Richard C. Retroactive inhibition of prose as a function of the type of test. *Journal of Educational Psychology*, 1972, *63*, 303-308.
Osgood, Charles E. The similarity paradox in human learning: A resolution. *Psychological Review*, 1949, *56*, 132-143.
Paris, Scott G. Integration and influence in children's comprehension and memory. In Frank Restle et al. (Eds.), *Cognitive theory* (Vol. 1, pp. 223-246). Hillsdale, N.J.: Lawrence Erlbaum Associates, 1975.
Slamecka, N. J. Studies of retention of connected discourse. *American Journal of Psychology*, 1959, *72*, 409-416.
Slamecka, N. J. Retroactive inhibition of connected discourse as a function of practice level. *Journal of Experimental Psychology*, 1960, *59*, 104-108. (a)
Slamecka, N. J. Retroactive inhibition of connected discourse as a function of similarity of topic. *Journal of Experimental Psychology*, 1960, *60*, 245-249. (b)
Slamecka, N. J. Retention of connected discourse as a function of duration of interpolated learning. *Journal of Experimental Psychology*, 1962, *62*, 480-486.
Slamecka, N. J., & Ceraso, J. Retroactive and proactive inhibition of verbal learning. *Psychological Bulletin*, 1960, *57*, 449-475.
Taba, Hilda. *Teaching strategic and cognitive functioning in elementary school children.* San Francisco: San Francisco State College, 1966.

Chapter 3

The Improvement of Learning in School Settings

The use of the word *improvement* can create mischief, for it implies both that there is a deficiency in the current state of affairs and that a program of known dimensions exists to rectify the present inadequacy. Although the claims on both of those scores are tenuous, a case can be made for considering the improvement of school learning. Whereas the goals of the preceding chapter were to identify and to elaborate the variables and processes involved in pupils' acquisition and retention of information, our concern in this chapter is with ways of modifying and manipulating relevant variables for the purpose of improving classroom learning. There are five principal issues under consideration.

1. Can introductory material be constructed to improve learning by providing clear and structured organization for the learner?

2. How can questions be used to control students' attention, thus increasing the chances that they pay attention to the right things and engage in those cognitive behaviors that are important for learning to occur?

3. Can questions be used to heighten learners' motivation for a task, for example, by arousing his curiosity about what he is to learn?

4. How can pictures and other graphic material improve learners' comprehension of ideas?

5. How much practice is necessary or useful with meaningful material? How should reviews and drills be spaced?

This chapter has two major sections. The first, and much the longer of the two, concentrates upon the modification of instructional materials or teaching procedures to improve student learning. This section is further divided into four related subsections, corresponding to the first four questions above. The second main section reviews the effects of practice on learning and retention. A third section, entitled "Potpourri," provides a brief discussion of the possible uses of overlearning and mnemonics, both of which may play small but definite parts in the improvement of learning.

Two different but not conflicting ideas carry the conceptual burden of the chapter. One of these is an extension of the principles of organization in learning delineated in Chapter 2. The other is the idea that people learn what they attend to in the environment, and procedures for improving learning must therefore try to ensure that the learner attends to the relevant and significant aspects of the learning task.

Improving Learning by Modifying Materials and Methods

Orienting the learner

In Chapter 2, great emphasis was placed on the role of selective attention in the learning process. Little learning will occur if the learner does not attend to the lesson, but it is also important that she or he pay attention to the right things. If the teacher or the teaching material can assist the learner in knowing what should be attended to, the process can be somewhat expedited. Most teachers recognize the appropriateness and importance of introducing learners to new ideas or content in a systematic way. To launch into the middle of a new topic, such as the political system of the Soviet Union, without laying some groundwork first would be foolish. Students become confused and unclear about what they are to learn. In the final analysis, their learning is bound to be harmed by such a procedure. Flanders (1965) has shown that teachers obtain better learning in arithmetic and social studies if they are indirect in their influence in the early stages of learning, when the goals of learning and the means for achieving them are not yet settled. The teacher is indirect when she encourages students to ask questions and helps them extend and clarify their ideas. Direct influence consists of the teacher presenting information to the students, as in a lecture, or providing explicit direction about how tasks are to be performed. Direct influence plays an important role in the learning process once the student has a clear conception of what he is trying to do, or of what he is supposed to learn from a particular block of subject matter.

How can the teacher orient students toward what they are to learn? Hartley and Davies (1976) suggested several classes of procedures, which with some modifications, have been followed here. In general, the purpose of orientation is to alert the learner to what is coming and perhaps to explain to him or her what is to be learned from the task. One way to do this is to provide the learner with *objectives*. Recently there has been great emphasis upon the statement of behavioral objectives which specify precisely the performance of which the learner is to be capable after instruction. As a steady diet, behavioral objectives are tasteless and hard to swallow. Well-constructed objectives are often more general and comprehensive. What is important is that the learner knows where his effort and attention are to be focused. If graphs or figures in a textbook are to be studied, toward what end should effort be directed? Perhaps the teacher wishes students to observe trends in American industrial production over the decades from 1900 to 1970. If the learner knows that this is the goal, he can pay attention to a definite learning task instead of dissipating his effort by aimlessly staring at a set of graphs.

A recent study illustrates the broader point. Rothkopf and Kaplan (1972) examined the effects on high school students' learning of text material brought about by variations in the density and specificity of instructional objectives. Density refers to the number of objectives per page of text. As density increases, the probability that any particular objective will be met decreases. Specific objectives were relevant to one sentence in the text, but general objectives were relevant to several. Here is an example from their study of one general objective, followed by three specific ones based upon the same content.

> *General objective:* Learn about the physical appearance of three kinds of type faces discussed!
> *Specific objectives:*
> 1. Learn about the physical appearance of Gothic type!
> 2. Learn about the physical appearance of Italic Type!
> 3. Learn about the physical appearance of Roman type! (Rothkopf and Kaplan, 1972, p. 296)

Learning was better for the students whose reading was guided by specific objectives. However, a more impressive finding resulted from a simple variation in experimental procedure. In addition to groups of students who were given either specific or general objectives, another group was given the Conventional Learning Direction—that is, the students were simply told to "learn everything." These students learned far less than the groups that received either specific or general objectives. Teachers often make assignments that are very close to Rothkopf and Kaplan's "learn everything" direction. When the teacher says, "Take the next ten pages for tomorrow, " or "Continue reading the section in the text on the Industrial Revolution," the parallel seems quite close. With all qualifiers and disclaimers aside, teachers probably can facilitate their students' acquisition of knowledge if they specify assignments with some care, taking special pains to clarify what the student should learn as a result of his study.

Pretests are another form of introduction that can be useful. A pretest can help students see where their weaknesses or gaps in knowledge lie. Of course, a pretest is of little use if students possess no background in an area.

Perhaps the orienting technique that comes most naturally to teachers (and to textbook writers) is the *overview*. For all practical purposes an overview is a summary that is presented before a lesson or block of content is studied rather than afterward. Overviews stress the major ideas and central themes or arguments that are to be learned. We tend to eliminate trivial or highly specific details from an overview in favor of getting to the heart of the matter. The language of an overview is ordinarily the same as that used in the lesson itself. No effort is made to present it at a higher level of abstraction or in language that is more general than the detailed material to follow. Overviews are usually verbal, and they may appear as informal introductions to a topic by the teacher, or as a paragraph or two in the textbook which introduces a new chapter or unit of instruction. There is no reason that overviews must be exclusively verbal, or even that they appear as passages of connected discourse. They may also be outlines, and graphic or pictorial material could in some cases be part of an overview.

Of the studies that have been done on overviews, many were investigations of adjunct materials used with instructional films. Little is known about how teachers use overviews or what their effects are. Although most of the studies have shown positive effects on student learning and retention, it is possible that those benefits could accrue through simple alternatives. For example, Hartley and Davies (1976) cite an early study in which the investigators used overviews with a filmstrip in one condition but showed the filmstrip a second time to learners in another group. The second viewing cost no additional time (beyond what was needed to present the overviews and the filmstrip) and yielded the same results. In short, we know less about the role of overviews on learning than we should, but they do seem to be useful for pupil learning and retention. Furthermore, teachers seem naturally to build something akin to overviews into their language in the classroom. Bellack (1966) discovered that teachers structure new content in their discourse. The high school teachers studied by Bellack used almost 8 percent of their language to structure the material to be discussed. This is not to say that structuring and overviews are identical, but that overviews may rather easily be generated by teachers, and if they are an effective device for the improvement of students' learning and retention, then the effort the average teacher may invest in expanding structuring into more systematic overviews of new content may be very productive.

Another type of orienting procedure is the *advance organizer.* The idea of an advance organizer, unlike the overview, grew out of a clear and systematic theory of meaningful learning. Ausubel (1960, 1963) argued that the learning of bodies of knowledge, such as those that are characteristic of school subjects, begins with the most general, abstract, and comprehensive propositions that represent the fundamentals of a discipline. Only as the student begins to develop this broad comprehension of the basic ideas of government, chemistry, biology, or history is he capable of understanding and incorporating less general concepts and particular details into his cognitive structure.

Advance organizers serve the purpose of providing a conceptual outline to be filled out by subsequent learning, or they help the learner to differentiate between information that he has learned and new information that is similar to the old and might therefore be confused with it. According to Ausubel's theory of meaningful verbal learning, new information can be retained in cognitive structure only if it is clear to the learner and thoroughly mastered. This includes the ideas that its relationships to other superordinate concepts must also be clear and stable, and the learner must comprehend what is distinctively different about his new learning. Otherwise it will sooner or later lose its discriminability, and the learner will remember only the original idea.

What Is An Advance Organizer? This question will be answered in two ways. First we will consider how advance organizers are to function in facilitating school learning, and then we will analyze the attributes or properties of advance organizers. In this connection an example of an organizer will be given, and how it might be used to facilitate learning will be analyzed.

The function of advance organizers is to provide an ideational scheme or system that the learner can use to assist him or her in the organization of subsequent and detailed learning passages. There are two general types of organizers, which Ausubel has labeled *expository* and *comparative.* When material that is new and completely unfamiliar to the learner is to be studied, an organizer can theoretically function as a facilitator by placing into cognitive structure a general conceptual framework which provides the learner with some benchmarks for classifying incoming information and for making a preliminary differentiation of important and less important information. That is the purpose of an expository organizer. It is probably more often the case, however, especially with more mature students, that some concepts or information about a topic are already known. This prior knowledge may either be directly related to what is subsequently to be learned or it may bear an analogous relationship to it. The function of a comparative organizer is to alert the learner to the basic similarities and differences between the old and the new. By doing that, appropriate discriminations are made available to the learner, who can then classify some elements of the new learning under concepts or rubrics already known to him, while at the same time retaining other information as distinct and separable from existing concepts.

An advance organizer is a statement given to the learner before the task to be studied. Relative to that task, it is much briefer, and it is written at a more general level and at a higher level of abstraction. An effective organizer has a variety of characteristics, some of which, at first glance, appear to conflict with others. For example, although the organizer must be general and abstract, it must also be learnable and written in language that is familiar to those who are to benefit from it. As we shall see when we examine experimental tests of organizers, there is some confusion about how an organizer is to be written, as well as what its functions are. Because the idea of the advance organizer is an important one theoretically, and because it has potential as a practical device to improve students' learning, it is worthwhile to try to identify and clarify the several properties required of an adequate advance organizer:

1. It is relatively brief, and it is written at a more general and abstract level than the learning passage to which it pertains.

2. The language used in the organizer should be familiar to the learner. It should permit him to learn the content of the organizer and to relate it to his existing knowledge.

3. Organizers to be used with children of elementary school age may require specific examples and concrete or diagrammatic models. Such aids are not ordinarily required with older students unless the material to be learned is very remote from anything they already know or extremely difficult.

4. Organizers are probably more effective with learning passages that are factual instead of conceptual. This is true because conceptual material by definition is organized. In general, the less well organized the learning passage, the greater should be the potential benefit to be contributed by the advance organizer.

Organizers Compared with Overviews. Teachers (and some investigators as well) sometimes assume that advance organizers are synonymous with overviews. The latter gives the learner a brief and highly condensed version of what he is about to study, as we have noted. Ausubel has explicitly observed that overviews achieve their effect mainly through repetition and condensation. The level of abstraction is not different in an overview from that of the material it precedes. Furthermore, the overview sets forth the most important terms of the passage to be learned. Although overviews may be beneficial at times, their purpose and structure are different from those of an advance organizer. The organizer, as its name suggests, establishes a scheme which the learner can employ to organize the basic ideas of the material to be learned, thus enhancing its acquisition and retention. It is *not* a brief and condensed form of the learning passage.

An Illustration. Suppose that in their science class, fifth-graders are about to undertake a study of trees. Among the many outcomes for pupils from such a study, let us focus upon their learning of the six major groups or classifications into which trees are placed, and the criteria that are used for assignment to each such class. Trees are designated as broadleaf, needleleaf, palms, cycads, tree fern, and gingko.

What information should be contained in the advance organizer? We might begin with a reference to the concept of classes or groups, recalling some common groups that children know, such as "boys and girls," "fourth-and fifth-graders," "number sets," or the like, and point out that trees, too, are placed into different large groups. The most important element of the organizer would deal with the presence or absence of seeds in the tree and the type of seeds the tree produces, since this is the overriding principle for the classification of trees. A second important point for the organizer to cover is that most trees which are grouped together resemble one another in several respects—they have leaves of similar sizes and shapes, or they grow in similar climates and regions of the world—but there are exceptions to classification on these grounds. For example, some trees look very much like those of one group, but they are classified with another because they have the same type of seeds.

Strictly speaking, we might not include anything of a more concrete or specific nature in the organizer, for we would want to know whether the abstract organization scheme it outlines facilitates children's learning of the more detailed passage. If we insert specific information into the organizer, and subsequently include test items based upon that same information, we would be precluded from attributing a superior outcome to the effect of an organizer, because of the students' additional exposure to the content to be learned.

Let us pursue the present illustration another step. After the children's study of the learning passage, questions could call for the number of broad classes of trees and for the name of each. The organizer as we have outlined it gives no information bearing directly upon those topics, but it does suggest that there are different groups (and presumably that these are to be learned and subsumed under the more general heading of "major groups of trees"). Similarly the organizer does not identify trees that reproduce through seeds as opposed to spores, or which groups are fruit bearing or cone bearing, and so forth.

How Effective Are Advance Organizers? The concept of the advance organizer has generated great research interest since Ausubel's first report of its successful use in 1960. If one considers doctoral dissertations devoted to the idea as well as research studies published in journals, a conservative estimate would be over 100 investigations. The idea is appealing—if students lack background in a field, build ideational scaffolding for them before you try to lay on all the lath and bricks of detailed facts. Furthermore, the organizer arises from one of the most original and detailed theoretical views of classroom learning ever promulgated: Ausubel's theory of meaningful verbal learning. When Ausubel and various of his associates conducted a vigorous program of research on organizers throughout the 1960s, their papers not only tended to demonstrate the success of organizers but also to elucidate the conditions under which they worked well and the types of students and content for which they were useful.

For all these reasons, advance organizers cannot be ignored in our consideration of procedures for orienting learners toward new material. However, there are major limitations and reservations which should be cited, and they unhappily dim the light of what earlier promised to be a remarkably efficacious means to facilitate classroom learning. The bulk of the criticisms can be summarized in two points.

First, there is a lack of direction for the preparation of advance organizers. We are told that organizers should be more abstract, general, and inclusive than the passages they precede, but this is hardly prescriptive. There is little specific information available to guide teachers' writing efforts. Such uncertainty, of course, reduces incentives for producing organizers. I have directed several doctoral dissertations in which one or another dimension of organizers has been studied, but the ambiguity which surrounded the specification of the task made these frustrating and not very definitive ventures. I have also asked teachers enrolled in courses in school learning to develop organizers for use with their own pupils. Although the task is greeted with enthusiasm, most teachers express their disillusionment and disappointment as they try to implement the guidelines for an organizer. These personal experiences are cited only because it is apparent that they are widely shared. Hartley and Davies (1976) lament that "this uncertainty (about constructing organizers) has led at least one researcher to complain, 'If it works, it's an advance organizer; if it doesn't work, it isn't' " (p. 256).

Second, the effectiveness of advance organizers has not consistently been demonstrated. As we indicated earlier, the experiments reported by Ausubel and his associates showed superiority in learning and retention for students who had received advance organizers, compared to control subjects who had only historical introductory material to study. However, studies conducted by other research workers have shown positive results for organizers with less frequency. Hartley and Davies (1976), for example, in summarizing the research history of organizers, indicate that they are effective more often with students in college than with those in the lower schools and that they provide little help for lower ability students, including the educable mentally retarded. Expository organizers appear to be useful with younger or lower ability students. They characterize the accumulated research as "confused." A few months before the Hartley and Davies review was published, one by Barnes and Clawson (1975) appeared that was even more pessimistic about the effectiveness of organizers. In 32 studies of organizers they reviewed, 12 yielded positive results but 20 did not. These two major reviews, plus my own evaluation of most of the same studies, leads to the following position.

The conception of the advance organizer is an excellent one. Ausubel's system is designed primarily to guide learning at the secondary school and college level and *not* at the elementary school level. He recognizes the need for concrete materials and direct manipulation by children below the developmental level of formal operations. For adolescents and adults, manipulation is not only unnecessary but redundant and wasteful. His theoretical scheme that learning progresses from the most abstract and general to the particular is sensible when the developmental constraints are considered. The organizer, as a means of facilitating learning, is, as we have noted before, an attractive conception. Research evidence has sometimes shown positive results for organizers, and these successes are not limited to studies by the "Ausubel group." Misconceptions of organizers by some investigators and serious flaws in the design of other studies have led to some of the negative results.

I do not fully agree with the gloomy prognosis for organizers laid down by some reviewers. However, the difficulties in providing guidelines for the construction of organizers is a serious hindrance to their use, especially if we wish teachers to develop organizers for their own classroom instruction. The lack of specification of how organizers should be developed has probably also contributed to the assortment of equivocal research outcomes. Despite the negative slant to the current interpretations of organizers, it is possible that a new examination will be made of the concept and effort will be directed to clarifying procedures for the development and testing of advance organizers. In short, the idea still seems to have sufficient merit that teachers and researchers alike should resist its abandonment.

How do questions affect students' learning?

It will be no surprise to teachers to be told that they ask many questions in the course of a school day. Questions can be a means to maintain the focus of attention upon the desired content or a way to progress from one aspect of a lesson to another. They can also help to review students' knowledge or provide a challenge to their thinking. Teachers use questions to achieve various ends. Given that fact, however, there may be raised eyebrows when we say that teachers appear to ask about 350 questions or more in a school day—an estimate based on Gall's (1970) review of teachers' practices as question askers. Several other salient facts from this review can be noted. In Gall's words,

> The findings in studies on teachers' questioning practices are fairly consistent. . . . It is reasonable to conclude that in a half century there has been no essential change in the types of questions which teachers emphasize in the classroom. *About 60% of teachers' questions ask students to recall facts; about 20% require students to think; and the remaining 20% are procedural.* (p. 713; Italics added.)

Contemporary research, most of which had its origins in places other than classrooms and therefore was not included in Gall's review, suggests two major new ways in which teachers can use questions. One variation is to intersperse one or more questions into text material on a systematic and frequent basis. In this method the questions should be based upon content that the learner has just read; that is, they should follow rather than precede his studying. When questions are employed in this manner, they have been found to assert control over the inspection of study activities of the learner. They may extend the amount of time spent in reading as well as expand the student's attention to what is read, more than if the same questions are encountered immediately before a study period.

The second variation (surely known to teachers, but not widely or effectively practiced) is to use questions in advance of study to heighten students' interest; in short, to spur the learner's curiosity about what is to come. Simply put, a good, intriguing question is hypothesized to broaden the learner's attention to, and the depth of processing he imposes upon, the material that follows. As we shall see, the term *question* in this sense need not always be in the form of a verbal interrogation but may take on other shapes as well.

One of the more anxiety-provoking experiences for a public speaker is to discover midway through his talk that his audience has become restless. People begin to look around, to converse with one another, and signs of boredom prevail. There is little chance that the speaker will communicate with the audience because its members are not listening; they have ceased to pay attention. Teachers, too, sometimes observe inattention on the part of pupils, and they realize, or ought to realize, that under that circumstance little learning is going to occur. Something must be changed to focus the students' attention once again upon the material to be learned.

On occasion teachers direct pupils' attention by giving them questions to answer. The pupil keeps these questions more or less in mind as the lesson progresses, paying attention particularly to those parts of it that help him to formulate answers. Let us analyze the events involved in this sequence. We shall suppose that pupils are to read an assignment that is several pages in length. The teacher wants their attention maintained throughout the task, on the assumption that learning will not occur without it. Questions are constructed (perhaps spaced so the answer to each one is on a different page of the text) for the pupils to answer as they read. The teacher may then believe that the pupil has learned what is contained in those pages. Is that what really happens? Anderson (1970) suggests that an effective strategy is to assume that the learner will do only those things that the teacher's instructions compel him to do. Will the desired learning occur under these circumstances?

First let us think of attending as a behavior or a response that the learner emits. The amount of attending or inspecting that occurs dependably is controlled by whatever the learner requires to answer questions. For example, Anderson found with programmed instruction that students learned less when the required responses in the material were underlined, presumably because students had to engage in minimal inspection and cognitive processing to locate the required material. Similarly Frase (1968a) discovered that learners fail to make crucial associations between stimuli (questions) and responses (answers) in reading. Thus, a question might ask, "What year was John born?" The learner scans the experimental text until he sees, "John was born in 1927." But his response is only "1927"; he does not connect it with the question. The work of both Anderson and Frase stresses the need to control the learner's inspection of material thoroughly enough that he processes the information that will later be required of him. If the processing is in a form that corresponds to what he will subsequently be asked to do with the information, that is all to the good. One solution to this problem is to give students more general questions which force attention to larger segments of content. However, if the questions are too general, the learner's attending behavior may be extinguished for lack of reinforcement.

Rothkopf (1965) coined the term *mathemagenic* behavior to describe the learner's inspection of written material. His phrase means behaviors that "give birth to new learning." Thus it is not restricted conceptually to the use of questions, although the experiments that have been conducted examine the role of questions in siring new learning. Rothkopf speaks of testlike events and adjunct materials to signify that his theoretical goals are much broader than demonstrating relationships between questions and reading comprehension. (For example, see Rothkopf, 1970.) For our purposes, however, that is an issue of great import, and we will not pursue all the theoretical ramifications. The learner's inspection behavior includes what the learner pays attention to, for how long, and at what level he processes it. We have identified these variables as significant for classroom learning. Since questions are a widely used technique to stimulate learning, they represent a practical means of trying to control study behavior.

Rothkopf makes an important distinction between *question-related learning* and *incidental learning*. The former refers to the learning of content that is covered by questions asked while the learner is reading; the latter to information that is not touched upon by the inserted or adjunct questions. The interest of these research workers lies primarily in finding and understanding the variables that influence incidental learning. Since 1965 several basic facts about how questions can be employed in conjunction with written instructional materials have been learned. It should be understood, however, that most of the investigations from which those facts have been induced imposed certain artificial restrictions upon how learners could handle their assignments. Once a learner had read a page of text material, he was not permitted to review it. That condition, of course, would not normally be imposed upon learners in typical classrooms. Also, the learners are not told whether their answers to questions are right or wrong.

One thing that has been learned is that students score better on tests given at the end of a reading assignment if they have been asked questions as they go along, compared with other students who have simply read the passages with no questions to answer. This probably happens because any question has a certain stimulating or incentive value, and also because the questions tell the learner something about what he should try to learn. The practical implications of this outcome are clear, and they also seem quite important.

In most cases, the questions have resulted in better learning if they are inserted immediately after passages that have been read, rather than before them. Questions that come before a learning passage tend to focus the learner's attention upon specific sections of the text. It has sometimes been found that questions before reading result in less incidental learning than is acquired by control subjects who have no questions at all. (For example, Rothkopf, 1966; Rothkopf and Bisbicos, 1967; Frase, 1967, 1968c, as well as others.)

Why should questions placed after text result in superior learning? We have already seen that questions given before learning are likely to narrow and limit the learner's attention. Let us attempt a similar analysis for questions that follow reading. Frase (1967) argues that questions which follow a reading passage provide a general test-taking orientation for the material that follows them. In other words, they do not initiate review behavior of the passage they follow. The function of the questions is altered to widen and extend the reader's surveillance of material in the yet-to-be-read portion of the assignment.

Frase (1968a) explored the role of questions following text, observing whether students perform increasingly better through the various sections of a reading passage. If they do, that would be evidence that a skill of reading or processing is developing as a result of the questions. However, the postquestion effect was apparent from the beginning, and it did not change appreciably over the course of the 20 paragraphs read. Frase concludes that the use of "post questions confirms and maintains the use of certain reading skills which are already in the repertoire of student responses. These skills do not show significant changes over reading passages of 2,000 words" (p. 188). Another way to express this idea is that the questions appearing at the ends of paragraphs serve as signals or cues to the reader for him to pay attention. The "attention-paying response" does not have to be developed because it is already under the learner's control. The response occurs under appropriate conditions, such as when questions follow instead of precede reading material. The available research does not specify what is involved in these behaviors nor how or when they develop. Research along similar lines with younger students, perhaps even in the primary grades, seems badly needed so that we can improve our understanding of the processes involved.

Frequency of Questions. How often should the learner encounter questions in his reading? Frase has found that the variable of frequency, or pacing, makes a difference in how well the students learn. In one study which may be used to illustrate the point, Frase (1968c) wrote a series of questions that were read by college students either before or after every 10, 20, 40, or 50 sentences of an introductory psychology book. All students encountered the same questions. Some students saw one every 10 sentences; others were given five questions for each 50 sentences as a block. Results for incidental learning showed that there was little difference between the before-and-after placement of questions if they were separated by 50 sentences. However, a large difference in favor of the postquestion placement occurred when the questions were spaced so that one appeared after each ten sentences. Overall retention for the question after ten sentences was about 40 percent better than that for the question before each 10 sentences.

Questions Asked by the Teacher. At least one investigation has been reported in which the effects were assessed of questions asked by a teacher and answered orally by the student. Rothkopf and Bloom (1970) were interested in how interpersonal interaction might be used in a self-instructional library. They invited high school students to read geology text material (about rivers and glaciers, and the geological features produced by both of them) which had been transcribed onto 35 millimeter slides and which the student could advance according to his own reading rate. The geology text appeared on 108 slides. All the students read the first 24 slides at their own rate. After that, students were subjected to one of three conditions. One third of them simply continued as before, reading the content without interruption. The other two thirds of the students were asked a question after each six slides, the question being based upon some informational point covered in the preceding six slides. The difference was that half those students encountered the question in printed form, and the other half were asked it individually by a young woman cast in the role of the teacher. The results are enlightening. Compared to the control students, those who answered questions made higher test scores. However, the students who were asked questions by the "teacher" and who provided their answers to her made scores still higher than the students who answered written questions.

Question Types. We have said little about the questions used in these studies. They appear to have been factual, testing readers' memory of the content. Watts and Anderson (1971) have shown that questions which are interspersed in reading passages and which require students to apply what they have read lead to superior results. They think this may be because the application forces readers to process the content more deeply, thus bettering their opportunity to comprehend and remember it. This experiment was conducted with high school students who read a series of paragraphs about five psychological concepts. These were followed by questions of a multiple-choice nature that could be answered by identifying an example exactly as it appeared in the text, or a new example that illustrated the concept, or by selecting the name of the psychologist closely associated with the concept. Any given student encountered one of these types of questions throughout the reading. There was also a control group who simply read the learning material. Afterward all the students took a test composed of all the earlier mentioned items. The best scores were earned by students who had practiced selecting new examples of the concept. They were followed by those who identified reproductions from the text. Even control students surpassed those who had selected the names of appropriate scientists.

These authors also examined the issue of how postquestions affect learning. If their influence is a forward one, as Rothkopf and Frase have suggested, one might expect to find that learners do progressively better in answering questions through the learning passage. The results show that no such increment occurs. Although Watts and Anderson did not have the data in this study that would be required to show it, they are disposed to believe that the application questions led to a review process of the material just read.

On balance, the evidence is strong that the regular and frequent use of questions in reading material improves students' mastery of the content. This is especially true when questions follow rather than precede the content to which they pertain. The effects are more dependable for retention (that is, answering questions on a posttest that were used as guides in the reading) than for incidental learning, although in some studies postquestions have also been found to facilitate incidental learning. Whether the postquestions function to shape the inspection behavior of readers for what follows, or whether they initiate a review process, is unsettled. It seems evident, though, that questions coming after reading encourage broader inspection of the content than when they precede study passages. Questions that call for application demand more thorough processing than simple recognition problems. That effect, of course, may not be limited to application questions per se but may occur whenever the questions instruct students to transform content from the printed page in order to answer the questions.

Classroom Application. How can teachers make use of the findings pertaining to adjunct questions? It is hard to be exact about this, but the following speculations probably do not depart far from the supporting evidence.

First of all, the teacher should note that simply using a set of questions with material to be read has important consequences for learning. This does not mean that the quality of the questions is a trivial consideration. They must be clear, and they should be related to the content under study. There is a parallel to the earlier observation that objectives have an orienting and alerting function for students. Most of the studies that have examined the role of adjunct questions have employed questions about specific facts and information in reading passages. The teacher should not have much difficulty in emulating that practice.

On occasion investigators have tried to write questions at a level that requires explicit kinds of cognitive operations. The study by Watts and Anderson was used to illustrate the point. It is more difficult for the teacher to prepare questions which involve application of principles or which lead to specific kinds of problem solving. However, as the earlier citation of Gall's review suggested, in teachers' questions there is a disproportionate emphasis upon specific information and facts. Efforts directed toward producing higher order questions seem especially desirable.

Where should the questions be located? The research evidence seems quite clear that better incidental learning, and overall retention as well, results when the questions are interspersed in reading material and are based upon the preceding rather than the following segments of it. The frequency with which questions should be encountered is a matter that the teacher may wish to give some thought. The rule of thumb seems to be that if questions come in smaller numbers but often, the results are better than if they are spread out (as in Frase's study cited above). On the other hand, Rothkopf and Bloom interjected a question only at the end of every six slides. This was constant across both conditions, of course, and it is not possible to determine how many sentences intervened between questions, but it must have been rather a large number. As a matter of classroom practice, it might be advisable to try using a question with every page or two of text material, depending upon its length and complexity. Modifications can be made as the teacher observes the consequences.

Does it matter whether the teacher writes questions to be answered after a specific amount of reading, or whether she or he asks the questions of students? Given the positive finding by Rothkopf and Bloom that interpersonal interaction facilitates high school students' study of text material, the temptation is to recommend oral questions be used in preference to written ones. As far as the specific results of that investigation are concerned, the recommendation is reasonable. However, it suffers from the defect we always encounter when procedures that have been tested with individual learners are to be extended to larger groups, such as a class of students. Note that in the Rothkopf and Bloom experiment, the "teacher" delivered each question individually to each student at the time the sixth slide had been completed. There are several unknowns. Does the obtained outcome depend upon exact timing between the completion of reading and presentation of the question? How important is the one-to-one contact of teacher with student? If the teacher attempted to present questions orally, for example, to a small group of students matched for their speed of reading, would the effect still occur? Furthermore, perhaps the contact itself between the teacher and the individual student is important. Were a general encouraging comment or simple direction to "read carefully" substituted for the question, would it make a difference? My guess is that the teacher can obtain quite good results by giving questions orally to each student as she or he finishes a predetermined amount of reading. A simple signal system ("Raise your hand when you get to the bottom of page 5") would probably be adequate.

In short, the use of adjunct questions in the classroom, either written or oral, should pose no insuperable difficulty for the teacher. They must, of course, be developed, but as we have suggested, that can be done directly from the text material itself. One of the beauties of this technique is that it can be used with many different types of existing text material. The teacher is not burdened with writing new materials or with large-scale alterations to what is already available in the classroom. The only modification required is the questions themselves.

Questions as arousers of curiosity

Not long ago the world became aware of the extraordinary longevity of certain citizens of the Soviet Union who live in remote reaches of that vast land. The headlines of feature newspaper articles read, "Why Has She Lived to 135?" and showed a picture of a grizzled but smiling great grandmother, a cigarette dangling from her ancient lips. The invitation to read about this woman and her compatriots was very appealing. Advertisers understand that questions can arouse curiosity which leads to reading their advertisements, and, they hope, to people purchasing their clients' products. So they ask questions such as, "Why don't people listen when you talk?", or "Does she—or doesn't she?" The implication is clear that we can learn the answers by reading the rest of the ad.

A theory of epistemic (knowledge-based) curiosity was propounded some years ago by Berlyne (1960). Arousal stems from a state of conceptual conflict. One's attention is mobilized to reduce that conflict, which means that the individual will observe the phenomena responsible for the conflict until he is able to understand and reconcile events to his satisfaction. Questions are one means to arouse the learner's curiosity. Although any question may produce some arousal, questions differ in their arousal value.

We shall pursue the issue of questions and arousal, but first let us examine a study by Levonian (1967) which analyzed the relationship between arousal and learning. Levonian took continuous readings of the skin resistance of 83 high school students as they watched a ten-minute film on traffic safety called *Seat Belt for Susie*. We are not given much detail about the film, but it appears to have several exciting sequences, at least one carnival sequence, and one auto collision sequence. (This is important because arousal seems to depend upon fairly intense stimulation. In a study to be reviewed shortly, the questions employed may not have had the arousal value they were intended to possess.) Levonian constructed a 15-item recognition test of events that occurred within a four-second interval of the film. Those students who had experienced an *increment* in arousal during the minute of which the four-second interval was the midpoint scored significantly higher than those who did not have a rise in their arousal level. These results were the reverse of the immediate recognition test. What the event was that mediated arousal did not matter. Levonian says that arousal is emotion dependent. The learner could be aroused by fear or joy, and the consequences for learning would be no different. (This should probably be modified to some intermediate range of intensity. Strong drives have the effect of restricting individuals' ability to respond to the environment.)

Levonian was quite concerned to speak to teachers about the meaning of his study. He stresses two points in particular. One is that the teacher should provide learners with the most critical information at the time of maximum arousal. The other point is that students are not all aroused by the same stimuli. This fact imposes a severe limitation upon trying to match arousal and learning in group instruction. A compromise procedure would involve identifying groups for instruction that are homogeneous with respect to conditions for arousal. Finally, as we observed above, short-term retention may not show the same relationship with arousal as long-term retention, which is ordinarily of more importance in school learning.

Bull (1973) observed that research on mathemagenic behavior, with its stress on questions that follow reading tasks, has overlooked the possibilities for improved learning offered by questions of high arousal potential. She says, following Levonian, that low arousal questions facilitate immediate retention, and high arousal questions facilitate long-term retention. As we said earlier, the questions used in mathemagenic research (with exceptions, such as the Watts and Anderson study) have been factual, and probably would have low arousal value. Bull indicates that questions with high arousal potential cause conceptual conflict. Thus to ask readers, "What do ants grow in their underground farms?" should have the effect, since it confronts them with incompatible and unusual ideas: "Ants as farmers?" "Farms that are underground?"

Bull and Dizney (1973) set out to test the idea explained above. College students read a 19-paragraph passage based on a paper by Mead. Besides a control group that was instructed to read carefully, subjects saw either questions of high arousal potential or low arousal potential in groups of four or five questions that appeared before each block of six or seven paragraphs. One week later all the students answered a 28-item multiple-choice test. Questions of both kinds covered the same content but were intended to vary in the degree to which they would arouse readers' curiosity. An example of a high-arousal question is, "If teachers are generally viewed as middle class, why was it the Balinese of high caste who sent their daughters to be educated?" This is contrasted with a low-arousal question such as, "Why did the Balinese send their daughters to be educated?" It was imperative that the questions in this study function as they were intended to, that is, as questions of low or high arousal. Subjective judgments of this, of course, would not suffice, so Bull and Dizney recruited other students to read each question and rate it on a five-point scale of interest. They had hoped to have 19 questions of each type, one for each paragraph in the learning task, but they were able to produce only 14 pairs of questions that were separated by as much as 0.40 on the rating scale. The equivocal results of this experiment may have as much to do with the minimal difference between levels of the independent variables as with the underlying theory.

Retention test scores were analyzed for relevant and incidental learning. Students learned more of the question-related content than of the incidental material. However, when the treatments were compared, no significant difference in their effect was seen. Bull and Dizney then used another procedure to compare pairs of treatments (that is, scores of the high-arousal question group were compared with those of the control subjects, and so forth). These analyses showed that students who had read the high-arousal questions scored significantly higher than the control students, but those with the low-arousal questions did not score significantly higher than the controls. However, there was no significant difference between the students in the high-arousal and those in the low-arousal groups. The high-arousal group made scores that were higher than the others (means were 14.70, 13.57, and 12.67 for high arousal, low arousal, and controls, respectively), but the differences are not significant. Perhaps other questions would have aroused more of the experimental students, or a replication of the study would provide positive results. We cannot safely conclude that questions designed to induce arousal, and coming before a reading passage, reliably improve students' long-term retention.

Another investigation adds an interesting dimension to the topic. Although it deals with different (and simpler) material, its results are germane to the preceding discussion, and they lend indirect evidence to Bull's belief that arousal can facilitate students' incidental learning. Paradowski (1967) used a simple set of materials to test the effects of curiosity arousal on incidental learning. He created two sets of animal pictures, five pictures per set. The novel set contained a picture of one imaginary animal and four rare ones: pichicigo, megatherium, elephant shrew, and hemigale. The common pictures were of a donkey, deer, dog, sheep, and muskrat. College students viewed all the pictures, read accompanying brief texts for each, and then took a test on that content. Later Paradowski gave each student a ten-page booklet which contained a smaller version of the pictured animals. Now the true purpose of the experiment emerged. Students were asked to tell what kind of background (for example, mountains, desert, jungle) and what color border each of the original ten pictures had had. This, of course, was the test of incidental learning. Paradowski found that the observers recalled more of the information about the unusual animals. He also reported that significantly longer periods of time had been devoted to looking at the unusual than at the common animal pictures. Is the effect of the novel or arousing stimulus just to lengthen the time learners will attend to a task, or, as seems more likely, is the explanation more complex? It is Paradowski's contention that interest and curiosity are positive, pleasant states of emotion, and therefore they tend to extend the individual's range of cue utilization. That would account for the greater time interval, since more time would be required to attend to and process the details of a picture, or presumably, of other types of material.

Nunnally (1971) has approached similar issues, but his explanation of why people spend more time looking at a stimulus such as the one on the lefthand side of Figure 3.1 than they do the one on the right is different. He found that adults prefer to look at pleasant rather than unpleasant slides. This finding would agree with Paradowski's interpretation and with the arousal model of Berlyne. However, studies of children's looking behavior have shown that children look longer at either pleasant or unpleasant pictures than they do at neutral ones. The hedonistic explanation that seems to account for adult behavior does not apply well to children in the years of concrete operational thinking.

As a broader explanation of selective visual attention, Nunnally suggests the construct of *information conflict*. In order to survive, animals engage in tropistic behavior of sorting objects into things to eat and those by which they might be eaten. When an object is seen that has conflicting cues, making classification difficult, the animal extends its search behavior. Nunnally hypothesizes that specific visual exploratory behavior is largely determined by information conflict and the motivation associated

84 Learning and Thinking

FIGURE 3.1
Example of a banal stimulus (cow on the right) and a highly incongruous stimulus

Source: Nunnally (1971), p. 73.

with the tropism. This is an interesting idea, and its interest is heightened by Nunnally's willingness to apply it to education.

Nunnally gives several examples of how information conflict can be used to facilitate classroom learning. When children encounter a drawing of a child riding on the back of a lion in a book about jungle animals, their interest is stimulated to read the book in order to find out about the conflicting cues. The same principle applies in an example from a physics text. Information conflict is initiated to stir students' interest and stimulate them to ask questions. "A cannon is so powerful that it can fire a shot all the way around the world and land back at the place of its origin. If that were possible, the ball would land at exactly the same time as one dropped from a man's hands positioned at the same height as the muzzle of the cannon" (Nunnally, 1971, p. 81). In geometry one form that appears to have a smaller area than another can be identified as having actually a larger one. Then the information conflict arises out of a visual perception that gives one message, and a verbal statement that offers a different and contradictory one. Again the result should be extended attention to the discrepancy and heightened receptivity on the part of the learner to resolving the information conflict.

In addition to the series of examples, Nunnally has also provided some suggestions for how information conflict can be used effectively for educational purposes.

1. Information conflict should have direct relevance to the topic under consideration.
2. The materials to which the learner has access, or his own processes of thought, should make it possible to reduce the conflict. Little learning is achieved if the stimulus is on the order of that in Figure 3.1. There is no way for the learner to resolve the conflict it induces.
3. Information conflict should be avoided in connection with highly personal and sensitive matters, such as a child's social acceptability, his health, ability, or personal adjustment. Nunnally believes that information conflict, if induced around such intimate issues, results in anxiety that debilitates the learner instead of having its desired stimulative effect.

Classroom Application. In this section, we have seen that in theory questions that occur before the presentation of new content may have a much more powerful effect on learning than postquestions dealing with mathemagenic behavior, as noted in the preceding section. The effect can be not only on immediate learning, but on retention as well. Whereas questions used to guide study behavior are often fairly routine and basically factual in nature, the questions that teachers compose to arouse curiosity or to induce information conflict have special properties. In addition, good questions for these purposes are not easy to develop. (Remember that *question* in this context may refer to a picture or drawing, film, or other graphic aid. It is not limited to the traditional verbal query.)

The examples of questions Nunnally provided cover a range of subject matters, and they give the teacher some guidance about what might and might not be suitable. Since teachers often spend preparation time in searching for materials, this discussion may help to focus the search. A good question or stimulating drawing, once located, can be used repeatedly with different groups of learners, of course. Also, since relatively few of them are needed, compared with the larger numbers of questions that are used to guide study behavior, the dimensions of the task are less formidable than might otherwise be true. Before the teacher can judge the adequacy of any question, it must be tried out with learners. As we saw in the study of Bull and Dizney, even though their questions were calibrated with care and had been written in accordance with their theory about arousal and curiosity, they were only marginally capable of inducing the level of drive that was predicted.

A final example of a kind of question material available for classroom use is the Inquiry Training Program developed by Suchman (1961). (This program is described in some detail in Chapter 7.) Suchman developed a series of brief, silent films, each of which demonstrates a basic physical principle but in a way designed to arouse children's curiosity. For instance, one film uses a metal ball and ring. The experimenter shows the viewer that the ball will not pass through the ring. Next the ball is held over a bunsen burner. Now it will pass through the ring. It is then doused in what appears to be a beaker of water. Once more the ball fails to pass through the ring. The film fades with the single question, "Why...?"

In this section, many of the illustrations were cast in forms other than strictly verbal material. The next section examines more explicitly the role of pictorial material in classroom learning.

The Use of Pictures to Improve Learners' Comprehension

One of the contributions research makes to our improved understanding of how people live and learn is to disabuse us of beliefs that "everyone knows are true." An example of this kind of contribution is to be seen in research by Dwyer (1967), who observed that pictures are valued for purposes of learning because they are realistic in a way that exposition or even sketches and diagrams are not. This position argues that the learner requires realism when the material to be learned is complex, and his understanding cannot be comprehensive if it is simplified. Dwyer conducted an interesting experiment with a group of college freshmen in which he tried not so much to confirm or to refute that idea in its totality as to assess how several sets of materials that depart increasingly from reality affect what the students learned.

The topic was the physiology of the heart. Students saw a series of slides that differed in their approximations to reality. An "oral" group was given the appropriate names of the various parts of the organ. A second group received that oral information and saw abstract line drawings. Another group observed more detailed, shaded drawings, and a fourth group saw realistic photographs of the parts of the heart being described. (See Figure 3.2 for an example of the material presented to the various

FIGURE 3.2
Examples of materials used in study of realism in media

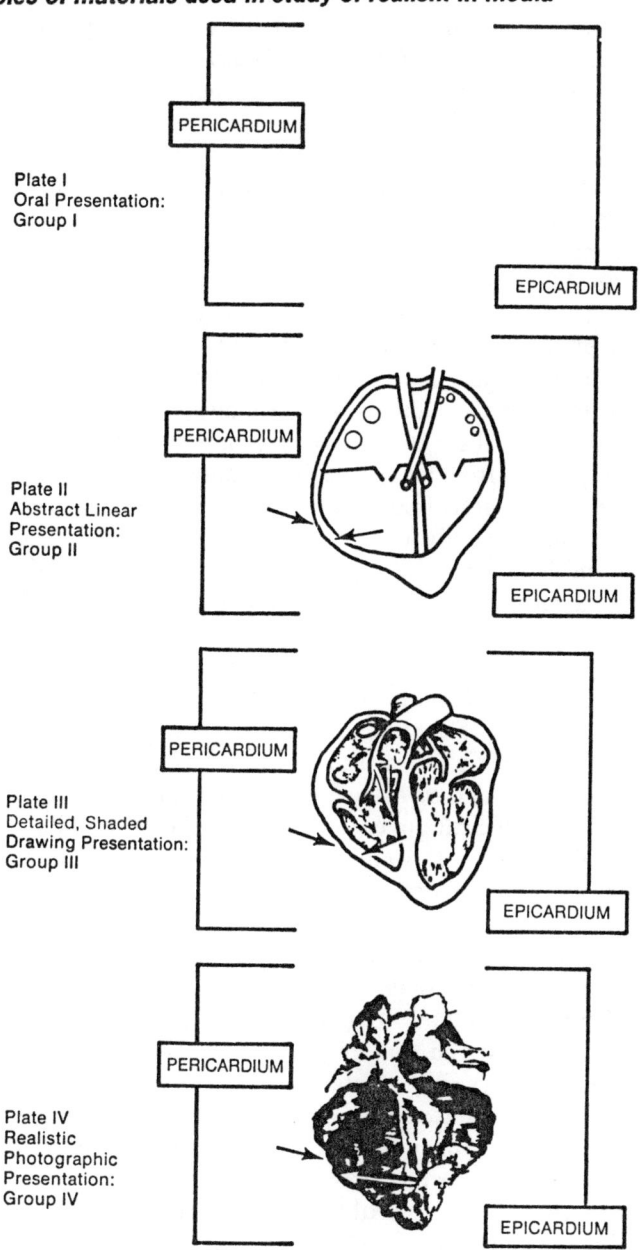

Plate I
Oral Presentation:
Group I

Plate II
Abstract Linear
Presentation:
Group II

Plate III
Detailed, Shaded
Drawing Presentation:
Group III

Plate IV
Realistic
Photographic
Presentation:
Group IV

Source: Dwyer (1967), between pp. 256 and 257.

experimental groups.) Dwyer administered to his learners four tests which differed in the medium in which they had to respond, as well as involving some variation in the content and the cognitive processing required for responding. The tests were (1) Heart Model Test, (2) Drawing Test, (3) Terminology Test, and (4) Comprehension Test. A fifth score was a composite of all scores.

The fundamental question is whether how the groups were instructed made any difference on the tests. The overriding outcome is that the students who saw the most realistic slides, that is, the photographs of the heart, performed the most poorly on the various tests. When each test is considered, the line drawings were never surpassed for their instructional effectiveness, though in some tests they were no better than the more detailed drawings. For the terminology test, only the realistic photographs were inferior to the other procedures. Finally, for the test of comprehension, all the treatment conditions were equally effective. The general finding that the more abstract line drawings of the heart were at least as effective as any others from an instructional standpoint, and in some cases the most effective, suggests that material which is highly realistic for an untutored and intellectually unsophisticated audience may provide too great detail and may render the burden of learning and the differentiation of content more difficult than the novice learner can handle efficiently.

Too pat a parallel is unnecessary, but it may be that the more schematic sketches function for this task much as an advance organizer does for verbal information. The sketches direct the learner's attention to the aspects of the heart he is to learn to recognize. They do not divert him with other detail, nor do they make it difficult for him to discriminate between the precise element to be learned and the surrounding tissue, chambers, and so forth. It would be an interesting extension of the Dwyer study to find whether learners who are initially trained on the more abstract schematic material can transfer knowledge more adequately as learning progresses than those who have dealt with the more realistic materials from the outset. We can think, for example, of medical students, whose ultimate knowledge of the physiology of the heart must be much more detailed and comprehensive than in the level of outcome represented in the Dwyer investigation.

Samuels (1970) conducted a review of research on the role of pictures in the reading process, including their effects on comprehension. The weight of the evidence does not show that pictures enhance a child's comprehension of what he reads. Neither do they, except in a minor way, interfere with the child's comprehension. We need to take into account, though, the kind of content, and therefore the types of pictures under discussion. Samuels's focus is principally upon the process of learning to read. The material in readers, for example, does not tend to be specific or detailed. Thus, drawings or pictures such as those in Dwyer's study are not considered. Nonetheless, Samuels points out that the absence of positive facilitation of pictures is not a sufficient reason to omit them from children's books. They frequently have aesthetic values, and they may also improve the child's attitude toward reading. Vernon (1953, 1954) reported two studies in which she examined the contribution of pictures to students' "understanding and remembering." The first study was conducted with older students, about equivalent in age to students in American secondary schools. Vernon's conclusion in this study, as with the second one using children of 11 and 12, is that the contribution of pictures accompanying informational text passages is minimal. Miller (1938) examined the effect of pictures on the reading of first-, second-, and third-grade children in one midwestern community. His study lasted the length of a school semester. The children all used the same reading series, but half the children in a class had a version with illustrations, and the other half had just the text. There was no evidence at the end of that time that students with the illustrated versions profited either more or less than the others.

Farnham-Diggory (1972) reminds us that children cannot operate with diagrammatic material at a level beyond that of their cognitive development. Adults often commit the error of believing that the child will understand content if it is reduced to a pictorial or graphic form. In the studies by Vernon referred to earlier, graphic material that was intended to help adolescents clarify relationships among sex, age, location, and frequency of tuberculosis confused many of them. The interpretation of graphs necessitates a period of definite instruction for most learners (instruction, incidentally, that few students appear to receive). Farnham-Diggory (1972) suggests the following practical hierarchy for instruction or for self-help when one encounters difficulty in the decoding of graphic material:

> 1. Clarifying the nature of the code—of what symbol stands for what concept.
> 2. Clarifying the nature of the relationships among the symbols—how this is more than that at one point in time, but not at another.
> 3. Clarifying a proper sequence of interpretative steps—what should be looked at first, second.
>
> We must therefore develop a verbal program for threading our way through academic visuals. We must learn to *say* about what we are seeing and in what order to say it. (Farnham-Diggory, 1972, p. 473)

If complex symbolic abstractions such as graphs require specific instruction in order to be comprehended, is this also necessary for us to understand pictures? Kennedy (1974) cites anecdotes of the explorers in primitive societies where natives are bewildered by photographs and are unable to decipher them. There is little direct evidence on this point, but the stories would lead one to believe that human beings must have a period of learning how to read pictures. However, as Kennedy points out, when the developmental process has been carefully controlled and studied, it appears that the child requires no instruction in order to recognize familiar objects depicted in flat two-dimensional photographs or line drawings.

Hochberg and Brooks (1962) conducted what can only be described as a courageous longitudinal study. The psychologists controlled the environment of their newborn son for 19 months to prevent him from seeing pictures or having labels applied to them. Anyone who has lived with babies in the months after they have learned to crawl and then walk can sympathize with the mother of this child. We can also be forgiven a mild skepticism about the degree of control possible, short of isolating the infant (which was not done). For example, picture books were gently taken away from him on the six occasions he picked one up. However, at 19 months the child was able to identify by name photographs and line drawings of such objects as a car, a shoe, a key, dolls, and other objects. The parents used judges in addition to themselves to make an independent confirmation of the child's performance. Hochberg and Brooks conclude that "It seems clear from the results that at least one human child is capable of recognizing pictorial representations of solid objects (including bare outline drawings) without specific training or instruction" (p. 628).

Of the large body of research and expert opinion on the use of motion pictures (or television) in the classroom, only one major study will be reviewed. Mark A. May had conducted a project on educational films at Yale University for many years. In 1958, he and Arthur Lumsdaine published a book entitled *Learning from Films* which reported the major investigations and results of this extensive project. Several of the studies inquired into the utility of "commonsense" properties of films; for example, they discovered that children neither learned less nor expressed less interest in films that were shot in black and white instead of color, or which lacked polished pictorial quality. Similarly, off-stage narration of an educational film compared favorably with a competitive version in which the film's characters engaged in dialogue.

Several of May and Lumsdaine's inquiries asked questions similar to those asked in studies already reviewed in this chapter. For example, in one slide-film study, soldiers were taught the phonetic alphabet (in which each letter is represented by a distinctive word to avoid communications errors; for example, a–alpha, b–baker, and so forth). The variable in this study was the type of review the men were to employ—either active or passive. The active review was uniformly superior to passive review. Reminiscent of Dwyer's study was the corresponding finding that a simple presentation was more conducive to learning than a condition in which the slides were embellished with humorous cartoons intended to enliven the slides. Apparently their effect was to divert the troops' attention from the association of c–Charlie and d–dog to the Sad Sack cartoon characters.

Other May and Lumsdaine studies considered the role of questions spliced into educational films. With 10th and 11th graders who viewed a film on how the human heart works, two kinds of questions were used, either "motivating" or "participation" questions. The former preceded a section of the film and were designed to arouse the learner's curiosity about what he was about to see. They asked questions such as, "Do you know exactly what parts of your heart make the sounds which the doctor hears in the stethoscope?" Participation questions immediately followed parts of the film. They provided learners an opportunity to respond actively to the content of the film as it was temporarily halted. Both types of questions, individually and in combination, yielded results superior to simply viewing the film.

One other effort by May and Lumsdaine deserves comment. They examined the effects upon learning of instructions that directed learners' attention to different aspects or elements of a film. In one experiment using a filmed version of Dickens's *David Copperfield,* the attention of high school students was directed either to the chronology of events or to such items as the names and places of characters and occurrences. Posttest results give some support to the hypothesis that students learn best those items that are based upon the dimension of the film to which they are specifically urged to attend. In another experiment in this series, the effects of different types of review prior to viewing the film a second time were examined. Some students were given the ten most difficult test items to review, whereas others reviewed their own errors following the first showing. Surprisingly, the students who reviewed the most difficult items scored higher than a control group, but the students given the chance to correct their own errors did not.

For many years the developers of teaching materials assumed that films or books fulfilled their functions for the learner if they provided clear and orderly, as well as accurate, presentations of their content. More recently, as the evidence amassed in this chapter attests, psychologists have reconsidered ways to maximize the effectiveness of these materials for learning. We have seen that these inquiries adopt various forms, and that they may grow from different theoretical bases. One position, espoused principally by Ausubel, stresses the facilitating power of organizational schemes which provide the learner with a general, conceptual guide in cognitive structure which enables him appropriately to process and integrate new information as it becomes available. Other psychologists have seized upon the importance of the learner's attention in the learning process. Two schools of thought predominate. Although both of them have employed questions to focus attention, their orientations are significantly different. For one group (whose conceptual base comes from the work of Berlyne) questions are used to arouse the curiosity of the learner and thus to heighten his attention to the learning task. For the other (represented by the initial formulation of Rothkopf and the detailed theoretical analysis of Frase, especially) learning is facilitated by sharpening and extending the inspection behavior of the learner. In a specific way, questions that follow passages of text have sometimes been found to have such a facilitating effect. Explanations about why this should happen remain in contention. Whether the postquestions serve as discriminative stimuli to expand inspection in the passage that follows, or whether they set up review processes of what has just been read is not known. Finally, we have seen that pictures accompanying text often do not have the facilitative effects on children's comprehension that are commonly assumed. Although available evidence seems to suggest that children can perceive and interpret pictures or line drawings of familiar objects without the benefit of instruction or experience, the opposite is true when they must decode and interpret graphs and other symbolic nonverbal material.

The ideas and their tests which we have examined in this chapter hold promise of leading to more effective designs for teaching materials than we have had in the past. However, none of these ideas has proven itself to the point that we know how to develop materials that will lead dependably to improved learning and retention. They represent, in my view, some of the most exciting scientifically based approaches to school learning to be seen since the conceptual basis for programmed instruction was described a generation ago by B. F. Skinner.

Practice

One of the oldest adages in the world about learning is that "practice makes perfect." This seems to apply particularly well to skilled performances: a champion figure skater practices daily between four and six hours, and the great composer and pianist Paderewski, even at an advanced age, declared that he could discern the effect on his own playing of a single day's absence from the piano. Athletes of all kinds also must practice their skills regularly if they are to perform at the highest possible level. Of course, improvement with practice is not automatic. It depends, for example, upon the performance being practiced as it is intended to occur. If errors are practiced, they are also learned and can become increasingly difficult to eradicate from one's repertoire.

Our interest, however, is less in skills with heavy motor components than it is with the tasks of the classroom. We must ask whether practice is required for material that has been learned with meaning. The answer is yes, because material tends to be only partly learned from a single reading or presentation (refer to the work of Meyer and McConkie described in Chapter 2), and because subordinate concepts and information lose their distinctiveness and are not remembered as separate items after the passage of time. Still, material that has been learned with meaning is less susceptible to forgetting than material that lacks meaning and therefore is learned by rote.

This point was well documented in an early investigation of the distribution of study time between reading the material and active recitation of it (Gates, 1917). Eighth-grade students were given nine minutes to memorize a list of 16 nonsense syllables, but they were given various instructions. Some were told to spend the entire time just reading the syllables; others were instructed to spend 20, 40, 60, or 80 percent of the available time *reciting* the syllables. (To illustrate the procedure, a student in the four-fifths recitation group would have about two minutes to read through the material to be learned. Then, upon a signal, he would devote the balance of the study time to actively reciting the syllables. He might look at the the first two or three, then look away and say them to himself, and so forth.) Immediately after learning, the amount of material that the students recalled varied directly with the proportion of time they had invested in recitation. These results ranged from 35 percent recalled by students who read all the time to 75 percent for those who had devoted as much as four-fifths of the learning time to recitation. When recall was measured four hours after original learning, the percentages recalled were still proportional to time spent in recitation, but the figures were much lower, reflecting the rapid decrement in recall for nonsense material. For example, only 15 percent of the material could still be recalled by those who had only read the material, but 48 percent was recalled by students who had committed as much as 80 percent of their time to recitation.

In a second part of the study, Gates had students read (and recite, using the same assignments of time as before) material that was at least somewhat more meaningful. The second task was to study five brief biographies. Although this consisted of connected sentences, there was not a great deal of meaning to be developed by the learner. The biographies of each individual were very short, and they contained dates, places, and some indication of major achievements. With this alteration in the learning task, although recitation still yielded the best recall, the range of differences is markedly less than with nonsense syllables. If all the learning time was spent in reading, immediate recall was 35 percent. When up to four fifths of the available time was used in recitation, recall advanced to only 42 percent. The level and range of recall after four hours was from 16 percent to 26 percent.

There is no doubt that the learner can markedly improve the amount of a task he learns and that he subsequently retains if he uses active recitation in his initial attack on the task. If the learner simply passively reads the material to be learned, it is doubtful that he will derive as much benefit from it. Of course it is impossible in practical situations to assess what the learner is doing. When one student "reads" an assignment he may be doing nothing more than scanning the words printed on the page, with no effort to process them. For another student, the reading process may represent an active and intellectually aggressive attack upon the material, one aimed at extracting and classifying and organizing information along the way. The gap between this consideration of the role of practice and our earlier discussion of arousal and of mathemagenic activities may not be as great as it first appears. The latter are efforts to build in control over the learner's attending and processing of the task. They are effective to the degree that they exercise such control and direct it to the proper stimuli and relations among stimuli. The use of active recitation by the learner has also been shown to be effective when it is utilized. Text materials and teachers can assist the process by instructing learners in how to recite—how to engage in the active process of responding during learning—but it is extremely difficult to monitor the process, for the learner retains control over his covert behavior.

The nature of practice

Whenever possible, practice should be conducted under the conditions that public or final performance will occur. Guthrie (1935) made this point eminently well in his practical treatise on the psychology of learning. He reasons that the performance to be expected is the last one practiced. Thus, when his mother wants eight-year-old Billy to hang up his coat on the way upstairs after school, she *must* make him perform that act. If he fails to do so on his own, he must be recalled halfway up the steps and compelled to hang up his wrap. Lectures or imprecations that instruct him in what to do but fail to ensure its enactment are futile. It becomes increasingly likely that tomorrow and the next day Billy will leave his coat on the hallway floor and charge upstairs, with his mother's protestations nipping helplessly at his heels.

There are many tasks in school which the learner must be able to perform upon demand and which cannot be learned at the moment they are needed. The ability to read and proficiency in the number combinations of arithmetic are good cases in point. An obvious analogy is to the drama company, which begins the preparation of a new play with the actors reading the parts of their respective characters. Day by day the play assumes a shape closer to what it will be on opening night. Well before the final rehearsals each player has thoroughly mastered his part; not only the lines to speak, but his positions on stage, his actions, and whatever enters into the finished performance. Ausubel (1968) makes the point that some educators contend that skills should be practiced in natural, nonartificial situations, such as those associated with the development of projects. Some years ago progressive educators asserted that the pupil, especially the child of elementary school age, should encounter situations which naturally demanded of him arithmetic computations and measurement and which depended upon his ability to read and follow instructions. This might happen, for example, in a science class where the child is to construct a window box of given dimensions so he can later assess the effects on plant growth of water and sunlight. Such events could represent excellent educative acts in the 1920s and 1930s, as they can today. The proponents of such methods in earlier years attempted to remind teachers that children are better motivated to learn the necessary skills and information offered by the school when they have a purpose for doing so. In our daily lives we rarely compute or measure or even read in the absence of some purpose to be served.

The difficulty with the position expressed here is that the learner must already possess the basic skills in usable form before he encounters such an opportunity for their application. A fourth-grader may better understand his study of the concept of area in arithmetic class when he has to determine how much seed to buy for a school vegetable garden. Then he has a real purpose to be answered by the textbook lessons he has had. However, it is not only the realism of such situations that makes them successful. This happens also because the learner has an opportunity to apply what he has already learned in a situation which calls for it. To suggest that such situations should serve as the context for the initial learning of arithmetic, reading, or other subject matter skills seems badly to miss an opportunity for learning of a different type.

The resolution of such issues, as most teachers are aware, is to see to it that pupils do possess mastery of needed skills at a sufficient level to use them when they are suitable, perhaps with brief review or simple modifications and additions. The role of drill in the educational psychology of learning is a long, inglorious, misunderstood, and important one. The two principal objections that are voiced to the use of drill in the classroom are that it is meaningless for learners and that it holds no interest for them; that is, they lack motivation (or purpose) for engaging in drill. But those objections are valid, if they apply, to many kinds of activity. In the recent past industry, the worker, and even society at large expressed concern about the individual whose productive working years are spent on industrial assembly lines in jobs that are endlessly repetitious and monotonous beyond endurance. Generations of specialists in the teaching of arithmetic, for example, have dedicated themselves to demonstrating that when children first learn number combinations with understanding, the drill then needed to make the combinations automatic is not meaningless. Similarly, many workers have shown that drills can be constructed in numerous forms which children are likely to find interesting. Among the more recent commentators on this scene is Brown (1972), who observed that drill must be preceded by understanding. In conclusion on this point, let us note that the learner's attention in this, as in so many other matters, is critical. If drill is designed with that consideration in mind, it can be effective.

The distribution of practice

After the initial learning, when should practice on the task occur? For some tasks or skills that are used frequently as elements in other tasks, the question is answered automatically, inasmuch as continuous practice occurs. Or for some few tasks that must be remembered well, at least for a limited time, the teacher may make the opportunity to review the material frequently. In the practical world of the classroom, however, the learner is confronted with numerous and competing demands upon his time. It quickly becomes impossible for the learner to review frequently all the things he is expected to learn, so some conception of when reviews will give the maximum benefit is important. Years ago several extensive studies of this question were conducted. We shall review briefly two of the largest scale investigations.

In 1939 Spitzer wrote two short factual passages of the kind of material sixth-graders are likely to encounter in their textbooks. Each of them was about 600 words long. One dealt with "Peanuts" and the other with

"Bamboos"; 3,605 sixth-graders read the "Peanuts" passage and took a test on it, which was used to sort the pupils into ten large groups. All groups then read the "Bamboos" paper and took a test based on it once, twice, or three times, spaced anywhere from immediately after reading the story to 63 days later. In this way Spitzer was able to evaluate the effects over extended periods of time of immediate retesting or retesting after a week, and so forth. Without exception, the groups that had an opportunity to recall the material (those who took the test either two or three times) recalled significantly more by the end of nine weeks than those who did not. For example, one group of children read the "Bamboos" passage, took the test immediately afterwards, one week later, and 63 days after the initial reading. The mean score of that group on the third test was 10.74. This was significantly higher than the mean of 6.38 scored by another group which took no test until the 63rd day.

Spitzer emphasizes the importance of a review test occurring immediately after initial learning. His evidence shows clearly that a group which took the test one day after the initial learning period scored only 9.56 on the average. Even with this relatively meaningful material, the decrement in retention that occurs within 24 hours without aided recall is large. For groups that had no recall test until two or four weeks following their reading of the passage, test scores ranged only around 20 percent. It is unfortunate that Spitzer used the same test throughout to provide aided recall and to measure the amount recalled. If he had used alternative forms of the test we should have a much more general picture of what children remember from the total learning passage rather than the specific points covered by this test.

Reviews, of course, need not always occur in the form of a test. Teachers frequently assign the rereading of a learning task as the means of review. Sones and Stroud (1940) found general confirmation for Spitzer's results with seventh graders when they used review tests. However, when the pupils read the material again, the effect upon recall at the end of a 42-day period was inconsequential, whether the review reading was done early or late in the interval. Their reasonable explanation is that a review test depends for its effect upon what the pupil can recall from his initial learning. If the test occurs early, of course his retention is best and can be buttressed by the opportunity to review. The longer he waits to review, the more forgetting occurs, and when the review test comes late in the retention interval, its effects are minimal. Review as reading the task again, however, permits a second opportunity for learning to occur. Whether this opportunity comes early or relatively late in the total interval seems to matter very little.

These studies, and most of what we have said about practice, pertain

98 Learning and Thinking

to the learning of factual information and simple skills. The role of practice and review on the recall of intellectual skills has not been studied much. Gay (1973) made an effort to extend the generalizations about factual reviews to the case of an intellectual skill. She conducted two experiments with eighth-graders, both involving four principles taken from algebra and geometry: raising an algebraic expression to the power indicated [$(2x^2y^3)^4 = ?$]; determining the measure of the third angle of a triangle (if A equals 70 and B equals 50, what is C?); determining the exponent of a product ($aa^2a^3 = ?$) and finding the geometric mean (what is the geometric mean of 16 and 4?). These particular principles were chosen because seventh-and eighth-graders have rarely encountered them, but the prerequisite learnings demanded are only the basic operations of addition, subtraction, multiplication, and division. Students were first taught the principles, and their ability to apply them subsequently to examples was the measure of recall. In Experiment I, she found, according to expectation, that when a single review was provided it made no difference whether it took place 1 day, 7 days, or 14 days after initial learning. However, all review conditions were superior to a control group that had no review. In Experiment II, two reviews were provided; occurring either early (on days 1 and 2), late (days 6 and 7), or in combination (days 1 and 7). The last combination of reviews provided the best results.

The results showed that the first and the second reviews each added a sizable percentage to what students remembered of the principles. For example, the first review added about 45 percent. The second review added even more, ranging between 75 and 150 percent. The results of this and other studies agree that an early review should occur shortly after original learning, and not more than a single day following it. It is not well demonstrated when a later review should occur for maximum benefit. Gay also observes that the functions of the second review are different from those of the first. The second review has a differential effect upon groups of students, so that differences between them that are initially small become magnified as the result of the later review.

Potpourri

Several additional techniques for the improvement of learning may be briefly mentioned. Each is limited in its usefulness, but may have applicability to classroom learning from time to time.

Overlearning

The term refers to the amount of practice or repetition in which the learner engages. Most teachers and students are aware that additional practice beyond the point at which a lesson has just been mastered will be beneficial for its retention. Krueger (1929) asked students to learn or to overlearn lists of words. Three groups of students participated in the experiment. One group quit practicing as soon as members could recite the word list without an error. Another group continued to practice 50 percent again as long as had been required to reach the errorless trial criterion. A third group practiced twice as long as necessary to reach mastery of the word list. Retention was measured at a variety of intervals between 2 and 28 days. Krueger found that overlearning yielded superior results, but that there is a limit to the efficiency of overlearning. Students who practiced twice as much as necessary to learn the task originally did not remember the words twice as well after 28 days as those who committed only half as much additional time to practice. In this particular study, 50 percent overlearning was optimal. Although students who devoted 100 percent to overlearning actually retained more, their additional practice yielded less retention per unit of time spent than those who were in the 50 percent overlearning group.

The effect of overlearning is not limited to lists of words. Reference was made in Chapter 2 to a study conducted by Ausubel, Stager, & Gaite (1968) in which high school students studied an experimental passage about Zen Buddhism. Half the students read the passage on two separate days (a measure of overlearning). They scored much higher on the final test of learning than other students who only read the passage once. Even when the material to be learned is meaningful, a second or perhaps a third reading of it may be valuable. Beyond that, additional sustained practice loses much of its effectiveness.

Isolation effects

When a particular point is especially to be remembered, it can be

ISOLATED

from its surrounding context. As long as the technique is not overused it can be effective with meaningful school content as well as with the types of lists used in the verbal learning laboratory. A recent experimental demonstration of that fact was made by Holen and Oaster (1976). Midway through a taped lecture, the members of an experimental class heard the instructor say, "This seems to be an especially significant point." The isolated information was presented immediately after that statement. On an end-of-lecture test, a question based on that point was correctly answered by students in the experimental class far more often than students in a control class who had not experienced the isolation or differentiation of that point from others in the lecture. Fundamental propositions, concepts, or facts that the teacher wants to be sure are learned can be differentiated from other elements of the lesson with good effect. However, the isolation of material must be done with restraint if the effect is not to be dissipated.

Mnemonics

Also called "artificial memory," mnemonics is one of those psychological techniques that has its roots buried in antiquity. Long abandoned in modern psychology, the topic has recently been the subject of renewed interest. Its origins lie in the work of a poet, Simonides, whose methods were later recounted by Cicero. In the fifth century B. C. Simonides had been invited to sing at a banquet given by an Olympic winner to celebrate his victory. During the banquet Simonides was called from the hall, and shortly thereafter the floors collapsed, killing all the guests. The bodies were crushed beyond recognition, but Simonides was able to help relatives identify their dead kinsmen by recalling who was seated at each place.

The method of location, as devised by Simonides, is still a fundamental technique of the mnemonist. The learner calls to mind places he knows very well, such as the rooms of his home. He then figuratively stores items he wishes to remember in those places. For example, a grocery list might be recalled in this way: a loaf of bread is stuffed in the hall umbrella stand; a carton of eggs laid on the banister of the stairs; a pound of bacon on top of the hallway clock, with a two-pound can of coffee perched on the closet shelf. A professional mnemonist divides rooms of a house into a series of squares. The floor of the room and the four walls are divided into nine squares. The ceiling above each wall receives a number, as does the center of the ceiling. This number (50) also serves as a transition to a second room. Thus, two rooms provide 100 spaces in which to store items. The mnemonist can do much more than reel off items in a series from 1 to 100. Each number has a specific and vivid location for him, and he can immediately identify the 12th item in the series, or the 79th. Conversely, he can indicate that the "giraffe" is number 33, and so forth. There are other, equally complicated schemes used by the professional. Obviously the typical student will rarely have occasion to use such devices.

An interesting review of the use of mnemonics to facilitate remembering tasks such as shopping lists, appointments, principal products of a country, or the major causes of a war was written by Bower (1973). His review deals principally with two types of mnemonics: method of location and pegword method. Based upon the results of his own work, Bower judges that the two methods yield comparable results.

Bower has found in his studies at Stanford University that a "pegword" system can markedly enhance learners' ability to recall lists of unconnected items or words for extended periods of time. The technique is also used by professional mnemonists as a means of remembering very lengthy lists or series, and also as a way of enabling them to break into a sequence and identify any item or subitem that may be requested. Put simply, the learner identifies a series of words to associate with the first 10 or 20 numbers. For instance, "one-bun," "two-shoe," "three-tree," "four-door," "five-hive," and so forth. The pegwords should be concrete because the learner is to build vivid images between them and the items to be remembered. This part of the procedure is the same as our earlier example from Bower's work about the dog who smoked cigars in his homburg hat while riding a bicycle. Figure 3.3 is an illustration of how the procedure might be used to remember a shopping list. The learner creates images between the items on the list and the pegwords. These items are then easily recalled because the student has clear associations between the number and the pegword, and between the pegword and the item to be recalled.

The results of Bower's studies show that the pegword method and the location method give comparable levels of recall, and both are far superior to homemade techniques that emphasize rote rehearsal of lists. The pegword method is also effective for recalling several lists which have to be learned at the same time. To illustrate the technique with multiple lists, suppose that the second item on the first list to be learned is dog, item two on list two is cigar, on list three it is hat, and on list four, bicycle. The visual sequence described previously can be constructed as the learner goes along. Results of experiments with college students show that students who learned by this progressive method recalled many more of the total number of items learned than other students who tried to learn four different lists by replacing the associations between pegwords and items between each list. When they learned one list they tended to forget items on the other lists.

Mnemonics can assist the student's retention of material that is low in meaningfulness. A mnemonic substitutes a more familiar or more easily learned expression, or a rhyme, for the learning task, which is then associated with it. I was once taught the following mnemonic to help me remember the order of the planets in our solar system. It begins with Mercury, which is nearest to the sun, and the initial letter of each word represents the planets in order, moving away from the sun. Thus,

FIGURE 3.3
Illustration of the peg word method

Item Number	Pegword	Peg Image	Item to Be Recalled	Connecting Image
1	bun		milk	
2	shoe		bread	
3	tree		bananas	
4	door		cigarette	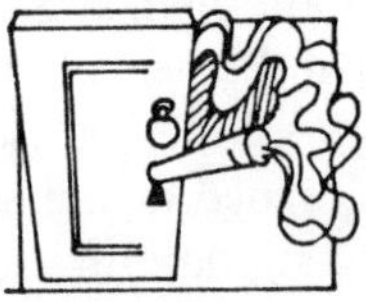
5	hive		coffee	

Connecting images:
1. *Milk* pouring onto a soggy hamburger *bun*
2. A *shoe* kicking and breaking a brittle load of French *bread*
3. Several bunches of *bananas* hanging from a *tree*
4. Keyhole of a *door* smoking a *cigarette*
5. Pouring *coffee* into top of a bee *hive*

Source: Bower (1973), p. 66.

The Improvement of Learning in School Settings

"Merry Virgil eats much jam sitting up nights playing" is easily translated into "Mercury, Venus, Earth, Mars, Jupiter, Saturn, Uranus, Neptune, Pluto." A second-grade teacher recently told me in an interview that her young pupils have trouble remembering how to use symbols to indicate "greater than" and "less than." She teaches them that the symbol "always points to the 'baby' (smaller) number."

As a final example, consider a digit-letter system, a 19th-century derivative of a much earlier prototype. Hunter (1964) reports that an English schoolmaster named Brayshaw published a collection of rhymes that contained over 2,000 dates and number facts from the curriculum of the middle 19th century. In an age when education consisted largely of rote memorization of specific facts, it was no doubt a great assistance to many a reluctant pupil. First the learner memorized consonants in association with numbers, as in Figure 3.4. These, in turn, were embodied in rhymes such as the one to help him remember the succession to the British crown which is also reproduced in Figure 3.4.

FIGURE 3.4
Example of a mnemonic system used in a Victorian school

1	2	3	4	5	6	7	8	9	0	00
B	D	G	J	L	M	P	R	T	W	St
C	F	H	K		N	Q	V	X		
			S		A					

1066 By *men,* near Hastings, William gains the crown;
1087 A *rap* in Forest New brings Rufus down.
1100 Gaul's *coast* first Henry hates, whose son is drowned;
1135 Like *beagle,* Stephen fights with Maude renoun'd.
1154 A *cloak,* at Becket's tomb, sec'nd Henry wears;
1189 And *brave* first Richard oft Saladin dares.
1199 John's *act* at Runnymede England pleased avows;
1216 His *face, in* Parliament, weak third Henry shows.

The verse continues in this way up to the last line, which gives the date of Queen Victoria's accession.

1837 Lastly, *our hope* rests on Victoria's will.

Source: Hunter (1964), pp. 298–299.

Questions for Review and Discussion

1. What does it mean to "improve" school learning? What criterion would you use to decide what required improvement? How would you know whether the intended or desired improvement had occurred?

104   Learning and Thinking

2. The first section of this chapter was called "Orienting the Learner." Why do you think the word "orienting" was used? Research evidence suggests that students learn more from a lesson or an assignment if they are aware of the objective, that is, if they know what it is they are intended to learn. How would you implement this knowledge in the classroom? Consider ways that are available to you to communicate with your students, and remember that what you say or write will be effective only if it is attended to and acted upon by the learner.

3. How is an "overview" different from an "advance organizer"? With what kind of content is the organizer most likely to be effective? Select one topic that is to be learned by students, and prepare an overview and an organizer to be used with it. If possible, try out one or the other with a class, or the overview with one group and the organizer with another. How well do they work? Analyze the reasons for your success or failure with these procedures.

4. Were you surprised to learn that teachers ask pupils 350 questions in a school day? That perhaps only one fifth or fewer of them require students to *think*? Are there implications in those data for your present or future behavior as a teacher? What are they?

5. The discussion of "questions after" reading and "questions before" exposure to new content is based upon different theoretical views of how questions can serve to stimulate learning. Express those views in your own terms. What are the relative merits of the two positions? Consider them from the standpoint of learning and of their utility for the teacher.

6. The ancient adage tells us "one picture is worth a thousand words." Does the review of classroom pictures, graphs, and films alter your belief in that adage? Why or why not?

7. We have tried to show that initial learning can be maintained at a high level by means of an appropriate schedule of tests and reviews, perhaps review in the shape of additional study of content learned at an earlier time. Would you advocate the repeated use of the same review test? What are the advantages and disadvantages? Teachers usually feel that their classroom schedule is quite crowded with knowledge to be taught and learned. If each newly learned body of content is placed into a review schedule, the time available for new material will gradually decrease. What criteria would you impose upon the selection of material for review?

8. What is a "mnemonic"? Can you think of any you have learned, or that you have used to help others remember? What place in classroom learning do mnemonics have? Would you ever use a mnemonic with content that is meaningful?

Readings for Further Reflection

Introductory level
The readings recommended at the end of Chapter 2 for this level are also appropriate to supplement and extend Chapter 3.

Advanced level
The advance organizer was presented in this chapter as a technique for the improvement of learning which is rooted in the learning theory of David P. Ausubel. For the student who wishes to obtain a more complete picture of how Ausubel developed and tested the conception of an organizer, the two papers listed below are suitable. They also provide a detailed look at research methodology and statistical analysis of a type frequently used by research workers in educational psychology.

Ausubel, David P. "The Use of Advance Organizers in the Learning and Retention of Meaningful Material." *Journal of Educational Psychology*, 1960, *51*, 267–272.

Ausubel, David P., and Fitzgerald, Donald. "The Role of Discriminability in Meaningful Verbal Learning and Retention." *Journal of Educational Psychology*, 1961, *52*, 266–274.

Two reviews can be cited that deal with issues on the role of questions in learning. These are intended for people pursuing research interests; although they deal with topics similar to those in the present chapter, their emphasis is research and theory rather than classroom applications.

Frase, Lawrence T. "Advances in Research and Theory in Instructional Technology." In Fred N. Kerlinger (Ed.), *Review of Research in Education*, *3*. Itasca, Ill.: F. E. Peacock Publishers, Inc., 1975.

Gagné, Robert M. "Learning and Instructional Sequence." In Fred N. Kerlinger (Ed.), *Review of Research in Education*, *1*. Itasca, Ill.: F. E. Peacock Publishers, Inc., 1973.

References

Anderson, Richard C. Control of student mediating processes during verbal learning and instruction. *Review of Educational Research*, 1970, *40*, 349–369.

Ausubel, David P. The use of advance organizers in the learning and retention of meaningful material. *Journal of Educational Psychology*, 1960, *51*, 267–272.

Ausubel, David P. *The psychology of meaningful verbal learning.* New York: Grune & Stratton, 1963.

Ausubel, David P. *Educational psychology: A cognitive view.* New York: Holt, Rinehart, & Winston, 1968.

Ausubel, David P., Stager, Mary, & Gaite, A. J. H. Retroactive facilitation in meaningful verbal learning. *Journal of Educational Psychology,* 1968, *59,* 250–255.

Barnes, Buckley R., & Clawson, Elmer U. Do advance organizers facilitate learning? *Review of Educational Research,* 1975, *45,* 637–659.

Bellack, Arno A., Kliebard, Herbert M., Hyman, Ronald T., and Smith, Frank L., Jr. *The language of the classroom.* New York: Teachers College Press, 1966.

Berlyne, D. E. *Conflict, arousal, and curiosity.* New York: McGraw-Hill Book Co., 1960.

Berlyne, D. E. Conditions of prequestioning and retention of meaningful material. *Journal of Educational Psychology,* 1966, *57,* 128–132.

Bower, Gordon H. How to remember. *Psychology Today,* 1973, *1,* 62–70.

Brown, John C. Learning theory applied to arithmetic instruction. *Psychology in the Schools,* 1972, *9,* 289–293.

Bull, Sheelagh G. The role of questions in maintaining attention to textual material. *Review of Educational Research,* 1973, *43,* 83–87.

Bull, Sheelagh G., & Dizney, Henry F. Epistemic curiosity-arousing prequestions: Their effect on long-term retention. *Journal of Educational Psychology,* 1973, *65,* 45–49.

Dwyer, Francis M., Jr. Adapting visual illustrations for effective learning. *Harvard Educational Review,* 1967, *37,* 250–263.

Farnham-Diggory, Sylvia. *Cognitive processes in education.* New York: Harper & Row, 1972.

Flanders, Ned A. *Teacher influence, pupil attitudes and achievement* (Cooperative Research Monograph No. 12). Washington D.C.: U.S. Office of Education, 1965.

Frase, Lawrence T. Learning from prose material: Length of passage, knowledge of results, and position of questions. *Journal of Educational Psychology,* 1967, *58,* 266–272.

Frase, Lawrence T. Questions as aids to reading: Some research and a theory. *American Educational Research Journal,* 1968, *5,* 319–332. (a)

Frase, Lawrence T. Some data concerning the mathemagenic hypothesis. *American Educational Research Journal,* 1968, *5,* 181–189. (b)

Frase, Lawrence T. Some unpredicted effects of different questions upon learning from connected discourse. *Journal of Educational Psychol-*

ogy, 1968, *57,* 197–201 (c)

Gagné, Robert M. Context, isolation, and interference effects on the retention of fact. *Journal of Educational Psychology,* 1969, *60,* 408–414.

Gagné, Robert M., & Wiegand, Virginia K. Effects of a superordinate context and retention of facts. *Journal of Educational Psychology,* 1970, *61,* 406–409.

Gall, Meredith. The use of questions in teaching. *Review of Educational Research,* 1970, *40,* 707–721.

Gates, Arthur I. Recitation as a factor in memorizing. *Archives of Psychology,* 1917, *40.*

Gay, Lorraine R. Temporal position of reviews and its effect on the retention of mathematical rules. *Journal of Educational Psychology,* 1973, *64,* 171–182.

Guthrie, E. R. *The psychology of learning* (Rev. ed.). New York: Harper & Row, 1952. (Originally published, 1935.)

Hartley, James & Davies, Ivor K. Preinstructional strategies: The role of pretests, behavioral objectives, overviews, and advance organizers. *Review of Educational Research,* 1976, *46,* 239–265.

Hochberg, J. E., & Brooks, V. Pictorial recognition as an unlearned ability. *American Journal of Psychology,* 1962, *75,* 624–628.

Holen, Michael C., & Oaster, Thomas R. Serial position and isolation effects in a classroom lecture simulation. *Journal of Educational Psychology,* 1976, *68,* 293–296.

Hunter, Ian M. L. *Memory* (Rev. ed.). Baltimore: Penguin Books, 1964.

Kennedy, John M. *A psychology of picture perception.* San Francisco: Jossey-Bass Publishers, 1974.

Krueger, W. C. F. The effect of overlearning on retention. *Journal of Experimental Psychology,* 1929, *12,* 71–78.

Levonian, Edward. Retention of information in relation to arousal during continuously presented material. *American Educational Research Journal,* 1967, *4,* 103–116.

May, Mark A., & Lumsdaine, Arthur A. *Learning from films.* New Haven, Conn.: Yale University Press, 1958.

Miller, William. Reading with and without pictures. *Elementary School Journal,* 1938, *38,* 676–682.

Nunnally, Jum C. Determinants of visual exploratory behavior: A human tropism for resolving informational conflicts. In H. I. Day, D. E. Berlyne, & D. E. Hunt (Eds.), *Intrinsic motivation: A new direction in education* (pp. 73–82). Toronto: Holt, Rinehart, & Winston of Canada, Ltd., 1971.

Paivio, Allan. *Imagery and verbal processes.* New York: Holt, Rinehart, & Winston, 1971.

Paradowski, William. Effect of curiosity on incidental learning. *Journal of Educational Psychology,* 1967, *58,* 50-55.

Rothkopf, Ernst Z. Some theoretical and experimental approaches to problems in written instruction. In J. D. Krumboltz (Ed.), *Learning and the educational process* (pp. 193-221). Chicago: Rand McNally, 1965.

Rothkopf, Ernst Z. Learning from written instructive material: An exploration of the control of inspection behavior by test-like events. *American Educational Research Journal,* 1966, *3,* 241-249.

Rothkopf, Ernst Z. The concept of mathemagenic activities. *Review of Educational Research,* 1970, *40,* 325-336.

Rothkopf, Ernst Z., & Bisbicos, Ethel E. Selective facilitative effects of interspersed questions on learning from written materials. *Journal of Educational Psychology,* 1967, *58,* 56-61.

Rothkopf, Ernst Z., & Bloom, Richard D. Effects of interspersed interaction on the instructional value of adjunct questions in learning from written material. *Journal of Educational Psychology,* 1970, *61,* 417-422.

Rothkopf, Ernst Z., & Kaplan, R. Exploration of the effect of density and specificity of instructional objectives on learning from text. *Journal of Educational Psychology,* 1972, *63,* 295-302.

Samuels, S. Jay. Effects of pictures on learning to read, comprehension and attitudes. *Review of Educational Research,* 1970, *40,* 397-407.

Sones, A. M., & Stroud, J. B. Review with special reference to temporal position. *Journal of Educational Psychology,* 1940, *31,* 665-676.

Spitzer, Herbert F. Studies in retention. *Journal of Educational Psychology,* 1939, *30,* 641-656.

Suchman, J. Richard. Inquiry training: Building skills for autonomous discovery. *Merrill-Palmer Quarterly,* 1961, *7,* 147-169.

Vernon, Magdalen D. The value of pictorial illustration. *British Journal of Educational Psychology,* 1954, *24,* 171-179.

Watts, Graeme H., & Anderson, Richard C. Effects of three types of inserted questions on learning from prose. *Journal of Educational Psychology,* 1971, *62,* 387-394.

Chapter 4

Conceptual Learning

Suppose you were unable to classify all the events and objects you encounter in everyday life into categories, as other people do. Everything you see or hear or touch would be new to you, because in some particular it would be different from anything you have seen or heard or touched before. The demand on your memory would be excessive. With no way to order objects, and consequently no means to establish a system of superordinate and subordinate relationships among them, your ability to think could never advance beyond the "booming, buzzing confusion" which William James ascribed to the existence of infants.

Fortunately, human beings do have the capacity to categorize and classify objects, so the perplexing and frustrating state of affairs described here is unlikely to exist. However, the hypothetical case can help clarify one of the central functions performed by concepts—they provide classes or categories into which events can be conveniently and productively filed.

What Is a Concept?

A concept is an abstraction which represents a general class of events but is not restricted to any specific example of that class. Concepts are man-made; they reflect people's efforts to systematize experience and knowledge and to reduce the amount of confusion in their world. Since people communicate principally through the medium of language, we manage to assign an identifying label and a description or definition to most concepts. These are not the concepts themselves but only ways we have devised to make it possible for people to talk and write to each other effectively.

Concepts range from very simple, concrete, "point-to-able" objects, such as a chair or a table, to complex, abstract, difficult to define concepts such as *beauty, democracy,* or *the good life.* In order to learn a concept, a person must, at some stage, have seen or had direct experience with objects or events that contribute to the concept. The experience need not occur at the time he is learning the concept. As no two people ever have precisely the same set of experiences to form their concepts, so no two people ever have exactly the same concepts. This can lead to great failures of communication, not only in the classroom but in the family, among friends, and, obviously, among people or groups from different cultures. This discrepancy is most notable among the nations of the world.

One thing which accounts for the variation in difficulty of concepts can be called the level of abstraction. Take the concept *table.* Tables have physical properties. They can be seen, and they can be touched. A small child may have very concrete experiences with tables, such as cracking his or her head on their edges or chewing on their legs. A table has a few invariant characteristics, or what can be called criterial attributes. It has a top or resting surface, and it has legs or some type of support. Other than that, tables may be high or low, wood or metal, light or dark, large or small, ad infinitum. Their functions may also vary; one may dine at the table, or be operated upon while lying on one. Or one may play bridge, do homework, or use a table for numerous other things.

For most of us tables are so abundant, and our experiences with them begin so early, that we have no memory of learning what a table is. We seem always to have known. In fact, we have not. We learn *table* through many experiences such as those illustrated above. Along the line we have heard the word *table* associated with the object so often that we come to make the appropriate designation with no trouble. To use the parlance of the psychologist who studies concept learning, we have seen plenty of positive instances, or examples of a table. The positive instances always entail the invariant or criterial attributes. By a process of generalization, we learn to apply the label "table" to all those objects that possess the proper attributes, while we ignore the irrelevant details; that is, the differences from one table to the next.

A second learning process is involved. We may have called a large tray, for instance the type used to serve meals in bed, a table. Our error is pointed out, however, and we learn to discriminate between trays and tables. Or we may erroneously identify a certain desk as a table. Again, we are told of the mistake, and we learn to discriminate between the two classes. Note the convenience that the categorizing function furnishes. As we generalize across examples, no further thought need be given to individual examples, even though they may in some particular be different from any other example we have ever encountered.

A concept such as *beauty* lacks the easily identifiable physical properties of *table*. There is beauty in the gold and violet of a summer sunset or in fields of autumn wheat undulating in a September breeze. There is the face of a beautiful woman, or the beauty of one's child tucked safely in his bed for the night. There is the beauty of Michelangelo's Pieta, and that of a Shakespearean sonnet. All are beautiful, but what is it about them that defines beauty? The learner must abstract meaning at a much higher level in order to generalize across examples.

Development, Concept Learning, and Cognitive Structure

How are concepts different from cognitive structure? The answer, of course, is that concepts are an integral part of one's cognitive structure. Cognitive structure incorporates the concepts of a field of study, and if the learner's cognitive structure is aptly delineated, the relationships among the concepts in a field will be organized so as to reflect its content structure adequately. Concepts do not represent the totality of one's cognitive structure, which also includes broader generalizations and principles, as well as specific facts and information, but they are the building blocks that enable a learner to think effectively in a field. They achieve this function in two ways. First, a concept itself, as we have already seen, permits the accurate subsumption or classification of examples or events which may not resemble each other in a great many ways, but which are categorized as equivalent because they share appropriate defining characteristics (criterial attributes). Second, principles or generalizations consist of explicit relationships between or among sets of concepts. This does not necessarily mean that a concept must be learned as a separate entity before it can be learned as part of a principle, although that frequently will happen. It may be learned as part of the principle. It is in these senses that we speak of concepts as the building blocks of thinking.

There is an additional question about the relationships among intellectual development, concept learning, and cognitive structures. In earlier chapters we have several times observed that one view of school learning (notably that adduced by Ausubel) is that large blocks of substantive content are learned through a process of continuous differentiation. The first thing the student learns about a field is its broadest generalizations and propositions. These are superordinate to less general concepts, which emerge somewhat later in the learning process, and also to the specific facts and details that are the last to be elucidated. The idea of the advance organizer is based upon this proposition. If the student knows little or nothing of a field, the teacher should not begin the learning process with the minutiae and specifics of it, but should start with the broadest ideas. The learner cannot master the details until he has the broader "ideational scaffolding" constructed. This seems to be an eminently sensible and reasonable position. Furthermore (as we saw in Chapter 2), when college students recalled what they heard in a tape-recorded lecture, the cognitive structure resembled Ausubel's conception.

Whatever concept is to be learned, the learner must have a background of concrete or direct experiences to undergird it. But we have concrete experiences with specific cases, examples, items, or objects, and not with the broadest propositions of a field of study. The notions of concrete experiences and broad propositions as prerequisites to learning seem to be in direct contradiction of each other. Do we simply have two different points of view, one of which must necessarily be wrong if the other is correct? Or can we reconcile the two positions?

To answer this question we must consider again the intellectual development of the learner. We saw in Chapter 1 that the child is engaged in finding out how the world is constructed, virtually from the first weeks of life. It is not until an age that conforms roughly to the close of the elementary school years that most children can reliably reason at abstract levels; that is, without the assistance of concrete objects. The first 11 or 12 years have been highly productive ones for the normal child, however, with regard to the learning of concepts. Just as an example, he will have been controlled, ordered about, and disciplined often enough by parents, teachers, and others to form clear if rudimentary concepts of *government, justice, democracy, totalitarianism,* and other concepts that pertain to social control. These basic concepts can be extended by the adolescent to more remote, abstract variations without the need for additional concrete experience. The adolescent's transition into a stage of formal thought enables him to manipulate relationships among sets of abstract concepts without further recourse to specific or concrete examples. This is not to say that illustrations are no longer of value, even to the adult learner. They may contribute to increased clarity, and especially to the level of interest, but they are no longer required as they are in the learning of the younger child.

This suggests that the responsibilities of teachers at elementary and secondary school levels may be different, as far as their roles in guiding students' concept learning is concerned. The elementary teacher must pay particular attention to identifying concepts that are central to the student's later learning as well as present enterprises. The teacher at this level must see to it that these concepts are clearly delineated for the learner, recognize that learning demands appropriate concrete experiences, and provide an opportunity to compare positive and negative instances. Conceptual development thus seems to be one of the principal contributions of the elementary school to the child's learning. In the secondary school, stress should shift to the development of abstract concepts and to the relationships of these concepts to one another.

How are concepts learned?

There are basically two ways in which a concept can be learned: by inductive means and by deductive learning. In their unelaborated sense, these methods differ in the following way. A concept is learned inductively when the learner observes a series of examples of the concept and is left to attain the concept for himself from the examples he observes. Learning occurs deductively if the learner is given a statement of the concept at the outset. Examples that confirm the meaning of the concept may also be presented, but they are subordinate in the sense of illustrating the concept. As we shall see a bit later, learning of school concepts might best be accomplished through a mixture of inductive and deductive learning.

Most studies of the inductive learning of concepts have been done in psychology laboratories. The interest of the laboratory psychologist has rarely been in how school learning can be improved; he is more concerned with isolating and understanding the process of concept learning as it goes on in the less structured world outside the school. The brief review of laboratory studies of concept learning which follows describes some of the ways in which the psychologist studies concepts and examines why he does so. It is also focused on two of the many findings of psychologists that seem relevant to school learning: the use of positive and negative instances, and the effect of establishing a set to learn concepts. A section analyzing concept learning in classrooms or school-type settings follows, and the chapter closes with the compilation of a series of steps or procedures for teachers to use as a means of improving concept learning in classrooms.

Procedures in the Laboratory Study of Concept Attainment

For more than 50 years, psychologists have conducted experimental studies of how people learn concepts. Because the behavioral scientist's interest is principally in the processes involved and in the course of learning, the concepts chosen for research have rarely been "real" concepts. More typically, college students have been asked to learn the meaning of nonsense words such as *kun, vor, bep,* and *yem,* or to decide what *silm* or *fard* mean. In still other investigations, the effects of various strategies have been analyzed as participants try to determine that the "concept" to be learned is "all red circles" or "green crosses with two borders."

The experimental psychologist is as interested as anyone in making sense of the learning process. His use of artificial tasks to study concept learning is dictated by the fact that he can safely assume no learner already knows that *kun* means animal, but if he selected *force, acceleration, price-earnings ratio,* or some other meaningful concept to study, all of his subjects would start at different points on the learning curve. He also wants to discover how human beings process and integrate information in direct and natural situations to attain concepts. For example, he is very much interested in how Ted or Mary learns about cats and dogs. Even if he watched the child day after day, the occasions on which the event of interest might occur would be rare and unpredictable. Although ultimately he might learn something about the phenomenon, he is more concerned with knowing the relevant variables that govern the learning process and how they can be manipulated to improve it.

For these reasons, laboratory studies have concentrated on finding answers to questions such as the following: How is concept learning affected by varying the number of relevant dimensions (critical or defining dimensions) included in the concept, or the number of irrelevant (nondefining) dimensions? Do positive instances (examples) of the concept teach it as well as negative instances (nonexamples)? What happens if the learner is told to learn concepts (given a learning set) compared with an instruction simply to learn the material? Are some kinds of concepts easier to learn than others? Do some strategies lead to better learning?

The effect of a set to learn concepts

Reed (1946) demonstrated the positive effect of instructing the learner to learn concepts rather than just trying to associate common words with nonsense syllables. He constructed 42 cards which represented six concepts to be learned. (*Kun* meant animal, *vor* meant love, *bep* meant vegetable, and so forth.) An experimental subject would be shown a card with the words *horn leaf monkey debt* on it. After a few seconds he would be informed that the name of the card was *kun.* Six other cards in the series were also *kun,* and each of them contained the name of an animal and three other words. Except for the animal word, the others varied from card to card, and all were irrelevant to the attainment of the concept.

College students saw the cards one at a time. If they did not give the correct name for the card, after three seconds they were told its name, and after an elapsed total of seven seconds, the next card was presented. Students were shown the cards as many times as necessary until they could identify all of them in one errorless trial. Thus their task was to learn the name of each card. Half of those who participated were given only that instruction: learn the name of each of the 42 cards. The other half of the students were given a set to learn concepts and not simply to associate each card with a syllable. They were told what a concept is, to look at all the words on each card, and to try to learn what each nonsense syllable meant.

Except for the difference in set given to the two groups, the tasks they were to perform were identical. The set, however, turned out to have a major consequence. Students without the set to learn concepts required about 41 prompts on the average before they could identify the cards errorlessly, but students who had been given the set needed only 31 trials. About a third more effort was demanded of the students without the set. Their retention of the cards on a later test was also poorer than for those who had learned the names as concept labels. Reed also included in his report some brief descriptions of the individual reactions of students. One bright girl in the names-only group found the task so massive and frustrating that she broke into tears and had to be excused from that session. Students with the set cannot be said to behave identically to one another, for there are individual differences, but Reed did specify some identifiable steps that all the learners tend to take:

> First, a period of doubt and orientation.
> Second, a period of search and trial solutions.
> Third, a period of evaluation and checking. (Reed, 1946, p. 84)

This adoption of a set to learn what the nonsense syllables mean is a special case of a more general principle. Learning is facilitated when the learner knows what the learning task is and what final performance is expected of him. This applies also to information about how to tackle the task. "Set" subjects were instructed to examine all four words on each card. This placed them in a much stronger position to see that each *vor* card contained one love-oriented word (such as precious, sweetheart). Other students, left to their own devices, had to try to associate the name of each card with some specific cue, such as the initial letter of the first word on the front of the card. As we know, such a rote approach makes the task of learning difficult, and more vulnerable to forgetting as well.

Type of instance: Positive or negative

When the learner is exposed to examples that are pertinent to a concept, does it matter whether they are positive or negative examples? A positive example, of course, is one that fits the class to be learned. Negative instances might technically be anything else, but in practice they tend to be similar to positive instances, with only one or two criterial differences.

The role of positive and negative instances in concept learning has probably had more prominence than it would have had if it were not for a paper published by Smoke (1933). Smoke asked college students to learn a series of six geometric-shaped concepts; for example, a *dax* was a circle accompanied by two dots, one inside and one outside the circle. Other concepts involved trisecting one line with two others, bisecting a triangle, and so forth. In this study, Smoke constructed large sheets with numerous examples of one of the concepts on each sheet. A subject saw either all positive instances of the concept or a variety of positive and negative instances. Smoke kept a record of the time it took his subjects to learn each concept and found that there were no particular differences in that time, whether the student had all positive instances or a mixed sample. However, he did find that students reached more false conclusions which they had to change when all the instances were positive than when they were mixed. (He did not perform a statistical test of significance.)

At the end of his paper, Smoke reports that of the 30 students who learned the concepts, 23 preferred working with the combination of positive and negative instances, six preferred all positive instances, and one said he didn't care. Smoke observed that the use of negative instances in the learning trials may not have reduced the time for learning, but it did increase subjects' accuracy. Thus, he said, the benefit of negative instances lies in preventing the learner from jumping to hasty and incorrect conclusions about the nature of the concept.

For example, as part of a study of African wildlife, a teacher might want children to learn to identify African elephants. Since elephants also live in Southeast Asia, it is important that the pupils be able to distinguish between them. If African elephants are treated as the positive instance, the teacher could present several pictures of such elephants, preferably including front and side views. He could also mention some of the prominent features of African elephants, such as their size, weight, and color and the largeness of their ears, trunks, and tusks. Then one or two pictures of Asian elephants could well be used as negative instances. The teacher would especially want to compare and contrast the salient points of difference between the two species; the much smaller ears of the Asian elephant, its coloration, which is much lighter than the African species, the smaller tusks and trunk, and so forth. Note that the distinguishing characteristics of the African elephant can be made salient by these contrasts with the Asian elephant (that is, with the negative instances). In this way, the learner can begin to fix in his mind the significant differences between the two. There is always the possibility of interference; that is, the learner may sort out the criterial attributes adequately but associate the labels incorrectly, or forget which is which. For that reason, the teacher would probably wish to use several positive instances of the concept before introducing the negative ones. (See the section of Chapter 2 on Interference.)

Since Smoke's investigation, psychologists have from time to time raised the issue of how learners use negative information in achieving concepts. Hovland and Weiss (1953) developed a procedure for equating the amount of information transmitted by positive and negative instances, but they still found that sequences of all positive instances led to better concept acquisition, and mixed series were intermediate between positive and all negative series. Bruner, Goodnow, and Austin (1956), in a careful experimental study of disjunctive concepts, discovered that, even under conditions when a negative instance eliminated many more competing alternative solutions than a positive instance, their learners preferred to choose positive instances. Bruner thinks one reason for the reluctance of subjects to use negative information is because of its indirectness. With regard to the learning of disjunctive concepts in general, he adds that Western scientific thinking traditionally associates common effects with common causes, an assumption that breaks down when the same effect can be brought about by numerous and apparently unrelated causes.

Freidbergs and Tulving (1961) demonstrated that, when instances are equated for the amount of information they transmit, subjects can be taught to use negative instances almost as effectively as positive instances. After 11 trials, the time required for subjects with negative examples to learn a concept was only slightly longer than for the positive-instance subjects, and after 20 trials, the differences were indistinguishable.

Learning Concepts in School Settings

Educational psychologists grew impatient with laboratory studies of concept learning for two reasons: the purely inductive or discovery approach employed in psychological laboratories is not typical of how concept learning in school proceeds, and many of the experiments do not teach concepts. Instead they look at the strategies a learner uses to attach a nonsense label to some constellation of figures or shapes, such as *all red circles* or *cards with green borders*. Not until the early 1960s, through the insightful and detailed analyses of Robert Gagné and John B. Carroll, did it begin to be demonstrated that concept learning and teaching could be studied as it actually occurs in schools. This section, therefore, deals largely with investigations of recent vintage. Our attention will be directed to investigations of concept learning, such as how students come to learn the definitions of words and how they infer the meaning of new and unfamiliar words from the context in which they are embedded.

Gagné (1970) observed that learning is hierarchically organized, and before we can learn concepts, other lower order learnings must first be mastered. He also pointed out that most concepts taught by the school are complex and relational; to comprehend one concept, the learner must have comprehension of others that combine in altered forms to provide the meaning of the overarching concept. In Chapter 1 we noted that information, concepts, and principles are organized in an hierarchical manner, and we shall see later how this hierarchy is organized.

A paper by Carroll (1964) analyzed the properties and requirements of school concepts and differentiated between laboratory studies and the requirements of investigations of school concept learning so persuasively that it can almost be said that the study of school concept learning began with the publication of Carroll's paper. Carroll pointed out that a principal task of teachers at all levels is to teach words and their meanings, and concepts. This may mean not just the assignment of a new word to a familiar meaning but the teaching of entirely new concepts, and this teaching is usually intuitive and unanalytic.

Although a vast experimental literature on concept learning exists, it seems to have very little to do with how people learn concepts in schools. Carroll cites five differences between concept-formation studies and the school learning of concepts:

1. The learning that occurs in school involves "new" concepts rather than an artificial combination of familiar attributes such as "three blue triangles," and so forth.
2. New school concepts usually involve attributes that are themselves complex concepts. The attributes are usually verbal and cannot be represented by simple sensory data.
3. School concepts are relational, not conjunctive. They deal with relations among attributes, not with their combined presence or absence.
4. School learning requires that labels or names for concepts be

learned. Since memory is involved in concept learning in this connection, it is probable that the rate at which concepts should be introduced is limited.

5. The most critical difference is that school concepts are primarily deductive, whereas the emphasis of the concept-formation research has been upon inductive learning. Perhaps teaching of school concepts should incorporate more elements of inductive learning than is presently the case.

However, there are similarities as well as differences between school and laboratory studies of concepts. For example, concept learning is continuous with out-of-school learning. Many concepts are learned partly deductively and partly inductively. A concept such as *dog* is learned according to procedures much like those used in the psychology laboratory. Concepts such as *tourist* and *immigrant,* which might be learned at school, can also be partly learned through the direct observation and reinforcement of the learner. So there are circumstances under which the cumulative knowledge of the laboratory has applicability for the more deductive learning of the classroom.

To illustrate his points about the combination of deductive and inductive learning, Carroll pursues the child's learning of *tourist* and *immigrant.* The two could have much in common, and in the ordinary course of events, if the child is learning the concepts only through direct observation, the achievement of clarity and accuracy can be a long-drawn-out affair. Instances of one or the other may come along rarely and unpredictably, and the child may have no source of feedback to help him differentiate between the two. The purpose of teaching is to short cut the capricious process of concept attainment in the natural environment. To that end, the teacher might properly tell the pupil that a tourist is a visitor, and one day he will go home again, whereas an immigrant has moved to a new place permanently. In order for the child to acquire the concepts adequately, he must possess other prerequisite concepts, such as *permanent home, country, foreign,* and so forth.

How are concepts taught at school? One frequently used method is definition. To illustrate our overview of the learning process in Chapter 2, we described a social studies lesson in which the students were to learn the meaning of such terms as *legislature, constitution, judiciary,* and others. The idea is that as students obtain meaningful definitions of these words, they begin to build concepts. Carroll suggests that dictionary definitions are of two kinds: they provide verbal equivalents or synonyms (*lethargic* means apathetic, drowsy, or dull), or they give the reader a formal definition. The definition consists of two elements: genus and differentia. The genus includes those attributes of the term that assign it to a general class or category, and the differentia indicates the subclass or species into which it falls under the more general category. For example, in the definition of a *tarn* as a small mountain lake or pool, the term *lake or pool* is the genus, and *small mountain* is the differentia. It literally differentiates the subclass of special lakes or pools that are to be classified as tarns.

Note that in both of these cases the student's learning is not advanced unless the terms in the definition, or the synonyms to which he is referred, possess meaning for him. Our imprecations about rote learning as compared to meaningful learning apply here. Furthermore, we must once again recognize the importance of direct experience in learning concepts, especially direct experiences in the early years of development. It is true that a student who has never visited mountains or lakes can learn the definition of a tarn, but his verbal conception is necessarily limited in contrast to that of the person who has gaped in awe at the majesty of the Rockies or the beauty of the Blue Ridge mountains. Without some background of direct experience, we can no more extract the full meaning of a concept than we can imagine a new color which lies outside the spectrum. Several investigations have been made of learning concepts from definitions.

Learning concepts from definitions

Johnson and O'Reilly (1964) view a concept as a hypothetical construct whose existence is inferred from a change in the learner's behavior, such as his ability to classify information or examples in categories according to certain rules. However, in their view, the child who possesses a concept should be able to demonstrate that possession in ways other than through classificatory behavior. He should be able to use it in communication and problem solving, to describe its common characteristics, and to define it. In short, there are several correlated indicators of concept mastery.

Johnson and O'Reilly used 60 11- and 12-year-old children to study the effects of variations in training on classifying and defining. Unfortunately, the task to be learned was an artificial one, but it does bear some resemblance to concept-learning tasks that children encounter in schools. They were to learn the difference between "bunkle birds" and "gunkle birds". Two groups of the children (20 in each group) saw a series of 27 drawings of birds. The birds' wings could be any one of three colors, as could their tails, and their beaks were either long, short, or hooked. The task was to classify each picture as a "gunkle" or "bunkle" bird, and the trials continued until ten pictures in a row were correctly classified. One of the groups (called pictorial-definition) tried to define the terms after every fifth picture card. Otherwise it and the pictorial group's task were identical. The third group, called verbal, saw not pictures but cards with verbal descriptions: "red wing, orange tail, hooked beak, two feet with toes," and so forth. They were also to classify the instances, but no practice in defining was involved. Practice trials for all three groups continued until the classifying criterion was achieved. (This required significantly fewer trials for the verbal group than for either of the pictorial groups. Given the verbal descriptions, children learned to classify accurately in about 87 trials, whereas those youngsters who classified the pictures required twice as many trials or more.)

Concept mastery was assessed in three ways. One was by classifying the examples, as already described. A second assessment was of the child's ability to define the difference ("Gunkle birds all have black tails"), and the third was a transfer test. The children were asked to classify ten cards in the medium (verbal or pictorial) which was other than their training condition.

The best definitions were provided by children in the pictorial-definition group. Of the 20 children in that group, 16 were judged to generate good definitions. Comparable figures for the other groups were 14 for the verbal group and only 9 for the pictorial. Only the difference between the pictorial-definition and the pictorial groups proved to be statistically significant. Even though the efforts of children in the pictorial-definition group were not evaluated during the learning session, judges assigned the highest ratings for definitions on the criterion test to children in that group. Johnson and O'Reilly attribute this result to the simple effects of practice at defining. As we shall see shortly, Anderson and Kulhavy (1972) obtained a similar result when they asked students to construct a sentence in which they could use a new word. Their interpretation is that the effort to be intellectually active in this context generated deeper processing of the definition. Finally, in the Johnson and O'Reilly study, children in all three training conditions earned scores on the transfer test somewhat above 8, on the average, out of a possible 10. The level of transfer was very high, and there was no difference among the three groups.

The experiment by Anderson and Kulhavy (1972) was a direct test of whether students learn concepts from definitions. A group of words that occur in normal English usage less than once in a million times was selected, and 13 were retained that were not known by a sample of 48 college students exposed to them. (The 13 included *atavistic, besprent,* and *cuprous,* for example.) Each word and a one-sentence dictionary definition of it appeared on a separate 5- by 8-inch card. Each student saw the defined term for six seconds at a time. At the end of a study trial, the student answered a 13-item multiple-choice test, one item based upon each word. The test items contained none of the same substantive words that were in the definition. For that reason, Anderson and Kulhavy contend that the learner must comprehend the items he answers correctly on the test.

Figure 4.1 is an illustration of the material to be learned by students and of the kinds of items they had to answer on the test. One of these questions appeared on each of the two tests. Each student went through two cycles: study trial 1, followed by a test. The student then studied the terms a second time and took another test. Half of the participants, selected at random, constructed sentences of their own for each word in the presence of the definition. An informal check led the investigators to conclude that college students were doing this effectively—for example, one student opined that "Mayor Daley's politics are atavistic." The remaining 24 students read each definition aloud three times during the brief period it was before them.

The results show two things:

1. There is a significant effect for trials; that is, students scored better on the second test than they did on the first.
2. The effect for treatments is also effective. Those who made up their own sentences scored better on the tests. This result cannot be the effect of practice or repetition alone, for half the students read each definition several times during each trial. Anderson and Kulhavy are probably correct in their conclusion that this forces more semantic encoding (or the search for what, in this case, the sentence means), as opposed to phonological or syntactic processing. The same analysis probably also applies to Johnson and O'Reilly's finding of superior results for the children who defined the critical attribute of gunkle birds, because of the deeper processing that would be required to construct the definitions.

At the risk of belaboring the obvious, we should nail down two points before we proceed to the next topic.

First, why do Anderson and Kulhavy speak of learning concepts from definitions? The answer concerns their notion of comprehension. In order to select a correct test response, the learner had to translate—better yet, to generalize—his definition of the term to specific examples that illustrate it. If his knowledge were limited to the explicit definition given him, his generalizations would be inaccurate most of the time. This study provides an excellent illustration of the generality of learning afforded by concepts.

FIGURE 4.1
An example of the material used to teach concepts by means of definitions

---

Definition:
    Atavistic means reversion to a primitive type.
Item 1: *atavistic*
A. The students complained that his approach to teaching was very old-fashioned.
B. Her main object in attending class was to flirt with every boy who sat next to her.
C. The photographs of the murder scene were so awful that the district attorney hesitated to use them as evidence.
D. Uncle Joe was as stubborn as they come.
Item 2: *atavistic*
A. Once the little boy had decided he wanted candy, there was no peace until he got some.
B. The stewardess smiled invitingly at the businessman.
C. The lion, although raised in the zoo, returned to instinctual behaviors when released in the African jungles.
D. The young boy was delighted by the bizarre characters in the horror movies.

Source: Anderson & Kulhavy (1972), p. 387.

Second, in both these studies we again encounter the important principle of learner activity and participation in the process of learning. When the learners, whether they were 12 or 20, had to assume an active role in processing and reorganizing the information to be learned, the highest level of learning resulted. But note that this participation is structured and disciplined. Simple repetition in the Anderson and Kulhavy study could certainly represent active participation. However, much better results ensued when the learner had the obligation to engage in meaningful processing of the definitions. Johnson and O'Reilly also do not tell us how successful the younger children were in their trial definitions. Is a task of that order easy for pupils of age 11, or is systematic instruction in how to construct a definition called for? An answer to that question would have practical consequences for the classroom teacher who wants to improve his students' mastery of subject matter concepts.

Although students learn concepts from definitions, there is also evidence that the learner's stage of intellectual development and the level of his knowledge must be taken into account in determining the substance of the definition with which he is supplied. Feldman and Klausmeier

(1974) tested this idea with fourth-graders and eighth-graders. All the children were to learn to use a definition of an equilateral triangle, either what the authors called a technical definition or a common-usage definition. The technical definition read as follows: "An equilateral triangle is a figure with three straight sides of equal length. It is plane, closed, and simple." The common-usage definition said: "An equilateral triangle is a figure with three sides which are all equal in length." Half the children at each grade level were given each of the definitions. The authors hypothesized that the fourth-grade children would perform better with the common-usage definition, on the grounds that the terms and relationships in the more detailed and technical definition would be confusing to them, and therefore of less use in guiding their classificatory behavior. The anticipated result did, in fact, occur. The idea underlying this study seems very sound; that is, to introduce concepts through definitions which are simple but correct, and to advance from them to more complex or more technical definitions at a later time.

In a sequel to that study, Klausmeier and Feldman (1975) investigated the effects of four different conditions for teaching fourth-grade children the concept of an equilateral triangle. Again, the criterion was classificatory behavior; that is, the children were tested after instruction for their ability to classify 38 examples and nonexamples of the concept.

One group of children was given the definition of the concept to study. Another was given what the researchers call a rational set of examples; in this study, that meant a set of three examples which reflected a broad range of triangles equilateral in form, and five nonexamples in which the negative examples differed from the examples in a small number of attributes. This helps learners to avoid misconceptions. The investigators had assumed that these two conditions would have about the same effect on learners, and they did. Both led to significantly better performance than control students, but no significant difference between the two treatments.

In a third group, children were supplied with the definition and a rational set of examples, and, although the combination provided some additional information to the learner, scores were only nonsignificantly higher on the criterion test. The fourth group of students received the definition and three sets of examples and nonexamples. This treatment resulted in significantly higher test scores. As an illustration, students in the definition-only group scored 76 percent on the test, and students in the last mentioned treatment scored 88 percent. The added rational sets appear to have provided the children with sufficient new information to enable them to classify somewhat more examples and nonexamples than the others were able to do. Klausmeier and Feldman point out that this approach improves concept learning constructed as classificatory behavior, but concept learning at a formal level may require different kinds of training. According to them, concept attainment at a formal level includes classification, and the learner can also discriminate the defining attributes of the concept, give the name of the concept and the defining attributes, classify examples and nonexamples on the basis of defining attributes, and define the word that labels the concept.

Learning meanings from context

Textbooks and teachers sometimes use words which are not known to the learner but whose meaning can presumably be determined from the context in which they appear. Through the years several studies have examined how such contextual learning occurs. It appears that the ability to infer meaning from context improves with age and that more than one use of the term in context is necessary for dependable meaning to be abstracted. Let us look briefly at the results of three investigations.

An early paper by Gibbons (1940) revealed that large proportions of a sample of college freshmen were unable to produce acceptable meanings for new words from a single use in context. Gibbons selected 24 words from an initial list of 50 that could not be defined by 85 percent or more of a group of 234 college freshmen. Each word appeared in a sentence or paragraph of text, and students were asked to determine its meaning. The words included *itinerant, myriad,* and *vicarious.* Overall, almost half the students were not able to derive meanings for the words. As an example, the word *vicarious* was presented in the following context:

> Part of our education is obtained directly through actual experiences; *vicarious* experiences which come through reading, pictures, lectures, art, and music are equally important, however, as a means of extending real experiences. (p. 31)

No answer or an incorrect answer was given by 91 percent of the students. For example, students suggested the meaning of vicarious to be "experiences obtained gradually," "indiscrete experiences," or "the act of feeling, seeing, learning," and so forth. Similarly, one third of the students could not adequately define the word *itinerant* after encountering it in the following sentence:

> In the beginning the teacher travelled from one locality to another to meet the students, thereby bringing into existence the *itinerant* school master. (p. 29)

Students described an itinerant teacher as "immoral," "a research schoolmaster," "intolerable," "humble," and so on.

Gibbons's analysis of what the student must do with the sentence provided in order to construct an acceptable definition is pertinent to our discussion. She identified three skills:

1. The student must perceive accurately the relationships among elements in the sentence; for example, he must see that *thereby* (in the schoolmaster sentence) establishes a relationship between the fact that early teachers traveled about the countryside to conduct classes and the meaning of the word to be defined.
2. The student must have the ability to infer meanings from those given in the sentence.
3. The student must be able to paraphrase the meanings given.

Gibbons suggests that instruction can be provided to teach these skills, but no program for doing so is indicated. We should also observe that, unlike Anderson and Kulhavy, whose tests of comprehension of terms were multiple choice, Gibbons apparently forced her students to construct and write their own definitions. This might inflate the percentage of inadequate responses, compared to other procedures.

Werner and Kaplan (1950) studied much the same issue with children of elementary school age. They invented words to represent common objects and embedded them in groups of sentences. For example:

A *corplum* may be used for support.

Corplums may be used to close off an open space.

A wet *corplum* does not burn. (p. 3)

Children eight years of age were unable to construct meanings that were not tied to an aspect of a given sentence. Werner and Kaplan discovered that the ability to infer more general meanings improved with advancing age, but not until age 11 were the pupils able to give meanings for the artificial words which were independent of any specific sentences.

Johnson and Stratton (1966), observing that teachers use numerous methods to teach concepts, compared five methods. One group of students studied definitions; another completed sentences using the words to be learned; still another learned a classification method; and others were given synonyms. The fifth group studied a program that had selected elements of all four of the other methods and there was also a sixth group which functioned as a control. The 200 students in an introductory psychology class received one of these six programs, distributed on a random basis. They were to learn the meanings of *alacrity, altercation, chide,* and *opulent.* Twelve minutes were allotted to study of the learning task. Nine days later a test was administered to all the students; this test consisted of items of all the types studied by the different groups. This made it possible to assess the amount of transfer that occurred from one method to another.

The investigators attempted to construct each of the methods to operate at its most effective level. A few examples of what the learners were exposed to will demonstrate these methods. Students who were in the definitions group saw material of this kind:

> When two or more people express different opinions, get excited, and contradict each other, the event is called an *altercation*. Thus an *altercation* is a social interaction characterized by heated exchange of opposing arguments. Now write a definition of *altercation* in your own words. (p. 50)

The mixed program required abridgements and reductions in the number of examples and synonyms that could be included. Students who used the mixed program had only as much time to study it as their peers in any of the other groups. Here is an example of what the students using the mixed program studied:

> To chide someone is to talk to him to get him to correct his mistakes. Chide means to criticize or reproach. Thus a mother might chide her children for fighting with each other. An example might be a group of fellows poking fun at a boy with dirty clothes. Now write in your own words what chide means. (p. 51)

The results of the tests after nine days were clear-cut. Students who had been given the single-method treatments scored better, on the average, than the group of control students who had received no instruction. However, the group who had studied the mixed program scored significantly better than the students in any of the four single methods. The investigators also indicate that transfer of learning from one task to another was complete. Even though Johnson and Stratton controlled the amount of study time for each group, students in the mixed program obviously received a great deal more information about the words they were to learn.

As a practical matter, the finding of the Johnson and Stratton paper is a helpful guide to teaching concepts, at least with college students. If the learner studies words as definitions, synonyms, and in other contexts, he has increasing access to their meaning. Notice also from the examples cited above that these students had to remain active in generating their own definitions of the terms, once they had an opportunity to acquire pertinent information.

The research studies reviewed here provide a valuable foundation of knowledge about how students learn one class of responses which are important in concept learning; that is, the meanings of words. As important as this is, it is but a fraction of what we mean by the learning of concepts in school. What is the course of learning when the acquisition of a new concept depends upon the learner having possession of one or more other concepts? How are relational concepts learned? Let us admit at the outset that we have many more questions about concept learning than we have answers at the present time. In the next section, we turn our attention largely to the work of Gagné and his associates and students.

Learning principles

Conceptual learning is one aspect of Gagné's (1970) delineation of the learning process. A brief sketch of how he views the entire process reveals both its order and its complexity. According to Gagné, learning proceeds through a series of eight stages or levels, and the learner's ability to perform at any level depends upon his mastery of those beneath it in the learning hierarchy. The lowest levels of learning correspond to classical conditioning and instrumental conditioning. The basic experiences that children require in order to operate at higher levels are acquired through direct contact with objects and with the environment in the years before formal schooling begins. The learner's direct contact with objects plays an important part in Gagné's system, even in conceptual learning.

The kinds of learning that are important in school are classified by Gagné as discrimination learning, the learning of concepts, rule learning, and problem solving. The hierarchical nature of the system should be evident from these labels. The learner can attain concepts only as he has developed capabilities for making discriminations; defined concepts and rules (the topics of this discussion) depend upon his conceptual learning, for rules are statements of the relationships which exist between two or more concepts. Finally, problem solving can be effective only if the student comprehends the rules that are to be applied to the problem.

We can apply part of Gagnés system to enhance our understanding of how complex concepts (what he calls rules or principles) are learned. We begin with an example from real life, one which is all too frequently played in homes and classrooms. A fifth-grade boy, seated at the kitchen table, is doing his arithmetic. "Dad," he says, to his father, engrossed nearby in the evening newspaper, "I don't know how to do these." The father walks over, looks at the arithmetic page. It is filled with drawings of cubes and other rectilinear solids, their dimensions neatly printed along their edges. The examples are different, but the questions asked are the same. "What is the volume?" and "What is the surface area?" Figure 4.2 sketches one solid upon which the discussion here is focused; actually the assignment ranged widely over a half dozen similar examples.

FIGURE 4.2
The learner's ability to apply rules to find area and volume of objects depends upon his mastery of subordinate concepts.

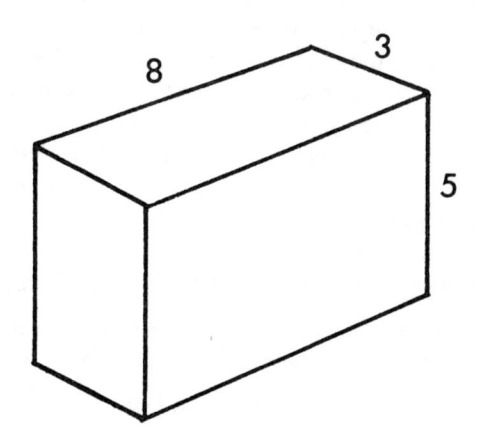

The father-son dialogue goes like this:

>Father: Okay, how do you find the volume?
>Son: I don't know.
>Father: Well, how do you get the area?
>Son: I don't know—just tell me, will you?
>Father: Do you know what the dimensions of this are?
>Son: Yeah—3, 5, and 8.
>Father: Good. Now, if you know the dimensions, can you find the volume?
>Son: (Very uncertainly.) I think—don't you multiply? It's 3 times 8 times 5.
>Father: That's very good. Why'd you tell me you don't know how? Okay, what does that give you?
>Son: (Multiplies.) 120.
>Father: 120 what?
>Son: 120 centimeters.
>Father: What?
>Son: 120—cubic centimeters.
>Father: Look, when I ask you for the volume, don't make me ask three questions. Give me the whole thing, understand?

By this time, the father has a strong suspicion that his son lacks understanding of the concept of volume, but like the novice skydiver, he's afraid to take the first step. He decides, instead, to retreat to the safer concept of area. He asks the boy whether he can now find the surface area, and after a moment's computation, the son gives him an answer: "240." Fortunately, he does not add "cubic centimeters." Father asks where the 240 came from. "Well, we had 120 and I doubled it." A glimmer of comprehension dawns on the father. The relationship which the arithmetic book has tried to teach the pupil between area and volume has been but vaguely, and altogether incorrectly, learned. What the child has concluded is that, since the surface area is found by summing the area of the six surfaces of the solid, he can get the proper result by multiplying the volume by two, since he used each dimension once in that computation. There is a strange, inchoate plausibility to this operation which makes its confusion difficult to overcome.

When all else fails, give the young child a concrete example to deal with. Father moves the discussion directly to the idea of area:

> Father: Now, wait a minute. Think about the vegetable garden we have in the backyard. Suppose I asked you to find its area. What would you do?
>
> Son: (Vaguely.) I don't know—measure it, I guess.
>
> Father: Fine, what would you measure?
>
> Son: I don't know—stuff—things.
>
> Father: Like what, the clumps of dirt?
>
> Son: (a gleam in his eye) No—I'd measure—I'd measure the vegetables, that's what I'd do. I'd measure the vegetables.

They look at each other and dissolve into laughter. The tasks posed by the youngster's arithmetic textbook provide extended opportunity to apply rules that are assumed to be well known. In the example above, the rules cannot be intelligently applied because the concepts upon which they are based have not been comprehended. That is an inference, of course, but it can be supported by the chain of events. Consider the opening interchange about the figure's volume. The rule that to find volume one multiplies the three dimensions was used correctly, but it is apparent that the boy did not have a conception that for each unit of all three dimensions that entered into his computation he was defining the boundaries of a cubic unit of measurement; that is, that the measurement of one centimeter of length, width, and height defines one cubic centimeter. Without that concept, however, can the student ever comprehend that when each dimension is increased to 2, this does not double the volume but increases it by a factor of 8? In another context this child has learned that $1^3 = 1$, that $2^3 = 8$, that $3^3 = 27$, $4^3 = 64$, and so on. Can he ever comprehend the relationship between the exponential expansion and the rate of increase in volume if he lacks that fundamental concept?

Gagné (1970) distinguished clearly between concepts and principles or rules. When a child can assign the numeral 3 to a set of three marbles, tops, or other objects, he possesses a concept of that number. But a fuller conception would include some of the relationships of three to other numbers; for instance, when you add 1 to 2 you obtain 3, the quotient of 6 divided by 2 is 3, the square of 9 is 3. The two kinds of learning demand different capabilities. In the case of three as a concept, only the application of the label is required. As a principle, the learner must use the concept in other combinations; for example, to add or subtract.

On the assumption that two kinds of learning are involved, Gagné argues, it is reasonable to suppose that the conditions for their learning are also different. One of the important differences lies in the role of language. He assumes (as we took pains to demonstrate earlier) that human beings can learn concepts much faster and better because of the use of language than they can without it. Not to use language to facilitate the learning of concepts would be to retard the process needlessly and to reduce severely the number of concepts the student would learn. Although language can also be used to teach students relationships or principles, Gagné is not as sure of the long-term efficacy of doing so. Whereas one can teach a young child the concepts of *liquid* and *solid* by means of a simple combination of demonstrations and verbal instruction, the role of induction or discovery may be of more importance for the child to learn a relationship such as "liquids pour." The evidence is not overwhelming, but he believes that retention and transfer may be somewhat enhanced if the student plays a more active role in discovering such relationships than if they are simply taught to him. Carroll's observation that school concept teaching perhaps should involve more inductive learning than is commonly the case makes much the same point.

Gagné's most important statement concerning the learning of principles is one we tried to illustrate in the case of the fifth-grade arithmetic lesson, on area and volume. Principles or rules can be learned meaningfully only when the concepts upon which they are based have been mastered by the learner. This is true precisely because the relationship stated in the rule is a relationship between or among concepts. If they are not known, the learner is left in the position of having to deal by rote and, in arbitrary ways with verbal or symbolic principles that have limited meaning for him. (Compare this with our discussion of meaningful and rote learning in Chapter 2.)

Gagné observes (as we have throughout this section) that principles are sometimes used for the purpose of teaching concepts. This is so, for example, when textbooks and teachers employ formal definitions to teach concepts. The success of that learning depends heavily upon the pupil's understanding of each concept that enters into the definition. In this connection, Gagné stresses the importance of direct experience by the learner in concept acquisition. Suppose he learns that the word *caliche* is "a crust of calcium carbonate formed on stony soil in arid regions." We would be much more confident that the student will correctly identify caliche when he sees it if direct contact with it has been associated with learning the definition. It is for this same reason that science educators stress direct experience and observation of substance and operations in science laboratories.

Retention of subordinate concepts

As part of an extensive study of mathematics learning, Gagné and Bassler (1963) studied the retention by sixth-grade pupils of topics in nonmetric geometry. The tests of retention were given nine weeks after the concepts had been learned originally. No specific problems were repeated from the instructional to the retention phase, but the concepts tested for were identical to those that had already been learned. The tests examined two general features of learning: the retention of the final performance, and retention of the subordinate learnings—items which did not appear in the final performance but which were nonetheless critical to its learning. The results show that, nine weeks after original learning, retention exceeds 100 percent for all but one of the original training conditions. (The authors point out that this occurs because the posttest served as an additional learning trial.) At any rate, it can be seen that these topics in nonmetric geometry are highly resistant to forgetting.

That is not true, however, for the subordinate learnings. Concepts such as *ray, line segment,* simple closed figures, or specifying intersections of various figures and identifying and drawing intersections were remembered much less well. Retention of those subordinate learnings ranged from 60 to 88 percent. Although of great importance to the original learning, their importance diminishes once the learning has been achieved. Furthermore which of the subordinate tasks will be forgotten and which remembered appears to be a random rather than a predictable phenomenon. No great harm ensues from this forgetting unless the learner needs to draw upon them in the future to learn a new task. The finding also demonstrates that the final product is not just the accumulation of the numerous subordinate concepts or skills.

Hierarchical structure of a nonmathematical concept

How important is the sequencing of learning tasks for the acquisition of a complex concept? Eustace (1969) showed that second-and third-grade children learned a concept better when they studied a program of high structure rather than programs of lower degrees of structure. Her study is interesting also because the concept taught was *noun* which does not lend itself particularly well to the task analysis of mathematics or the physical sciences, which have clearer structures. Eustace designated eight levels of knowledge of the concept. Level VIII, the top one, was:

> understanding of the concept "noun" as being a combination of related factors which include definition and use. Illustrated by the student's ability to identify a concrete or abstract noun and as a subject in a simple sentence.

The lower levels in Eustace's program are somewhat restricted statements of the same concept. For example, Level IV reads as follows:

> Understanding of the limited concept "noun." Illustrated by the student's ability to use the limited definition, "a noun is a name of a person or something you can touch" to identify nouns as isolated words as opposed to non-nouns as isolated words."

The eight levels were collapsed into four by combining adjacent pairs. For purposes of the research, 208 second-and third-graders received one of four programs of study. The items to be learned were the same in all programs, but the sequence, and therefore the degree of structure, differed among the four programs. Programs were designated as Hi Hi; Hi Lo (there were two of them), and Lo Lo. (As examples, children in the Hi Hi program studied the material in sequence, beginning with Level I and ending with Level VIII. The Lo Lo program had exactly the opposite sequence. Hi and Lo were different but intermediate degrees of structure between the extremes.) In accordance with her hypothesis, the residual gain scores decreased as structure of the training program decreased. A trend test showed significance at the .05 level.

Eustace interprets her basic finding as evidence that the definition of a concept advances and becomes more complex at different levels. Thus we can say that a pupil can "have" a concept of noun at a variety of levels. Her or his ability to advance to higher levels depends upon systematic sequencing, not random exposure to additional aspects of the definition or characteristics of the concept. The data and interpretation are congruent with Gagné's explanation that subordinate learnings transfer positively to, and therefore facilitate the learning of, the next higher item in the hierarchy.

The Improvement of Concept Learning

Concepts are obviously important in education; they have been called the building blocks of thinking. They should be as clear and accurate in the learner's cognitive structure, and as comprehensive and well delineated, as possible. People learn concepts in the natural world outside the school, to be sure. However, there the learner has no control over the quality of examples he encounters, or their frequency, or how well they help him to attain a good concept. The school, principally through the teacher's action, can aid concept learning.

We have reviewed several bodies of research in this chapter about how people learn concepts. Now we will translate some of the findings and generalizations of that research into a set of suggestions or procedures for the teacher's guidance. There are two parts to this: First, a series of steps that should be generally helpful for concept learning is suggested. This list is derived from studies reviewed before in the chapter, as well as from Clark (1971) and Hudgins (1972). Second, the steps are applied to the biological concept of *cell* to provide a somewhat more realistic illustration of how they can assist the teacher and the learner.

The steps in concept learning are as follows:

1. The student should know that he is expected to learn a concept, or group of concepts. What the concepts are should be made explicit, as well as why they are to be learned; that is, how they will contribute to his understanding of a larger field of knowledge. This point, of course, is not restricted to the learning of concepts, but it is applicable to them.

2. Appropriate recognition should be given to the intellectual development of the student who is to learn the concept. This does not mean only taking account of the complexity of the language that is suitable, or the need for concrete illustrations, although both of these considerations are involved. It also means assessing what the learner knows about the concept, or conceptual network, so that new learning can be geared to his or her existing knowledge.

3. The learner should begin with a clear, positive example of the concept. Whether the example is verbal, pictorial, or in some other form will depend upon the nature of the concept. But the first several examples should be unmistakably clear and simple examples of what the concept label identifies, points to, or incorporates.

4. As the learner studies these examples, the defining or criterial attributes should also be identified: "One reason this is x is because it contains 1, 2, and 3."

5. Positive examples should include as little distracting or irrelevant material as possible. They should be selected so as to *vary* the distractors they provide. If the learner repeatedly observes examples that contain a common element, he will conclude that it is a defining part of the concept,

even though it may not be. A child in the hospital was cared for by a succession of women nurses. When a male nurse came on the ward, the child identified him as a doctor.

6. If it is possible to do so, the learner should have access to all examples at the same time. This greatly reduces the load he has to remember (and the possibility of recalling information erroneously). It also makes point-by-point comparisons and contrasts among the examples possible.

8. As learning progresses, examples should be expanded to define the limits of the concept. In the beginning, all the examples are typical, conventional, "good" examples. Most concepts can be cast in more complex forms, and the learner must be able to identify them. Examples should become more realistic or more detailed, perhaps less clear. The learner should again be challenged to identify examples and give reasons. Feedback should continue.

9. For some concepts negative examples may play an important role in learning. Sometimes two very different concepts may easily be mistaken for one another, except for an identifying characteristic or two. These should be clearly pointed out, and the learner should understand how the concepts are different and how to identify the differences. Examples of both concepts should be provided in conjunction with each other. The learner should have a chance to inform himself of where the defining differences lie.

10. How the learner is to use the concept should guide the preceding steps, as well as the teacher's effort to assess the learner's mastery of the concept. If it is important for the learner to be able to recognize and make use of a concept which is often embedded in text or otherwise difficult to discern, or to identify it correctly when it is perceived, then the steps that guide his learning must be sequenced so that practice continues until he has mastered the concept as he will have to use it. The occasions in elementary and secondary schools when that would happen should be infrequent. On the other hand, some concepts can be easily communicated by a definition or by one or two offhand examples. How the teacher goes about guiding the learner's practice with a concept must be determined by its importance to a body of knowledge; whether it is a superordinate concept without which others would be meaningless, or a simple idea, or one that most people at a given educational level will already have learned.

Application of these steps or general procedures to the learning of a particular concept can be only illustrative of the methodology for that single concept. The broad concept considered below is: "The cell is the basic unit of living things." The development of the concept is aimed at the middle grades of the elementary school, but it was selected because it may appear in the school child's curriculum at several times during her or his educational career: in the primary grades, and again in the high school biology class. Obviously, at each of these times, the treatment would differ in its complexity and extensiveness.

As an introduction the teacher should make clear to pupils what they are to learn: *cells* are the basic building blocks of plants and animals. How are cells constructed, and what do they do? The evidence is clear that if the learner begins with an idea of what his or her study is to yield, the irrelevant or tangential aspects of the task can be discarded or ignored.

The learner must acquire a good, clear image of what a cell looks like. For this purpose, microscopic examination of cells is probably not the best introduction to the concept. The teacher would do better to draw the learner's attention to a textbook drawing if one is available; if not, one can be drawn on the chalkboard or any convenient place. The particular type of cell used for the introduction is not critical. It is essential, however, that the invariant aspects of cells (or their criterial attributes) are clearly identified and that the name of each part is labeled and made clear as well. Thus the teacher may see to it that the child pays attention to a clearly drawn and well-marked illustration of a cell. The location of the *nucleus,* the *cytoplasm,* and the *membrane* should be unequivocal. In the parlance of concept learning, the process should begin with a positive instance or example. A step should be taken to ensure that the three basic parts of the cell have been identified and that the student is able to name each of them.

This might be followed by the presentation of additional drawings. Some of these may demonstrate to the child that the location of the nucleus varies from one cell to another. Such a series of drawings or microscopic photographs should become increasingly realistic. If possible, each child should examine cells through a microscope. Through a series of progressive steps, it becomes possible for the learner to see what he is after more easily than if we initiate the learning process with all its attendant complexities.

Since there are many different types of cells, the learner's concept is limited by whatever examples he has seen. Unless we widen the array to which the learner is exposed, we run the risk of restricting or distorting his concept. The process of discrimination now takes an active part in the learning process. Each example the learner sees will contain the basic parts of the cell. This enables the learner to generalize across all cases. However, the various types of cells differ greatly in appearance. The learner should see several different ones: for example, skin cells, nerve cells, red blood cells, and muscle cells. They exemplify the broad range of differences, yet all possess the basic characteristics of cells. They also perform the cell's functions of taking in food and oxygen and giving off carbon dioxide and wastes. The learner should see these different examples of cells simultaneously. Direct comparisons and contrasts among them are then possible.

So far the student's learning has been guided primarily by perception and by varying the range and number of positive examples of the concept to which he is exposed. Although the learning of this concept demands visual observation, including the examination of models and of specimens under the microscope, the concept cannot be comprehensive if it is limited to observation. The student must learn what the cell's functions are and how they are carried out. We observed earlier that concepts can sometimes be taught by means of definitions or through the use of context. In order for the child to understand how energy is released and used in the cell, he must have a concept of *oxidation*. This concept can be amply clarified by the use of example and analogy, drawing upon phenomena with which the learner has had previous acquaintance. Oxidation occurs when a candle burns. Oxygen combines with a substance to produce light and heat. An oxide results, such as carbon dioxide. But oxidation does not require a flame. If the child leaves his bicycle outside overnight, it may be rusty the next morning. Oxidation has occurred in that case, too.

How far to continue examples depends finally upon how complex and refined we expect the learner's concept to be at a given time. The fifth-grade teacher will create a foundation upon which the secondary school science teacher can build.

Research literature has shown that the use of negative examples can contribute to concept learning. Negative examples of cells are not numerous, but plant and animal cells can be discriminated on the basis of the presence or absence of a cell wall. Plant cells have cell walls, but animal cells do not. This difference represents a major division between plant and animal cells. Pupils should see examples of both types side by side, and they should learn what the function of the cell wall is. The cell walls are composed of cellulose, and that is what gives greater rigidity to plants compared to animals. There are other distinctions between the cells of the two; for example, the presence of chloroplasts in the cells of green plants, and so on. Again, the objective for a lesson or a unit must define how extensive the examples and the range of discriminations is to be.

As concept learning progresses, there should be opportunity for the learner and the teacher to interact with one another. This is important especially because interaction affords the teacher the chance to monitor and assess the learner's concept and to provide feedback to the learner, as well as additional information about the concept. Tests for the accuracy of the learner's concept ought not to be postponed until learning is supposed to be complete. For example, if the teacher projects a slide of a cell on the screen, she may direct pupils' attention to a vacuole and ask what it is. If a child identifies it as the nucleus, it is important that the error be corrected and that the learner be given an opportunity to compare the appearance of the two more closely.

Later examples should include one or more characteristics that do not define the class. These examples might include plant cells; green plant cells with their chloroplasts, or protozoa; paramecia, amoebas, and so forth. At a still later stage, the characteristics that differentiate one major type of cells from others should be systematically discriminated.

Finally the teacher must bear in mind that the pupil's learning of concepts bears a close relationship to the conditions under which the learning occurred and the range of examples to which the learner was exposed. It may be that the teacher wishes to restrict the learner's practice to the recognition of drawings or models of typical cells. That may be a legitimate goal for young children, but the teacher ought not then to expect the learner to be able to identify cells on slides under a microscope, or paramecia floating in a drop of pond water. If, as teachers, we seem to make one major collective error about the relationship between learning and instruction, it is that we anticipate broader and more extensive outcomes for learners than is warranted by the amount and quality of instruction they are provided. Our next concern, to which we turn in Chapter 5, is with the conditions of learning that promote or inhibit transfer of one thing we have learned to the learning of something else.

Questions for Review and Discussion

1. What is a concept? Are definitions and concepts the same thing? Why is it more difficult to attain a concept of *equality* or *liberty* or *justice* than one of *chair* or *airplane* or *teacher?*

2. We speak sometimes of "concept formation" and other times of "concept attainment." What is the difference? How do processes of generalization and discrimination enter into concept learning?

3. According to Carroll, laboratory studies of concept learning are very different from how concepts are learned in the classroom. What do you think are the principal differences? Can you think of a concept that would be better learned deductively than inductively? What about the reverse?

4. Select any concept you might wish students to learn. Compose several positive examples of it. Can you construct some negative examples as well? Compare your positive and negative examples. How are they different?

5. Pick another concept of your choice that could be learned adequately from a definition, or in the context of a textbook or teacher exposition. Express it in terms that would be used with learners. Reflect on why you selected the particular concept you did to answer Question 4 and this one. Are the concepts of different orders in a conceptual hierarchy? Is one more important than the other?

6. Try to sketch an application of the steps outlined in the final section of the chapter to any concept you wish to teach. Be clear about what the learner is to know when he has mastered the concept. List any less general concepts the learner will require, and suggest how they are to be learned. Estimate how many examples would be required for the concept to be learned. How would they be placed in sequence? Would the perception occur in a single lesson? Several? How much time would be required?

Readings for Further Reflection

Introductory level

The collections listed here include one or more good papers in the area of concept formation or concept learning.

DeCecco, John P. (Ed.). *The Psychology of Language, Thought, and Instruction.* New York: Holt, Rinehart, & Winston, 1967.

Shulman, Lee S., and Keislar, Evan R. (Eds.). *Learning By Discovery: A Critical Appraisal.* Chicago: Rand McNally & Co., 1966.

Advanced level

As indicated above, one of the definitive papers on the nature of concept learning in school was written by John B. Carroll. Any teacher who is serious about improving the quality of conceptual learning in his or her classroom should read:

Carroll, John B. "Words, Meanings, and Concepts." *Harvard Educational Review,* 1964, *34,* 178–202.

Other interesting readings include the following:

Bruner, Jerome S. "Some Elements of Discovery." In Shulman and Keislar (Eds.), *Learning by Discovery.*

Bruner, Jerome S., Goodnow, Jacqueline J., and Austin, George A. *A Study of Thinking.* New York: John Wiley & Sons, 1956.

Martorella, Peter H. *Concept Learning: Design for Instruction.* Scranton, Pa.: Intext Educational Publishers, 1972.

Klausmeier, Herbert J., and Harris, Chester W. (Eds.). *Analysis of Concept Learning.* New York: Academic Press, 1966.

References

Anderson, Richard C., & Kulhavy, Raymond W. Learning concepts from definitions. *American Educational Research Journal,* 1972, *9,* 385–390.

Bruner, Jerome S., Goodnow, Jacqueline J., & Austin, George A. *A study of thinking.* New York: John Wiley & Sons, 1956.

Carroll, John B. Words, meanings, and concepts. *Harvard Educational Review,* 1964, *34,* 179–202.

Clark D. Cecil. Teaching concepts in the classroom: A set of teaching prescriptions derived from experimental research. *Journal of Educational Psychology,* 1971, *62,* 253–278.

Eustace, Barbara. Learning a complex concept at differing hierarchical levels. *Journal of Educational Psychology,* 1969, *60,* 449–452.

Feldman, Katherine V., & Klausmeier, Herbert J. The effects of two kinds of definition on the concept attainment of fourth and eighth graders. *Journal of Educational Research,* 1974, *67,* 219–223.

Freidbergs, V., & Tulving, E. The effect of practice on utilization of information from positive and negative instances in concept identification. *Canadian Journal of Psychology,* 1961, *15,* 101–106.

Gagné, Robert M. *The conditions of learning* (2nd ed.). New York: Holt, Rinehart, & Winston, 1970.

Gagné, Robert M., & Bassler, O. C. Study of retention of some topics of elementary nonmetric geometry. *Journal of Educational Psychology,* 1963, *54,* 123–131.

Gibbons, H. The ability of college freshmen to construct the meaning of a strange word from the context in which it appears. *Journal of Experimental Education,* 1940, *9,* 29–33.

Hovland, Carl I., & Weiss, W., Transmission of information concerning concepts through positive and negative instances. *Journal of Experimental Psychology,* 1953, *45,* 175–182.

Hudgins, Bryce B. The portrayal of concepts: An issue in the development of protocol materials. In *Acquiring Teaching Competencies:*

Reports and Studies (Report No. 2). Bloomington: Indiana University, School of Education, 1972.

Johnson, Donald M., & O'Reilly, C. A. Concept attainment in children: Classifying and defining. *Journal of Educational Psychology,* 1964, *55,* 71–74.

Johnson, Donald M., & Stratton, R. P. Evaluation of five methods of teaching concepts. *Journal of Educational Psychology,* 1966, *57,* 48–53.

Klausmeier, Herbert J., & Feldman, Katherine V. Effects of a definition and a varying number of examples and nonexamples on concept attainment. *Journal of Educational Psychology,* 1975, *67,* 174–178.

Reed, Horace B. Factors influencing the learning and retention of concepts. I. The influence of set. *Journal of Experimental Psychology,* 1946, *36,* 71–87.

Smoke, Kenneth L. Negative instances in concept learning. *Journal of Experimental Psychology,* 1933, *16,* 583–588.

Suchman, J. Richard. Inquiry training: Building skills for autonomous discovery. *Merrill-Palmer Quarterly of Behavior and Development,* 1971, *7,* 148–169.

Werner, Heinz, & Kaplan, Edith. The acquisition of word meanings: A developmental study. *Monograph of the Society for Research in Child Development,* 1950, *15* (51).

Chapter 5

The Generality of Learning: Issues in Transfer

When something which has already been learned plays a part in subsequent learning, we say that transfer of learning has occurred. For example, a beginning student of French may be told to learn to conjugate the "-ir" verbs. To do this, he need not identify and learn the conjugations for all the verbs of the "-ir" form. Rather, he learns one, and it is then assumed that he can use that knowledge to conjugate others. In other words, transfer is anticipated from the first situation to some later and unspecified situations. Similarly, when the child in the primary grades practices number combinations through exercises such as 48 + 36, there is an implicit assumption that the knowledge of these combinations can also be used to add 86 + 34 or 68 + 43, and so forth.

Both of these simple examples illustrate positive transfer, which enables the student to benefit from her or his previous learning without having that learning interfere with something that is to come later. Also, the transfer of these examples is near rather than remote. The term *near transfer* refers to applications that are like the original learning in important regards. In the addition examples, notice that the first one, or what we might call the training example, involves carrying from the ones to the tens column. The two transfer examples also involve carrying from the ones to the tens columns, a good example of what we mean by near transfer, since if the learner can reliably perform such an operation with his training examples, he should be able to easily transfer it to test examples. But unlike the training case, the two later examples also demand carrying from the tens to the hundreds column and reporting the sum in the answer. This operation was not included in the learner's training, and although no new principle is involved in the test items, they approach what we mean by the term *remote transfer*. The learner would have to extend the principle of carrying to another column of numbers and add the specific variation of reporting that sum in the addend. Without additional training, this leap is too broad for most learners.

The evidence available about transfer of school learning does not support an argument for remote transfer. The learner can better extend his previous learning to a new task when the two of them have some clear relationships, as illustrated in the introductory examples.

Anderson and Anderson (1963) reported a well-designed study with sixth-grade boys in which they tested carefully for remote transfer. The researchers were investigating originality training and wanted to find out the extent of transfer to be expected from such training. To do this, 36 sixth-grade boys were randomly assigned to three groups, two of which were experimental; the other was a control group. The boys in the experimental treatments met with one of the experimenters in groups of three for a series of 30-minute training sessions. The investigator would show an object to one of the small groups and ask the boys to provide novel uses for it. When their suggestions were exhausted, he would mention an attribute of the object to spur them on. He also used verbal reinforcement to encourage their responses. The difference between the two experimental treatments was in the degree of variety of the objects to which they were exposed. One group had 30 different objects; the other studied 30 objects that were classified into six categories: fruits, boards, tin cans, lubricants, ropes, and abrasives.

Two transfer tests were given. The first was a Novel Uses Test which gave each subject four *new* objects for which he was to create novel uses. The scores for both the experimental groups were superior to those for the control group, but there was no significant difference between the two experimental groups. The second transfer test presented the subject with three insight problems. For example, one problem asked the boys to tie two suspended strings together when the distance between them surpassed the subjects' reach. If the learner solved the problem in four minutes, the item used in that solution was removed, and the learner was asked to invent a new solution. These problems were extremely difficult for the sixth-graders. The high-variety condition learners provided slightly fewer than three and one-half solutions for the three problems; the low-variety subjects just over three and one-half, and the control subjects averaged three solutions for the total insight problems. These differences were not statistically significant.

The authors concluded that "massive generalized transfer of training" in the area of creativity and imagination training is not forthcoming, and to obtain such transfer probably would demand very careful training programs. We can add to this the observation that the insight problems depended for solution upon something more than the child's ability to see new uses for objects. Whereas the transfer of that training for the experimental subjects was clear in the first transfer test, it did not extend to the more elaborated and complicated insight problems.

The teacher and the learner will do well to remember that positive transfer can occur in school learning, but it is easy to anticipate greater transfer across tasks than is warranted by the limits of original training. If this is a disappointingly conservative view of transfer, it seems better justified by the available evidence than a less critical application to remotely connected situations.

Another issue in transfer which will bear examination concerns what material transfers, or the generality of transfer. It is customary to categorize transfer as specific or general. Specific transfer would occur in the introductory examples given above. The child learns number combinations, and these can be used again and again, perhaps in altered form, to answer an infinite number of specific arithmetic or daily-use problems. General or nonspecific transfer occurs when the learner applies a rule or a principle to a case that has not been previously encountered. For instance, Chapter 6 indicates that one characteristic of a critical thinker is that he or she requires evidence in support of conclusions. That is a very general disposition. If the school child evaluates television commercials, his friends' rumors, his teachers' statements, and his parents' edicts alike on the basis of the evidence that can be adduced to support them, he may lead the happy but short life of the critical thinker. In addition, his action would be an example of what we mean by general transfer.

Many people believe that transfer is the principal learning outcome of schooling. In that view, learning is important not only because it represents an immediate end but also because it paves the way for subsequent learning, and even because what is learned in school today will transfer to later learning outside of school. At a concrete level, we teach young children to read, not because we value the content of their beginning readers but because of the obvious transferability of their reading skills to all kinds of substantive and pleasure reading both within and outside the school. Furthermore, we know that beginning reading skills furnish a basis upon which the child can build other and more complex skills as he goes along. This, too, is an important kind of transfer in school learning. Gagné (1970) has labeled this vertical transfer, a topic to which we shall return later in the chapter.

Transfer of training has a long and interesting history, perhaps more than most topics in the educational psychology of learning. In the first pages of this chapter we take a brief look at some of that history and then examine more contemporary theories of transfer, especially those espoused by educational psychologists, notably Ausubel and Gagné. At the same time this chapter considers issues and presents information about the nature of the transfer of learning, it also serves somewhat as a transition between the first and second halves of this book. Until now, our attention has been directed toward how students learn the types of information and concepts they encounter in their elementary and secondary classrooms. Now we will shift to questions pertaining to students' roles as thinkers and to improving their ability to solve problems, to reason about the validity of an answer, to generate alternative solutions to problems, or to think creatively.

The role that transfer plays in improving students' thinking is probably a more general one than the examples so far have suggested. The learner's knowledge of how to conjugate one class of verbs should have rather specific and direct transferability to other verbs of that class, and once the child can add simple numbers, their transfer is explicit, if limited. But situations that demand thinking do so, in large part, because they will not yield to the overtures of such specific and explicit skills, habits, and techniques as the learner already has at his fingertips. Apparently what transfers, or what may transfer, in situations that call more for thinking, and less for the running off of specific behavioral repertoires, is general skills, principles, attitudes, and approaches to situations. To illustrate how such general transfer can be achieved, reference will be made in some detail to the Productive Thinking Program as an example of an outstanding curriculum for children in the middle grades of the elementary school, an effort that has as its unabashed objective "teaching children how to think." In closing the chapter, some concrete suggestions for teachers about facilitating transfer in the classroom are given.

Early Views of Transfer of Learning

The position our academic forefathers held about transfer of learning was a more comfortable one than present-day beliefs make possible. Throughout the 19th century educators persisted in the view that human intellect was composed of a variety of faculties: for example, memory, will, reasoning, judgment, attention, and the like. The goal of education was to discipline and train these faculties. Any subject that vied for a place in the curriculum of that day had to make a case for its disciplinary value. Classical languages were given the first rank on those grounds, and mathematics was not far below. A passage from Kolesnik (1958) based upon a report written by the faculty of Yale in 1828 demonstrates the control which the doctrine of formal discipline exercised in higher education at that time:

> According to the Yale committee, "The two great points to be gained in intellectual culture are the discipline and furniture of mind," that is, "expanding its powers and storing it with knowledge." The committee felt that of these, the former was the more important. It recommended, therefore, that those subjects be required and those means of instruction be adopted "which are best calculated to teach the art of fixing the attention, directing the train of thought, analyzing a subject proposed for investigation; following with accurate discrimination the course of argument; balancing nicely the evidence presented to the judgment; awakening, elevating, and controlling the imagination; arranging, with skill, the treasures which memory gathers; rousing and guiding the powers of genius."
>
> Such habits of thinking, the report continued, are not to be formed by a "light and hasty course of study," by reading a few books, or hearing a few lectures, but by long continued close application. "A commanding object, therefore, in a collegiate course should be to call into daily and vigorous exercise the faculties of the student." Moreover, "in laying the foundation of a thorough education, it is necessary that all the important mental faculties be brought into exercise." Toward this end the Yale faculty insisted upon the value of the study of the classical languages, but maintained that English, mathematics, the physical sciences, logic, philosophy, rhetoric and oratory also had their disciplinary values. (pp. 11–12)

Whatever grip the doctrine of this faculty psychology held on the shapers of higher education in the middle years of the 19th century, it was gradually but perceptibly loosened as the century drew toward a close. Challenges to the doctrine appeared from numerous sources, but only a few of the most famous and influential will be identified here. An early one was in William James's classic *The Principles of Psychology*, published in 1890. In his discussion of memory, James disputed the then widely accepted belief that training of the memory yields any general facilitation of a memory faculty. He made an important distinction between the improvement of a faculty and the improvement of thinking. People remember things better because they pay more attention to them and develop associations between new information and existing ideas, and not because a mythical faculty is strengthened.

James reported several brief experiments on memorizing poetry. Little or no improvement occurred in people's ability to memorize, even with considerable practice. The results are of no scientific merit, but they reveal something of the growing belief by 1890 that the case for faculty psychology had been vastly exaggerated. At the hands of a scholar of William James' stature, such repudiation must have sounded a warning for assaults that were yet to come.

Principal among those were two by Edward Lee Thorndike. Thorndike's two studies of transfer were conducted almost a quarter of a century apart. The first was a series of three reports by Thorndike and Woodworth (1901) which attacked the general theory of faculty psychology. "If it is true that a general faculty such as judgment exists," they argued, "then training people to make judgments of one kind should result in their being able to make improved judgments of another kind." Students were trained in many ways. As an example, individuals would first be tested for their ability to estimate the diameter of circles that varied, say, between four and seven inches. They would then be trained in estimating diameters of very small size (perhaps two to five centimeters). Subsequently they would estimate the sizes of the larger circles once more. Many types of tasks were tested, and improvement as a function of training was very slight. Thorndike and Woodworth concluded that no general improvement in a faculty was possible. The fact that some small gains often occurred tended to be overlooked, probably because of the expectation that, if faculties worked as the prevailing theory suggested, the transfer across tasks should have been very large.

Theory of identical elements

By 1903 Thorndike had formalized a statement about transfer of learning that became known as the theory of identical elements. Transfer was possible from one task to another if they contained elements that were the same. Thus, a young child was helped in learning to add 46 + 23 if he already knew how to add 6 + 3 and 4 + 2. It was not only skills and specific information, however, that were capable of transfer. This could also be true for such things as general procedures and techniques, or for attitudes. Thorndike's position is usually interpreted very narrowly, but it seems probable that he intended a more open interpretation when he included such characteristics as procedures and attitudes among the sources for transfer. It was during these early years of the 20th century that psychology offered its most pessimistic view about transfer to the educator. Even so, the theory of identical elements did not rule out the possibility of transfer among many general and important aspects of teaching. Thus, if a child learned efficient methods of studying and organizing his school tasks, these might apply to more advanced study or even to his work as an adult. The same would be true for general procedures, such as using facilities of the library; or reference materials, maps, and globes; or general skills in deciphering graphs, charts, and diagrams.

The second major study by Thorndike, published in 1924, was more specifically addressed to issues of mental discipline and subjects studied in high schools. As we have already seen, advocates of faculty psychology argued that intellectual functioning is improved when students take certain courses, notably classical languages, mathematics, and others identified as having strong disciplinary value. Thorndike's attack on this claim was characteristically straightforward and bold. He organized and analyzed records of thousands of secondary school students to compare the measured intelligence, over the course of a year of secondary school, of students whose curriculums had varied by degrees from what should be the optimum arrangement of courses to provide mental discipline. The idea was to take intelligence measures at the beginning and end of the year and determine which changes were greater for students taking such courses than for others who were in less academic programs. For example, comparisons would be made among those who took a selection from each of the following two groups of courses:

Greek, Latin or Hebrew—4 years
Mathematics—4 years
French or German—4 years
English—4 years
Ancient History—4 years
Science—4 years
Typing—4 years
Shopwork—4 years
Mechanical drawing—4 years
Art—4 years

Thorndike's plan was much more ambitious than such overall comparisons, however. He wished to be able, for example, to assess the contribution to a pupil's intellectual growth of studying one particular subject versus another: "For example we compare the gains for the pupils who studied English, history, geometry, and Latin during the year with the gains for the pupils who studied English, history, geometry and shopwork" (Thorndike, 1924, p. 7). The programs of students were so diverse that his lofty aim could not be realized. Instead, large blocks of studies had to be treated as equivalents. From his analyses of the test results, allowing for differences among students' programs, Thorndike concluded that, contrary to what traditional psychological theory predicted, the effect of studies on general improvement is small, and differences among studies are small.

The Generality of Learning: Issues in Transfer

Languages were found to have no special disciplinary value. In fact, Thorndike found, the value of any study is better determined by the knowledge and skills it will give to a particular pupil. This latter point was to have a tremendous impact upon curriculum construction for many years to come. It was part of a major effort at that time to simplify the curriculum and make the tasks of the school more directly related to the things children growing up in American society during the 1920–40 era needed to learn. In many ways this was a refreshing and healthy change. Educators began to look at questions of content selection, and even to pedagogical issues, more in terms of children's intellectual, societal, and personal needs than as studies to improve a largely mystical mental discipline. The curriculum in arithmetic, for one, underwent radical change. Esoteric and little-used topics were removed. Somewhat later the curriculum of the secondary school was expanded sufficiently to make room for such pursuits as driver education. Given the theory that transfer is minimal and that education should speak to the needs of the populace, and given the burgeoning slaughter on the nation's streets and highways, the logic that led to such decisions was valid. However, the same logic was capable of leading to educational decisions that are shortsighted and surely not in the best interest of the students toward whom they were directed.

Cronbach (1962) makes an excellent point in this regard:

> There is a risk that precisely topical curriculum development may omit fundamentals of a field of knowledge. In 1940, a high school chemistry teacher who believed in meeting students' future needs for specific information would have taught units on scrap alloys used in home and industry and the refining of petroleum. Such a curriculum would anticipate concerns of adult life. The topic of atomic structure would not have seemed useful to this teacher. "The nonscientist," he would have said, "faces no situations where understanding of atoms and electrons would help." The release of atomic energy in 1942 changed all that. Today, few scientific matters are of wider public concern than the atom and its use. (p. 318)

At the end of his lengthy report on mental discipline and high school studies, Thorndike (1924) cautions about inferring cause and effect from correlational data. Studies such as physical culture and the arts would appear to produce accomplished scholars if they were taken by the most able students. Indeed, that is precisely what happened in some ancient cultures. Particular attention should be paid to the concluding sentence in his paper (italicized for emphasis):

> *The chief reason why good thinkers seem superficially to have been made such by having taken certain studies, is that good thinkers have taken such*

studies, becoming better by the inherent tendency of the good to gain more than the poor from any study .... Disciplinary values *may be real and deserve weight in the curriculum, but the weight should be reasonable.* (Thorndike, 1924, p. 98)

General Transfer

One of the themes that has been developed throughout this book is that learning which is meaningful is superior to rote learning or learning without understanding. To the extent that we adopt a theory of transfer that is limited to specific and identical elements, we reduce the chances of synthesizing knowledge under broad organizational principles. Most of us have experienced the power of a principle or law that is applicable to a wide series of divergent cases. For example, every high school student of geometry knows the Pythagorean theorum that the square of the hypotenuse of a right triangle is equal to the sum of the squares of the other two sides. We need not engage in manual measurement of the unknown side of any right triangle once the general proposition is known to us. In the same way, other theorems and scientific rules have broad applicability. Even such definitions as those of the parts of speech help the learner to identify words in sentences without having to learn specifically the function of each new word he or she encounters. Less dependable, but still serviceable, is a host of rules about spelling and pronunciation; children learn "i before e except after c" and its major exceptions, such as *neighbor* and *weigh.*

Among the early noteworthy studies of transfer was one by Charles H. Judd (1908). Judd believed that the learner's knowledge and retention, and his ability to think, were facilitated by having information classified and organized in appropriate ways. This would include knowledge of general principles that can be applied to a host of specific situations. To demonstrate the validity of this belief, Judd arranged for a group of fifth- and sixth-grade boys to practice throwing darts at a submerged target. Half the boys were instructed in the principle of refraction of light, and the other half were not. At first, knowledge of the principle had little effect upon the boys' success, but when the target was subsequently moved to a different depth, superior performance was achieved by those who understood the principle.

This "experiment" appears to have had the informality almost of a Saturday afternoon boys' club activity, and it is not clear from Judd's account that any true difference emerged. However, later and somewhat more rigorous experiments (Hendrickson & Schroeder, 1941, Overing

& Travers 1966, 1967) have documented the essential points. Judd was reminding an educational community in shock at the loss of long-standing beliefs about the transfer value of education, and besieged by evidence that seemed to say "you must teach every specific response you want students to learn," that general principles had not lost their generality. When a student comprehends the range of conditions under which a principle is applicable, he has a powerful intellectual tool at his command.

Although Judd's work is something of a classic in educational psychology, other psychologists were beginning to ask similar questions and sometimes to provide more systematic answers than Judd did. A case in point is an early study by the British psychologist W. H. Winch (1923). The question he raised is still of importance to teachers today:

> Does improvement in Arithmetical Problematic Reasoning involve an improvement in Logical Reasoning which is not arithmetical? Are we, in teaching problems in arithmetic, not only helping the pupil to perform the arithmetical operations which will confront him in his daily life, but also helping to make him a better reasoner in other ways? The vast majority of teachers have no doubt that we are; much current psychology would assert that we are not. (p. 371)

Winch provided ten weeks of special instruction and practice in analyzing and solving arithmetic problems to one group of 12-year-old girls. A control group that had done equally well on tests of arithmetic and logical reasoning received no special training. (Examples of both types of problems are given in Figure 5.1.) When both sets of tests were repeated several weeks after the end of the special training period, the improvement for the experimental group of girls on the logic tests was much greater than the gain for the control group. (Mean score for experimental subjects increased from 35.0 to 49.5; that for the controls from 34.8 to 38.8.) As Winch expressed it, speaking of the girls in the practice group, "a differential improvement of about 150 percent in Problematic Arithmetic is accompanied by a differential improvement of about 30 percent in Logical Reasoning" (Winch, 1923, p. 386). In Winch's study, there appears to have been a considerable amount of generalized transfer from the training in arithmetic problem solving to the related but still different problems in logic.

However, the training in analysis provided by Winch may have stressed the same kinds of comparisons and drawing of inferences that are needed to solve the logic problems successfully.

An effort by Barlow (1937) was even more general than Winch's in that he attempted to measure gains in reasoning on the kind of material

FIGURE 5.1
Examples of two types of problems used in studies of arithmetic and reasoning

Samples of Winch's Logic Problems

Alice is taller than Kate and Kate is taller than Mary. Is Alice taller than Mary, or just as tall as Mary, or shorter than Mary, or can't you tell? You must say what makes you think so.

There were four clocks in a house which for a long while kept correct time. By-and-by three of them appeared to be faster than the other one, and all these three clocks seemed to gain the same amount each day as compared with the other one. Which do you think was more likely to be right, the three clocks which were faster, or the one which was slower? You must say why you think so.

If the only places in a town where you can buy marbles are toyshops, and all the toyshops in that town are on Burton Road, would it be true to say that the only places in that town where you can buy marbles are on the Burton Road?

Sample of Winch's Arithmetic Problems

Two men, Jones and Brown, set out together to walk to a town 160 miles away. Jones walked 10 miles a day, while Brown walked 8 miles a day. How many days' journey would Brown be behind Jones, when Jones reached the town?

Source: Winch (1923), p. 371.

brought about by training on altogether different material. Seventh- and eighth-graders (and some adults also) were first tested for their ability to state the moral taught by each of 15 of Aesop's fables. One of the fables was "The Widow and the Hen":

> A widow kept a hen that laid an egg every morning. Thought the woman to herself, "If I double my hen's allowance of barley, she will lay twice a day." So she tried her plan and the hen became so fat and sleek that she left off laying at all.

Barlow regarded "Figures are not always facts" as the best answer, and unsatisfactory paraphrases included statements such as, "Be patient" and "One hen can't do the work of two."

Half his subjects received a set of 12 special lessons, each 20 minutes in duration. Four of the lessons were on analogies of the following form: "Prince is to Princess as King is to_____ ." The exercises called for providing one, two, or three missing terms. Pupils wrote out their reasoning. Four other lessons dealt with abstractions and generalizations from the concrete to the general and from the general to the concrete. The other four lessons stressed reading comprehension and the analysis of behavior situations. It is too bad that Barlow gave no examples of the material used in this training program except for the single simple analogy repeated above. However, after the twelve lessons were taught, all subjects read and stated the moral for each of 15 different Aesop fables. The elementary school control pupils did no better at all on this second test, whereas the experimental group easily surpassed their pretraining performance (with a 5.35 average score after training compared to 3.28 before training). Barlow reports this as a 64 percent gain in transfer, which, of course, sounds good but is not very meaningful. In fact, the 38 seventh-and eighth-graders who received the 12 special lessons gave, on the average, two more correct morals than they were able to provide before the training.

Barlow gave the same final test one year later to as many of the elementary pupils as he could locate. By then any differences between the experimental and control groups had disappeared (E = 5.72, C = 5.81). Barlow makes the interesting point that his two-week course of instruction induced approximately the same gain in abstracting morals from fables as the control group achieved in a year as the results of general education and maturation. Of course, the groups may have been equal long before the lapse of a year. We cannot know this, because the follow-up test was not given until a year later.

Transfer, according to Barlow, occurs because the pupil learns general intellectual skills, such as analyzing, abstracting, completing analogies, and so forth, which can be applied to a range of specific materials. He also assigns some place to the role of "intentional efforts to apply learning methods." This is probably a critical point in transfer, and it deserves more careful study. Barlow's view of transfer, although it antedated contemporary cognitive views by a generation, is quite congruent with them. Transfer is seen as the product of integrated activities. Ways of processing and organizing information are integrated into structures which can be applied to new but related issues, as in thinking and problem solving.

Certain parts of the curriculum have for years been justified on the grounds that they produce transfer to important educational outcomes. As an example, at the upper grades of the elementary schools sentence diagraming has been held to improve pupils' sentence mastery. On the contrary, Greene and Petty (1971), in the latest edition of their standard text on language in the elementary school, observe that studies (not particularly recent ones, either) have shown that pupils can be taught diagraming rather efficiently, but there is very little benefit in terms of sentence mastery. In fact, one of the studies cited evidence that the control children actually improved a bit more in sentence mastery than the children who had been taught diagraming.

Contemporary Transfer Theory

The discussion of interference effects on retention introduced in Chapter 2 should help make it clear that interference and transfer are closely related concepts. *Interference* refers to the positive or negative effects of learning a second task upon retention of a first task, whereas *transfer* refers to the reverse circumstance: the effects of prior learning upon the acquisition or retention of a subsequent task. Transfer can be positive, that is, helpful, or negative, that is, it can make a new task more difficult to learn. The term *zero transfer* simply indicates that learning one task has no effect we can discern upon the learning of something else.

As part of our discussion in Chapter 2 we observed that the stimulus-response theory of interference is the dominant explanation of decrements in performance. The same thing can be said about contemporary transfer theory. Some of its major points are represented by Osgood's (1949) formulation of a transfer and retroaction surface.

FIGURE 5.2
Osgood's transfer and retroaction surface

Source: Osgood (1949), p. 140. Figure adapted by Hilgard & Bower (1975), p. 294.

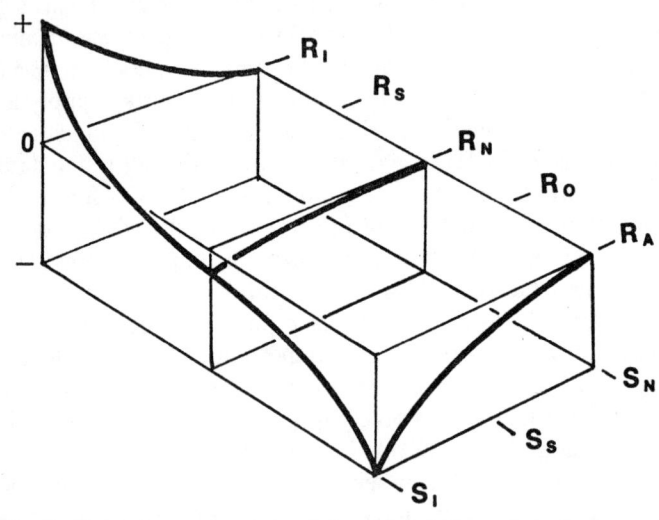

Vertical dimension, amount of transfer (+) or interference (−), with neutral zone represented by a plane (0). Left to right, amount of shift in response similarity between original task and new task, from identify (R_I) to antagonism (R_A). Front to rear, amount of shift in stimulus similarity between original and new task, from identify (S_I) to neutrality (S_N).

Osgood's surface has not been supported on all points by subsequent investigations, and some psychologists, for example, Martin (1965), have suggested additional surfaces that need to be tested. However, Osgood's formulation remains the most comprehensive, and it summarizes much of what was known about transfer and retroaction at the time of its development. The surface summarizes transfer outcomes for a universe of relationships between stimuli and responses. These relationships were deduced from laboratory studies of paired associate tasks, which provides the great advantage of clear distinctions between stimuli and responses. However, the relationships and outcomes expressed are restricted to comparable learning situations. Unfortunately, as far as transfer theory is concerned, only a few learning tasks of the school are classifiable as paired associate tasks. Included might be such things as learning a foreign language vocabulary, authors and titles, countries and products, and other similar items, clearly a limited cut into the total range of diverse learning tasks employed in schools.

The Osgood surface theorizes that maximum positive transfer will result when both the stimulus and the response elements of a new learning task are identical to those of the original task. Since that condition simply represents continued practice of the original word pairs, it is easy to understand why positive transfer would occur. As stimulus and response similarity diminish, transfer and retroaction between tasks becomes negative rather than positive. The region of maximum negative transfer is found where a new response must be learned to an old stimulus. Although the data of paired associates learning fit this formulation, its applicability to school learning is not clear. Recall the statement by Myrow and Anderson (1972) cited in Chapter 2 that we do not frequently teach students two different answers to the same question.

Several writers (for example, Deese & Hulse, 1967; Hilgard & Bower, 1975) have observed that current psychological transfer theory is not general enough to handle questions about school learning very adequately. This reduces the chances that studies of transfer in school, in turn, will be general enough to contribute to psychological theory. You may have noted that the accounts of general and specific transfer above reflected a vigorous interchange between educational and psychological theory.

However, Ausubel's (1968) theory of cognitive organization argues for a different interpretation of transfer phenomena when meaningful school-type learning is involved. When subject matter content is organized so that the fundamental laws, generalizations, or propositions of a study are introduced and mastered at the outset of learning, they provide conceptual frameworks which facilitate the learner's acquisition and retention of lower order concepts, and specific episodes or facts, which are associated with the broader framework. The availability in the learner's cognitive structure of the encompassing ideas of what he or she is to learn provides a series of ideational categories or networks into which less general information can be fitted. Again, as was stressed in Chapter 2, it is the meaningful nature of the school's learning tasks that makes such categorizations possible. In this cognitive view of transfer, concepts such as stimulus and response, and the similarity between them, lose much of their meaning. The effective variables are, instead, the meaningfulness of the material to be learned and its organization, including the degree of organization represented in the learner's cognitive structure.

It is interesting and important to note that both approaches to transfer (and retroaction) share an insistence upon mastery of the original learning. If the initial ideas are not thoroughly learned and comprehended, they do not play the central role in transfer—or subsequent learning—that the theory specifies for them. Ausubel stresses that point by saying that initial ideas must be clear, stable, and discriminable. These terms seem to set the task aptly. If an original idea is clear to the learner, it means that he has abstracted its basic meaning; if discriminable, there is no confusion between that idea and others that may be much like it in some respects. Ideas that are stable are not easily forgotten, nor are they susceptible to juxtaposition with other ideas that belong appropriately at lower or higher places in the hierarchy.

For the learner, it is these broad generalizations —when they are clear and well retained, and perceived as distinct from other propositions or competing concepts that furnish the background of knowledge—which makes the acquisition of new but related knowledge easier than it would be in the absence of such subject matter generalizations in cognitive structure. That is precisely what we mean by transfer; existing knowledge affects new learning for better or for worse.

Learning hierarchies as a source of transfer

Gagné (1970) conceives of school-type learning tasks as hierarchically organized, an idea which was introduced in the preceding chapter. Now we want to stress the notion that the learner's progress from one level to the next, to the highest one in a learning hierarchy, is facilitated by positive transfer. For example, before a child can add mixed numbers such as 3½ and 2⅝, an impressive number of lower order skills, concepts, and operations must have been mastered. These, too, at least in theory, are in hierarchical order, and thus no individual step or transfer is very large. The hierarchy for this example might look something like Figure 5.3.

The Generality of Learning: Issues in Transfer 157

FIGURE 5.3
Example of a learning hierarchy for addition of mixed fractions

```
        (6)    Add              3 1/2
               mixed numbers   + 2 5/8
                               -------

               (5)   Add whole number      5
                     and mixed number   + 1 1/8
                                        -------

               (4)   Convert improper
                     fraction to        9/8 = 1 1/8
                     mixed number

               (3)   Obtain least       3 1/2 = 3 4/8
                     common denominator 2 5/8 = 2 5/8
                                        -----   -----

(2)  Add whole numbers     (2a)  Add proper fractions
          3                          1/2       5/8
        + 2                        + 1/2     + 3/8
        ---                        -----     -----

(1)  Identify whole numbers  (1a)  Identify proper fractions
          1, 2, ... 10                 1/4, 1/2, 5/8
```

Theoretically the learner cannot perform the final (topmost) step unless each preceding level has been mastered.

The hierarchy in Figure 5.3 can be read in this way. The child must be able to read or identify common numbers and fractions, such as 2, 5/8, and so forth, as shown in stages 1 and 1a. Stages 2 and 2a require the child to be able to add whole numbers and fractions respectively, and so on. The creative notion of Gagné is to observe that the child can only add fractions if he knows that the denominators of each fraction must be the same. That knowledge undergirds the next highest skill (not shown in the hierarchy example) of converting the denominators and multiplying the numerators appropriately before adding. The hierarchy is a convenient, graphic way of portraying vertical transfer from one step to the next in the school learning process. It tends also to reinforce our earlier point that near transfer occurs more easily and more often than remote transfer.

Gagné's formulation of the learning hierarchy was established through a series of experimental studies in which children studied arithmetic learning tasks. The tasks were, of course, placed in a sequence that was determined always by asking a question of this sort. What would the learner already have to know in order to learn the new skill, if she or he is only given directions? After the instructional programs were completed, Gagné would identify four possible categories of learners. The first would be children who had mastered a new task and also the elements beneath it in the learning hierarchy. The second would be students who failed a higher order task but had learned the lower elements. The third would be composed of those who had learned the higher order task but not the underlying ones, and the fourth, those who failed on both. Theoretically, there ought not to be any subjects in the third category, that is, those who can perform a task high in the hierarchy without also being able to demonstrate mastery of the preceding elements. The basic idea of the hierarchy, of course, is that positive transfer results at each stage of it. If students can perform the presumably more demanding task in the absence of mastery of the lower tasks, then the argument that positive transfer occurs upward in the hierarchy starts to break down. Gagné's studies always resulted in some failures of this sort, although the proportion of such learners was relatively low.

A critic of Gagné's research on hierarchies, White (1973), observes that any of three sources may account for these damaging cases: (1) errors of measurement, (2) the forgetting which occurs between the time lower order elements and higher ones are learned, and (3) errors in the construction of the initial hierarchy. He adds that until each of these sources can be ruled out or their effects accounted for, it is impossible to determine whether the concept of the learning hierarchy itself is a tenable one.

Despite these criticisms, the learning hierarchy seems to be both a meaningful and a highly practical way for classroom teachers to think about and to plan for positive transfer in many types of learning.

General Transfer in a Contemporary Curriculum

Many excellent "new curricula" found their way into schools during the 1960s. Most of these conformed to existing subject matter divisions of traditional schools: social studies, mathematics, science, English, and so

The Generality of Learning: Issues in Transfer   159

on. Some of the curriculum efforts, however, did not fall into a readymade category. One of these, *The Productive Thinking Program* (Covington, Crutchfield, Davies, & Olton, 1972), is subtitled *A Course in Learning to Think*. Its basic and overarching goal is to teach children of fifth- and sixth-grade age a wide array of skills of thinking which can subsequently be applied to many problems in the more standard curriculum of the school.

This program, developed by Martin V. Covington, Richard S. Crutchfield, and others at the University of California at Berkeley, is of interest to us in two respects. First, it represents a rare, major effort to teach general intellectual skills to children for their transfer value. Although its developers use somewhat different language than we have used, the Productive Thinking Program fits nicely into the rhetoric of general transfer. The program attempts to teach children such collections of skills as:

> Take time to reflect on a problem before you begin work. Decide exactly what the problem is that you are trying to solve.
> Keep an open mind. Don't jump to conclusions about the answer to a problem.

Our second interest in the program is for what it tells us about the nature of thinking, especially "creative problem solving." The principal discussion of the program here is designed to make it meaningful by providing some detail about the lessons and their format. Its pertinence to the analysis of creative thinking is pointed out in Chapter 8.

At face value, the Productive Thinking Program consists of 16 basic lessons, each contained in a magazinelike booklet which uses a format similar to a comic book. The lessons revolve around the adventures of a sixth-grade boy, Jim Cannon, and his fifth-grade sister, Lila. These children encounter a series of mysteries, puzzles, and problems that are designed to be of interest to the 10- to 12-year-old set. In addition, there is a supplementary problem-set book which provides more problems for practice. The Teachers Guide for the program outlines the activities of the basic lessons and the problem sets and offers suggestions to teachers on guiding discussions and helping the student to solve the numerous problems.

To illustrate the activities and what the children do, one of the mysteries encountered midway in the program is "The Riddle of the Rare Coins." In the story, a collection of rare coins is on display in an office. A suspicious individual views them, and as he is leaving, the owner notices two rare nickel coins are missing. He chases the subject, who bumps into a third party. They grapple with the thief and the owner sends the third man to call the police on the pay phone in the hall. A search of the sus-

160 Learning and Thinking

pect reveals no coins. Windows were closed, so he could not throw them out. The problem: What happened to the coins?

The learner is not left to his own devices to search for or guess at the solution. In this lesson, emphasis is placed upon *conjectural thinking*. When the normal search patterns fail to disclose the mystery, Jim and Lila entertain the conjecture that the supposedly innocent bystander was involved. If this were true, how could he have stolen the coins? Where are they hidden? The children are led to *recall crucial facts* (for instance, he struggled with the suspect, he left the office unobserved, he used the hall telephone, etc.). Finally, the learner is taught how to *draw inferences* from these facts to determine where the coins are hidden.

In classroom use, the teacher might have children work on an activity such as the Riddle of the Rare Coins on one day. This would be followed on the second day by class discussion and activities which use different specific materials but which help to strengthen and extend the cognitive skills introduced on the first day. To continue the illustration, the Teachers Guide for the program suggests the following questions to launch class participation.

> 1. Why is it important to have a plan in mind before you begin working on a problem? Can't you just go ahead and start, using any one of the [thinking] guides?
> 2. In order to start work on the rare coins problem, Jim and Lila decided to make a plan —what they would do step by step. What were the important steps in their plan?

Other questions are aimed at allowing pupils to express flagging interest in the program or frustration at their inability to solve the problems. The authors are no doubt wise to recommend a "ventilation" period at this midway point, but teachers would appreciate more specific suggestions about how to handle and correct any complaints that arise.

The same week's work includes a class exercise which gives practice in predicting the consequences of events and speculating about the remote implications of such an event. The following problem serves as the vehicle for the discussion.

Controlling the Weather

During your lifetime, it is very likely that man will be able not only to predict the weather, but actually to control it in important ways. Already there have been experiments in which chemicals were dropped into clouds to make rain fall in one place instead of in another. In the future man will probably be able to control the weather in a much more complete way. He may be able to make it warmer in one place and, consequently, colder in another, windier in this place and calmer in that, sunnier here and rainier there.

This degree of weather control will certainly have an enormous number of consequences. Before man starts controlling the weather to such a degree, he needs to think about what these consequences might be. For example, if the Arctic and Antarctic regions were made warmer by only a few degrees, gigantic masses of ice would melt, and the level of all the oceans would rise by quite a few feet. So if weather control was used to warm these regions, there would be many, many consequences, such as these:

Many cities would be flooded.
Map makers would have to draw new maps.
Some inland cities would become seaports.
People would live and work in Antarctica.

Now try to think of the many other consequences of man's future ability to control the weather.

Two principles about thinking are used to guide the discussion. First, the children have earlier learned how to use the idea-tree method, in which general categories are identified and more particular consequences are elaborated beneath them. Second, a scanning method is employed in which the children are to scan a wide array of aspects of life in the world and select ideas from each of the aspects. Additional questions are available for the teacher who wishes his or her pupils to continue practicing these skills. For example:

The population of the world suddenly tripled in size.
It became possible for animals to 'talk' or to communicate directly with man.
People became able to read one another's minds.

A correlated problem set for this lesson provides more systematic and in a sense more traditional practice on the topic of general and particular ideas. This is accomplished by having children develop topical outlines, with the main headings serving as general solution possibilities and the subheadings as particular solutions. The activity is organized so that children advance from simple to more complex outlines. One problem that can be used for individual or group analysis concerns waste disposal. Children are informed that no particular outline is the correct one, and a limitless number might be produced. Here is the problem and part of one possible outline by way of solution:

Our country is faced with the problem of what to do with the increasing amounts of garbage, trash, and other waste produced in our houses and factories. How can these problems be solved?

I. Destroying the waste.
   A. Crush it under high pressure.
   B. Grind it up.
   C. Dissolve it with chemicals.
   D., E., F., etc.
II. Turn the waste into something useful.
   A. Make fertilizer from garbage containing chemicals necessary for the growth of plants.
   B. Heat the garbage to a very high temperature to kill the germs and then use it as food for farm animals.
   C. Heat the garbage slowly to a high temperature so that the different chemicals it contains can be trapped and used over again.
   D., E., F., etc.
III. Make less waste in the first place.
   A. Develop new forms of vegetables that are completely edible, including the skin and leaves, so nothing ends up in the garbage.
   B. Develop boxes, wrappings, and packaging materials that can be eaten along with the food.
   C., D., E., etc.
IV., V., etc.

(Teachers Guide to Productive Thinking Program, p. 42)

Do children who pursue the Productive Thinking Program succeed better in solving problems that demand thinking than their untutored peers do? Put somewhat differently, is there positive transfer from the training program to subsequent problem solving? This question must be subdivided into a consideration of "general," or nonspecific, problem solving, and to an examination of transfer effects to particular curricular areas, such as arithmetic, science, and social studies. The available evidence supports the contention that children who have been trained in productive thinking surpass control pupils in solving problems that are similar in form and content to those encountered in the program. Although Covington, Crutchfield, Davies, & Olton (1972) claim that the transfer extends to problems like those encountered in normal curriculum areas, no evidence is presented that children do a better job of such things as solving arithmetic problems or designing better experiments in science class. The extent to which the program's claims of transfer can be substantiated requires analysis.

Olton and Crutchfield (1969) reported on the results of an investigation in which an effort was made to achieve maximum learning and transfer among fifth- and sixth-graders. The supplementary exercises described above were added to the content of the basic 16 lessons to help extend transfer to school-related problems. Further, the teachers whose classes used the program were encouraged to participate heavily by guiding and stimulating discussion.

The pupils upon whom the analysis focuses were a subsample of the total research sample, 50 fifth-graders drawn from two classes. Half the children in each of these classes received instruction, and the other half were controls. The two groups were closely matched for IQ and achievement scores. All of the children took tests at three different times, the first one just before the instructional period. Then for eight weeks the experimental group children studied the materials for about one hour a day, and the control pupils had a program which consisted of general educational activities such as movies, stories, and other interesting projects, none of which were judged to utilize productive thinking. A posttest was given at the end of the eight-week period and a follow-up test six months later. Several of the items on these latter two tests, drawn from the account written by Olton and Crutchfield (1969) are given below. The posttest contained the following problems:

> Black House problem. Student attempts to solve a puzzling problem in which he must make an insightful reorganization of the elements of the problem.
> Bird Migration. Student reads an account of the migratory behavior of a hypothetical flock of birds. He is asked to note anything about the behavior of the flock that seems puzzling and to try to account for these puzzling facts.
> Poverty essay. Student writes an essay in which he has the opportunity to demonstrate his thinking ability in connection with the problem of poverty.

The follow-up tests, administered six months after the instructional period, consisted of these five problems:

> Missing Jewel problem. Student attempts to solve a puzzling mystery problem in which he must make an insightful reorganization of the elements of the problem.
> The Nameless Tomb. Student works on a hypothetical problem in archeology in which he must discover which of ten possible suspects is buried in a nameless ancient tomb.
> The Lost Colony. Student reacts to the challenge of a problem which requires thinking about the puzzling failure of the first attempted English colony in the New World.
> Understanding Thinking. Student indicates what thinking strategies are useful at various stages of work in a complex problem.
> Natural Resources essay. Student writes an essay in which he has the opportunity to demonstrate his thinking in connection with the problem of conserving natural resources.

Since none of the posttest or follow-up test items had previously been encountered by the pupils, they can be regarded as tests of transfer for the instructed group. When the two test scores are combined for all pupils and a composite median is identified, 72 percent of the instructed pupils, but only 24 percent of the control children, scored above the median. These differences are graphically reflected in Figure 5.4. It is also worth

Figure 5.4
Composite productive thinking score

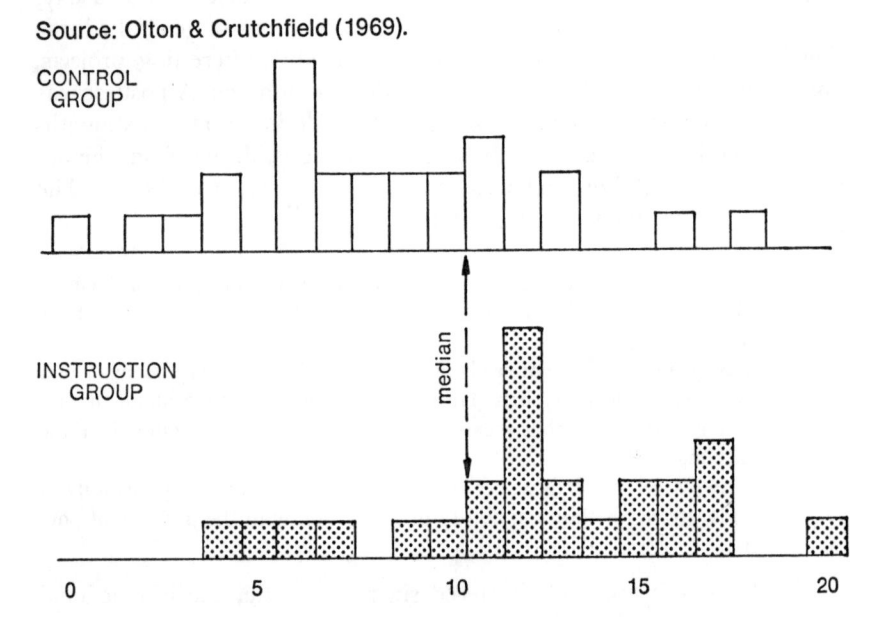

Source: Olton & Crutchfield (1969).

Distributions of 23-item productive thinking composite scores for instruction and control groups. The median of the combined groups is shown. A significantly higher proportion of instruction than of control students score above this median.

noting that superior performance was maintained by the instructed group over the controls in the follow-up test, six months after the completion. This finding lends support to the contention that the skills of thinking are well retained. Our principal interest is in the degree of transfer the program generates, and it may be well to recall the earlier distinction between near and remote transfer.

A good amount of near transfer is evident for the instructed pupils. This can be seen from the overall statistical results cited earlier, but also by reference to the children's performance on some of the follow-up test items. For example, the Nameless Tomb problem challenges the child to determine which one of ten people is buried there. Simple facts in the problem statement can eliminate seven of the ten, and a single clue makes one person the obvious choice, but the learner has to be flexible enough to break a mental set, or he is unlikely to respond to the clue. Of the control students, 37 percent eliminated the seven possible occupants and 58 percent went on to solve the problem correctly. Corresponding scores for the instructed group were 69 percent and 91 percent.

Perhaps more impressive, in what it says for the transfer power of the program, is the result of pupils' work on the poverty essay. The child was left free to write whatever he felt about the topic, and the essays were scored on three variables: (1) the number of descriptions of poverty given, (2) the number of causes of poverty mentioned, and (3) the number of suggestions about how poverty might be ended. The instruction and control groups did not differ in the number of descriptions of poverty given; their basic fund of knowledge about the problem was about the same. But the instruction group listed on the average almost five causes of poverty, three times as many as named by the control pupils. Since the learners were not asked to cite causes, this suggests a more active role of thinking by the instruction group. Only 5 children from the total group of 50 proffered suggestions for the eradication of poverty. This is a small fraction of those who might have done so, but it is noteworthy that four of the five came from the instructed group. All in all, the evidence, even though it is limited in amount, speaks well for the positive impact the program has on the active thinking skills of children. The results suggest that, much more often than control pupils, those who have been through the program make use of the skills that have been developed or sharpened.

The case for remote transfer from the Productive Thinking Program has been strengthened by the results of two recent investigations. Baker (1975) discovered improved reading comprehension for fourth-and fifth-grade children who suffered reading disabilities and were given an opportunity to study the Productive Thinking Program. Similarly, Hogan and Garvey (1975) found that gifted seventh-and eighth-graders who had access to the program made larger improvements on tests of their ability to think creatively than control pupils did.

Covington, in personal communications in 1976, agreed with me that to date there has been little evidence aimed at showing remote transfer from the program to standard curricular areas. This point is somewhat weakened by the Baker and Hogan and Garvey data cited above. Still, questions bearing upon whether children who study the program are helped to solve arithmetic problems more effectively or to design better science experiments, and so forth, have not been answered. In Covington's view, several legitimate answers to those questions can be given. With respect to a curriculum area such as arithmetic problem solving, the rule-bound content of the subject is too narrow to expect much transfer from general problem-solving skills. That is, if you want improved arithmetic problem solving, work on that. I would agree (given the data to be reviewed in Chapter 7) that this is probably a valid solution. Covington also observes that, although some of the problems used to test the efficacy of his program are not like the standard materials of the curriculum, the curriculum materials ought to be altered to be more like the tasks used in the Productive Thinking Program. To the extent that the tests used by the Berkeley group are superior to standard curricular tasks as measures of thinking, I would also agree with this assertion. In fact, Covington may be right to a considerable extent. On the other hand, it seems doubtful that large numbers of schools are going to move very quickly away from the types of materials they use to extend or measure children's thinking skills.

The Productive Thinking Program has adduced some evidence which demonstrates its potential for general transfer; that is, for the development of general thinking skills. To the extent that its authors can continue to develop evidence which suggests its transferability to those intellectual skills the schools are trying to produce, teachers may perceive it as a body of curriculum material that is germane to their educational objectives. Otherwise, they may regard it only as an interesting and desirable additive, for which it is difficult to find room in already overburdened instructional schedules.

Suggestions for Teaching for Transfer

Throughout this chapter we have seen that transfer is not automatic, and what we have called near transfer is more attainable than remote transfer. We have also seen that transfer is possible, and that both specific and general transfer occur in certain circumstances. Teachers interested in means to increase the transfer their students achieve can consider the following suggestions. Each teacher, however, must evaluate their applicability to his or her teaching situation and adapt or modify the suggestions accordingly.

First, no other learning variable appears to influence subsequent learning (transfer) as much as the degree of mastery of the original learning. When the ideas to which new learning is to be attached are well learned, one of the basic limiting factors affecting transfer is in place. If prior learning has been partial or inaccurate, and if the variety of its meanings and possible extensions is not well understood by the learner, the chances are sharply diminished that positive transfer will occur; indeed, there is even a possibility for negative transfer.

Second, the more explicit the applications of learning can be made, the greater is the possibility of positive transfer. In this connection, the mathematics teacher should point out to the learner the role that a skill or operation will play in later work. The language arts teacher should stress that knowledge of how to construct an outline and skill in doing so will be of continuing value throughout life, whenever a writing chore more complex than a shopping list is necessary. Then the teacher should check that all written assignments have been outlined, or that the student sees the lack of an outline as responsible for inadequacies in the final product. In such arrangements as team teaching or the departmental structure of secondary schools, some objectives are achieved best when the science or social studies teacher, for example, requires students to apply outlining skills to work in these subject matter areas. Transfer is more likely to occur, and with higher frequency, when such opportunities are extended and when students perceive teachers' expectations for the application of prior learning to new situations.

Third, the learner should be led to expect his learning to transfer to proximate tasks. If what he learns today seldom has to be recalled for application at a later time, it becomes less likely that he will search for opportunities to transfer his knowledge.

Fourth, an attitude of flexibility toward transfer by the learner should be encouraged. Applications of learning cannot always be straightforward; often problems must be perceived in a different way, or a principle must be modified if it is to transfer effectively. For example, Wertheimer (1959) observed an arithmetic class in which children were taught how to find the area of a rectangle. They correctly solved numerous application problems, all of which involved simple use of the formula they had been given. When he drew a parallelogram on the board, however, he found they were unable to make use of what they knew about the area of a rectangle to find the area of the parallelogram.

Fifth, consideration should be given to the correspondence between the situation in which something is to be learned and that in which it is to be applied or to which it is to transfer. Dwyer (1967; see Chapter 3) found line drawings more effective for teaching novices about cardiac functioning than complex photographs, but Overing and Travers (1966) found that learners applied their knowledge of the principle of refraction of light better if the complexity of the training system matched that of the transfer test conditions. It seems probable that many learning tasks require at least a two-stage approach when transfer to a very complex task is important. The first (or first series of steps) would be similar to Dwyer's point, that is, would require a sufficiently simplified situation for the task to be appropriately learned. The second stage (which again might be cast as a series of lessons or trials) would involve learning how to adapt a basic principle or operation to more complex phenomena.

Sixth, simply reminding students to transfer previous learning to a new task can result in transfer. Barlow (1937) had confidence in such a technique, as we saw earlier, but no evidence. In an early study, Dorsey and Hopkins (1930) divided three different groups of college students into experimental and control halves. The first group was composed of freshmen students who were failing in college work and were therefore taught a special study method. The second was a group of students of college Latin who had studied four years of Latin in high school. Their task was to choose the correct Latin derivative of 100 Latin words, 50 that had previously been studied and 50 that had not been studied. The final group, composed of 100 male engineering students, had just finished a course in descriptive geometry, and the task was to solve certain geometric problems. The experimental half of each group was instructed, before the experimental task, to apply what they knew to the new task. For example, the students who were taught a special method of study were told, before reading about a task on which they would be subsequently tested, to "Use the method of study which you have learned in studying these paragraphs." The other two experimental sets of students were advised to use their knowledge of Latin or descriptive geometry, respectively. In all three cases, the experimental subgroups produced higher test scores than the control students who were not given an explicit prompt to make use of relevant knowledge or method.

In summary, the suggestions made on how to promote transfer all point to an overarching principle to the effect that transfer is more probable when the learner perceives the tasks he is learning to be meaningful, and when he understands that lessons lead over time to a larger, comprehensible whole. Teachers often have conceptions of this wholeness and of the relationships among the several parts. However, it is one thing for the teacher to possess such a model or design and quite another to impart it to the learner. Students not uncommonly regard their school tasks as small, separate activities, lacking continuity, and not as building in a cumulative way. The odds favor transfer for the student who discerns meaning in what he is to learn and who expects his present knowledge to be advantageous in his continuing pursuit of new learning.

Questions for Review and Discussion

1. It is not uncommon, even today, to hear someone say that a particu-

lar subject, such as Latin or mathematics, provides intellectual discipline. How would you answer such a statement?

2. We defined transfer as the impact of prior learning upon the acquisition of a subsequent task. Identify two or three examples in a subject you teach or are studying which represent good opportunities to provide transfer.

3. Why were the 1901 studies by Thorndike and Woodworth instrumental in bringing down the idea of formal discipline?

4. Compare and contrast Thorndike's theory of transfer by identical elements with Judd's conception of general transfer.

5. Gagné and Ausubel use different models and different language to account for transfer. Would they also differ about the conditions under which transfer occurs? Would they agree on when and when not to expect transfer?

6. You have read the description of the Productive Thinking Program, and some of the array of research evidence that supports its ability to foster general problem solving. If you taught at a grade level for which it is appropriate, would you use the program? Why or why not?

7. A series of suggestions was made at the close of the chapter for promoting positive transfer in the classroom. Consider a single lesson you will teach in the near future. See if you can incorporate some of those suggestions into your plans. If you are not teaching, select a lesson of interest to you and attempt the same application.

Readings for Further Reflection

Introductory level

Ellis, Henry. *The Transfer of Learning*. New York: Macmillan, 1965.

Ellis devotes the first 85 pages of this brief paperback to a clear and simple exposition of concepts about transfer, including its measurement, and the theory of transfer. The second part considers six psychological studies of transfer, including the paper by Osgood referred to in this chapter.

All books on the psychology of learning contain one or more chapters devoted to the topic of transfer. A particularly good treatment is to be found in:

Deese, James, and Hulse, Stewart H. *The Psychology of Learning* (3rd ed.). New York: McGraw-Hill Book Co., 1967.

Advanced level

A comprehensive review and analysis of the history of mental discipline, including an assessment of its role in contemporary education as of 20 years ago, is:

Kolesnik, Walter B. *Mental Discipline in Modern Education*. Madison, University of Wisconsin Press, 1958.

A detailed and technical discussion of serial and transfer phenomena is found in Chapter 12, pages 495–548, of:

Osgood, Charles E. *Method and Theory in Experimental Psychology*. New York: Oxford University Press, 1953.

For an original formulation of transfer phenomena, see:

Haselrud, George M. *Transfer, Memory, and Creativity: After-learning as a Perceptual Process*. Minneapolis: University of Minnesota Press, 1972.

References

Anderson, Richard C., & Anderson, Richard M. Transfer of originality training. *Journal of Educational Psychology*, 1963, *54*, 300–304.

Ausubel, David P. *Educational psychology: A cognitive view*. New York: Holt, Rinehart & Winston, 1968.

Baker, Linda S. *The effect of cognitive style training on students with reading disabilities*. Unpublished M. A. thesis, California State University, Haywood, 1975.

Barlow, M. C. Transfer of training in reasoning. *Journal of Educational Psychology*, 1937, *28*, 122–128.

Covington, Martin V., Crutchfield, Richard S., Davies, Lillian, & Olton, Robert M. *The Productive Thinking Program: A course in learning to think*. Columbus, Ohio: Charles E. Merrill Publishing Co., 1972.

Cronbach, Lee J. *Educational psychology* (2nd ed.). New York: Harcourt, Brace, 1962.

Deese, James, & Hulse, S. H. *The psychology of learning* (3rd ed.). New York: McGraw-Hill Book Co., 1967.

Dorsey, Mettie F., & Hopkins, L. Thomas. The influence of attitude upon transfer. *Journal of Educational Psychology*, 1930, *21*, 410–417.

Dwyer, Francis M., Jr. Adapting visual illustrations for effective learning. *Harvard Educational Review*, 1967, 37, 250–263.

Gagné, Robert M. *The conditions of learning* (2nd ed.). New York: Holt, Rinehart, & Winston, 1970.
Greene, Harry A., & Petty, Walter T. *Developing language skills in the elementary schools* (4th ed.). Boston: Allyn & Bacon, 1971.
Hendrickson, Gordon, & Schroeder, William J. Transfer of training in learning to hit a submerged target. *Journal of Educational Psychology,* 1941, 32, 205-213.
Hilgard, Ernest R., & Bower, Gordon H. *Theories of learning* (4th ed.). Englewood Cliffs, N.J.: Prentice-Hall, 1975.
Hogan, Robert, & Garvey, Catherine. *Study of verbally gifted youth,* 3rd annual report to the Spencer Foundation. Baltimore: Johns Hopkins University, 1975.
James, William. *The principles of psychology.* New York: Dover Publications, 1950. (Originally published, 1890.)
Judd, Charles H. The relation of special training to general intelligence. *Educational Review,* 1908, 36, 28-42.
Kolesnik, Walter B. *Mental discipline in modern education.* Madison: University of Wisconsin Press, 1958.
Martin, Edwin. Transfer of verbal paired associates. *Psychological Review,* 1965, 72, 327-343.
Myrow, David L., & Anderson, Richard C. Retroactive inhibition of prose as a function of the type of test. *Journal of Educational Psychology,* 1972, 63, 303-308.
Olton, Robert M., & Crutchfield, Richard S. Developing the skills of productive thinking, 68-9. In P. Mussen, J. Langer, & M. V. Covington, *Trends and issues in developmental psychology.* New York: Holt, Rinehart, & Winston, 1969.
Osgood, Charles E. The similarity paradox in human learning: A resolution. *Psychological Review,* 1949, 56, 132-143.
Overing, Robert L. R., & Travers, Robert M. W. Effect upon transfer of variations in training conditions. *Journal of Educational Psychology,* 1966, 57, 179-188.
Overing, Robert L. R., and Travers, Robert M. W. Variation in the amount of irrelevant cues in training and test conditions and the effect upon transfer. *Journal of Educational Psychology,* 1967, 58, 62-68.
Thorndike, Edward L. Mental discipline in high school studies. *Journal of Educational Psychology,* 1924, 15, 1-22, 83-98.
Thorndike, Edward L. & Woodworth, Robert S. The influence of improvement in one mental function upon the efficiency of other functions. *Psychological Review,* 1901, 8, 247-261, 384-395, 553-564.
Wertheimer, Max. *Productive thinking* (enlarged ed.). New York:

Harper & Bros., 1959.

White, Richard T. Research into learning hierarchies. *Review of Educational Research*, 1973, 43, 361–375.

Winch, W. H. The transfer of improvement in reasoning in school children. *British Journal of Psychology*, 1923, 13, 370–381.

Chapter 6

The Pupil As Thinker: Critical Thinking

Despite the vagueness of the term, *critical thinking* remains an important educational goal for most teachers. In everyday parlance, the reference is in part to the student's ability to attend carefully to and to comprehend the meaning of material. In part, also, it refers to his disposition to compare one claim or argument against another, to weigh evidence, and to accept conclusions based on reason rather than on authority. Both of these aspects are important, but since the former has been considered a basic condition for learning throughout this book, the latter meaning comes closer to the more differentiated conception of critical thinking to be discussed in this chapter.

In this chapter, first will come a definition of critical thinking. Second, we will review available reports of what has happened when experimenters or teachers have tried to teach students to do critical thinking. This review is separated into studies conducted with elementary students and those that have examined critical thinking at the secondary school level. Then the outcomes of that work will be assessed in order to indicate the kinds of activities and instruction that have been most successful. The basic question will be: If a teacher wishes to improve his students' ability to do critical thinking, how should he go about it?

A Concept of Critical Thinking

There are certain limitations we must work with in an attempt to define critical thinking. A formal and simple definition in which critical thinking is defined as a process, or in which it is seen as equivalent to another already known process, does not seem possible. To prepare a definition that gives such an appearance might be momentarily satisfying, but difficulties would continuously ooze through the definition, like flood water through the sandbags of a crumbling levee. To begin, we might take Ennis's (1962) definition that critical thinking is the reasonable assessment of statements. "Reasonable assessment," of course, requires careful definition, but we begin to see that the learner must engage in some generic evaluative behavior upon statements, with evaluation broadly conceived. The statements (or arguments, conclusions, experimental results, and so forth) may have been created by him or by someone else. If they are his, his role as a critical thinker is different from that as a creator.

Our first effort to get at what the critical thinker does entails the specification of some sets of attributes. They are not set out in any particular order, as it would be difficult to demonstrate that one is more or less important than the others. Under each of the general topics some of the more obvious examples of the behavior have been identified.

Attributes of critical thinking

If the learner is to make a reasonable assessment of an argument, she or he would be expected to know what the argument is about.

1. *The learner comprehends the essential elements of the argument.* Critical thinking cannot occur when the learner is unaware of or is unable to understand what the argument is about. People who want to pursue their own goals at the expense of or to the detriment of other people or the public at large endeavor to prevent others from reaching an impartial and independent understanding of the topic. Political campaigns are notorious for "campaign oratory" in which little effort is made to identify and analyze the fundamental issues that affect people's lives. Such campaigns deal in slogans and bandwagon psychology. A salesman whose income will advance directly at the expense of the customer is not eager for the fine print of a long-term payment contract to be scrutinized.

What does it mean to say that the learner must understand the argument? Primarily, that he must have a background of concepts and information sufficient to enable him to determine the probable truth of an argument or the likelihood of a predicted outcome. It also means that he must possess the appropriate skills to assess the argument. The learner who does not have the concepts, skills, and knowledge to perform in this way is disqualified as a critical thinker. Surely it is a basic function of the educational system to provide these tools of thinking in abundance. Of course all of us confront occasions when we do suffer this disqualification. Should we vote to allow a nuclear power plant to be constructed near our city? If we allow it and a nuclear accident occurs, we will have contributed to a major disaster. If we prevent it, we may be dangerously postponing the development of badly needed new sources of energy. When surgeons tell us that our child must have a risky heart operation or suffer the possibility of poor health and an early death, we cannot make an independent judgment of the wisdom of their advice. In that sense we are disqualified as critical thinkers, but we are not prevented from making partially informed judgments. To become informed, we can attend city council debates between advocates and opponents of the nuclear plant, we can read the available literature pertaining to the risks, and we can examine reports from other communities which have permitted such power plants to be built. Or we can seek additional medical opinions about the advisability of surgery for our child. In short, when we cannot exercise autonomous decision making, we can often compel those who wish to influence our decision to disclose, clarify, and explain their reasoning. (See Hudgins, 1960, and especially Hudgins and Smith, 1966, for information about how groups of children monitor problem solutions of their more knowledgeable peers.)

This raises an important question pertaining to the education of critical thinkers. Some instructional efforts have attempted to build thinking directly into a curriculum in social studies, science, mathematics, or some other area of study. Others have been more general, with the emphasis placed upon the intellectual skills involved. The content of the instruction is selected because it permits practice on the skill and not because it is part of a systematic and coordinated study of biology or physics or geometry. We will return to this issue later.

2. *The learner seeks out evidence that bears upon the argument or the conclusion advanced.* This covers so many possibilities about the drawing of conclusions that if the assertion is to have any meaning, some of them must be identified in more detail. What constitutes evidence for or against a proposition is often difficult to decide, for interpretation and inference are involved in all but the most clear-cut case. However, we would expect a critical thinker to check for evidence in at least the following ways.

First, is there a body of facts, information, observations, or other kinds of data that lies behind the advocated conclusion? Henry VIII was able to have his wife Anne Boleyn beheaded on the charge of treason, but there was scant evidence in support of it. Hitler and his supporters conspired to place German Jews in the role of scapegoats (and to murder millions of them before the end of World War II) on the pretext that Jews were responsible for the social, economic, and political woes that faced Germany in the 1920s. Throughout the ages, totalitarian leaders have used unsupported conclusions to gain territory, to destroy their enemies, and otherwise to increase their own power.

Thus an important and fundamental aspect of critical thinking is to find out whether *any* evidence is available to support a conclusion. Of course, this concern is not limited to the arena of social life. The success of the experimental natural sciences from the time of the Renaissance is in no small part due to their recognition that ideas about the earth and the universe must be tested against observations, and that theories (conclusions) unsupported by reality must be modified or changed.

Second, are there sources of bias in the evidence adduced? Bias in the information intended to support conclusions can be of many types. Among the more frequently occuring biases we can include unreliability of observations or reports and overgeneralization (or overcaution). In the Cornell Critical Thinking Test (1966), a hypothetical situation is set up in which space explorers are sent to a planet to determine what happened to a previous expedition. In one set of questions the student is asked to judge whose observations are more reliable; for example, the conflicting reports given by a soldier and the health officer on the potability of the local water. Athletic contests usually have umpires who make crucial decisions about "safe" or "out", "in" or "out", and so forth, because contestants' perceptions are affected by their interest in the outcome, whereas the umpire's role is defined as disinterested and his competence is judged according to his neutrality.

Overgeneralization is defined as the tendency to accept a conclusion based on insufficient evidence or on an insufficient number of examples to prove the point. The critical thinker must learn to identify and assess the impact of various sources of unreliability leading to conclusions, as he must establish criteria for determining under- or overgeneralization. Does a given conclusion, if it is to be accepted, demand that the event always occur under given conditions, or is a probability model more adequate to account for observations? If so, what proportion of the observations made must fall within specified limits? With younger children, such formal techniques and training are impossible, but even very young pupils should be taught the dangers of accepting an idea based upon one occurrence or a very limited number of cases.

3. *The learner will weigh and evaluate both the evidence available and the line of reasoning offered before he accepts the conclusions.* This principle implies a general attitude of skepticism on the part of the critical thinker, and a disposition to avoid reaching a conclusion until enough evidence can be found to lead to a reasonable decision. Thus the thinker is

not only concerned with whether the available evidence is reliable and essentially unbiased, he must also ask whether it is germane to the argument. In Arthur Miller's *The Crucible,* a play about the Salem witch trials of 1692, the testimony of a group of hysterical teen-aged girls, controlled by the malice of their leader, succeeds in condemning several local citizens to death by hanging. Although some of their testimony was pure mischief, other parts of it were reported with some accuracy but interpreted with dubious logic. For example, one woman was accused of witchcraft because she was seen in the pasture of a neighbor whose cow subsequently quit giving milk. Logically, this is the error of affirming the consequent. We may say that "If x occurs, then y will occur," or in the present case, it would be said that "If Goody x is a witch, then cow y will go dry." The fallacy occurs when we conclude that "Since cow y went dry, Goody x must be a witch."

Recognizing the danger in making judgments too quickly or based on too little evidence, the attributes of critical thinking are expanded to include suspended judgment and calls for evidence. But these must be tempered with an understanding that for many issues of practical and scientific or intellectual significance, there will never come a time when all the evidence that might pertain to an issue is available. To postpone a judgment beyond the point when the predominant weight of evidence is available is as serious an error as leaping to conclusions. In fact, both may signify the lack of any reasoned thought at all. Similarly, while we want the learner to ask for evidence in support of conclusions, we do not want to encourage endless (and mindless) cries of "What's your evidence for that?" To succeed as a critical thinker, the learner must know what is relevant data and when an argument has sufficient evidence pertaining to it to be either accepted or rejected. Critical thinking is sometimes equated with negativism, but this is an erroneous conception. The learner who cannot be convinced, no matter how complete and compelling the evidence, is no better a critical thinker than the one who accepts any assertion placed before him.

4. *Finally, the learner should note and take account of what is not said in an argument or conclusion.* This statement refers to such aspects of critical thinking as detecting assumptions, interpreting ambiguous or equivocal statements, and drawing inferences. Life is filled with assumptions, mostly unstated. We assume when we leave for work in the morning that we will return home safely at night. We plan our lives on the assumption that we have a future. Without the ability to make such an assumption, most of us would find daily living very difficult to cope with. The algebra teacher assumes his students can perform basic algebraic operations of combining terms inside and outside parentheses when he

proceeds to teach them factoring; every teacher assumes his students have prepared for class in a way that makes today's lesson feasible, and he (and they) pay a price if the assumption is untenable.

An important characteristic of the critical thinker is that he analyzes arguments for the assumptions upon which they are based and tries to determine what will happen if the assumptions are not met. Teachers are justifiably indignant when academicians or others suggest that new ideas for teaching or the results of research are applicable to the teachers' situations, when they can identify differences that would militate against such application. For example, if a method of teaching has succeeded with children of a different age, ability level, or social class, or who otherwise differ drastically from the children being taught by those who are expected to apply the method, it is quite true that the violation of assumptions may destroy the method's efficacy.

The language of an argument often is not specific as to the intended referent. Is only x implied, or can one argue as well that x, y, and z could be included? The critical thinker may not be able to reduce or to resolve the ambiguity, but he should detect it, and he should be aware of its effects upon conclusions. In the same way, inferences are to be drawn from statements in which the referent is not specified. Except in very simple and direct cases, it is possible for more than a single inference to be drawn.

This introduces the notion that critical thinking often involves awareness that alternative ideas are available in a given argument. Once more, it may not always be possible for the learner to select an unequivocally best conclusion in an argument. However, he should be able to identify the possible interpretations and the conditions under which each might hold.

An effort at definition

We can now attempt to define what we mean by critical thinking. The concept involves, in the first place, *an attitude or a disposition to search for evidence* which bears upon an argument or the conclusions drawn from argument. Such an attitude should pervade the behavior of the learner whenever he is asked to accept a conclusion, and so we identify this attitude of wanting to know what evidence is available as a hallmark of critical thinking. *Knowledge and information* is another significant aspect of critical thinking. When a heretofore unknown Renoir is brought to officials of the Louvre, their search for evidence of its authenticity is immediately translated into a series of technical questions; some of these involve the chemistry of dating, some the unique style of the artist, his whereabouts at the period the new painting dates from, and more. In Scotland, reports of the Loch Ness monster are heard from time to time, sometimes even accompanied by photographs. To date when the right technical questions have been asked and alternative explanations of the ominous shapes have been given, the arguments for the existence of the monster have collapsed. Finally, *critical thinking involves a complex set of intellectual skills,* to which we have referred above. These include the ability to detect obvious biases in reports, overgeneralization or overcaution, and the ability to sort out and take account of assumptions and inferences.

To summarize, we can say that critical thinking is a general attitude of searching for evidence relevant to conclusions. The attitude must be supported by an array of intellectual skills that are germane to the analysis and evaluation of arguments. These skills are broadly known as inferential reasoning, detecting assumptions, identifying sources of bias in arguments, and so forth. Frequently, and particularly for advanced students and adults, effective utilization of these skills depends upon specialized systems of reasoning such as logic, mathematical deduction, the statistics of inference, and other techniques. It may also depend upon the thinker's background of knowledge and experience. Thus our definition includes a developmental question. Whether younger children of elementary school age can engage in critical thinking, or whether this is a dimension of education and learning that must be postponed until the attainment of the state of formal reasoning, or approximately the time that the child enters the secondary school, is in part, but only in part, a matter of how one construes the preceding definition.

There are many who argue the latter position, that is, that critical thinking depends upon the emergence of formal operations of reasoning, and before the age of 11 or 12 the child is incapable of such propositional logic. This is Piaget's position, and within the past decade there have probably been more people willing to agree with it than disagree. However, Ennis (1975) has challenged Piaget's logic and has countered it by presenting evidence from his own work that children of six and seven years are capable of performing certain classes of conditional reasoning. In addition, there is evidence, to be reviewed in the following section, that some aspects of critical thinking are susceptible to training in elementary school children. I find perhaps most persuasive the hypothesis that a general critical attitude, a style or approach to thinking, will bear greater fruit if it is learned in the early years of life than if we attempt to superimpose it only through the standard curriculum of the secondary school. Obviously the critical thinking of third- or fourth-graders will lack the formal logic and the detailed knowledge base available to high school or college students, but there seems to be no evidence to preclude the possibility that a foundation for critical thinking can be learned by children in the elementary school. Some evidence to support that contention is offered below.

Studies of Critical Thinking

At the elementary school level

The attempts that have been made to examine critical thinking of children before the age of adolescence can be conveniently divided into two types: those that look at the ability of children to reason and the developmental sequence through which such ability travels, and those that are reports of efforts to provide instruction in one or more aspects of critical thinking. Studies of the first type are for the most part of more recent origin and are more focused in that they tend to examine children's ability to engage in formal, logical reasoning. What we may call the instructional studies are often more diffuse and, lamentably, suffer from a variety of flaws. However, they do tend to show that explicit instruction can improve children's ability to do certain kinds of critical thinking.

Development of Ability to Reason. The first adequate test of intelligence developed by Alfred Binet in the early 1900s contained items that demanded reasoning. Since the Binet test is age graded, these items provided a rough scale for the development of reasoning. However, it was not until after World War I that Cyril Burt published his famous papers (1919) on the development of reasoning in school children. Burt had developed a large number of items or problems designed to test different reasoning abilities. He was dismayed to find others making extensive use of only one type of his items (analogy), which he regards as limited in scope. However, in his large-scale test with London schoolchildren he also discovered that some kinds of content and problems repeatedly survived as test items better than others did. Items that were passed by between 40 and 60 percent of the children in the sample at a given age were retained. In Figure 6.1 we have reproduced one of Burt's items for each age he studied, that is, from 7 to 14. Burt concluded that the seven-year-olds seem to possess all the fundamental abilities required to reason successfully but that the informational content of many of the problems was beyond their knowledge. The fact remains that Burt by no means found children even as young as seven unable to reason with logical forms.

FIGURE 6.1
Sample items from reasoning tests for children, ages 7—14

---

7 years: Tom runs faster than Jim. Jack runs slower than Jim. Who is the slowest—Jim, Jack, or Tom?

8 years: Ethel has twice as many apples as John. Lucy has half as many as John. Lucy has ten. How many has Ethel?

9 years: C is smaller than B; and B is smaller than A. Is A greater than C?

10 years:
"I sprang to the saddle and Joris and he; I galloped, Dirck galloped, we galloped all three."
What was the name of the person referred to as "he" in these lines of poetry?

11 years: A man was found nearly dead with his throat cut, and on the back of his left arm there was a blood-stained mark of a left hand. The policeman says he tried to kill himself. Do you think that the policeman was right?

12 years: My birthday is on December 27, and I am just four days older than Tom. This year Christmas is on a Tuesday. On what day of the week is Tom's birthday?

13 years: Explain how the following code is worked:

Message (in code) dpnf up Mpoepo bu podf.
The same (translated) Come to London at once.
What is the secret letter for "x" in this code?

14 years: When you enter my house you will find a window on your right in the side wall of the passage. When the sun sets it shines straight through this window onto the wall opposite. What direction are you facing when you stand in the doorway and look across the street?

Note: Items that were selected for these reasoning tests were successfully passed by 40 to 60 percent of the London schoolchildren of a given age who were selected at random by Burt (1919).

Source: Burt (1919), pp. 70—72.

Several more recent studies provide additional information about schoolchildren's logical reasoning abilities. Their conclusions are at some variance, but nonetheless they demonstrate with greater clarity which logic problems are easier or more difficult for children to solve. Two related studies (O'Brien & Shapiro, 1968; Shapiro & O'Brien, 1970) demonstrated that elementary schoolchildren earn significantly better scores on a test of logical reasoning when they must decide simply whether a given conclusion is valid or invalid than when a third option ("can't tell") is added to the items.

182   Learning and Thinking

In the first of these studies, younger children in the first three grades of elementary school were given a 100-item test in which each of the three choices, "yes", "no", and "not enough clues" was correct one third of the time. The pupils selected "not enough clues" significantly less often on the appropriate "opened up" items than they did the other two choices. In the later study, Shapiro and O'Brien extended their sample to include children through the age of 13, using the same test as before, 100 logical items, but in two forms. At each grade level, first through eighth (ages 6 through 13) half the pupils were given Test A and asked to answer items in which the conclusion was either valid or invalid. The other half of the children were given Test B, which had 33 items to be answered "not enough clues," and all 100 items had all three options. The scores on Test B were lower than those on Test A, which the investigators interpret to mean that elementary-age children are better able to recognize a conclusion than they are to test for it. Using Test B results, they also found a definite pattern of growth across the age range, with no ceiling effect. Significant differences appeared between the age groups of 6–8, 9–12, and 13, but there were not significant differences within those ranges. Scores for these pupils were especially low on the 33 "opened up" items; that is, those where the correct answer was "not enough clues."

Roberge (1970) administered three tests of reasoning to 263 pupils in grades four, six, eight, and ten. The tests varied in the principles involved and the type of reasoning (class or conditional) called for. Roberge found developmental patterns emerging; that is, older children tended to reason more successfully than younger ones, but he also found that certain principles, especially those which lead to invalid conclusions (affirming the consequent and negating the antecedent) are especially difficult. An example of the former type is:

All As are Bs
x is a B
∴ x is an A

Of the latter,

All As are Bs
x is not an A
∴ x is not a B

Only a small percentage of even the oldest pupils were capable of correctly answering these items.

These three groups of studies suggest some of the developmental topography of the logical landscape, but they do not inform us as to whether logical reasoning might be improved as a result of instruction, or how this could be done. However, Shapiro and O'Brien stress that their results do not rule out the possibility that improvement could occur through instruction and that, in fact, it is important to discover what the effects of deliberate manipulation may be upon children's reasoning. Roberge adds to this the explicit suggestion, based upon his findings, that classroom instruction could profitably begin as early as the fourth grade in the case of some of the valid principles that have been found easiest to master, such as *modus ponens* (all As are Bs —x is A; ∴ x is B). As of this writing, no studies could be located which reflect the results of instruction, but the zeitgeist is such that studies of this type will surely appear in the near future.

Effects of Instruction in Critical Thinking. There have been, as was indicated earlier, some attempts to improve children's critical thinking. These studies have generally been isolated in time and in intellectual origin from one another, and their cumulative impact is negligible. The sample sizes are small, and some of the reports are almost informal testimonials by a teacher of the values of instructing children to think critically. Perhaps the most critical indictment to be leveled against this work is the failure by its authors to investigate the transfer effects of their instructional programs. That is, teachers are likely to be much more concerned with whether a course of instruction in logical reasoning or using data leads to improvement in their pupils' abilities to evaluate biased arguments or to reject the conclusions of an ill-designed experiment than with whether the same instruction elevates their test scores on material like that used in the course of instruction.

There is one study (Morgan & Carrington, 1944) which bears quite closely upon the foregoing discussion. It was conducted long before the current interest in children's logic and therefore lacks the theoretical base which later studies ought to possess. The investigators wished to answer the question of whether simple diagrams can be used to help children solve relational problems. All the pupils in grades two through six of a large elementary school were given a pretest of ten three-term series problems. (Example: Dorothy has a bigger book than Marie; Alice has a bigger book than Dorothy. Who has the smallest book?) The school had three classrooms at each grade level. After the pretest two rooms of each grade were given a brief lesson (about 20 minutes in length) which showed pupils how to diagram three-term series problems. For example, in the problem,

> John has fewer marbles than Bill.
> Tom has fewer marbles than John.
> Who has the fewest marbles?

184   Learning and Thinking

the children were instructed to sketch piles of marbles for each boy, corresponding to his relationship to the others:

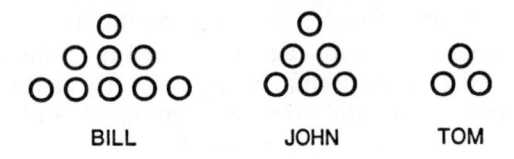

```
          O              O
         OOO            OO              O
       OOOOO            OOO            OO
                                        O
        BILL            JOHN           TOM
```

The diagram points out to the child in concrete terms the answer to the problem. Altogether the experimental groups received six problems by way of training, after which they and the third class of each level (the control classes) took a ten-item posttest. Morgan and Carrington conclude that the instructed classes at all levels showed improvement, but the real impact occurred at the third and fourth grades. The older children seemed to solve the problems reasonably well, even without the instruction. The investigators suggest that the teaching procedure should be extended to other types of relationships. That seems to be an excellent idea, and the study, for all of its flaws, is most provocative, but seems never to have been repeated or extended as the authors recommended a generation ago.

Arnold (1938) developed a series of 25 stories to be used by teachers of fifth- and sixth-graders to teach the intelligent use of data, defined as "the ability to *recognize relevance, dependability, bias in source,* and *adequacy of data* in regard to a particular problem, question, or conclusion" (pp. 256–257). All of these fit comfortably with the attributes of critical thinking set forth above. The Arnold study is valuable for several reasons, beyond the abilities he tried to teach. For one thing, he designed his story-lessons to be used in a convenient problem-discussion format. The teacher read the story to the children and then guided the discussion by means of a series of questions. The only restriction Arnold imposed on the teachers was that they avoid answering the questions for the class. Then, too, the instruction was accomplished by the children's regular teachers, rather than by Arnold or other outsiders, which eliminates certain threats to the generalizability of the results. And the instruction continued over a long enough period (three months) that the lessons were no longer a novelty by the end of the unit. On the posttest, the 90 experimental pupils scored significantly higher than the 83 control pupils.

A large proportion of the content in the Arnold study would have to be rewritten if teachers wished to use it today, because many of the stories dealt with stereotypes about Germans or Japanese immediately before World War II. In the main, however, the content is of little consequence;

it is the principles of relevance, bias, and the rest that Arnold tried to teach. For example, in one case pupils are led to see that the report of an incident given by a third party is probably more dependable than that of either antagonist whose interests are directly concerned. Another case illustrates the increased dependability of a conclusion based on a large number of observations rather than on hearsay or on one or only a few observations. In the lesson one person reports that he knows a baseball team is good because he has been told so; another says he saw them play once, and they were good. Still another observer has often seen the team play well. The discussion is then set up to permit children to discuss the situation and draw a conclusion.

During the 1960s, Hilda Taba and her associates developed and tested a curriculum in elementary social studies which had special objectives with regard to the improvement of children's thinking. The Taba effort is particularly noteworthy because the curriculum itself, including texts and other materials in use by teachers and pupils, as well as the in-service training given to the teachers, were designed to work on a variety of children's intellectual skills. These had to do particularly with conceptualizing and generalizing. The principal objective of the Taba work was to examine the development of thinking processes under optimal conditions where the curriculum and the teaching strategies employed fostered thinking skills and reinforced one another, and where pupils had ample time in training to develop the skills. Another objective was to examine the relationships between teaching strategies and measures of thinking (specifically, in Taba's research, the drawing of inferences and the application of principles; special measures were developed during the project for these purposes).

In an effort to determine whether the combined curriculum–in-service education offered by her project was having the kinds of effects upon children's thinking that she anticipated, Taba launched a yearlong field experiment. Participating classes were at the fourth-, fifth-, and sixth-grade levels, although the total project included classes with younger children also. The intermediate grades were selected for research purposes for the simple reason that the older children were better prepared to handle the written testing materials. Four treatment conditions were identified: E–1 classes were to be those where the children had used the special curriculum (the Contra Costa County Social Studies Curriculum) the year before the experimental year, as well as during that year, and where the teachers had had the special training and had also taught the curriculum previously. In other words, the E–1 classes would be the best representatives of how well children improved in thinking when given maximum access to the Taba materials and program. E–2 classes would be one step removed; the children in E–2 classes would be new to the Contra Costa materials, and their teachers would receive special training during the experimental year. E–3 classes would also be composed of children who would experience the new social studies curriculum for the first time, but whose teachers would receive no special training in its use. C (control) classes would not use the Contra Costa curriculum, and, of course, their teachers would not have the training. Each condition was to consist of two classes at the fourth-, two at the fifth-, and two at the sixth-grade levels, for a total of 24 classes.

Taba predicted that the pupils who had had the most experience with the Contra Costa County Social Studies Curriculum, and whose teachers were both trained and experienced in its use, would improve most in their ability to draw inferences and to apply principles. Conversely, control classes which were not studying the same social studies curriculum would fare least well on those measures between the beginning and the end of the school year. The results of the tests did not support those predictions. The children who had the most direct experience with her curriculum did only middling well compared with other pupils.

The results of the Taba experiment reflect some of the great difficulties involved in field experiments in education when the experimenter hopes to find changes in rather narrowly defined variables, which have to be isolated from the whole complex series of learning and life events to which the pupils have been exposed for a period of a school year. Unless the effects of a specific treatment are very strong, and those of all other influences on the child are minimal in their impact, such isolated variations are extremely difficult to produce.

Furthermore, field experiments in education have built-in booby traps. Taba observes ruefully that the six classes which were to have represented her most powerful treatment (that is, the E–1 classes) were reduced from six to two. Each of the six was to consist of pupils, promoted as a unit, who had experienced the special curriculum the year before the test. Despite promises from principals that they would create such classes, the mobility of the children involved was such that in only the two fourth-grade classes was this criterion even approximated. In those two classes, a majority of the pupils had had the prior experience, but even here not all the children met the basic condition for the experimental treatment. Taba clearly suspected, also, that there was a contaminating influence at work in some of the schools. Some teachers without the training, or who were not using her curriculum, were able to learn about the strategies and materials being employed in the experimental classes. Whether that knowledge had the effect of modifying their behavior to become more like the experimental teachers is not easily determined, but, of course, any adaptation in that direction would tend to nullify differences among the treatments. It also is not clear that efforts were made throughout the year to monitor the behavior of the participating teachers, except on four occasions when each of them tape-recorded a demonstration lesson as part of the research project. The question raised is that of implementation: Were the teachers, as a matter of fact, continuously behaving throughout the year in the way that their experimental or control treatments dictated they ought to behave? When such careful monitoring is lacking, and when differences among groups that are anticipated fail to develop, large, unanswerable questions about the causes emerge. Did the E groups in the Taba study fail to surpass C classes in an educationally significant way because the curriculum and the training of the teachers were not sufficiently different, or at least effective enough, to bring about sizable changes? Or did most or all of the teachers over time shift toward more typical, and perhaps cognitively less demanding roles, so that at the end of the year the experimental treatments had not really been fully implemented, thus resulting in only weak outcomes? In the absence of good monitoring data, it is not possible to answer these questions, which must haunt the investigator or the curriculum decision maker who wishes firm answers about the improvement of children's skills in thinking.

At least two investigations have been reported in which certain types of logical reasoning constituted the curriculum for the experimental classes (White, 1936; Hyram, 1957). Compared to Taba's elaborate field experience, both are very small in scale. It should also be pointed out that although these studies were conducted in elementary schools, the participants would, in most contemporary school systems, be attending some form of secondary school. White's pupils, on the average, were only one or two months away from their 13th birthdays. Hyram's study was done with seventh- and eighth-grade pupils in a large urban system which has maintained a kindergarten through eighth-grade elementary school organization.

The study done by White (1936) employed two classes of twelve-year-old boys attending school in central London. The study was designed to see whether grammar, if supplemented by instruction in reasoning, could improve the learner's quality of written expression, which is one of the ostensible but usually unachieved objectives of grammar. One of the classes continued with its regular grammar lessons, and the experimental class received one hour each week of instruction in logic; this continued for three months. The logic program consisted of three major units: (1) classification, (2) inference, including induction and deduction and the syllogism, and (3) emotional or affective thinking.

188   Learning and Thinking

At the end of three months several measures were taken. One was a reasoning test much like the instruction given to the experimental class, which did significantly better than the control group, a result which is not surprising since the test was so similar to their training. Of more value was White's decision to have all 78 of the boys (experimental and control) write a composition. This was a better test of the pupils' ability to apply the lessons in thinking to a task of their own construction. White took some elaborate but necessary precautions to see that the compositions were scored without bias. He trained two others to work with him in scoring the papers for clarity of thought and for connectedness and coherence of reasoning. Penalties were assessed for incoherent thought and unrelated ideas. All the papers were disguised and shuffled so no one would know whose paper he was reading. Furthermore, all the essays were retyped and their spelling was corrected so that the scorers would not inadvertently reward good spelling or punish illegibility. Although the scores for the experimental pupils' papers were higher than the others, White describes the difference as "probably significant," an equivocal conclusion, to say the least. Still the evidence suggests some applicability by the boys who received the logic instruction, and the demonstration of transfer from the training material to a typical school task (composition) which involves reasoning is a positive feature of this early study that is lacking in many later ones.

Hyram (1957) evaluated the gains made in logical thinking by a group of upper elementary school pupils (in seventh and eighth grades) to whom he presented a seven-unit program. The experimental treatment consumed 50 minutes of each school day for four months in the teaching of the following units: (1) nature of thinking in general, (2) tools of thinking, (3) nature of definition, (4) nature of inductive inference, (5) nature of deductive inference, (6) nature of experimentation, and (7) common errors in thinking. Experimental pupils were matched with controls on IQ (all pupils scored 110 or better on a measure of intelligence), mental age, reading ability, and initial reasoning ability. The end-of-term test revealed highly significant gains for the experimental pupils. This finding is useful as far as it goes, but it fails to indicate whether such a heavy instructional investment helps pupils to evaluate scientific or historical material more adequately, to detect fallacies in others' arguments, or to avoid them in their own. All the questions we might wish to ask about the effects of this program, even the simple one of how lasting the gains are, remain unanswered.

Two other older studies can be briefly mentioned. Barlow (1937) gave a course of lessons to older children who analyzed the morals of fables, studied the conclusions of arguments, and performed other tasks aimed at improving general reasoning ability. Some retention remained a year later, but transfer across tasks was poor. Grener and Raths (1945) describe Grener's efforts to improve the thinking of her third-grade pupils. This is not a scientific report, since it is based only on her own class and through anecdotal records, but it does suggest that a dedicated teacher can bring about important changes for the better in pupils' thinking when he or she states the goals explicitly and designs activities and materials that can be employed to achieve the goals. Their paper is a convincing statement that Grener did construct a total immersion atmosphere which stressed children's thinking. Their final conclusion, although it is much too general to provide a guideline for learning, is still of some importance. "A continuing emphasis throughout all the school years on improvement in the thinking process might be the greatest contribution we could make to the improvement of instruction in the elementary school" (Grener & Raths, 1945, p. 42).

At the secondary school level

Most of the efforts to teach critical thinking to students of secondary school age, as might be expected, have employed subject matter vehicles such as geometry or social studies. The increasing differentiation of studies for older students renders it improbable that general approaches to critical thinking will have much practical value, although they may be useful as an outline or a guide to planning instruction in critical thinking. For example, if a high school senior is asked to judge the adequacy of inferences in an argument about the future level of the gross national product, he cannot do so effectively unless he possesses some of the basic concepts and analytical tools of the economist. But neither is it necessarily true that instruction in a subject, be it economics, English, geometry, or geography, will automatically improve the students' ability to reason about the subject. The weight of the available evidence suggests that improvements in reasoning emerge as the instruction provided to the student is aimed at critical thinking about a particular branch of knowledge. At the height of the progressive movement in education, extreme positions on this topic were sometimes expressed. One of them was that improvement in students' thinking ability is independent of the content being studied and depends rather on how the subject is organized than what is organized. Any content could be an effective vehicle for teaching thinking. Thus, lessons in baking a cake or other very practical and domestic tasks could provide the occasion for lessons in thinking. No doubt the extreme position was stated for the sake of emphasis; thought is not the automatic and natural by-product of any subject. The history of mental discipline was reviewed in the preceding chapter, and there is no need to do so here, but it is foolish to argue that one content is the equal of another as the vehicle for teaching thinking.

Numerous studies appeared in the literature, most of them in the 1930s and 1940s, which demonstrated the possibility of improved thinking in such studies as English, geometry, and chemistry when instruction in the subject was planned with objectives of improved thinking as an integral part of the curriculum. Let us examine several of the better known of these experiments, and then one that failed to produce the expected positive outcomes, to provide some conception of the linkages that must be made between instruction in thinking and desirable changes in students' behavior.

Among the earliest studies, and one of the most comprehensive as regards describing instructional method and detailing of the outcomes, is Fawcett's (1938) monograph on the nature of proof. This report of a two-year project in teaching geometry to high school students reflected Fawcett's recognition that if students' critical thinking ability was to be improved and extended to nonmathematical activities, as well as to problems in geometry, the experiences in his classroom must highlight the basic continuity of thinking processes across activities. He assumed that the content of the geometry class could be nicely adapted to achieve objectives of critical thinking, but that these would not occur unless his goals were defined and arrangements were made for working toward them. The characteristics of a pupil who understands the nature of deductive proof were delineated in the following terms:

1. He will select the significant words and phrases in any statement that is important to him and ask that they be carefully defined.
2. He will require evidence in support of any conclusion he is pressed to accept.
3. He will analyze that evidence and distinguish fact from assumption.
4. He will recognize stated and unstated assumptions essential to the conclusion.
5. He will evaluate these assumptions, accepting some and rejecting others.
6. He will evaluate the argument, accepting or rejecting the conclusions.
7. He will constantly reexamine the assumptions which are behind his beliefs and which guide his actions.

(Fawcett, 1938, pp. 11–12)

Fawcett's monograph makes it evident that this was a teacher who had a very clear conception of what he wished to accomplish with his students, and who also had definite and carefully reasoned strategies and tactics for achieving these ends. At the beginning of school in the first year of his study (which encompassed two years with the same group of students) Fawcett arranged class discussions on nonmathematical topics that would be likely to elicit from the students a recognition of the fact that in debate, if disagreements are ever to be resolved, antagonists must come to the point of defining the terms being used. Fawcett seized upon the topic of awards for "outstanding achievements" which was then a controversial issue at the high school. Under his guidance (which apparently was gentle but unmistakable in its impact), students began to identify their need for better definition. Later this same need was transferred to mathematical terms when Fawcett and the students set out to develop "A Theory of Space." The record of the two-year project shows continuous shifting from mathematical to nonmathematical topics, and the clear conveyance of the concept that reasoning is important in reaching intelligent decisions of all kinds. To this end the students analyzed advertisements, newspaper editorials, and political speeches, as well as solving problems in geometry. The unity of knowledge was stressed rather than the differences, as so often occurs.

Evidence of several interesting kinds is available to help us decide whether Fawcett's original objectives were achieved. First, he showed that his students scored at the 80th percentile among students in the state of Ohio who took a geometry achievement test at the same time. (However, since the mean IQ of his students was 115, higher than average achievement would be anticipated.) The point is that, although less time was devoted to the study of traditional topics in geometry, students' achievement in mathematics did not suffer as a consequence. Fawcett also developed a test of the nature of proof applied to nonmathematical topics. When he compared the before and after achievement of his students with those of others in the same high school and in different high schools, only those in his class demonstrated significant improvement over the course of the school year. Finally, the reports of students and their parents, although they probably reflect a strong halo effect, tended to confirm his reports that the course was successful in advancing students' critical thinking skills. Many of the pupils were able to cite examples of how they had applied improved reasoning to other classes at school and to out-of-school problems as well. Parents reported, sometimes rather unhappily, a variety of occasions on which their sons' and daughters' critical thinking was evidenced within the family or the community. We must not overlook the fact, however, that Fawcett seems to have been a gifted teacher who likely built solid and effective working relationships with his students. Enough of his analysis comes through in the monograph to provide some outline of why his procedures led to improvement in students' skill as critical thinkers.

At nearly the same time Fawcett reported his experiences with high school students in the demonstrative geometry class, Ulmer (1939) demonstrated that the ordinary geometry teacher, working within the normal limits of his or her classroom, can induce marked improvement in the reasoning skills of pupils, and that it can be done with no sacrifice in the mastery of the traditional mathematics knowledge. Ulmer's study lacks the depth and the detailed account of procedures that Fawcett provided, but it contributes other information of importance. Fawcett's results, as we have already observed, may depend heavily upon his idiosyncratic talents as a teacher. From the single case reported, it is impossible to separate the general effects of his procedures from the impact of his personality and his rapport with students. Ulmer's studies employed several experimental teachers, not just the investigator, to implement the objectives and the activities designed by Ulmer to provide reflective thinking. When the predicted outcomes of instruction are achieved broadly by a group of teachers who represent the general population of teachers, we can have more confidence in the effects of the program. Furthermore, Ulmer compared the results of his experimental classes with those of other geometry classes whose pupils were not studying geometry at all. Improvement in reasoning scores was significantly better for the experimental classes than for either set of controls.

Thelen (1944) developed a method for teaching chemistry to college freshmen which was designed to improve certain aspects of their critical thinking, compared to other classes of chemistry students who followed a more standard curriculum. Thelen's experimental treatment emphasized group processes in the study of chemistry. He tried to reduce the dependence of students on the authority of the teacher, the textbook, and the expected outcomes of laboratory exercises, and to substitute direct experience by the students with the phenomena under study and intense group interaction. Thelen's experimental students earned better test scores than the controls on some outcome measures, but not on all. The improvements in abilities such as generalizing beyond available data, or being overcautious, were related more to the proportion of time devoted in the course to relevant activities (such as planning experiments or interpreting data) and the extent to which the content was "rationalized." Today we would express the latter term as comprehension and the integration of ideas into the learner's existing cognitive structure.

Another of the early efforts to improve adolescents' critical thinking was undertaken by Glaser (1941), whose experiment was conducted in high school English classes. He inserted his experimental program into a semester when the regular English curriculum called for the study and analysis of essays and newspapers, but even so, the instruction and materials were but tangentially related to English. The units stand alone as a program to teach critical thinking.

Glaser's program consisted of eight units, each designed to teach an aspect of critical thinking to adolescents. The units were: (1) "Recognition of Need for Definition," (2) "Logic and the Weight of Evidence," (3) "The Nature of Probable Evidence," (4) "Deductive and Inductive Inference," (5) "Logic and the Method of Science, and Some Characteristics of Scientific Attitude," (6) "Prejudice as a Factor Making for Crooked Thinking," (7) "Values and Logic," (8) "Propaganda and Crooked Thinking." (Note the similarity, in labels at least, among a variety of the programs we have reviewed at elementary and secondary levels; for example, White's teaching of logic, the units of Hyram's program, Taba's efforts to teach inferential reasoning, and so forth.) It is important to observe that Glaser provided a complete set of materials and references for reading to the teachers. With careful planning on their part, the materials enabled the teachers to present a self-contained program for critical thinking.

To test the efficacy of his teaching program, Glaser arranged an experiment in which eight 12th-grade English classes participated, four as experimental and four as control groups. All eight of the classes were taught by different teachers. An effort was made to identify teachers with good reputations for competence in teaching, and there was no basis for believing that the experimental and control teachers were much different from each other in this respect or in their ability to relate effectively to students. Similarly, the students in the two sets of classes were comparable in ability. Some slight differences in initial ability favored the control groups. The experimental period lasted eight weeks, with one week devoted to each of the units. One week was given over to testing before and after the experimental period. Test scores revealed a marked advantage for students in the experimental classes. The mean gain for the experimental classes was 71 points, and the mean gain for the control classes was only 41 points. (One of the objectives of the standard English curriculum was the development of critical thinking. This was done chiefly through reading and discussion of the English essayists, such as Bacon, Addison, and Steele, and through the study and analysis of newspapers. Thus the differences between experimental and control classes reflect differential success with which this goal was achieved by the two programs.)

Deliberate programs of instruction do not necessarily achieve the goals their authors intend. A well-known effort to teach students at the senior high school level resistance to propaganda (Osborn, 1939) is a good case in point. Osborn employed 20 pairs of 11th- and 12th-grade social studies classes. Each pair was taught by the same teacher, one class receiving the special instructional unit on propaganda and the other continuing its normal class work, which did not include any such instruction. Three weeks after the close of the six-day instructional period, all the students took a variety of attitude and achievement measures. These included, in sequence, a measure of their attitude toward capital punishment, a test concerning knowledge about capital punishment, an article on "Why Capital Punishment Is Necessary" to be read, and a post-measure of attitude toward capital punishment. The last measure was repeated two weeks later.

We are told very little about what the teachers did with their experimental classes to induce resistance to propaganda, except that they read and discussed a variety of papers and topics. However, the measures listed above reflected that students in the experimental classes were no more successful than the control students in resisting the propagandistic overtures of the one-sided presentation about the need for capital punishment. This finding must, however, be seen in context. The experimental students did learn the basic propagandistic devices and how to detect them. What they did not appear to learn was to apply them to a given situation. Osborn's conclusion that a longer instructional unit would have done no good is probably correct. Instruction that was directed at understanding how the propaganda in what one reads and hears can directly alter one's attitudes or beliefs would probably have been more to the point.

The Birmingham studies

Since 1965, studies at the University of Birmingham (England) which focus upon the development of adolescent thinking (judgment) have been underway. This work was initiated by and has been continued under the direction of E. A. Peel. Peel's work on adolescent judgment began with the conviction that studies of their verbal comprehension were needed because virtually all the instructional materials used in secondary schools are in the form of connected prose. Several problems were formulated and tried out on groups of pupils ranging in age from ten to midadolescence. The responses students give to questions based upon those problems range from *descriptive* at the lower age levels (10 or 11) to *explanatory* on the part of the older pupils (age 14 plus). Descriptions are limited to relating the parts of a phenomenon with each other, whereas explanation involves relating the current phenomena to other previously experienced phenomena and to other generalizations and concepts which have been previously formed.

Peel has found that his test problems elicit a variety of responses from pupils which can be reliably classified by trained raters. Two of the often used problems and the categories of responses they stimulate are examined below.

> Only brave pilots are allowed to fly over high mountains. This summer a fighter pilot flying over the Alps collided with an aerial cable railway and cut a main cable causing some cars to fall to the glacier below. Several people were killed, and many others had to spend the night suspended above the glacier.
> 1. Was the pilot a careful airman? 2. Why do you think so?

Peel's scoring of the responses to this story by 78 New Jersey pupils, ranging in age from 9 to 15 fell into four categories:

Category C: Yes, No, Maybe, taking account of extenuating possibilities, vision, weather, state of the plane.

Category Bii: No, because if he was careful he would not have cut the cable.

Category Bi: No, beause he hit the cable, and so on.

Category A: Yes or No, with irrelevant comment or denial of the premise, e.g., Yes, he was brave; yes, the cable shouldn't be there; no, he was a show off.

The categories of answers are closely related to advances in age of the pupils. Answers assigned to Category C, which involves thinking that goes beyond the information given in the passage, are rare before the age of 14. The more limited circumstantial responses of the Bi and Bii categories occur principally among pupils at ages 12 to 13½. Such Category A responses as occur are given by the younger pupils, but these answers are rare.

A second problem, similar to the one about the flyer, has been found to yield comparable results:

> Jane is a very clever 15-year-old girl who is preparing for her final examinations. One evening as Jane was doing her homework, her mother asked her to look after her younger brother, Teddy, while she went out. Teddy wandered from the living room into the kitchen, got hold of a jar of jam, ate a lot of it, covered his clothes with it, and spilled it on to some clean washing in a basket so that it was ruined.
> 1. Was Jane a careless person? 2. Why do you think so?

Analyses of the responses by pupils to these story problems reveals not only a developmental shift from irrelevant or tautological responses, to circumstantially prescribed ones, to those that introduce hypothetical explanations, although such a progression is clear in Peel's data. Of even greater interest is the logic which children of similar ages use in responding to the different problems. For example, to both stories, responses in Category Bi (that is, the first level of response above the irrelevant answers of some of the least mature pupils) conform to *modus ponens* (in which the presence of *a* implies the presence of *b*). In the "Jane" problem, "Teddy wandered" is chosen as the single piece of evidence to which the child responds; therefore, the fact that Teddy wanders implies that Jane is careless. In the "pilot" problem, the fact that the plane crashes implies that the pilot was careless.

At the next highest level (Bii), the form of the responses changes to that of *modus tollens* (denial of the consequent means denial of the antecedent): "She should have watched Teddy, if she had been careful she would not have . . ." "If the pilot was careful, he would not have crashed the plane. He should have been careful." These expressions, which also mark the use of the more sophisticated conditional form, are given by children who are between six months and a year older than the first group. (It is interesting to speculate on the possible relationship between the ages at which Peel's pupils use *modus ponens* and *modus tollens,* and the development of ability in children to reason with various logical forms as revealed in the work of Roberge (1970) which we examined earlier in this chapter. Recall Roberge's suggestion that formal school instruction in the easier logical forms, such as *modus ponens,* might begin at the fourth grade.)

The first hints of explanation which draw upon outside events or possibilities appear in the responses of pupils at age 14 and afterward. Their responses are of the form, "Although Jane was doing her homework, she should have watched Teddy." This may be a practical implication that Jane ought to abandon her homework to concentrate upon her younger brother, or it may signal the logical possibility that homework and child watching are not incompatible, and that watching would prevent wandering. It is not until the age of 14 that pupils can break away from the circumstances provided in the situation to make more circumspect and comprehensive judgments by realizing the limited nature of available evidence and invoking alternative possibilities. "This transition," says Peel (1966, p. 83), "from partially descriptive to imagined explanatory responses marks the major change in the quality of the pupils' judgment during mid-adolescence."

Since our interest in this book is more focused on learning (and teach-

The Pupil as Thinker: Critical Thinking   197

ing) than it is on development, we shall pursue one of Peel's major hypotheses about the forces that determine the level or category of pupils' responses. It is his position that readiness plays an important role in this determination. We have seen that the more mature responses involve the pupils' introduction of outside events or ideas to help explain or judge what has occurred. It would usually be the case that older students would possess more information than younger ones. Perhaps, therefore, the introduction of additional information into the story situations would alter the level of responses that students generate. Peel's test of this seems a peculiar one. One of the problems (developed and used by one of his students) concerned the flood damage in Florence, Italy, in the autumn of 1966. For purposes of testing the readiness hypothesis, an additional paragraph of information was added to the original. (Both are reproduced below.) The argument is made that if a student who answers the original inquiry at the imaginative level of explanation does so purely on the basis of added information, he will produce essentially the same response when given more information, and the latter response would then be scored as circumstantial or content bound. Here is a sample of the material used to test the idea of readiness versus added information:

> All large cities have art galleries and Italy is exceptionally rich in art treasures. Many people travel to Italy especially to enjoy these old paintings, books and sculptures. Floods in the Florence area have recently damaged many of these great works. Old paintings are rare, valuable and beautiful and should be kept safely stored.

This represented the original presentation of the problem. The second form added the following paragraph:

> The authorities knew the river was going to flood within the next day, and the Florentines knew that many of their churches, museums, and art galleries stood below flood water level.

The following question was asked on both occasions:

> Are the Italians to blame for the loss of the paintings and art treasures?

When several groups of adolescents were tested under both conditions, no significant difference appeared among the three categories of responses under the alternative conditions. That is, students who gave imaginative responses to the original paragraph also gave them to the stimulus situation with the added information. Peel interprets this as evidence tending to confirm his readiness hypothesis. He argues that you can give added information to younger pupils, but it is extraneous if they are not prepared to make use of it. Furthermore, Peel has observed that the younger pupils (at least to the ages of 11 or 12) not only fail to take account of all the information available in a situation, but they tend to seize upon one aspect of it and to make their judgments as though that portion were the whole. This behavior seems to be analogous to the centering upon one dimension (length or width) that Piaget reports with preoperational children. It is an open question whether instructional programs can be designed which will be instrumental in teaching children to broaden the amount of information they process or to suspend judgment while they consider more evidence. It should constitute a worthy challenge to those who believe that children can be taught to think.

The Birmingham program has also undertaken to examine the development of students' ability to follow (from a logical standpoint) strictly what is given in a problem situation without assuming points not in evidence or erroneously implying cause-and-effect relationships from contiguity or association of events. The results of tests with two problems of different logical construction are of interest. In the first, three logical conjunctions are given but a fourth is withheld. It is about the fourth one that the question is asked of the learner:

> I've seen Mary standing at the edge of the skating rink with skates on her feet. I often see her walking and running to school and standing about. I've seen her watching the skating at the rink and she is always talking about skating.
> 1. Can Mary skate? 2. Why do you think so?

The ablest and most mature students left the answer open, on the apparent grounds that not all had been told. Others who followed the passage rigorously but who said "No, Mary can't skate" tended to elaborate their responses in the explanation of their answers. Most of those who concluded that Mary is able to skate were among the youngest and least able of the group.

The following problem is very similar to situations faced by science students in the upper elementary as well as secondary grades when asked to interpret the data of scientific observations.

> I was looking at my friend's rose garden. He had been spraying his rose leaves with a chemical to kill a leaf disease. I saw sprayed leaves which were healthy and I saw unsprayed leaves, some of which were diseased and some healthy.
> 1. Can I say anything definite about the effect of the spray on the disease?
> 2. Why do you think so?

What inferences do students draw from the reported (and unreported) implications? Three of the four possible conjunctions are specified: unsprayed leaves may be either healthy or diseased. Sprayed leaves that were healthy were seen. No indication is given whether sprayed leaves that were diseased also occur. Students' answers were classified into five categories:

1. Logically adequate.
2. Recognizing ambiguity; e.g., looking for alternative explanations for the phenomenon.
3. *Assuming* the problem to be a statement of implication; thus, it was decided, no leaves were sprayed but unhealthy. Subjects tended to cite one or more of the conjunctions specified if they gave this answer.
4. Ignoring the logical nature of the problem in favor of its content. The responses in this category dealt with the act of spraying (he missed some of the leaves) or with the nature of the disease.
5. A small number of responses reflected misunderstandings, tautologies, irrelevances, and other failures to cope with the problem.

In an exploratory study (1973) Peel used two quite dramatically different samples of students, postgraduate students and school pupils. Despite the fact that some overlapping occurs between these samples, the effects of age and sophistication upon the learners' ability to respond to and utilize logical aspects of verbal problems is vividly illustrated (see Table 6.1).

TABLE 6.1
Responses of two samples of students to the rose garden spray problem

Answer Categories	Main features	Postgraduate students	School pupils
1.	Logically adequate	25	1
2.	Logical-causal; looking for other causes	26	15
3.	Assuming implication; linguistic restriction	9	44
4.	Content-circumstance dominated		10
5.	Restricted		14

Source: Peel (1973), p. 63.

The effects of educational programs designed to improve judgments

Although Peel's major interest has been in the course of development of adolescent judgments, and he adopts a readiness position with regard to development, he is at the same time open to seeing educational efforts made to improve adolescents' thinking. His writings also indicate a cautious optimism that such programs can be successful if they take proper account of the stages of development through which thinking passes. Because the three principal types of responses, *restricted, circumstantial,* and *comprehensive-imaginative,* have occurred repeatedly across many types of tasks, Peel urges that any program of instruction must take care to assist pupils in their transition from one level to the next, particularly in moving from the circumstantial or content-bound response to the comprehensive-imaginative. This would not be a simple task to be accomplished by instruction; involved at a minimum would be the following elements. First the learner must be able to generate and to make explicit possible hypotheses or explanations for the judgment to be made. He must also be capable of retaining the most plausible of those and eliminating the inferior ones.

To do this demands the ability of deductive thinking, "and may invoke the power of sustained argument." Specific ingredients of such arguing are:

1. Detection of inconsistencies and partialities.
2. Ability to examine a situation formally and structurally, as opposed to circumstantially and merely contentwise.
3. The capacity to relate the test material to the offered hypothesis.
4. A capacity to reason propositionally.
5. A mastery of language in relation to reason.

(Peel, 1973, p. 115)

Peel (1973) describes two efforts conducted by his students to improve the judgments of secondary school pupils. One student, Anderson, developed a course of four topics based on teaching pupils how to recognize inconsistencies, incompatibilities, irrelevances, and partialities. Eight groups of secondary school students, with eight members in each group, studied and discussed the instructional material. There was also a control condition with an equal number of pupils. Some examples of the materials Anderson used are reproduced here. For example, in studying inconsistencies, pupils answered questions such as the following:

Can you be obedient and disobedient at the same time to the same person?
Can you be obedient and clumsy at the same time?
If you are judging a girl's dancing, does it matter whether she can cook?

Other exercises dwelt upon the relevance of reasons, for Peel's results showed that irrelevance of information frequently interrupt pupils' reasoning:

If a man causes an accident you should consider whether he was
 (rich   clever   old   careless)

Activities in a third topic dealt with implication and the quantifiers *all* and *some*. An example of these activities is given in Figure 6.2.

FIGURE 6.2

Doctors have discovered that people who have a disease called scurvy have swollen gums and painful sores. You are not likely to catch this if you have plenty of fresh fruit and vegetables in your diet.

		Yes	No	Can't say
(a)	Jane has scurvy. Are her gums swollen?	___	___	___
(b)	John has swollen gums. Has he got scurvy?	___	___	___
(c)	Jean's gums are not swollen, but she has several painful sores. She likes apples. Has she got scurvy?	___	___	___
(d)	In the old days of sailing ships, sailors lived for months on a very salt diet with no fresh food. Were they likely to get scurvy?	___	___	___
(e)	Can you be ill through eating too much fruit?	___	___	___
(f)	A man has sailed round the world on his own and apart from a few accidents has been healthy all the time. Did he carry fresh food with him?	___	___	___

At the end of the instructional period, he gave pupils an eight-item test, with each response scored on one of three levels. The levels reflect increasing maturity of judgments. Very few of the lowest level responses occurred. These are partial or unrelated answers, and there were only 16 of them in the total 1024 responses scored. When the responses on the final test are organized to show a percentage of gain of the instructed pupils over the uninstructed ones in the control groups, the gains are very large. The largest increases occur among the younger pupils, as might be expected. Unfortunately no average ages or mean differences in age between the groups are given. Among the younger pupils, the greatest gains are made by the least able subgroup, but the opposite happens with the older students. However, the difference is much less marked (300 percent vs. 207 percent in the younger, with the larger gain for the less able; 100 percent vs. 81 percent for the older students, with the more able subset achieving the larger gain.)

Other efforts at improving adolescent judgments have employed the technique of branching programs. Gray, another of Peel's students who is an experienced programmer, wrote five instructional programs of this sort in which he used actual responses given in earlier studies as the alternatives which pupils were to select. The pupil was then directed to a different page in the program, where the adequacy or inadequacy of his selection was discussed. If his original response were wrong, he had to make a new one. The power of the branched program is that (in theory at least) it enables the student always to work only upon the problem with which he needs help. The five programs were based upon problems like the "pilot" problem discussed above. The students—secondary school pupils—studied one program a day for five consecutive school days, after which they and the control students took six tests. Three of the tests involved judgments, and on these the experimental students significantly outscored the control students. There were no experimental-control differences on the other three tests, two of which involved problem solving and the other a measure of divergent thinking. The training program appears to have achieved its basic purpose of improving adolescents' judgments, but its transfer does not extend to the more remote topics of problem solving and idea generation.

Brief mention may be made of another programmed instruction effort by Stones, a history teacher and a student in the Birmingham group, because it demonstrates that judgments in subject matter areas may be improved by careful instruction. She gave experimental students a 62-frame program on the concept underlying historical content to be read (on the development of the American railway system). Control students were given a list of concept definitions; all then read the three passages of historical material (and answered three questions on each passage. Stones had developed a sensitive six-point scale to assess the level of reasoning of each response. Experimental students' reasoning scores were significantly higher than those of control students. However, the results are rendered equivocal by the fact that the effects of students' intelligence and verbal fluency are stronger than the instructional effects.

Suggestions for Teaching Critical Thinking

In giving some suggestions to the teacher who wishes to improve the critical thinking of his or her students, there are many specific things the teacher might do that we will not touch upon. In fact, the suggestions given will be more general than specific, for any teacher will have to adapt them to the particulars of the instructional setting in which he works. The main trouble with specificity is its specificity; once you alter the environment in which it is to be used, it may no longer be useful. Be that as it may, one of the first and most important issues which confronts the teacher is to decide what objectives he holds for critical thinking. The teacher must determine what his students are to be able to do (or how they are to be able to think) at the conclusion of the instruction. Thought and effort invested at this stage of teaching will be well repaid, for the clearer the teacher can be about the objectives, the more likely his students are to achieve them. Objectives, and the procedures that will be used to work toward them, must be formulated with the developmental characteristics of the pupils in mind. For instance, the teacher of first- or second-grade pupils will court failure if he casts his critical thinking objectives largely in terms of logical operations to be achieved. As we have seen repeatedly in this chapter, children who are concrete thinkers have not yet developed the cognitive structures necessary to allow logical thinking of any formal sort to occur. However, certain objectives are more likely to be achieved, given appropriate experiences and guidance. These are objectives which are aimed at teaching the child to view conclusions from more than a single point of view, to understand that a single experience with another person is usually a poor basis on which to reach a conclusion about that individual, or to recognize that one's own likes and dislikes can distort one's judgment. By the same token, teachers should strive not to underestimate the level of thinking of which their students are capable. Beyond the years of junior high school, students are capable of formal propositional reasoning, and limited amounts of direct experience with the environment are sufficient basis for reasoning to proceed.

An additional point concerns the time perspective the teacher adopts for the achievement of objectives. The time frame must be long rather than short. Since critical thinking involves a constellation of attitudes and intellectual skills, we ought not to expect dramatic changes in critical thinking as the result of minor, brief units or exercises. This brings us to a significant issue for the teacher who wishes to pursue an objective of improved critical thinking with his students. The issue involves distinguishing between critical thinking as a complex, integrated set of intellectual performances, and critical thinking as a series of discrete skills. What view the teacher takes of this issue will go a long way toward determining how he goes about trying to teach students to think in a critical way.

Let us try to clarify the issue. Many of the reports on critical thinking we have reviewed focused upon teaching children or adolescents one or more intellectual skills. Thus, in one or more studies, students were taught how to detect bias in a source, drawing inferences, reasoning deductively and inductively, detecting assumptions, identifying emotional appeals, the use of propagandistic devices, and others. All of these intellectual skills can be fitted into a conception of critical thinking in a reasonable way. To teach these skills, the investigator developed activities for students; a measure was made afterward of their achievement of the skill, which was normally compared to that of some kind of a control group. Growth or improvement of critical thinking was inferred from these comparisons.

Although it is a somewhat artificial division, we can separate the activities of these studies into *training* and *application*. When the teacher assigns material that provides practice in identifying assumptions or drawing inferences, students are receiving training in those intellectual skills. To be sure, such training or practice is important. This is as far as many studies carry the issue of critical thinking, and they achieve positive results because, as with any learning, students who are instructed and given opportunities to practice a skill almost always surpass an untutored group of pupils, at least if achievement is measured shortly after the periods of instruction and practice. A simple analogy may drive home the point. Suppose the baseball coach gives one of his players instruction and practice in throwing a ball from the outfield. After several days of this, a marked improvement is noticed in how far the ball travels. Has the boy become a better baseball player? Of course he has in a sense, for any outfielder wishes to throw as well as possible. We would not expect, though, that this would improve his hitting, or his ability to bunt or to run the bases. More pertinently, we would not necessarily even anticipate that the training would make the boy a more intelligent thrower; that is, would improve his judgment about where to throw the ball depending upon where the base runners are when he retrieves it, and so forth. To put the issue simply and bluntly, one probably does well not to anticipate large amounts of lateral or vertical transfer across intellectual skills, such as critical thinking, unless there is ample evidence to justify such optimism. As was stressed over and over in Chapter 5, near transfer is much more likely to occur than far transfer.

A more stringent test of the effects of what we call training can be seen in White's (1936) study discussed above. At the application stage, he searched for signs that his experimental students' compositions would reflect their measured improvement in reasoning. Some application was evident, but the overall differences with the products of the control class were not impressive. The results of Osborn's (1939) effort also help to clarify this point. Students in his experimental classes evidently had learned satisfactorily how to detect and classify the various common types of propaganda—"bandwagon", "glittering generalities", and the rest. What they lacked was the recognition that these techniques, embedded in the biased article on capital punishment, were capable of altering *their* attitudes, and in fact did so, no less than for the control students. In short, if we are to teach students to have a "critical quality" in their thinking, it appears that teachers need to provide situations that call for appropriate transfer or application. The weight of evidence suggests that, failing this, many students are unable to make applications of their own accord.

Fawcett's (1938) study is an excellent illustration of how a teacher can extend meanings and applications for his students. Recall that the activities in his geometry class were extremely diversified. Students learned to define mathematical concepts, but they also learned that definitions of terms can be of critical importance in nonmathematical issues as well. Fawcett did not assume that adolescents are capable of generating these applications independently of the teacher and the curriculum. Neither did he assume that *telling* the students that skills learned in geometry may apply rather broadly, given some adaptation to a variety of other situations, such as analyzing editorials, political speeches, or policies to govern awards for outstanding achievement. Instead, these situations were utilized directly as part of the instructional program, and students learned how to define the terms of their own arguments as well as the concepts of the mathematician. In Chapter 5 we saw that one good basis for transfer is the similarity between what has been learned first and a second task. By focusing upon issues mathematical, social, political, and economic, Fawcett helped students to see the underlying similarity among them and to recognize that methods of logic—definition of terms, seeking out assumptions, and so on—can be as helpful in analyzing the motives of the local trucking industry's opposition to highway-use taxes as to following the proof of a geometric theorem. Fawcett was also able to help students understand that nonmathematical issues may arouse human emotions and that particular care is necessary to avoid unreason in thinking when we become emotionally involved.

In summary, there is a series of questions the teacher needs to answer about critical thinking and issues that require careful consideration and planning. The major questions are listed below.

1. What is the teacher's conception of critical thinking? How is it modified to take account of the age, educational level, and stage of intellectual development of his or her students?

2. Is the time perspective adopted adequate to allow for systematic instruction and development of critical thinking?

3. The teacher should make appropriate plans for *training* and for *application*. Programs of critical thinking that provide only for instruction in relevant skills of critical thinking may fail because students do not recognize situations to which their training can be applied, or because they do not have sufficient skill in thinking to adapt what they have learned to new situations.

4. The teacher must have appropriate instructional materials for use in the improvement of critical thinking. An inventory by the teacher can assist in identifying materials available to him which can be organized to achieve program goals. Similarly the teacher needs to consider which parts of the courses he teaches lend themselves most adequately to critical thinking; for example, historical events that are open to different inter-

pretations are more suitable for this purpose than chronological accounts of a nation's development.

5. An attitude of critical thinking becomes pervasive. It is not turned on and off to correspond to the periods in which the teacher distributes worksheets on data analysis or the interpretation of evidence. If critical thinking is taught well, students apply it to a wide range of circumstances, including the teacher's statements, decisions, and proposed courses of action. The irony of this is not so difficult to live with when one considers that he has helped the students take one sure step down the road to reason.

Questions for Review and Discussion

1. How would you define critical thinking? Several types of skills were identified in the chapter as requisites for critical thinking. If these are learned, is the student a critical thinker? If not, what is missing?

2. In what ways would the critical thinking ability of a first-grade child be different from that of a junior high school pupil? A college student? What are the principal sources of those differences? The work of Peel reviewed in this chapter provides a partial answer to the question in terms of developmental changes in logical thinking.

3. Is logical thinking synonymous with critical thinking?

4. As you consider the various efforts that have been made to improve schoolchildren's critical thinking, what common elements can you identify which have tended to be associated with success? How would approaches to teaching critical thinking differ between elementary and secondary school classes?

5. How general is the ability to do critical thinking? Does a student learn to think in a critical way independently of the content about which he is to think? Or conversely, is critical thinking closely tied to the specific tools of thinking of a discipline, such as physics, anthropology, or mathematics? (The discussion of general and specific transfer in the preceding chapter should be germane to your thinking about this topic.)

6. What are the major tasks and decisions that face a teacher who wants to help his or her students become better critical thinkers? Consider these especially with regard to (a) objectives, (b) the time perspective and materials and activities for teaching critical thinking, and (c) means for evaluating or judging improvement in students' critical thinking ability.

Readings for Further Reflection

There are some especially interesting and rewarding books to be recommended in the area of critical thinking. For the reader who wishes to achieve an introduction to logic, with special reference to its applicability to thinking in schools and in daily life, the first two books listed would be particularly valuable.

Dewey, John. *How We Think* (Gateway edition). Chicago: Henry Regnery Co., 1971.

Dewey's famous book for teachers was published originally in 1910. A revised and extended version was reissued in 1933 and reprinted in 1971 in paperback, which makes this fine volume readily accessible to teachers. The three parts are devoted to the nature of reflective thinking, logical considerations in thinking, and the training of thought.

Thouless, Robert H. *How to Think Straight.* New York: Hart Publishing Co. (no date).

This book appeared in two earlier versions years ago. First published in 1932 under the title of *Straight and Crooked Thinking,* it was revised and published under its present title in 1939. The edition cited here is in paperback form and is of fairly recent vintage, but unfortunately the title page does not carry a publication date. References within the book suggest that it was revised after 1939.

The author, a British philosopher-psychologist, provides a most interesting introduction to how people apply and misapply logic to the problems of daily life and arguments. The book was written for the public at large, not for teachers, but it is a good source for the teacher who is more interested in the applications of logic than in logic as a formal study.

Two books that were written for teachers about critical thinking are:

Aylesworth, Thomas G., and Reagan, Gerald M. *Teaching for Thinking.* Garden City, N.Y.: Doubleday & Co., 1969.

Burton, William H., Kimball, Roland B., and Wing, Richard L. *Education for Effective Thinking.* New York: Appleton-Century-Crofts, 1960.

Two additional references at a more advanced level are:

Black, Max. *Critical Thinking* (2nd ed.). Englewood Cliffs, N.J.: Prentice-Hall, 1952.

Ennis, Robert H. *Logic in Teaching.* Englewood Cliffs, N.J.: Prentice-Hall, 1969.

Finally, two research monographs may be cited that, although technical in their content, are meritorious because of their effort to analyze the ways in which teachers and students employ logic in their daily classroom interaction.

Smith, B. O., and Meux, M., et al. *A Study of the Logic of Teaching.* Urbana: University of Illinois, Bureau of Educational Research, 1962.

Smith, B. O., Meux, M., Coombs, J., Nuthall, G., and Precians, R. *A Study of the Strategies of Teaching.* Urbana: University of Illinois, Bureau of Educational Research, 1967.

References

Arnold, O. L. Testing ability to use data in the fifth and sixth grades. *Educational Research Bulletin,* 1938, *17,* 225–259, 278.

Barlow, M. C. Transfer of training in reasoning. *Journal of Educational Psychology,* 1937, *28,* 122–28.

Burt, Cyril. The development of reasoning in school children. *Journal of Experimental Pedagogy,* 1919, *5,* 68–77, 121–128.

Cornell Critical Thinking Tests. Ithaca, N.Y.: Cornell University, Department of Education, 1966.

Ennis, Robert H. A concept of critical thinking. *Harvard Educational Review,* 1962, *32.*

Ennis, Robert H. Children's ability to handle Piaget's propositional logic: A conceptual critique. *Review of Educational Research,* 1975, *45,* 1–41.

Fawcett, H. P. *The Nature of Proof.* 13th Yearbook, National Council of Teachers of Mathematics. 1938.

Glaser, Edward M. An experiment in the development of critical thinking. *Teachers College Contributions to Education,* No. 843, New York: Bureau of Publications, Teachers College, Columbia University, 1941.

Grener, Norma, & Raths, Louis. Thinking in Grade 3. *Educational Research Bulletin,* 1945, *24,* 38–42.

Hudgins, Bryce B. Effects of group experience on individual problem solving. *Journal of Educational Psychology,* 1960, *51,* 37–42.

Hudgins, Bryce B., & Smith, Louis M. Group structure and productivity in problem solving. *Journal of Educational Psychology,* 1966, *57,* 287–296.

Hyram, George H. An experiment in developing critical thinking in children. *Journal of Experimental Education,* 1957, *26,* 125–132.

Morgan, John J. B., & Carrington, Dorothy H. Graphical instruction in relational reasoning. *Journal of Educational Psychology,* 1944, *35,* 536–544.

O'Brien, Thomas C., & Shapiro, Bernard J. The development of logical thinking in children. *American Educational Research Journal,* 1968, *5,* 531–542.

Osborn, W. W. An experiment in teaching resistance to propaganda. *Journal of Experimental Education,* 1939, *8,* 1–17.

Peel, Edwin A. Intellectual growth during adolescence. *Educational Review,* 1965, *17,* 169–180.

Peel, Edwin A. A study of differences in the judgments of adolescent pupils. *British Journal of Educational Psychology,* 1966, *36,* 77–86.

Peel, Edwin A. *The nature of adolescent judgment.* New York: Wiley-Interscience, 1973.

Roberge, James J. A study of children's abilities to reason with basic principles of deductive reasoning. *American Educational Research Journal,* 1970, *7,* 583–596.

Shapiro, Bernard J., & O'Brien, Thomas C. Logical thinking in children ages six through thirteen. *Child Development,* 1970, *41,* 823–829.

Taba, Hilda. *Teaching strategies and cognitive functioning in elementary school children.* Cooperative Research Project No. 2404, San Francisco State College, 1966.

Thelen, Herbert A. A methodological study of the learning of chemical concepts and of certain abilities to think critically in freshman chemistry. *Journal of Experimental Education,* 1944, *13,* 53–75.

Ulmer, Gilbert. Teaching geometry to cultivate reflective thinking: An experimental study of 1,239 high school pupils. *Journal of Experimental Education,* 1939, *8,* 18–25.

White, Ernest E. A study of the possibility of improving habits of thought in school children by a training in logic. *British Journal of Educational Psychology,* 1936, *6,* 267–273.

Chapter 7

The Pupil as Thinker: Problem Solving

The history of psychological research on problem solving, although intrinsically interesting, has less relevance to the classroom than we would wish. There are several reasons for this. One is that, despite the existence of hundreds of studies of problem solving, there is little agreement about the underlying variables which govern such thinking. The development of theory to explain problem solving has been slow, and most efforts in this direction are fragmentary. Most discouraging to the educator is the nature of the problems psychologists have studied. D. M. Johnson (1966) wrote that anagrams were the most thoroughly studied problem in the psychology of problem solving. For the teacher who hopes to find guidance for her or his own instructional practices from the work of experimental psychology, this is cold comfort; the generality of anagrams is so limited that it tells us little about how people solve problems of other types. In a similar vein, Niemark and Santa (1975) upbraided scholars in their review of the field for the "deadeningly low level of empiricism" in problem solving research.

Despite the fact that the applicability of psychological studies of problem solving to educational issues is imperfect, there are lessons to be learned from the work. By no means are all the studies concerned with anagrams. Other tasks have also been investigated, and while they are not the problems of the schoolroom, nevertheless they are challenges to the learner's ingenuity and his ability to modify and apply his knowledge in order to solve the problem. Such tasks are related to the work that teachers perform, even if they are not the same thing, and the educator should be capable of extending them to his own concerns.

Furthermore, there is a renewed interest in psychological studies of arithmetic and mathematics problem solving. It would be hard to imagine an area of research that could have more direct bearing upon the classroom work of many teachers. We shall review the research in this field, both the old and the new, in detail. The 1970s have also witnessed the publication of a monumental treatise on human problem solving. This classic study by Newell and Simon (1972) views problem solving from the standpoint of an information-processing system. The work concentrates on the analysis and synthesis of adults' struggles to solve three types of problems: cryptarithmetic, logic, and chess. The translation of this work—especially the emerging theory—to educational problems is manageable.

What Is a Problem?

A problem exists when the learner is confronted with a situation he cannot resolve by the direct application of any response immediately at his command. Suppose you come home late on a dark night and have to unlock the door. Even though you must fumble for the key and guide it into the lock, we would not consider this problem solving. Some trial and error might be involved as you attempt to unlock the door with first one key and then another, but a door is opened by inserting the correct key and turning it in the lock. A different situation that does represent a problem involves a hungry chimpanzee locked in a cage; just beyond his reach outside the bars lies a banana. This is a problem for the animal because none of the patterns of behavior that are available to him—reaching, jumping, and grasping—provide the extension of his reach that is required to procure the food.

Most of the problems in which we are interested have a more cognitive or intellectual flavor. Here is one you will probably find challenging. (Later we will reveal the standard solution for this problem; for now, try to solve it independently.) You are seated at a small table, and two metal balls are presented which are identical, to all appearances, and which are of equal weight. However, you are told that one ball is made of a much heavier metal than the other. Without doing anything, such as cutting, peeling, or opening the balls, how could you determine, quickly and easily, which is made of the heavier metal?

Or consider this problem: "A school playground is rectangular, 273 feet long, and 21 feet wide. What is the total length of the fence around the playground?" Sixth-grade pupils in two studies conducted by Suppes and his co-workers found this to be a difficult problem. Compared to other problems, this one was hard for pupils who were good in arithmetic as well as for those whose arithmetic achievement was low. Later in the chapter we will analyze what makes arithmetic problems hard or easy for schoolchildren.

What makes a good problem for the classroom? Perhaps there is no way to set firm criteria for the purpose, because the teacher or other educational authority is the final arbiter in such matters. However, several points are worth considering as we consider the issue.

1. Is the situation which is posed for the learner really a problem? Psychologists sometimes distinguish between *productive thinking* and *reproductive thinking*. Problem solving has to demand productive thinking that calls upon the learner to select and organize his knowledge to generate potential solutions. Productive thinking signifies aggressive intellectual action in which the thinker may reconstruct or redefine what he knows to fit the strictures of the given situation. Reproductive thinking amounts to the continual application of a principle or formula to the solution of type-problems. This is legitimate to help fix a relationship, or when the purpose is to provide practice so that applications can be made faster and more smoothly. Once the activity is reduced to sheer "plugging in" of data in a routine way, it no longer is problem solving.

2. Some concept or principle which is an integral part of the structure of the subject should be taught through problems, or there should be reason to expect that students will better comprehend a rule if it is applied to the solution of problems, rather than taught by expository means. This is the reason that tasks such as anagrams or parlor games of the "twenty questions" type give little help to the educator. These tasks are to be contrasted with physics problems that demand application of the laws of motion, or problems in mathematics that depend upon the students' knowledge of theorems, properties of numbers, and the like.

3. Classroom problems should possess capability for transfer of training. This transfer can be of two kinds. Either the problem can assist the learner in seeing further extensions of a principle, such as the applicability of statistical laws of probability to voting behavior or consumer purchasing, or a given class of problems should exhibit transfer by improving the learner's chances of solving new problems.

4. Finally, classroom problems should have a strong incentive value for students. In large measure, the teacher's artistry is necessary to ensure this condition, but there are some ways that make it more or less probable. The student must feel that he has a good, but not certain, chance of solving the problems. If only reproductive thinking is called for, his or

her incentive diminishes. There must always be the prospect of a challenge—something he has to add to the situation from his store of knowledge—to succeed. The chance that a student will be motivated to work on a problem is tied to its pertinence for the student. Problems must be real to the learner. This does *not* mean that problems must pertain to an aspect of the growing child's or adolescent's personal or social life. On the contrary, when problems are well constructed, children are fascinated, and they become actively involved in searching for ways to solve them.

A good case in point is made by Richard Suchman's Inquiry Training Program, to be discussed somewhat later. Suchman (1962) reversed the traditional process of teaching basic physics to intermediate-grade children. By means of film, they are shown well-known phenomena and then taught to use questions to find out why events unfold as they do on the film. For example, children see the experimenter hold a spatula in the flame of a Bunsen burner. The blade bends downward; it straightens when plunged into a beaker of water. When turned over and reinserted in the flame, the blade bends upward. The film ends with the question, "Why does the blade first bend one way, and then the other?"

If the student has a clear conception of what the problem is about and how concepts and principles in his cognitive structure can be applied to find a solution, then his estimate of success will be high. Problem-solving activities encounter difficulties with students when they represent repetitive activities in the guise of problems, or when the students see them as intellectual games that do not make sense. When that happens, the potential benefits to the learner may be more than offset by the price he pays in aimless or resentful activity.

A General Description of Problem Solving

Imagine yourself in the following situation. You have agreed to participate in a psychological experiment, and you report to a large, bare room —a gymnasium or auditorium. While you wait, you are asked to lend a helping hand to the research assistant, and you spend the next few minutes at a table off to one side of the room where you nail boards together into frames, as directed. The nails, boards, and hammer, as well as the table, are provided. Before very long, the assistant stops you, and you move to the middle of the room, where, some distance from each other, two ropes dangle from the ceiling to the floor. This time the assistant asks you if you would please tie the ropes together so the experiment can begin, and off he goes again. The thought may cross your mind that these psychologists want a lot of free help, but you seize the end of one of the ropes and start off toward the other one. You are brought up short by the realization that you can't reach the second one unless you release the first. That would be foolish, so you hold on to the first rope and stretch as far as possible for the second, but it is obvious that you cannot reach it! In a moment the assistant will return, expecting this simple chore to be completed, and there you stand, flailing at the rope like a hooked trout. What do you do?

Change the scene. It is rural northern Virginia, 50 miles from Washington, D.C. The time is midway through World War II. You are an aspirant for the Office of Strategic Services, the then-renowned U.S. intelligence branch. On a field problem you reach a large, deep shell hole, which your instructions forbid you to circumnavigate. The hole is too steep to be walked across, and it is much too wide to jump over, even though you are young, athletic, and well conditioned. Fortunately, you see some wooden planks not far away, and quickly you pick up the longest of the lot to place over the hole. To your dismay, this board turns out to be several feet too short. You realize that critical eyes are trained on you, and what you do in the next two minutes may determine your immediate future.

Here is still a different problem designed for adults. It is not as dramatic as the two previous ones, nor does it require any physical equipment. This is the famous "ray problem" posed by Duncker (1945). "Given a patient with an inoperable stomach tumor, and a ray which, at the proper intensity, will destroy tissue. The problem is, how to use the ray in order to reduce the tumor without damaging healthy tissue." Presented with this problem, you are asked to talk aloud about how you would solve it.

Two more problems will be considered here, but the first is for children and the second for chimpanzees, so in these you are in the role of observer rather than participant. Loftus and Suppes (1972) report that sixth-grade pupils find problems of the following order very difficult: "Charles is 20 years old. In two years he'll be twice as old as Philip. How old is Philip now?" In famous studies of chimpanzees made by the German psychologist Wolfgang Kohler during his internment on the island of Tenerife in World War I, the psychologist posed the following problem for the apes. Outside the cage, and slightly beyond their most extended reach, lay a banana. Inside the cage lay two notched sticks, neither of which is long enough to reach the pole, but if joined they will make an adequate tool to rake in the prize. Can a chimpanzee learn to do this, short of having the doubled pole handed to him?

Let us examine these situations for their commonalities. We have noted that a problem exists when the learner confronts a perplexity for which he has no ready-made response. None of our examples would seem to be disqualified on these grounds. If one makes appropriate allowances for developmental or species differences, it is unlikely that first responses would very often solve the problem. We can illustrate a number of useful principles about problem solving using the array of examples. Since, by definition, first responses do not solve problems, our first principle is that the learner must remain an active and goal-oriented seeker after effective means to achieve solution. As soon as he ceases actively responding to the challenge of the problem, all hope of achieving success is gone. It should be added that random or purposeless trial-and-error behavior is only slightly better than cessation of activity. It may keep the learner somewhat involved, but the generation of an effective solution is remote.

A corollary of this principle is that the active responding of the learner must involve variability. This in turn implies, although it is not always the case, that the learner constructs one or more hypotheses to be tested, based upon his definition of the problem. Several of our examples illustrate this corollary, but it is perhaps seen most clearly in the case of the Duncker ray problem. Duncker's summary interpretation of the protocol of one student who solved the problem aloud appears as Figure 7.1.

FIGURE 7.1 Progressive solutions to the ray problem given by one subject

Treatment of tumor by rays without destruction of healthy tissue

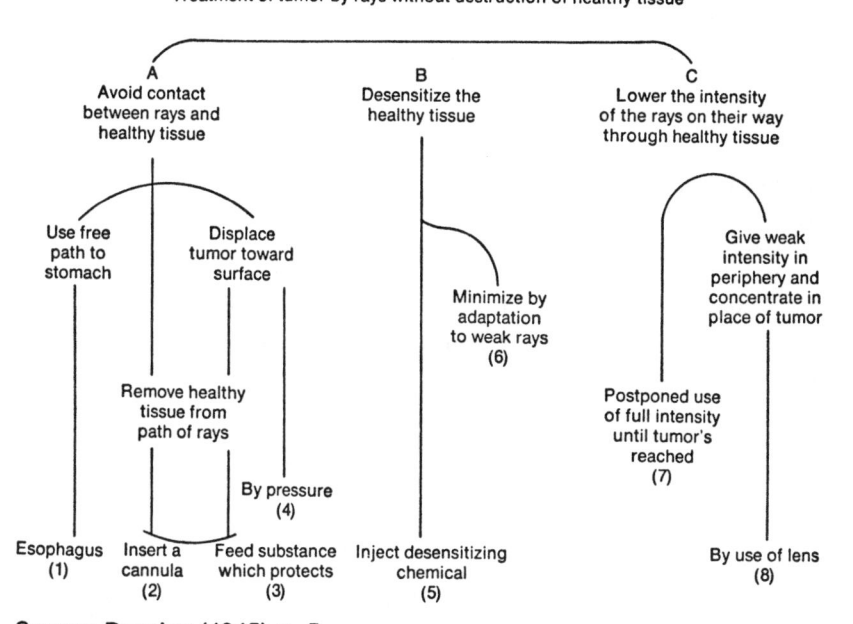

```
                                        A                          B                          C
                                 Avoid contact            Desensitize the           Lower the intensity
                                 between rays and         healthy tissue            of the rays on their way
                                 healthy tissue                                     through healthy tissue

              Use free           Displace                                           Give weak
              path to            tumor toward                                       intensity in
              stomach            surface                                            periphery and
                                                          Minimize by               concentrate in
                                                          adaptation                place of tumor
                                                          to weak rays
                                                              (6)

                                 Remove healthy                                     Postponed use
                                 tissue from                                        of full intensity
                                 path of rays                                       until tumor's
                                                                                    reached
                                                                                       (7)
                                       By pressure
                                           (4)
   Esophagus   Insert a    Feed substance    Inject desensitizing        By use of lens
      (1)      cannula     which protects       chemical                     (8)
                 (2)            (3)                (5)
```

Source: Duncker (1945), p. 5.

As the student attacked the problem, three separate general possibilities (labeled A, B, and C) were considered in turn. The first one, that contact between the destructive ray and healthy tissue should be avoided, proved untenable. All of the extensions of that hypothesis would necessitate some kind of manipulation of the stomach or tumor, conditions that are prohibited by the statement of the problem. The second possibility, that of desensitizing the healthy tissue, was also in itself unsatisfactory, but note that its elaborations, such as (6), "minimize by adaptation to weak rays," begins to suggest the third and successful idea: to lower the intensity of the rays on their way through healthy tissue. Of course, Hypothesis C is too general to constitute a solution to the problem, but it provides a framework within which possible solutions can be formulated and against which they can be tested. Notice the increasing specificity of these provisional solutions as they appear at the right in Figure 7.1. It is necessary to find a way to keep the ray's intensity weak (that is, below the threshold of tissue damage) both before and after the tumor is attacked by the ray, and the use of a lens is suggested as a means of accomplishing this. According to this reasoning, a special lens can be ground so that when the rays pass through it, it will disperse them in the periphery of the body but focus them at an appropriate intensity precisely at the site of the tumor. It is interesting to point out, in passing, that a similar solution was actually arrived at for the conduct of certain types of radiation therapy. Heavy particle or high proton beam radiation, for example, does not employ lenses, but it depends on two factors that are similar to the principles of Duncker's early problem. First the trajectory of the beam is calibrated so that its point of maximum intensity can be specified. That projection is coupled with highly precise and mechanically controlled rotation of the affected part of the patient's body, which is also slowly rotated. The end effect is very much that suggested by solutions to the Duncker ray problem.

Problem solving demands variability of behavior, which may also mean that the learner must modify or abandon hypotheses that do not move him toward solution. Often the solution lies in the learner's ability to adapt something in his environment to a purpose for which it is not ordinarily used. If a draft keeps closing our door, a heavy book or perhaps a shoe may be placed against it to serve as a doorstop. In the illustration where you were left trying to seize the two ropes, you might return to the table in the corner, pick up the hammer, and tie it to the end of one rope. You swing it, pendulumlike, while you pick up the second rope, and then you tie the two together. When we use an object in some accustomed way, we are less likely to perceive other purposes for it. Psychologists call this disability *functional fixedness*. As we shall see in

Chapter 8, one of the talents of the creative individual is overcoming the boundaries that normally restrict us in our approach to solutions. The good problem solver, similarly, has to be able to view things as if for the first time. Many of us do not do this particularly well, but we can profit by having another individual review the situation with us. Often a fresh eye sees possibilities for solution that we have overlooked simply because we have already classified or defined them in a particular and, as it happens, inappropriate way.

The learner not only needs to remain alert to the environmental possibilities in problem solving; he often must redefine the problem so as to make it solvable. Consider the O.S.S. candidate gaping into a shell hole in the example above. The availability of planks strongly suggests laying one across the hole to provide a bridge. An adequate solution is unlikely to occur until the learner perceives that some of the planks can be used to reduce the diameter of the circle; for example, one board can be used as a secant. If it is one of the longer ones, it will reduce the diameter sufficiently that the longest board can then cover the major distance across the gap. Numerous similar solutions of this problem are possible. In his fascinating book *The Five Day Course in Thinking,* Edward DeBono (1967) confronts the student with a problem that in principle is much like the one above. Starting with three bottles and four kitchen knives, one is to form a platform on the bottles with the knives that is stable enough so a full glass of water can be placed on it without spilling.

Sometimes, too, the learner's ability to solve a problem depends upon seeing a new relationship among the elements of the problem. In the example of Kohler's chimpanzees and their frustrating efforts to seize fruit outside their cages, when the relationship between placing two notched sticks together and using the resulting pole to rake in the food was perceived, the problem was quickly solved. It is true that the animals required large amounts of assistance to comprehend the point, but that is much less important than the fact that, once comprehended, the principle led to the physical solution of the problem quickly and easily.

From our consideration of these diverse problems, a series of more general principles emerges about how problems are solved.

1. The learner must be prepared to vary his approaches to the problem. This in turn implies an attitude of reflective thought in selecting and evaluating possible methods of attack. Haphazard shifting from one random pattern to another avails the learner little.

2. Although a problem is not solvable by any immediately available means, the learner may succeed if he considers how older ideas, methods, or materials may be altered or employed in effective but unusual ways.

3. Conversely, the learner must be able to redefine or to restructure the problem. A problem as given may defy solution, but if it can be reinterpreted, often existing materials or ideas can be adapted to provide the basis for a solution.

4. The solution to a problem often depends upon the learner's understanding of a new relationship he has not previously perceived. When that happens, his available responses can frequently be recombined in a new way to solve the problem.

5. Much problem solving proceeds on the basis of an idea, hunch, or hypothesis, which the learner holds about how the problem is to be solved. Dewey (1933) observed that the adequacy of hypotheses needs to be tested so that the learner can modify his behavior when the models he uses as a guide fail.

In the final analysis, problem-solving behavior is characterized by a thoughtful awareness that new approaches to problems are required and that solutions are favored by systematic attacks upon problems in an environment which makes detachment possible. This in turn implies that the learner must be free to try new ideas, even though many will be unsuccessful. If failure is viewed as weakness to be avoided or punished, the learner loses his most important avenue for generating new ways of learning about the world and for overcoming obstacles in his intellectual path. If there is one overarching principle for problem solving, it is the need for the learner to have freedom to explore and invent alternative solutions for existing problems in an environment which evaluates his behavior on the basis of its ingenuity and its intelligence, and not alone upon the quick attainment of correct and expected answers.

Instruction in Methods for Solving Problems

Teachers are naturally interested in knowing what effects upon their students' ability to solve problems may result from instruction. The issue involves two questions: What kind of instruction should students be provided? To what extent is their problem solving improved by having to work their own way through the problems, as opposed to being assisted in the process? These are not easy questions to answer, but some guidelines can be provided. The second question concerns practice to improve problem solving. We would expect a certain amount of practice to be helpful, but practice of the wrong kind may reduce the learner's sensitivity to better ways to solve problems and may result in rigid, mechanized ways of doing things.

To open our discussion of instruction in problem solving, let us return to a problem we introduced before, the one which asked the reader to determine which of two identical balls was made of heavier metal. Szekely (1950) demonstrated that the transfer effect of physics text material to the solution of the "two-sphere problem" was greater for a group of students who were first given a different problem, who then read the text, and finally tried to solve the two-sphere problem. The students in that group were shown a torsion pendulum, with two weights suspended from it near the middle of the bar, and two others suspended from it near the two ends. They were asked to predict under which condition it would spin more rapidly after being rotated and released. They were told that the physics text they were subsequently to read would provide a basis from which they could derive an answer. A second group of students, labeled the "traditional" group by Szekely, read the text but did not have the pendulum problem presented to them. Several days later, members of both groups were asked to solve the two-sphere problems, and a larger number from the first group were able to do so.

Szekely's conclusion was that a modern, problem-solving orientation produced more transfer than a traditional textbook approach to problem solving. However, an effort to replicate this study revealed that approximately half of all the subjects who read the pertinent physics text went on to solve the problem. The replication, performed by Maltzman, Eisman, and Brooks (1956), involved some modifications of Szekely's original design. Three experimental groups were constituted. The first two were the same as the two groups used by Szekely, and the third introduced a variation in which students read the physics text first and *then* received the demonstration with the torsion pendulum. None of these modifications made any significant difference. However, significantly more of the students in the three experimental conditions combined solved the problem than a control group whose members did not have an opportunity to study the text. The group scores were 50, 50, and 40 percent correct for the three experimental groups, and only 20 percent for the control. The correct solution involves two steps, the first of which college students seem to deduce with little trouble: the fact that one of the balls must have a hollow center. The text, then, enables about half of those who read it to make the further deduction that if the table before them is tilted slightly to form an inclined plane, the heavier ball will accelerate faster than the one made from the lighter metal.

Psychologists and teachers alike probably expect too much from the instruction they give to their experimental subjects or their students, respectively. To put the emphasis differently, we often underestimate the directness required in instruction and the assistance in making applications to new problems that most students need. If a principle is to be applied to the solution of a problem, the principle must be thoroughly known by the student, and the range of conditions under which it is applicable must also be known. When the learner recognizes that, as in the Maltzman, Eisman, and Brooks study, a principle given in the instructional material can be applied to the solution of a problem, then its use becomes probable.

There is a limited amount of evidence available which supports the contention that principles must be thoroughly learned, but the range of applications must also be known to the learner. Morrisett and Hovland (1959) trained groups of high school students to solve a class of problems. All subjects received the same amount of practice, but they studied different numbers of practice problems: 1, 3, or 24. Their hypothesis was that with equal but limited amounts of practice, students who were exposed to 24 different practice problems would have the greatest difficulty in applying their practice to new problems, because none of the problems could be well learned. Students with three problem types had the advantage of sufficient opportunity to learn all three thoroughly, plus the fact that they sampled the range of applicable problems to an extent. These students solved new problems most effectively, but even the students who were trained on only a single problem type fared better on the transfer tests than those given 24 problems.

How much information should the student be given?

A persistent issue in the study of problem solving is whether individuals solve new problems more easily if they induce the applicable principle for themselves during the training series or are provided with the principles while they are learning to apply it. The results of studies that have examined such questions are frankly conflicting. Some investigators have reported that subjects perform best if given the principle; some do best under "discovery" conditions; others report that subjects who were given some assistance in discovering the principle solve transfer problems better than those who were given no help or those who were given the principle. Part of the conflict seems to stem from the different ways in which investigators have defined their experimental variables, but some of the difficulty seems to lie also in the logic of the interpretation of the findings.

Haselrud and Meyers (1958) hypothesized that greater positive transfer would occur if subjects were forced to induce a principle for themselves from concrete instances than if they were provided with a statement of the principle, which they were then to apply. To test this hypothesis, they used an experimental group of 76 college students and a control group of 24. The experimental subjects worked on two tasks, both of which were problems in learning codes. The first task consisted of a list of 20 sentences written in English. Each sentence was followed by its code translation. Above half the code sentences, a statement of the key to the code appeared; no such statement was given for the other sentences. The statements appeared above alternate sentences in the task. The control subjects did not work on the first task.

Both groups then attempted the transfer task, which was administered a week after the training series. Again 20 sentences were given, each followed by four possible translations; the subjects were to check the correct translation. Since the control group did not have an opportunity to work on the first lesson, any difference between their scores and those of the experimental subjects could be attributed to the influence of the first task. The mean score on Test 2 was significantly greater for the experimental subjects than for the control subjects, so it was concluded that practice in translating English sentences into code does transfer to a similar task.

However, the principal interest of the investigators lay in determining whether a difference in transferability occurred between the two conditions under which the experimental subjects had been trained. Four scores were computed for the experimental subjects: (1) the number of correct translations on the guided exercises of Test 1, (2) the number of correct translations on the unguided translations of Test 1, (3) the number of translations correct on Test 2 which were like the guided examples of Test 1, and (4) the number of translations correctly completed on Test 2 which were like the unguided examples of Test 1. This made it possible to compare the effect of each training condition upon the subject's ability to translate the sentences in the second task.

Significant transfer occurred for both training conditions. The percentage of increase was greater from Task 1 to Task 2 for the unguided examples (46 percent, to 10 percent for the guided examples). The investigators interpret this difference to provide support for their hypothesis. While at first glance this seems to be a reasonable enough interpretation, it leaves at least one important question unanswered. The subjects solved more of the code problems on the first task when they were given the principle than when they were not. Although the proportion of correct choices made on Task 2, which were based on codes like those for which the subject was given no guidance on the preliminary task, is significantly greater, there is no difference on the transfer task in the total number of correct solutions. When we look at the number of correct solutions on the second task of problems like the guided examples of Task 1, and compare this number with the correct solutions on Task 2 based on the unguided examples of Task 1, no difference is apparent.

Haselrud and Meyers's interpretation needs to be qualified by the question about transfer of a principle that teachers are most likely to want answered. If that question simply concerns which method leads to maximum transfer, the answer seems to be: Any method which allows pupils an opportunity to practice using the principle. Whether the pupil is given the principle or is forced to induce it during practice makes little difference if the criterion is the number of problems he can solve on a transfer test. On the other hand, if the teacher is also interested in the conditions under which pupils are likely to perform in a superior way on the practice material as well as on a transfer task, the results seem to favor a method of guided practice, since the sentences on Task 1 that provided the principle were more frequently solved than those that did not. It may very well be, of course, that if the subjects had practiced with the unguided sentences until they were as successful as with the guided ones, a significant difference in transfer would have resulted. Unfortunately, Haselrud and Meyers did not design their study in a way that sheds much light on this speculation. At any rate, the teacher would have to consider whether the additional time in training on principle induction would be warranted by the possible gain in transfer since, presumably, equal additional time spent on practicing the application of the principle would also facilitate transfer.

Kersh (1958) explained the superiority of a discovery method in problem solving, not in terms of learning per se but as a consequence of an increment in motivation which appears to lead to increased independent practice on the task. In a subsequent study (Kersh, 1962), designed to examine differences in retention and transfer of principles between a directed group and a discovery group, Kersh employed a control group which was given the principle to be learned and a series of examples to which it was to be applied. When transfer tests were administered to all subjects over periods ranging from three days to six weeks, the major finding was totally unanticipated by the investigator. The control group, which had memorized the principles and practiced their application, was better able than either the directed or the discovery group to use the principles to solve new problems and to state the substance of the principles. This is a significant result, not only in its implications for the teacher's role in guiding problem-solving behavior but also because of what it suggests about the utilization of instructional time.

Hendrix (1947), in a frequently cited study, reported that subjects who discovered the rule but did not immediately formulate it (method of unverbalized awareness) took greater advantage of opportunities to apply the rule than subjects who discovered the rule and verbalized it, or subjects who were first given the rule and then practiced its use with various examples. On the strength of these findings, Hendrix suggests that pupils' ability to transfer or apply a generalization from the context in which it is originally learned to a new one will not be materially improved by first specifying the principle and that, in fact, such verbalization may impede the desired use of the principle. This is a startling recommendation, but examination of Hendrix's results casts great doubt upon the reliability of her findings. She replicated her methods on three separate but small samples (a total experimental sample of 40 persons). Each time the results were the same, that is, more applications were made by the unverbalized awareness subjects. However, the differences among her subjects, while always in the direction predicted, are not statistically significant. In fact, the difference between the unverbalized awareness subjects and those who verbalized the rule as part of their experimental treatment is so small as to occur by chance about one time in three.

Corman (1957) conducted an experiment with a group of senior high school students in which he examined the influence of providing different amounts of information about principles or methods for solving problems on the success the pupils enjoyed. The general hypothesis Corman tested was that guidance in problem solving, to be effective, must be highly related to the task. More explicitly, he predicted that when the criterion is the solution of a problem, guidance about the method to use in attaining solution would be of help, and that when the criterion is not solution itself but stating the rule to be used in solution, guidance relevant to the rule would facilitate such verbalization.

The task used by Corman was in the form of a puzzle. Subjects were confronted with five adjacent squares composed of a total of 15 safety matches. By moving only three of the matches, they were to reduce the number of squares to 4. Several limitations were placed upon the way in which these changes could occur. For example, the matches could not be stood on end, only one match could serve as the side of a square, and all the squares were to be of the same size, one-match length.

Subjects of this experiment were 233 twelfth-graders from selected suburban New York and New Jersey high schools. The total sample was divided into high-ability and low-ability groups. Pupils who scored above the median on a group-administered intelligence test were identified as high ability; those who fell below the median were designated as low ability. Each subject was provided with some information about the method for solving the problems and about the rule to use in arriving at solutions. For the rule or principle, three degrees of information were provided: (1) no information, (2) some information—there is a rule which will be of use in solving the problems, and (3) much information—every match should be the side of only one square. Three similar kinds of information were provided with respect to the method to be used in solving the problems: (1) no information, (2) some information—subjects were directed to shade certain squares of the test problem, and (3) much information—subjects were told which matches to move and to practice these moves. A total of nine combinations of guidance were used, varying from the case where the subjects were given no information about either the principle or the method, to the case where subjects were given complete information about both rule and method.

The experiment itself consisted of having subjects solve three guided problems called the instructional problems. These were followed by three simple transfer tasks and five complex transfer tasks. Complexity was defined in terms of the similarity of the transfer problem to the instructional problem. Thus the simple transfer tasks were more similar to the instruction problems, the complex tasks were more remote. The subjects' final task was to write the rule they had used in solving the problems.

Corman had hypothesized that pupils of lower and higher mental ability would not profit differentially from the several kinds of guidance, that is, that the type of guidance which was helpful to high-ability students would also be effective with pupils of lower mental ability. His results did not support that hypothesis. Therefore, it is necessary to consider the results separately for the two subsamples.

If we consider first the results for the above-average pupils, we find that information about the rule was of no help in solving the instructional problems; that is, when these pupils were given no information about the method to use in solving the problem, whatever amount of information they were given about the rule did not change the frequency with which the instructional problems were solved. Pupils who were given some information about the method performed more adequately on the instructional problems, and, as might be expected from what has been stated earlier, the greatest facilitation occurred for pupils who were given maximum information about the method.

For the simple transfer tasks, two combinations yielded results superior to the other seven combinations. Pupils did best in solving the simple transfer tasks when they were either given maximum rule information and intermediate guidance about the method, or when these conditions were reversed and they were given some information about the rule and maximum method information. For the complex transfer tasks, those pupils who were given information only about the method or intermediate information about the rule only fared best. At first glance these findings are difficult to integrate with those about the instruction problems and the simple transfer problems. However, the complex transfer tasks were different from the other tasks in many specifics. It may be that a great deal of information about the rule and method which were useful for the solution of the earlier simple problems resulted in negative transfer, or interference, with the more complex problems, whereas the intermediate conditions, either for the rule or for the method, provided the pupil with an entering wedge, a way to make an intelligent attack on the problems without arbitrarily committing himself to a plan of action which was not totally suitable for solving the new problems.

When the results are examined for the other half of the experimental sample, the pupils whom Corman identified as low in ability, the most obvious finding is that information about the rule, in any amount, was of no assistance to the pupils in solving any of the tasks. The low-ability pupils performed best when they were given either intermediate or maximum amounts of information about the specifics of the method to use.

Corman employed two kinds of dependent variables. The first, success in solving three kinds of problems, we have already discussed. His other interest lay in observing which of the pupils would be most successful in learning the rule. The result is straightforward: the more information the pupil had been given about the rule, the better he was able to write it. This result was significantly different, however, only for the comparison between pupils who were given maximum information about the rule and those who were given no information about it. Although subjects who had been provided with intermediate information did some better than the no-information group, the difference between them was not significant.

It is possible to place the results of Corman's investigation in a broader context of research results and educational practice. Ordinarily, less talented pupils require more direct, concrete experience with learning materials than do above-average or gifted students. Corman's finding that his low-ability pupils performed best under the conditions where they were given information about the method to use in solving problems, and that no amount of information about the rule to apply appreciably altered the level of their performance, would seem to fit this generalization. The more able pupils in Corman's sample also profited from information about method, but for the transfer problems, rule guidance, either in combination with information about the method or by itself, was equally efficacious. Corman's other findings, that success in learning to write the rule was dependent upon the amount of information provided about the rule and that success in solving the problems and in writing the rule were independent of each other, are evidence that the two kinds of tasks did not transfer to each other.

The role of verbalization in problem solving

Instructions to verbalize each move they made in solving practice problems transferred positively to students' attempts to solve a more complex form of the same problem. Gagné and Smith (1962) investigated the effects of verbalization upon the problem-solving ability of a group of ninth- and tenth-grade boys of above-average ability. They wished to determine whether stating the underlying principle in an adequate form would also lead to improved ability.

The problem called for the boys to move different numbers of aluminum discs from one circle to another. A third circle was also available on the board, and it could be used as an intermediate step if required. The discs were graduated in size, and one of the rules was that a disc of larger diameter could never be placed on a smaller disc. Thus the subject might start with three discs, and he had to move them from the starting point to the designated circle in the minimum number of moves. Practice problems included two, three, four, and five discs. The final performance was a six-disc problem. The principle was: "If the number of discs is odd, move first to the circle to which you want to go eventually; if even, move first away from this circle. Continue by moving discs with odd numbers always in a clockwise direction, and the discs with even numbers always in a counterclockwise direction." The investigators also wanted to find out whether their instructions would improve the boys' ability to state the underlying principle.

After the 28 subjects had tried the three-and four-disc problems, they were assigned to one of four groups: (1) Group V–SS (verbalizing, solution set); (2) Group V (verbalizing; no solution set); (3) Group SS (no verbalizing; solution set); (4) Group No (no verbalizing; no solution set). Verbalizing demanded stating each move aloud; solution set was an instruction to try to formulate a general rule for the solution. Did it make a difference whether the student verbalized about his procedure in moving the discs? The results show emphatically that it made a large difference. Differences favoring the boys who verbalized their moves began to appear as early as the three-disc practice problem. By the final performance (that is the six-disc problem) the mean number of moves in excess of the minimum required was as follows: for the group that verbalized and had a solution set, the mean was 7.9; for the group that was to verbalize but had no solution set, it was 9.3. The mean number of moves for the two groups without verbalization increased dramatically—48.1 for the solution set group, and 61.7 for the group which, in effect, had no operating instructions whatsoever. No significant difference resulted, however, from the instruction to try to abstract a principle.

Gagné and Smith made a further analysis to see whether the treatment combinations to which the boys were assigned affected their ability to state the principle for solving these problems. They categorized the statement attempted by each of the subjects into one of three rubrics: (1) inadequate, if no sensible principle emerged; (2) partial, if one of the two components of the principle was present; or (3) complete, if both of the elements were present in a decipherable form. Table 7.1 shows that the verbalization groups were superior to the others. In fact, the No group produced only one response accurate enough to be classified as partial.

TABLE 7.1 *Number of inadequate, partial, and complete verbal principles stated by subjects*

		\multicolumn{4}{c}{Number of instances of principles judged as}
Group		N	Inadequate	Partial	Complete
V—SS	(verbalizing, solution set)	7	0	3	4
V	(verbalizing, no solution set)	7	0	5	2
SS	(no verbalizing; solution set)	7	1	6	0
No	(no verbalizing; no solution set)	7	6	1	0

Source: Gagné & Smith (1962), p. 16.

The major finding of this study is the striking effect of an instruction to subjects to state aloud why they were making each individual move at the time they made it. The actual substance of what the boys said during practice was rather pedestrian, and not particularly revealing of their internal processes of thought. Gagné and Smith do not have a theory to fall back upon in explaining the effects of verbalization, except that it may have "forced the SS to think." Since they had to come up with reasons frequently, and may have grown weary of always giving the same ones, they perhaps searched for new explanations from time to time, thus extending their understanding of the principle. We should add a word that the particular type of problem used in this study was well adapted to Gagné and Smith's procedures, since the identical principle was applicable to each new extension of the problem. Whether verbalization in the solution of problems in science of mathematics would yield transfer in the same way is not known, but with the studies we have reviewed here as background, the effort to study the conditions of transfer under such an instruction would seem to be a good investment of time and energy.

Set and rigidity

Some of the most interesting and provocative information about the relationship between set and rigidity in problem solving comes from a series of experiments reported by Luchins (1942). The general question Luchins sought to answer was of the form: If you teach an individual a specific method for solving a problem, then allow him to solve a series of problems where that method is appropriate, what will happen to his behavior when he confronts problems which can be solved more directly than by the prescribed method? Luchins was also interested in the potential effect on behavior of a warning to be alert. For most of his experiments he used "water jar problems" as experimental tasks. The subject is instructed that from three jars, A, B, C, he is to get a specified amount of water. An illustrative problem is constructed so that the subject (hypothetically) fills jar B, then subtracts enough water to fill jar A once and jar C twice. For example, the problem might read, "Jar A contains a 6-quart capacity, jar B contains a 128-quart capacity, and jar C contains a 1-quart capacity. Obtain 120 quarts of water." The formula B–A–2C is applicable. A series of problems, all solvable by the same method, follows. After a half dozen or so of these problems, others are inserted which can be solved by the earlier learned formula, but for which a simpler method is applicable, for example: "A = 15, B = 39, C = 3; obtain 18." While 39 minus 21 will yield the required 18 quarts, the subject need only add A and C to reach the desired quantity. Frequently subjects, well-educated adults as well as elementary school children, fail to note the more direct solution and proceed with the B –A –2C formula.

To some subjects, Luchins provided a clue before the beginning of the experiment. This clue consisted of a reminder to subjects to write the words "Don't be blind!" on their answer sheets following the completion of the sixth problem. As indicated, the first six problems usually were introduced to build up the set or to blind subjects to the fact that a change in procedure was coming. However, the "Don't be blind!" instruction tended to have differential effects, depending upon the subject's interpretation of its meaning. When the subject made the appropriate interpretation, that is, "Be alert now, I'm going to throw you a curve!" the set frequently was broken. Subjects scanned the array of jars for cues which would suggest an alternative means of attaining the solution. Other subjects, typically those with whom the instruction was ineffective, apparently thought it meant, "Don't be blind! The method I have taught you still works, even if the problems look different." Some subjects, under this instruction, proceeded to apply the B –A –2C formula even to subsequent problems which were not solvable by the formula given.

A number of the experimental subjects used by Luchins in his investigation of the role of *Einstellung,* or rigidity in problem solving, were elementary school pupils. Luchins observed that the environment to which pupils had become accustomed in the classroom was instrumental in influencing their responses to the water jar problems. Particularly prone to the *Einstellung* effect were the pupils of teachers who stressed classroom routine and drill. Postexperimental reactions of such pupils included expressions of surprise or indignation that a teacher (the experimenter) would expect pupils to use a different method to solve problems than the one he had explicitly taught them.

It seems reasonable to extrapolate two principles of practice for the classroom from Luchin's findings, although there is not specific evidence currently available to support them.

1. If pupil problem-solving behavior is to avoid the inhibiting effects of stereotype, the classroom atmosphere must reinforce (or at least must allow) attempts to vary strategy in seeking solutions.

2. When the teacher provides a series of problems, even though these are primarily intended to furnish practice on a recently taught principle or operation, it seems advisable to insert an occasional problem which demands the application of a different principle. The value of practice is questionable if the pupil knows from previous occasions that tomorrow's homework is invariably based on today's lesson.

Conversely, if pupils are aware that problems are likely to demand a variety of applications, including recently as well as earlier learned operations, there should be an additional value beyond merely breaking down response rigidity. Such foreknowledge might also be expected to induce pupils to analyze problems carefully, inasmuch as they cannot rely upon correspondence with recent teaching.

A study by Miller (1957) furnishes at least indirect support for these contentions. Miller tested a group of 120 boys in a British secondary school which included both "modern" and "technical" streams. The boys in the modern stream complete their formal education at the secondary school level, while most of the boys in the technical stream are headed toward advanced training. Apparently there are quite different expectations held by the teachers for classes in the two streams. The same teachers in this school instruct classes from both streams, but they report that they employ different instructional techniques. Drill procedures are, according to the teachers' statements, used more extensively with classes from the modern stream than with those in the technical stream.

Since Miller was interested in determining whether there are relationships between intelligence and rigidity, and between rigidity and teaching methods, he administered the Luchins water jar problems to boys in both streams of the school. He then computed a rank-order correlation between their scores on the water jar problems (a measure of rigidity) and intelligence. This yielded a negative but significant relationship (rho = −.304). A negative correlation indicates that the two factors under examination vary with each other, but one decreases as the other increases. In this case, the negative correlation suggests that the higher a pupil's measured IQ, the lower his score on rigidity is likely to be.

Miller also attempted to answer the question: Is rigidity related to the type of instruction pupils receive in school? This seems to be an interesting and important question, and it is unfortunate that Miller's answer to it is not definitive. He selected students from the middle IQ range of both streams, so that there was no significant difference in intelligence between the two groups. This gave him a sample of 29 boys from the modern stream with a mean IQ of 100.6, and a group of 41 technical-stream boys with a mean intelligence test score of 102.8. When these two groups are compared with respect to their rigidity, the differences are quite dramatic. Of the boys from the modern stream, 83 percent were high on *Einstellung*, whereas only 49 percent of the boys in the technical stream had high rigidity scores.

Miller argues on the basis of these data that, since the boys all shared the same general school environment and the groups were of equal intelligence, the differences in rigidity must be accounted for by some additional factor or factors. He suggests that, although the boys are in contact in their classes with essentially the same group of teachers, the teachers report that they handle the classes differently. His interpretation is a long way from providing evidence that routine drill methods of teaching contribute to the development of rigidity in pupils, but it does raise the possibility that teaching methods may be more important in the development of *Einstellung* than has been thought in the past.

Luchin's comments about the reactions of pupils in classes where instructional procedures are highly routinized are no more definitive than Miller's supposition. The two independent reports placed together, however, do suggest a trend. Until further evidence is available on the point, it seems reasonable to hypothesize that methods of teaching and rigidity are related to each other.

Effects of training pupils in alternative methods of solving problems

The teacher's goal in the development of problem-solving skills is broader than teaching pupils to solve any given set of problems successfully. He must also be concerned with developing flexible but usable strategies that enable pupils to attack problems independently, that is, when cues ordinarily available from the context of the lesson or from the teacher's guidance are missing.

Ackerman and Levin (1958) attempted to train elementary school children not to form a set in problem solving or to abandon it once it becomes evident that the mode of attack they are using is not going to be successful. The investigators divided their sample of sixth-grade pupils into two groups, an alternative group (A) which was taught two methods by which to solve a set of training problems, and a no-alternative group (NA), which was taught only one method for solving the same set of problems. The items in the training series were the familiar Luchins water jar problems, modified so that they were susceptible to solution by either of the methods in which the A group received instruction. Ackerman and Levin were interested in the effect the alternative method of training would have on pupils' behavior when they encountered new problems which would not yield to either of the methods previously practiced. A transfer test was also given to both groups of pupils, consisting of a set of problems different from the Luchins water jar items.

For both of the tests following the training session, the results were essentially the same. No statistically significant differences occurred between the A group and the NA group in the total number of problems solved correctly. However, the difference between the two groups was in the direction predicted, that is, the A subjects did solve more problems than the NA subjects. Despite the failure of the training in alternative methods of solution to yield significant differences in total solutions, other important differences between the two groups appeared. Members of the group trained with alternative solutions were more variable in choosing alternative methods of working on the problems than were the members of the NA training group. Also, the A-group pupils persisted in working on the problems for longer periods of time than the NA subjects.

The interpretation of Ackerman and Levin's findings for classroom practice is complicated by their failure to report significant differences in the total number of correct solutions between the pupils in the two training conditions. Obviously, if we knew that there was a direct correspondence between an instructional method which concentrated on exposing pupils to multiple approaches to problems and the number of problems pupils could subsequently solve, we could feel relatively certain about the wisdom of incorporating such methods into the practice of teaching.

The training period the pupils experienced in this experiment was relatively brief; the problems with which they were dealing were highly proscribed. It may be that, as a consistent practice in the classroom, careful training in selecting alternative ways of seeking solutions to problems will result in the kind of increment in solutions which Ackerman and Levin were hopeful of demonstrating.

A Science Curriculum Emphasizing Problem Solving

When an entire curriculum is focused upon problem solving, the achievement of cognitive objectives should be enhanced, in contrast with the ordinary case in which the teacher attempts to use existing instructional materials, adapting them to his or her purposes as that is possible. A curriculum that may be said to have a problem-solving orientation— the Inquiry Training Program developed by Suchman (1961) to which we referred earlier—concentrates on the field of elementary science, specifically upon the discovery of a number of basic physics principles. Children are taught an explicit set of procedures that are designed to assist them in the process of inquiry. Suchman leaves no doubt, however, that the child's preoccupation in this curriculum is upon learning why certain curiosity-arousing phenomena occur, as pictured in the films he views. At a theoretical level there is a clear relationship between the structure of this curriculum and the hypothesis presented in Chapter 3, that discrepant or unusual events arouse curiosity, which in turn energizes the learner and focuses his attention on the task to be learned or, in this case, explained. The process of inquiry as such, although it has been carefully and systematically incorporated into the curriculum, is clearly subordinate to the science content.

Suchman developed this program because he believed that the child's school life should have more active intellectual inquiry built into it than is usually the case. The program consists of a series of filmed demonstrations of physical phenomena which the students first view and then are challenged to explain. The inquiry training consists essentially of instructing the children to ask disciplined questions and encouraging them to do so. An ingenious characteristic of the program is that it avoids the necessity of transactions that involve manipulation of concrete materials and the attendant and often unproductive experimentation with them.

Preoccupation with materials frequently catches students up in the mechanics of laboratory work at the expense of careful, reflective thought about the phenomena studied. In the Suchman program of inquiry training, questions replace such maneuvers, and teachers' responses become substitutes for environmental feedback. An added dimension is that the teacher will answer only those questions that lead to meaningful yes or no responses. One of the difficult early lessons the child has to learn is to formulate questions that are meaningful and that can be productively answered in that manner. Suchman's reports of early pilot studies show that question asking of the disciplined type required is extremely difficult, even for children of superior intelligence and scientific dispositions. Preliminary individual interviews with children quickly demonstrated that a program of inquiry training would have to concentrate upon teaching children how to ask meaningful questions. Consider the following example.

One of the films in the series portrays what Suchman labeled "The Bimetallic Strip." (Children are not given titles of the films.) A spatula is made of two thin pieces of metal fused together, one steel and the other brass. The film shows the spatula being held by a wooden handle, with the steel side down, in the flame of a Bunsen burner. Almost immediately after being placed in the fire, the strip begins to bend downward, forming almost a 90-degree angle with the horizontal. The strip is then plunged into a beaker of water and straightens out. The experimenter reverses the strip in his hand (the side that was originally down is now up) and again places the strip over heat. Again it bends, but this time upward; again the strip is dashed in water and straightens out. The children are left with this question: "Why does the strip bend and then straighten out again?"

One of the first things Suchman learned in the formative stages of his program is that many children 10 or 11 years of age are, in the beginning, simply incapable of knowing how to find an explanation for this physical phenomenon. The excerpt of an interview with Mark reproduced below illustrates the need for systematic instruction in problem solving.

> Examiner: What made it go up? I'm here to answer questions.
> Mark: Yes, I know. I can't think of any to ask.
> Examiner: I see. Think. Try.
> Mark: (Pause) Well I can't think of any questions.
> Examiner: What is it you want to know? What would you want to know?
> Mark: Why it bended upwards.
> Examiner: What could you do to find out what things were necessary.
> Mark: Try it. Ask someone who knew.
> Examiner: Yes, you could ask someone that knew, but that would just be getting somebody else to tell you, wouldn't it? I mean, finding out for yourself.
> Mark: Just try different things.
> Examiner: What?
> Mark: Well, you could get the materials and things, and then try holding the thing at a different angle.

Examiner: What do you think would happen?
Mark: I don't know.
Examiner: Can you ask me some questions to find out?
Mark: No I can't ask you any questions.
Examiner: You're completely stumped? You have any ideas now for any rules at all that would explain it?
Mark: No.
Examiner: None at all. It's a complete mystery to you? No hunches? And no ideas as to what you could ask me to get some hunches?
Mark: No.

(Suchman, 1969, p. 321)

Let us see how the program is used in a classroom. The children first see a brief silent film which demonstrates the phenomenon they are to explain and usually lasts no more than a minute or two. As an example, we shall sketch the development of a lesson around the topic "The Ball and Ring." The series of sketches in Figure 7.2 will give you an idea of the basic action that occurs in the film. At first the ball passes easily through the ring. After heat is applied to the ball, it catches in the ring for a brief time and then once again drops to the table surface below. The film closes with two questions: "Why does the ball get stuck in the ring? Why does it fall through again?"

Note the fundamental contrast between this approach to the discovery of explanations and that of the more traditional way of presenting science findings to children. In the Inquiry Training Program, each phenomenon is presented to the watching student. He is not given a verbal explanation of what happened or why it occurred. On the contrary, it is only through his own ability (and that of his classmates) to organize functional questions that progress toward identifying precisely what did transpire can be established. Beyond that, additional thought and questions can move him toward explaining the phenomenon, a goal which is not often achieved by students in this setting, but which, on the other hand, is seldom attempted by students who are more accustomed to textbook assignments and demonstrations dictated in laboratory manuals. The central idea of Suchman's procedure, whatever its limitations so far in practice, is an especially creative one for helping teachers to develop a climate in which productive thinking can emerge. This is aided by the use of a set of simple films, which also means the elimination for the teacher of burdens of locating sets of demonstration materials, supervising numerous groups of children as they manipulate them, worrying about inadequate demonstrations by teacher or pupils, and concern for the myriad other obstacles to good science teaching, particularly in the elementary school.

The Pupil as Thinker: Problem Solving 235

FIGURE 7.2 *Example of a problem posed by the Inquiry Training Program*

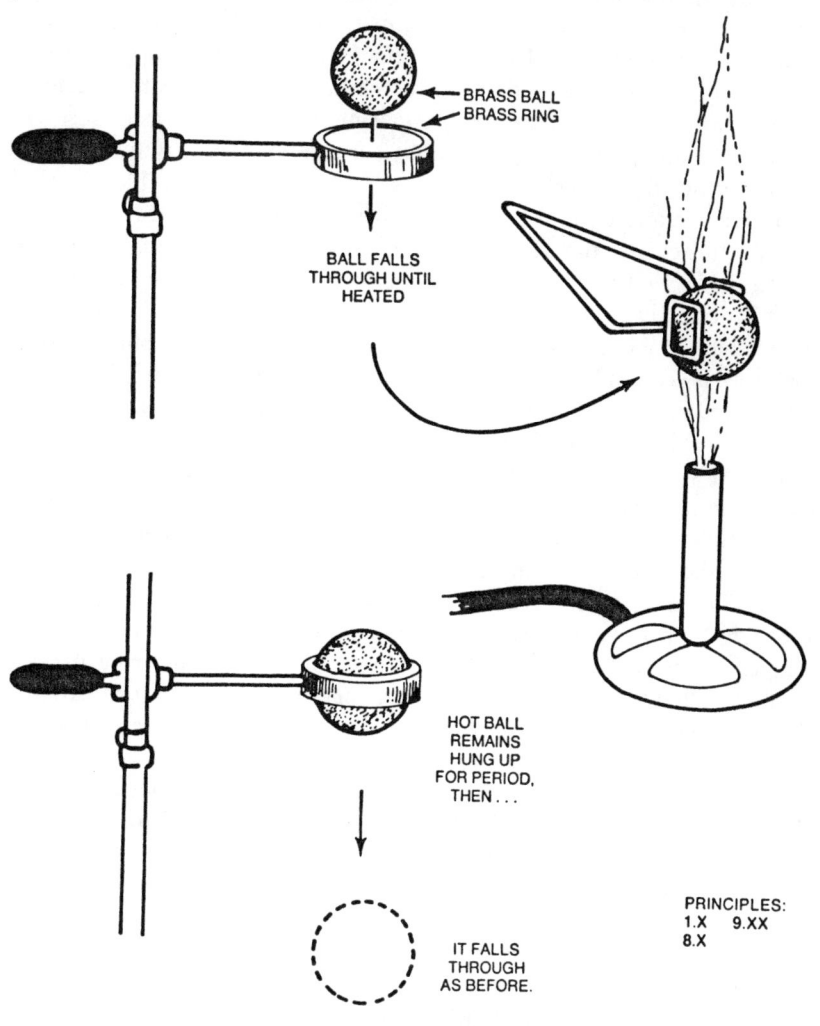

BRASS BALL
BRASS RING

BALL FALLS THROUGH UNTIL HEATED

HOT BALL REMAINS HUNG UP FOR PERIOD, THEN...

IT FALLS THROUGH AS BEFORE.

PRINCIPLES:
1.X   9.XX
8.X

FILM NO. 16   PROBLEM NO. 8
BALL AND RING

WHY DOES THE BALL GET STUCK IN THE RING? WHY DOES IT FALL THROUGH AGAIN?

Source: Suchman's Teacher's Manual for the Inquiry Training Program, p. 36.

The program consists of three stages: (1) episode analysis, (2) determination of relevance, and (3) induction of relational constructs. The purpose of episode analysis is to compel the child to verify what happened in the experimental demonstration: "Was the flame applied to the ring?" "No." In the second stage, the child asks questions to determine the relevant variables, and the conditions necessary for the result observed to occur. In the third stage, the child's job is to explain why the observed events occurred. As Suchman suggests, this stage imposes a high level of cognitive demand upon the child, and it is obviously beyond the grasp of many children. At the same time, the information and hypotheses produced in the first two stages contribute to the child's chances of generating scientifically valid explanations.

A model of what episode analysis for the ball and ring problem should look like is seen in Table 7.2. The question and answer session between pupils and teacher continues through a series of analyses. In the organization of episode analysis shown in the table, the pupils are working toward a systematic examination of the conditions and events that account for the behavior of the ball and ring. Among other things, they must establish the conditions that are necessary for the ball to become stuck in the ring; for example, the diameter of the ball must exceed the inner diameter of the ring. At the outset, since the ball passed easily through the ring, one of two changes must have occurred. Either the diameter of the ball expanded, or the inner diameter of the ring became smaller. The fact is that the ball was heated, which caused it to expand, therefore increasing its diameter. The diameter of the ring remained unaltered.

Conditions necessary for the ball to pass through the ring once more must also be identified. Basically the diameter of the ball must become smaller than the ring's inner diameter. When the ball is seated in the ring, heat is conducted from the ball to the ring. The ring subsequently expands as it becomes heated; the ball contracts as it loses heat to the ring. When the temperature of the two are equal, the ball slips through the ring.

The success of this approach depends upon systematic progression through the conditions and events that characterize the phenomena. As we shall see shortly, an ultimate explanation of the phenomenon depends upon several basic physics generalizations. Their application by sixth-grade children demands a comprehension of them that far exceeds simple memorization of the rules. It is obvious also that many children in the intermediate or junior high school grades will not make the connections between such principles and the simple demonstration of the ball and ring. That is, their comprehension may be limited to an understanding of the

TABLE 7.2 Model of episode analysis for the ball and ring problem

Systems and objects	Starting conditions	Events — conditions		
		After ball is heated	After ball is placed in ring	When brass ball falls through ring
Ring (brass)	Temperature: Room temperature	Temperature: Room temperature	Temperature: Increases	Temperature: > Normal; equals temperature of ball
	Inner diameter: Normal—just large enough to accommodate ball	Inner diameter: Normal	Inner diameter: Starts to increase	Inner diameter: > Normal; equals diameter of ball.
Ball (brass)	Temperature: Room temperature	Temperature: > Room temperature	Temperature: Starts to decrease	Temperature: > Normal; equals temperature of ring
	Diameter: Normal—able to fit through ring.	Diameter: > Normal; > inner diameter of ring	Diameter: Starts to decrease	Diameter: > Normal; equals inner diameter of ring.
Bunsen burner	Not heating ball or ring	Directly under ball; not heating ring	Removed from ball and ring	Removed from ball and ring

Source: Suchman's Teacher's Manual for the Inquiry Training Program, p. 37.

events that occurred and the circumstances associated with them, without an extension of the broader principles to subsume the empirical events.

Once again, it must be stressed that children learn disciplined ways of asking questions which can be answered with a yes or no by the teacher, and which also provide information to the learner that advances his knowledge and understanding of the events he has witnessed. Thus, a question that asks, "Why did the ball stick in the ring after it was heated?" would be ruled out of order. An answer to that question would place the onus for identifying, classifying, and explaining events on the teacher and not on the student, which is what the program is designed to do.

A basic explanation of the ball and ring phenomenon, as with each of the other demonstrations, rests upon several basic principles. The three principles involved in this demonstration, as they appear in Suchman's Teacher's Manual (p. 39), are:

Newton's First Law of Motion:
An object at rest tends to remain at rest, and, when in motion, tends to remain in motion in a straight line and at the same speed unless acted upon by an unbalanced force.

Conduction of Heat:
Heat may be conducted through objects or from one object to another by direct contact. Materials vary in the rate at which they will conduct heat. (May be explained in terms of molecular motion.)

Temperature-Volume Relationship in Liquids and Solids:
Objects generally expand when heated and contract when cooled. (There are certain exceptions at or near the fusion point.)

The Inquiry Training Program was developed in four phases. The first involved the specifications of the physics principles to be studied and the ensuing development of the film clips and attendant materials for teachers. The second phase was devoted to the training of teachers. Teachers who were to teach the experimental program in inquiry were provided with an eight-week seminar the summer preceding their entry into the teaching aspects of the program. The third phase involved the direct instructional period, which was 24 weeks in length. This period included time for orientation to the program and pretesting and posttesting of the participating children, with the bulk of the time being given over to specific practice in inquiry. This sequence of events is mentioned here in order to emphasize the care with which this program was designed. Teachers were provided with an extensive period of in-service training, in contrast to the occasional one- or two-day seminars most public school systems offer for the introduction of new textbook series or new curricula.

Similarly, the 24 weeks of instruction given to the children represents a curriculum intervention that can be characterized as of at least moderate length. The final phase of the program involved measurement of its outcomes.

For purposes of the experiment, two sixth-grade classes were identified in each participating school. One served as an experimental class, the other as a control. For the most part, the inquiry program was taught by someone other than the children's regular classroom teacher. Sometimes the same teacher instructed both the experimental and control classes in the same school. The major difference in the instructional treatment was the presence or absence of inquiry training. The control groups viewed the same science films, but instead of engaging in the inquiry process they were taught the underlying physics principles. The amount of time devoted to the program was about the same for all groups, experimental and control (that is, approximately one to two hours a week for the duration of the 24 weeks).

Results of the program for the most part failed to produce significant differences between experimental and control classes. With the exception of two experimental classes who scored higher than their control counterparts, no significant differences occurred between the two sets in their conceptual mastery of physics. Nor, in general, was there much difference in the ability of the pupils to apply principles to new situations. The most striking differences occurred in the *process* of inquiry. For these comparisons, 60 experimental and 57 control subjects each were given 25 minutes to ask questions about an episode. These protocols were tape-recorded and analyzed for question fluency and the types of questions asked. The only major difference in question types favoring experimental subjects was in the asking of verification questions. However, experimental subjects as a group asked many more questions than control subjects; means were 50.23 for experimentals and 32.67 for controls.

Suchman observes that the outcomes of the study are not conclusive, and that inquiry training must not be an isolated curriculum subject if it is to be successful in improving children's thinking. He also comments that the children's interests lie not in becoming more proficient inquirers but in finding out what the explanation is that causes the surprising event they witness on the screen. It might be added, in connection with the discussion earlier about general and specific training in thinking, that Suchman's experimental subjects were at a great disadvantage providing complete explanations of the phenomena they witnessed. Such explanations tend to hinge upon well-known physics laws and principles which are found in high school textbooks, but whose independent discovery by normal children of 11 or 12 is scarcely to be expected.

The Inquiry Training Program is instructive and interesting to us for at least two reasons:

1. It provides a sample of a science curriculum at the level of upper elementary school children which confronts them with real phenomena and demands explanations for them, in contrast to the typically puerile discourse of intermediate-grade science textbooks.

2. It illustrates the specificity of outcomes to be expected from training programs.

The crux of the training lay in the generation of disciplined questions. The one clear positive outcome of Suchman's study is that the children who received instruction and abundant practice became clearly and significantly more fluent in the asking of questions germane to the phenomena under study. This improved fluency did not, however, also lead to better ability to apply scientific principles or to construct basic explanations for the observations.

Solving Arithmetic Problems

Research papers and monographs on the topic of arithmetic word problems typically open with a recognition that children have difficulty solving such problems. If the author can believe what arithmetic teachers who have attended his courses through the years say, it is indeed the case that such problems represent an instructional challenge to the teacher, as well as a mathematical challenge to their pupils. In this section we will analyze the processes involved in the solution of word problems in arithmetic, consider what research has contributed to our knowledge of why certain problems are more difficult than others, and look at some efforts to improve children's performance. Finally, a modest and tentative proposal is made for the teaching of problem solving.

Since the recent excellent research by Suppes and his colleagues (Loftus & Suppes, 1972) will figure prominently in the discussion, let us begin with one of the simple problems they submitted to sixth-graders as a first illustration: "A bushel of corn weighs 56 pounds. How much do 44 bushels weigh?" At the simplest level we can say that the child must identify the unit (pounds) in which the answer is to be expressed. Since the total weight of 44 bushels is called for and the weight of one is given, his next step is to identify the correct arithmetic process, compute the product, and express the answer as 2,464 pounds, If the problem is to be solved correctly, the pupil must handle two basic tasks. One is to comprehend the relationship between "44 bushels" and "each bushel weighs 56 pounds". If the language is not interpreted as calling for multiplication, the problem will not be solved. The second task is to accomplish the computation correctly. Although that aspect is not of paramount concern to us, there are some points to be made later about pupils' approaches to computation and the need for teachers to diagnose pupils' behavior.

What makes arithmetic problems hard?

Loftus and Suppes (1972) have given probably the most comprehensive answer to that question to date. Their interest was in the structural variables that make problems hard or easy. Structural variables characterize individual problems and the relationships between individual problems, such as the structural similarities between two successive problems. Two classes of structural variables were investigated.

The first class of variables investigated are those that are either present or absent; for example, a problem either demands that conversions be made, or it does not. (A *conversion* is something like having to convert or change days to weeks in order to work the problem.) Other variables of this in or out variety that were examined by Loftus and Suppes are sequence, verbal clues, and order. *Sequence* refers to the relationships or similarities between sequential problems. The criterion for inclusion is whether the same or different arithmetic operations are involved in successive problems. *Verbal clues* constitute a small dictionary of terms which point to the operation to be used. Thus *and* denotes addition; *left* or some other comparative signifies subtraction, and so forth. The *order* variable asks whether numbers given in the problem enter into computations in the same order as they appear in the problem.

The second class of variables investigated by Loftus and Suppes includes those that assume a finite set of values, but in which the value is greater than 2. Such variables include the *length* of the problem (the number of words it contains), *operations* (addition, subtraction, multiplication, or division), the number of *steps* (if one has to add three numbers, and then find the average of them, the number of steps would be four, and the number of operations, two), and the problem's *depth*. This last variable comes from linguistic analysis in which depth is a measure of the embeddedness of terms in sentences. Theoretically the greater the depth, the more complex is the statement of the problem.

The Loftus and Suppes study is part of an extensive inquiry into the teaching of elementary mathematics via computers. For this study a group of sixth-graders from a school in an economically and socially disadvantaged region of the San Franscisco Bay area first received extended training in how to use the computer console to solve problems. Subsequently they were given a set of 100 arithmetic problems (a sample of which you read at the beginning of this section) which were solved over a period of several weeks. The analyses of interest here are those pertinent to the variables that render problems easier or more difficult for these children to solve. Five of the previously defined variables were found to contribute significantly to problem difficulty. They are sequence, operations, depth, length, and conversion. As the investigators interpret their findings,

> ... a word problem will be difficult if it differs from the problem type that preceded it, if its solution requires a large number of different operations, if its surface structure is complex, if it has a large number of words or if it requires a conversion of units. The predictive results of this analysis are rather impressive. (p. 541)

In a previous study in which the subjects were good problem solvers, a similar subset of variables turned out to determine problem difficulty. The variables were operations, sequence, and conversion. Loftus and Suppes regard the most suggestive findings of both studies to be the importance of the operations and sequence variables, which extend to the problem solving of pupils at both ends of the ability continuum.

> Whether students are bright or dull they are more likely to solve a problem correctly if it is similar to the problem that preceded it, or if its solution requires a small number of different operations. The implication is that many aspects of the internal processing done by students when they solve problems do not differ for children of differing mental ability. (p. 541)

Order was not a significant variable affecting problem difficulty by Loftus and Suppes, but it did influence the problem-solving success of third-graders studied by Rosenthal and Resnick (1974). They constructed problems so three dimensions could be identified and varied:

1. The order of mention of chronological events.
2. The identity of the unknown set or element of the problem. This could be the starting or ending set (that is, $5 + 2 = ?$, versus $? + 2 = 5$).
3. The type of verb associated with the change set. The verb expressed either a gain or loss, suggesting an initial equation involving addition or subtraction.

The last variable was not significant, but the other two were. When numbers were mentioned in the reverse order to that used in solution, problem difficulty increased. However, as Rosenthal and Resnick see it, the underlying variable that accounts for greater difficulty in the problems they constructed is to start with an unknown set. For third-graders at least, this seems to demand additional reading of the problem and more complex processing of information than when it is the ending set that is withheld.

Efforts to improve children's problem solving

Advice (often) and investigations (sometimes) about the improvement of children's performance with arithmetic problems date back as far as the recognition that problems are a problem. Riedesel (1969) reduced the results of 50 years of research on arithmetic problem solving to a short set of procedures that do or do not improve it. For example, despite the idea that computational skill is important in getting the right answers to problems, direct practice on computation does not improve the pupil's ability to reason or solve problems, a rather obvious point. In general, improvements have resulted when a pupil's motivation for working on problems has been kept high, the problems are at a level of difficulty commensurate with his or her current ability, and direct help is available as needed; for example, help in translating problems into mathematical statements or tape recordings to aid pupils who have reading problems.

Research workers have long been aware that problem-solving success depends upon the learner's ability to decode the language in which the problem is stated. Numerous studies have appeared through the years which have examined one or another aspect of language and problem solving. One type of study that has consistently demonstrated improvement in children's problem solving provides direct instruction in the vocabulary used in the problems. Among the more comprehensive studies of this kind is one by H. C. Johnson (1944) who worked with 28 seventh-grade arithmetic classes and their teachers. Over half the pupils were in experimental classes, and the smaller number served as controls. Johnson matched groups before the study and gave tests at three points during it. There was also a retention test three months later, and pupils' knowledge of arithmetic vocabulary which was not directly taught was also measured. In this way Johnson hoped to find out what the limits were of the instruction.

The experimental teaching was accomplished by the regular classroom teachers, which tends to increase the study's validity. Johnson had prepared worksheets to teach 60 of the words pupils would encounter during the 14 weeks of the experiment (a sample of the worksheet material is given in Figure 7.3). The teachers of all 28 classes agreed to teach five chapters of their common text. The instructional material was not extraordinary in conception, seeking only to teach basic meanings of arithmetic terms clearly. Experimental teachers agreed to spend several minutes each day (apparently only three to eight minutes were consumed daily on the average) with the material. Control pupils received only whatever instruction was supplied by their textbook.

Figure 7.3 *Example of material used to teach mathematical vocabulary to seventh-grade pupils*

Area refers to *surface*, and is measured in *square units*, such as square inches, square yards, etc.
　Perimeter means *distance around*, and refers to *length*. It is measured in inches, feet, miles, etc.
　Volume refers to the amount of *space*, or *contents*, or *capacity*. It is expressed in terms of cubic inches, cubic feet, etc.
　Exercises: Opposite each of the following, write *volume, area,* or *perimeter,* as the case may be:

(a) 350 square feet _____　(c) 3 square miles _____

(b) 40 yards _____　(d) 35 cubic inches _____

Tell whether each of the following refers to *volume, area,* or *perimeter*:

(a) Amount of molding for a picture frame _____

(b) Amount of wallpaper for a room _____

(c) Length of curbstone around a city block _____

(d) Amount of water in an aquarium _____

(e) Size of a state or county _____

(f) Truckload of sand _____

Source: H. C. Johnson (1944), p. 102.

　Results of tests given at three intervals during the experiment showed the experimental pupils to be significantly better in the directly taught arithmetic terms than the control pupils, but there were no reliable differences between the two groups on the transfer to similar but untaught words. Scores on the problem-solving tests were significantly higher for the experimental pupils after the first two intervals, but not the third. However, a retention test three months later continued to show significant gains for those pupils who had studied the worksheets, compared with those who had not. This study gives us reasonably good assurance that direct instruction in the arithmetic vocabulary which appears in conjunction with the problems pupils are to solve improves their problem-solving performance. Probably what happens is that the instructed students have a better conception of the terms than those without the instruction, which enables them to determine more often the correct process or processes to employ in solving a problem. For example, referring to

Figure 7.3, we can reason as follows. Pupils in the experimental group learned the meaning of *perimeter,* both as the distance around something, with reference to length, and by means of practical examples: the amount of molding needed for a picture frame, or the extent of curbstone around a city block. When they encounter a problem that asks for perimeter, they can translate the term at two levels. One is as the length around an area, such as the particular problem calls for. Or, if the problem asks a question such as "How much fence will be needed to go around the garden?" they can translate this into perimeter. This second translation of the term constitutes a check that they will make the appropriate computations.

Do contemporary texts do a better job of teaching vocabulary than they did over 30 years ago, at the time of Johnson's study? Although a definite answer cannot be given, there are indications that teacher efforts of the same kind made by Johnson's teachers would still be beneficial. Twenty years after Johnson's study, Vanderlinde (1964) conducted a very similar investigation, except that the effective span of time was almost an entire school year, and the participants were fifth-graders. The teachers of the experimental classes taught a quantitative vocabulary of 242 words to their pupils during the course of the school year. Compared to children in the control classes, they improved significantly in problem solving and in knowledge of mathematics concepts, but the differences did *not* extend to either vocabulary or arithmetic achievement in general. One other study is pertinent. Olander and Ehmer (1971) tried to determine whether intermediate-grade pupils of 1968 knew more or less arithmetic vocabulary than their 1930 forebears. This comparison is difficult to make because the vocabulary in use in 1968 was considerably different from that of 1930. However, the fourth- and fifth-graders of 1968 did somewhat better on the 1930 vocabulary than the pupils of that era had done, while the sixth-graders of the recent era scored slightly lower than the 1930 sample had.

The role of structure in problem solving

Despite the clear effect of instruction in vocabulary, we would expect even greater benefits to emerge in programs which stress such tasks as translation of the ordinary language of the problem into mathematical statements and which are aimed at teaching pupils to identify and comprehend relationships between elements of a problem. Surprisingly little evidence is available on these points, and, for one reason or another, the existing information is inconclusive. A study by Wilson (1967) at the elementary school level examined one aspect of these concerns. He taught problem solving to groups of children for nine weeks. One group was

246   Learning and Thinking

taught a problem structure which emphasized the actions and events of the problem. A second and more successful experimental group was instructed in what Wilson termed a *wanted-given* problem structure. The training consisted of teaching children (1) to recognize the wanted-given structure of the problem, (2) to express the relationship in an equation, and (3) to compute the answer by using the operation indicated in the equation. The control group received practice in solving problems, but no special training. At the end of the nine-week instructional period, and on a retention test nine weeks after that, pupils who had learned the wanted-given analysis outscored others to a significant degree.

At the secondary school level, Kennedy, Eliot, and Krulee (1970) studied the error patterns of algebra students. Their initial hypothesis was that the more able algebra students (those in the advanced class) would be superior in their identification of language relationships in problem statements. This did not turn out to be the case. Students from the average class did this equally well. The difference that was discovered between them was the better ability of the advanced class members to identify necessary logical or physical inferences in the problem statements. This is an interesting observation that is similar to Paige and Simon's (1966) conclusion that the better problem solvers in their college and high school samples clearly recognized the conservation requirements of the problems and their implications. However, the students in the study by Kennedy, Eliot, and Krulee, even the less able ones, were well above the average of high school students in the population at large. It may be that students of average or below-average ability would benefit by improved problem solving from instruction that helps them to identify and work out the meanings of mathematical relationships.

Teachers of arithmetic and mathematics are, of course, not without ideas which they have developed through the rigors of daily experience with pupils. An interesting example has been formulated by Dahmus (1970); he calls it the DPPC method, which stands for "direct, pure, piecemeal, complete." The key feature of the method is its attempt to guide the student through a concrete translation of all the facts in the problem. Since this method might well be a preliminary to the analysis of relationships, empirical evidence bearing upon its effectiveness or that of similar methods would be extremely valuable.

Dahmus's instructions to pupils are explicit: They are to translate the English of the problem into a series of mathematical statements. Operations are not to be performed, each element is to be translated as it occurs, and all facts and ideas are to be translated. The following examples from Dahmus's report show how students are instructed in the method (a translation is inserted beneath the portion of the problem it represents).

1. The sum of 6 and a number is the same as the difference of 32 and the
number. Find the number.

6 plus n = $32 - n$

$? = n$

4. Mark is twice as old as John. In two years the sum of their ages will be 5 times as much as John's age was 4 years ago. How old is each now?

$M = 2 \times J$ (M plus 2) plus (J plus 2)

$5 \times (J - 4)$

$M = ?$ $J = ?$

Pace (1961) studied the relationships between children's understanding of basic processes and their ability to do arithmetic problems. Two classes of fourth-grade pupils were matched with respect to chronological age, IQ, and arithmetic achievement. One was an experimental, the other a control class. The basic experiment continued over eight weeks of the school year. Children in both classes were given 24 special sets of problems at the rate of three sets each week. The basic treatment difference was the emphasis in the experimental class on discussion, such as: "What must you do to solve this problem?" "Why do that?" Pupils in the control class just worked the problems.

Results at the end of eight weeks showed that children in the experimental class solved significantly more problems than they were capable of prior to the study, but the control pupils did not. However, another test administered eight weeks *after* the end of the training showed that children from both the experimental and the control class were solving significantly more problems than they had been able to do eight weeks earlier. Pace built in a demanding and productive technique during the course of her experiment. She interviewed children from time to time during the experimental eight weeks to determine how well they understood the work they were doing. These interviews showed that the abundant amounts of problem-solving practice helped to improve the understanding of control subjects, but the impact on the understanding of the experimental children was even greater.

Of course, one reason this study is of some practical importance is because of its close correspondence to what goes on daily in the lives of fourth-grade children and teachers. The problems were especially constructed for the experiment, but they are similar to ordinary arithmetic problems. (The one criticism which might be made in this regard is that the problem examples given in Pace's research report seem quite simple for fourth-grade pupils.)

The Pace study makes some excellent points about training children in problem solving. First, just providing many problem-solving opportunities for subjects may be the most important thing to do. Furthermore, pupils should be allowed to find and to use their own procedures to solve the problems. Ordinarily each problem can be solved in a variety of ways. The use of discussion to force children to clarify and structure their problem-solving practices was an additional help, as judged by the significant differences in experimental results over control subjects. An important but unanswered question is whether the children in the experimental class developed or abstracted any more general principles and procedures for solving these classes of problems which they are able to apply at a later time.

Need for clinical and diagnostic studies of problem solving

Some years ago Bloom and Broder (1950) compared the problem-solving processes of college students at the University of Chicago who were successful and effective in problem solving with those of other students who were in serious academic difficulty. Despite the fact that their work did not deal explicitly with mathematics problems, their approach has much to say about how programs of remedial problem solving might operate. The investigators gave good and poor problem solvers a series of problems to solve in which they were asked to vocalize. This permitted a written record to be maintained which probably was a reasonably accurate representation of students' actual processes of thinking as they went about solving the problems. Bloom and Broder abstracted from the protocols four major categories which characterize the differences between the effective and the incompetent problem solvers:

1. Understanding of the nature of the problem.
2. Understanding of the ideas contained in the problem.
3. General approach to the solution of the problems.
4. Attitude toward the solution of the problems.

With respect to *understanding the nature of the problem,* the students differed on two major points. First, the unsuccessful students frequently failed to comprehend or to follow the directions given in the problem or to be guided by the constraints that the directions tried to impose. For example, if a problem says, "Assume for purposes of this problem that the following is true," the learner who fails to make the assumption will be unlikely to solve the problem correctly. Second, the unsuccessful students sometimes reasoned their way well through a problem and arrived at a solution, but along the way they changed the conditions that were stated in the original problem. Consequently, the problem they solved was different from the one they were given.

Failure to *understand the ideas contained in the problem* was a major source of difficulty for some unsuccessful students. Naturally we all may encounter problems which demand technical information and modes of thinking that are foreign to us. However, the problems used by Bloom and Broder, although they were drawn from one or another subject matter field, were not terribly technical; that is, highly specialized training in a given area was not mandatory for successful solutions. At the same time, it was true that the less successful students had lower levels of general and specific knowledge than the more successful solvers. They also were less often able to examine the language of a problem and say, "I don't know exactly how that would work, but I am acquainted with *x*, which should be similar, and therefore. . . ." The poorer students were more disposed to look at a problem, decide they did not know the answer to it, and abandon their effort. The better students consistently searched their memories for things they *did* know that might be of value to them in solving new and unfamiliar problems.

There were three dimensions along which the good and poor solvers differed in their *approach to problems*. These are:

1. *The extent of thought given to the problem.* The better students invest more time and energy in planning their attack upon the problem.

2. *Systematic analysis of the problem.* Again, the less effective students tend to assume that problems have pat solutions; if they are unable to see the solution quickly, they abandon the problem. The more successful students are more systematic in their approach; they subdivide the problem into manageable elements and apply their knowledge to the smaller parts.

3. *Completion of a process of reasoning.* The less successful problem solvers tended to be more distractible; extraneous words in the problem could divert them from their original plan for solution. Although they frequently began with an adequate approach to the problem, they were much less likely than their successful counterparts to follow through on the line of reasoning with which they began.

Finally, the two groups differed heavily in their *attitude toward the solutions of problems*. One group expected to achieve little success; the other clearly felt their chances of solving new problems were good. All these factors no doubt worked together to lead to success or failure. Personal biases also entered into the thinking of the unsuccessful solvers more often than they did with the other students. A student might comprehend the correct answer, but, because he disagreed with it or favored another solution, the correct one was rejected.

As Duncan (1959) pointed out in his exhaustive survey and analysis of problem-solving research through the 1950s, Bloom and Broder offered a prototype for the study of problem solving that, unfortunately, has received little further attention. The potential benefits for the educational psychology of learning and for classroom instruction that could accrue from systematic efforts to have school children "talk" their way through problems of many kinds, including perhaps arithmetic and algebra, seem well worth the effort involved. Similarly, a technique developed by Rimoldi (1955, 1960) and used by him and others could be easily modified to reveal similarities and differences in the problem-solving behavior of good and poor solvers in arithmetic. Rimoldi's technique consists of presenting the subject with a problem. His first applications were for medical diagnosis made by students in medical school. The subject is confronted with an array of cards with a question on the visible side of each. The student is free to ask any of the questions he thinks will help him to solve the problem. When a card is turned over, the answer is provided, and a record can be kept of the questions the student asked, their total number, and the sequence in which they occurred. Our knowledge of the educational psychology of learning is sufficient, coupled with clinical diagnostic methods such as the two briefly described here, to discover patterns that will reliably differentiate between good and poor arithmetic problem solvers, and so lead to effective instructional programs to correct existing deficiencies. This is one important area of school learning in which there no longer seems to be a justification for lamenting the continuing difficulties and lack of achievement of pupils.

Questions for Review and Discussion

1. Identify several problems which you ask students to solve or which you have been asked to solve as a student. Evaluate them against the four criteria for classroom problems that were stated in the opening pages of the chapter.

2. One of the interesting aspects of Duncker's work in problem solving was his technique of asking research subjects to talk aloud about their efforts at solution. Would this be a source of information for you as a teacher to understand students' difficulties in solving problems? How could you arrange to have sessions in which individuals talk their way through a problem? Sometimes teachers tape-record such problem-solving episodes so they can analyze a student's cognitive processes at leisure and without the on-the-spot pressure of the classroom.

3. How much general direction or instruction about how to solve problems can be given effectively to students? How much guidance of problem solving is specific to the content of a subject, and even to the particulars of a problem on which one is working?

4. You have undoubtedly found yourself at one time or another falling under the spell of what Luchins labels *Einstellung*. Can you think of tasks commonly taught in school that make students susceptible to such intellectual blindness? How can a teacher help students avoid such mechanical approaches to problem solving?

5. Our discussion of Suchman's Inquiry Training Program again stresses the impact of curriculum materials upon the approach to learning which can conveniently be taken in the classroom. Do you find the results reported at the end of the experimental year surprising? Do you think they reflect failure of the program to achieve its goals, or evidence of the difficulty with which intellectual behavior is changed? Or something else?

6. If you teach arithmetic or mathematics, try your hand at estimating the relative difficulty of problems à la Loftus and Suppes. The studies of H. C. Johnson (1944) and of Vanderlinde (1964) both showed positive effects of special lessons in arithmetic vocabulary on children's arithmetic problem solving. But note that the effects are limited. What are the limits, and why do they occur?

7. How could the diagnostic techniques, such as those used by Bloom and Broder, or by Rimoldi, be adapted for use in an average classroom? What benefits could be expected from successful adaptations of such procedures?

Readings for Further Reflection

Introductory level
Davis, Gary A. *Psychology of Problem Solving: Theory and Practice.*
   New York: Basic Books, 1973.

Davis brings together reviews of two distinct bodies of research literature. The first is a review of psychological theory and research on problem solving; the second deals with research and training programs from education and industry. Much of the research that Davis places under the heading of training is reviewed in this book in the final chapter on creativity.

DeBono, Edward. *The Five Day Course in Thinking.* New York: Basic
   Books, 1967.

The title is a bit misleading in that the book contains not *one* five-day course in thinking, but three. The first deals with insight thinking, and the other two are devoted to sequential and to strategic thinking. This is a do-it-yourself book; each problem requires a few simple props and a considerable amount of thinking. I have from time to time used one of De Bono's easier problems as a means of introducing a unit on problem solving to classes of college students or teachers. The activities are absorbing and worthwhile. DeBono's orientation is to encourage what he calls lateral in contrast to conventional vertical thinking.

Advanced level

Kohler, Wolfgang. *The Mentality of Apes.* New York: Humanities Press, 1925.

This is the classic book on animal problem solving, written about Kohler's extensive experiments with chimpanzees while he was interned on Tenerife during World War I. The struggles of the chimpanzees to solve problems leading to food are probably the most often cited studies of problem solving in the history of psychology.

Wason, Peter C., and Johnson-Laird, Philip N. *Psychology of Reasoning: Structure and Content.* London: P. T. Batsford, Ltd., 1972.

This volume is a report of numerous investigations of human thinking conducted by the authors. The studies are tied closely to standard topics of logic, such as deductive reasoning, induction, and syllogistic reasoning. The experiments described are interesting, and many of them are related to daily problems of reasoning, as in the chapter on understanding of regulations. The writing is good, but the book on the whole, is technical and fairly difficult. If you want a more penetrating look at the psychology of thinking, oriented to research methodology, it is an excellent volume.

References

Ackerman, Walter I., & Levin, Harry. Effects of training in alternative solution on subsequent problem solving. *Journal of Educational Psychology,* 1958, *49,* 239–244.

Aiken, Lewis R., Jr. Language factors in learning mathematics. *Review of Educational Research,* 1972, *42,* 359–385.

Bloom, Benjamin S., & Broder, Lois J. Problem-solving processes of college students: An exploratory investigation. *Supplementary Educational Monographs,* No. 73, Chicago: The University of Chicago Press, 1950.

Corman, Bernard R. The effect of varying amounts and kinds of information as guidance in problem solving. *Psychological Monographs,* 1957, *71* (Whole No. 431).

Covington, Martin V., Crutchfield, Richard S., Davies, Lillian, & Olton, Robert M., Jr. *The Productive Thinking Program: A course in learning to think.* Columbus, Ohio: Charles E. Merrill Publishing Co., 1972.

Dahmus, Maurice E. How to teach verbal problems. *School Science and Mathematics,* 1970, *70,* 121–138.

De Bono, Edward. *The five day course in thinking.* New York: Basic Books, 1967.

Dewey, John. *How we think.* Boston: D. C. Heath Co., 1933

Dewey, John. *How we think* (new ed.). Boston: D. C. Heath & Co., 1933.

Duncan, Carl P. Recent research in human problem solving. *Psychological Bulletin,* 1959, *56,* 397–429.

Duncker, Karl. On problem solving. *Psychological Monographs,* 1945 (Whole No. 270).

Gagné, Robert M., & Smith, Ernest C., Jr. A study of the effects of verbalization on problem solving. *Journal of Experimental Psychology,* 1962, *63,* 12–18.

Haselrud, G. M., and Meyers, Shirley. The transfer value of given and individually derived principles. *Journal of Educational Psychology,* 1958, *49,* 293–298.

Hendrix, Gertrude. A new clue to transfer of training. *Elementary School Journal,* 1947, *48,* 197–208.

Johnson, Donald M. Solution of anagrams. *Psychological Bulletin,* 1966, *66,* 371–384.

Johnson, Harry C. The effect of instruction in mathematical vocabulary upon problem solving in arithmetic. *Journal of Educational Research,* 1944, *38,* 97–110.

Kennedy, George, Eliot, John, & Krulee, Gilbert. Error patterns in problem solving formulations. *Psychology in the Schools,* 1970, *7,* 93–99.

Kersh, Bert Y. The adequacy of "meaning" as an explanation for the superiority of learning by independent discovery. *Journal of Educational Psychology,* 1958, *49,* 282–292.

Kersh, Bert Y. The motivating effect of learning by directed discovery. *Journal of Educational Psychology,* 1962, *53,* 65–71.

Loftus, Elizabeth F., & Suppes, Patrick. Structural variables that determine problem-solving difficulty in computer-assisted instruction. *Journal of Educational Psychology,* 1972, *63,* 531–542.

Luchins, Abraham S. Mechanization in problem solving—the effect of Einstellung. *Psychological Monographs,* 1942, *54* (Whole No. 248).

Maltzman, Irving, Eisman, Eugene, & Brooks, Lloyd O. Some relationships between methods of instruction, personality, variable, and problem solving behavior. *Journal of Educational Psychology,* 1956, *47,* 71-78.

Miller, K. M. Einstellung, rigidity, intelligence, and teaching methods. *British Journal of Educational Psychology,* 1957, *27,* 127-134.

Morrisett, Lloyd P., Jr., & Hovland, Carl I. A comparison of three varieties of training in human problem solving. *Journal of Experimental Psychology,* 1959, *58,* 52-55.

Newell, Allen, & Simon, Herbert A. *Human problem solving.* Englewood Cliffs, N.J.: Prentice-Hall, 1972.

Niemark, Edith D., & Santa, John L. Thinking and concept attainment. *Annual Review of Psychology, 1975* (vol. 26, pp. 172-206).

Olander, Herbert T., & Ehmer, Charles L. What pupils know about vocabulary in mathematics—1930 and 1968. *Elementary School Journal,* 1971, *71,* 361-367.

Olton, Robert M., & Crutchfield, Richard S. Developing the skills of productive thinking. In P. Mussen, J. Langer, & M. J. Covington (Eds.), *New directions in developmental psychology.* New York: Holt, Rinehart, & Winston, 1969.

Pace, Angela. Understanding and the ability to solve problems. *Arithmetic Teacher,* 1961, *8,* 226-233.

Paige, Jeffrey M., & Simon, Herbert A. Cognitive processes in solving algebra word problems. In Benjamin Kleinmuntz (Ed.), *Problem solving: Research method and theory* (pp. 51-119). New York: John Wiley & Sons, 1966.

Riedesel, C. Alan. Problem solving: Some suggestions from research. *Arithmetic Teacher,* 1969, *16,* 54-58.

Rimoldi, H. J. A. A technique for the study of problem solving. *Educational and Psychological Measurement,* 1955, *15,* 450-461.

Rimoldi, H. J. A. Problem solving as a process. *Educational and Psychological Measurement,* 1960, *20,* 449-460.

Rosenthal, Daniel J. A., & Resnick, Lauren B. Children's solution processes in arithmetic word problems. *Journal of Educational Psychology,* 1974, *66,* 817-825.

Suchman, J. Richard. The elementary school training program in scientific inquiry. Washington, D.C.: U.S. Office of Education, 1962.

Suchman, J. Richard. Inquiry training: Building skills for autonomous discovery. *Merrill-Palmer Quarterly,* 1961, 7, 147-169. Reprinted in Paul E. Torrance & William F. White, *Issues and Advances in Educational Psychology,* p. 321. Itasca, Ill.: F. E. Peacock Publishers, 1969.

Szekely, L. Productive processes in learning and thinking. *Acta Psychologia*, 1950, *7*, 388–407.

Vanderlinde, Louis F. Does the study of quantitative vocabulary improve problem solving? *Elementary School Journal*, 1964, *65*, 143–152.

Wardrop, James L., & others. The development of productive thinking skills in fifth grade children. *Journal of Experimental Education*, 1969, *37*, 67–77.

Wilson, John W. The role of structure in verbal problem solving. *Arithmetic Teacher*, 1967, *14*, 486–497.

Chapter 8

The Pupil as Thinker: Creative Thinking

Every spring I teach a course at Washington University, designed for classroom teachers, in which the major topics conform roughly to the final three chapters of this book. The pupil as thinker is studied in three aspects: critical thinking (Chapter 6), problem solving (Chapter 7), and creative thinking (this chapter). Discussions of creativity usually center upon its measurement, the nature of creative acts, and means for stimulating and nurturing it. Study of this skill work usually has been *about* creativity and has fallen short of active participation in the process of creation. However, as this chapter was being written, I gave the class the following assignment:

> Create something—anything you like, but do it in an area that is new for you. If you paint for fun on weekends, write a poem. If you write short stories for relaxation, sculpt something. When you have finished your product, write a one-page essay about your reactions to the process and your accomplishment. Then select one individual—husband or wife, friend, colleague; it doesn't matter—and let him or her react to your creation. Then write one more page on which you reflect upon that reaction.

A deadline one month later was set, and an agreement was made that those who wished to share their reactions would have an opportunity to do so. Although the assignment was required, no grade was to be given, nor would the instructor evaluate the creative products. When the day for sharing the experience with others arrived, all the students except one participated.

What, if anything, the students learned from this exercise would be difficult to say. The author learned a great deal, some of which is worth sharing. First, several of the teachers in the group reported that the afternoon the assignment was given, it struck terror into their hearts. This was something different and challenging. Would they be able to do it? There was no way I could detect this emotion from their reactions at the time; pens and pencils glided across paper, scribbling notes, in the dispassionate manner students have as they play "please the professor." Then the reactions to exposing their creations to the gaze of another person emerged. Because they are intelligent and mature adults, teachers in their own right, I reasoned that they would share their products with someone else in a spirit of disinterested observation in the reaction.

Excerpts from several of the teachers' essays reveal just how wrong that assumption was. One said:

> ... I visited a friend whom I consider to be of high intelligence and good taste. When I showed her my sculpture she asked which one of my (very young) daughters had carved it. This confirmed my opinion of her mind and taste.
>
> My reaction to my friend's comment was one of intense discouragement. I didn't think my confidence level could go much lower while I was working on the project, but this brought it down even more.

Another student received favorable reaction but was not reassured: "In the back of my mind is the gnawing fear she is not giving a truthful opinion." An intense expression of apprehension about coming face to face with the evaluation of another was this statement by a teacher who had written a moving and revealing poem: "I could not help but feel a tremendous fear that a very deep and personal part of me was being exposed; my defenses would be worthless, for this person was viewing my innermost thoughts."

Several of the teachers' reactions were of the order, "Who is he to criticize my work?" "I know what's wrong with it; I don't need him to tell me." No one seemed indifferent to or emotionally neutral to the experience of opening himself or herself to the reaction of another person. The teachers' reactions reveal an overwhelming feeling of sensitivity on the part of their critics, of anxiety to avoid hurt feelings and desire to offer positive support to the amateur creator. The unspoken question fairly rang out in the classroom: "Are we, as teachers, equally sensitive to the feelings of our students when they offer their creative products to us?"

It is of interest that not a single student referred in a positive way to his own creativity. (We can anticipate later discussion to the extent of saying that highly creative people are very confident of their talent and not unwilling to acknowledge it, at least when asked.) Any number of the students, on the contrary, reported that they do not consider themselves to be creative. Typical of the feeling expressed was this evaluation from a preschool teacher:

> This entire project was painful. I felt totally inadequate the whole time. I've given very little thought to it, but I've never thought of myself as a "creative person." I can't ever remember being encouraged to "do something different," "take a chance with an idea," "be creative," by parents, teachers, or bosses.

These people did not think of themselves as creative, but they are bright, and they know it. Furthermore, most of them recognized and commented on the uniqueness of an opportunity or a challenge to behave in a creative way. This brought home to me, with some dramatic impact, the validity of arguments that creative thinking is seen to be something different and apart from our everyday lives as students, teachers, and people. These same teachers would bristle at an insinuation that they do not think in a critical way or that they are unable to cope effectively with problems, but they plead "no contest" when they are pressed to be creative.

This chapter entertains a series of questions about creative thinking.

1. What does "creativity" mean? What do educational psychologists refer to when they talk about creativity? Can it be measured? What are some of the ways to do it? Can teachers achieve measures of creativity on their pupils?
2. What is the creative person like? How does he see the world? What sets him apart from the rest of people? How smart is he?
3. Psychologically, what happens when an individual engages in a creative act? Is the process the same for everyone, the gifted painter as well as the school child struggling with a creative writing assignment?
4. Can the school do very much about making people creative? Does it matter what kind of social environment or "climate" the teacher attempts to set? Are there specialized programs or curricula that contribute to children's creative thinking? What kinds of training programs or techniques have been found most successful?

The chapter ends with a consideration of reasonable classroom goals in the area of creativity. The position that creativity is a rare and qualitatively different trait is considered in opposition to the more environmental and teachable orientation that predominates throughout most of the chapter.

The Concept of Creativity

The attention of psychologists was dramatically drawn to the topic of creativity in 1950 by Joy P. Guilford. Guilford pointed out that conceptions of human intelligence have been unduly narrow in focusing principally upon factors such as memory, evaluation, and ability to reason toward a specific and predetermined answer to a problem. A major lack in those conceptions is the recognition of divergent thinking, the kind that follows different directions. This is of major importance in creative thinking. By the close of the 1950s Guilford had elaborated his conception of human intelligence to the point of presenting a theoretical model of the Structure of Intellect. In the Structure of Intellect, every factor is independent, but some clusters resemble each other enough to permit classification. The Structure of Intellect represents intersections of three such bases; according to intellectual abilities or types of intellectual *operations*, according to *content*, and the types of outcomes or *products* that emerge. Five types of operations or abilities intersect with four types of content and six classes of products to yield the cube depicted in Figure 8.1, the Structure of Intellect. A total of 120 intellectual factors is posited.

For purposes of our discussion of creative thinking, the slice of factors associated with divergent thinking in this model is of paramount importance. Its unique feature is the production of a variety of responses. The breadth of the divergent thinking factors can be seen from the examples that have been incorporated into Table 8.1. You may find it stimulating to ponder your own responses to the sample tests.

The basic divergent-thinking factors central to creativity, then, are *originality, fluency, flexibility*, and *elaboration*. (Note that for Guilford, originality is equated with certain flexibility factors. Refer to Table 8.1.) There are other factors which lie outside the divergent category and which are also important. One of these, evaluative in nature, is *sensitivity to problems*. The creative person tends to perceive inadequacies in products or the incompleteness of a painting or story and to be restless until the deficiency is corrected. His uncreative sister or brother may or may not exhibit awareness and will almost surely lack a drive to repair or alter the existing situation. Guilford also stresses the importance of memory factors in creative thinking. Good memory in itself is no guarantee of creative ability, but the original thinker who has a large store of information is in a strong position to think creatively. Others have also recognized the importance of memory in creative thinking. Mednick (1962), whose associative theory of creativity stresses the ability to tie together superficially unrelated ideas by means of remote associations, notes that the greater the array of experiences the learner has had, that is, the larger the

260   **Learning and Thinking**

FIGURE 8.1
Structure of intellect model

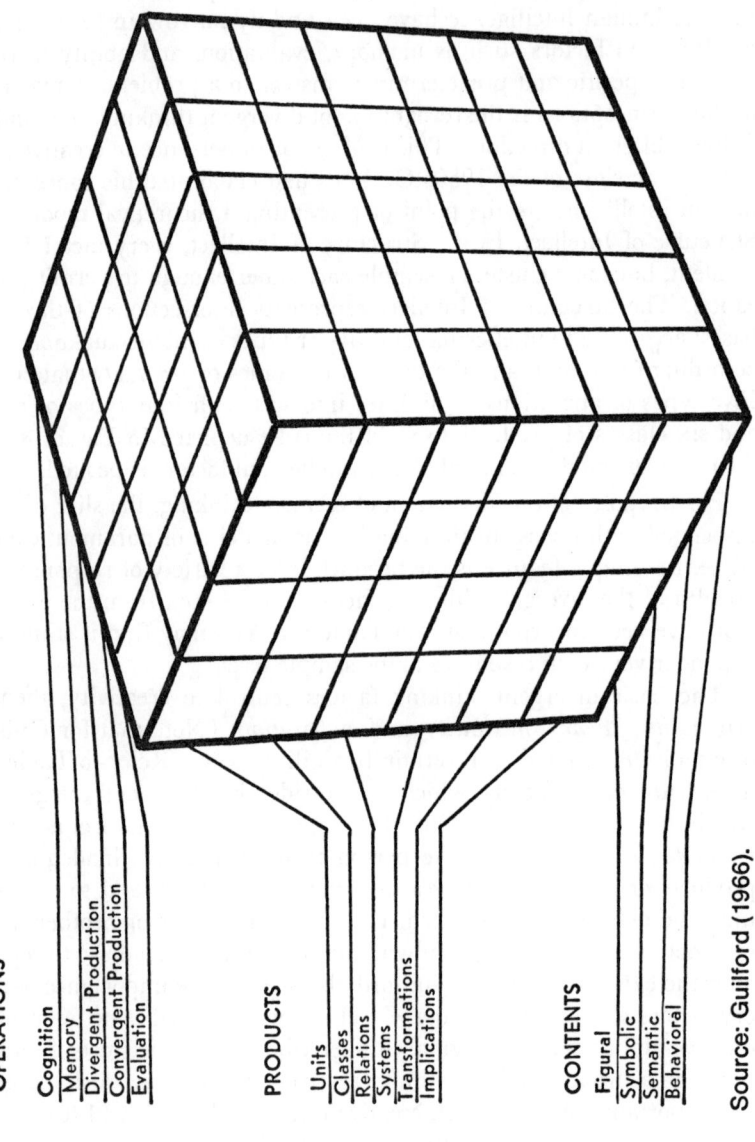

OPERATIONS
Cognition
Memory
Divergent Production
Convergent Production
Evaluation

PRODUCTS
Units
Classes
Relations
Systems
Transformations
Implications

CONTENTS
Figural
Symbolic
Semantic
Behavioral

Source: Guilford (1966).

TABLE 8.1
Divergent-thinking factors involved in creative thinking

Factors	Sample tests
Fluency factors	
Ideational fluency—the rate of generation of a quantity of ideas	List objects that are round and edible. List all things you can think of that are solid, flexible, and colored.
Associational fluency—the completion of relationships. May also apply to the construction of analogy	List words that mean about the same as "good." List words that mean about the opposite of "hard."
Expressional fluency—the ability to construct sentences	Write as many four-word sentences as possible using the same initial letters, without repeating any words. Use these letters: W____ c____ e____ n____.
Flexibility factors	
Spontaneous flexibility—the ability to shift classes of responses without direction to do so	List all the uses you can think of for a common brick. (Score is only for the number of classes; e.g., *build* something, *drive* a nail, *grind* up for red powder.)
Adaptive flexibility—originality is interpreted to be adaptive flexibility with verbal material	Plot titles. Subject hears a very short story and then is to make up as many titles for the story as he can. Commonplace titles contribute to score for ideational fluency. Responses rated as "clever" are scored for originality.
Elaboration—production of a variety of implications	Given the bare outline of a plan, the subject is asked to produce the detailed steps required to make it work.

Source: Guilford (1962).

number of associations he has had an opportunity to make, the greater the chance that an appropriate but remote relationship will be achieved. Guilford has also made clear his belief that instruction can be useful in stimulating people's creativity and in assisting them to make the best possible use of the abilities they possess. This, of course, is an issue that will occupy our attention through much of this chapter.

The Torrance Tests of Creative Thinking

Probably the best known effort to measure creativity is that of E. Paul Torrance (1963, 1965, 1966, 1972). Work on these tests continued over a span of a decade and resulted in the middle 1960s in the publication of two types of tests, one verbal, the other figural. Both tests emerge from a single conception of creativity, and both attempt to measure the same four variables. Torrance's definition of creativity emphasizes sensitivity to the existence of problems, awareness that a gap needs to be filled. The creative person generates multiple ideas or hypotheses about the solution to problems or the filling in of gaps. Torrance's critics claim that his conception is narrowly biased toward scientific productivity and takes little account of the abilities demanded for creativity in other areas, such as music and the fine arts.

Although both test types have alternate forms, only one of each will be described. The figural test, called Thinking Creatively with Pictures, consists of three subtests or activities. In the first, Picture Construction, the student is given a green egg-shaped object made of construction paper and told to locate it anywhere he chooses on the page of his test booklet. It is to serve as part of the picture he is then to draw. Instructions stress drawing an idea that "nobody else will think of." The second activity, Picture Completion, confronts the student with ten apparently randomly drawn combinations of lines. The task is to complete pictures incorporating each of the given configurations. In Part 3 of the test, called Parallel Lines, 30 pairs of vertical parallel lines are to be converted into separate drawings, and the learner is to avoid repeating himself.

The verbal test, called Thinking Creatively with Words, is quite different. The first three parts, labeled Ask and Guess Activities, engage the learner in constructing hypotheses, causes, and consequences. These activities are clearly related to productive thinking in scientific areas. A fourth activity is Product Improvement. Either a drawing or a model of a stuffed toy elephant is provided, and the learner is asked to indicate how it could be improved so it would be more fun for children to play with. Other activities, Unusual Uses and Unusual Questions, are also closely derived from Guilford's uses of a brick test. Torrance asks us to generate all the uses we can think of for either a tin can or a cardboard box, and subsequently to ask all the questions we can think of about the same object. The final part of the test is a Just Suppose Activity. For example, the student may see a sketch of clouds with strings attached to them, descending toward the ground. He is told this is a pretty unlikely situation, but just suppose clouds did have strings. What would all the consequences of the phenomenon be? Torrance inserted this task to generate more spontaneous responses and to engage children's interest in particular. He argues that creative people enjoy the playfulness of an improbable situation, whereas the uncreative reject such a task on the grounds of its unreality or absurdity.

Each part of the test has a ten-minute time limit, and, with a brief interval between sections for directions and questions, it is possible to administer the figural test within about 40 minutes. On another day, to complete the battery, the verbal test can be taken in about the same length of time. The format of the instrument, together with its strict time limits, tends to stress its test properties, yet most people contend that creative responses cannot be hurried and that testing situations inhibit creativity. With elementary school children, very different outcomes on one section of the test resulted when it was administered in school under the typical time constraints, compared with an occasion when the children were allowed 24 hours in which to add any items they wished.

Torrance's conceptualization of creativity is clearly related to Guilford's. His tests are scored for originality, fluency, flexibility, and elaboration. Since elaboration scores do not correlate well with scores on the other factors (Crockenberg, 1972), and since elaboration seems to be trivial in creative thinking, we shall dismiss it from further consideration. Originality lies at the heart of the creative act. To be original, a response or a product must be rare or unique, but it must also be pertinent to the situation. The latter criterion can help us to discriminate between true originality and drivel. If we ask a man what follows today, and he tells us "airplanes" or "apples," we may have lunacy, but if he writes, "Tomorrow and tomorrow and tomorrow creeps in this petty pace to the last syllable of recorded time," we have poetry. Originality demands a relationship between the answer given and the issue or use for which it was originated. (This leaves unresolved the fact that your contemporaries may be too time and place bound to recognize your originality, which must remain to be discovered by future generations.)

How to score the Torrance Test or any test of creative thinking presents problems. Since for the most part, divergent responses are solicited, how can a scoring key be worked out? To do this, the psychologist makes good use of the statistical frequency with which various responses occur. This is particularly true in scoring the originality of ideas, but the concept is also applied to measuring other factors as well.

If you produce idea A, let us say, and it turns out that 10 percent or more of other people produce the same idea, you would not receive credit for an original idea. If, however, you also produce idea Z, which occurs to few other people, then your response is considered original. Although conceptually this seems to be clear enough, there are in fact two major difficulties with the approach. One of these is the nature of the norming sample, the people who took the test in the beginning and from whose performance inferences are made about originality. If the norming group is somehow a biased sample, it can happen that subsequent responses are scored as original when, in fact, they are not. The second problem is how to deal with a rare but inappropriate response. Torrance developed the concept of "creative strength" to handle this problem. The scorer makes a judgment whether the response shows evidence of a high level of intellectual energy or whether it is simply a superficial and indifferent response. The idea of creative strength allows the scorer to lower originality scores, despite the uniqueness of the response, if the second criterion is not met. This approach presumably works well, since reported reliability of scoring on the test is very high.

Torrance has continuously attempted to study the validity of his own tests, and he has reported upon a range of short-term as well as long-term validity studies. Only the longest and most prodigious effort at validation will be cited here. In 1959 all students then attending the University of Minnesota High School (grades 7 through 12) took the Torrance Tests of Creative Thinking. Several other measures were taken at about the same time. One was called Inventive Level, which follows the criteria for patents laid down by the United States Patent Office; another was a measure of IQ. The students as a whole were bright high achievers whose parents were successful professionals or business people. Mean IQ for the sample was 118, and achievement averaged at the 84th percentile. Other measures included peer ratings of creativity and grade point averages in high school.

The most recent study of the tests' validity was done in 1971, or after 12 years, when the former students ranged from 25 to 31 years of age. Torrance and his associates gathered information from them about a variety of creative activities; for example, scientific papers published, books or poems written, and prizes awarded for scientific or artistic contributions. Responses to these inquiries were subdivided into three categories: quantity of creative products, quality of the products, and aspiration, which is an estimate of the degree of creativity demanded for accomplishment of one's aspirations. Presumably more creativity enters into earning a doctorate in experimental physics than in being a short-order cook.

For the 12-year validity study, six measures taken in 1959 were correlated separately for men and for women with the three creative categories described above. The six measures were those for fluency, flexibility, originality, and elaboration from the Torrance tests, plus inventive level and IQ. This generated 18 correlation coefficients for each sex subsample. For the men, all 18 of the coefficients were significant at the .01

level. One immediate and interesting interpretation of this result is that the IQ score from 1959 was a significant predictor of early adult creative achievement. IQ was weakest as a predictor of the quantity of creative output. The best predictors for men were originality and inventive level.

The results for the sample of women are less clear cut. IQ is not as highly correlated for the women with creative output as for the men. Inventive level and originality, although yielding the highest overall correlations, are lower than they were for the male sample. Some of the most salient coefficients have been listed in Table 8.2.

TABLE 8.2
Predictive validity (after 12 years) of selected creative measures and IQ with categories of adult creative achievements

Selected variable measured in 1959	Men: Predictive validity of 1959 measures with productive achievement measured in 1971		
	Quantity	Quality	Aspiration
Inventive level	.42	.43	.42
Originality	.41	.45	.45
IQ	.24	.40	.37

Note: All the correlation coefficients reported above are significant at the .01 level.

Selected variable measured in 1959	Women: Predictive validity of 1959 measures with productive achievement measured in 1971		
	Quantity	Quality	Aspiration
Inventive level	.28	.41	.32
Originality	.37	.40	.30
IQ	.06**	.29	.18*

* Significant at .05 level.
** Not significant.

Source: Torrance (1972), p. 249.

Correlation coefficients of .40–.45 may be regarded as low, but compared to other validity coefficients in education and psychology, they are at least moderately high. Teacher's ratings or peer evaluations obtained at the same time as Torrance's originality measure later correlated essentially zero with adult creativity.

Other measures of creative thinking

There are numerous other formal and informal measurements of creative thinking that have appeared in research projects or in professional

266   Learning and Thinking

journals or which are commercially available. We will consider only two, both available in published form. They are different from the Torrance Tests, and from each other.

One interesting contrast with Torrance's work is found in the Remote Associations Test developed by Mednick (1962). Whereas Torrance's theory of creativity is derived from Guilford's factor analytic approach to human intelligence, Mednick's effort assesses the associative basis of creativity. The fundamental idea is simple, and the theory is among the oldest in the history of psychology. In our culture, at least, it is possible to make reasonably good predictions about associations between certain words. For example, if I say "bacon," you will probably answer, "eggs." These words are closely associated, since we have heard them together and used them in conjunction with each other over and over since childhood. Mednick reasoned that uncreative people probably have only a few associations for each word, but these are very strong, whereas more creative individuals have a flat distribution of associations. That is, the creative individual might be expected to associate one word with another that would not commonly be linked with it. He refers to these as remote associations; his hypothesis is that the ability to see remote associations might be a good indicator of creative ability.

Mednick subsequently developed tests in the verbal domain which present a trio of superficially unrelated words. The thinker's problem is to identify a fourth word that links the three he has been given. In its finished form, the Remote Associations Test consists of 30 such trios of words. The test taker is given 40 minutes in which to formulate his answers, and his score is simply the number of correct remote associates he produces. It is interesting that Mednick has developed a test of creative thinking that is convergent in nature. The correct answers have been worked out in advance, and although this procedure avoids some of the ambiguity of the Torrance scoring systems, it raises some doubts at the conceptual level about what Mednick's test measures. A few examples of the kind employed in the RAT are reproduced here. The answers to these sample items are given in a footnote at the bottom of the following page.

Remote associations test sample

				Fourth Word
1.	stool	powder	ball	
2.	house	village	golf	
3.	card	knee	rope	
4.	plan	show	walker	

Answers in footnote on next page.

In his original formulation of the test, Mednick (1962) reported that research supervisors' ratings of the creativity of graduate students tends to conform with their ranking on the Remote Associations Test. Mednick (1968) has also reported that the reliability of the test is quite high.

A third commercially available instrument is the Alpha Biographical Inventory. Designed explicitly for use with juniors and seniors in high school, it is a survey of 300 items. These probe the adolescent's life history, his family background, academic development, and areas pertaining to his life plans and interests. The inventory yields two scores, one for creativity and another for the prediction of academic success in college. The instrument had a long history of development and validation based upon life histories of NASA scientists and high school and college students before its publication in 1968.

Davis and Belcher (1971) conducted a small-scale study of high school seniors in which they examined correlations between scores on the Torrance tests, RAT, the college academic success portion of the Alpha Biographical Inventory, and a measure of IQ. The intention was also to determine the validity of the measures as tests of creativity for this adolescent sample. No good outside criterion of creative thinking was available, but the creativity portion of the Alpha Biographical Inventory contains a set of questions in which students rate their own creative ability relative to others in their class, and in general. Student responses to those questions were used as the outside criterion of creativity. (Naturally the creativity portion of the ABI was not used subsequently, since it would have correlated very highly and artificially with the subset of questions taken from it to serve as the criterion of creativity.) Davis and Belcher reported correlations separately for boys and girls. For the boys, none of the measures related significantly to the creativity self-ratings. For the girls, the Torrance tests were significantly correlated with the criterion, but none of the other measures were.

The sample in this study is small, and we probably ought not to depend too heavily upon its results. However, it appeared that the RAT was too difficult for these high school students. They scored only about 12 on the average of a possible 30. More important are the correlations between the RAT and IQ; .76 for the boys, and .60 for the girls. Davis and Belcher conclude that the Alpha Biographical Inventory is probably the most valid measure available for anyone who wants to estimate the creative potential of high school students. That conclusion obviously is based not on the data of their study but on their conviction that the instrument was carefully validated, using life-history data of NASA scientists.

Answers to Remote Associations Test examples: (1) foot, (2) green, (3) trick, (4) floor.

However, the ABI is not very useful if the effects of a training program or other sources of change in creative functioning are to be looked at. The Torrance tests *are* suitable for such purposes. Furthermore, the ABI was developed for a limited range of educational levels, whereas the Torrance tests can be used with very young children and with adults, as well as with students at the upper elementary, secondary, and college levels. For the teacher who wishes to measure her or his students' creativity and to be able to assess the effects of a creative thinking course or the equivalent, the Torrance tests appear to be the best instrument available at this time. Davis and Belcher suggest that an interest or personality test should be used in conjunction with the measure of creative thinking, because students' attitudes and interests are so intricately bound with creative performance. The well-known Adjective Check List developed by Gough (1961) would be one possibility.

The Creative Individual

What is a creative person like as an individual? The question has received much attention, and has provided some interesting answers. Given our principal interest in children and adolescents, perhaps it is unfortunate that most of the best analyses of creative people have been done with adults. We do not as yet seem to have as many penetrating analyses of the creative child at age five or when in junior high school as we have of established creative adults. We can try to reason backward from adult characteristics to what the creative individual was like at younger ages, but such speculation obviously has risks.

One of the major sources in this country for the development of knowledge about creative people is the Institute of Personality Assessment and Research at the University of California at Berkeley. Its procedure for learning about creative adults was to identify a sample of the most creative members of a given art or science, recruit them to participate in the study, and then invite them in groups, usually ten people at a time, to spend a three-day weekend on the university campus. During that period, the participants solved problems, took batteries of standardized and other tests, were interviewed by staff psychiatrists, and conversed with creative peers as well as with the assessment staff. The aim of these weekends was to collect for analysis as broad and as deep a slice into the intellectual and emotional functioning of the creative person as possible.

The director of the institute at this time was Donald W. MacKinnon. It was MacKinnon's belief that the only way to ensure that the studies would focus upon highly creative people was to select mature adults whose creative achievement was outstanding and recognized. This precluded working with children or adolescents, for rarely would sufficient evidence be available to ensure that an individual of great talent was under study. MacKinnon also avoided the use of psychological measures of creativity (such as the Torrance tests) as a way of identifying the people to be investigated. In the procedure adopted, an occupational group, one that characteristically calls for a degree of creative ability, was selected to be studied. All in all, the institute assessed representatives from architecture, mathematics, painting, writing, and several other areas. Nominations of the most creative members of an occupation or art were solicited from people in the best position to know the talent available; for example, when architects were to be studied, five distinguished professors of architecture were asked to name the top 40 architects in the United States. More than double that number were named, which shows that, although no unanimity exists in the field, there was a considerable amount of agreement among the five judges. Subsequently the editors of architectural journals and the architects in the sample were asked to rank the people named on the basis of their creativity. Those rankings resulted in a very high correlation. Then 40 of the architects were invited to the Berkeley campus to participate in the study. The characteristics discussed below are based upon results of the study of the creative architects and of groups of other creative people who were also studied.

Creativity and intelligence

Among creative individuals, the correlation between measured intelligence and creative ability is low. Some care must be taken in the interpretation of this statement, however. For virtually any creative endeavor, a fairly high level of general intelligence is required. Beyond the level of intelligence required for competent performance, as in science or writing, IQ loses its power to predict who will be more and who less creative. Let us illustrate the point. Barron (1963, 1971) studied creative writers. The average score made by the 30 outstanding writers studied on the Terman Concept Mastery Test was 157. Although this score does not translate directly into IQ points, a sample of U. S. Air Force captains averaged 60 on the same test. Given this example, one can begin to see why variations in intelligence within a sample such as the gifted writers would not be helpful in ordering them on creativity.

Some writers have suggested that an IQ of about 120 is sufficient for most creative enterprises and that additional intelligence does not differentiate among individuals who are more or less creative. We would seldom find a creative person who has low intelligence. Given sufficient intelligence to master the necessary knowledge and skills of a field, then other kinds of abilities, such as originality and flexibility in thinking, become more important to creativity than additional IQ points.

Guilford and Christensen (1973) have taken one of the most recent looks at the question of a change in the relationship between IQ and creativity at the level of 120 IQ. They tested several hundred fourth-, fifth-, and sixth-grade pupils in two schools to correlate their divergent production scores with intelligence. In general, the correlation coefficients were low, ranging around .25, and they found no evidence of a threshold at or near the 120 IQ level.

> In a number of writings on the main problem of this report, reference is made to threshold hypothesis. This hypothesis is that below a critical IQ level, usually said to be about 120, there is some correlation between IQ and creative potential, and above it there is not. In neither (an earlier) study nor in this one, do the scatter plots show any breaks. The degree of apparent relationship shows a continuous gradual shift, from low to high IQ. It is more correct to say that the higher the IQ the more likely we are to find at least some individuals with high creative potential. (Guilford & Christensen, 1973, p. 251)

Personality characteristics

Several traits characterize the highly creative individual. MacKinnon (1962) observed fundamental differences in self-descriptions provided by architects of the highest reaches of creativity compared with those of less creative architects. The most creative of the group described themselves as "inventive, determined, independent, individualistic, enthusiastic, and industrious." The less creative architects stressed more sociable characteristics, rating themselves as "responsible, sincere, reliable, dependable, clear thinking, and understanding." The independence and autonomy of the creative individual stand out. This is not limited to self-reports. Crutchfield (1962), for example, measured the willingness of people from different occupational groups to resist group pressures toward conformity.

Crutchfield presented individuals with information about decisions purportedly made by four of their peers in such items as the longest in a set of lines, the largest of a group of geometric shapes, and so forth. After a few trials the individual observed that all of his group mates had presented the same answer, but it was clearly wrong. The individual being studied then had to decide whether he would go along with that judgment or give what he knew to be the correct answer in the face of a unanimous majority against him. This situation was called a critical trial;

12 of those occurred for each participant, so it was possible to obtain a range of scores on independence. The average conformity score was computed for each group. Air force captains earned the highest conformity score of any group tested. This makes sense, for military officers are selected for their ability both to give and to take orders. Research scientists were at the opposite end of the distribution of scores on conformity; they rarely yielded. Many of the scientists were able to resist the pressures of the group on all 12 critical trials, and presumably they could have continued to do so indefinitely.

Creative people are also open to experiences, and they are in touch with their own feelings to an extraordinary extent. This often enables the creative person to deal with ideas and information in an intuitive way. By the same token, certain personality tests reveal creative males to have much higher than average scores on some dimensions that, in American culture at least, are considered to be feminine. This is not so much an indication of a lack of appropriate sex role identification as it is of the intuitiveness and sensitivity of the creative being. These and other identifiable traits are more associated with the *anima* of the female than they are with the *persona* of the male figure.

Barron's work (1963, 1971) has been especially illuminating of the inner life of the creative individual. In his study of outstanding creative writers, for example, Barron found their commitment to communicating the truth as they see it their most dominant characteristic. Although great financial success had come to some members of that group, notably the authors of best-selling novels, there are others who must work in the most menial jobs to support themselves. Barron even tells of encountering a distinguished but improvident poet on the university campus one evening. This man, whose latest volume of poetry had just won international acclaim, did not have bus fare to return to San Francisco from Berkeley. Unwilling to accept a donation, he autographed a copy of his book and "sold" it to Barron for a dollar. Whether the truth such individuals write earns millions or pennies is of less consequence than the drive to determine and to tell what life means. This was true for all of the highly creative groups studied. Their strongest values are in the aesthetic and theoretical domains, their lowest interest in economics.

Barron's analysis of highly creative individuals is based in part upon a series of dichotomies: *perception* vs. *judgment; intuition* vs. *sense perception*, and preference for *complexity* vs. preference for *simplicity*.

In theory, use of the mind always involves either perception or judgment. Perception involves awareness and may lead to openness to experience, and flexibility and spontaneity. Judgment means evaluation and drawing conclusions. It stresses orderliness and planning, but these occur within a fixed set of principles and a closed universe. Barron observes that, except for the scientists of their studies, the Berkeley group consistently found creative individuals perceptual rather than judgmental. In all groups studied, including the scientists, the more creative people are perceptual, the less creative ones more judgmental.

Similarly, perception may involve either direct and simple sense perception, or intuition, which involves awareness of deeper meanings and the symbolism of events. Creative individuals are intuitive. Interviews with the creative people continuously revealed the occurrences of mystical experiences, or of "feelings of utter desolation and horror." Some individuals reported that they had been caught in hailstorms of disconnected words or had seen the world suddenly take on a new brightness. Compared to control groups, the creative people dream with much greater frequency, and they report that their dreams are in color.

Creative people also prefer complexity to simplicity. This preference emerges in several ways. The creative writers, when shown a large number of paintings, consistently expressed a preference for those that were asymmetrical and more rather than less complex. In this they were similar to architects and artists.

MacKinnon and Barron have provided brief but definitive statements about the creative people studied at the University of California. Barron's analysis is restricted to creative writers, but MacKinnon's is expanded to summarize the dominant characteristics of all the groups. Their statements are presented in Figure 8.2.

Characteristics of creative children

Getzels and Jackson (1963) studied the similarities and differences between adolescents they identified as either creative *or* highly intelligent. The mean IQ of the latter group was 150, which is extraordinarily high. The average IQ of the creative group was 127, which is at least as high as the mean we would find for most of the good secondary schools in the nation. In other words, although the members of that group scored lower in IQ than those in the highly intelligent group, they are nonetheless very bright young people, as well as more creative than their friends in the other group. This is a good point to keep in mind as we review some of the distinctions made by Getzels and Jackson.

First, they report that the groups did not differ from each other in academic achievement. Getzels and Jackson suggest that intellectual creativity accounts for the superior achievement of the creative group. However, these students were intelligent enough to achieve well in any academic environment. It seems superfluous to invoke an alternative explanation.

FIGURE 8.2

Summary statements about characteristics of highly creative individuals

---

Mackinnon (1966), p. 156:

> If ... one still insists on asking what most generally characterizes the creative individual as he has revealed himself in the Berkeley studies, it is his high level of effective intelligence, his openness to experience, his freedom from crippling restraints and impoverishing inhibitions, his esthetic sensitivity, his cognitive flexibility, his independence in thought and action, his high level of creative energy, his unquestioning commitments to creative endeavor, and his unceasing striving for solutions to the ever more difficult problems that he constantly sets for himself.

Barron (1966), p. 158:

> ... the five items most characteristic of the group of thirty creative writers were:
> Appears to have a high degree of intellectual capacity.
> Values intellectual and cognitive matters.
> Values own independence and autonomy.
> Is verbally fluent, can express ideas well.
> Enjoys esthetic impressions, is esthetically reactive.
> The next eight characteristic items were:
> Is productive, gets things done.
> Is concerned with philosophical problems; e.g., religion, values, the meaning of life, etc.
> Has high aspiration level for self.
> Has a wide range of interests.
> Thinks and associates to ideas in unusual ways, has unconventional thought processes.
> Is an interesting, arresting person.
> Appears straightforward, forthright, candid in dealing with others.
> Behaves in an ethically consistent manner, is consistent with own personal standards.

A second question is, Which of the two groups was preferred by teachers? (Getzels and Jackson, 1963, p. 165.) The answer is that teachers preferred highly intelligent students to the average student, but they did not significantly prefer the creative group to the average. Neither were the high IQ students given significant preference over the creative group by the teachers. No difference in achievement motivation was found between the two groups.

Some differences do appear between the two categories when they were asked to rank order a set of qualities (1) as they prefer them for themselves, (2) as they make for adult success, and (3) as they are valued by teachers. The bright students produced rankings that were very similar for all three questions. What they want by way of personal qualities is seen as highly congruent with characteristics they believe teachers like to see in students, and also with what the gifted adolescents regard as traits that contribute heavily to adult success. The creative students' list of personal preferences was independent of what they perceived are likely to make them successful in the future, and actually negatively related to how they believed teachers would rank the qualities. Table 8.3 lists the qualities in question and the ranking assigned to them by each of the two groups. (You can decide for yourself how you believe the qualities should be ranked.)

TABLE 8.3
Rankings of eight qualities in their order of personal preference by two groups of gifted adolescents

Qualities ranked	High IQ Group	Creative group
Character	1	3
Emotional stability	2	1
Goal directedness	3	4.5
Creativity	4	6
Wide range of interests	5	4.5
High marks	6	7
IQ	7	8
Sense of humor	8	2

Source: Based on data in Getzels & Jackson (1963), p. 167.

The creative students are much more likely to consider a wide range of potential occupations, especially unconventional ones. They are also less likely to make an early commitment to an occupation. In short, educational and occupational goals of the type, "I'm going to college and then to medical school (law school, business school)" are more typical of the group whom Getzels and Jackson labeled as high IQ than they are of the creative students.

When these students were asked to write stories in a very short time (three or four minutes) in response to picture stimuli, the creative students made much greater use of stimulus-free themes, unexpected endings, humor, incongruities, and playfulness. Overall, the impression is that the adolescents who were identified as creative share much in common with the proven creative adults of the Berkeley studies. Long-range, longitudinal studies of the development of creative people are not available, but this cross section gives us a glimpse of such individuals when they are between 15 and 18 years of age.

Torrance (1972) also compared highly creative with highly intelligent pupils, but with two important differences. His studies were done with elementary school children, which helps us to sketch the developmental picture somewhat more fully, and they constituted a group that included children who were both creative and of high IQ. This is an important addition, since it would be from such a population that we would expect the truly creative people to emerge.

In Torrance's tests at the University of Minnesota Laboratory School, samples of children were identified as creative or intelligent. The two groups were not significantly different in academic achievement as measured by two well-known sets of standardized achievement tests. It was found that the high IQ children were better known to their teachers than the creative children, and the teachers considered them to be more desirable students. The preference extended to high IQ–low creativity pupils compared to those who were high on both variables. Teachers see the children who are both bright and creative as more unruly and dominant, more independent and ambitious, but also as friendlier and more studious and hardworking than either of the other two groups: creative or intelligent alone.

The highly creative and intelligent children are also perceived by their teachers to be the most talkative and to have unusual but good ideas. They are the children who can quickly generate new ideas if original plans go awry. Furthermore, their peers pay attention to them for their ideas. These perceptions are shared by the children's classmates, who nominate them as being talkative and having good ideas, but often wild or silly ones. The bright but not so creative children have the most friends, the creative but less bright ones the fewest.

Wodtke and Wallen (1965) tried to observe boys at the fourth- and fifth-grade level, some of whom were identified as creative and others as not creative. The purpose of the observations was to try to confirm contentions of such writers as Torrance that creative children are more nonconforming. The observers had a good deal of difficulty in observing behaviors reliably, but their findings showed that the manifest behaviors of creative children do not fit as neatly into conceptual packages as some questionnaire studies suggest. For example, Wodtke and Wallen did not find creative pupils to be any more nonconforming than their less creative classmates. However, their measure of nonconformity seems closer to misbehavior than what such writers as Crutchfield or Torrance would mean by nonconformity (that is, autonomy or independence). The observers did rate creative pupils as more alert and as initiating less talk in the classroom than the noncreative students. They conclude that advice about permissiveness and acceptance of creative children's unusual behavior has little evidence to support it.

The Creative Process

What happens when a person is in the act of creativity? We may have the impression that the novelist sits down at his desk in a calm and businesslike manner and emerges several hours later with a satisfying clutch of manuscript. Or we may subscribe to the movie version of the frantic scientist who deduces earthshaking conclusions from the bubbles passing through a retort. Neither of these stereotypes seem to come very close to the reality of creativity. When Thomas Edison was asked the secret of his creativity, he is said to have answered "Invention is 99 percent perspiration and 1 percent inspiration."

Wallas (1926) long ago introduced the idea of a series of stages of thought involved in creative production. He called them preparation, incubation, illumination, and verification. Despite the rather pat-sounding terminology, these concepts have been well accepted among students of the creative process for over half a century. *Preparation* includes not just specific organizing of information for a given problem but extends to the idea of the wide-ranging background of knowledge, skills, and even ways of looking at the world that are possessed by the creator. Congruent with Mednick's (1962) notion that creativity is a matter of remote associations, the role of preparation is to supply both extensive and unusual materials to the learner which may ultimately assist him in the creative enterprise. *Incubation,* as we shall see, is a well-documented phenomenon, although its psychological causes and how it comes to pass are not at all well understood. Nonetheless, it frequently happens that when individuals who are renowned for their creative successes reflect upon the process of creativity, they refer to a period in which they put the entire issue out of mind. The stage of incubation is followed by a flash of *illumination,* or what some have called insight. At that moment, the solution to the problem or the missing stanza of the poem suddenly comes to the creator, with no further effort on his part. Finally there is the phase of *verification,* or testing or revision, in which the initial product is altered or improved to better satisfy whatever requirements govern it.

Rugg (1963) provided a fascinating series of accounts of creative insights or discoveries as they have been reported by famous scientists, mathematicians, and poets. Although the accounts are autobiographical and subjective, they, too, tend to confirm the stages of thought identified earlier. The creative productions were carried on over periods that ranged into months or even years. Two points are very clear. One is the absolute requirement that an extended period of preparation is required. Often the creator finds that despite his best efforts day after day, the problem will not yield to solution. The mathematical function remains obscure, the poem does not flow, the plot does not develop. Furthermore, conscious effort to force solution does not pay dividends. Again and again, however, the autobiographical accounts also tell of the sudden recognition of solution or discovery that comes after a time away from the problem.

The mathematician Poincaré, for example, reported that he had given up his mathematical investigations for a time to participate in a geological expedition. One day as he boarded a bus, engaged in a conversation, it came to him with certainty that the transformations he had used in his earlier work were identical with those of non-Euclidean geometry. At the time of this insight he had not been thinking of his mathematical work. Indeed it did not seem to be connected to the illuminating flash. Poincaré did not so much as interrupt the conversation in which he was engaged. He knew that the solution which came to him was right, and he delayed verifying it until a later time when he could do so at leisure. Yet the verification seems to be a process of recording what he already knew, rather than one of testing whether his flash of insight would survive critical analysis.

Examples of this sort abound. The British poet A. E. Housman tells how he would sometimes drink a pint of beer at lunch and then take a walk in the afternoon for two or three hours. Sometimes a line or two of poetry would come to him during his walks, accompanied by some notion of the broader poem of which they would be a part. Rugg quotes Housman's recollection of how the last poem in his first volume was composed. Two of the four stanzas came to him in finished form as he crossed a London intersection. With a bit of coaxing another one emerged after tea. The fourth one, however, as Housman puts it, he had to write himself. The effort was extremely laborious. It required 13 drafts and occupied the poet off and on for over a year.

We are indebted to Catherine Patrick for a series of painstaking investigations into the creative processes of different types of people. Patrick really had two questions she was trying to answer. The first was whether Wallas's four stages mentioned above could be justified. The second asked about the generality of the phenomena. If they do occur, is it only among individuals who are creative, or are they characteristic of the creative process itself? Patrick conducted three investigations during the middle 1930s, in each of which a sample of about 100 mature adults was identified.

In the first study (1935), half of these people were successful poets, and the other half were nonpoets. Each person was individually interviewed and tested by Patrick. First a painting of a landscape was shown, and each participant was instructed to compose a poem based upon the painting or on something suggested by it. In addition, all were asked to think out loud as they worked. Patrick kept a record of how long each person worked, and then divided the elapsed time into quarters. More than two thirds of the total number of lines were composed in the second and third quarter, thus providing evidence in support of a period of illumination. Similarly, about two thirds of all changes or revisions were made in the last quarter, which she construed as evidence of verification. The stages of thought are seen as distinct but overlapping. Most of the poets and would-be poets also showed a period of incubation. In fact, this appeared for a somewhat larger proportion of the control subjects than poets. Several findings were similar for the two groups. We have already mentioned that the several aspects or stages of thought emerged in very much the same form for the two groups. Patrick suggested these are characteristic of the process of creativity, independent of the quality of the product or the gifts of the "creator." Both groups took the same average time to compose their poems (21 minutes) and produced poems of the same length (six lines, on the average). Several raters judged the quality of the poems. Happily, the professional poets' work was judged superior.

Patrick's second study (1937) was done with a sample of painters and nonartists. In outline it was very similar to the first one, but this time a copy of a poem was supplied, and the individuals were invited to draw a picture based upon the poem. The stages of thought à la Wallas were once again discernible, and the groups (painters and nonpainters) were remarkably alike in such aspects as the frequency with which they began work on the background or the foreground, the total elapsed time, whether they worked from left to right, and where they placed the center of interest of their drawing. Again raters easily found the professionals' work superior to the amateurs, although several of the nonpainters received ratings about as high as those given to some of the artists' work.

In both these studies, the differences in creative talent and training were manifested in other ways besides the rating of superior products. For example, Patrick notes explicitly that the poets, after they viewed the landscape painting, searched for deeper meanings within it to base their poems upon. Their emotional involvement was extensive. The amateurs, on the other hand, worked directly from the stimulus offered by the painting. Both artists and poets were more apt to follow the conventions of their respective crafts than were their nonprofessional counterparts. This is an extremely important point. Their knowledge and training in the art gave them a degree of discipline and a choice of means of expression that were not available to the control subjects. There is not a hint of conformity here. Instead what comes through is the increased precision and opportunity to express oneself in intended ways that is made possible by the mastery of the art. Teachers who are afraid that providing standards of excellence for children and giving them basic skills and techniques may rob them of creative spontaneity should take heart from those findings.

Patrick's third study (1938) was of a somewhat different nature. She identified a sample of about the same size as before but divided it into two groups, differentiated not on the basis of training or giftedness but on the basis of the conditions under which they were to construct an experiment to study the relative importance of heredity and environment. Half of these people were told the problem and then asked to design the experiment on the spot, again using the "talk out loud" method. The other people were given a two-week period in which to think about what to do and a notebook in which to record their ideas. At a subsequent interview they explained to Patrick how their experiment would be designed. The difference in time perspective is an interesting variation, inasmuch as we have seen that creative thinking often extends over long time intervals. No effort was made to study the fourth stage of creative thought, verification, since that would have required an impossible effort to execute the experiments and check the results. Once again the first three stages of creative thinking were observed. Several differences between the immediate and delayed groups emerged in their final plans. What they seem to indicate is that the longer preparation and incubation periods allow initially poor decisions to be revised. For example, the delayed group often suggested in the beginning that subjects of the experiment should be adults. Two weeks later, their final plans usually shifted to children as subjects. The delayed group specified a sample three times the size of the immediate design group. Also the group given more time to plan was five times as likely to use more than one method in its final plan.

Efforts to Improve and Support Creative Thinking

For the teacher who wants to play an instrumental role in enabling her or his students to make effective use of whatever creative ability they have, there are two major steps to be taken. One of these consists of trying to help students express themselves creatively; to stimulate ideas; to seek new and effective ways of solving problems; to write the best poems and stories they can; to draw, paint, compose, or otherwise perform at the highest level their intelligence and creative talent permit them to do. The second step is to provide an environment or a "classroom climate" that is psychologically and emotionally safe and secure enough that students are willing to unveil their inner thoughts and to try out new ways of acting.

Most of us are likely to make some rather bizarre mistakes when we attempt to strike out in new directions. If the net effect is that the student winds up feeling embarrassed or humiliated, or just plain dumb, he may not make further efforts at divergent production for a long time into the future. This climate is probably less important for the highly creative student a teacher may occasionally encounter than it is for the great majority of those whose lesser talents he wants to cultivate. As we have seen, people who are truly creative have an independence and self-confidence that makes them not necessarily impervious to criticism or impossible to be understood by others, but basically capable of operating effectively despite what others say or feel.

Within the past generation countless efforts have been launched to teach people how to think creatively. Many of these have been one-time shots which have frequently succeeded in bringing about a certain creative outcome in a limited time. However, whether the thinkers were subsequently able to generalize from such limited experiences and apply them to future and perhaps more realistic situations has received little attention, and we will not concern ourselves with these endeavors.

"Brainstorming" is a technique for encouraging creative thinking which has been used in group and individual settings. The term is associated with Alex Osborn, who suggested the procedure as a way of generating multiple ideas about a topic or problem. In general, whether working alone or in a pair or a much larger group, people list ideas or suggestions as they come to mind. In the brainstorming period, emphasis is solely upon the production of ideas; any form of criticism or other behavior that might inhibit the flow of ideas is strictly ruled out. Evaluation occurs at some later time when the creative juices have subsided. The gist of the evidence on this topic points to superior quality of ideas when the brainstorming technique is used by individuals. A group often produces a much larger number of ideas altogether, but the solitary thinker will typically come up with better ones. Brainstorming can clearly play a role in the classroom whenever the occasion demands a variety of new ideas on a problem.

Despite the fact that there are many examples of creativity training, it seems unlikely that taken together they would add up to a coherent whole which teachers could apply in classroom situations. Therefore, we will discuss present programs or courses which have been used to promote creative thinking and about which considerable information exists. Three programs will be considered, one each for elementary education, the secondary school, and the college or adult level. The Productive Thinking Program described and analyzed in Chapter 5 represents an additional excellent example. The middle grades of the elementary school have been a particularly rich environment for investigation and curriculum development in this area. Teachers of the fifth- and sixth-grades are more fortunate than most to have available for their use programs such as the Productive Thinking Program and the Purdue Creativity Program, to be introduced below.

Programs Designed to Stimulate Creative Thinking at Different Levels

At the elementary school level

The Purdue Creative Thinking Program was originally used as a series of 28 radio broadcasts, each 15 minutes long. The first three to five minutes of each program were devoted to explaining a principle of creative thinking or an idea for the improvement of creativity. Another seven to ten minutes were used in the dramatization of the life of an explorer, discoverer, or inventor. The program closed with instructions for the written exercises that were to follow. Children, with the teacher's help, then worked on verbal and nonverbal activities pertinent to ideational fluency, flexibility, originality, and elaboration. Figure 8.3 summarizes the program and gives examples of the kinds of material the children hear and write about.

A first study to determine the general effectiveness of the Purdue Creative Training Program (Feldhusen, Bahlke, & Treffinger, 1969) compared scores on sections of the Torrance Tests of Creative Thinking of 129 children in six classes at the third-, fourth-, and fifth-grade levels (two classes at each grade level) who participated in the program with those of six other comparable classes of children who did not. Significant differences in these test scores favored the experimental classes. An important finding was that boys and girls scored about equally well on all the tests, and the results also showed that the program's principal impact was upon fifth-graders. This was explained as a matter of the demands for reading and writing imposed by the exercises and the complex thinking demanded by the programs. The third- and fourth-graders were a bit too immature to benefit fully from the program, even though here too the experimental classes outscored the control classes.

Somewhat later an analytical study (Feldhusen, Treffinger, & Bahlke, 1970) was made to determine the effectiveness of each component of the program: the presentations, stories, and exercises. Classes of fifth-grade pupils studied one, two, or all three parts of the program in an effort to determine their differential effectiveness. In general the exer-

FIGURE 8.3

Purdue Creativity Program: Summary and examples

The program consists of 28 segments, each subdivided into an audiotape portion and a concluding set of written exercises for the children. The audiotape in turn has two parts: The presentation, which explains one principle or technique of creative thinking, and the dramatized history of a pioneer, explorer, or someone else whose ideas represented a frontier.

Taped Segment

1. Presentation. Usually this takes three or four minutes at the opening of the program. On one segment the announcer discusses the use of creative thinking outside of the classroom. It is suggested that children who come up with new ideas for games have more fun, and, with humor, techniques are suggested for synthesizing ideas to solve a problem.
2. Story. The content of the stories is historical. The 28 stories in the series are divided into four equal groups:
   a. Early explorers—Columbus, Cortez, Magellan, Lewis and Clark are examples.
   b. Famous Americans—Samuel Morse, Lincoln, Alexander Bell.
   c. Statesmen—Thomas Jefferson, George Washington, Simon Bolivar.
   d. Modern inventors and explorers—Marconi and the radio, polio vaccine, astronauts and space exploration.

Exercises

The exercises, based on the content of each story, emphasize the need for many solutions. The examples here are taken from a story about the Pony Express and exercises in which the children are asked to place themselves in the role of participants. Other exercises stress verbal originality and nonverbal skills as in the third example.

> a. Suppose that you were a Pony Express rider. You are riding across the country with a bag of mail. It is a warm afternoon. Suddenly, off in the distance on a mountain ridge, you see two Indians mounted on horses. They are standing still, looking in your direction. What would you do?
> b. Suppose that the telegraph and the railroads had not come along and replaced the Pony Express. The Pony Express would probably have continued to carry the mail. How could the Pony Express Service have been improved? List as many ways as you can think of that would have improved it.
> c. Draw a picture of a Pony Express rider crossing a dusty desert. Give your picture as many good and clever titles as you can think of.

Source: From Feldhusen, Treffinger, & Bahlke (1970), pp. 86 and 87.

cise and the stories, singly or in combination with each other, produced good results. The presentations (the introductory statements of principles of creative thinking) were generally the least effective component.

Another study of the Purdue Creativity Program (Treffinger, Speedie, & Brunner, 1974) was conducted a few years later. In this one the effects of distribution of training, the divergent thinking ability of teachers, and the extent of peer and teacher participation were all assessed. Furthermore, the Purdue program was pitted in head to head competition with the Productive Thinking Program. Treffinger and his associates wanted to learn whether children's creative thinking would be affected by certain pronounced differences in program utilization. The distribution of training was defined as either four or eight weeks of study; children were exposed to the total program under both conditions, and only the time span differed. Teachers were identified as high or low in their ability to think divergently. Half the teachers using each program were instructed to lead discussions and otherwise participate actively in the class sessions. A more passive role, distributing materials and answering routine questions, was assigned to the others.

The results are complex and do not reveal a single pattern which would be described as "the best one." However, the Purdue program was most effective when it was used over the longer time period by teachers who are good divergent thinkers and who both stimulated discussion among their pupils and participated in the discussions themselves. The Productive Thinking Program showed greater stability. It was also effective in the four-week period and when a minimum of teacher involvement was allowed. Treffinger and the others suggest that the Berkeley program was designed as a self-instructional curriculum, and the design is affirmed by these results.

The outcome measures of this study are of interest in relation to our earlier distinction between near and remote transfer. Children were tested after they had studied the programs on several subtests of the Torrance Tests of Creative Thinking, on the Black House problem developed to evaluate the Productive Thinking Program (see the discussion of this problem in Chapter 5), on two real-life problems based on conflict at school, and on two verbal problem-solving tasks, one an anagram and the other a word-generation task.

The instructional variables differentiated the groups, as we have already seen, on the Torrance subtests. Scores on the Black House problem were higher for both instructional groups than for control pupils, but the children who had studied the Productive Thinking Program also scored significantly higher than the Purdue-trained pupils.

Of the remaining tasks, significant differences occurred only for the anagram problem. The Purdue program produced a significant outcome on the anagram only for the four-week training group with no discussion, and when teachers of low divergent ability did the teaching. The Productive Thinking Program led to significant outcomes on a much broader basis; four-and eight-week training groups, when teachers were either high or low in divergent thinking ability.

The real-life problems and the word-generation tasks did not produce results for trained subjects that were significantly different from those for control children. The investigators observe (and I agree) that those problems were so different from the instructional programs, or so general in their content relative to the training the children received, that they may have represented a very difficult criterion of transfer from the instructional programs. Why the investigators included such remote transfer tasks in their array of measures is not made explicit. They may simply have wished to determine at what point transfer from the programs would approach zero.

Whatever their intention, we have one more bit of evidence that transfer is limited in its scope. Apparently there must be some discernible degree of similarity between training and test tasks, or a common relationship between the two, for positive transfer to occur. In making this point, however, we must not obscure the basic findings of the study, which are that both programs foster creativity as measured by selected subtests from Torrance, and they improve children's ability to solve problems which call upon the same kinds of abilities that are strengthened in the training programs. There are also differences between the programs in the extent of their effectiveness and the range of conditions under which they are superior to no special instruction.

At the secondary school level

Davis (1969) describes a program to train creativity in adolescence that was developed by him and Houtman (1968). The program, entitled *Thinking Creatively: A Guide to Training Imagination,* provides systematic instruction for students of high school age in the use of idea-generating techniques. The program is based upon several assumptions about the behavior of adolescents. These include the assumptions that high school students must be made aware of the fast-changing pace of developments in contemporary society, and that the students must adopt attitudes that are conducive to creative thinking in themselves and in others. Students are taught to value unusual ideas, whether they are their own or those of classmates. Another important assumption is that adolescents are especially vulnerable to criticism, which shuts off the flow of creative ideas. Since humor and playfulness are characteristics manifested by most creative people, Davis and Houtman attempted to build them into the program.

Four basic techniques of creative thinking are used.

1. *Attribute listing.* The basic parts of an object or process are identified, and ideas are generated to improve each of them.

2. *Morphological synthesis.* Two or more dimensions of an object are identified, and their attributes are listed. The thinker then combines attributes from each dimension. For instance, if you are seeking ideas for new pop-up toasters, you can start with the existing five sizes, 20 colors, and 15 shapes. All the values of these dimensions immediately yield 1,500 combinations. This is a brute force, rather than an elegant technique, for generating many new combinations. If used with care, it can produce both good and new ideas.

3. *Checklist.* A prepared checklist is examined as a source of ideas. Davis developed one to use for changing a product which includes only seven items; add or subtract something, change the color, change parts, vary the shape, vary the size, alter the design.

4. *Synectics.* The emphasis is on analogies, particularly from nature. Remote free associations are encouraged. These often lead to wild and unusable ideas that in turn lead to more practical solutions.

These techniques are incorporated into the program through its four characters: Mr. I., a backyard scientist-inventor; Dudley Bond, a relative of agent 007; Dudley's friend, Maybelle; and Max, a professional bear. Max provides comic relief and is the vehicle for expressing creative techniques and attitudes with humor. Knowledge about the techniques and attitudes of creative thinking is communicated by Mr. I., and the other three members of the cast participate in the solution of problems, applying the various techniques. The Davis and Houtman program can be used in various ways, either as the core of a creative thinking course or in a supplementary capacity. It can also be used as the focus of teacher and pupil discussions, or adolescents can work with it on an independent basis. Information about the effectiveness with which the attitudes and techniques are taught by the program would be welcome.

At the college or adult level

Without doubt the best known work designed specifically to develop creativity at the college level is the course in creative problem solving taught at the University of Buffalo by Sidney J. Parnes (Parnes & Meadow, 1963; Parnes, 1971). The course imparts the concepts of Alex

F. Osborn's book *Applied Imagination* (1963); brainstorming, one of the most famous techniques in creative thinking, was discussed above. The book also stresses the generality of creative thinking in all types of occupations.

The course also alerts students to perceptual, emotional, and cultural blocks to thought. These include errors such as failing to see problems or defining them too narrowly. An important principle taught is that of deferred judgment, separating the process of idea generation from that of judgment or evaluation. Several of the techniques in the Davis and Houtman program are also used in the Buffalo Creative Problem Solving Course. These include attribute listing, checklists, and a technique similar to morphological synthesis.

Students are encouraged to practice creative thinking extensively and to apply it to problems that arise in their daily lives or in their work. The climate and procedures stress informality. For group discussions, chairs are arranged in a semicircle instead of in the rows more typical of lecture rooms. Small groups are used frequently, and students have the opportunity to lead them.

Parnes's course has undergone continuous evaluation to determine how well objectives are achieved, which cannot be said of many educational activities at any level. The standardized achievement batteries usually employed at elementary and secondary schools reveal an overall picture of achievement, but they provide no help in identifying potential causes or remedies. Preliminary evaluations of the course in creative problem solving examined changes in students' ability to produce quantity and quality of ideas. Students who had been through the course improved in quantity of production and showed significant gains on three measures of the quality of ideas, but not on two other measures. Assessments were also made of three personality traits: dominance, self-control, and need to achieve. Measurement showed that course graduates became more dominant, a trait stressed by the course because of the belief that creative people are more than normally dominant.

It is a fair question to ask whether the course contributes to students' creative development. Most of the measures of quantity and quality of ideas stressed such things as new uses for broomsticks and coat hangers. Two other tests that have marginal relationship to creative writing (clever story titles and original plots) did not show significant gains. The gains that occurred were shown on subtests of creative thinking of the type discussed earlier; for example, originality, flexibility, and fluency. Whether the improvements that are obviously generated by the course transfer to creative productivity in such terms as short stories, inventions, or other tangible outcomes, we do not know.

Parnes's data showed that gains accrue to individuals who differ in IQ, initial creative level, and sex, and that gains are retained. Measures repeated up to a year and a half after course completion showed trained students could outperform new students on both the quantity and quality dimensions.

One important principle that has emerged from research on this course is that many more good ideas appear later rather than early in a person's thinking on a problem. Parnes suggests that the noncreative thinker settles for the first idea which seems capable of solving his problem, whereas the creative thinker continues to probe and generate new ideas in the knowledge that better ones come later rather than early.

Climate for creativity

There is an interesting parallel to the classroom in Kaplan's (1963) observations of creativity in industrial scientific laboratories. He distinguishes between directors of laboratories who value productivity and those who attach more importance to creativity. For example, if the director is responsible for testing 500 substances for antibiotic effect, he must have scientists working for him who will hew to those tests, and do it in an intelligent and not perfunctory way. If the scientists are highly creative, the routine work may be abandoned, as each of them pursues his or her original ideas. Of course the director cannot tolerate that, for his own mission and, ultimately, his future with the company, are contingent upon the productivity of the laboratory. In such cases, the creative scientist is not highly prized by the director, because the goals and achievements of the latter are jeopardized by the autonomy of the creative worker.

One may see pressures toward conformity of the same sort in classrooms when teachers stress the routine completion of sets of mathematics problems or chemistry experiments on a set schedule, and according to the formulas set up by textbooks and laboratory manuals. Individualistic approaches to problems, even though they might occasionally lead to genuine insight for a student, tend to be discouraged for the understandable reason that they interfere with the classroom equivalent of industrial productivity. Perhaps the best approach in the classroom is to set aside some occasions when students are both permitted and encouraged to strike out on their own; that is, to look for new solutions and new approaches that are not prescribed by the teacher or by the textbook. There are few subjects or classrooms where occasionally arrangements could not be made to foster such divergent and exploratory behavior. When we fail *ever* to find such opportunities for students to explore, manipulate, wonder, invent, or propose, the effect is stultifying to the student's imagination. This may account more than any other single thing for the preschool teacher quoted in the opening pages of this chapter who confessed that she could *never* remember being asked to be creative!

De Bono (1969) distinguishes between vertical and lateral thinking. *Vertical* thinking is analogous to boring one hole deeper and deeper. Much of our thinking is of this sort, including the thinking done in school. *Lateral thinking* involves drilling a series of shallow holes, all in different places. The point of lateral thinking is to generate as many alternative ideas as possible—and not to pursue the most promising one. De Bono sees our fear of being wrong as the greatest single deterrent to our ability to come up with new ideas. We learn, from our earliest years, that being mistaken is shameful. Teachers intensify these feelings with their needs to maintain classroom productivity and to emphasize correctness. Again, at least occasionally, if the teacher wishes to promote creative thinking, there should be a chance to try out ideas in a psychologically safe setting.

Torrance (1965) identified five specific principles that teachers can use to reward creative thinking in the classroom. He also undertook a series of small-scale studies to see how teachers use them. The principles seem to be widely accepted, but perhaps more at the level of lip service than of action.

1. Be respectful of unusual questions.
2. Be respectful of imaginative, unusual ideas.
3. Show your pupils that their ideas have value.
4. Occasionally have pupils do something "for practice" without the threat of evaluation.
5. Tie in evaluation with causes and consequences.

(Torrance, 1965, p. 43)

Torrance concluded that, despite his being criticized variously for promoting "principles" that are only untested hypotheses, or for belaboring educators with truisms that are obvious to everyone, teachers rarely apply the principles at all in their daily work with young people. One could do much worse than to hold before himself these questions: Am I committed to helping people realize whatever creative potential they have? Does my behavior reflect that concern, and does it convey an attitude of respect for their ideas; of willingness to listen, to watch, and to encourage? With all the cares and obligations we fall heir to as teachers, are any more important to our role than these?

Creativity and the Classroom

Finally we must consider these questions: Can teachers improve the creativity of their students? Is it wise to invest time and resources in trying to do so? Most teachers complain that they have insufficient time to accomplish what they are now striving to do. Many believe that results would be better if there were fewer activities in the curriculum, not more.

To determine whether schools can improve the creative functioning of their students depends partly on how we define terms. Ausubel (1968), for example, finds the idea ridiculous. He conceives of the creative person as an extraordinarily rare individual with great gifts concentrated in a single field, such as painting, writing, or mathematics. The creative person has not simply more of the creative abilities that are universally shared. He is *qualitatively* different from the rest of us. The creative person is a Mozart or Tschaikowsky; a Shakespeare or Goethe; a Wren or Wright. He is a rare breed, and few teachers will encounter such a creative genius as a first-grader or as a student in a junior or senior high school class. Given his interpretation, Ausubel is right that programs of creative training will do little to produce such gifted people.

He is right in another sense as well. The expression of creativity is never general. It results in the writing of novels and plays, or in scientific discovery, or the design of new buildings. Yet few of our measures of creativity are so directed, and suggestions for the improvement of creativity have a general and all-encompassing quality, rather than a single-minded approach to teaching a talented child how to paint, to sculpt, to write, or to compose. The general approaches, such as those we have reviewed in this chapter, are of little use for the improvement of specialized talents.

The intention of programs for the improvement of creative thinking such as the ones we have examined is to do something different than providing specialized training for the highly creative individual. Their purpose is to remind us that all children have some seeds of creativity within them, and part of the educational process is to allow these to flower as fully as possible. Young children engage in imaginative play. Self-expression in music, dance, art, and story telling and writing are natural and wholesome extensions of their intellectual and emotional development. The teacher, like the parent, who encourages and cherishes such expression is helping the child to become whatever he is capable of becoming. The drive to create is one of the most natural drives we know. Schools accept the legitimacy of placing children in "discovery" situations in which they can better understand how scientists work or how mathematicians discover generalizations. We do these things simply because they are one way to expand the child's intellectual and emotional horizons, to help him see and understand an aspect of life that is challenging and exciting, even though one that he may not ordinarily engage in. Analogously, schools can provide the child with chances to think creatively and to experience, insofar as he is capable, the satisfactions and the thrills of creating. It is in this sense that the school can contribute to the child's creative development, without the delusion that creative people, in Ausubel's terms, are being produced.

Two basic principles stand out for the teacher who wishes to encourage the emergence of students' natural creativity. One of these, as we have already stated, is the establishment of a climate which encourages creative performance. At the same time, there must be an emphasis upon divergent thinking: the student's ability to propose alternatives, to see multiple solutions, to find new ways to behave. But if these are to have any value for the learner, they must be disciplined. The child poet must learn some of the standards of writing poetry as he expresses himself. His school days should improve his expression by giving him the tools that are needed to communicate inner feelings to a waiting world, even if that world is populated only by the child across the aisle or the teacher or the mother of the writer. The principle, then, can be simply stated. Creativity demands continuing emphasis upon divergent thinking, coupled with discipline. The teacher's aim is to foster the learner's creative development by encouraging alternatives that might never occur to the teacher, at the same time providing the necessary skills—in science or art, as the case may be—and holding the expectation that they are incorporated into the learner's burgeoning talent. Far from stifling the learner's creativity, such dedicated care is the finest contribution the teacher can make to the student's creative development.

Questions for Review and Discussion

1. How important do you think it is for schools to try to foster their students' creativity? Are you more inclined to agree with Ausubel, who holds that true creativity is so rare that to talk about teaching children to think creatively does not make much sense, or with someone like Parnes, who has devised a curriculum for teaching creativity? What evidence can you bring to bear on your position?

2. Can you identify the creative people in your classes? What criteria do you use? If you had the freedom to use tests to select creative students, which would you use?

3. We sometimes hear the opinion expressed that highly creative people suffer from aberrations—the "mad scientist" syndrome. Would accounts of the creative person, such as those given by MacKinnon or Barron, support that opinion? Why do you think so or think not?

4. Have you ever had an "illuminating flash" such as in the descriptions of the work of Poincaré or Housman? If not, try to locate someone who reports having had such an experience. How does his or her account tally with those in the chapter?

5. I believe that whatever contribution a teacher can make to a student's creativity depends on two qualities in the classroom environment: it must be one in which trials and inevitable failures can be safely carried out, but at the same time, teacher discipline and standards of excellence will prevail. What do you think? Would you suggest different qualities? Is it possible to combine these, or are they incompatible?

Readings for Further Reflection

The *Journal of Creative Behavior*, published since 1967 by the Creative Education Foundation, Buffalo, New York, is a quarterly journal devoted to creative education. Contents vary from poems to lengthy research reports; articles are of variable quality. The journal is an excellent vehicle for keeping up with current publications in the field of creativity.

Introductory level

For brief and nontechnical but definitive statements about creative people, see two articles, referred to in the chapter, both of them in the same issue of *Theory into Practice:*

Barron, Frank. "The Psychology of the Creative Writer." *Theory into Practice*, 1966, 5, 157–159.

MacKinnon, Donald W. "What Makes a Person Creative?" *Theory in Practice*, 1966, 5, 152–156.

The book of readings cited below is particularly useful because it includes papers that were written for use in industrial, engineering, and corporate settings as well as educational ones. For teachers and prospective teachers, a glimpse into some of these other organizations and their procedures for coping with creativity is enlightening.

Davis, Gary A., and Scott, Joseph A. *Training Creative Thinking*. New York: Holt, Rinehart, & Winston, 1971.

Finally, we would mention at the introductory level the widely publicized book that popularized the idea of brainstorming:

Osborn, Alex F. *Applied Imagination* (3rd rev. ed.). New York: Charles Scribner's Sons, 1963.

Advanced level

Harold Rugg was a professor at Teachers College, Columbia University, during a long and sometimes controversial career. His final years after his retirement were spent largely in reflecting about the process of creativity. His book, incomplete at the time of his death, is a provocative synthesis and interpretation of a wealth of knowledge about the topic.

Rugg, Harold. *Imagination.* New York: Harper & Row, 1963.

Arthur Koestler is a renowned writer and scholar. The book cited below is a fascinating series of essays on activities which explore the area deeply from a variety of scientific and scholarly points of view. It is an outstanding, readable volume well worth one's time to read in its totality, but sections of it can also be read independently.

Koestler, Arthur. *The Act of Creativity.* New York: Macmillan Co., 1964.

References

Ausubel, David P. *Educational psychology: A cognitive view.* New York: Holt, Rinehart, & Winston, 1968.

Barron, Frank. *Creativity and psychological health.* New York: D. Van Nostrand, 1963.

Barron, Frank. The psychology of the creative writer. *Theory into Practice,* 1966, *5,* 157–159.

Barron, Frank. An eye more fantastical. In Gary A. Davis and Joseph A. Scott (Eds.), *Training creative thinking.* New York: Holt, Rinehart, & Winston, 1971.

Crockenberg, Susan B. Creativity tests: A boon or boondoggle for education? *Review of Educational Research,* 1972, *42,* 27–45.

Crutchfield, Richard S., Conformity and Creative Thinking. In Gruber, Howard E., Terrell, Glenn, and Wertheimer, Michael, (Eds.), *Contemporary Approaches to Creative Thinking.* 120–140. New York: Atherton Press, 1962.

Davis, Gary A. Training creativity in adolescence: A discussion of strategy, *Journal of Creative Behavior,* 1969, *3,* 95–104.

Davis, Gary A., & Belcher, Terence L. How shall creativity be measured? Torrance Tests, RAT, Alpha Biographical, and IQ, *Journal of Creative Behavior*, 1971, *5*, 153–161.
Davis, Gary A., & Houtman, S. E. *Thinking Creatively: A guide to training imagination.* Madison: Wisconsin Research and Development Center for Cognitive Learning, University of Wisconsin, 1968.
De Bono, Edward. Information processing and new ideas—lateral and vertical thinking. *Journal of Creative Behavior*, 1969, *3*, 159–171.
Feldhusen, John F., Bahlke, Susan J. & Treffinger, Donald J. Teaching creative thinking. *Elementary School Journal*, 1969, *70*, 48–53.
Feldhusen, John F., Treffinger, Donald J., & Bahlke, Susan. Developing creative thinking: The Purdue Creativity Program. *Journal of Creative Behavior*, 1970, *4*, 85–90.
Getzels, Jacob W., & Jackson, Philip W. The highly intelligent and the highly creative adolescent: A summary of some research findings. In Calvin W. Taylor & Frank Barron (Eds.), *Scientific creativity: Its recognition and development* (pp. 161–172). New York: John Wiley & Sons, 1963.
Getzels, Jacob W., & Jackson, Philip W. *Creativity and intelligence: Explorations with gifted students,* New York: John Wiley & Sons, 1962.
Gough, H. G. *The adjective check list.* Palo Alto, Calif.: Consulting Psychologists Press, 1961.
Guilford, Joy P. Creativity. *American Psychologist*, 1950, *5*, 444–454.
Guilford, Joy P. Intelligence: 1965 model. *American Psychologist*, 1966, *21*, 20–26.
Guilford, Joy P., Factors that aid and hinder creativity. *Teachers College Record*, 1962, *63*, 380–392.
Guilford, Joy P., & Christensen, P. The one-way relation between creative potential and IQ. *Journal of Creative Behavior*, 1973, *7*, 247–252.
Kaplan, Norman. The relation of creativity to sociological variables in research organizations. In Calvin W. Taylor, and Frank Barron (Eds.), *Scientific creativity: Its recognition and development* (pp. 195–204). New York: John Wiley & Sons, 1963.
MacKinnon, Donald W. The nature and nurture of creative talent. *American Psychologist*, 1962, *17*, 484–495.
MacKinnon, Donald W. What makes a person creative? *Theory into Practice*, 1966, *5*, 152–156.
Mednick, Sarnoff A. The associative basis of creativity. *Psychological Review*, 1962, *69*, 220–232.

Mednick, Sarnoff A. The Remote Associate Test. *Journal of Creative Behavior,* 1968, *2*, 213–214.

Osborn, Alex F. *Applied imagination* (3rd ed.). New York: Scribners, 1963.

Parnes, Sidney J. Can creativity be increased? In Gary A. Davis and Joseph A. Scott, *Training creative thinking.* New York: Holt, Rinehart, & Winston, 1971.

Parnes, Sidney J., & Meadow, Arnold. Development of individual creative talent. In Calvin W. Taylor and Fred Barron (Eds.), *Scientific creativity: Its recognition and development* (pp. 331–320). New York: John Wiley & Sons, 1963.

Patrick, Catherine. Creative thought in poets. *Archives of Psychology,* 1935 (No. 178), pp. 1–74.

Patrick, Catherine. Creative thought in artists. *Journal of Psychology,* 1937, *4*, 35–73.

Patrick, Catherine. Scientific thought. *Journal of Psychology,* 1938, *5*, 55–83.

Rugg, Harold. *Imagination.* New York: Harper & Row, 1963.

Torrance, E. Paul. Explorations in creative thinking in the early years: A progress report. In Calvin W. Taylor, & Frank Barron (Eds.), *Scientific creativity: Its recognition and development* (pp. 173–183). New York: John Wiley & Sons, 1963.

Torrance, E. Paul. *Rewarding creative behavior: Experiments in classroom creativity,* Englewood Cliffs, N.J.: Prentice-Hall, 1965.

Torrance, E. Paul. Predictive validity of the Torrance Tests of Creative Thinking. *Journal of Creative Behavior,* 1972, *6*, 236–262.

Torrance Tests of Creative Thinking. Princeton, N.J.: Personnel Press, 1966.

Treffinger, Donald J., Speedie, Stuart M., & Brunner, Wayne D. Improving children's creative problem solving ability: The Purdue Creativity Project. *Journal of Creative Behavior,* 1974, *8*, 20–30.

Wallas, Graham. *The art of thought.* New York: Harcourt, 1926.

Wodtke, Kenneth W. and Wallen, Normal E., Teacher classroom control, pupil creativity, and pupil classroom behavior. *Journal of Experimental Education,* 1965, *34*, 1, 59–65.

Name Index

Ackerman, Walter L., 231, 232
Adams, J. A., 61
Anderson, Richard C., 30, 56, 57, 58, 74, 77, 78, 79, 81, 121, 122, 123, 126, 143, 155
Anderson, Richard M., 143
Arnold, O. L., 184, 185
Austin, George A., 43, 117, 140
Ausubel, David P., 21, 36, 37, 39, 56, 57, 58, 60, 68, 70, 71, 72, 92, 94, 99, 105, 109, 110, 145, 155, 156, 289, 290
Aylesworth, Thomas C., 207

Bahlke, Susan, 281, 283
Baker, Linda S., 165
Barlow, M. C., 151, 152, 153, 168, 188
Barnes, Buckley R., 72
Barron, Frank, 269, 271, 272, 273, 291
Bartlett, Frederick, 44, 45, 46, 47, 48, 61
Bassler, O. C., 132
Belcher, Terence L., 267, 268
Bellack, Arno A., 67, 68
Berlyne, D. E., 80, 83, 92

Binet, Alfred, 180
Bisbicos, Ethel, 76
Black, Max, 207
Blake, E., Jr., 62
Bloom, Benjamin, 248, 249
Bloom, Richard D., 77, 79
Bousfield, W. A., 40
Bower, Gordon H., 17, 41, 42, 43, 61, 100, 101, 102, 154, 155
Bransford, John D., 48, 49
Briggs, Leslie J., 36
Broder, Lois J., 248, 249
Brooks, Lloyd O., 219, 220
Brooks, V., 90
Brown, John C., 96
Bruner, Jerome S., 43, 117, 139, 140
Brunner, Wayne D., 283
Bull, Sheelagh, 81, 82, 83, 86
Burt, Cyril, 180, 181
Burton, William H., 207

Carmichael, Leonard, 46, 48
Carrington, Dorothy H., 183, 184
Carroll, John B., 118, 119, 131, 139
Ceraso, J., 55
Christensen, P., 270

Name Index

Cicero, 100
Clark, D. Cecil, 134
Clark, Michael C., 42
Clawson, Elmer U., 72
Coombs, J., 208
Corman, Bernard R., 223, 224, 225
Covington, Martin V., 159, 162, 165, 166
Crockenberg, Susan B., 263
Cronbach, Lee J., 149
Crutchfield, Richard S., 159, 162, 163, 164, 270, 275

Dahmus, Maurice E., 246
Davies, Ivor K., 66, 67, 72
Davies, Lillian, 159, 162
Davis, Gary A., 251, 267, 268, 284, 285, 286, 291
DeBono, Edward, 217, 251, 288
DeCecco, John P., 139
Deese, James, 155, 169
Dewey, John, 207, 218
Dizney, Henry, 81, 82, 86
Dorsey, Mettie F., 168
Duncan, Carl P., 249
Dunker, Karl, 214, 215, 216
Dwyer, Francis M., Jr., 86, 87, 88, 89, 91, 167, 168

Ebbinghaus, Herman, 33, 34
Edison, Thomas, 276
Ehmer, Charles, 245
Eisman, Eugene, 219, 220
Eliot, John, 246
Ellis, Henry, 169
Ennis, Robert H., 17, 174, 179, 207
Entwistle, Doris R., 55
Eustace, Barbara, 133

Farnham-Diggory, Sylvia, 89
Fawcett, H. P., 190, 191, 192, 204, 205
Feldhusen, John F., 281, 283
Feldman, Katherine V., 123, 124

Fitzgerald, Donald, 105
Flanders, Ned A., 65
Flavell, John, 22
Franks, Jeffrey J., 48, 49
Frase, Lawrence T., 74, 76, 78, 79, 92, 105
Freidbergs, V., 117

Gagné, Robert M., 61, 105, 118, 128, 131, 132, 133, 144, 145, 156, 157, 158, 226, 227
Gaite, A. J. H., 56, 99
Gall, Meredith, 73 79
Garvey, Catherine, 165
Gates, Arthur I., 93
Gay, Lorraine R., 98
Getzels, Jacob W., 272, 273, 274
Gibbons, H., 125, 126
Ginsburg, Herbert, 22
Glaser, Edward M., 193
Goodnow, Jacqueline, 43, 117, 140
Gough, H. G., 268
Greene, Harry A., 153
Grener, Norma, 189
Guilford, Joy P., 259, 260, 261, 262, 263, 266, 270
Guthrie, E. R., 94

Harris, Chester, 140
Hartley, James, 66, 67, 72
Haselrud, George M., 170, 220, 222
Hendrickson, Gordon, 150
Hendrix, Gertrude, 222, 223
Hilgard, Ernest R., 17, 61, 154, 155
Hochberg, J. E., 90
Hogan, Robert, 165
Holen, Michael C., 99
Hooper, Frank H., 22
Hopkins, L. Thomas, 168
Housman, A. E., 277
Houtman, S. E., 284, 285, 286
Hovland, Carl I., 117, 220
Hudgins, Bryce B., 140, 175

Name Index 297

Huggins, W. H., 55
Hulse, S. H., 155, 169
Hunter, Ian M. L., 44, 46, 48, 52, 55, 57, 61, 102
Hyram, George H., 187, 188, 193

Inhelder, Barbel, 13, 14, 15, 17, 21, 22

Jackson, Philip W., 272, 273, 274
James, William, 30, 109, 146, 147
Johnson, Donald M., 120, 121, 122, 123, 126, 210
Johnson, Harry C., 243, 244, 245
Johnson-Laird, Philip N., 252
Judd, Charles H., 150, 151

Kaplan, Edith, 126
Kaplan, Norman, 287
Kaplan, R., 66
Katona, George A., 38, 46
Keislar, Evan R., 139
Kennedy, George, 246
Kennedy, John M., 90
Kersh, Ben Y., 222
Kimball, Roland B., 207
Klausmeier, Herbert J., 123, 124
Koestler, Arthur, 292
Kohler, Wolfgang, 214, 217, 252
Kolesnik, Walter B., 146, 170
Krueger, W. C. F., 99
Krulee, Gilbert, 246
Kulhavy, Raymond W., 121, 122, 123, 126

Lesgold, Alan M., 42
Levin, Harry, 231, 232
Levonian, Edward, 80, 81
Loftus, Elizabeth, 214, 240, 241, 242
Luchins, Abraham S., 228, 229, 230, 231
Lumsdaine, Arthur, 90, 91

McConkie, George W., 38, 39, 93

MacKinnon, Donald W., 268, 269, 270, 272, 273, 291
Maltzman, Irving, 219, 220
Mandler, George, 40
Martin, Edwin, 155
Martorella, Peter H., 140
Mathews, Ravenna, 41
May, Mark A., 90, 91
Meadow, Arnold, 285
Mednick, Sarnoff A., 259, 266, 267, 276
Meux, M., 208
Meyer, Bonnie J. F., 38, 39, 93
Meyers, Shirley, 220, 222
Miller, Arthur, 177
Miller, George A., 41
Miller, K. M., 229, 230
Miller, William, 89
Morgan, John J. B., 183, 184
Morrisett, Lloyd P. Jr., 220
Myrow, David L., 56, 57, 58, 155

Newell, Allen, 211
Niemark, Edith D., 210
Nunnally, Jim C., 83, 84, 85
Nuthall, G., 208

Oaster, Thomas R., 99
O'Brien, Thomas C., 181, 182, 183
Olander, Herbert T., 245
Olton, Robert M., 159, 162, 163, 164
Opper, Sylvia, 22
O'Reilly, C. A., 120, 121, 122, 123
Osborn, Alex, 280, 286, 287, 292
Osborn, W. W., 194, 204
Osgood, Charles F., 54, 154, 155, 170
Overing, Robert L. R., 150, 167

Pace, Angela, 247
Paderewski, 93
Paige, Jeffrey M., 246
Paivio, Allan, 61
Paradowski, William, 83

Name Index

Paris, Scott G., 40, 49, 50, 51, 52, 53
Parnes, Sidney J., 285, 286, 287
Patrick, Catherine, 277, 278, 279
Peel, E. A., 15, 16, 194, 195, 196, 197, 199, 200, 201
Petty, Walter T., 153
Piaget, Jean, 4, 10, 11, 12, 13, 14, 15, 16, 17, 18, 19, 20, 21, 22, 179, 198
Poincaré, 277
Pollio, Howard R., 21
Precians, R. A., 208

Raths, Louis, 189
Reagan, Gerald M., 207
Reed, Homer B., 36
Reed, Horace B., 114, 115
Resnick, Lauren B., 242
Riedesel, C. Alan, 243
Rimoldi, H. J. A., 250
Roberge, James J., 182, 196
Robbins, Lillian C., 56
Rosenthal, Daniel J. A., 242
Rothkopf, Ernst Z., 66, 75, 76, 77, 78, 79, 92
Rugg, Harold, 276, 292

Samuels, S. Jay, 88, 89
Santa, John L., 210
Schroeder, William J., 150
Scott, Joseph A., 291
Shapiro, Bernard J., 181, 182, 183
Shulman, Lee S., 139
Sigel, Irving E., 22
Simon, Herbert A., 211, 246
Simonides, 100
Skinner, B. F., 92
Slamecka, N. J., 55
Smedslund, Jan, 20
Smith, B. O., 208
Smith, Ernest C., Jr., 226, 227
Smith, Louis M., 175
Smoke, Kenneth L., 116, 117
Sones, A. M., 97

Speedie, Donald J., 293
Spitzer, Herbert F., 96, 97
Staats, Arthur W., 21
Stager, Mary, 56, 99
Stratton, R. P., 126
Stroud, J., 97
Suchman, J. Richard, 86, 213, 232, 233, 234, 235, 236, 237, 238, 239, 240
Suppes, Patrick, 212, 214, 240, 241, 242
Szekely, L., 219

Taba, Hilda, 43, 185, 186, 187, 193
Thelen, Herbert A., 192
Thorndike, Edward Lee, 147, 148, 149, 150
Thouless, Robert H., 207
Torrance, E. Paul, 262, 263, 264, 265, 268, 274, 275, 288
Travers, Robert M. W., 151, 167
Treffinger, Donald J., 281, 283
Tulving, E., 117

Ulmer, Gilbert, 192

Vanderlinde, Louis F., 245
Vernon, Magdalen D., 89

Wallas, Graham, 276, 277
Wallen, Normal E., 275
Wason, Peter C., 252
Watts, Graeme H., 77, 78, 79, 81
Weiss, W., 117
Werner, Heinz, 126
Wertheimer, Max, 167
White, Ernest E., 187, 188, 193, 204
White, Richard T., 158
Wilson, John W., 245, 246
Winch, W. H., 151, 152
Wing, Richard L., 207
Winzens, David, 42
Wodtke, Kenneth W., 275
Woodworth, Robert S., 147

Subject Index

Abstract thinking, 17, 30, 112
Active learning, 2–3, 20
Adjective Check List, 268
Advance organizers, 37, 68–73
  compared to overview, 69–70
Alpha Biographical Inventory, 267 268
Anagrams, 210
Application, 204, 205
Applied Imagination, 286
Arithmetic problem solving, 240–248
  DPPC method, 246
  structural variables, 241
  transfer, 166
  vocabulary, 243–245
Arousal, 80–86
  curiosity, 80
  learning, 80–83
  retention, 81, 82
Ask and Guess Activities, 262
Assumptions, 177, 178, 179
Attention, 73
  questions, 74
Attention-paying response, 76
Attribute listing, 285

Behavioral objectives, 66
Bias, 176, 179
Biological nature of intellectual development, 17
Birmingham studies, 194–199
Brainstorming, 280, 286
Buffalo Creative Problem Solving Course, 285, 286

Categorization, 40–43
  cognitive organization, 156
  conceptual, 42, 43, 109
  recall, 40–41
Centering, 12, 13
Checklist of ideas for creative thinking, 285
Circumstantial stage of thinking development, 199–200
Clustering, 40–43
Cognitive development, *see* Intellectual development, stages of
Cognitive organization, theory of, 155–156
Cognitive structure, 29, 36
  concepts, 111
  organization of knowledge, 37
Comparative organizer, 68, 69

Subject Index

Comprehensive-imaginative stage of thinking deevlopment, 199–200
Concept, 109–111
Conceptual learning, 109–138
  context, 125–128
  definition, 119–125
  improvement of, 133–138
  laboratory study of, 113–117
  principles, 128–132
  school setting, 117–120
Concrete operational thinking, 11, 14–15
  conservation of matter, principle, 13
  meaningful material, 30
Conservation of substance, principle of, 13, 18, 19
Conservation of volume, 13, 14, 18, 19
Conservation of weight, 13, 14, 18, 19
Construction, 11
Contextual learning, 125–128
Contra Costa County Social Studies Curriculum, 185, 186, 187
Conventional Learning Direction, 66
Conversion variable of arithmetic problems, 241, 242
Cornell Critical Thinking Test, 176
Creative process, 276–279
  stages of, 276–279
Creative thinking, 256–291
  children, 272–275
  classroom aspect, 289–290
  climate for, 287–288
  correlation with intelligence, 269–270
  improvement and support of, 279–281
  measures of, 262–268
  personality characteristics, 270–272, 273
  process, 276–279
  stimulation of, 281–287
Critical thinking, 173–206
  definition, 178
  elementary school level, 180–189
  secondary school level, 189–194
  teaching suggestions, 202–206
Crucible, The, 177
Curiosity, 80–86, 92
Curriculum, 149
  critical thinking, 185–194
  problem solving, 232–240
  transfer theory, 153, 158–166

Deductive learning, 113, 119
Definition, 119–125
Depth variable of arithmetic problem, 241, 242
Digit–letter system, 103
Discipline of faculties, 146–147
Discovery method in problem solving, 222–223
Discrimination learning, 128
Divergent thinking, 259
DPPC method of arithmetic problem solving, 246
Drill, 98
Duncker ray problem, 215

Education, 19
Educational psychology, *see* Psychology of learning
Einstellung (Rigidity) in problem solving, 228–230
Elaboration, 259, 261
Environmental events in learning, 25, 26, 27
Epistemic curiosity, 80
Equilibration, 20
Evidence, 175, 176, 177, 178
Experience, 18, 19
Experimental spirit, 16–17
Expository organizer, 68, 69, 72

Facilitation, 56, 58

Subject Index

Faculty psychology, 146–147, 148
Films
　learning, 90–92
　overviews, 67
　questions, 86
Five Day Course in Thinking, 217
Flexibility, 259, 261
Floating bodies, law of, 13–15
Fluency, 259, 261
Forgetting, 52–57
Formal operational thinking, 11, 16–17
　conceptual development, 112, 125
　critical thinking, 179
Functional fixedness, 216–217

General (Nonspecific) transfer, 144, 150–154
　curriculum, 158–166

Hierarchy of learning, 118, 128
　nonmathematical concept, 132
　organization of school learning, 23–24
　transfer, 156–158

Identical elements, theory of, 147–150
Illumination stage of creative process, 276, 277, 278
Implied instruments, 51
Incidental learning, 75, 76, 78
Incubation stage of creative process, 276
Inductive learning, 113, 119
　problem solving, 220, 222
Inferred consequences, 51
Inferring, 51, 125, 126, 177, 178, 179
Information conflict, 83–85
Inquiry Training, Program, 86, 213, 232–240
　episode analysis, 236, 237
　teacher training, 238

Inspection behavior, 74, 75, 92
Institute of Personality Assessment and Research (University of California at Berkeley), 268
Instructional objectives, 66, 67
Intellectual development, stages of, 10–20
　biological nature of, 17
　concept learning, 111
Intelligence correlated with creativity, 269
Intelligence tests, 180
Interference theory, 25, 117
　forgetting, 52–59
　transfer, 154
Intuition, 271
Inventive Level test, 264
IQ test, 264, 265, 267, 270
　creativity in children, 272–275
Isolation effects, 99-100

Judgement, 271–272
Just Suppose Activity, 262–263

Learning, 2
　activity, 2–3, 20
　classroom examples, 5–9
　conceptual, 109
　developmental stages, 4, 10–20
　hierarchy, *see* Hierarchy of learning
　meaningful, *see* Meaningful learning
　meaning of, 9
　objectives, 66, 67
　organization, *see* Organization of learning
　principles, 128–132
　psychology of, 20, 146, 151
　retention, *see* Retention of learning
Learning from Films, 90
Length variable of arithmetic problem, 241, 242

Location method of mnemonics, 101
Logical–mathematical experience, 19
Logical reasoning, 181, 182–183
Luchins water jar problem, 230, 231

Mathemagenic behavior, 75, 81
Maturation, 18
Meaningful learning, 23, 150
  concrete referent, 30
  material, 29–37
  organization, 37–40
  retention, 35–37
  specific examples, 31–32
  transfer, 156
  verbal, 71
Memorizing, 9, 36, 146
Memory, *see* Remembering; Retention
Mnemonics, 100–103
  digit–letter method, 103
  location method, 101
  pegword method, 101, 102
Morphological synthesis, 285

Near transfer, 142, 158, 164–165, 166
Negative instance (Negative example), 116–117, 137–138
Negative transfer, 154, 155, 167
  problem solving, 225
Nonsense material, 32, 33
  retention, 33, 34, 35, 93
Novel Uses Test, 143

Operation, 12
  reversibility, 13
Operations variable of arithmetic problems, 241–242
Order variable of arithmetic problems, 241, 242
Organization of learning, 3–4, 23–24, 40–43

hierarchy, *see* Hierarchy of learning
  meaningful material, 37–40
  recall, 40
  transfer, 155–156
Orientation to learning, 66, 67, 68
  advance organization, 68
  overview, 67
Originality, 259, 263
Osgood surface, 154–155
Overgeneralization, 176, 179
Overlearning, 56, 98–99
Overview, 67, 68
  compared to advance organization, 69–70

Parallel Lines test, 262
Pegword method, 101, 102
Perception, 271–272
Phonological storage, 49
Physical experience, 18, 19
Piagetian system of cognitive development, 10–20
Picture Completion Test, 262
Picture Construction Test, 262
Picture use in comprehension improvement, 86–89, 92
  reading, 89
  realism, 86–88
Positive instance (Positive example), 116–117
Positive transfer, 142, 144, 154, 155, 156, 167
  problem solving, 220–221
  Productive Thinking Program, 162
Postquestion, 78
Practice, 92–98, 204
  distribution, 98–99
  nature of, 94–96
  overlearning, 98–99
  recall, 93
Preoperational thought, 11–14
Preparation stage of creative process, 276

Subject Index

Presuppositions, 51
Pretests, 67
Principles, 128, 131
  induction of, 220, 222
Principles of Psychology, 146
Problem, 211
Problem solving, 128, 210-250
  arithmetic, *see* Arithmetic problem solving
  clinical and diagnostic studies of, 248-250
  discovery method, 218-232
  instruction method, 218-232
  rigidity, 228-230
  set, 228-230
  structure, 245
  training in alternate methods, 230-232
  verbalization, 226-227
Product Improvement test, 262
Productive thinking, 212
Productive Thinking Program, 145, 159-166, 280-281, 283, 284
  Teacher's Guide, 159, 160, 162
Propositional operations, 16-17
Prose comprehension, 51-52
Psychology of learning, 20, 146, 151
Purdue Creative Thinking Program, 281-284

Question-related learning, 75, 76
Questions, 73-86, 92
  curiosity arousal, 80
  films, 91
  frequency, 76-77
  learning, 75
  location, 79
  types, 77-78

Ray problem, 214, 215, 216
Realism, 86, 87, 88
Reasoning, 180-189
  tests, 180, 181, 182, 188

Recall, *see* Retention
Recitation, 93-94
Reconstruction, 11-12
Remembering, 44-51
  mnemonics, 100-103
  psychology of learning, 146
  see also Retention
Remembering, 44
Remote Association Test (RAT), 266-267
Remote transfer, 143, 158, 165
Reproductive thinking, 212
Restricted stage of thinking development, 199-200
Retention, 23, 25
  arousal, 81, 82
  categorization, 40-43
  interference, 52-59
  meaningful material, 35, 36
  nonsense material, 33, 34
  organization of learning, 37, 40-44
  practice, 92-98
  subordinate concepts, 132
  see also Remembering
Retroaction, 154, 155, 156
Retroactive facilitation, 56
Retroactive inhibition, 54, 55, 56, 57
Reversibility of operations, 13
Review, 96, 97
Rigidity (Einstellung) in problem solving, 228-230
Rote learning, 35, 36, 37, 150
Rule learning, 128
Rules, 128-131

School-type learning, 23, 26
  improvement, 64-103
  meaningful, 23
  organization of, 23-24, 256
  processes of, 26-28
  see also Learning
Selective attention, 65
  visual, 83

Subject Index

Semantic entailment, 51
Semantic memory, 49
Sensimotor stage of intellectual development, 11–12
Sensitivity to problems, 259
Sentence memory, 48–51
Sequence variable of arithmetic problems, 241, 242
Serial reproduction, 44–46
Set to learn concepts, 114–115
Set in problem solving, 228–230, 231
Social transmission, 19
Specific transfer, 144
Stimuli and response, 155
Structure of Intellect (model), 259, 260
Synectics, 285
Syntactic memory, 49

Terman Concept Mastery Test, 269
Thinking, 10
 developmental stages, 199–200
Thinking Creatively: A Guide to Training Imagination, 284
Thinking Creatively with Pictures test, 262
Thinking Creatively with Words test, 262
Torrance Tests of Creative Thinking, 262–265, 267, 268, 281, 283
 children, 275

 scoring, 263–264
 validity, 264
Training, 204
Transfer and retoaction surface, 154
Transfer of learning, 142–168
 contemporary theory, 154–156
 critical thinking, 183, 204–205
 generality of, 144
 negative, *see* Negative transfer
 positive, *see* Positive transfer
 problems, 121, 220–221, 222, 223, 224, 225
 teaching suggestions, 166–168

Unverbalized awareness, 222–223

Verbal clues to arithmetic problem solving, 241
Verbalization, 222–223
 problem solving, 222–223, 226–227
Verbal learning, theory of, 71
Verbal transfer, 144, 157
Verification stage of creative process, 276, 277, 278
Vertical thinking, 288
Vocabulary, 243

Wanted–given problem structure, 246

Zero transfer, 154

THE BOOK MANUFACTURER

Learning and Thinking: A Primer for Teachers was typeset, printed, and bound at R. R. Donnelley & Sons Company, Elgin, Illinois, and Crawfordsville, Indiana. The cover was designed by Harvey Retzloff; cover material is Kivar 6. The type is Baskerville with Vega Medium display.

ON SPECIAL SUBJECTS

ter understanding of the work and problems of his family doctor, the specialists he may consult from time to time, and the private and public agencies concerned with his health and the health of the community in which he lives.

The articles will be found under their alphabetical headings in the encyclopedia.

I **KEEPING YOURSELF WELL**
PREFACE TO THE SECOND VOLUME
II **YOUR EMOTIONAL PROBLEMS**
PREFACE TO THE FOURTH VOLUME
III **YOU AND YOUR CHILD**
PREFACE TO THE SIXTH VOLUME
IV **PROBLEMS OF YOUR HOME**
PREFACE TO THE EIGHTH VOLUME
V **YOU AND YOUR DOCTOR**
PREFACE TO THE TENTH VOLUME
VI **YOU AND YOUR LATER YEARS**
PREFACE TO THE TWELFTH VOLUME

AND YOUR DOCTOR

tions and training. Surgical specialties. Urgent, or emergency, surgery. Elective surgery. Before the operation: hospital arrangements and the preparation of the patient. The operating room and personnel. The recovery room. How soon can the patient be visited after surgery? Postoperative care.

ANESTHESIA VOLUME 1
The modern science of anesthesia and the development of new anesthetics. General anesthetics: putting the patient to sleep. Spinal and local anesthetics. The newest techniques, including refrigeration anesthesia.

NURSING VOLUME 8
The skilled profession of modern nursing. Registered nurses, practical nurses, and nurses' aides. Nurses' training. Specializations. The opportunities for nurses, male and female.

DENTISTRY VOLUME 4
Tooth decay, the world's most prevalent disease. Avoiding serious dental problems. It doesn't hurt: recent advances in the practice and equipment of dentistry. Examinations. About fillings, crowns, caps, root-canal therapy, extractions, and dentures. The dentist's training and specialties.

HEALTH INSURANCE VOLUME 6
Protecting yourself and your family against the cost of illness or accident. The five basic types of health insurance. The insurance companies and the service organizations, Blue Cross and Blue Shield. Prepaid group-practice plans. Group versus individual plans. Over-65 plans.

PUBLIC HEALTH VOLUME 9
Safeguarding the health of the community as a whole. Public health organizations. The services of community health departments. The many jobs of the U. S. Public Health Service. Protecting the purity of food and drugs. The World Health Organization. What the individual citizen can do.

FLUORIDATION VOLUME 5
A controversial question of public health. What is fluoride? Fluoride and the elimination of tooth decay in children. Fluoridation of water: tests and testimony. Providing fluoride protection in communities where the water is not fluoridated.

AIR POLLUTION VOLUME 1
A growing health problem. About smog. What causes air pollution? What can be done to control and eliminate air pollution?

Other articles concerned with the medical profession and specialties include DIAGNOSIS, PREVENTIVE MEDICINE, CONVALESCENCE, HOME NURSING, LATER YEARS, BRAIN SURGERY, HEART SURGERY, OPERATION, OCULIST, OPHTHALMOLOGIST, PSYCHIATRY, PSYCHOANALYSIS, PSYCHOTHERAPY, CHIROPRACTOR, OSTEOPATH, FAITH HEALING, MENTAL HOSPITAL, and QUACK. Subjects related to public health include WATER POLLUTION, IMMUNIZATION, and RADIATION HAZARDS.

ADVISORY BOARD

CHARLES D. ARING, M.D.
Prof. and Chairman, Dept. of Neurology, Univ. of Cincinnati College of Medicine; Director of Neurological Services, Cincinnati General Hospital; past President, American Neurological Society.

LEONA BAUMGARTNER, M.D.
Asst. Administrator for Technical Cooperation and Research, U.S. Government; Prof. of Pediatrics, Cornell Medical College. Formerly Commissioner of Health, New York City.

HENRY BRAINERD, M.D.
Prof. of Medicine, Univ. of California Medical School; Director, Medical Service, San Francisco General Hospital. Coauthor: CURRENT DIAGNOSIS AND TREATMENT.

HARRY F. DOWLING, M.D.
Prof. and Chairman, Dept. of Medicine, Univ. of Illinois School of Medicine; Member, Advisory Council, Inst. of Allergy and Infectious Diseases (1960-63). Author: THE ACUTE BACTERIAL DISEASES; THAT THE PATIENT MAY KNOW.

FRANK FREMONT-SMITH, M.D.
Visiting Prof. of Psychiatry, Temple Univ. School of Medicine, Philadelphia; Member, Board of Trustees, Academy of Religion and Mental Health; Consultant, Natl. Inst. of Child Health and Human Development.

BERNARD LOWN, M.D.
Inventor, Lown Cardioverter; Director, Coronary Clinic, Peter Bent Brigham Hospital, Boston; Member, Dept. of Nutrition, Harvard School of Public Health. Coauthor: CURRENT CONCEPTS OF DIGITALIS THERAPY; ATRIAL ARRHYTHMIAS, DIGITALIS, AND POTASSIUM.

IRVINE H. PAGE, M.D.
Editor, MODERN MEDICINE; Director, Research Division, Cleveland Clinic; past President, American Heart Assoc.; Lasker Award. Author: HYPERTENSION; CHEMISTRY OF THE BRAIN; RENAL HYPERTENSION; ARTERIAL HYPERTENSION—ITS DIAGNOSIS AND TREATMENT.

JOHN H. PETERS, M.D.
U.S. Veterans Admin., Dept. of Medicine and Surgery, Washington, D.C. Formerly Director Medical Research, U.S. Veterans Hospital, Atlanta; Assoc. Director for Research, American Heart Assoc.

CHARLES A. RAGAN, M.D.
Prof. of Medicine, College of Physicians and Surgeons, Columbia Univ., New York; Director, First Medical Service, Bellevue Hospital, New York; Member, Natl. Research Council Comm. for Survey of Research on Rheumatic Diseases.

ALBERT B. SABIN, M.D.
Developer, Sabin Oral Polio Vaccine; Distinguished Service Prof. of Research Pediatrics at the Univ. of Cincinnati College of Medicine; Legion of Merit; Theobald Smith Award in Medical Science; Corresponding Member, British Pediatrics Assoc. and Royal Academy of Medicine, Belgium.

LEONARD A. SCHEELE, M.D.
Former Surgeon General, U.S. Public Health Service; Life Member, Assoc. of Military Surgeons of the U.S.; Honorary Fellow, American College of Surgeons; Consultant in Public Health, Morristown Memorial Hospital, New Jersey; Visiting Lecturer, Harvard School of Public Health.

MYRON E. WEGMAN, M.D.
Dean, School of Public Health and Prof. of Pediatrics, School of Medicine, Univ. of Michigan; Chairman, Editorial Board, PEDIATRICS (1961-63). Contributor: ENCYCLOPEDIA OF CHILD CARE AND GUIDANCE; ADVANCES IN PEDIATRICS.

PAUL DUDLEY WHITE, M.D.
Consultant Cardiologist to former President Dwight D. Eisenhower; Emeritus Prof. of Medicine, Harvard Medical School; Physician, Massachusetts General Hospital, Boston; past President, American Heart Assoc.; Legion of Honor, France; Member, Royal Soc. of Medicine, England. Author: HEART DISEASE; CLUES IN THE DIAGNOSIS AND TREATMENT OF HEART DISEASE; HEART DISEASE IN GENERAL PRACTICE.

VOLUME **10** Ra/Sm

THE MODERN MEDICAL ENCYCLOPEDIA

AN ILLUSTRATED FAMILY GUIDE ANSWERING QUESTIONS OF ILLNESS AND HEALTH, PHYSICAL AND MENTAL FITNESS, FIRST AID AND HYGIENE; INCLUDING ADVICE ON PERSONAL AND FAMILY PROBLEMS AND THEIR RELATION TO GOOD HEALTH

EDITOR-IN-CHIEF
BENJAMIN F. MILLER, M.D.

Assoc. Prof., Univ. of Pennsylvania School of Medicine, Philadelphia. Former Director, May Inst. for Medical Research, Univ. of Cincinnati College of Medicine; former Lecturer on Medicine, Harvard Medical School. Francis Amory Prize, 1962; Member, Medical Advisory Board, Council on High Blood Pressure Research, American Heart Assoc. Author: THE COMPLETE MEDICAL GUIDE; YOU AND YOUR DOCTOR; *coauthor:* MAN AND HIS BODY; GOOD HEALTH: PERSONAL AND COMMUNITY; *coeditor:* WHEN DOCTORS ARE PATIENTS.

GOLDEN PRESS · NEW YORK

THE STAFF

EDITOR-IN-CHIEF
Benjamin F. Miller, M.D.

DIRECTORS
Tom Torre Bevans
George Wolfson

MANAGING EDITOR
Jonathan Bartlett

ART DIRECTOR
William Sayles

PRODUCTION
Martin Connell

PICTURE EDITOR
Ronald Buehl

SPECIAL CONSULTANTS
Bertel Bruun, M.D.
Myles A. Greenberg, D.V.M.
David Harris, M.D.
Charles Pinckney Horton, D.D.S.
Charles W. Lester, M.D.
Louis Miller, M.D.
Paul Schneck, M.D.

ARTIST & TECHNICAL CONSULTANT
Neil Hardy

EDITORS
Arlette Brauer
Ruth Goode
R. Tinker Greene
Richard Harkins
Theodore Kamholtz, M.D.
Roger Menges
Elaine Rabins

ASSOCIATE EDITORS
Marion Bates
Nunzia Bongiorno
Edith Firoozi
Roland C. Gask
Judith Goode
Iris Kim
Mary Lambert
George McHugh Nicholson
James L. Steffensen

EDITORIAL ASSISTANTS
Robin Berry
Louise Fox
Miriam Lowe
Margaret Thompson

INDEX
Burton Lasky Associates

WRITERS
Don Abarbanel
Robert C. Casto
Ormonde de Kay, Jr.
William Dial
Douglas Wood Gibson
Alex Gordon
John Hopewell
Michael Knibbs
Morris Krieger
Eva La Salle
Ruth Lescher
Ian McMahan
Ellen Nodelman
Michael Rubin
Thaddeus L. Smith
Jane Sutter
George Trinkaus
Devereux P. Wight
Jerome Wyckoff

ARTISTS
Robert Beane
Remo Cosentino
Dick Dodge
Ben Goode
Enid Kotschnig
Libra Studio
Andrew Mudryck
Harriet E. Phillips
Erwin Schachner
Helen E. Speiden
Hans Zillessen

HOW TO USE THIS ENCYCLOPEDIA, *a page of suggestions for quick and easy reference, appears inside the back cover of every volume.*

© COPYRIGHT 1965 BY GOLDEN PRESS, INC., AND BENJAMIN F. MILLER. ALL RIGHTS RESERVED INCLUDING THE RIGHT OF REPRODUCTION IN WHOLE OR IN PART IN ANY FORM. DESIGNED AND PRODUCED BY ARTISTS AND WRITERS PRESS, INC. PRINTED IN THE U.S.A. BY WESTERN PRINTING AND LITHOGRAPHING CO. PUBLISHED BY GOLDEN PRESS, INC., NEW YORK.

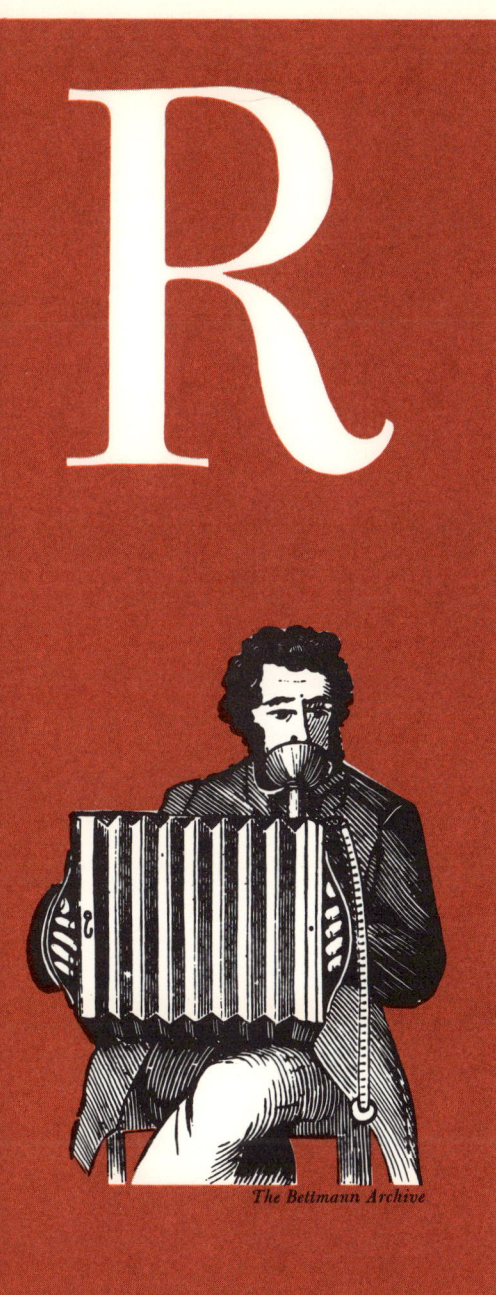

Respiratory accordion designed about 1880 for the inhalation of rarified or condensed air. If drawn apart, the instrument rarified the air within; if compressed, the air was condensed.

RABBIT FEVER

A serious but rare infectious disease carried by wild animals, mainly rabbits and ground squirrels, which can be transmitted to man; its medical name is *tularemia.*

Only about 600 cases of rabbit fever occur in the United States each year, almost exclusively among hunters, butchers, and farmers. Until the recent development of antibiotics, the disease was frequently fatal. Now, with early treatment, the mortality rate has been sharply reduced.

The illness can be contracted by handling diseased animals, eating infected wild game, or being bitten by insects, such as horseflies and deer flies, which have fed on infected animals.

Symptoms and Treatment. Rabbit fever begins with a sudden onset of chills and fever, accompanied by headache, nausea, vomiting, and severe weakness. A day or so later, a small sore usually develops at the site of the infection. This then becomes ulcerated and infected and drains pus. The lymph nodes can also become enlarged and ulcerate. There may also be a generalized red rash. In some forms, rabbit fever resembles TYPHOID FEVER, while in other forms it resembles PNEUMONIA. In untreated cases, the fever may last for weeks or even months. Tests done on the blood or draining pus help make the diagnosis.

Treatment is by antibiotics, such as tetracycline, streptomycin, and chloramphenicol.

Prevention. Rabbit fever is usually thought of as an occupational disease. Among those who may be exposed to it, such as game wardens and hunters, certain precautions may be taken. Wild animals, particularly rabbits and squirrels, should be handled only when gloves are worn. Wild game must be especially well cooked before being eaten, in order to kill the tularemia organism. When frequenting woods, the body should be covered as much as practicable to prevent the bite of insects that might be carriers of this disease.

RABBIT TEST

A test to determine whether or not a woman is pregnant. The test is performed by injecting a sample of the woman's urine or blood into a female rabbit. If the hormone *chorionic gonadotrophin*, produced during pregnancy, is present, the rabbit's ovaries will show swelling and bleeding, indicating that the woman is pregnant.

For information about such tests, see **PREGNANCY TESTS; PREGNANCY.**

RABIES

A serious virus disease affecting the brain and the nervous system; also called *hydrophobia*.

Rabies is transmitted to people by warm-blooded animals, especially dogs, that have the disease. The virus is often present in the saliva of affected animals and is transmitted chiefly through bite wounds and occasionally through open wounds or sores.

After the virus enters the body it travels along the nerve trunk to the brain; the farther the bite is from the head, the longer it takes to reach the brain. It may take from two weeks to as long as a year. The bitten person must start treatment with vaccines and serum before the virus reaches the brain. In the early stages the rabies germ can be conquered by injections; after the virus reaches the brain the disease is always fatal in animals or man. *Always have an animal bite treated by a doctor.*

Prevention

Some important measures will reduce the chances of being exposed to rabies. One is to have all warm-blooded family pets—including dogs, cats, and monkeys — vaccinated periodically against rabies by a veterinarian. Other animals likely to carry rabies are foxes, skunks, squirrels, horses, cattle, and bats. Another measure is to take any pet that is behaving strangely to a veterinarian.

It is also essential to learn to recognize a rabid animal. In the early "anxiety" stages, a rabid animal may have a change of temperament. Many, including wild animals, may become unusually friendly; it is wise to be cautious with overfriendly wild animals. The rabid animal may next enter a "furious" stage in which it wanders about biting everything that moves, and even some things that do not move, such as sticks and stones. It then develops paralysis of the throat, which makes swallowing difficult. The name hydrophobia, which means "fear of water," was given to the disease because it was observed that stricken animals avoid water. Actually, they do not do so because of fear, but because they cannot swallow. Saliva often drips from the animal's mouth and may be whipped into a foam. (Foaming

---

FIRST AID FOR RABIES

What to do in case of animal bite

1. Wash out wound thoroughly with soap and water, and bandage with sterile gauze.

2. Take bitten person to a doctor immediately.

3. Arrange to have animal that did the biting observed by a veterinarian.

4. If this is not possible, inform doctor so that bitten person can be treated for rabies immediately.

at the mouth can also occur during convulsions caused by other diseases).

Some animals pass directly from the anxiety stage to paralysis without becoming violent. This is called the "dumb" form of rabies. The animal may appear to have something caught in his throat. When a dog acts in this way, its owner is tempted to put his hand in the dog's mouth and try to remove whatever seems to be choking the dog. This should be avoided unless it is certain that the dog actually is choking on something. Usually, a dog with something in his throat tries to remove it himself, but a rabid dog will not. Eventually all of the rabid animal's muscles become paralyzed and it dies.

Treatment

When a person is bitten by an animal the wound should be washed thoroughly with soap and water, then treated like any other wound. It is extremely important to go to a doctor immediately. If at all possible, steps should be taken to find out if the biting animal has rabies. The most reliable method of determining this is to have the animal observed by a veterinarian. The animal's owner should be asked to put the animal in a veterinary hospital, but if the owner is unknown or refuses, the police and public health officials should be notified so that they can confine the animal for observation. When the biting animal must be killed in order to capture it, care must be taken to see that the head is not damaged, so that the brain can be examined by a health department to establish a diagnosis.

A veterinarian will watch the animal for the development of rabies symptoms for 7 to 14 days, depending on local health laws. If rabies does develop, the person who was bitten will be treated for rabies. There are times when the biting animal cannot be caught for observation. If so, the bitten person must be treated immediately, in case the animal did have rabies.

Preventive treatment of suspected rabies is based on **IMMUNIZATION**. In general, this involves immunizing the bite victim by a series of vaccine injections before the virus reaches the brain. If the treatment is successful, the disease will not develop. When bites are in areas close to the head or in areas with many nerve endings, such as the hands, the virus may reach the brain very quickly. In such cases treatment should start immediately, even though the suspected animal is still being observed. Along with the vaccine, such patients are often given a serum made from the blood of horses that have been made immune to rabies.

Treatment for rabies, while usually effective, occasionally has undesirable side effects on some people. Rabies is a deadly disease, however, and treatment is essential in spite of the side effects. Veterinarians and others who run a high risk of being exposed to rabies can be vaccinated against it in advance.

RADIATION HAZARDS

The dangers of highly penetrating radiation, such as X-rays, gamma rays, and cosmic rays, for human beings and other living organisms exposed to them.

Radioactive substances can be dramatically useful when carefully controlled. X-rays are used in medicine to retard the growth of cancer, and for X-ray photography. Radium and radioactive cobalt are also used in treatment of cancer, while radioactive iodine and many other radioactive substances are useful in medicine, industry, and research (see **RADIOISOTOPE**).

Excessive amounts of radiation, however, pose great hazards, because they

To minimize the possible hazards from exposure to radioactivity for medical, technical, and scientific personnel who work with radioactive materials, institutions maintain what is called a "hot laboratory." Here, radioactive material is handled by adjustable remote control manipulation. The scientist is protected behind a wall of lead bricks and lead glass through which radioactivity cannot penetrate.

tend to destroy tissues of the body. It is possible for a person to receive a large dose of radiation, as from atomic fallout, without feeling it. Harmful effects of uncontrolled radiation include serious disturbances of bone marrow and other blood-forming organs, skin burns, and sterility. There may be permanent damage to the *germ plasm*, or *genes*, which are the biological units that control heredity. Large doses of radiation produce **RADIATION SICKNESS**, which can be fatal.

People who are constantly subjected to radiation because of their work observe painstaking precautions to guard against overexposure. Physicians and X-ray technicians, for example, wear heavy protective aprons or stand outside the X-ray room when the machine is turned on. In nuclear plants, hospitals, and other places where dangerous exposure may occur, radiation can be detected by means of instruments such as the Geiger counter, and the quantity of radiation to which a person is exposed can be measured by devices such as the film badge, which measures radiation by means of photographic film.

Man's everyday environment exposes him to a certain amount of background radiation in the form of cosmic rays, atmospheric radiation, and particles emitted during the breakdown of naturally occurring radioactive substances, such as uranium, in the earth's crust. To this is added radiation received through medical treatments and incidental exposure to radioactive paints, nuclear reactions, and other sources. Medical authorities agree that these types of radiation doses received during the average person's lifetime are harmless.

Pollution of the world's atmosphere by nuclear explosions is cause for concern, however. Some of the fallout remains radioactive for many years, and although most of it is scattered very widely through the atmosphere, dangerous quantities may by chance fall upon certain areas. All authorities agree that prolonged nuclear warfare would seriously threaten the health and even the future existence of mankind.

RADIATION SICKNESS

A disease resulting from the penetration of the body by radiation. Its severity varies with the individual and his physical condition, the body areas exposed, and the amount, kind, and intensity of the exposure. The disease may be so slight that the exposed person scarcely notices it, or it may be so acute that death results in a few hours or days. Since radiation cannot itself be seen or felt, an individual can receive a harmful dose without being aware of it.

All persons during their lifetimes are exposed to radiation at various times (see RADIATION HAZARDS), but the exposures are usually too slight to be harmful. (For discussions of the therapeutic uses of radiation, see RADIOLOGY and RADIOTHERAPY.)

Some cases of radiation sickness result from intensive radiotherapy for cancer. The symptoms are generally nausea, vomiting, diarrhea, and a feeling of general weakness. The intensity of the therapy, and therefore the symptoms, can be controlled by the doctor. He will also guard against the development of complications. Some radiation sickness may have to be accepted as a price for the advantages of the therapy.

Much publicity has been given to radiation injuries from nuclear explosions. Radiation sickness was widespread among survivors of the atomic bombing of Japan in World War II, and these survivors have suffered long-term effects. Today radiation sickness in acute form occurs as a result of rare accidents in factories or power plants that use large quantities of nuclear materials. Acute radiation sickness is of general interest, however, in view of the possibility of any future war between major nations in which nuclear weapons with world-wide effect might be used.

Effects of Massive Radiation

An exposure of the entire body to several thousand roentgens at one time will cause death within a few days. About 600 roentgens is enough to be fatal over a longer period. Within a few hours after such a dose the victim will show signs of shock, nausea, and generalized distress. Often there follows a period of seeming recovery, but after several days the damage to internal organs becomes apparent. Symptoms may include soreness of mouth and throat, bloody diarrhea, progressively increasing fever, loss of hair, and general weakening of the body. Coma may follow, and then death, within about two weeks of the exposure.

Around 450 roentgens is considered enough to cause serious radiation sickness with a 50 percent chance of recovery. Symptoms appear and the disease progresses as in fatal cases, but if the victim does not contract a secondary disease such as pneumonia, and if he can survive as long as three months, recovery is likely.

In cases of milder exposure, the immediate symptoms may be totally absent. After several weeks, mild forms of the symptoms already described may appear. Barring complications, the victim should then recover gradually.

Generally speaking, the more intense the first symptoms, the less likely is the patient to survive. The length of the period before the onset of the second stage of the disease also indicates the severity of the case. If this period lasts but a day or two, an unfavorable outcome can be expected.

Though a person may recover from radiation sickness, he may suffer long-term effects, including damage to the *germ plasm,* or *genes,* that control heredity, as well as scars and deformations of internal tissues. There is also in radiation sickness apparently a greater-than-average susceptibility to cancer. Women pregnant at the time of excessive exposure may produce deformed children.

RADIOISOTOPE

A *radioactive* form of an element. A radioisotope consists of unstable atoms that emit rays of energy or streams of atomic particles. Radioisotopes occur naturally, as in the cases of radium and uranium, or may be created artificially.

Scientists create artificial radioisotopes by bombarding stable atoms of an element with subatomic particles in a nuclear reactor or in an atom smasher, or *cyclotron*. When the nucleus of a stable atom is charged by bombarding particles, the atom usually becomes unstable, or radioactive. A number of radioisotopes have important uses in medicine, industry, research, and other fields.

Radioisotopes in Medicine

Radioisotopes are used in medicine for both diagnosis and treatment. In general, the therapeutic use of radioisotopes is reserved for older groups, aged 40 and over.

The most widely used radioisotopes in medicine are forms of iodine, phosphorus, gold, iron, and cobalt.

Radioactive Iodine. When taken into the body, iodine salts concentrate in the THYROID GLAND. Doctors put this fact to use in various ways with the aid of radioactive iodine (I^{131}). The amount of I^{131} absorbed by the gland, as observed by a Geiger counter or similar instrument, can reveal whether the gland is functioning normally or is underactive or overactive. In toxic GOITER, or *hyperthyroidism*, a form of overactivity of the thyroid, radiation from I^{131} is used to destroy excessive gland tissue. Similarly, I^{131} is used to destroy malignant cells in some kinds of CANCER of the thyroid.

Radioactive Phosphorus. Radioactive phosphorus (P^{32}) gravitates to actively growing tissues, particularly those involved in manufacturing BLOOD cells; its radiation is therefore used to destroy red blood cells in *polycythemia vera,* a disease marked by excessive manufacture of red blood cells. P^{32} is useful in the treatment of chronic LEUKEMIA and some other forms of cancer.

Radioactive Gold. A radioisotope of gold (Au^{198}) is used to relieve some types of cancer that are not subject to surgery, such as inoperable cancer of the PROSTATE GLAND. A further use is the treatment of certain cancerous conditions in body cavities of the chest and abdominal regions. Au^{198} may also be used to reduce or destroy a tumor of the PITUITARY GLAND that is a cause of ACROMEGALY, or gigantism.

Radioactive Iron. Since iron forms part of *hemoglobin,* one of the principal components of red blood cells, radioactive iron (Fe^{59}) is useful in studying certain blood conditions, including iron-deficiency anemia.

Radioactive Cobalt. Radioactive cobalt (Co^{60}) has largely replaced radium in radiotherapy for localized cancer, since it can be produced relatively cheaply and in compact equipment, and provides radiation of high intensity. Co^{60} is also used in measuring vitamin B_{12} absorption in pernicious anemia.

RADIOLOGY

The branch of medicine concerned with diagnosing and treating disease through the use of X-rays, radioactive substances, and other forms of radiant energy. Radiology is a modern science that had its origin in 1895 when the German physicist Wilhelm Konrad Roentgen announced his discovery of X-rays. Roentgen reported that he had produced a new kind of ray by sending a high voltage current from a filament to a target sealed in a glass vacuum tube. He announced that these rays could penetrate through matter that is opaque to other rays, and that they could be used to make photographic images of bones and other structures situated within the body.

Soon the rays were being used as an aid in diagnosing internal conditions in the body. It was also found that the rays, if given in large doses or repeatedly, had the power to injure tissue. This power is used to destroy unwanted tissue, such as that of cancer. In the early days, primitive equipment limited the use of X-rays for treatment. Radium, the highly radioactive element first discovered by Pierre and Marie Curie in 1898, provided a more flexible technique. Subsequently great improvements were made in X-ray apparatus, and X-rays came into wide use in treatment as well as in diagnosis.

Today specialized X-ray devices have been developed for many specific purposes, and there are few branches of medicine in which X-rays are not used for diagnosis or treatment. In every hospital and in most doctors' and dentists' offices, X-ray apparatus is routine equipment. In addition, radioisotopes, or radioactive forms of various elements that are used in diagnosis and treatment, have broadened the scope of radiology. Such forms of treatment, whether administered by X-rays or radioactive

Radiological health is a new field in the science of public health for which highly trained specialists are needed. These public health workers from all over the country are learning to use radiation detection instruments at a U. S. Public Health Center. A source of radiation has been put in the center of the circles and the instruments are read and checked from specified known distances.

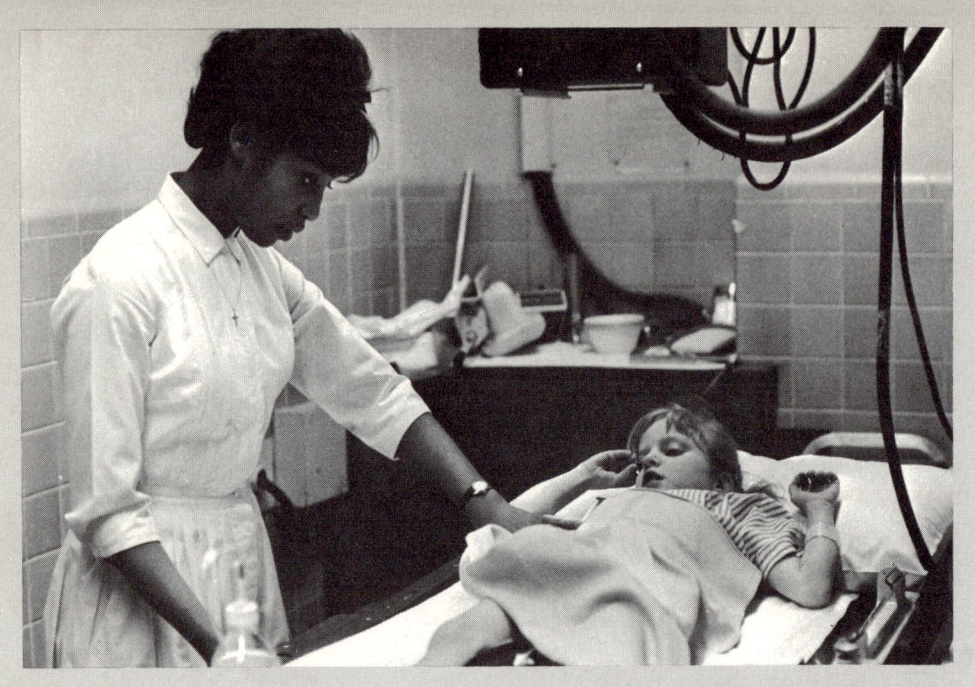

A radiological technician prepares to take a photograph of this young girl's knee with an X-ray camera. After photographing the knee from the front, she will turn the girl and photograph the joint from the back and sides. The X-ray pictures will help in diagnosis of the knee ailment.

substances, are known as **RADIOTHERAPY** or *radiation*.

The Nature of X-rays

X-rays are energy waves of very short wave length, which gives them their special penetrating power. They are produced by bombarding a tungsten target with high-speed electrons in a vacuum tube. They are not visible to the human eye, but, like ordinary light, they may be captured as a visible image on film, or on the specially coated screen of a **FLUOROSCOPE**.

The degree of penetration of X-rays depends partly on the density of the matter at which they are aimed. This is the reason why X-rays directed through the body produce a picture of internal structures. Because the tissues of the body are of varying densities, they permit different amounts of the rays to pass through them. On the film or screen, these different ray intensities produce a shadow picture. The lungs, for example, show up because of the great difference in density between the air in the lung spaces and the solid tissues.

Some structures in the body have a density similar to adjacent or surrounding structures, and cannot be seen in an ordinary X-ray. These structures can, however, be clearly visualized by techniques in which the organs are filled with material that X-rays cannot penetrate. A familiar example of this technique is the gastrointestinal series (GI series), a **BARIUM TEST** in which a chalky compound called barium sulfate is introduced into the digestive tract. This substance makes the organs stand out in silhouette in the X-ray image.

With highly developed modern tech-

ATOMIC MEDICINE AGAINST DISEASE
Highlights in the History of Radiology

X-RAYS were discovered in November 1895 by the German physicist Wilhelm Konrad Roentgen while he was experimenting with cathode tubes. He produced short electromagnetic wave radiations that could penetrate many substances, including body tissues. Four months later the first American photographic plate made exclusively for X-ray use was tested in a Philadelphia maternity hospital to diagnose an immobility of the finger joints.

ROENTGEN

NATURAL RADIOACTIVITY was discovered in uranium in 1896 by Antoine Henri Becquerel. Two years later Pierre and Marie Curie discovered polonium and radium. They isolated one gram of radium salts from about eight tons of pitchblende. For their work they shared a Nobel Prize with Becquerel in 1903. In 1934 their daughter Irène Joliot-Curie and her husband, Frédéric Joliot-Curie, discovered that substances could be made artificially radioactive by bombarding them with alpha particles from the new element polonium.

MARIE AND PIERRE CURIE

PORTABLE X-RAY APPARATUS invented by Thomas Edison was used by the United States Army during the Spanish-American War. Edison also made a fluorescent screen from calcium tungstate with which Professor Michael I. Pupin of Columbia University made the first efficient fluoroscopic picture in 1896.

THE TREATMENT OF DISEASE with radiation began as early as 1896 when John Daniel of Vanderbilt University used X-rays to cure patients with dermatoses. In 1939 radioactive phosphorus was first used to treat leukemia. Today powerful radiation can be concentrated into needles called bombs which are applied directly to an area to destroy the agents of disease without endangering surrounding tissues. Radioactive substances such as phosphorus 32, iodine 131, gold 198, yttrium 90, cobalt 60, cesium 137, radon 222, and strontium 90 are used to treat diseases of the skin, lymph glands, uterus, the gastrointestinal tract, and other organs.

THE DIAGNOSTIC USE of radioactive elements has greatly increased since 1946 when radioactive medical materials first became available in useful amounts. Today radioactive materials, along with X-ray photographs, help physicians to determine the nature and extent of cancers and diseases of the thyroid gland, blood, and liver. These "tracers" are given by mouth or by injection and their pathways through organs of the body can be followed and analyzed by Geiger or scintillation counters.

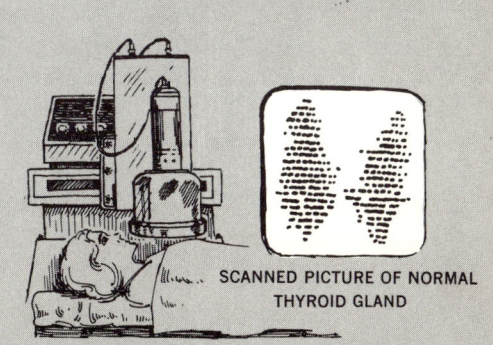

SCANNED PICTURE OF NORMAL THYROID GLAND

RADIOLOGY

A nurse attends a betatron used in cancer treatment. The beam is carefully controlled from a shielded control booth. The betatron provides radiation of high intensity, useful in treating deep-seated cancers.

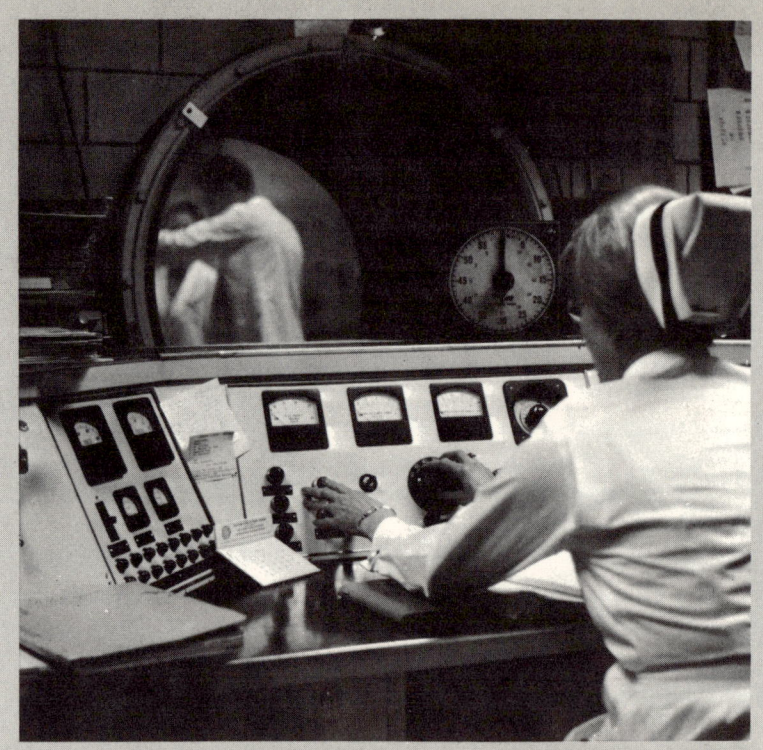

niques and equipment, it is possible to detect and diagnose many disorders within the body by X-rays. These disorders range from fractures and tooth decay to tumors and infections.

Radioactive Substances

Radium, the first radioactive substance to be used in medical treatment, produces spontaneously several kinds of rays that check the growth of tissue. It has been used successfully in the treatment of various diseases, notably cancer. One type of rays called *beta rays* may be used to treat conditions on or near the surface of the body, while the more penetrating rays called *gamma rays* may also be used in the treatment of deeper conditions.

Radium is usually used in the form of one of its salts. The salts are confined in various airtight containers that are inserted into body cavities and tumor tissue. Platinum or gold needles are sometimes employed; tiny tubes called seeds may be filled with *radon*, a gas given off by radium, and inserted in growths temporarily or sometimes permanently.

Many radioisotopes consist of substances which are not ordinarily radioactive but which have been made radioactive by artificial means (see RADIOISOTOPE). These emit beta and gamma rays and are used in many ways. One of them, radioactive cobalt, provides radiation of a very high intensity and has largely replaced radium in treatment for localized cancer. Radioactive cobalt-60 machines, delivering one of the most powerful of the artificially produced nuclear radiations for cancer treatment, have given encouraging results. Radioisotopes used in

RADIOLOGY

tracer studies are valuable diagnostic aids in such diseases as hyperthyroidism.

Radiotherapy and Cancer

Among conditions that are treated by radiotherapy, by far the most important is CANCER. Several forms of cancer have been treated successfully in this way. Of the many living Americans who have been cured of cancer, at least half have been treated with radiation. Other cancerous conditions have been improved by such treatment. Often radiotherapy is used in conjunction with surgery, medicines, or a combination of the two.

The success of radiotherapy has been increasing steadily. The reasons for this are many; they include the development of new equipment and techniques.

Therapeutic radiation ordinarily does not destroy cancer cells directly; only the very highest dose will kill the cells outright. Radiation somehow alters the cell so that it cannot reproduce. The irradiated cell eventually ages and dies, leaving no new cells behind.

Not all forms of cancer are suitable for radiation treatment, and the decision as to whether or not it is to be used and what technique is suitable must be made by a physician. He will also be able to recommend a radiologist.

The Radiologist

The training required of the radiologist, as of any specialist, is long and rigorous. It includes college and medical school, where the candidate earns his doctor of medicine degree (M.D.), fol-

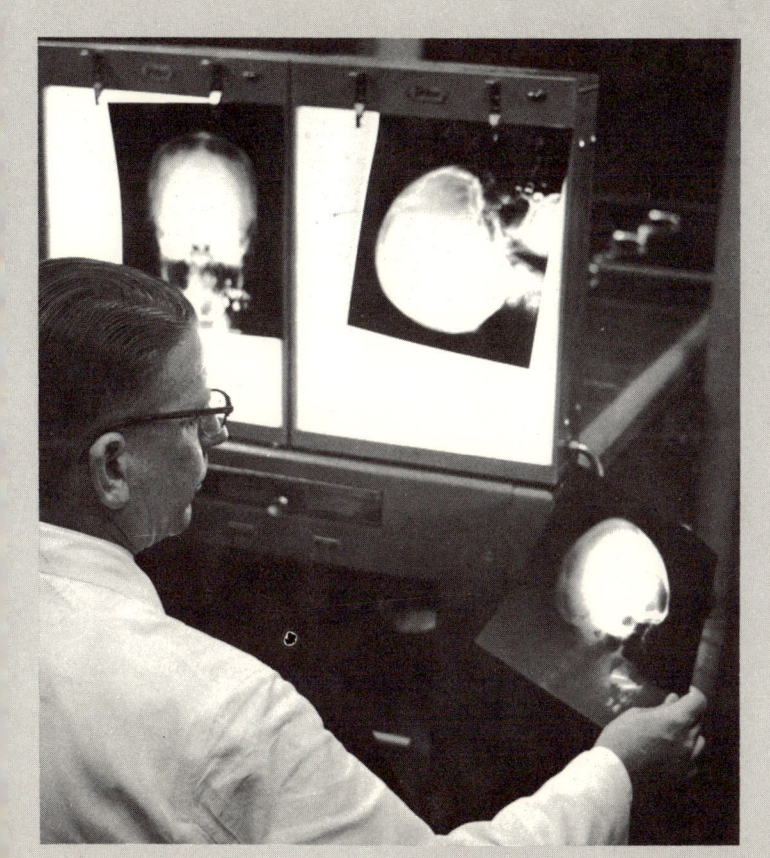

A radiologist is a physician who specializes in the medical science of using radioactive energy in the diagnosis and treatment of diseases. An important part of his work is the interpretation of X-ray photographs. This radiologist is studying X-ray photographs of a patient's head taken from three angles.

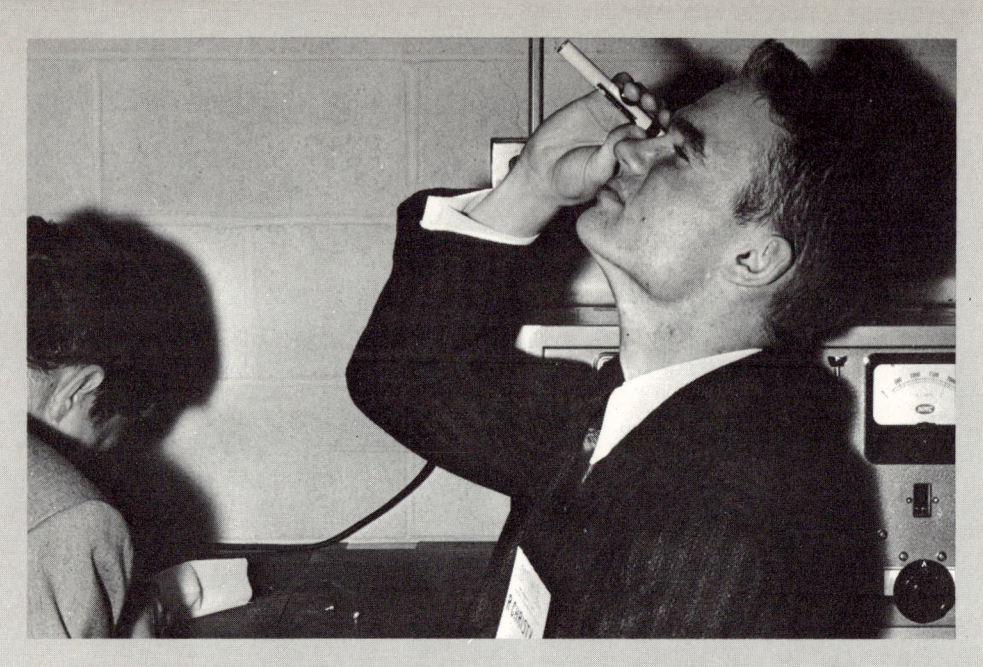

A dosimeter, which this young man is reading, is an instrument which helps radiotherapists and other scientific personnel protect themselves from possible exposure to dangerous radiation. Worn in a breast pocket like a fountain pen, it registers the wearer's cumulative exposure to radiation.

lowed by internship, and a three-year residency (for a general discussion on the training of a DOCTOR, see the article under that heading). A year after completing his residency in radiology, the doctor is eligible to take the qualifying examination given by the American Board of Radiology. His practice usually includes both X-ray diagnosis and radiotherapy.

The radiologist himself does not necessarily perform every radiological procedure. If a patient is having an ordinary X-ray examination, he may not see the radiologist. The examination is usually conducted by an X-ray technician, who positions the patient for the particular area to be filmed and carries out the physician's directions in such matters as the number of films to be taken. The interpretation of the completed films remains the responsibility of the radiologist.

RADIOTHERAPY

The use of X-rays, radiation from radioactive substances, and other similar forms of energy in the treatment of cancer and other diseases.

X-RAYS are energy waves of very short wave length which have many properties, including the power to injure or destroy tissue, such as the growths produced by cancer. *Radium*, the first radioactive substance to be used in medical treatment, spontaneously gives off rays that affect the growth of tissue. Other substances not normally radioactive, such as *cobalt*, can be made radioactive (see RADIOISOTOPE), and are widely used in medicine.

Radiotherapy is often used in conjunction with surgical treatment or with medicines, or with a combination of the two, when cancer is present.

For a broader discussion of radiotherapy, see RADIOLOGY.

RADIUM

A highly radioactive metallic element found in pitchblende and other uranium minerals.

Radium is used in several ways in the treatment of certain kinds of cancers. In the form of needles or pellets, it can be inserted in the diseased or tumorous tissue and left there until its rays have destroyed that tissue. It can be used in the form of plaques applied to the cancer. Large amounts of radium are also used as a source of gamma rays, much like a cobalt machine.

For additional information, see RADIOLOGY; CANCER.

RASH

A visible inflammation of the skin, usually temporary.

There are so many kinds of rashes and such a variety of causes that usually only a doctor can identify them accurately; even he may be puzzled in some cases until he has checked the patient for other symptoms. Laboratory tests may be required. In appearance, rashes range from the rosy-colored spots of GERMAN MEASLES to the scaly patches of PSORIASIS or the more uniformly scarlet skin in SCARLET FEVER. Some rashes may result from disease involving only the skin, or may be symptoms of diseases elsewhere in the body.

Other rashes are not related to any disease and are relatively innocuous, as, for example, the rash caused by chafing of tight clothing. Infants' DIAPER RASH is another instance of chafing, although it sometimes may have more complex causes. PRICKLY HEAT is another harmless, although annoying, common rash.

In CONTACT DERMATITIS, the rash or eruption may be due to direct contact with an object to which a person is sensitive, or allergic. Many people are sensitive to POISON IVY, OAK, AND SUMAC. Some are allergic to certain substances which make them "break out"—the metal in a piece of costume jewelry or a wrist watch, for example, or the rubber in a girdle or the leather in a hatband. Food allergies also can cause rashes, and at times skin eruptions seem to result from tension or other emotional difficulties. HIVES and ECZEMA are rash-producing diseases which in some cases appear to have been caused, at least in part, by allergies or emotions. Identifying these special sensitivities can be difficult. In complex or persistent cases, doctors may refer patients to dermatologists.

Bacteria, viruses, and infectious funguses are common causes of rashlike inflammations, such as RINGWORM and ATHLETE'S FOOT. Still other rashes are caused by contagious diseases within the body, such as MENINGITIS and MEASLES. In these diseases, the rash is an outward result of the internal disorder. The spots or blotches are warnings calling for diagnosis and treatment of the disease which caused them. SYPHILIS may make itself known by a rash which initially can mimic many other types of rashes; the disease can be identified by a *Wassermann* blood test.

Though most rashes are not serious and often disappear quickly, it is not wise to let them go without medical attention unless the cause is obvious, familiar, and not serious (a light exposure to poison ivy, perhaps, or a reaction to a substance to which a person is known to be allergic). Certainly any rash accompanied by fever or a general feeling of illness calls for immediate notification of the doctor. Minor outbreaks of rashes, especially if they persist or recur, should also be seen by a physician, who can prescribe medication to soothe and cure the inflammations and, if necessary, test for allergies that may cause them.

RAT CONTROL

Of all animals, rats have had one of the most profound effects on mankind. They live in man's houses and eat his food. Not only have they caused great economic losses, but they have changed the course of history by the diseases they have spread.

The most terrible of all these diseases is *bubonic plague* (see PLAGUE), which at various times in history has ravaged large areas of the world in great pandemics (widespread epidemics). It is believed that more people died in these pandemics than in all the wars of history. Bubonic plague is actually a disease of rats, spread among them by the bites of infected fleas and then to man when the fleas leave the dying animals in search of other hosts. So virulent is the disease that in former times it was nearly always fatal; in epidemics the mortality rate was as high as 90 percent. Today, however, with the discovery of antibiotics, the mortality rate has been reduced to 5 percent, and the disease occurs extremely rarely, except in the more remote parts of the world.

Weil's disease, an acute infection frequently accompanied by jaundice and other disorders, is also carried by the rat; it spreads to humans through food contaminated by rat urine or through broken skin which may have come in contact with the urine. The disease is present in wild rodents in some parts of the United States, but only rarely is it transmitted to humans.

RATBITE FEVER is the name given to either of two similar diseases caused by bacteria in the mouths of rats and transmitted when the rodents bite. Both diseases cause inflammation of the lymph glands, and though less serious than some of the other rat-borne diseases, can be extremely debilitating.

To avoid these and other diseases spread by rats, constant vigilance must be maintained against rats. Cleanliness is essential, especially where food is served. Food should always be stored in closed containers to prevent rats from getting into it. Refuse and garbage should also be put in closed metal containers until it is suitably disposed of. In buildings known to be infested with rats, special care must be taken to protect young children and invalids. Any rat bite should be reported to a doctor without delay.

Rat-proofing. The existence of rats in substandard housing emphasizes the relationship between HOUSING AND HEALTH. Since rats depend largely on human habitations for shelter, buildings should be kept as ratproof as possible. In new buildings, ratproof construction is commonly employed. Older buildings, especially deteriorating ones, should be ratproofed with materials such as concrete, hollow tile, sheet iron, tin, and hardware cloth. The breaks at the foundation and roof require special attention. All holes through which rats might enter should be plugged. At floor and ceiling levels, pipes should be tightly fitted with metal shoulders to close off possible openings.

Rat-killing. In the countryside, animals such as snakes, owls, hawks and skunks—natural enemies of rats—are nature's way of controlling rats. In domestic areas, dogs and cats are useful as rat-killers. Traps are often useful, although rats learn to avoid them.

The most effective means of eliminating rats is with one of several proven poisons. Ideally, a rat poison should be harmless to humans and domestic animals. One widely used and "safe" preparation is red squill; mixed with food bait, it causes heart failure and respiratory paralysis in rats. Rats retain the poison, whereas most domestic animals and humans immediately vomit it. Another widely used poison is Warfarin, which causes rats to bleed internally and die.

Phosphorous poison is effective, but presents a danger to man and to other animals. Barium carbonate is also effective, and has the added advantage of making rats thirsty, so that they will go back to their drinking place to die.

When any form of rat poison is used, it is absolutely essential to protect children from coming in contact with either the poisoned bait or the container (see POISONS AND POISONING).

RATBITE FEVER

Either of two distinct diseases that may be transmitted to man by the bite of an infected rat and less commonly by the bite of an infected squirrel, weasel, dog, cat, or pig. The more common of the two fevers in the United States is *Haverhill fever,* so named because the first epidemic to be studied occurred in Haverhill, Mass. The other form, *sodoku,* rarely occurs in the United States but is observed frequently in Japan and other Eastern countries. Although both diseases were originally identified following the bite of a rat or similar animal, there are also other ways of transmission. Both diseases require prompt medical treatment.

Haverhill fever is caused by a type of bacteria called *Streptobacillus moniliformis.* If the disease follows a rat bite, a fluid-filled sore appears at the site of the bite within 10 days. High fever alternates with periods of normal temperature at intervals of 24 to 48 hours, and there is swelling of regional lymph nodes. The joints—usually the large joints—become reddened, swollen, and painful. There may be back pain, and a spotty, measles-like skin rash.

Sodoku, or *spirillar* ratbite fever, is caused by *Spirillum minus* bacteria. The original bite heals promptly but within 5 to 28 days the site becomes swollen and takes on a dusky, purplish hue. In sodoku, there is usually no joint inflammation and the rash is patchy rather than spotty. Otherwise the symptoms resemble those of Haverhill fever.

Treatment for both forms of ratbite fever is with penicillin, streptomycin, or other antibiotic compounds. The diseases are prevented by exterminating rats and by ratproofing houses. The methods are discussed under RAT CONTROL. There are no vaccines.

RECTAL EXAMINATION

A medical examination of the RECTUM to ascertain if there is a rectal or prostatic disorder. Such an examination forms part of every thorough MEDICAL EXAMINATION, or check-up; in addition, it will be performed by the doctor at any time when his patient shows symptoms of rectal difficulty.

The examination consists of a direct visual inspection of the anus and of the interior of the rectum and *sigmoid* (the looped segment of the intestine above the rectum) by means of the *sigmoidoscope* or PROCTOSCOPE—a lighted tube which the doctor inserts into the rectum and through which he can see the tissues. Ordinarily this is a simple and painless examination.

He will also insert a gloved and lubricated finger into the rectum to determine whether there are masses in the rectum or in the pelvic region, and to determine the size and texture of the PROSTATE GLAND in men.

RECTUM

The lowest segment of the INTESTINE. It ends in an opening to the outside of the body, the anus. Through this opening pass the feces, the solid waste prod-

RECTUM

ucts of DIGESTION. These are formed in the large intestine and are gradually pushed down into the rectum by the intestine's muscular action. The distention of the rectum by the accumulating feces sets up nerve impulses that indicate to the brain the need to empty the bowels (see BOWEL MOVEMENT).

The rectum itself is between 6 and 8 inches long, with the anal canal making up the last inch. The anus is kept closed —except during the evacuation process —by a muscular ring, the *sphincter*.

REDUCING

Overweight can affect physical and mental health. Too many extra pounds are a strain on the body, and can eventually shorten the span of life. Overweight is also unattractive, and this may create psychological problems.

Today we are more aware of the dangers of overweight than in the past. We know that the overweight person is inviting a number of unnecessary complications. Some of these are an overworked heart; shortness of breath; a tendency to hardening of the arteries and high blood pressure or to diabetes; chronic back and joint pains from increased strain on joints and ligaments; a greater tendency to contract infectious diseases; and a reduced ability to exercise or enjoy sports. We know, too, that carefully compiled statistics show that mortality from circulatory conditions is about 45 percent higher in seriously overweight men than in those whose weight is reasonably close to normal, and death from such conditions is apt to occur sooner. Because of this increased risk, life insurance companies are reluctant to grant insurance to people greatly overweight.

Psychologically, too, the overweight person is at a disadvantage. The show of good cheer sometimes associated

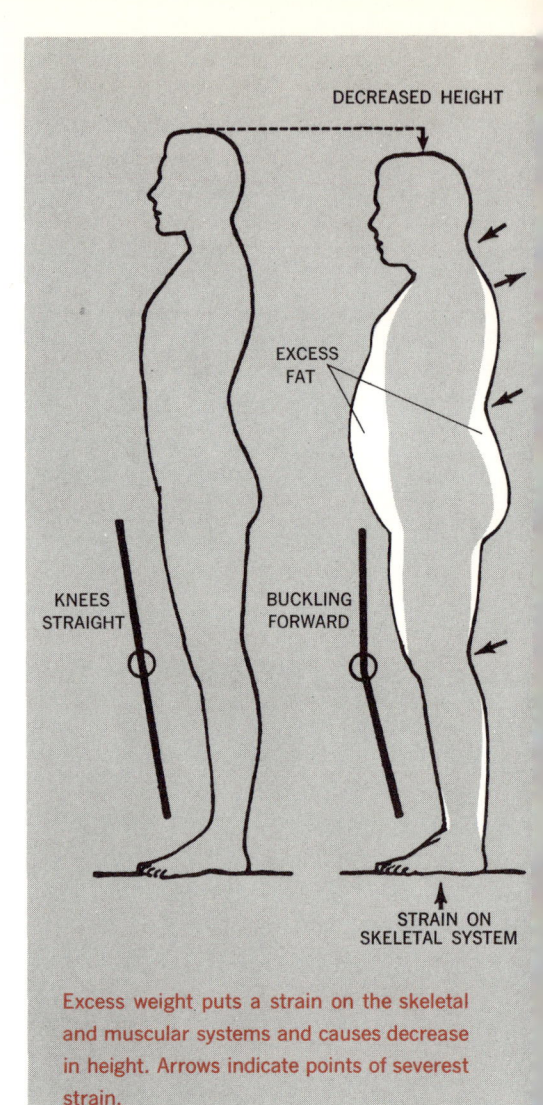

Excess weight puts a strain on the skeletal and muscular systems and causes decrease in height. Arrows indicate points of severest strain.

with obese people usually masks unconscious—or even conscious—unhappiness and disappointment. Overweight can cause personality problems; in turn, emotional difficulties such as those caused by persistent loneliness, tension, or boredom sometimes find an outlet in compulsive overeating. Talking these problems over with the family doctor may be helpful; in extreme cases he may recommend PSYCHOTHERAPY.

HEIGHT—WEIGHT CHARTS
WEIGHT IN POUNDS ACCORDING TO FRAME (IN INDOOR CLOTHING)

MEN, AGED 25 YEARS AND OVER

HEIGHT (with shoes on) 1-inch heels Feet / Inches	SMALL FRAME	MEDIUM FRAME	LARGE FRAME
5 2	112-120	118-129	126-141
5 3	115-123	121-133	129-144
5 4	118-126	124-136	132-148
5 5	121-129	127-139	135-152
5 6	124-133	130-143	138-156
5 7	128-137	134-147	142-161
5 8	132-141	138-152	147-166
5 9	136-145	142-156	151-170
5 10	140-150	146-160	155-174
5 11	144-154	150-165	159-179
6 0	148-158	154-170	164-184
6 1	152-162	158-175	168-189
6 2	156-167	162-180	173-194
6 3	160-171	167-185	178-199
6 4	164-175	172-190	182-204

WOMEN, AGED 25 YEARS AND OVER

HEIGHT (with shoes on) 2-inch heels Feet / Inches	SMALL FRAME	MEDIUM FRAME	LARGE FRAME
4 10	92- 98	96-107	104-119
4 11	94-101	98-110	106-122
5 0	96-104	101-113	109-125
5 1	99-107	104-116	112-128
5 2	102-110	107-119	115-131
5 3	105-113	110-122	118-134
5 4	108-116	113-126	121-138
5 5	111-119	116-130	125-142
5 6	114-123	120-135	129-146
5 7	118-127	124-139	133-150
5 8	122-131	128-143	137-154
5 9	126-135	132-147	141-158
5 10	130-140	136-151	145-163
5 11	134-144	140-155	149-168
6 0	138-148	144-159	153-173

METROPOLITAN LIFE INSURANCE COMPANY

Causes of Overweight

Many overweight people delude themselves into believing that their extra pounds are caused by glandular disturbances. This is very rarely the case, although some types of obesity do result from improper functioning of glands that secrete the hormones which control metabolism, appetite, and the body's utilization of fat. Such cases can usually be controlled or cured by hormones given under a doctor's direction.

Most often, however, obesity is caused simply by eating or drinking too much. Unable to "burn" all the "fuel" it takes in and does not eliminate as waste, the body stores the surplus as fat. And fat, it has been discovered, is not simply inactive stored material; fat works busily making more fat. The common observation that "the more you eat, the more you need to eat" is true enough, superficially, since the heart and other muscles of an obese person have to work harder than those of a person of normal weight, and consequently require more "fuel." Thus overindulgence leads to further overindulgence in a vicious circle.

Factors in Reducing

There are a number of approaches to reducing. These should be considered and discussed with a physician, who will suggest the method most suitable to the patient's particular needs. Because the family doctor knows the physical condition and special requirements of the people under his care, he is in a position to guide a person toward the best reducing program.

The most important factor in losing weight is the determination to do so, and the will to remain reduced when weight has been lost. In general, it is unwise to try to lose a great deal of weight in a short time. The right procedure depends largely on how much overweight one is. If it is only a few pounds, and the program has been worked out with the doctor, a person can usually succeed on his own. He should inform his doctor at once of any unusual symptom, such as diarrhea. On the other hand, one who is seriously overweight should keep in close touch with the doctor throughout the recommended reducing course.

The accompanying tables may serve as a useful guide for judging the extent of overweight. Compiled by the Metropolitan Life Insurance Company, they list the weights considered desirable for men and women of various heights and builds. The minimum and maximum figures, in pounds, are for persons wearing their regular indoor clothing, including shoes.

A person who weighs a few pounds more than the higher figure given for his height and build should discuss the matter with his doctor on his next visit. Anyone who exceeds the given limit by at least 15 pounds, however, should arrange for a medical check-up without delay. The average person tends to put on weight as the years go by, and the hazards of being overweight increase with age.

Dieting

Practically everybody can achieve and maintain an ideal weight, regardless of family history. Healthy individuals gain or lose weight according to the amount and kind of food they eat and the amount of energy they expend. Thus diet and exercise are the keys to reducing; of the two, diet is the more important.

Just as an automobile engine burns gasoline, the human body burns food for heat and energy, and just as a car uses more fuel going fast or uphill, the body needs more food when it works hard. The amount of energy obtained from food is measured in calories, a word which comes from the Latin *calor,* meaning heat. The number of calories a person needs varies not only with his weight but with his occupation. A lumberjack may burn up 6,000 calories a day, while a stenographer uses only 2,000. (For a guide to calories consumed in various activities, consult the chart in the article on CALORIE.)

But quantity—the number of calories —is not the only guide to an adequate diet. Quality counts, too. In proportions which vary greatly from one kind of food to another, food is made up of carbohydrates (including sugars and starches), fats, proteins, vitamins, and minerals (see NUTRITION). Each of these plays its own role in supplying the body with the materials it needs for energy and growth and for the never-ending process of repairing and replacing tissue. In a well-planned diet these nutritional elements are in proper balance with one another so as to meet the body's various requirements. This is why a doctor's advice about a diet is so important.

Calorie Diets

For most overweight people, a balanced low-calorie diet provides the most straightforward way to lose weight. Diets of this kind vary according to the food preferences and special requirements of the individual; for example, some people need more than the average amount of bulk to keep the intestinal tract clear.

The following menu for one day, totaling 995 calories, is taken from a typical reducing diet. Vitamin supplements may be required with some low-calorie diets. For guidance on any full reducing program, it is always advisable to consult a physician.

CALORIE CHART

Food and Measures*	Approximate Calories
Apple, baked, 1 large and 2 tbs. sugar	200
fresh, 1 large	100
Asparagus, fresh or canned, 5 stalks, 5 in. long	15
Avocado, ½ 4-in. pear	265
Bacon, 2-3 long slices, cooked	100
Banana, 1 medium, 6 in. long	90
Beans, lima, fresh or canned, ½ cup	100
green or yellow, fresh or canned, ½ cup	25
canned with pork, ½ cup	175
Beef (cooked), corned, 1 slice, 4 by 1½ by 1 in.	100
hamburger, 3 oz.	300
round, lean, 1 medium slice (2 oz.)	125
sirloin, lean, 1 average slice (3 oz.)	250
tongue, 2 oz.	125
Beets, fresh or canned, 2, 2-in. in diam.	50
Bread, corn (1 egg), 1 2-in. square	120
rye, 1 slice, ½ in. thick	70–75
white, enriched, 1 slice, average	75
whole wheat, 100%, 1 slice average	75
Broccoli, 3 stalks, 5½ in. long	100
Brussels sprouts, 6 sprouts, 1½ in. diam.	50
Butter, 1 tbs.	95
Cabbage, cooked, ½ cup	40
raw, 1 cup	25
Cake, angel, 1/10 large cake	
choc. or vanilla, with icing 2 by 1½ by 2 in.	155
	200
cupcake (med.), choc. icing	250
Cantaloupe, ½ 5½-in. melon	50
Carrot, 4 in. long	25
Cauliflower, ¼ of head, 4½ in. in diam.	25
Celery, 2 stalks	15
Cheese, American cheddar, 1 cube 1⅛ in. square	110
cottage, 5 tbs.	100
cream, 2 tbs.	100
Chicken, ½ med. broiler	270
Chocolate, milk, sweetened, 1 oz.	140
malted milk, fountain size	460
syrup, ¼ cup	200
Cocoa, half milk, half water, 1 cup	150
Cod steak, 1 piece, 3½ by 2 by 1 in.	100
Cola soft drinks, 6-oz. bottle	75
Collards, ½ cup, cooked	50
Corn, ½ cup	70
Corn flakes, 1 cup	80
Cracker, graham, 1 square	35
saltine, 2-in. square	15

Food and Measures*	Approximate Calories
Cream, light, 2 tbs.	65
heavy, 2 tbs.	120
whipped, 3 tbs.	100
Custard, ½ cup	130
Egg, medium	75
Eggplant, 3 slices, 4 in. diam., ½ in. thick, raw	50
Flour, 1 tbs., unsifted	35
Frankfurter	125
Gelatin, fruit flavored, ready to serve, ½ cup	85
Grapefruit juice, unsweetened, 1 cup	100
Grape juice, ½ cup	80
Griddle cake, 4 in. diam.	75
Halibut, 1 piece, 3 by 1⅜ by 1 in.	100
Ham, lean, 1 slice, 4¼ by 4 by ½ in.	265
Hominy grits, cooked, ¾ cup	100
Ice cream, ½ cup	200
Ice cream soda, fountain size	325
Jellies and jams, 1 rounded tbs.	100
Lamb, roast, 1 slice, 3½ by 4½ by ⅛ in.	100
Lettuce, 2 large leaves	5
Liver, 1 slice, 3 by 3 by ½ in.	100
Liverwurst, 2 oz.	130
Macaroni, cooked, ¾ cup	100
Maple syrup, 1 tbs.	70
Margarine, 1 tbs.	100
Milk, buttermilk, 1 cup	85
condensed, 1½ tbs.	100
evaporated, ½ cup	160
skim, 1 cup	85
whole, 1 cup	170
yogurt, plain, 1 cup	120–160
Mushrooms, 10 large	10
Noodles, cooked, ¾ cup	75
Oatmeal, cooked, ¾ cup	110
Oil, corn, cottonseed, olive, peanut, 1 tbs.	100
Olives, green, 6 medium	50
ripe, 4-5 medium	50
Onions, 3-4 medium	100
Orange, 1 medium	80
juice, 1 cup	125
Parsnip, 7 in. long	100
Peach, fresh, 1 medium	50
canned in syrup, 2 lg. halves, 3 tbs. juice	100
Peanut butter, 1 tbs.	100
Peanuts, shelled, 10	50
Pear, fresh, 1 medium	50
canned in syrup, 3 halves, 3 tbs. juice	100

Food and Measures*	Approximate Calories
Peas, canned, ½ cup	65
fresh, shelled, ¾ cup	100
Pepper, green, 1 medium	20
Pie, apple, 3-in. sector	200
mincemeat, 3-in. sector	300
Pineapple, fresh, 1 slice, ¾ in. thick	50
canned, unsweetened, 1 slice, ½ in. thick, 1 tbs. juice	50
juice, unsweetened, 1 cup	135
Pork chop, lean, 1 medium	200
Potato chips, 8-10 large	100
Potato salad with mayonnaise, ½ cup	200
Potatoes, mashed, ½ cup	100
sweet, ½ medium	100
white, 1 medium	100
Prunes, dried, 4 medium	100
Pumpkin, ½ cup	50
Raisins, ¼ cup	90
Rice, cooked, ¾ cup	100
Rutabagas, ½ cup	30
Salad dressing, French, 1 tbs.	90
mayonnaise, 1 tbs.	100
Salmon, canned, ½ cup	100
Sauerkraut, ½ cup	15
Soup, condensed, 11-oz. can, mushroom	360
tomato	230
vegetable	200
Spaghetti, cooked, ¾ cup	100
Spinach, cooked, ½ cup	20
Squash, summer, cooked, ½ cup	20
winter, cooked, ½ cup	50
Sugar, brown, 1 tbs.	50
granulated, 1 tbs.	50
Tapioca, uncooked, 1 tbs.	50
Tomato juice, 1 cup	60
Tomatoes, canned, ½ cup	25
fresh, 1 medium	30
Tuna fish, canned, ¼ cup, drained	100
Turnip, 1, 1¾ in. diam.	25
Veal, roast, 1 slice, 3 by 3¾ by ½ in.	120
Waffle, 6 in. in diam.	250
Wheat flakes, ¾ cup	100

Alcoholic Beverages

Beer, 8 oz.	120
Gin, 1½ oz.	120
Rum, 1½ oz.	150
Whisky, 1½ oz.	150
Wines	
champagne, 4 oz.	120
port, 1 oz.	50
sherry, 1 oz.	40
table, red or white, 4 oz.	95

* 1 cup equals 8 ounces (oz.); 3 teaspoons (tsp.) equal 1 tablespoon (tbs.); 4 tablespoons (tbs.) equal ¼ cup.

COURTESY OF THE METROPOLITAN LIFE INSURANCE COMPANY

MENU FOR ONE DAY: 995 CALORIES

Food	Number of calories
Breakfast	
Orange juice (½ cup)	85
Soft-boiled egg	75
Toast, 1 slice	75
Butter (1 teaspoonful)	30
Coffee	0
with cream (1 tablespoonful)	30
	295
Luncheon	
Consomme (1 cup)	25
Lamb chop	130
Broccoli (1 large stalk)	40
Carrots (½ cup)	25
Pineapple slice	50
Coffee or tea	0
with cream	30
	300
Supper	
Crabmeat (3 ounces)	90
Green peas (½ cup)	55
Cole slaw	15
with vinegar	0
Apple	75
Cookie	75
Skim milk (1 cup)	90
	400

If using sugar to sweeten coffee or tea, remember that one teaspoonful contains 16 calories. A dieter can safely drink coffee or tea in moderation at any time; they may satisfy his hunger for the time being and give him the quick energy he needs. He can even nibble food between meals, particularly if this cuts his appetite at mealtimes. But when he does, he should carefully check the calorie content of his snack. Most snack foods contain many more calories than most people realize. While a handful of cheese tidbits has only about a dozen calories, a sweet pickle 15, and a raw carrot 25, an ice cream sundae may contain from 300 to 400 calories. It is better to eat the total allowance of calories over an entire day than at one time.

Whittling Calories from Meals

There are many ways in which housewives can lower the calorie content of foods in preparing and serving them. Here are a few.

Fats. Skim milk or powdered milk can take the place of cream in beverages, on cereals and fruit, and in soup, mashed potatoes, and gravy. Cottage cheese is a versatile nonfattening substitute for butter; it is especially good as a spread on thin, dry Melba toast with chives or onion or celery salt. In cooking chopped spinach or other greens in very little water, the addition of a bouillon cube gives flavor so that butter can be omitted. Fried foods, especially French fried potatoes, should be avoided, as all oils and greases are fattening. Eggs boiled or poached instead of fried or scrambled make a delicious breakfast dish; poached eggs are appetizing on a slice of unbuttered toast or on a toasted English muffin. If a stew is cooked ahead of time and allowed to cool, the hardened fat can be removed. In preparing and eating meat in any form, the fat should be trimmed off.

Starches. These should be largely avoided. Leafy green vegetables can provide the bulk that starches ordinarily supply. Salad served ahead of the main course can be a boon to dieters, for it takes the edge off their hunger before the higher-calorie foods appear. To save on calories, dieters can use wine vinegar with herbs or lemon juice as salad dressing instead of mayonnaise. Bread and rolls are best avoided altogether or eaten sparingly, and if served, should be eaten without butter.

Additional points for a dieter to keep in mind are: A hearty, high-protein breakfast will usually allay hunger pangs during the morning and prevent overeating at midday; small, frequent meals are better than one or two very large ones. Alcoholic beverages are high in calories and often stimulate the appetite. Dieters should drink only in moderation.

The dieter should not try to get rid of extra pounds too fast. Fat lost at the rate of half a pound to a pound a week stays off much more surely than fat lost rapidly. When a person loses weight slowly, moreover, his skin can adjust to the loss, and he does not take on a haggard, loose-skinned appearance.

Crash Diets

New diets that promise to take off excess weight in a hurry are constantly appearing. While a crash diet may fulfill its authors' claim, it may also undermine a dieter's resistance to the point where his health is endangered. Too often, a crash diet will give quick results but the dieter does not develop the habit of eating moderately. He usually returns to his former habits—and to his former weight. A limited number of crash diets have been thoroughly tested, however, and have produced remarkable, even if temporary, results. It is of the utmost importance that any crash diet be undertaken only with the advice of a doctor and under his supervision.

Low-calorie Food Substitutes

What applies to crash diets applies also to the various low-calorie food substitutes on the market: Their use on a regular basis should always be under medical supervision. These preparations are mostly in canned liquid form, and are sold in drugstores, grocery stores, delicatessens, and other retail outlets. Many people find them a convenient and economical means of reducing. However, they may lack some of the essential ingredients of a properly balanced diet, particularly bulk. Relying on them exclusively can be as dangerous as overdoing any diet.

Quality and Quantity

In their quest for the ideal reducing formula, many people overlook the fact that almost anyone can lose weight simply by consuming less of the food he ordinarily eats. The prospect of cutting down on the quantity but not sacrificing the quality of their food intake should appeal particularly to overweight men and women who relish fine food, together with its sauces, seasonings, and other trimmings. By substantially reducing the sizes of their portions and using a few substitutions that are scarcely perceptible even to the most sensitive palates, they can continue to enjoy the same varied, high-quality fare while they lose weight, slowly and safely.

Diet and Exercise

While EXERCISE can be very beneficial to health, it is not in itself an effective way to lose weight. It has been estimated, for example, that the average overweight person would have to walk 36 miles to lose a single pound. On the other hand, exercise can be a valuable adjunct to dieting, as it keeps the dieter fit and helps him lose weight in the right places. Many doctors recommend a course of exercises along with a diet, varying the program according to the patient's age and physical condition.

Other Reducing Methods

A variety of pills, powders, and other preparations sold commercially do curb the appetite, making it easier for overweight people to refrain from overeating. Such preparations should never be taken except on the prescription or advice of a doctor; some contain thyroid extract, which can be harmful to the heart and other parts of the body. Furthermore, even preparations that are harmless to most people can harm a few.

REDUCING

In this connection, smoking, particularly of cigarettes, undeniably dulls the appetite. Smoking more for the sake of reducing, however, could provide a cure worse than the complaint (see SMOKING).

Massage may tone up the skin and muscles and help the body of a dieter adjust to its new, slimmer contours, but it does not reduce weight. Hot baths, such as steam, Turkish, and sauna baths, are likewise worthless as weight reducers; they simply remove water, in the form of sweat, which is almost immediately regained. They accomplish nothing and at the same time may cause positive harm by putting a dangerous strain on the heart and circulation.

REFLEX

An involuntary, automatic act or movement performed in response to a stimulus. Two of the most familiar reflexes are the knee jerk, which the doctor tests with his hammer, and the "hot-stove reflex," by means of which the hand pulls away from a hot surface even before the person feels the sensation of burnt fingers.

A reflex is different from an *instinct* in that it is built into the NERVOUS SYSTEM and does not need the intervention of conscious thought to take effect. An instinct is a patterned response in the brain itself.

The knee jerk is an example of the simplest type of reflex. When the knee is tapped, the nerve that receives this stimulus sends an impulse to the spinal cord, where it is relayed to a motor nerve. This causes the muscle at the front of the thigh to contract and jerk the leg up. This reflex, or *simple reflex arc*, involves only two nerves and one *synapse*, or connection between them. The leg begins to jerk up while the brain is just becoming aware of the tap.

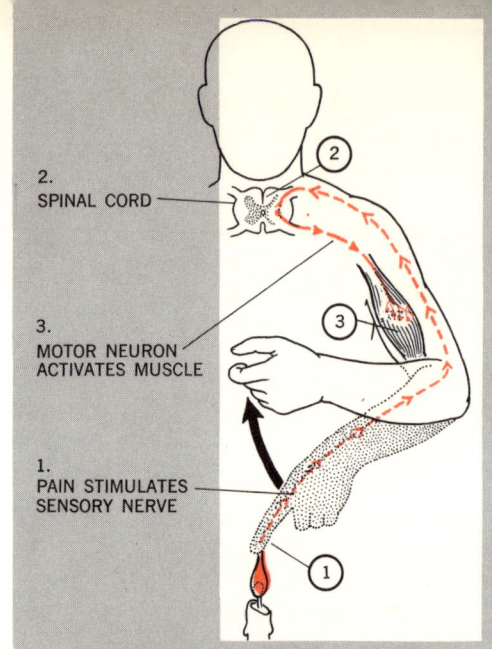

2. SPINAL CORD

3. MOTOR NEURON ACTIVATES MUSCLE

1. PAIN STIMULATES SENSORY NERVE

A reflex is achieved when the nervous system transmits sensory information that the arm is near a candle, and the brain transmits motor instructions back through the nervous system that cause the arm to withdraw.

Other simple reflexes, the *stretch reflexes*, help the body maintain its balance. Every time a muscle is stretched, it reacts with a reflex impulse to contract. As a person reaches or leans, the skeletal muscles tense and tighten, tending to hold him and keep him from falling. Even standing still, the stretch reflexes in the skeletal muscles make many tiny adjustments to keep the body erect.

The hot-stove reflex is more complex, calling into play many different muscles. Just to pull the hand away, an impulse must go from the sensory nerve endings in the skin to a center in the spinal cord, from there to a motor center, and then out along the motor nerves to shoulder, arm, and hand muscles. Trunk and leg muscles respond to support the body in its sudden change of position, and the head and eyes turn to look at the cause of the injury. All this happens while the person is becoming aware of the burning sensation. A reflex that protects the body from injury, as this one does, is called a *nociceptive reflex*. Sneezing, coughing, and gagging are similar reflexes in response to foreign bodies in the nose and throat, while the wink reflex helps protect the eyes from injury.

Far different from these reflexes is the CONDITIONED REFLEX, first identified in 1911 by the Russian physiologist Ivan Petrovich Pavlov in a famous experiment. Pavlov rang a bell each time he gave food to a dog, and showed that in time the dog would salivate at the sound of the bell alone, without the food. This occurred because the repeated association of the bell with food built what can be considered a new reflex into the dog's nervous system.

REHABILITATION

The process of restoring a person's ability to live and work as normally as possible after a disabling injury or illness. It aims to help the patient achieve maximum possible physical and psychological fitness and regain the ability to care for himself. It offers assistance with the learning or relearning of skills needed in everyday activities, with occupational training and guidance, and with psychological readjustment.

Rehabilitation is an integral part of *convalescence*. Proper food and medication, hygiene, and suitable exercise provide the physical basis for recovery. The patient is encouraged to be active physically and mentally to the extent recommended by the doctor. Entertainment and other recreation, such as reading, enjoying radio or TV, and seeing visitors, help to keep up the convalescent's spirits. Easy work activities, such as painting or sewing, also help. If the patient is depressed, psychological counseling may be needed. For more guidance on patient care during CONVALESCENCE, see the article of that title.

Physical Therapy. Most hospitals have a physical therapy department staffed by professionally trained men and women. Its primary purposes are to relieve the physical discomfort of disabled persons and to help them recover muscular function. Physical therapy is especially important for those who are recovering from illnesses or injuries such as poliomyelitis, muscular dystrophy, stroke, and broken limbs which affect body movement. Bed exercise, massage, heat treatments, and hydrotherapy may be used. During this period or later, as part of the physical restoration of the patient, reconstructive surgery may be performed—for example, the repair of a hip joint so that the patient can walk again.

After the patient is discharged from the hospital, physical therapy may be continued on an outpatient basis, or it may be given at home by a trained therapist or a properly instructed member of the patient's family. See also PHYSICAL THERAPY.

Learning Self-care. The training of disabled persons to care for themselves begins as early as is practicable during convalescence. People with serious physical handicaps, such as blindness or loss of both legs, must learn new methods of getting around, dressing and undressing, bathing, eating, and going to the toilet. They may have to learn the proper use of wheel chairs, orthopedic braces, artificial limbs, or other mechanical aids. Speech therapy may be necessary for persons who have suffered strokes or undergone throat surgery.

Occupational Therapy. As their ability in self-care increases, convalescent persons are able to take advantage

REHABILITATION

Physical therapy is a form of rehabilitation for patients recovering from diseases. This boy, whose walking was hampered by a disease affecting his legs, learns to walk again with help from a therapist.

of *occupational therapy*. This is designed to restore or develop skills in various kinds of work and hobbies that are within the ability of the patient, such as sewing and painting, light carpentry and weaving, modeling, and ceramics. These activities not only afford good mental and physical exercise but prevent boredom and bolster the patient's morale. Some occupational therapy centers have arranged for the sale of objects made by their patients, and the proceeds are of great help both financially and psychologically. Occupational therapy is available in some hospitals and also at certain private and community-operated agencies staffed and equipped for highly specialized service.

Disabled persons must be educated and trained for maximum competence and self-reliance, for their own welfare and for the welfare of others. A housewife who has lost one arm can learn how to run her household again successfully, despite the handicap. A child partly crippled by poliomyelitis can be taught to handle the details of household chores and to cope with school activities. A paraplegic father can learn to drive a specially equipped car that will get him to and from his place of business. Today there are available many service agencies, as well as a remarkable assortment of mechanical devices, to aid the handicapped toward greater independence.

In some instances an accident or illness makes it impossible for a disabled person to return to his former occupation. A shop foreman who has become blind, or a bus driver who has lost both

REHABILITATION

legs, obviously will need training for a new occupation. For persons with such problems, rehabilitation centers are available with specially trained occupational therapists. Under their guidance the disabled person can learn a new trade, making the most of his natural interests and talents.

Training courses of many kinds, especially in manual occupations, are available at rehabilitation centers. Many partially disabled persons take correspondence courses or attend technical, business, and other schools to qualify for new occupations. Rehabilitation agencies often are able to place their clients with business firms or other organizations where they can get on-the-job training. See also OCCUPATIONAL THERAPY.

Rehabilitation Centers and Programs. During and after convalescence,

Art therapy can be an important guide to rehabilitation of mental patients. By interpreting the patients' work, trained psychologists gain insight into their progress toward recovery.

Vocational therapy is a form of rehabilitation that teaches new types of work. Under the guidance of a therapist, this woman is learning how to operate an electric sewing machine.

REHABILITATION

a disabled person or his family can get information about rehabilitation programs from the hospital or from his physician. Some programs may be available locally or from the hospital itself. Among the nationally known independent, nonprofit centers are the following: The Institute for the Crippled and Disabled, New York City; the Cleveland Rehabilitation Center; the May T. Morrison Center for Rehabilitation, San Francisco; the Rehabilitation Institute, Kansas City; the Kessler Institute for Rehabilitation, West Orange, N.J.; and the Kaiser Foundation Rehabilitation Center, Vallejo, Calif.

Some centers, such as the Institute of Physical Medicine and Rehabilitation in New York City, are integral parts of medical centers. Other rehabilitation units are operated by state and local governments and by independent charitable agencies, such as the Goodwill Industries. Institutes for the training of the blind, such as the Lighthouse, in New York City, also are available.

RELAPSING FEVER

Any one of a group of similar infectious diseases transmitted to man by the bites of **LICE** and **TICKS,** and marked by alternating periods of normal temperature and periods of fever relapse.

The diseases in this group are caused by several different species of a type of bacteria called *spirochetes.* Relapsing fevers are divided into those transmitted to man by ticks and those transmitted by head and body lice; but there is little difference between the two.

Symptoms and Diagnosis

Generally, relapsing fever starts with a sudden high fever of 104° to 105°, accompanied by chills, headache, muscle aches, nausea, and vomiting. There may also be jaundice (yellowing of the skin and eyes) and skin rash. The attack lasts two or three days, after which the symptoms disappear by crisis, which means that they end suddenly, with profuse sweating accompanying the rapid drop in temperature. In elderly people this may be accompanied by collapse, in which the heart and respiratory systems function poorly. After three or four days there is a relapse and the symptoms return in their former severity. The cycle continues through four or five attacks, or even up to ten, before the disease has run its course. Relapsing fevers are rarely fatal, but they can be serious and a doctor should be consulted as soon as possible. Laboratory tests are performed to verify the diagnosis.

Treatment and Prevention

Treatment is with antibiotics. Sponge baths and aspirin help to control the fever and comfort the patient.

While tick-borne relapsing fever still occurs in the western United States as well as in other parts of the world, the louse-borne fever is now largely confined to underdeveloped parts of Asia, Africa, and Latin America. Improved public sanitation and louse and tick control account for the decline of the disease. Lice can be destroyed by insecticides such as DDT. Sometimes it is necessary to treat clothing with the chemical. Tick repellent, such as dimethylphthalate, should be applied to clothing and exposed parts of the skin when it is necessary to enter tick-infested areas.

RELAXATION

Relaxation is one of the fundamental human needs, in its way as necessary as sleep. Everyone needs frequent periods of rest and diversion so that he can return to his daily tasks refreshed. The positive use of the time available for relaxation, however, is an art not everyone has mastered.

True relaxation involves both the mind and the body. It cannot be achieved simply by being inactive or killing time in some meaningless activity. Instead, relaxation should provide a pleasant change from ordinary activity.

Physical and mental tension are closely connected, and proper relaxation can eliminate both. Many people whose work involves severe mental tension find that they can relax their minds by having someone massage their neck and shoulder muscles, which are very sensitive to tension. Others whose work is more physically active can best relax through some passive activity, such as watching television, listening to music, or reading.

Hobbies and sports provide another approach to relaxation. They offer the widest range of physical and mental demands, from the intense physical activity of tennis and the heavy mental demands of chess to the much lighter demands of fishing or stamp collecting. The most important consideration in choosing a sport or hobby is that it should be a relaxation from the stresses of ordinary tasks, and not another field in which these tensions are reflected.

For example, a person whose work involves keen competition with others will probably find it easier to relax if he avoids leisure-time activities that are highly competitive. In the same way, a person who works alone might find a group activity refreshing. And for a person who leads an active life, a simple and leisurely activity like whittling may be an effective way to relax.

For a complete change of pace, the annual vacation is not only desirable, but is almost a necessity.

The articles on SPORTS AND HEALTH and VACATIONS contain further discussion about ways to make one's leisure time meaningful. Inability to relax can lead to physical and emotional problems. How this can happen is discussed in the articles on EMOTIONS AND HEALTH, PSYCHOSOMATIC ILLNESS, STRESS, and TENSION.

REPRODUCTION

The process by which individuals produce offspring. The sex glands, or gonads—the ovaries in the female and the testes in the male—create the germ cells that unite and grow into a new human being inside the mother. Reproduction begins when the germ cells unite, a process called fertilization.

Production of Germ Cells. The germ cells are the male sperm and the female ovum, or egg. The mature ovum is a comparatively large, round cell that is just visible to the naked eye. Sperm can be seen only under a microscope, where each appears as a small, flattened head with a long whiplike tail used for locomotion.

The ability to have children begins at puberty during the teens. Many psychological, physical, and metabolic changes accompany puberty in the growing boy and girl, including maturation of the gonads and other sexual organs (see REPRODUCTIVE ORGANS, FEMALE, and REPRODUCTIVE ORGANS, MALE). Adolescents are able to produce children when the girl begins to have regular menstrual periods and the boy is able to ejaculate seminal fluid containing sperm from the erect penis.

Menstruation means that the girl's reproductive organs are probably producing ova, although several years may be required before these organs attain full maturity. She will normally continue to produce one egg capable of fertilization with each menstrual cycle until the menopause, the "change of life," which usually occurs in the mid-forties. When menstruation ceases, so does the ability to conceive children. There is no such sudden loss of fertility in the male, who, from puberty on, may produce viable sperm for his entire life.

The maturation of an ovum in the woman to the point where it can be fertilized by a sperm is a remarkable process controlled by hormones secreted by the female's endocrine glands. The menstrual cycle is ordinarily 28 days long, measured from the beginning of bleeding—caused by the discharge of blood and tissue from the uterus—until the next bleeding (see MENSTRUATION). During the first two weeks of the usual cycle, one of the ova becomes mature enough to be released from the ovary. When the mature ovum ruptures through the capsule of the ovary, we say that OVULATION has occurred. At this point, the ovum can be fertilized.

The ovum is released into the abdominal cavity. Somehow, by mechanisms that are unclear, it moves into a FALLOPIAN TUBE, one of which lies near each ovary. Then it begins the descent toward the UTERUS, or womb, where the baby is to be developed. If the ovum remains unfertilized, menstrual bleeding occurs about two weeks later.

There is no sexual cycle in the male comparable to the cyclical activity of ovulation in the female. Mature sperm are constantly being made in the testes of the adult male and stored there in the duct system.

Fertilization, or Conception. Fertilization of the ovum, or conception, results from sexual intercourse. For this act, the male penis becomes engorged with blood so that it is erect and hard enough to enter the female vagina. After stimulation, seminal fluid is ejaculated from the penis into the back of the vagina near the cervix of the uterus.

About a teaspoonful of semen is discharged with each ejaculation, containing several hundred millions of sperm, together with the secretions of several sexual glands. Of this enormous number of sperm, only one is needed to fertilize the egg. Yet the obstacles to be overcome are considerable before this one sperm reaches the egg. Many of the sperm are deformed and cannot move. Others are killed by the acid secretions of the vagina, even though the semen itself is alkaline. The sperm must then swim against the current of secretions flowing out of the uterus.

The sperm swim on the average between one eighth of an inch to one full inch in a minute. When one or more vigorous sperm are able to reach the egg, which is normally in the outer half of the Fallopian tube, fertilization occurs. The head end of the sperm plunges through the thick wall of the egg, leaving its tail outside. The genetic materials, the chromosomes, are injected into the egg, where they unite with the chromosomes inherited from the mother (see HEREDITY). The sex of the child is determined at this instant, according to the particular types of chromosomes carried by the sperm.

If by chance two eggs have been released and are fertilized by two sperm, fraternal TWINS are formed. Identical twins are produced by a single fertilized egg that divides into two eggs early in its development.

Ovulation and Fertilization. Fertilization can occur only on the average of four days out of every menstrual cycle. The mature ovum lives only about one or two days after ovulation, and the sperm have only about the same amount of time before they perish in the female reproductive tract. To fertilize the ovum, intercourse must take place within the period which begins one or two days before ovulation and lasts until one or two days after

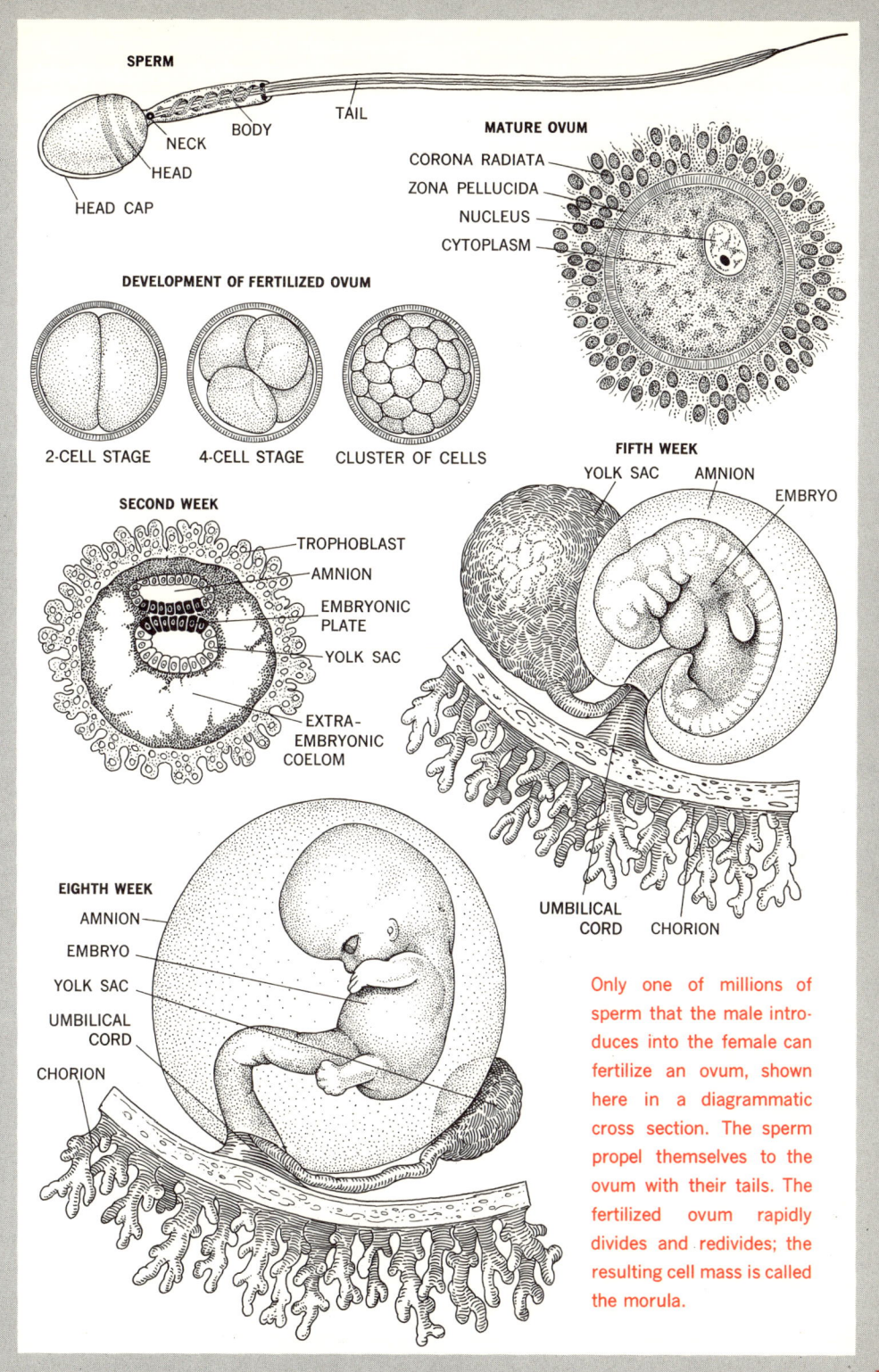

REPRODUCTION

SPERM
- HEAD CAP
- HEAD
- NECK
- BODY
- TAIL

MATURE OVUM
- CORONA RADIATA
- ZONA PELLUCIDA
- NUCLEUS
- CYTOPLASM

DEVELOPMENT OF FERTILIZED OVUM
- 2-CELL STAGE
- 4-CELL STAGE
- CLUSTER OF CELLS

SECOND WEEK
- TROPHOBLAST
- AMNION
- EMBRYONIC PLATE
- YOLK SAC
- EXTRA-EMBRYONIC COELOM

FIFTH WEEK
- YOLK SAC
- AMNION
- EMBRYO
- UMBILICAL CORD
- CHORION

EIGHTH WEEK
- AMNION
- EMBRYO
- YOLK SAC
- UMBILICAL CORD
- CHORION

Only one of millions of sperm that the male introduces into the female can fertilize an ovum, shown here in a diagrammatic cross section. The sperm propel themselves to the ovum with their tails. The fertilized ovum rapidly divides and redivides; the resulting cell mass is called the morula.

ovulation. There is much variation, however, in the time when ovulation occurs. Most women ovulate between the 12th and the 16th days after the beginning of the last period, but others ovulate as early as 8 or as late as 20 days after the first day of the period.

For couples who are trying to have children, and for those who are using the rhythm method of CONTRACEPTION, it is important to know just when ovulation occurs. Then the couple may regulate intercourse according to their desire to have or avoid having children. A method for determining the time of ovulation is described in the article on FERTILITY.

The Problem of Infertility. About 10 out of every 100 American couples fail to have a child even after trying for a year or more. This difficulty, called infertility, has many causes (see FERTILITY). Sometimes the problem is merely an improper technique of intercourse, which is easily remedied by advice. Or the fertility of either the husband or the wife may be affected by organic disease.

Whatever the problem, the couple should not assume that one or the other is to blame, or that there is something shameful about infertility. It may be a temporary condition. The couple should visit the family physician for a check-up and a discussion. The doctor may want to do certain tests on the woman and analyze a sperm specimen from the man. If the man's sperm is found inadequate, even after sustained medical efforts to remedy the physical condition which may be responsible, the couple may decide to adopt a child (see ADOPTION). Or they may prefer ARTIFICIAL INSEMINATION, a technique in which healthy sperm from a donor unknown to the couple are artificially placed into the female's reproductive system.

Pregnancy. During the first two weeks of pregnancy, the product of conception is often still called an ovum. During the third to eighth weeks, it is called an *embryo*. The organs are being formed in this period, and the embryo assumes a definite shape. After the eighth week the embryo is called a *fetus*.

The egg begins to change immediately after the sperm has fertilized it. The membrane surrounding the egg becomes impenetrable to other sperm. Soon the egg is dividing into a cluster of two, then four, then more cells, as it makes its way down the Fallopian tube toward the uterus. At first it looks like a bunch of tiny grapes stuck together. By the time the egg reaches the uterus, in three to five days, the cells are formed in the shape of a minute ball, hollow on the inside with an internal bump at one side where the embryo will form. This aggregation of cells, called a *blastocyst,* quickly buries itself in the lining of the uterus. On rare occasions, the blastocyst does not implant in the uterine lining, but elsewhere in an *ectopic,* or abnormal, site. This produces an *ectopic pregnancy,* a serious condition involving loss of the fetus (see ECTOPIC PREGNANCY).

As soon as the blastocyst is implanted, its wall begins to change into a structure that eventually develops into the placenta. Through the placenta the fetus secures nourishment from the mother and gets rid of waste products. Essentially the placenta is a filtering mechanism by which the mother's blood is brought close to the fetal blood without the actual mixing of blood cells.

During the early stages of pregnancy, the future child is growing at an extremely rapid rate. The mother's body must undergo profound changes to support this organism. The muscles of the uterus grow, vaginal secretions change,

REPRODUCTIVE ORGANS, FEMALE

the blood volume expands, the work of the heart increases, the mother gains weight, the breasts prepare for nursing, and other adjustments are made throughout the mother's body. When the time of labor and delivery approaches, the pituitary gland at the base of the brain secretes a hormone that causes the contractions of the uterus known as labor. Other hormones regulate lactation, the production of milk. For more information on these aspects of reproduction, consult the articles **PREGNANCY** and **CHILDBIRTH**.

Many women first realize they may be pregnant when they miss a menstrual period, but there are many other symptoms that may appear early in pregnancy, such as soreness of the breasts, a tendency to tire easily, a slight abdominal enlargement, and sometimes nausea or vomiting. When it seems that a patient may be pregnant, a doctor usually recommends one of several **PREGNANCY TESTS**, which are highly accurate.

Usually by the 18th to 20th week, or earlier, the mother can feel a "quickening" in her abdomen, caused by very slight movements of the fetus that cannot yet be felt externally. The physician cannot be 100 percent sure of the diagnosis until after the fourth month. At this time, he can hear the fetal heart with his stethoscope and feel the fetal movements.

As soon as a woman believes she is pregnant, she should consult her physician, who may refer her to an obstetrician if he does not perform deliveries.

Women who have an unwanted pregnancy should never attempt to produce abortions by themselves or with the aid of friends or others. Many of the techniques passed on by word of mouth are useless, and some are extremely dangerous, leading to great pain, deformity, infection, or death. Infection with a very high mortality is one of the great dangers of such abortions. The subject of unwanted pregnancy is covered in the articles **ABORTION** and **UNWED MOTHER**.

REPRODUCTIVE ORGANS, FEMALE

A woman's reproductive system includes a number of different organs. Included in the system are the ovaries, which produce the *ova*, or eggs, to be fertilized; the Fallopian tubes, which convey a ripened ovum to the uterus, or womb, in which a fertilized ovum grows through pregnancy to an infant ready to be born; the vagina, or birth canal, through which it is born, and the vulva, comprising the external sex organs. The breasts are a secondary sex characteristic, enclosing the mammary glands which produce milk to nourish the newborn infant.

The reproductive system is linked to the body's system of endocrine, or ductless, glands by the **OVARIES**, the female sex glands. Besides producing the egg cells to be fertilized, the ovaries secrete

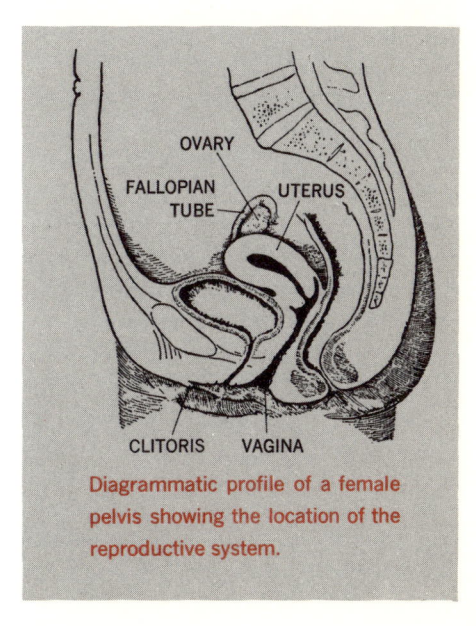

Diagrammatic profile of a female pelvis showing the location of the reproductive system.

the female sex hormones which influence the body's development and general functioning as well as the sexual function. The master gland of the endocrines, the **PITUITARY GLAND,** in turn plays an important role in the reproductive system, although it is not part of the system.

The two ovaries, each about the size of a small plum, lie one on each side of the pear-shaped uterus at its wide upper part. When a girl baby is born, her undeveloped ovaries already contain the specialized cells that can eventually become eggs. At puberty these eggs begin to ripen one at a time, and usually the ovaries alternate in producing one egg a month. As the undeveloped egg cell, called a *follicle,* begins to ripen, it makes its way to the ovary's surface, breaks through its own outer covering, and is released. The release of an egg cell, called **OVULATION,** occurs about once in 28 days, and approximately 400 ovulations take place between the onset of puberty and the end of a woman's childbearing years at the menopause.

After its separation from the ovary the egg is drawn into the nearby **FALLOPIAN TUBE** through its fringed, flared opening, and is moved along by rhythmic contractions of the tube's walls and by the *cilia,* or hairlike cells, of its mucous lining. In the course of its passage the egg ripens fully, and if fertilization occurs it usually takes place while the egg is moving through one of the two Fallopian tubes.

The other end of the tube opens directly into the **UTERUS.** This muscular organ is capable of stretching to contain a fertilized egg as it grows through the nine months of pregnancy from the size of a pea to a fully grown baby. Its mucous membrane lining is also specially adapted to hold the unborn infant securely and to nourish it. When the egg arrives, the hormones **ESTROGEN** and **PROGESTERONE** produced in the ovary have already stimulated the uterus to prepare its lining with extra blood vessels. If the egg has not been fertilized, it loses its vitality, the hormone supply ceases, and the egg and the extra blood and tissues are discharged from the body through the vagina, in the menstrual flow (see **MENSTRUATION**). If fertilization, or *conception,* has taken place, the growth of a new life has begun; menstruation does not occur, and in fact ceases entirely during the nine months (approximately 270 days) of pregnancy. At the end of that time the uterus begins rhythmic contractions, called *labor,* which move the baby out and down the birth canal to its independent life in the world.

The lower end of the uterus forms an opening called the **CERVIX,** or neck, which protrudes into the birth canal or **VAGINA.** Enclosed by muscles and lined with mucous membrane, the vagina measures on the average about three inches in length. In sexual intercourse it receives the male copulatory organ, or **PENIS,** and the male's discharge of sperm during ejaculation. Like the uterus, the vagina undergoes changes during **PREGNANCY** that enable it to stretch to many times its usual size, allowing the infant to pass through the vagina in childbirth.

The exterior opening of the vagina and the surrounding organs make up the vulva. The vulva consists of the *labia majora* (the major lips), the *labia minora* (the minor lips), the vestibule, and the clitoris. To the front of the vulva lies a triangular fatty pad covered with pubic hair, the *mons veneris.* Between the clitoris and the entry to the vagina is the opening of the urethra from which urine is excreted. The anus lies to the rear of the vaginal opening. In a virgin, or a woman who has not experienced sexual intercourse, a membrane called the **HYMEN** usually closes off a part of the opening to the vagina.

The labia majora envelop the labia minora, and these join together at the clitoris. This is a rudimentary, diminutive, penis-like organ which has a purely erotic function. Like the penis, the clitoris has a foreskin and many nerve endings. The area that surrounds the entry to the vagina and lies within the labia minora is the vestibule. At each side of the vaginal opening and elsewhere in the vestibule, glands secrete lubricating fluids to facilitate intercourse.

A woman's **BREASTS** serve to provide milk for the newborn baby. At puberty the breasts increase in size; during pregnancy they again become much larger and start to secrete milk shortly after **CHILDBIRTH**. Following weaning, the breasts generally regain their former size. Hormones secreted by the pituitary gland and the ovaries govern the development of the breasts, which in turn secrete fluids during their milk-producing periods (lactation) that hasten the shrinking of the uterus after childbirth.

Disorders

Bacterial and other infections, tumors, and birth injuries can affect the female reproductive organs.

Growths, or tumors, can develop in all parts of the female reproductive organs. These are most often benign, and may not require treatment, but they should be periodically examined without fail in case they grow large and affect the organs, or become malignant (see **CANCER**).

An ovarian growth may be a cyst or a tumor, and either can develop without symptoms of distress. When diagnosed, an ovarian tumor is usually removed surgically; cysts, however, often remain without excessive harm or pain. The neighboring Fallopian tubes may also be the site of growths, though such tumors usually result from the involvement of some other organ. The uterus, particularly the cervix, is one of the most frequent locations of tumors. In the uterus they are usually fibroid tumors which may attain considerable size. These are, however, quite readily diagnosed and, when found early enough, are treated successfully by surgery.

Any unnatural bleeding or discharge from the vagina may be a symptom of a dangerous growth and should have medical attention. Twice-yearly medical examinations, including the cancer-screening **PAP TEST**, will enable the doctor to detect growths in time in a high percentage of cases. Growths may occur in the vagina and vulva but they are rare.

In the reproductive system, the breasts are the most common site of growths of all kinds, both cysts and tumors, the latter both benign and malignant. A variety of sores and abscesses may afflict the breasts, especially in their milk-producing periods. Any lump or other irregularity within or on a breast should receive prompt medical attention (see also **BREAST TUMOR**).

The most prevalent bacterial diseases of a woman's reproductive organs are the venereal infections. Of these the most serious are **SYPHILIS** and **GONORRHEA**, but several other, less dangerous diseases are also in the same category (see **VENEREAL DISEASE**). Venereal diseases are usually, but not necessarily, contracted through sexual intercourse. When left untreated, both syphilis and gonorrhea gravely affect the reproduc-

REPRODUCTIVE ORGANS, FEMALE

tive system: syphilis may ultimately bring death; gonorrhea may cause permanent sterility. The onset of these diseases may be especially treacherous, since first symptoms may not be at all noticeable. Therefore, any sexual act that might have led to infection should be followed by a medical examination.

A number of bacterial protozoa and yeastlike infections can occur within the vagina or in the area of the vulva. These cause varying discharges and irritations and can usually be readily treated following a correct diagnosis (see LEUKORRHEA).

Difficult childbirth can produce deformations of the reproductive organs, particularly of the uterus. This is one of many reasons for regular prenatal care and delivery by an obstetrician or family doctor who can often anticipate possible difficulties and either prevent or control their effects. In some cases, the uterus is displaced so that the cervix drops too far into the vagina. In others, the uterus is moved forward or backward and bent. The wearing of supportive pessaries or surgery may be necessary to relieve this condition.

In rare cases a fertilized egg fails to enter the uterus and begins to grow within a Fallopian tube. This is an ECTOPIC PREGNANCY. When the condition is discovered, surgery is necessary to remove both the tube and the embryo. In some cases no symptoms appear until the tube breaks, causing an internal hemorrhage and requiring prompt surgery.

Care and Hygiene

For protection during menstruation most women wear either an external pad held by a supporting belt or a tampon inserted within the vagina. The choice is largely a matter of individual preference. Some women choose not to use a tampon till after marriage, but some also find it possible to use tampons without rupturing the hymen (see MENSTRUATION).

It is widely, but wrongly, believed that washing the vagina (douching) is needed to keep the area clean. Frequent bathing and normal body cleanliness provide all the necessary hygiene for the genital area. The body produces secretions that make the organ normally self-cleansing, and frequent douches may be irritating. If occasionally desired, a douche should consist of about three tablespoonfuls of household vinegar mixed in two quarts of warm tapwater. It is never wise to use any strong antiseptic or vaginal medication except under the doctor's orders. In particular, douches should not be used to treat undiagnosed vaginal discharges.

In rare instances the circular muscles enveloping the vaginal canal will contract abnormally and uncontrollably to prevent or inhibit intercourse. This condition is due usually to psychological and emotional difficulties and PSYCHOTHERAPY is usually advised.

REPRODUCTIVE ORGANS, MALE

The male reproductive organs include the external genitals, accessory glands that secrete special fluids, and the ducts through which these organs and glands are connected to each other and through which the sperm, or spermatozoa, are ejaculated during sexual intercourse.

External Genitals. The penis, testes, and scrotum (the sac that contains the testes) are together known as the external genitals. The *penis* is the organ through which semen is transferred into the female during sexual intercourse. Semen is a carrier for the sperm, which are produced in the *testes*. The testes also produce the male hormone testosterone, which gives a sexually mature male his distinctively masculine characteristics and his sexual energy and drive. In fact, sexual maturity is impossible without this hormone.

The testes are suspended from the spermatic cord, which also connects the testes with the other parts of the reproductive system. This cord consists of blood vessels, nerves, and ducts, all enclosed in connective tissue.

Accessory Glands. The accessory reproductive glands include the prostate gland, two seminal vesicles, and two bulbo-urethral glands, also known as Cowper's glands.

The *prostate gland* is located below and against the urinary bladder. It completely surrounds the urethra, the tube through which urine passes from the bladder. The prostate gland produces a thin, clear, slightly alkaline fluid that neutralizes the normal acidity of the urethra caused by the continual passage of urine. This fluid enables the sperm to pass through the urethra unharmed.

The *seminal vesicles* are two glands located just above and to the rear of the prostate gland. These glands consist of many small sacs, or pockets, in which is produced and stored the thick, milky fluid that is ejaculated during the male orgasm. This fluid serves as the carrier for the sperm and is the major constituent of the semen, which also consists of secretions, produced in the ducts, that facilitate the journey of the sperm from the testes.

Cowper's glands, which are about the size of peas, secrete a clear, sticky fluid that lubricates the urethra, thus making it easier for the semen to pass through it during an ejaculation.

Ducts. The sperm are led from the testes to the urethra through a system of ducts. First, there are two convoluted tubes, one lying on top of each testis and connected directly to it. Each tube is called an *epididymis*. Mature sperm produced in the testes are stored in each epididymis.

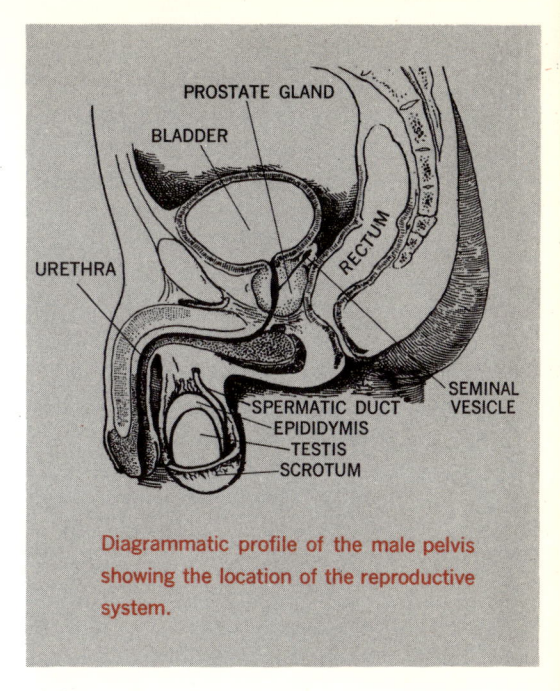

Next come two *spermatic ducts*, each of which is also known as a *vas deferens*. Each duct is the continuation of the corresponding epididymis. The spermatic ducts are part of the spermatic cord and conduct the sperm to the duct lying close to the bladder.

The spermatic ducts join with ducts leading from the seminal vesicles just before the urethra. The combined duct is called the *ejaculatory duct*. This duct passes through the prostate gland and joins with the urethra. The urethra then conducts the semen through the penis.

Discharge of Semen. The tissues that form the mass of the penis are called *erectile tissue*. This tissue is spongy in nature and filled with innumerable hollow spaces. There is also a network of veins and arteries within the penis. Sex-

Diagrammatic profile of the male pelvis showing the location of the reproductive system.

ual excitement causes the muscles surrounding the veins to contract, thereby restricting the flow of blood from the penis. At the same time, the muscles surrounding the arteries relax, permitting the free flow of blood into the penis at the full pressure of the circulatory system. The result is that the spongy tissue fills with blood and the penis swells in size and becomes stiff and erect.

The sexual excitement also stimulates the accessory glands to secrete a larger amount of their fluids. When the sexual tension becomes acute enough, as a result of sexual intercourse or other factors such as purely mental stimulation (as in "wet dreams"), there is a series of reflex convulsive contractions of the reproductive organs.

The muscles surrounding the seminal ducts, the prostate gland, and the seminal vesicles contract convulsively, which causes the semen to be ejaculated forcibly from the penis. There is first an ejaculation of the fluid from the prostate gland, followed immediately by the semen. About two or three cubic centimeters of semen (something less than a teaspoonful) are ejaculated. This volume of semen is believed to contain between 200 and 500 million sperm, only one of which is necessary to fertilize the ovum.

Disorders

Disorders that affect particular organs are described separately in the articles on the PENIS, TESTES, and PROSTATE GLAND. Since these organs are connected so closely with each other, however, an infection in one is likely to spread throughout the entire reproductive system. This is particularly true of VENEREAL DISEASES, such as *gonorrhea*, which are contracted almost entirely through sexual intercourse.

Care of the Genitals. As part of one's ordinary hygiene, the genitals should be washed frequently. It is especially important that the *foreskin* covering the head of the penis should be pulled back and the inner fold washed thoroughly. The warm, moist conditions within the fold of the foreskin easily lead to irritations.

For related information, see also REPRODUCTION; REPRODUCTIVE ORGANS, FEMALE; SCROTUM; TESTOSTERONE; URETHRA.

RESIDENT

A physician serving in his medical specialty at a hospital. A period of residency, which follows his internship and usually lasts three to five years, is required of all physicians specializing in a particular branch of medicine, such as internal medicine, surgery, pediatrics, obstetrics, or psychiatry. After he completes his residency, he is usually qualified to take the examination held by a national board in his respective specialty for certification as a specialist in his field. The resident physician may or may not live at the hospital.

For additional and related information, see the article on DOCTOR.

RESPIRATION

The process by which the body breathes in and distributes oxygen and exhales carbon dioxide. Oxygen is essential to the life processes of all the body's cells, and carbon dioxide is one of the major waste products of these activities. Thus respiration is a continuous activity. Even in a state of rest, the body still needs 300 quarts of oxygen a day. In a single minute of ordinary activity, half a pint of oxygen has to be transferred from the air to the blood, and to get this half-pint the lungs must process about five quarts of air every minute. An athlete running a race at sea level must breathe as much as 120 quarts of air a minute.

Running or resting, every living cell of the body must have a steady supply of oxygen. Every cell must also get rid of its carbon dioxide waste.

The RESPIRATORY SYSTEM is the specialized system that makes the exchange of oxygen and carbon dioxide with the outside world for all the body's cells. Its principal organs are the lungs and the breathing apparatus.

The Respiration Sequence

The sequence of the respiration process begins as air enters the corridors of the nose or mouth, where it is moistened and warmed. The air then passes through the pharynx, the larynx, the trachea or windpipe, and on into the bronchial tubes, which branch off into the twin lungs.

The bronchial tubes branch into the lungs in smaller and smaller bronchioles, ending in clusters of tiny air sacs. There are 750 million of these *alveoli,* as they are called, in the lungs. The blood flows through the lungs in a special circulatory system, called the *pulmonary system,* branching into minute blood vessels called capillaries. Through the thin membrane of the network of capillaries around the alveoli, the air and the blood make their exchange of oxygen and carbon dioxide. The carbon molecules migrate from the red blood cells in the capillaries through the porous membrane into the air in the air sacs, while the oxygen molecules cross from the air to the cells.

The red blood cells proceed through the circulatory system, carrying the oxygen in loose combination with the HEMOGLOBIN and giving it up to the body cells that need it. (The course of the blood cells through the body is described in CIRCULATION; the way in which hemoglobin picks up and conveys oxygen is explained under BLOOD.) The lungs dispose of the carbon dioxide, left there by the red blood cells, in the process of breathing. With each breath, about one sixth of the air in the lungs is exchanged for new air.

Breathing

The lungs inflate and deflate some 16 to 20 times a minute. Their elastic tissue allows them to expand and contract like a bellows worked by the diaphragm and the rib muscles. The diaphragm contracts, flattening itself downward, and thus enlarges the chest cavity. At the same time the ribs are pulled up and outward by the action of the narrow but powerful rib muscles that expand and contract the rib cage. As the chest expands, the air rushes in.

Exhaling comes about when the diaphragm and rib muscles relax and the chest returns automatically to its minimum size, expelling the air.

The rate of breathing varies: sometimes it is rapid, sometimes slow; sometimes it is deep and sometimes it is shallow; but it continues all the time, waking and sleeping. Breathing stops only at the moment of swallowing. Breathing can be controlled voluntarily as, for example, in singing and speaking. It can also be stopped for 45 seconds or more as happens when we are snapping the shutter of a camera, aiming a rifle, swimming under water, and in various other familiar situations in which we consciously hold our breath. Breathing is partly automatic and partly conscious.

Automatic Breathing Controls

The automatic control of breathing stems from certain nerve centers of the brain, which send impulses down the spinal cord to the nerve that controls the diaphragm, and to the rib muscles. Chemical and reflex signals control these nerve centers.

The chemical controls of breathing are mainly dependent on the level of carbon dioxide in the blood. The response is so sensitive that if the carbon dioxide in the blood increases only two tenths of 1 per cent, breathing speeds up automatically to double the amount of air taken in per minute, until the excess of carbon dioxide is eliminated. It is not lack of oxygen but excess of carbon dioxide that causes this instant and powerful reaction.

Breathing and Strenuous Exercise

Want of oxygen makes breathing faster and deeper, without a rise in the carbon dioxide level. This can be observed at altitudes of 10,000 feet or higher where air pressure is low and there is less oxygen. To keep the supply normal, breathing is speeded up. (See ALTITUDE SICKNESS.)

When a particularly strenuous exertion is demanded as in running a race, the lungs cannot possibly supply, or the blood cells pick up and carry, enough oxygen for the sharply increased needs of the muscles. The muscle tissue cannot even absorb the oxygen that rapidly.

What happens is that the muscles do their work and the body goes into debt for oxygen for the emergency. Lactic acid, a waste product of muscle metabolism, builds up. When the race is run, the panting athlete takes in enough air to complete the metabolic cycle of reconverting the lactic acid to usable energy fuel.

In longer exertions, such as a distance race, the runner will slip into a new gear known as "second wind." From this point, he can go on smoothly and easily with almost no feeling of strain. His breathing becomes deeper and more rapid, the heart accelerates and enlarges, and the blood pressure rises so that the blood is circulated more rapidly. This makes the transfer of oxygen and carbon dioxide faster both with the air in the lungs and within the muscle tissues. The speeding up of respiration and circulation, together with the expansion of blood vessels, increases the actual quantity of oxygenated blood carried to the muscles, until it becomes equal to the muscles' oxygen need. A balance is established. The athlete who has made a marathon run or a distance swim, or played a match of tennis, will of course be tired, but he may not be panting at all—unless he has finished with a sprint and incurred an oxygen debt at the end.

Protective Respiratory Mechanisms

The lungs are exposed constantly to the surrounding atmosphere. Twenty times a minute, more or less, they take in a gaseous mixture, along with whatever foreign particles happen to be floating in it and at whatever temperature it may happen to be. To compensate, the lungs have some remarkable protective devices.

On its way through the nasal passage the cold air from outside is preheated by a large supply of blood, circulating like hot water in a radiator, giving off warmth through the thin mucous membrane that lines the respiratory tract. This same mucous lining is always moist, and dry air picks up moisture as it passes.

Dust, soot, and bacteria are filtered out by a barrier of *cilia*, or tiny threadlike growths that line the passageways to the bronchial tubes like a fine fuzz. These catch not only foreign particles but also mucus produced by the respiratory passages themselves. Since the movement of the cilia is always toward the outside, they push the interfering matter upward, away from the delicate lung tissues, so that it can be expectorated or swallowed. Particles that are too large for the cilia to dispose of usually stimulate a sneeze or a cough, which forcibly expels them.

Sneezing and coughing are *reflexive acts* in response to stimulation of nerve endings in the respiratory passages. The stimulus for a cough comes from the air passages in the throat; for a sneeze, from those in the nose.

Yawns and Sighs

In addition, there is the long gape-mouthed inhalation called the yawn, and its counterpart, the sigh, which is nothing more than a prolonged exhalation. Probably the yawn has to do with a need to liven up a weary or bored mind and body by accelerating the exchange of oxygen and carbon dioxide between the blood and the lungs, thus sending a more stimulating mixture through the body.

A sigh is usually psychologically stimulated. We sigh in relief after a tense experience, or to unburden ourselves of an emotional weight of grief or anxiety. The deep inhalation and the prolonged exhalation serve to relax muscle tensions.

Another common respiratory phenomenon is hiccups. They occur when the normal rhythm of respiration is broken by a spasmodic contraction of the diaphragm. (A description of the cause and cure of HICCUPS is presented in the article under that title.)

RESPIRATOR

A device in which changing air pressure artificially expands and contracts the lungs of a patient whose breathing, or respiratory, muscles are paralyzed; also called an *iron lung*.

Inhalation and Exhalation

In a normal individual, the rhythmic movements of the *diaphragm* (the muscular floor of the chest cavity) and of certain muscles in the chest produce breathing. The lungs themselves have no muscles. When a person takes a breath, the diaphragm drops. At the same time, the chest muscles draw the ribs upward and outward. These movements enlarge the chest cavity. Just as when a bellows is expanded, this enlargement reduces the air pressure inside the cavity. Outside, the normal air pressure of approximately 15 pounds per square inch pushes air into the cavity.

Within the chest cavity lie the lungs, made of millions of tiny sacs of elastic tissue, each able to expand and contract like a minute balloon. Since air passages connect the lungs to the nose and mouth, the external air rushes into the lungs, causing them to inflate to the limits of the cavity walls. This is the *inhalation* phase of breathing. *Exhalation* takes place when the chest and diaphragm muscles relax, letting the chest cavity shrink. The elastic sacs of the lungs contract, pushing out the air. The diaphragm may be brought into play to push out still more air.

When the breathing muscles fail temporarily (as in SHOCK, for example), their functions can be roughly duplicated by the techniques of artificial respiration. This method in effect substitutes the muscle power of the person giving first aid for the breathing function of the patient.

How the Respirator Works

The mechanical respirator bypasses the muscular processes of breathing altogether. It is used for long-term treatment of patients whose respiratory muscles are paralyzed, a condition which occurs primarily in some forms of PO-

LIOMYELITIS and also in some types of **BRAIN** injury.

The machine operates on principles borrowed from the mechanics of air pressure in normal breathing. The patient is placed in an airtight, cylindrical chamber from which only his head protrudes through a leakproof foam-rubber collar. The chamber is similar to the chest cavity which houses the lungs. Pressure in the chamber is reduced by mechanical means—in some respirators by extending a large leather or rubber diaphragm, in others by expanding a bellows. In each case the mechanism is driven by an electric motor. The extension of the diaphragm or the expansion of the bellows has the same effect as the enlargement of the human chest cavity. Reduction of pressure within the chamber permits air to rush in through the patient's nose or mouth, and the lungs in turn inflate (inhale).

The lungs are made to exhale simply by relaxing the diaphragm or contracting the bellows as the case may be, to return the air pressure in the chamber to normal. At normal pressure, the lungs contract by the force of their own elasticity and expel the breath. The respirator can be adjusted to between 14 and 36 inhalations per minute to meet the breathing needs of the patient; the depth of breathing can also be regulated.

The conventional cylindrical respirator chamber used in hospitals has glass portholes so that the patient can be observed. Openings surrounded by airtight rubber cuffs enable a nurse to attend the enclosed body of the patient without pressure leakage around her arms.

Bedside Respirators

In addition to the conventional respirator just described, there are two bedside versions. One encloses the patient from waist to neck in an airtight tank. The tank is connected to pumping equipment beside the patient's bed. This type is able to handle the same cases as the conventional respirator. Another similar, portable bedside respirator is used for milder cases of respiratory failure needing only slight help. In this model an airtight shell, or *cuirass,* covers the chest and is connected to pumping equipment beside the patient's bed. Other types have also been developed.

These bedside models enable patients to remain in the respirator for an extended period of time, or for as long as it takes until they recover enough muscle power to breathe by themselves.

RESPIRATORY SYSTEM

The group of specialized organs that does the breathing for the body. Its specific function is to provide for the transfer of oxygen from the air to the blood and of waste carbon dioxide from the blood to the air. The organs of the system include the **NOSE**, the **PHARYNX**, the **LARYNX**, the **TRACHEA**, or windpipe, the *bronchial tubes,* and the **LUNGS**. The way in which the respiratory system works is described under **RESPIRATION**.

How well these organs function is dependent upon several factors. The air itself is a factor in respiratory health. The polluted air of cities, for example, contains irritants which may interfere with the functioning of the system and harm the organs (see **AIR POLLUTION**.) Climate is also a factor. Some people seem to breathe better in the warm dry climate of the Southwest; others find the extreme dryness an irritant. Some people are invigorated by the clean briny wind of San Francisco, while others find that the ocean dampness leads to chronic sinus trouble. People also react differently to changes in altitude.

RESPIRATORY SYSTEM

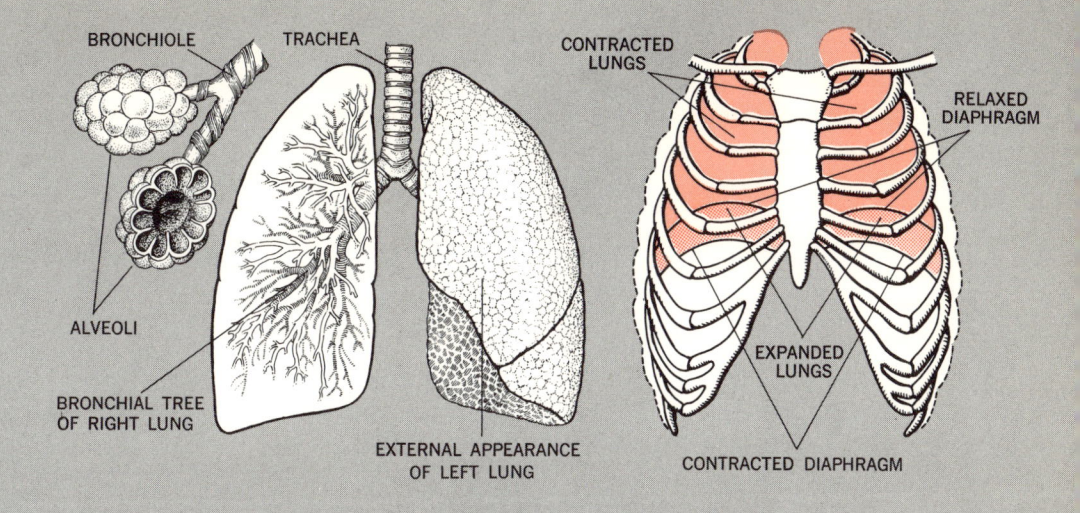

The respiratory system consists of the nose and mouth, through which air enters and leaves the body; the larynx, trachea, and bronchi, through which air passes to and from the lungs; and the lungs, where oxygen and carbon dioxide are exchanged in the blood. The larynx and the vocal cords are the mechanisms that enable the body to produce sound.

The choice of occupation may present certain hazards. The breathing of irritants, such as silica dust (see SILICOSIS), in the course of daily work over a long period of time may have an adverse effect on the lungs or air passages (see JOBS AND HEALTH).

Cigarette SMOKING is believed by most medical authorities to be a major cause of lung cancer, as well as of other serious respiratory ailments such as EMPHYSEMA.

Respiratory Disorders

Of the numerous disorders that affect the respiratory system, the most frequently experienced is the COMMON COLD, a virus infection of the upper respiratory tract. Common upper respiratory disorders also include HAY FEVER and other allergic reactions (see ALLERGY). The early symptoms of colds and allergic reactions are somewhat similar; they include watery eyes, runny nose, and SNEEZING. In allergic conditions, the eyes may almost stream with water and may also itch. Generally speaking, allergic symptoms appear rather suddenly in full force, while those of a cold develop more gradually.

Other diseases that affect the respiratory tract include INFLUENZA, WHOOPING COUGH, and DIPHTHERIA. Some more generalized diseases, such as MEASLES, are also accompanied by respiratory symptoms. A respiratory inflammation or infection, such as a cold, may spread to other parts of the respiratory system and may be a cause of a number of related symptoms and disorders. For example, one condition that may stem from a cold or from other causes is SINUSITIS, an inflammation of the mucous lining of the sinus cavities.

1143

RESPIRATORY SYSTEM

Children in particular may be bothered by enlarged ADENOIDS, which block the rear of the nasal passages and make breathing through the nose difficult. The tonsils at the sides of the throat are also very susceptible to infection and enlargement (see TONSILLITIS). The inflammation of a SORE THROAT, usually accompanied by a COUGH, may be a symptom of a variety of disorders. When inflammation affects the larynx, or voice box, the condition is known as LARYNGITIS, and if it attacks the bronchial tubes that connect the windpipe and the lungs, the result is BRONCHITIS. Another disorder that affects the bronchial tubes is ASTHMA, which causes contraction of the tubes and hinders breathing. Asthma is frequently an allergic reaction.

Some of the most serious respiratory disorders arise as complications in a number of types of heart disease. Blood clots known as *pulmonary infarcts* also cause serious respiratory distress.

An infection of the lungs is known as PNEUMONIA, while PLEURISY occurs when the coverings of the lungs, the *pleurae*, become inflamed. A serious infectious disease that may attack the lungs is TUBERCULOSIS. A LUNG ABSCESS, an inflammation in which there is localized accumulation of pus and destruction of tissue, may sometimes be a complication of tuberculosis or pneumonia.

A very serious disease that has become increasingly prevalent in the 20th century is LUNG CANCER. Other parts of the respiratory system may also be affected by cancer. For information on other respiratory disorders, see the separate articles on the various respiratory organs.

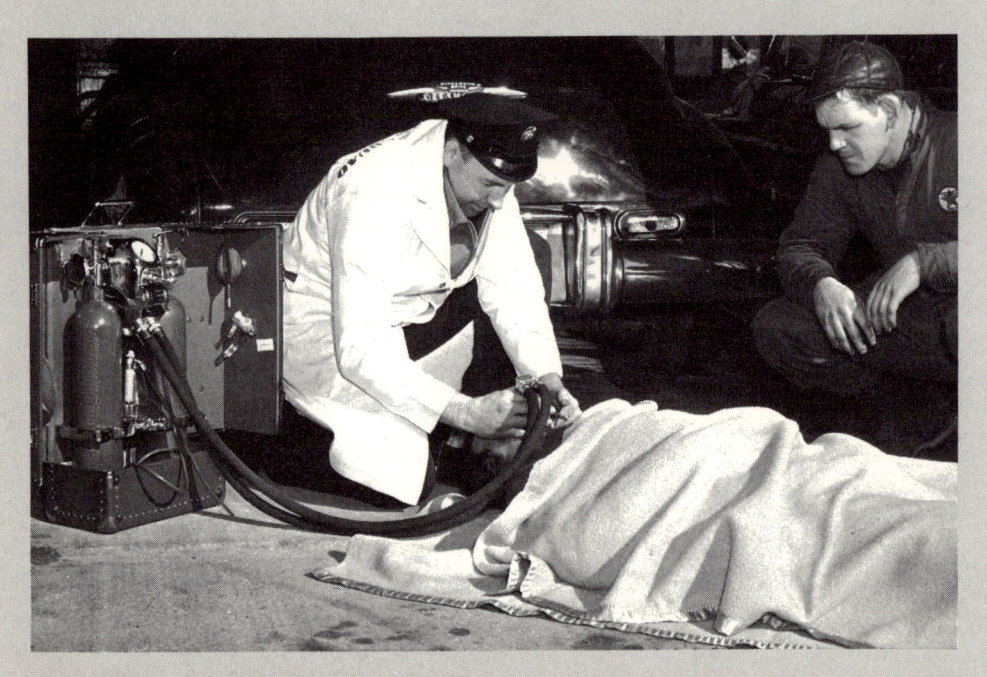

A member of a police rescue squad uses a portable resuscitator to revive a victim of carbon monoxide poisoning. Instructions for three methods of artificial respiration that do not require any equipment are given in the article ARTIFICIAL RESPIRATION.

RESUSCITATION

Revival of a person whose breathing has stopped. This can be carried out directly by *artificial respiration*, a technique for which no equipment is necessary. When available, a RESUSCITATOR or other device for forcing oxygen or air, or a mixture of both, into and out of the lungs may be used.

Various methods of ARTIFICIAL RESPIRATION are described in the article of that title. One of them, preferably the mouth-to-mouth method, should be begun *immediately* if breathing has stopped. This may be the result of accident or emergency such as near-drowning, electric shock, choking, gas poisoning, drug poisoning by overdosage of medicine, chest injury, or suffocation. It is essential to be familiar with first-aid techniques *before* an accident occurs.

RESUSCITATOR

A portable apparatus used to restore respiration in a person whose breathing has stopped. Such an emergency may result from various causes, including smoke suffocation, electric shock, near-drowning, gas poisoning, hanging, respiratory paralysis, or heart attack.

A typical resuscitator apparatus has three parts: (1) A resuscitator which pumps oxygen into the lungs through a hose and mask and withdraws the used gases in a continuous cycle; this part of the apparatus is used until the victim resumes breathing. (2) An inhalator which supplies the person, once he has resumed breathing, with a flow of oxygen of greater concentration than that contained in the atmosphere. (3) An aspirator, or tube, for removing fluid from the upper air passages.

Resuscitators are used by police and fire departments, beach lifeguards, and other rescue personnel (as at coal mines). They must be operated by trained persons. They are frequently used in conjunction with artificial respiration.

RETICULO-ENDOTHELIAL SYSTEM

A network of cells and tissues found throughout the body, especially in the blood, general connective tissue, spleen, liver, lungs, bone marrow, and lymph nodes. Some of the reticulo-endothelial cells found in the BLOOD and in the general CONNECTIVE TISSUE are unusually large in size. These cells are primarily responsible for protecting the body from harmful foreign particles. Some are *motile*—that is, capable of spontaneous motion—and *phagocytic*—they can ingest and destroy unwanted foreign material. They rush to the scene of a wound or body infection and devour the enemy bacteria before extensive damage can take place.

The reticulo-endothelial cells inhabiting the SPLEEN possess the ability to dispose of disintegrated red blood corpuscles. They do not, however, destroy the valuable HEMOGLOBIN, which is liberated in the process.

The reticulo-endothelial cells located in the blood cavities of the LIVER are called Kupffer cells. These cells, together with the cells of the general connective tissue and bone marrow, are capable of transforming the hemoglobin released by disintegrated red blood corpuscles into bile pigment.

Disorders

The reticulo-endothelial system can be the site of a variety of diseases, all of which are rare. These are generally treated through X-ray therapy and the administering of steroids (certain types of hormones), among other methods. The prospects for recovery cannot always be predicted.

In *Gaucher's disease*, unusual

amounts of special fats are stored in the cells of the reticulo-endothelial system. The signs of this slowly developing disease, usually seen in childhood, are abnormal expansion and tenderness of the abdomen. The enlarged Gaucher cells of the spleen are responsible for this excessive growth.

Letterer-Siwe disease is also mostly restricted to children. Symptoms are purplish patches or inflammations on the skin, fever, anemia, and the enlargement of the spleen, liver, and lymph nodes caused by a rapid and widespread multiplication of reticulo-endothelial cells.

Eosinophilic granuloma is a disease of bone, not serious in nature, which again occurs largely in children or young adults. It is characterized by damage to bone in various areas. The patient is likely to experience pain and swelling and to run a slight fever.

A rare illness called *Niemann-Pick disease* mostly strikes children of Jewish origin. Excessive deposits of special types of fats, called phospholipids, in the reticulo-endothelial cells cause inflammation of the spleen, liver, and lymph nodes. Retardation in mental development and malnutrition are further effects experienced in this serious disease.

Hand-Schüller-Christian disease is another rare threat to children. Bulging of the eyes, defects of the skull, and inability to concentrate the urine are prominent symptoms.

RETIREMENT

Retirement can be the beginning of a highly rewarding period of life, but, unfortunately, for many people it is merely a prelude to gradual decline. The difference often lies in advance planning. To make the most of retirement and of the

These older people have retired from their jobs or businesses but still remain active. At left, a retired couple spend their leisure traveling to places they never had time to visit before. The man at right has turned his hobby of woodworking into a small business.

How Rh FACTOR Works

Rh+ POSITIVE — Rh+ RED BLOOD CELLS contain Rh ANTIGEN

Rh− NEGATIVE — Rh− RED BLOOD CELLS contain no Rh ANTIGEN

1. When Rh+ BLOOD is given to → an Rh− person, ANTIBODIES are formed.

2. When Rh+ BLOOD is again given to → the Rh− person, the Rh ANTIGEN reacts with the Rh ANTIBODIES dissolving the Rh+ RED BLOOD CELLS.

An Rh+ FATHER and an Rh− MOTHER can have an Rh+ CHILD.

During pregnancy, some of the child's Rh ANTIGENS may pass across the placenta into the mother's Rh− BLOOD and start ANTIBODY formation. If, or when, these ANTIBODIES cross the placenta into the baby's blood, they react with the ANTIGEN and dissolve the baby's red blood cells. Then the baby has an ANEMIA.

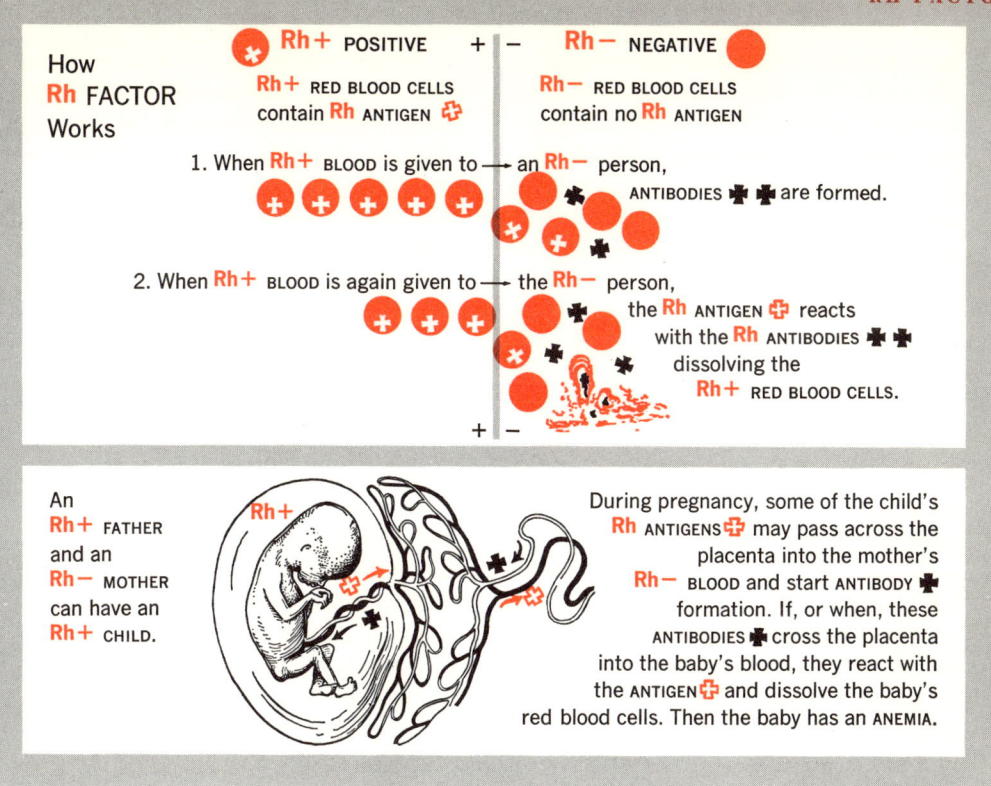

leisure hours it offers, one must plan ahead.

First there are the practical plans, such as making sure that income will be adequate and deciding where to live. But by far the most important preparation for retirement is to develop strong interests or activities that will carry over into later life. A few people find it possible to continue doing the same kind of work after retirement, as when a city newspaperman retires to publish a village weekly, or when a retired lawyer serves as a legal consultant. But most people, upon entering retirement, must turn to entirely different fields of interest to occupy their time, and this is not easy unless these interests are already firmly rooted.

For a further discussion of retirement, as well as other problems and pleasures of older people, see the article on the **LATER YEARS**.

RH FACTOR

A special inherited substance found in the red blood cells of most people. Those who have it are called *Rh positive* while those who lack it are *Rh negative*. About one in seven persons among the white population are Rh negative while absence of the Rh factor in other races is quite rare. Although individuals may have any of four **BLOOD TYPES**, A, B, AB, and O, their blood may, in addition, be Rh positive or Rh negative. The presence or absence of the Rh factor is especially important in blood **TRANSFUSIONS** and in **PREGNANCY**.

Dr. Karl Landsteiner, a Nobel prize winner, and Dr. Alexander Wiener discovered the Rh factor when they injected the red blood cells of Rhesus monkeys into rabbits. The rabbits developed antibodies against the monkey cells; these antibodies, called Rh after the Rhesus monkeys, were then tested against human red cells from many individuals. In about 85 percent of the individuals, the red cells were agglutinated or clumped by the rabbit serum. Thus it was learned that the blood of humans also had a substance similar to the Rh factor in the monkey blood.

The Rh-negative person should never receive a blood *transfusion* with Rh-positive blood. There may be no difficulty in the first transfusion, but by the time the second transfusion is given, the recipient's body has manufactured antibodies against the Rh-positive red cells, and the outcome may be fatal.

In *pregnancy*, there is rarely a problem if the father and mother are both Rh positive or both Rh negative. The trouble may arise if the mother's blood is Rh negative, and the father's Rh positive. Should the baby inherit the father's Rh-positive blood, the unborn child's blood may flow into the mother's blood stream, and trigger the formation of antibodies to the Rh-positive blood. This occurs in about 5 percent of Rh-negative mothers. Although the mother is not harmed, her antibodies may then attack and destroy the baby's red blood cells, both before and after birth. This condition in the baby is called *erythroblastosis fetalis*.

If the baby develops the condition, its early hours after birth are marked by anemia and a weak heart, and it may also develop a type of jaundice called *kernicterus*. The mortality in this situation is 50 percent, and the survivors usually suffer permanent brain damage.

Scientific advances have helped reduce the risk to Rh-positive babies. BLOOD TESTS taken in advance indicate whether the mother is Rh negative and the father Rh positive. During pregnancy the doctor can also examine the mother's blood for signs of Rh antibodies. Even if the Rh antibodies of the mother attack the baby's red cells before birth, an exchange transfusion at the proper time can frequently protect the baby. This type of transfusion withdraws the baby's damaged red blood cells and substitutes Rh-negative fresh blood of the baby's correct blood type.

Should the Rh factor incompatibility be so severe that the baby might die before birth, a new technique permits an exchange transfusion to be performed while the baby is still in the womb.

RHEUMATIC FEVER

A disease that attacks the connective tissues of the body. It is a relatively common disease and occurs particularly among children between 5 and 15 years of age. Young adults in the early twenties are also susceptible, although less so. It is called rheumatic fever because two of the commonest symptoms are a fever and a pain in the joints similar to that of RHEUMATISM. Most cases are mild and have little or no aftereffects, although in a small percentage of cases there is damage to the heart.

Causes

Rheumatic fever is not an infection in itself but a complication of an infection. This infection is from the same family of streptococcus bacteria that causes such common childhood illnesses as scarlet fever, tonsillitis, "strep" throat, and ear infections. Rheumatic fever is only one of several complications that can result from a streptococcal infection. Fortunately, this particular complication is comparatively rare.

The connection between rheumatic fever and a previous streptococcal infection has been proved only indirectly. That is, in almost all cases of rheumatic fever there is evidence of a previous streptococcal infection; and when these infections have been treated promptly, the occurrence of rheumatic fever has declined sharply. But exactly why rheumatic fever does occur after a streptococcal infection is unknown.

Rheumatic fever occurs most commonly in damp, cold climates, especially in sea-level cities in which the population lives closely together in indigent and unsanitary conditions. Therefore it has the reputation of being a poor child's illness. Where living conditions have been improved, as they have in Western Europe and the United States during the 20th century, cases of rheumatic fever have decreased considerably.

Rheumatic fever also tends to run in families, but whether this is primarily due to economic and environmental conditions or heredity is unknown.

Symptoms

The initial symptoms of the disease usually appear from one to four weeks after the streptococcal infection has occurred. The actual onset of the disease may be either gradual or sudden. The symptoms can vary widely and be of any degree of severity. They may be so slight as to escape attention. This makes diagnosis difficult. Many cases of what has later proved to be rheumatic fever are so mild that the disease goes completely unnoticed at the time.

The commonest initial complaints are a slight fever, a feeling of tiredness, a vague feeling of pain in the limbs (often mistaken for GROWING PAINS), and nosebleeds.

If the disease takes an acute form, the fever may reach 104 degrees by the second day and continue for several weeks, although the usual course of the fever is about two weeks. On the other hand, the fever may be quite mild.

At any stage of the disease, pain may develop in the joints and will last from a few hours to several weeks. The joints swell and are tender to the touch. The pain and swelling often travel about the body, subsiding in one group of joints and arising in another. As the pain subsides, the joints return to normal.

Other symptoms may include spasmodic twitching movements known as *chorea* or, more commonly, as St. Vitus's dance. This symptom most often affects children between the ages of 6 and 11, particularly girls. A rash caused by the fever may appear upon the body. Hard little balls (or *nodules*) may be seen or felt under the skin at the elbow, knee, and wrist joints, as well as along the backbone. Among the most serious symptoms is the development of a heart murmur, discussed later in this article.

Treatment

The main purpose of treatment is to reduce the fever and pain; no means have yet been discovered for fighting the disease directly. Until the introduction of the antibiotics and hormone extracts, the chief medications were aspirin and other kinds of salicylates. Antibiotics are now prescribed if there is evidence of a continuing streptococcal infection or the chance of exposure to streptococcal sore throat. Adrenocorticotrophic hormone (ACTH) or cortisone may be prescribed to reduce the pain and swelling in the joints. If pain is severe, medicines such as codeine may be given.

Bed rest is an important part of the treatment, particularly if the disease has injured the heart. Depending upon the severity of the disease, the patient may be kept in bed for months, and prolonged convalescence may be needed.

The convalescent period needs special consideration because of its psychological effects upon a child. Since the child cannot be physically active, it is important to keep his mind as occupied as possible. He should be given special projects to keep him busy. If possible his schoolwork should be continued at home. The illness should be talked of in matter-of-fact terms. A cheerful, confident atmosphere without anxiety should be maintained. It is particularly important to keep alive his interest and expectation of the normal active life he will return to, so that being sick and enjoying extra attention does not become an attractive way of life.

Heart Murmurs

The seriousness of rheumatic fever lies primarily in the permanent damage it can do to the HEART. The disease tends to recur and these recurrent attacks may further damage and weaken the heart and prevent the child from leading a normally active life.

When rheumatic fever damages the heart, it usually does so by inflaming the heart's inner lining (*endocarditis*) and its valves. As a valve heals, its edges may become so scarred and stiff that they fail to close properly. As a result, blood leaks through the valve when it is closed. The valves themselves may become thickened with scar tissue, restricting the amount of blood that can flow through the heart. In either case, the heart's efficiency decreases and the strain upon it increases.

By listening to the heart through a stethoscope, a doctor can hear distinctive murmuring sounds made by the blood as it passes through defective valves. Not all heart murmurs are cause for alarm. Some are functional, a peculiarity of the individual that does him no harm. But if the murmur is an organic one, the result of a disease, the doctor can determine which valves have been damaged and often how badly. If there is any doubt, an electrocardiogram, X-ray, or other procedure will clarify the diagnosis. More information will be found in the article on HEART MURMUR.

Prevention

Preventive care is extremely important, especially when rheumatic fever has already once occurred, since it tends to return unless precautionary steps are taken. Most important is that the child be kept in basic good health, with a good nutritious diet and sufficient sleep. Parents should be particularly watchful for unusual behavior for a month following a streptococcal infection. If suspicions are aroused for any reason, the doctor should be consulted immediately. It is believed that prompt treatment of "strep" sore throat will prevent many cases of rheumatic fever. Therefore it is important to inform the doctor when a child has a sore throat or a fever. If a streptococcal infection has become established, the doctor will be likely to administer or prescribe penicillin to help clear up or combat spread of the infection. Conditions should be avoided that may predispose a child to chilling and a possible streptococcal infection, such as sleeping on the ground during a camping trip, or selling newspapers in bad weather. Care must also be taken to prevent the child from becoming an invalid or feeling excessively protected. If the heart has been damaged, the doctor will prescribe the amount and kinds of activity that the patient may engage in.

He may also prescribe penicillin or sulfa medicines for regular long-term use to prevent recurring attacks of streptococcal or other infection.

RHEUMATISM

A general term loosely applied to any painful disease or disorder of a JOINT or of its muscles, bones, ligaments, tendons, and nerves.

"Rheumatism" or "rheumatic disease" are laymen's terms: they are not exact enough for a doctor to use in making a diagnosis. Among the rheumatic disorders are such totally unrelated conditions as bone tumors, fractures involving joints, and all the joint inflammations that come under the general heading of ARTHRITIS.

Doctors distinguish between *articular* rheumatism, or diseases that attack the joints themselves (for example, RHEUMATOID ARTHRITIS, OSTEOARTHRITIS, and RHEUMATIC FEVER), and *nonarticular* rheumatism, or disorders that affect connective tissue near the joints but not the actual joints. Nonarticular rheumatism includes such diseases as BURSITIS, or inflammation of a *bursa*, one of the small fluid-filled sacs that enable joints to function smoothly; SCIATICA, or pain along the lengthy sciatic nerve; and TENOSYNOVITIS, or inflammation of a tendon sheath.

Joint diseases are often chronic: They persist for a long time, or come and go with varying intensity. They are so common that they constitute a major health problem in the United States.

Persons having painful joint conditions should consult a physician for a complete diagnosis and for treatment.

For information on rheumatic diseases and assistance available for those who cannot afford private treatment, write to the Arthritis Foundation, 10 Columbus Circle, New York, N.Y. 10019.

RHEUMATOID ARTHRITIS

A form of *arthritis*. Its cause is unknown, though infections, hypersensitivity, hormone imbalances, and psychological stress have been suggested as possible causes. Usually the disease develops in persons 20 to 40 years old (it is relatively uncommon in children), and more than two thirds of the patients are women.

Symptoms. Rheumatoid arthritis is marked by stiff, sore joints, usually in the fingers, wrists, knees, ankles, or toes. Swelling, redness, and tenderness occur in the soft tissue surrounding the affected joints. These symptoms vary according to the stage and severity of the condition. In acute stages, the patient may feel severe pain, fatigue, and general weakness caused by rheumatoid changes in the muscles, and may develop fever. The affected joints become painful, swollen, and stiff, and the pains tend to migrate to other joints. Later many patients develop nodules under the skin at sites of bony prominences.

The course of rheumatoid arthritis is unpredictable. Symptoms may stop abruptly for reasons as little understood as the causes of the disease; they usually recur just as unexpectedly. In general, joint and muscle symptoms are particularly troublesome after the patient has been inactive physically, and lessen

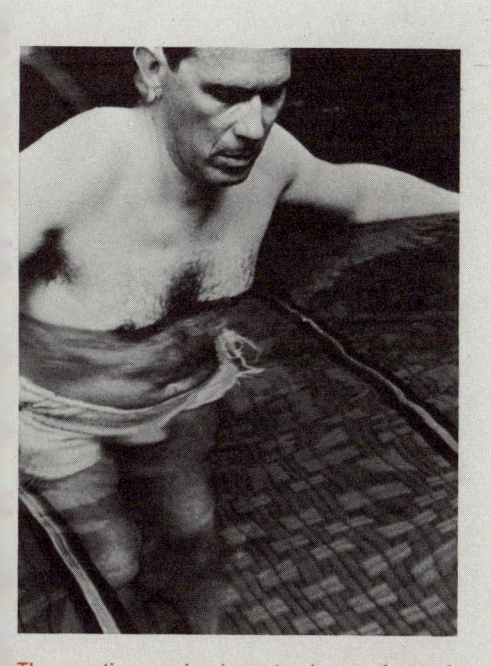

Therapeutic exercise in water is one form of treatment for rheumatic joint disorders. The buoyancy of the water relieves pressure on the joints, making movement easier.

when he resumes his normal activity.

Diagnosis is made on the basis of careful study of the patient's symptoms over a period of time and observation of the course of the disease, in order to eliminate the possibility of other diseases with similar symptoms. Laboratory tests are useful as is X-ray examination of the affected joints.

Treatment. Proper care and early treatment are essential to recovery and to the prevention of permanent damage to the joints. Though no specific cure has been found for rheumatoid arthritis, most patients respond well to treatment involving medication and carefully regulated programs of alternating rest and therapeutic exercise (see ARTHRITIS). Cortisone preparations or other medicines give dramatic relief in some cases but are in no sense curative. The disease is progressive and likely to recur, sometimes with increasing intensity. In about 15 percent of the cases, some degree of permanent stiffness eventually develops. However, most patients, especially those who begin treatment early, avoid stiffness.

With modern treatment, most rheumatoid arthritis patients can expect to lead full and normal lives, and to continue earning a living well into old age.

RHINITIS

Inflammation of the mucous membrane of the nose. It may be mild and chronic, or acute and of short duration, as in the common cold.

Viruses, bacteria, or allergens (see ALLERGY) are responsible for the varied manifestations of rhinitis. A virus is responsible for the common cold, for example. Often a *virus rhinitis* is complicated by a bacterial infection caused by streptococci, staphylococci, and pneumococci or other bacteria. HAY FEVER, an acute type of *allergic rhinitis,* is also subject to bacterial complications. Factors aiding bacterial invasion of the mucous membranes include allergens, excessive dryness, exposure to dampness and cold, dust inhalation, cigarette smoking, or injury to the nasal *cilia* (hairs) due to viral infection.

In general, rhinitis is not serious but some forms may be contagious. The mucous membrane of the nose becomes swollen and there is a nasal discharge. Some types are accompanied by fever, muscle aches, and general discomfort with sneezing and running eyes. Breathing through the nose may become difficult or impossible. Often rhinitis is accompanied by inflammation of the throat, sinuses, and middle ear. If bacterial infection develops, the nasal discharge will be thick and will contain pus.

In *acute rhinitis,* the medical term for the COMMON COLD, the best treatment consists of rest, preferably in bed, a well-balanced diet, and sufficient fluids. Aspirin will relieve headache and fever if these are present.

Prolonged and Chronic Forms. Repeated attacks of acute or chronic *sinusitis* may result in a permanent thickening and swelling of the mucous membrane, causing a nasal obstruction. This is known as *chronic hypertrophic rhinitis.* In addition to difficulty in breathing, there is a mucous discharge, including postnasal drip, as well as headache, sore throat, occasional hoarseness, and impairment of the sense of smell. Treatment consists in correcting whatever causes can be found, especially if they are allergies. There are also methods which can be used to shrink the enlarged, inflamed membranes.

Occasionally, a prolonged nasal infection accompanied by pus formation may lead to *atrophic rhinitis,* also called *ozena,* in which there is a wasting away of the mucous membrane. A thick discharge, with excessive, foul-smelling crusts, makes blowing the nose and coughing difficult. A doctor should be consulted for treatments.

There are various other forms of rhinitis including the *fibrinous*, or *croupous* type, in which there is the formation of a false membrane, and the *scrofulous*, or *tuberculous*, type, in which there is ulceration and a diseased condition of adjacent bones.

Although a simple inflammation of the mucous membrane of the nose is not serious, prolonged and chronic rhinitis should have the attention of a doctor so that the more complicated forms may be avoided.

RIBOFLAVIN

A vitamin known also as vitamin B$_2$, or *lactoflavin*.

Symptoms of a deficiency of this vitamin include general weakness, soreness at the corners of the mouth, reddening and soreness of the tip and edges of the tongue, and deterioration of the tissues of the eye, with impairment of vision. Prolonged riboflavin deficiency can result in permanent damage to health.

Foods with the highest content of riboflavin are liver, brewer's yeast, milk, greens, and enriched cereals. Riboflavin deficiency is most common among people of the southeastern United States and other regions, such as Asia and the West Indies, where the diet is likely to contain relatively large quantities of corn, potatoes, and rice, which lack riboflavin. A well-balanced diet will prevent riboflavin deficiency; it will also correct the disorder with the help of supplementary doses of riboflavin and other vitamins.

For a general discussion of **VITAMINS**, see the article under that title. See also **NUTRITION**.

RICKETS

A disease affecting the bones of infants and children and caused by a deficiency of vitamin D in the diet, which leads to altered calcium and phosphorus metabolism. Because of the widespread use of vitamin D-fortified milk, together with the additional vitamins that most babies are given, the disease is now uncommon in the United States.

Since the action of sunlight on the skin produces vitamin D in the human body, rickets often occurs in parts of the world where the winter is especially long, and where smoke and fog constantly intercept the sun. Negroes and other dark-skinned people are somewhat more susceptible to the disease if they live in areas with little sunlight, since the pigment in the skin blocks absorption of the sun's rays.

When a deficiency of vitamin D occurs in adults, it produces a condition known as *osteomalacia*, or softening of the bone.

Symptoms

Vitamin D is essential for the body (see **VITAMINS**). It aids the proper absorption and functioning of calcium and phosphorus, which are needed by cartilage, teeth, and newly formed bone. A major symptom of rickets is a softening (decalcification) of the bones. In children, this can produce various degrees of deformities such as nodules on the ribs, and flexible and bent bones. Bowlegs and an improperly developed or misshapen skull of a squared or boxed appearance are typical. The ability of the bones to support the body is seriously impaired.

Some cases of rickets are so mild that the effects are barely noticeable. In more severe cases, a child may sit with thighs apart, one leg crossed over the other, and the hands pressed flat on the ground or on the thighs to help the weakened spine hold the body erect. Potbelly may develop. Temporary, or baby, teeth may be slow in growing through the gums, and malformations can occur in the unerupted permanent teeth behind them.

Prevention

A proper diet that includes vitamin D-fortified milk is usually sufficient to prevent rickets. Ordinary milk contains adequate amounts of calcium but is a poor source of vitamin D. Small amounts of the vitamin are present in eggs, and in such fish as cod, herring, tuna, sardines, and salmon. Sunlight and other sources of ultraviolet light are beneficial.

Treatment

Treatment of an active case of rickets involves the administration of vitamin D. This is generally given in the form of the vitamin concentrate. Cod-liver oil, which was once widely used for this purpose, is less commonly used nowadays. The response to treatment is usually rapid.

There is a type of *vitamin D-resistant rickets* in which excessive loss of calcium and phosphorus does not respond to the usual doses of vitamin D. This condition is often characteristic of a particular family. Treatment involves massive doses of vitamin D and calcium supplements in the diet.

Rickets has no relation whatsoever to the *rickettsial diseases*, which are infections caused by a group of micro-organisms named after Howard T. Ricketts (1871–1910), an American microbiologist and pathologist.

RICKETTSIAL DISEASES

A group of infectious diseases caused by *rickettsia* micro-organisms, so called after their discoverer, Howard Taylor Ricketts (1871-1910), American pathologist. These micro-organisms, smaller than bacteria but larger than viruses, are found in rats, mice, and other rodents and are transmitted to man by ticks, lice, mites, and fleas.

Different types of rickettsiae cause different diseases. A number of insect CARRIERS, or *vectors*, transmit the germs; there is also considerable variety in the way the body is affected and in the symptoms. Nevertheless, it is possible to characterize the diseases as a group. Generally, the parasites invade the cells that line the walls of small blood vessels, where they multiply and ultimately burst the cells by sheer force of numbers. This damages the blood vessel walls. Sometimes toxins produced by the rickettsiae do additional damage. Allergic reactions may also occur.

The resulting symptoms usually consist of slight to high fever, a rash which appears on various parts of the body, depending on the specific disease, and perhaps a crusted sore at the site of the insect bite. Chills, nausea, and vomiting are common. Some rickettsial diseases are mild, but a few are extremely serious.

Rickettsial diseases are not common in communities with high sanitary standards, since prevention depends on controlling the rodent and insect populations. Major epidemics have occurred, especially in times of war when standards of sanitation drop.

Kinds of Rickettsial Diseases

Before the rickettsiae were identified and the diseases appropriately grouped, many names were given to the rickettsial "fevers," such as Rocky Mountain spotted fever, Kew Garden fever, camp fever, tick fever, African fever, and the nine-mile fever of Montana. The survival of these names today creates confusion. Doctors generally accept the following breakdown of the "fevers" into six major diseases.

Typhus fever, transmitted by the body louse, starts with a sudden high fever, chills, severe headache, constipation, and muscle pains. On about the fifth day a rash appears and spreads to the limbs and trunk. One of the more serious rickettsial diseases, typhus fever sometimes occurs in epidemics (see TYPHUS).

Rocky Mountain spotted fever is transmitted by the bite of the wood tick in the Rocky Mountain region and elsewhere. The symptoms are similar to those of typhus fever except that the rash appears later, begins on the limbs, and extends to the trunk and also to the palms, soles, and scalp (see ROCKY MOUNTAIN SPOTTED FEVER).

Q fever appears to be transmitted by ticks. It is also thought that the disease can be contracted by breathing airborne dust particles carrying the dried micro-organisms from the hides of sheep and cattle. Q fever affects the lungs, causing a dry cough and often mild to moderate chest pains. Other symptoms include pain behind the eyes, fever, chills, nausea, and vomiting. A comparatively mild disease, Q fever is seldom fatal. In the young it may last only a few days, but in older people it may go on for many weeks.

Tsutsugamushi, or *scrub typhus,* is transmitted by the bite of the larvae of certain mites. There is a small, crusted sore at the site of the bite and in about a third of the cases a rash appears, mostly on the trunk. Fever lasts about two weeks. Those who recover from this disease are often left with some permanent damage to the circulatory system and to hearing.

Trench fever is a relatively mild fever transmitted by the feces of the body louse. The disease is so named because it occurred mainly among field troops during World War I and II. In addition to fever, there are chills, muscle pain, pain behind the eyes, and a red rash.

Rickettsialpox is transmitted by the bite of the rodent mite. A round sore about one half of an inch in diameter appears at the site of the bite, grows into a blister, and later turns into a black, crusted sore. A few days after the sore appears there is a sudden onset of fever, chills, muscle pain, and headache, and the eyes are abnormally sensitive to light (*photophobia*). In another few days, the body becomes covered with a rash characterized by blisters and small solid eruptions called *papules.* When the rash and fever disappear, usually in one to two weeks, the patient recovers.

Diagnosis

Since the symptoms of rickettsial diseases at times resemble those of many other infectious diseases, it may be difficult for the doctor to make the diagnosis on the basis of symptoms alone. However, laboratory tests can be of great aid in many cases.

Treatment and Prevention

The rickettsial fevers generally respond quickly to treatment with tetracycline antibiotics and chloramphenicol. Cold, wet compresses help to comfort the patient during attacks of high fever.

The control of rodents and insects which carry the disease micro-organisms is essential to prevention. Patients suffering from the louse-borne rickettsial fevers should be thoroughly deloused with appropriate chemicals (see LICE). Other methods for avoiding and exterminating lice, mites, ticks, and other disease-bearing insects are discussed under INSECT BITES AND STINGS and LICE.

Vaccines are available that give partial immunity to epidemic typhus and Rocky Mountain spotted fever. Typhus fever immunization is required for travel to some parts of the world.

RIGOR MORTIS

The scientific term (Latin, "rigor of death") for the stiffening of the muscles in the body after death. It is caused by the accumulation of lactic acid and other substances in the muscles after circulation has ceased. Rigor mortis begins five to six hours after death in an adult who was in normal health, and disappears after about 36 hours.

RINGWORM

The popular name for a type of fungus infection of the skin, even though it is not caused by a worm and is not always ring-shaped in appearance.

Ringworm is caused by a group of related funguses of different types. These parasites feed on the body's waste products of dead skin and perspiration. They attack the skin in various areas, especially in body folds, such as the armpit and crotch. One type found between the toes is called ATHLETE'S FOOT; another affects the soles and toenails.

Some forms of ringworm, usually found in children and frequently traced to exposure to infected pets, attack the scalp and exposed areas of the body, particularly the arms and legs. These infections appear as reddish patches, often scaly or blistered. They sometimes become ring-shaped as the infection spreads out while its center heals or seems to heal. There is itching and soreness.

Highly contagious, the funguses are spread by humans, animals, and even objects, such as combs or towels handled by infected persons. Scratching is almost certain to pass the infection from one part of the body to another.

Ringworm in any form calls for the attention of a doctor, who can prescribe effective medication. Prevention is largely a matter of cleanliness. All parts of the body should be washed with soap and water, especially hairy areas and body folds where perspiration is likely to collect. Thorough drying is as important as bathing, for the funguses thrive in warm dampness.

ROCKY MOUNTAIN SPOTTED FEVER

An infectious disease marked by fever, headache, muscle pain, and rash; also called *tick fever.*

Rocky Mountain spotted fever belongs to a group of insect-borne fevers called RICKETTSIAL DISEASES, caused by microscopic parasites known as *rickettsiae,* which attack the cells lining small blood vessels. Rickettsia micro-organisms are found in rats, mice, and other rodents. The strain responsible for Rocky Mountain spotted fever is transmitted from rodent to man by the *wood tick.* In the eastern and southern states, it is transmitted by the *dog tick,* and is sometimes called *Eastern spotted fever.*

Symptoms. After the bite of the infected tick, there is an incubation period of three days to a week before the major symptoms set in. Within a day or two after the bite, the victim may feel somewhat ill and lose his appetite. The actual onset is marked by chills or chilly sensations, fever, headache, pain behind the eyes, joint and muscle pain, and hypersensitivity to light (*photophobia*). Other symptoms are nausea, vomiting, sore throat, and abdominal pain. Some patients become highly irritable and delirious or else so lethargic that they may lapse into a stupor or coma. Usually three to five days after the onset a rash appears on the wrists and ankles, then spreads to the trunk and limbs and occasionally to the face.

The appearance and progress of small red spots that eventually become larger sores distinguish Rocky Mountain spotted fever from the several diseases which it resembles in its other symptoms (measles, typhoid fever, typhus fever).

Treatment and Prevention. Like other rickettsial diseases, Rocky Mountain spotted fever responds readily to treatment with tetracycline antibiotics and chloramphenicol. If untreated, it can be extremely serious and often fatal.

Vaccines reduce the chance of infection and lessen its severity when it occurs, but since the advent of effective medicines they are rarely used. Preventive measures are directed mainly against the disease-carrying ticks and rodents.

Ticks should be pulled off the body, but the utmost care must be used to insure that the head and mouth parts are not left behind. A drop or two of chloroform, gasoline, or turpentine applied to the tick for a few minutes beforehand will cause it to loosen its jaws from the skin. The tick should not be crushed with the fingers for this can transfer the infection almost as effectively as a bite. It should be burned or dropped in a dish of gasoline, kerosene, or turpentine.

In endemic regions, fields of high grass and other tick-infested areas should be avoided; when it is necessary to enter them a repellent such as rotenone dust or spray should be applied to the clothing. (See **INSECT BITES AND STINGS**.)

ROSE FEVER

Formerly a popular term for what is now generally called *hay fever* (or, by physicians, *allergic rhinitis*). It is marked by watery discharge from the nose, itching of the eyes, sneezing, and swelling of the mucous membranes of the nose. In severe cases, the respiratory tract may be affected enough to make breathing difficult.

In a strict sense, hay fever is an allergic reaction to pollen which the afflicted person has breathed in. Many types of plants and trees (not just roses or grass) can produce these reactions in certain persons. Sometimes the term hay fever is loosely and inaccurately applied to reactions to other substances such as house dust, animal hair, and certain foods.

For more information, see **HAY FEVER; ALLERGY**.

ROSEOLA INFANTUM

A fairly common acute virus disease that usually occurs in children less than 24 months old. Also known as *exanthema subitum*, it attacks suddenly but disappears in a few days, leaving no permanent marks.

Diagnosis is difficult because the sole symptom at first, beyond irritability and drowsiness, is **FEVER**. There may be convulsions, and generally the fever is very high; 104° is not unusual, although the child is less sick-looking than his fever would lead one to expect. Despite the high fever, the disease is quite mild. Treatment consists only of such standard measures as aspirin and tepid sponge baths to allay the fever.

As the fever subsides, in three or four days, and the disease is apparently at an end, the child breaks out in a pink-reddish rash, usually on the body. This is completely unlike the course of other childhood diseases, such as measles, scarlet fever, and chicken pox, where the rash is present during the most intense phase of the illness.

The rash of roseola infantum does not persist for more than a few days, and, in fact, may disappear in a few hours. Very often it is so transitory that it is entirely missed. Once the disease is over, the child is believed to be immune for life against further attacks.

ROUND SHOULDERS

Shoulders that are hunched forward, so that the back is rounded. Habits of poor posture or faults in the body structure are sometimes responsible for this faulty position. It should be corrected, if possible, because it can have a detrimental effect on health. The hunching forward of the shoulders tends to impair breathing and to restrict normal action of the heart. Round shoulders are also physically unattractive, both in men and women.

Although round shoulders are often attributed to psychological factors, such as feelings of defeat, such factors are probably less important than is popularly believed. A round-shouldered posture may result from habit or occupation—for example, in children who carry a load of schoolbooks with both arms in front, and in persons who spend long hours leaning forward over desks.

Concerned parents often criticize children for poor posture. Continued criticism usually achieves little success and may do harm. A more positive approach is to encourage activities that will tend to strengthen the child's physique and increase his confidence and self-respect. Some specific suggestions are given in the articles on POSTURE and EXERCISE.

If round shoulders are due to a structural defect, such as a deformity of the spine, this defect is usually evident at birth. Occasionally it develops later. When they are observed early enough, defects can be corrected by a specialist in orthopedics. The sooner this can be done, the greater is the likelihood of improvement.

Defective VISION or HEARING, though less obvious than structural abnormalities, can often lead to round shoulders and generally poor posture. A tendency toward round shoulders often develops in aging persons as a result of changes in bone and muscular structure. Older persons, however, can generally maintain good posture through suitable exercise and other sound health habits.

ROUNDWORMS

Various types of parasitic nematode worms, somewhat resembling the common earthworm, which sometimes invade the human intestines and multiply there. Very common among them are the pinworm, or seatworm, which infests ten percent of the population of North America. Others include the ascarides, the hookworm, and the trichina, which causes TRICHINOSIS.

These worms can all impair health to varying degrees, but proper treatment will generally eliminate them. For more information, see WORMS.

RUPTURE

Any tearing or breaking apart of body tissue.

Doctors often speak of ruptured parts of the body, such as a ruptured appendix, meaning an appendix that has broken under the pressure of infection within it. Also, the word may indicate rupture of the membrane, or sac, in which a baby about to be born is contained. Used alone, the word rupture usually refers to the type of hernia in which a portion of the intestine is bulging into a weak spot in the wall of the abdomen or diaphragm. For further information, see HERNIA.

RUPTURED INTERVERTEBRAL DISK

The partial slipping-out of one of the disks from between the vertebrae of the backbone. The condition is commonly called a SLIPPED DISK and is described under that title.

Engraving of a 17th century French surgeon decked out with his instruments. Some of them were useful; many were fantastic.

SABIN VACCINE

A vaccine against **POLIOMYELITIS** developed by Dr. Albert B. Sabin. It contains live polio virus which has been attenuated—that is, sufficiently weakened so that it is unable to cause the disease—but which stimulates the production of disease-fighting antibodies in the person vaccinated. (For an explanation of this process of developing antibodies, see **IMMUNIZATION.**)

The Sabin vaccine can be taken by mouth and is as safe and effective as the **SALK VACCINE,** which must be given by injection. Experiments show that the attenuated viruses do not turn into paralytic ones. Especially convenient for administration to children and large groups of people, the vaccine can be given in a capsule, in candy, on a lump of sugar, in milk, or by medicine dropper.

A unique advantage of the Sabin vaccine is its potential effectiveness in checking the transmission of paralytic viruses from one person to another. The germs' first home in the body is the intestinal tract, from which they spread to other areas, eventually reaching the nervous system and causing paralysis. In a person who has been vaccinated by injection, the viruses are destroyed by antibodies before they reach the nervous system but after they have moved out of the intestine; viruses in the intestine are not destroyed and, still infectious, pass out of the body.

Sabin vaccine, taken orally, stimulates the production of antibodies in the digestive system as well as in other systems of the body; viruses in the intestine are destroyed, not passed on. Thus persons who have received the Sabin vaccine neither become infected nor carriers, whereas those who have received the Salk vaccine can be carriers of the viruses even though they are not themselves infected. Scientists see the

SABIN VACCINE

Dr. Albert B. Sabin demonstrates the Sabin oral polio vaccine, which he developed. It can be taken on a lump of sugar, as here, or in liquid form.

hopeful possibility of the drastic reduction of the reservoir of live paralytic viruses—the number of persons harboring them—in communities in which Sabin vaccine is used extensively.

Sabin vaccine is particularly recommended for the immunization of children, because they are exposed to the virus more frequently than are adults and are much more likely to become carriers.

SACROILIAC

Pertaining to the bony structures called the *sacrum* and the *ilium*, and the joint formed by these two bones, or to the lower part of the back where these bones meet on both sides of the back. The ilium is the upper part of the PELVIS. The sacrum, near the end of the SPINE, forms a wedge-shaped joint within the open portion of the ilium.

The tight joint allows little motion and is subject to great stress, as the body's weight pushes downward and the legs and pelvis push upward against the joint. The sacroiliac joint must also bear the leverage demands made by the trunk of the body as it turns, twists, pulls, and pushes. When these motions, especially during weight lifting, place an excess of stress on the ligaments that bind the joint and on the connecting muscles, strain may result.

Sacroiliac Strain

Sacroiliac strain is most often caused by an action that involves twisting to one side and bending forward and downward, while at the same time exerting leverage force through the muscles on the opposite side. Digging a garden or shoveling snow, for example, may cause injury in this way.

The pain centers in the lower back and spreads down the back of the thigh and outer borders of the leg and thigh on the affected side. In some patients, pain focuses on the lower back and hip. The pain is accompanied by stiffness, and the motion of the lower back is limited. The patient will be forced to limp, as it is too painful to put weight on the affected side, and he will also sit crookedly, on the buttock opposite the strain. Even in bed he may be uncomfortable, although tucking a pillow under the affected side often helps.

In any case of BACKACHE, it is advisable to try a bedboard between the mattress and springs for at least a week. Following certain simple rules when LIFTING AND CARRYING any heavy object will greatly lessen the chances of sacroiliac injury. Correct POSTURE habits are also vitally important.

Any pain in the back should be reported to a doctor. He will examine and test the legs and back, and he may consider it necessary to X-ray the back. Many cases of back strain which are at first blamed on the sacroiliac joint are later found to be due to injury to some other joint of the back, particularly the lumbosacral joint. This is the junction of the fifth lumbar vertebra with the sacrum, and strain of this joint often produces symptoms similar to sacroiliac strain.

The sacroiliac joint is also subject to other disorders, including ARTHRITIS. For a general discussion of joints, see JOINT.

SADISM

A form of sexual perversion in which sexual satisfaction is gained by inflicting pain on others, although it can manifest itself in many ways other than during the sexual act. Sadism is a mental disturbance and should be treated psychiatrically. For further information, see SEXUAL DEVIATION.

SAFETY

Many accidents can be prevented by taking proper safety precautions on the job, in the home, on the highways, and at vacation spots.

For information on many steps that can be taken to help prevent accidents, see the following articles: FARM SAFETY, JOBS AND HEALTH, HOUSING AND HEALTH, HIGHWAY SAFETY, WATER SAFETY.

SAINT ANTHONY'S FIRE

An infection of the skin and of the tissues just below the skin; also called *erysipelas*.

St. Anthony's Fire is so called because the skin turns an intense red and becomes hot to the touch as the infection develops and spreads. The disease can be serious, especially in the very young and very old, and may be accompanied by vomiting, chills, fever, and prostration. The patient is put to bed and treated with penicillin or other antibiotics.

For more information, see the separate article on ERYSIPELAS.

SAINT VITUS'S DANCE

A nervous disturbance in which the muscles twitch involuntarily; also called *chorea*. It generally attacks during childhood. St. Vitus's dance is caused by a hypersensitive allergic reaction identical to that which causes RHEUMATIC FEVER, which occurs in the motor control sections of the brain.

Symptoms are aimless movements of the head, arms, and legs. In addition, the victim may show other symptoms of rheumatic fever, such as fever, swelling of the joints, heart murmurs, and anemia.

St. Vitus's dance clears up and does not cause epilepsy or serious brain damage. Because of its close relationship to rheumatic fever, a physician should be consulted at the first signs of the disease.

SALINE SOLUTION

Any solution of a salt in water. Generally, the term means a solution of common table salt (sodium chloride) in the proportion of about one teaspoonful of salt to a quart of water (about the same concentration as is found in body fluids). Such a solution has many uses in medicine.

Often a saline solution, perhaps containing some other chemical such as glucose, is injected into the veins of a person suffering from severe blood loss, shock, or dehydration (abnormal loss of body water).

The solution increases the volume of the blood and, depending upon the chemicals it contains, may contribute certain needed nutrients.

SALIVARY GLANDS

The glands in the mouth that secrete *saliva*. The major ones are the three pairs of glands known as the parotid, submaxillary, and sublingual glands. There are other smaller salivary glands within the cheeks and tongue.

The largest of the salivary glands are the parotids, located below and in front of each ear. Saliva secreted by these is discharged into the mouth through openings in the cheeks on each side opposite the upper teeth. The submaxillary glands, located inside the lower jaw, discharge saliva upward through openings into the floor of the mouth. The sublingual glands, beneath the tongue, also discharge saliva into the floor of the mouth.

The saliva is needed to moisten the mouth, lubricate food for easier swallowing, and provide the ENZYMES necessary to begin food breakdown in the preliminary stage of digestion. All the salivary glands together produce about three pints of saliva daily.

The salivary glands are controlled by the nervous system. Normally they respond by producing saliva within two or three seconds after being stimulated by the sight, smell, or taste of food. This quick response is a reflex action, which can become conditioned in such a way that various stimuli associated with food, such as the ringing of a dinner gong, can start the secretion flowing (see CONDITIONED REFLEX).

In MUMPS, the major salivary glands, the parotids, become swollen. Occasionally, salivary glands produce too much saliva, for a number of reasons which vary from local irritation caused by dental appliances, to disturbances of digestion or the nervous system. Certain diseases, medicines such as morphine or atropine, or a nutritional deficiency of vitamin B can result in too little saliva.

SALK VACCINE

The vaccine against POLIOMYELITIS (infantile paralysis) developed by a group of medical scientists under the leadership of Dr. Jonas E. Salk. Like other vaccines, it causes the body to build up defenses against disease before a serious infection can occur (for further information on vaccination, see IMMUNIZATION).

The Salk vaccine is administered in a series of injections, the first of which can be given at any time after a child has reached the age of 6 weeks. A second injection is given 4 to 6 weeks after the first, a third 7 to 12 months after the second, and a fourth 12 to 18 months after the third. Then a booster is given annually. Frequently Salk vaccine is combined with those for diphtheria, whooping cough, and tetanus.

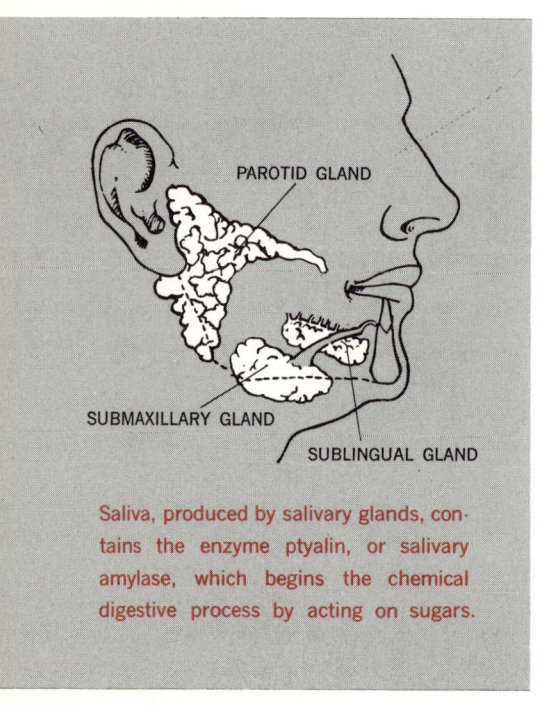

Saliva, produced by salivary glands, contains the enzyme ptyalin, or salivary amylase, which begins the chemical digestive process by acting on sugars.

In many regions, the Salk vaccine has been replaced by the Sabin vaccine, which is given orally. In some cases, immunization is begun with the Salk vaccine and continued with the Sabin vaccine.

For additional and related information, see POLIOMYELITIS; SABIN VACCINE.

SALMONELLA

A type of BACTERIA which causes a wide variety of intestinal diseases, including paratyphoid and TYPHOID FEVER and certain kinds of FOOD POISONING, of which diarrhea is apt to be a symptom. Any one of the many varieties of salmonella bacteria may be transmitted by contaminated water or food. Often food is contaminated through handling by a person who is a CARRIER of the particular disease.

For additional information, see FOOD POISONING; BACTERIA.

SANATORIUM

An establishment for the treatment of sick persons, especially a private hospital offering treatment for specific diseases or for mental disorders, or providing facilities for convalescents. The term is often used to designate institutions which specialize in treatment of TUBERCULOSIS.

The term *sanitarium*, as distinguished from *sanatorium*, was originally coined to distinguish other sanitoriums from those treating tuberculosis; in popular usage, however, the two terms have become synonymous.

For related information, see also HOSPITAL; MENTAL HOSPITAL.

SANITARY NAPKIN

A cloth pad used to absorb the flow from the vagina during menstruation; also called a *sanitary pad*. It is applied externally and held in position by means of a belt or girdle. There is also a smaller kind of pad, called a *tampon*, which can be inserted internally into the vagina.

For further information on the various types of sanitary protection, see MENSTRUATION.

SANITATION

The establishment, preservation, or restoration of hygienic conditions. Sanitary measures are designed to promote health by preventing disease and conditions in which disease can thrive or in which accidents can occur. This is done by controlling the environment.

The practice of sanitary measures is called *sanitary engineering* and covers a wide area. Included are garbage collection and waste disposal, sewerage and plumbing, air and stream pollution, water supply, swimming pools and bathing areas, street cleaning and snow removal, milk and shellfish sanitation, the sanitation of eating and drinking establishments, and insect and rodent control. Sanitary engineering, moreover, should result in a pleasant and comfort-producing environment as well as a healthy one.

The responsibility for maintaining proper sanitation lies with occupants of houses and apartments, and with industry, communities, and state and Federal governments. Private homeowners and apartment dwellers must do their share in keeping living areas free from dirt, rubbish, and obstruction. This includes sweeping sidewalks, burning leaves, and properly disposing of garbage. For more information about private and municipal responsibility for sanitation, see HOUSING AND HEALTH.

Besides ensuring that working conditions are sanitary, many industries have a special problem in the disposal of industrial waste. They must guard against

SANITATION

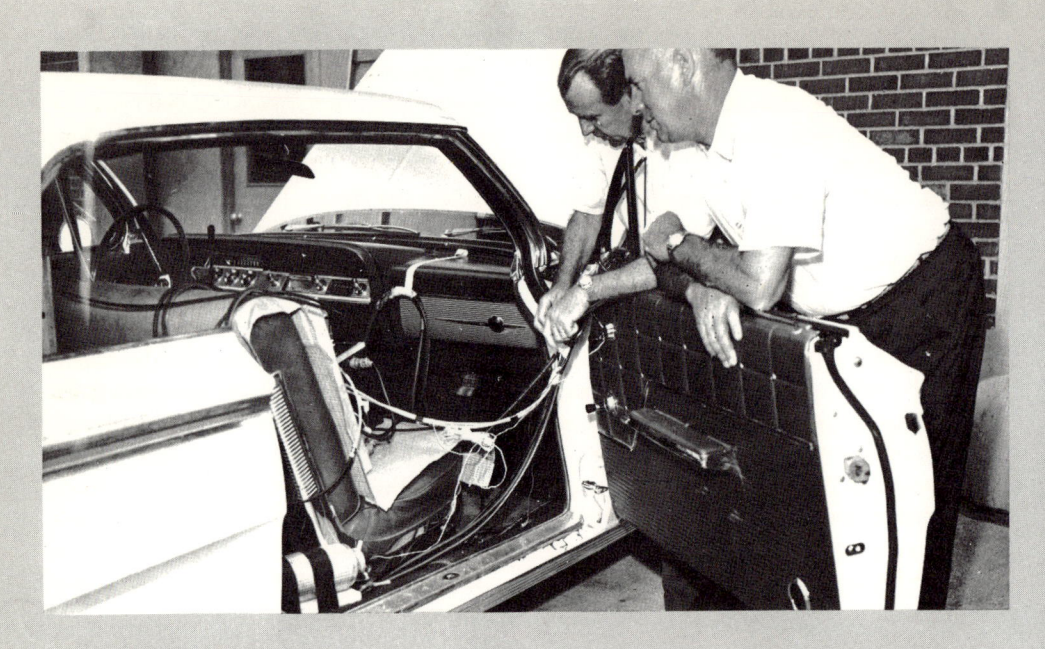

An increasingly important part of sanitary engineering is the control of air pollution, especially in large cities where there are many automobiles and industries. This automobile, at a United States Public Health Service Sanitary Engineering Center, is being used in a study of the causes and prevention of smog. It has special instruments that collect exhaust fumes for scientific study.

the pollution of the air, soil, and water. Some industries employ sanitary engineers and other scientists to study and solve the problem of what to do with industrial waste or how to improve industrial processes so that less waste is formed. Sometimes chemicals are added to neutralize waste, or other processes such as filters and screening devices are used.

Public health organizations in the United States exist at the Federal, state, and local levels, and are devoted to combating such problems as disease, environmental and occupational hazards, and unsanitary conditions which adversely affect the health of the public. For example, standards for safe drinking water have been established by the United States Public Health Service and are accepted by almost all areas as the minimum standards required. Also under the regulation of the Public Health Service are the problems of the disposal of both human and industrial wastes and the safeguarding of foods. Sanitary regulations are laid down by this agency for milk and foods served by restaurants, and sold in retail stores and vending machines, in order to prevent the transmission of diseases. For more information see the article on PUBLIC HEALTH.

SANITY

Soundness of mind and of judgment. A sound person is responsible for his actions; a person judged mentally unsound or ill, or *insane,* is not. The latter cannot be held responsible for his actions, or for his decisions, and may have to be institutionalized. The term insane is used primarily in social and legal terminology; psychiatrists prefer to use more precise definitions in referring to mental illness.

For additional and related information, see MENTAL HEALTH, MENTAL ILLNESS, PSYCHOSIS.

SARCOMA

One of the two main groups of CANCER, the other group being CARCINOMA. Sarcomas are relatively much rarer than other forms of cancer. A sarcoma is composed of cells derived from connective tissue such as bone and cartilage, and from muscle, blood vessel, and lymph tissue. These tumors usually develop swiftly and spread to other parts of the body by traveling through the lymph channels.

The different types of sarcomas are named after the specific tissue they affect: *fibrosarcomas* develop in fibrous connective tissue; *lymphosarcomas* in the lymphatic glands; *osteosarcomas* in bone; *chondrosarcomas* in cartilage; *rhabdomyosarcomas* in muscle; and *liposarcomas* in fat cells.

Treatment includes special medicines, radiation, and surgery.

SCAB

A crust formed over a sore or wound. A scab consists of dried-up discharge and forms a protection during the healing process. The scab will come off by itself when the tissue has healed. It should not be pulled off prematurely, as this may lead to infection.

If a scab happens to be scraped or pulled off too early, the area should be washed and treated with hydrogen peroxide or a mild tincture of iodine, and then covered with a bandage, to prevent reinfection.

SCABIES

A contagious skin infestation caused by insectlike parasites called itch mites.

Scabies, sometimes called merely "the itch," is most likely to erupt in folds of the skin, as in the groin, beneath the breasts, or between the toes or fingers. However, almost any part of the body may be affected.

The adult itch mite has a rounded body about one fiftieth of an inch long. Scabies is caused by the female, which burrows beneath the skin and stays there long enough to dig a short tunnel parallel to the surface, in which it lays its eggs. The eggs hatch in a few days, after which the baby mites fight their way to the skin surface, where they live their brief lives until they too are ready to burrow and lay their eggs.

Symptoms. While the initial tunnel digging and egg laying are going on, the human host may be oblivious to what is happening. There is little itching. The very slight skin discoloration may be mistaken for any one of numerous other skin disorders. In fact, it may be a week or more before the person notices his rash, by which time the mites may have spread considerably.

At this point, the itching is likely to become intense because the skin develops a hypersensitivity (or allergy) to the mite. The itch is much worse at night. The tiny tunnels in the skin can now be discerned as slightly elevated grayish-white lines. The mite itself can often be seen—with the aid of a magnifying glass—as an infinitesimal white speck at the end of the tunnel. Blisters also may develop on the skin near the tunnel, sometimes filled with pus. The scratching can lead to a secondary bacterial infection of the skin such as IMPETIGO.

Transmission. Anyone can be infected (or reinfected) with scabies. It is easily transmitted from person to person by direct skin contact or to a limited extent by contact with clothing of infected individuals. Epidemics are fairly common in such places as camps, barracks, and institutions. It is unusual for one member of a family not to communicate it to the others.

The period of communicability lasts until the itch mites and eggs are totally destroyed, a period that varies from one to two weeks depending on the effectiveness of the treatment used.

Treatment and Prevention. When scabies is first noticed or suspected, the doctor will look at the skin for the distinctive tunnels. He will verify the diagnosis by removing the mite for examination under a microscope. The usual therapy begins with a hot bath and thorough scrubbing to open and expose the burrows. This is followed by the application of one of several effective medicines as directed by the doctor.

The patient's underwear and bedclothing must be changed and laundered daily until all the itch mite eggs are hatched out and the mites eliminated, so as to prevent reinfection of the patient or infection of others.

In general, keeping the body clean by the abundant use of soap and water, plus equal attention to wearing fresh and clean clothing, are the two most effective ways to keep the itch mite away. This is all the more true if one is living in crowded quarters where close proximity invites the easy transmission of such parasitic disorders. (See also LICE; TICK.)

SCALD

A burn caused by hot water or steam. Scalds can be extremely painful. If they cover a large area, they can be serious and should receive prompt medical attention.

Ordinarily pain can be relieved by immersing the affected area in clean cold water or applying ice cubes for ten minutes each hour. Or apply a sterile gauze pad or clean cloth soaked in a solution of two tablespoonfuls of baking soda (bicarbonate of soda) dissolved in a quart of lukewarm water. The area should then be bandaged loosely. For minor scalds, a paste of baking soda and water or a dressing of petroleum jelly can be used; cover with a sterile gauze.

For further information, see BURNS.

SCAR

New tissue formed in the healing of a wound. The wound or skin break may be caused by injury, illness, smallpox vaccination, surgery, or other factors.

Beneath the skin, or covering tissue of the body, is a fibrous connective tissue known as *subcutaneous tissue*. It is composed of cells called *fibroblasts*. Fibroblasts are located throughout the body between tissues and lining cavities and organs.

Whenever there is a tissue injury, fibroblasts are stimulated to grow tissue which knits the wound together. Dense masses of this forms scar tissue. Scarring is part of the HEALING process. If a wound is severe, there will often be INFLAMMATION and the formation of pus and scabs while the scar is forming. The size and shape of the scar is determined by the extent of the destruction. Scars vary from the small round scar of a vaccination to the large irregular scar caused by a major burn. A scar may be discolored or the same shade as the skin. Although usually permanent, a scar will recede a little over the years. A scar on the skin usually causes no trouble other than the unsightliness of its appearance. A single unattractive scar,

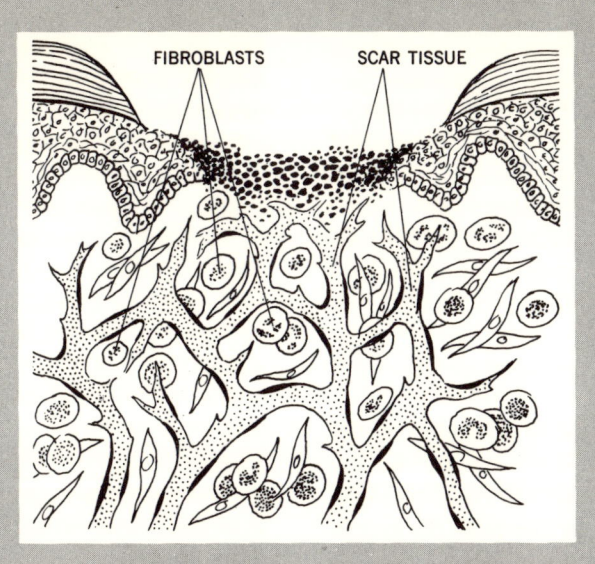

Fibroblasts repair an extensive wound by bridging the area of the wound and then hardening into white scar tissue.

however, frequently can be removed by an operation which will convert the scar into a barely discernible line.

Many skin diseases, such as boils, carbuncles, and the acne of adolescence, produce scars. Scarring is not inevitable in every case, especially if the disease is promptly and properly treated, and if the patient refrains from scratching and squeezing the sores (see articles on ACNE and BOIL).

Treatment

Often scars of acne or other conditions can be removed through planing with a rotating high-speed brush. This removes the outer layer of pitted skin (epidermis), leaving intact the inner portion (dermis), which contains the glands and hair follicles (see SKIN). New skin, rosy at first but fading to a normal color, replaces the skin that was planed off. Planing must be performed by a competent dermatologist, rather than by a beauty specialist. Medical knowledge is necessary to prevent injury, and planing requires the same aftercare that follows any operation.

Scars left by surgery usually cause no complications. But occasionally surgery will leave a large, somewhat swollen scar known as a KELOID. This is seen more in people with dark complexions. Often a keloid can be removed.

Extensive burns can create dangerous, disabling, or disfiguring scars. For burn scars, PLASTIC SURGERY is often advisable. Disfigurement is lessened or completely removed by processes such as grafting new skin.

Scars in the tissue within the body, whether from surgery or injury, usually cause no damage. Occasionally a scar can, by contracting, cause obstruction; for example, an ulcer scar may obstruct the outlet of the stomach (*pylorus*). Scar tissue may cling to the surface of adjoining organs forming ADHESIONS. These also usually cause no difficulty but may produce obstruction or malfunction. A scar which changes greatly or one that develops a chronic sore should be seen by a physician.

SCARLET FEVER

A contagious childhood disease; also called *scarlatina*. Scarlet fever is caused by members of the *streptococcus* family of germs. These same micro-organisms also cause "strep throat." In fact, scarlet fever may be contracted if there is any streptococcal infection of the throat, skin, middle ear, or any part of the body. There are approximately 75,000 cases of scarlet fever reported in the United States each year. The disease is most common in late winter and spring.

Scarlet fever is usually spread by droplets of moisture from an infected person's nose or throat. Objects the infected person has used, such as clothes, dishes, or toys, may carry the germ but this does not happen often. Occasionally a widespread outbreak may be caused by milk or food which has been infected by a person carrying the streptococcus.

Scarlet fever was formerly a very common and serious disease. In recent years, the number and severity of cases has greatly decreased. What is more important, complications are much less common, largely as a result of the development and use of antibiotics.

Symptoms

The incubation period of scarlet fever, from the time of exposure to the first appearance of symptoms, is usually two to five days, although it may be as few as one or as many as seven days.

The symptoms of scarlet fever vary a great deal. Many who catch the disease suffer only from a sore throat and swollen lymph glands of the neck. The tonsils may be covered by a patchy layer of pus. This is usually the first symptom. Because of the different varieties of streptococcal germs which can cause scarlet fever, the illness may or may not be accompanied by a rash. The child may feel nauseated, and may even vomit. The skin will usually feel hot and dry, and there also may be headaches and chills. In mild cases the temperature may rise to about 101 degrees and in severe cases to 103 or even 105 degrees.

Scarlet fever can vary from very mild cases without a rash to severe cases with one. In a classical (moderately severe) attack, a rash appears on the neck, behind the ears, and on the back. Frequently it will make its first appearance in the armpits and groin. The rash is composed of tiny spots, and is usually bright red. It spreads rapidly down the back and chest until it covers almost the entire body. The rash does not usually spread to the face, but the cheeks may be flushed, with a pale ring around the mouth. The skin blanches and turns whitish on pressure. The tongue becomes heavily coated, and then peels, becoming a very bright red.

If there are no complications, the temperature will slowly return to normal. The rash fades in about a week, and the skin peels; this peeling is usually most pronounced on the palms and soles. In all, the active and contagious part of the disease lasts about seven days.

Treatment

As soon as the first symptoms of scarlet fever appear, the patient should be put to bed, and the doctor notified immediately. Because of the contagious nature of the disease, the patient should be isolated as far as possible. The child will be given **ANTIBIOTICS**, usually *penicillin*. This treatment is continued for about ten days to avoid relapse. Aspirin may be used to relieve headache, fever, and sore throat.

Contact with the patient or any objects which he uses should be avoided. The scarlet fever germ is very hardy. The patient's clothes and bedding should be washed separately immediately after use, or soaked in a disinfectant for two hours if they are to be washed with those of other members of the family. Any toys, books, or other objects that the patient uses should be thoroughly aired or washed with soap and hot water.

The active stage of scarlet fever is over as soon as the fever is gone. The patient's skin may peel during the convalescent period but he can no longer pass the disease on to others. If the case was mild, the patient can usually return to his normal activities in seven to ten days.

If there is any persistent discharge from a body opening, such as a running ear, the disease may be still contagious. However, if the patient is treated properly with antibiotics, the streptococci will usually be destroyed and the patient will no longer be contagious. Even the discharge from the runny ear may not contain streptococcal organisms.

After the child has recovered, his room should be thoroughly cleaned and aired. Any dust-catching surfaces, such as floors, tables and window sills, should be washed with soap and hot water. If the patient has been using a private bathroom, it should be washed and disinfected as well. (For general information and advice on caring for a sick child at home, see HOME NURSING.)

Complications

Among the possible complications of scarlet fever are swelling of the *lymph glands* in the neck, infected ears and sinuses, kidney disease, pneumonia, and rheumatic fever. Any of these complications may be serious. However, since the development of antibiotics, they have become increasingly rare. Prompt and adequate treatment greatly reduces the danger of complications.

Prevention

If a child who has not had scarlet fever is exposed to it, prompt treatment with antibiotics may prevent the disease altogether. The short incubation period of scarlet fever makes immediate treatment necessary.

A person who has been exposed to scarlet fever and has not developed symptoms by the end of seven days can assume that he was not infected. If symptoms do develop, he should be treated immediately. Cases of scarlet fever must be reported to local health authorities, who have set up regulations concerning quarantine. This may vary depending on the area. The doctor treating the case will be familiar with the regulations in his particular area.

A *vaccine* which gives some immunity to scarlet fever has been developed but it confers immunity for only about six months. Since scarlet fever has become a much less serious disease, this vaccine is not often necessary.

SCHISTOSOMIASIS

A parasitic disease, caused by blood flukes, or *schistosomes*. Larvae of these worms enter the human body through the skin and migrate via the blood stream to various organs, usually concentrating in the small blood vessels of the lower intestinal and the urinary tracts, where they mature into adults. The disease is rare in North America but two forms are common in Egypt, other parts of Africa, and the Middle East (one of these forms also occurs in Puerto Rico). A type widely prevalent in the Nile Valley is called *bilharziasis*. A third variety is a significant health problem in Japan, China, and the Philippines.

The Schistosome Life Cycle. The life cycle of the schistosomes is similar to that of many parasitic WORMS which depend on two hosts, one human and one nonhuman, during their development. The larvae of the flukes hatch from eggs in water contaminated by infected urine or feces. For a time, they live in the bodies of certain types of snails, then move to human hosts, entering the skin of persons coming in contact with the water. Moving through the body, the larvae come eventually to certain blood vessels in which they grow into adult worms and deposit eggs. The eggs may be carried to the bowel wall or to tissue of the bladder or uterus, where they lodge, causing inflammation and ulceration. With one form of schistosomiasis, eggs lodge in the liver, producing such serious disorders as CIRRHOSIS. Many eggs pass out of the body in urine or feces and, when they come into contact with water, the cycle of development begins again.

Symptoms. In the human body, schistosomiasis infection usually develops in three stages, each marked with its own symptoms. Penetration of the skin by the larvae is likely to produce skin irritations. After four or five weeks, as the larvae move through the body, a variety of symptoms can develop, depending on what organs are invaded; usually there are fever and fatigue, and often respiratory trouble. These symptoms disappear in two weeks to two months, but about six months after the first infection renewed symptoms indicate that new eggs have been deposited in tissue of the intestinal or urinary tract. If the disease is not treated, symptoms become increasingly severe and debilitating, and ultimately the infection can lead to a fatal disorder of one of the affected organs.

Diagnosis and Treatment. Diagnosis of schistosomiasis usually involves analysis of the symptoms and laboratory tests for eggs in urine or feces. A BIOPSY or SKIN TEST usually makes possible the positive identification of the disease.

Treatment with different medications, if begun early, can bring about a complete cure but becomes increasingly difficult if the disease is allowed to progress.

SCHIZOPHRENIA

A form of mental illness in which the patient suffers from an emotional disorder so severe that he retreats into a world of fantasy and is unable to distinguish between it and reality. In this type of psychosis, the inability to think logically and the deeply disturbed emotional states are often accompanied by hallucinations and delusions. In extreme cases, the patient may develop *catatonia,* a condition in which there may be unco-operative or impulsive behavior, alternate periods of stupor and excitement, and sometimes the assumption of rigid physical positions that may be maintained for a considerable time.

Schizophrenia, formerly called *dementia praecox,* usually develops between the ages of 15 and 30. It can vary from a mild disorder, at times undetected, to one so severe as to require prolonged hospitalization. The chances of recovery are best if the condition is treated early.

For further information, see PSYCHOSIS.

SCIATIC NERVE

Either of two nerves extending from the base of the spine down the thigh, with branches throughout the lower leg and foot. They are the body's widest nerves and among the longest. A sciatic nerve sometimes becomes inflamed and causes leg pains, or SCIATIC NEURITIS. For other disorders affecting the sciatic nerve, see SCIATICA.

SCIATICA

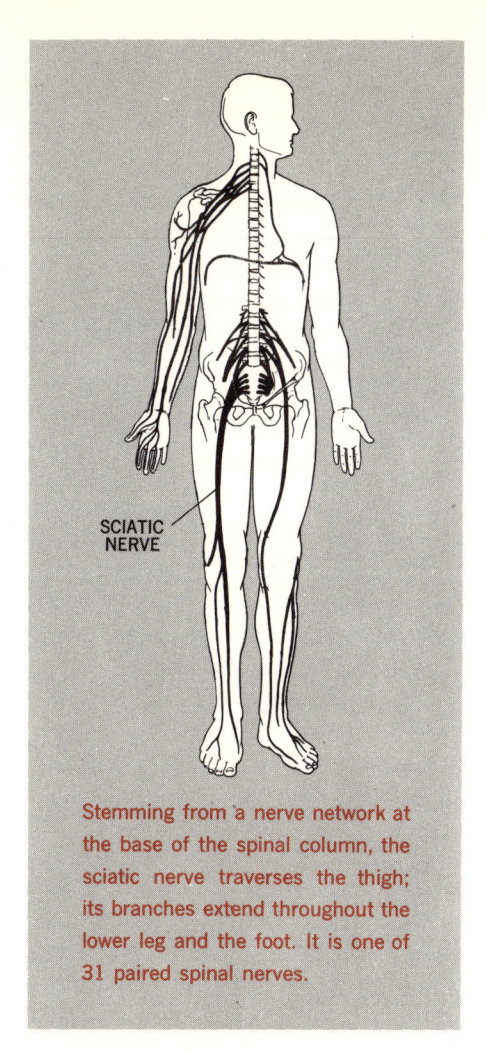

Strictly speaking, a term used to describe *sciatic neuritis*, or inflammation of the *sciatic nerve*. The term is also popularly used, however, to describe a number of disorders directly or indirectly affecting the sciatic nerve.

Extending from the spinal cord down each thigh, with branches throughout the lower leg and foot, the SCIATIC NERVE is the widest nerve in the body and one of the longest. It is exposed to many different kinds of injury to the back, in the pelvis, and along its course in the legs. Inflammation of the sciatic nerve or injury to it causes pain that travels down from the back or thigh into the feet and toes. Certain muscles of the legs may be partly or completely paralyzed by such a disorder. When this occurs, the doctor makes a careful search for the origin of the sciatica.

True SCIATIC NEURITIS is comparatively rare. It can be caused by certain toxic substances, such as lead, by alcoholism, and occasionally by various other factors (see NEURITIS).

Sciatic pain can, however, be produced by a number of conditions other than inflammation of the nerve. The most common cause is probably a SLIPPED DISK, or herniated disk, of the spine. A back injury, irritation from arthritis of the spine, or pressure on the nerve from certain types of manual work may also be the cause. Occasionally certain diseases such as diabetes, gout, and vitamin deficiencies may be the inciting factor. In rare cases, pain may be referred over connected nerve pathways to the sciatic nerve from a disorder in another part of the body.

Some cases of sciatica are idiopathic —that is, without known cause. However, because of the long, painful, and disabling course of severe sciatica, it is worth considerable time and money to

Stemming from a nerve network at the base of the spinal column, the sciatic nerve traverses the thigh; its branches extend throughout the lower leg and the foot. It is one of 31 paired spinal nerves.

SCIATIC NEURITIS

Inflammation of the SCIATIC NERVE, causing pain usually in the back of the thigh and leg, and sometimes paralysis of the leg. This is a comparatively rare disorder, caused by certain toxic substances such as lead, by alcoholism, and by various other factors more fully described under NEURITIS.

The term sciatica, when used in a strict sense, means sciatic neuritis. But it is often loosely applied to pains in the sciatic nerve not caused by sciatic inflammation. For a discussion of such pains, see SCIATICA.

have every possible cause investigated and the underlying cause corrected.

Sedatives and physiotherapy may be needed to relieve the pain and disability.

SCLEROSIS

Any hardening of tissue. It occurs in diseases of various kinds; therefore the term *sclerosis* usually appears as part of a more specific name of a disease.

Arteriosclerosis and *atherosclerosis*, commonly known as HARDENING OF THE ARTERIES, involve a thickening of the artery walls. A sclerosis of arteries in the kidney (*nephrosclerosis*) occurs in some types of NEPHRITIS. A sclerosis of the liver occurs in CIRRHOSIS.

In *amyotrophic lateral sclerosis*, a chronic, progressive disease of the nervous system, there is a degeneration of brain and spinal cord cells controlling certain groups of muscles. Symptoms include increasing weakness, tremors, wasting of the upper extremities, and paralysis. The cause of this disease is unknown, and no successful treatment has as yet been found. Amyotrophic lateral sclerosis is to be differentiated from *multiple sclerosis*, a disease which is characterized by hard patches on parts of the brain and spinal cord. This disease also is chronic and progressive, with a wide variety of signs and symptoms (see MULTIPLE SCLEROSIS).

Scleroderma is a chronic disease marked in early stages by hardening and thickening of the skin. In the generalized form of this disease, degeneration of other body tissues, including bone and the tissues of the heart, lungs, and kidney, occur progressively. For more details, see COLLAGEN DISEASES.

SCOLIOSIS

A sideward curvature of the spine.

Normally the spine curves slightly forward and backward but not from side to side. When a spine curves to the right or left, the condition is called *scoliosis*. The disorder may be noticed in infancy when the most likely cause is a defect in the development of the spine. More often, however, scoliosis develops during childhood, sometimes as the result of faulty posture, and becomes noticeable at about the age of 12. Diseases which affect the spine, such as RICKETS, or which weaken the muscles supporting the spine, such as POLIOMYELITIS, may also cause scoliosis.

Treatment varies according to the causative factor and the extent of the curve, but should be begun as early as possible. For a more detailed discussion of scoliosis, see the article on CURVATURE OF THE SPINE.

SCRAPE

An abrasion of the outer layers of the skin. An effective, simple treatment for a mild scrape is to run lukewarm water over the area. If foreign particles remain, remove by rubbing gently with an absorbent cotton pad with water and soap. Superficial small wounds do not usually require an antiseptic, although a mild one, such as hydrogen peroxide, may be used. Boric acid ointment or petroleum jelly may then be applied and the area covered with a bandage.

If an abrasion is sufficiently deep, a doctor may consider giving tetanus antitoxin or toxoid.

SCRATCH

A surface wound caused when something sharp or jagged tears the outer layers of the skin. Small scratches normally heal by themselves. In order to prevent infection, a scratch should be thoroughly cleansed with soap and water and then rinsed with clean water. It should be dried gently with sterile cloth, gauze, or tissue. A mild antiseptic such as tincture of iodine or hydrogen peroxide may be applied, and the scratch covered with a sterile gauze or bandage. For additional information, see CUTS AND SCRATCHES.

SCROFULA

Tuberculosis of the lymph nodes in the neck (see SWOLLEN GLANDS). The term also sometimes refers to TUBERCULOSIS of bones and joints. In its acute form it is marked by abscesses and breakdown of tissues in the affected areas.

Formerly scrofula was called "the king's evil," because of the belief that the touch of a king's hand would cure it. The conquest of TUBERCULOSIS by modern medicine has made scrofula uncommon today.

SCROTUM

The skin-covered sac in which the TESTES are contained. Each testicle is connected to a muscle (the *cremaster* muscle) descending from the abdominal wall. During cold weather, the muscle draws the testicle closer to the body to maintain the temperature of the testes. In hot weather, the reverse occurs. The scrotum usually follows this movement (see also SEX GLANDS).

The scrotum is subject to the same diseases as the rest of the SKIN, including cysts and cancer. Edema, whether caused by heart disease or the tropical disease ELEPHANTIASIS, can cause great enlargement of the scrotum by filling its loose tissues with fluid.

SCURVY

A disease caused by a lack of vitamin C, or *ascorbic acid,* in the diet. Essential for the health of bones, cartilage, connective tissue, and teeth, vitamin C is found chiefly in citrus fruits and certain vegetables. Scurvy was once common aboard ships during long voyages, when these foods were not available.

Today scurvy is a rare disease because we know that the daily diet should include some vitamin C. It still occurs occasionally in bottle-fed babies between 6 and 18 months old who have not been getting fruit juice or some other source of vitamin C to supplement their formula. Breast-fed babies seem to get sufficient vitamin C from their mothers' milk. Symptoms of infantile scurvy include poor appetite, digestive disturbances, failure to gain weight, and increasing irritability. Black and blue spots may be scattered over the skin. A severe deficiency may cause changes in bone structure.

The only adults in the United States likely to develop scurvy are older people who live alone and neglect their diet for months on end. In adults, scurvy symptoms are swollen and bleeding gums, loose teeth, easy rupture of small blood vessels, and small black and blue spots on the skin. Later symptoms may include anemia, extreme weakness, sore arms and legs, rapid heartbeat, and shortness of breath.

Treatment for scurvy consists of supplying the missing vitamin in dosages prescribed by the doctor, and of restoring the proper diet, including fresh fruits and vegetables. When this is done, the symptoms of the illness quickly disappear.

Fruits and vegetables that are rich sources of vitamin C include the following: grapefruit, oranges, lemons, limes, cantaloupes, strawberries, raspberries, turnips, raw cabbage, potatoes (baked), and tomatoes. Commercial orange-flavored drinks do not always contain the vitamin C that orange juice does; in some cases vitamin C is added.

For more information about NUTRITION and VITAMINS, see the articles under those titles.

SEASICKNESS

Discomfort caused by the motion of a boat under way. The unusual motion disturbs the organs of balance located in the inner ear. The symptoms of seasickness are nausea and vomiting, dizziness, headache, pallor, and cold perspiration.

There are a number of ways to help ward off seasickness. It is best to stay in the fresh air instead of in a stuffy room, to eat lightly, and to avoid fatty, fried, or spicy foods. Antinausea medicines prescribed by a doctor may be effective. If seasickness occurs, the sufferer should rest lying down with his head low, in a comfortable well-ventilated place.

For more information on this subject, see **MOTION SICKNESS**.

SEBACEOUS GLANDS

Lubricating glands situated in the inner layer of the skin. There are thousands of these tiny glands, which may number as many as 15 to a square inch of skin. The number varies in different areas of the body and from one person to another.

The sebaceous glands exude an oily, odorless, colorless fluid called *sebum*. This oily fluid seeps constantly from the skin pores and lubricates the skin surface. Too little sebum means a dry skin; too much, an oily skin.

Skin lubrication goes on automatically and reliably throughout most of a person's lifetime. The sebaceous glands seldom give trouble except during adolescence or pregnancy. During adolescense the sebaceous glands are prone to become overactive as a result of changes in hormone secretion; this overactivity causes **ACNE**, with its pimples, whiteheads, and blackheads. Acne affects about nine out of ten youngsters of both sexes and is particularly active in girls at their menstrual period. Usually the embarrassing pimples disappear by the time the adolescent reaches maturity.

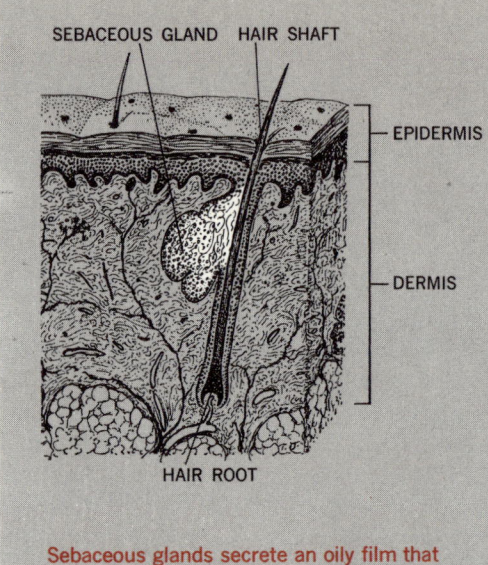

During pregnancy, the hormonal balance may again be disturbed and the sebaceous glands may become overactive, although not to the same extent as may happen during adolescence. It is important to keep the skin clean by taking regular baths.

DANDRUFF is attributed to malfunction of the sebaceous glands. There may be other contributing causes, such as an infection, but the sebaceous glands are always involved. For the prevention and cure of dandruff, scalp cleanliness is of the utmost importance.

A deficiency of vitamin A in the diet can cause the sebaceous glands to become clogged, making the skin rough and scaly. This condition is rare today in the United States because of generally high nutrition standards.

Sebaceous glands secrete an oily film that lubricates the skin and protects it by limiting water evaporation from, and absorption by, its surface.

SECOND WIND

A colloquial phrase for the ability to exert muscular effort after initial breathlessness.

As the muscles use up OXYGEN at an increased rate, breathing becomes deeper and more rapid, the heart accelerates and enlarges, and the blood pressure rises so that the blood is circulating more rapidly. This accelerates the transfer of oxygen and carbon dioxide both in the lungs and the muscle tissues. The quantity of oxygenated blood carried to the muscles becomes equal to the oxygen need of the muscles, and a balance is established (see RESPIRATION).

SECRETION

Any substance manufactured by glands or other tissues for use by the body. One example is the fatty substance produced by the SEBACEOUS GLANDS to lubricate the SKIN. Saliva, which is produced by the SALIVARY GLANDS, and gastric juice, secreted by specialized glands of the stomach, are both used in DIGESTION.

The secretions of the ENDOCRINE GLANDS, or ductless glands, include various hormones that are important in the overall regulation of body processes.

SEDATIVE

A medicine that calms nervousness, irritability, and excitement. In general, sedatives depress the central NERVOUS SYSTEM and tend to cause lassitude and reduced mental activity.

The degree of relaxation produced by a sedative varies with the kind of sedative, the amount of the dose, the way it is given, and the mental state of the patient. By relaxing a patient, a sedative may help him go to sleep, but it does not put him to sleep. Medicines that compel sleep are known as *hypnotics*. A medicine may act as a sedative in small amounts and as a hypnotic in large amounts.

The BARBITURATES, such as phenobarbital, are the best-known sedatives. They are also widely used as sleep producers. Other effective sedatives are the *bromides, paraldehyde,* CHLORAL HYDRATE, and *alcohol* (usually in the form of whisky or brandy).

Sedatives are useful in the treatment of any condition where rest and relaxation are important to recovery. Some sedatives are also useful in treatment of convulsive disorders or epilepsy and in counteracting the effect of convulsion-causing drugs. They are used in calming patients before childbirth and before surgery. Restlessness in invalids, profound grief in adults, and overexcitement in children can be controlled by medically supervised sedation. Because many sedatives are habit-forming, they should be used only under the supervision of a doctor.

Among drugs related to sedatives are the TRANQUILIZERS. These also have a calming effect, but unlike the sedatives they usually do not suppress body reactions. Certain tranquilizers are useful in the treatment of MENTAL ILLNESS.

SELF-MEDICATION

The safest rule to follow about medications of any sort is to take only those recommended by a doctor. Even though a medicine is sold without a PRESCRIPTION, the doctor is the best person to judge which one is right for the patient and for his situation.

It is true that certain common medications, such as aspirin, are considered safe for most people. However, even aspirin should not be taken indiscriminately because in some persons it seems to cause stomach irritation and even lead to peptic ulcer. Sodium bicarbonate, often used to counteract the dis-

SELF-MEDICATION

comfort of simple indigestion, is another medication which should not be taken regularly because occasionally it may cause toxic **ALKALOSIS**.

Symptoms that persist require medical diagnosis to be sure that they are not caused by a serious disorder. Medications a doctor has prescribed should always be taken according to his instructions. No one should take medications prescribed for another person, no matter how similar their symptoms may be.

SEMICIRCULAR CANALS

The passages in the inner ear which control the sense of balance. Each ear has three semicircular canals situated approximately at right angles to each other—forward, backward, and to the side. The canals are tiny tubes filled with fluid and have enlarged portions at one end, called *ampullae,* which contain nerve endings.

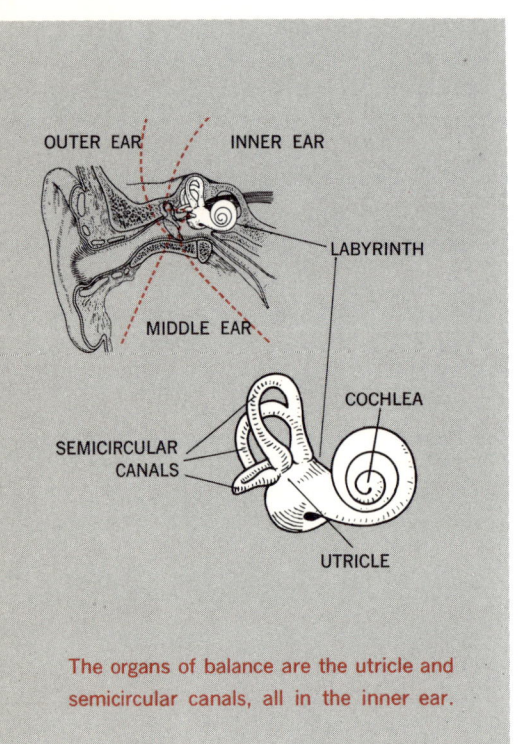

The semicircular canals respond to changes in the position of the head. When the head changes position in any direction, the fluid in the corresponding canal lags behind the movement because of its inertia. Thus the fluid presses against the delicate hairs of the nerves in the ampulla, and these nerves then register the fact that the head is turning in such a direction. Any movement is noted in this way by the fluid in the canals that lie in the same plane as the movement (see **BALANCE**).

It is the semicircular canals which cause the feeling of **DIZZINESS** or vertigo after spinning. When the spinning stops, the fluid in the horizontal canal continues to move for a moment in the direction of the spin, giving a temporary false reading that the head is turning in the other direction. **MOTION SICKNESS** is caused by the unusual and erratic motions of the head in an airplane, car, or ship, and the resulting stimulation of the semicircular canals.

SENILITY

A pronounced and abnormal loss of mental and emotional control in aged people, caused by physical or mental deterioration or a combination of the two. Certain types of **PSYCHOSIS**, a severe mental illness, are associated with senility.

By the age of 70, many people normally experience some degree of physical change, such as a slowing of the reflexes and a greater susceptibility to fatigue. In senility, however, changes are psychological and often extreme in nature. The patient may suffer lapses of memory and confuse the present with the past. Sudden uncontrolled outbursts of joy, rage, or despair may occur for no apparent reason. In severe cases, the

The organs of balance are the utricle and semicircular canals, all in the inner ear.

SENILITY

In most cases, senility is of psychological or emotional origin. Often it is caused by a feeling of being useless, especially among old people, like this woman, who need help in performing the simplest tasks, such as eating. Among important factors in preventing senility is an atmosphere of warmth and sympathy in which the person feels loved, needed, and useful.

patient may suffer from delusions of persecution, or fall into depression and apathy.

Doctors formerly believed that most cases of senility were caused by damage to the brain. However, it now appears that relatively few cases result from brain damage. The majority of cases of senility are of psychological and emotional origin.

Advances made in *geriatrics*, the branch of medicine which deals with the problems of the aged, are increasingly effective in preventing and controlling the symptoms of senility. Medical care, certain new medicines, psychiatric treatment, and especially a new concern with the social, psychological, and emotional environment of older people, are all helpful in this task.

Psychological Causes

Senility of psychological origin is believed to be a reaction to loss of interests and stimulation and to the insecurities, frustrations, fears, and stresses of old age. There may be no physical damage to the brain. The patient may have reason to feel that he has become worthless or useless in his old age, and as a result he withdraws from everyday life. In recent years, increased efforts have been made by local communities through various social organizations to give the aged a more interesting, enjoyable, and comfortable life, but these efforts are still far short of their goal. The period of old age makes necessary great adjustments to new physical conditions and living patterns, adjustments which many people are not able to make without professional help.

Physical Causes

The most common physical cause of senility is cerebral *arteriosclerosis* or

HARDENING OF THE ARTERIES of the brain, which can cause slow, progressive damage. This may lead to a *cerebral hemorrhage* or *thrombosis* (see **STROKE**), which can damage or destroy tissue in important areas of the brain. In this form the onset is usually sudden. There may be intervals of apparent marked improvement, followed by a return of symptoms. These symptoms depend largely on the area of the brain which is damaged. If the area which controls body movements is injured, this form of senility may be accompanied by a severe loss of co-ordination or by paralysis and in some cases loss of speech.

Symptoms

The onset of senility is often marked by severe depression or anxiety. The patient may become obsessed with physical ills, real and imaginary. His memory, especially for recent events, may suffer, although this is often a result of his not being actively involved in the life of the family or community. As the condition develops, the patient may lose interest in his surroundings and become inattentive and confused. Other symptoms may include sudden outbursts of rage, fits of joy or depression, personal untidiness, and neglect of appearance. If the patient becomes severely depressed, his condition should be evaluated by a doctor, since there may occasionally be some danger of suicide.

Senility is a form of illness, not a necessary part of aging. A great many of the elderly live full and active lives and take a continuing interest in their surroundings, participating in many activities and making useful contributions to their families and communities.

Treatment

Early detection of illness is an important part of treating senility. If the patient has hardening of the arteries, for example, the physician can usually treat this condition and possibly prevent or retard damage to the brain.

Senility as a result of psychological factors can be treated by **PSYCHOTHERAPY,** a branch of medicine that helps the patient understand and deal with his personal problems. The techniques of psychotherapy can be very effective in many cases, not only in treating senility but also in preventing it. The psychological problems that lead to senility exist long before the stresses of old age bring them out so strongly. If they are properly treated before the symptoms appear, the patient will have no psychological need to withdraw from the world.

If senility advances to the point at which the patient's behavior requires constant attention, care in an institution may be necessary. Such a step should be discussed thoroughly with the patient's doctor. In some cases it may be necessary to place the patient in a **MENTAL HOSPITAL** for his care and protection.

Prevention

It is important to remember that senility is not inevitable and that a person need not become helpless and out of touch with his surroundings. Poor mental health, like poor physical health, can be prevented in many cases. If attention is given to psychological preparation for old age, the adjustment can often be made with comparatively little difficulty.

Both the patient's family and his doctor have important roles to play in preventing senility. Proper nutrition, exercise, and rest are extremely important factors. Proper attention to any physical illness is also vital. Beyond this, however, a warm, sympathetic environment in which the patient feels loved, useful, and needed can prevent senility which has no physical cause, and can greatly reduce the psychological effects of physical disabilities.

In the past, many elderly people were needlessly sent to mental hospitals where little care or attention was given them because of their advanced age. This had the effect of rapidly accelerating their deterioration. Today, efforts are being directed toward providing proper attention, recreation, and rehabilitation. As a result, many elderly people are able to regain considerable self-sufficiency and return to relatively normal living at home. With help in understanding the emotional problems of adjustment, as well as proper attention to good health habits, senility can be prevented and, in many cases where it occurs, it can be overcome.

For a broad discussion of the subject of aging, see LATER YEARS.

SENSES

The means by which a person becomes aware of his own body and the world around him. The five major senses comprise those of vision, hearing, smell, taste, and touch; other senses include those of balance, pain, cold, and heat.

The operation of all senses involves the reception of stimuli by sense organs. Each sense organ is sensitive to a particular kind of stimulus. The eyes are sensitive to light; the ears, to sound; the olfactory organs of the nose, to odor; and the taste buds of the tongue, to taste. Various sense organs of the skin and other tissues are sensitive to touch, pain, temperature, and other sensations.

On receiving stimuli, the sense organ translates them into nerve impulses which are transmitted along the sensory nerves to the brain. In the *cerebral cortex* of the brain, the impulses are interpreted, or perceived, as sensations. The brain associates them with other information, acts upon them, and stores them as memory.

For more information on the part played by the nervous system and brain in the perception of sensation, see the articles on NERVOUS SYSTEM and BRAIN. For information on individual sense organs and senses, see the following articles: BALANCE, EAR, EYE, HEARING, MOUTH, NOSE, PAIN, SKIN, SMELL, TASTE, TOUCH, VISION.

SEPTICEMIA

A severe illness caused by the entry of germs into the blood stream; also called *bacteremia*. Popularly, septicemia is known as BLOOD POISONING (for

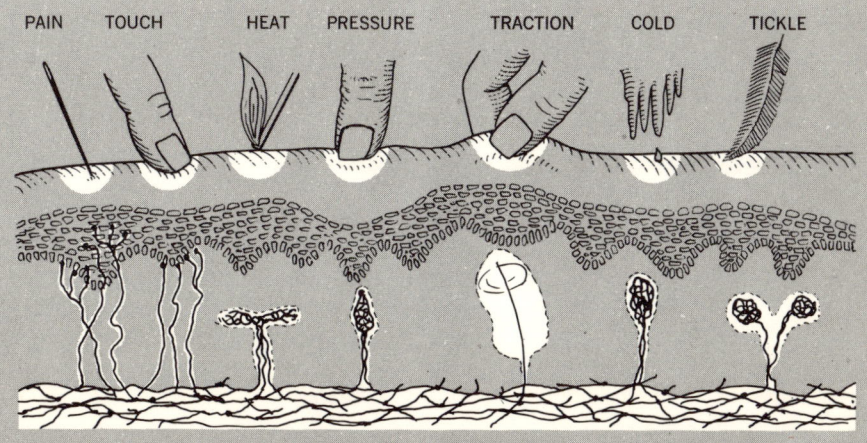

Below the skin surface are different types of sense organs. Each registers a different sensation—pain, touch, and so on. In this diagram, the section of the skin below the surface has been enlarged and simplified to show the sense organs.

more information on this subject, see the article under that heading).

SEPTUM

A wall or partition dividing a bodily space or cavity. Some septums are membranes, some are composed of bone, some of cartilage, and each is named according to its location. The wall separating the *atria*, or *auricles* (upper chambers), of the heart, for instance, is called the *septum atriorum*.

Usually, however, the term septum is used to refer to the *nasal septum*, a plate of bone and cartilage covered with mucous membrane, which divides the cavity of the NOSE. An injury or malformation of this septum can produce a DEVIATED SEPTUM, in which one part of the cavity is smaller than the other.

Usually this condition results from damage to the nose caused by a fall or a sharp blow. If the consequent blockage of the air passage through the nose proves to be permanent and troublesome, the condition may aggravate the problem of colds and other respiratory diseases. In such cases, the doctor may recommend corrective surgery, a relatively simple procedure.

SERUM

The clear portion of any animal or plant fluid that remains after the solid elements have been separated out. The term usually refers to *blood serum*, the clear, straw-colored liquid which separates from the blood cells and plasma in the process of *coagulation*, or CLOTTING. Along with the red and white blood cells and the blood platelets, *plasma* makes up the composition of the BLOOD. It contains vital substances, one of which is *fibrinogen*, the agent necessary for clotting to take place. Serum is actually the portion of the plasma which does not contain fibrinogen and remains fluid when the clot has formed.

Blood serum from persons or animals whose bodies have built up immunization in the form of *antibodies* to fight a disease is called an *antiserum*. Inoculation with such an antiserum provides temporary, or *passive*, immunity against the disease, and is used when a person has already been exposed to or has contracted the disease, as in tetanus and botulism. A fraction of one of the proteins in the serum, GAMMA GLOBULIN, has been found to contain the antibodies and can be extracted from the serum and used for the inoculation.

Active immunity against a disease is conferred by injection of some form or product of the disease bacteria into the body. This causes the person's own protective mechanisms to build up antibodies against the disease, providing immunity for a number of years, and in some cases for life. Smallpox, diphtheria, and poliomyelitis are among the diseases for which this kind of IMMUNIZATION is given.

SERUM SICKNESS

An allergic reaction to injections of SERUM. It is marked by HIVES (itchy swellings), fever, and enlarged glands.

Reactions to the horse serum of TETANUS antitoxin are especially common. When the serum-sensitive person is injected for the first time, the reaction is usually delayed for a period of 6 to 12 days. Once a person has had a serum reaction, the serum responsible should be avoided, since a second reaction will be more severe and perhaps dangerous.

It is customary for a doctor to test a patient's sensitivity with a small amount of serum before injecting the full dose. This precaution is especially important for patients with other allergic susceptibilities. See also ALLERGY.

SEX EDUCATION

Attitudes toward sex—and therefore toward sex education—have been transformed in the last fifty years. Partly because of systematic psychological investigations into the mysteries of human personality, our era recognizes the value of a frank attitude toward sex information. Today all authorities, religious, medical, and educational, consider a good sexual relationship the cornerstone of a successful marriage; and they regard knowledge about the mechanisms and functioning of sex as essential to this relationship.

Much misinformation about sex still exists, as do some prejudices against open discussion of sex matters. Yet many schools, churches, and social agencies today follow the trend of offering accurate scientific information and advice about sex to young people or adults who seek it.

The basis for sound, healthy attitudes toward sex is acquired by children at home, even before they go to school. From a child's earliest years until he grows up, he should be able to ask his parents questions about sex and receive frank, direct and simple answers.

It is not always easy for parents to maintain an objective point of view in giving sex information. They are frequently tempted to fall back on the methods by which they themselves were raised. They may also be put under some pressure by neighbors, relatives, and others who have other ideas about the needs of a child. If parents persevere, however, they will find that, as the child grows, they will have gained his trust and confidence. As they learn to understand their own attitudes and feelings toward sex, they learn how to shape and direct their child's attitudes in a healthy direction. Without this mutual trust established in childhood, it is difficult for parents to help their child through the problems of adolescence.

Sex Education for Young Children

The very youngest child, in the process of discovering all the parts of his body, shows an interest in his sex organs as he does in his nose, ears, or fingers. This is a natural instinct, and should not worry parents. Parents often tend to reflect their concern in their facial expressions or tone of voice, and this focuses the child's curiosity on this area of his body. A child will rapidly turn his interest to other things in his environment if parents understand that play with genitals is part of the natural growing-up process and reveal no particular interest in it themselves.

A Child's Questions. As the child learns to talk, he begins to ask many questions about himself and about the world around him, including questions about reproduction. It is important to answer these questions truthfully, though not necessarily in detail. A child will ultimately resent deception or evasion.

One of a child's first questions of this sort is: "Where did I come from?" The best answer is a simple and truthful one. The child's curiosity will usually be satisfied if he is told that he grew in a special place in his mother's body. There is no need to give long, complicated explanations; these would only confuse him. If he asks further questions, such as how he got there, the answers should be on the same simple level—for example, that he grew from a seed that was already there.

The parent's manner in answering the question is as important as the words he uses. He should be as casual and matter-of-fact as in answering a question about anything else in the world which the child is discovering.

At the same time, the child can understand, even at an early age, that some subjects are personal and that it is better to discuss them in private than in public. In the same way, children come to have a sense of modesty about their bodies from seeing that other people wear clothes. For the very young child, clothes seem to be a needless burden that hamper his activity. As the child reaches the toddler years he may sometimes have to be told that clothes are necessary. This should again be stated in a matter-of-fact way, and pointed to as something to be observed by a child who is growing up rather than a baby. The parents must try to set up a balance in their own behavior between being unselfconscious and yet maintaining the right to some personal privacy.

Difference Between Boys and Girls. One important aspect of the child's sex education is learning the difference between boys and girls. The earlier this is learned, the better; it is best if the child thinks of it as something he has "always known." In a family with children of both sexes, this usually occurs as a matter of course. If there is only one child in the family, or if the children are all of one sex, they will probably observe the difference in nursery school or under natural circumstances—for example, in a wading pool or watching a baby being bathed.

This will be a surprising lesson for the child, who has probably assumed that all children are like himself. His questions should be answered simply and directly. It should be explained to him that all little boys or girls are like that, and that is why some grow up to be fathers and some to be mothers.

Sexual Development. As mentioned before, at some time about the age of two, a child will go through a phase where he will handle his genitals, or masturbate. This is almost universal in children of both sexes until about the age of six. Masturbation is a normal stage in the child's sexual development, and does not harm the child. He will normally grow out of the habit until it is possibly picked up again during adolescence.

Another stage in the child's development that often worries parents is expressed in sex play. One common form of sex play is "playing doctor." This is also considered by authorities on child development a normal and natural expression of children's interest in themselves, and parents are advised not to be troubled when it occurs. However, it is suggested that parents can quite casually limit this kind of play, perhaps by taking the child aside later to suggest that too much of such games is not good for him. The parent's manner should be casual, much as it would be if he were telling the child not to swim right after eating.

The Rude Joke Phase. School-age children almost always go through a phase when they pick up slang words from their friends and use them in an attempt to shock their parents. Later most children become fascinated by jokes which concern excrement. The most effective way to deal with these passing phases is to tell the child firmly but goodhumoredly that this conduct is not "grown up" but babyish, and that grownups do not use this kind of language. Otherwise there is little the parents can do but realize that the fad will be outgrown and try to bear it in good humor.

For another discussion of sex education for young children, see the article on CHILD CARE, the section on *Sex.*

Sex Education for Adolescents

Even parents who have been very close to their children, welcoming their questions, may find that, with adolescence, a barrier seems to rise between them. The adolescent is in the difficult process of breaking his childhood ties to his parents, and for a time he may be unwilling to bring his personal problems to them. However, if the family is one in which questions about sex have always been discussed frankly and without embarrassment, the adolescent is more likely to confide in his parents and seek their help and advice.

Preparing for Puberty and Adolescence. A child should be prepared for adolescence before the physical changes in his body begin. In girls, PUBERTY usually begins between the ages of 12 and 14, although the normal range spreads from 10 to 18. Boys usually enter puberty one to two years later. A child who enters puberty noticeably before or after his friends should be assured that there is nothing abnormal about this.

It is difficult to say exactly when a child should be told about the physical and emotional changes of adolescence. A parent will often know when the child's curiosity and interest have developed enough. In any case, both boys and girls should understand the workings of the body and the process of sexual reproduction before they enter puberty. The article on REPRODUCTION can be given to the child to read as a useful supplement to the explanations of the parent.

It is especially important that all girls, and boys as well, be told about menstruation before they and their friends reach the age of puberty. The attitude of the mother in explaining menstruation is very important. She should make it clear in words and tone of voice that it is not a sickness but a milestone in the process of becoming a woman. If the child has heard others call menstruation "the curse," it is important for the mother to correct this attitude. She should explain it in relation to the process of reproduction as given in the article on MENSTRUATION. The girl who is about to menstruate should know exactly what to expect.

Some adolescent girls feel shy or even ashamed of their breast development. They may try to walk with their shoulders hunched over to conceal it. Mothers should encourage them to feel proud of their developing womanhood. They can also be helpful in choosing clothes suitable to the girl's new figure. Mothers should also explain that shortly before or during the girl's menstrual period, there may be some swelling or tenderness of the breasts, and that this should not cause concern.

In the same way, boys should be told in advance about nocturnal emissions. These are a natural part of adolescence and should not be a cause for shame or concern. The father should assure his son that the dreams and emotions which often accompany nocturnal emissions are normal and not a reason to feel guilt or anxiety.

As part of the process of sexual development during adolescence, a fair percentage of both boys and girls practice some form of self-stimulation. This may cause emotional damage if the child is made to feel guilty or if he is frightened by false accounts of the damage it will do to him. However, if these practices continue or are carried over into adult life, it may be a cause for concern, and should be discussed with a doctor.

Many boys and girls in early adolescence indulge in some form of homosexual play with a friend or friends. Such practices are a natural part of growing up and they usually stop as the boy or girl matures. But children should understand that, while a preference for others of one's own sex is natural in late childhood and early adolescence, its continuation into adulthood is a sign of an immature and emotionally disturbed personality. This preference usually overlaps for a short time with the development of attraction to the opposite sex. The normal adolescent then grows up emotionally, transferring his interest to the opposite sex.

Sexual Conduct. The questions about what constitutes proper sexual conduct for young people are difficult ones, on which the child's doctor, teachers, and religious adviser can all be helpful. As children enter the later stages of adolescence, the direct suggestions of their parents tend to have much less influence on their sexual behavior. The standards and attitudes of their friends seem much more realistic and meaningful to them. Direct intervention by his parents may arouse the child's rebelliousness.

However, the parents' own mature attitudes can still play a large role by setting standards and values which influence a young person indirectly. Ways of helping a young person develop healthy sexual attitudes are discussed in the article on ADOLESCENCE.

SEX GLANDS

The glands that regulate human reproduction and manufacture the hormones that give men and women their special sexual characteristics. These glands are the TESTES in the male, and the OVARIES in the female. They are also known as the gonads, from the Greek *gonos*, meaning seed.

The sex glands, or gonads, perform many functions. They produce the male sperm and the female *ova* (eggs) that combine to conceive babies. In addition, they manufacture HORMONES that circulate in the blood stream and stimulate a great variety of organs throughout the body. These hormones influence the development of the sex organs at puberty. They also control other physical traits which differentiate men from women in such characteristics as voice, bodily form, and size.

The gonads belong to the ENDOCRINE GLAND system, consisting of various ductless glands which secrete their hormones internally. Of all the endocrine glands, the gonads are the only ones that differ in structure and location in men and women, though other ductless glands may vary in the two sexes in their functions. For example, the pituitary gland in the female directly controls the production of milk for nursing mothers.

The Testes

The testes manufacture semen, which contains *sperm* for reproduction, and *testosterone,* one of the two main ANDROGENS, the male sex hormones that determine masculine characteristics. Sperm and testosterone, unrelated to each other chemically and produced by different cells of the testes, control virtually all male sexual activity.

The Testes and the Scrotum. The testes lie enclosed in the *scrotum* just behind the *penis.* The curiously unprotected site of the testes, suspended outside the body in a vulnerable sac of skin, is necessary for the production of *sperm,* which requires a temperature three or four degrees lower than that of the body. The scrotum has its own temperature-controlling mechanism: In warm weather, the sac is soft and relaxed, offering its largest surface for evaporation and cooling, but in cold weather muscle tissue tightens the sac, making it smaller, and at the same time brings it closer to the warm trunk of the body.

The testes of a male child develop within the groin and drop down into the scrotum in most instances before birth, but in some boys not until puberty, and

SEX GLANDS

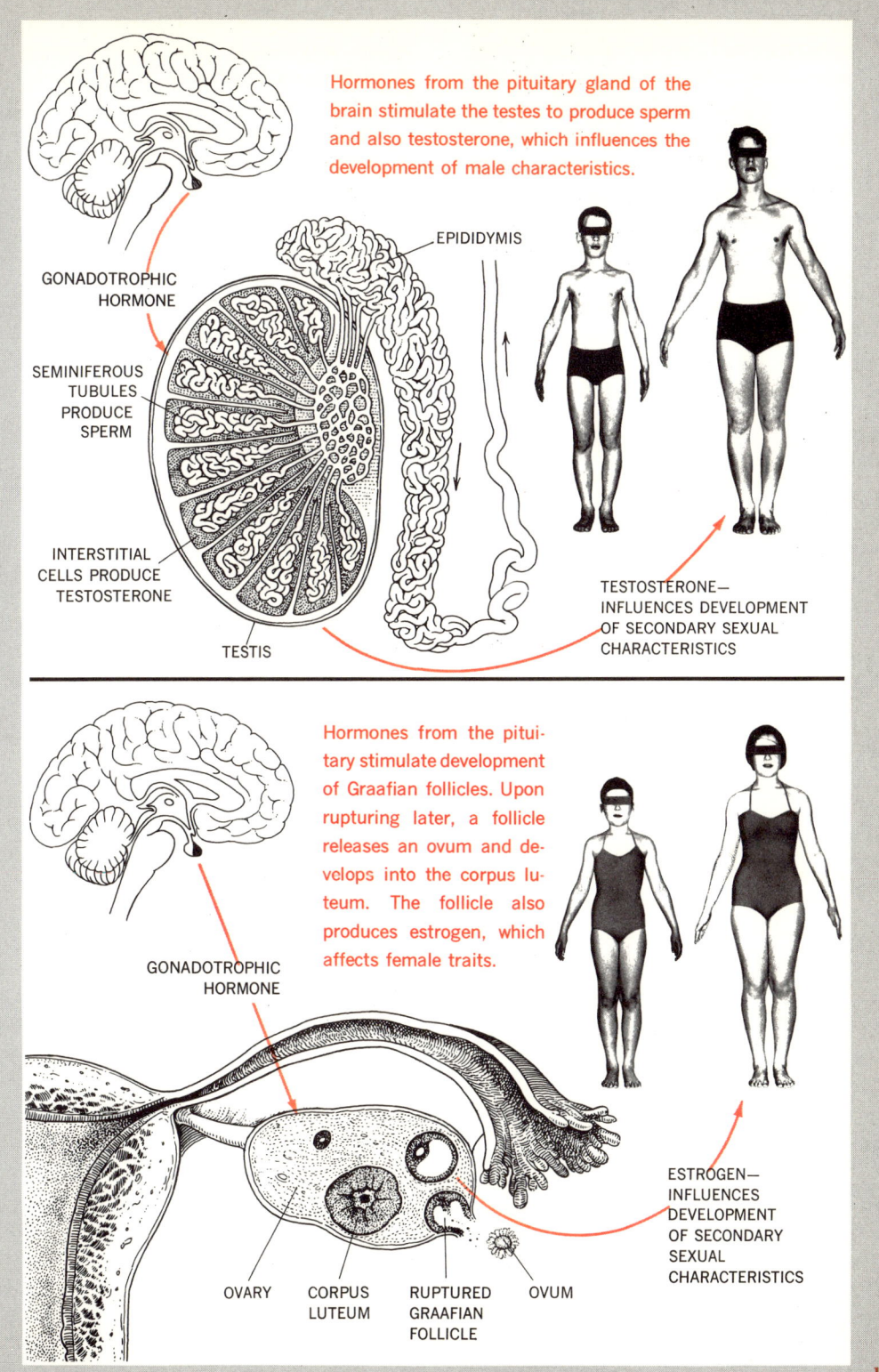

Hormones from the pituitary gland of the brain stimulate the testes to produce sperm and also testosterone, which influences the development of male characteristics.

GONADOTROPHIC HORMONE

SEMINIFEROUS TUBULES PRODUCE SPERM

INTERSTITIAL CELLS PRODUCE TESTOSTERONE

EPIDIDYMIS

TESTIS

TESTOSTERONE— INFLUENCES DEVELOPMENT OF SECONDARY SEXUAL CHARACTERISTICS

Hormones from the pituitary stimulate development of Graafian follicles. Upon rupturing later, a follicle releases an ovum and develops into the corpus luteum. The follicle also produces estrogen, which affects female traits.

GONADOTROPHIC HORMONE

OVARY

CORPUS LUTEUM

RUPTURED GRAAFIAN FOLLICLE

OVUM

ESTROGEN— INFLUENCES DEVELOPMENT OF SECONDARY SEXUAL CHARACTERISTICS

1185

very occasionally not at all. The failure of testes to descend does not affect normal sexual development or behavior, but it does affect *fertility*, because the sperm cells will not live if produced within the body, and without living sperm conception is impossible (see UNDESCENDED TESTICLE).

Testosterone and Its Functions. The testes produce testosterone through special cells called the *interstitial cells of Leydig*. This hormone controls the development of the male sex organs and the secondary masculine sexual characteristics such as body build and voice pitch. It also stimulates the growth of bones and muscles, and helps maintain the strength of muscles. The effect of this hormone is seen clearly in those cases where testosterone is not present in a young boy's system because of removal or destruction of the testes. When this happens before puberty, the boy fails to develop natural masculine characteristics in his body build and sexual organs.

When the testes are permanently missing or are not producing testosterone, injections of testosterone obtained from animals can help restore masculinity. But because the effect of injected testosterone is purely transitory, the treatments must be maintained throughout the subject's life.

The use of testosterone is not recommended for aging men who are seeking "rejuvenation" but whose testes are intact. Such use is not only ineffectual, but it sometimes leads to tumors of the prostate gland.

Actually, many men can reproduce at the age of 70 or older. The feeling of IMPOTENCE or sexual decline that some elderly men experience is more apt to be caused by a factor other than the sex glands—perhaps a physical ailment or a psychological difficulty. A thorough medical check-up is advisable rather than costly and perhaps dangerous hormonal injections. *Sterility,* the inability to have children (see FERTILITY), poses a somewhat different problem than impotence (inability to have sexual intercourse) because it involves not so much a lack of hormones as an insufficient supply of vital, active sperm.

The Ovaries

Like the testes, the *ovaries* are paired. Besides producing eggs, they also manufacture hormones that are necessary for the development of secondary sexual characteristics, and for reproduction.

The ovaries are ductless glands that vary greatly in size but usually are about the size and shape of small plums. They lie in the side portion of the abdomen below the navel, each ovary being connected with the womb by a Fallopian tube, through which the eggs travel down to the womb every month.

The Ovarian Hormones. The ovaries' principal hormone, ESTROGEN, is responsible for the female characteristics of a woman: the breasts and rounded buttocks; the feminine voice; the relatively delicate facial features, and smaller overall proportions.

There is very little secretion of the female sex hormones before puberty and after the menopause, but they are produced abundantly during the years between puberty, around the ages of 12 to 14, and menopause, between 40 and 50. This is the period during which a woman has her regular monthly cycles of MENSTRUATION and OVULATION. Without the hormones there would, in fact, be no ovulation.

If the ovaries produce an overabundance of hormones, there may be menstrual irregularities. If there is an appreciable undersupply, there may be premature menopause.

The Female Sex Cycle. The sexual cycle in women is regulated by a complex balance of estrogen and another hormone, **PROGESTERONE**. About every 28 to 32 days in the reproductive cycle, ovulation occurs. Following ovulation, the lining of the uterus increases in thickness and blood supply in preparation for receiving and nourishing the fertilized egg. These changes in the uterus are the result of the action of estrogen and progesterone. Progesterone is produced by the shell (*corpus luteum*) of the egg that is discharged from the ovary during ovulation. If pregnancy takes place, the *placenta,* or afterbirth, gradually acquires the ability to produce progesterone.

Soon after the egg has been discharged by the ovary, the production of estrogen decreases. When pregnancy does not occur, the corpus luteum disintegrates and the production of progesterone ceases. The uterus sheds its extra tissues and blood and these are discharged by menstruation, or the monthly menstrual period.

When a woman reaches her climacteric age, the eggs no longer mature in the ovaries, and the supply of estrogenic hormones dwindles too. She has now reached the **MENOPAUSE,** but even though this spells the end of reproductive activity, it need not affect sexual activity or the enjoyment of a full, vigorous, happy life. Some women may temporarily suffer some side effects, such as hot flashes or nervous tension. But if these conditions are at all troublesome, they can be helped by hormonal tablets or estrogen injections administered under a physician's care.

Role of Pituitary Gland

The sex glands in the male and female have the help of the **PITUITARY GLAND** in producing hormones. The anterior lobe of the pituitary gland secretes *gonadotrophic hormones* that stimulate the development of sex organs and control the production of sex hormones in the ovaries and testes.

Stimulated by the gonadotrophins, the testes and the ovaries produce the male and female hormones which control the reproductive processes.

The rate of production of gonadotrophins by the pituitary is influenced by the production of sex hormones by the ovaries and testes.

For further information on the functions of the sex glands, see **REPRODUCTIVE ORGANS, MALE,** and **REPRODUCTIVE ORGANS, FEMALE; REPRODUCTION; PREGNANCY.**

SEX HORMONES

Glandular secretions involved in the regulation of sexual functions. The principal sex hormone in the male is *testosterone,* produced by the testes. In the female, the ovaries produce *estrogen* and *progesterone* hormones.

These male and female hormones control the secondary sex characteristics, such as the shape and contour of the body, the distribution of hair on the body, and the pitch of the voice. The male hormones stimulate production of sperm in men, and the female hormones control ovulation, pregnancy, and the menstrual cycle in women.

For further information, see **SEX GLANDS.**

SEX ORGANS

The organs used for reproduction. In the male, these include the external genitalia, or the penis, testes, and scrotum. Also involved are the accessory glands that secrete fluids necessary to the reproductive process and the ducts through which the sperm cells travel when ejaculated.

SEX ORGANS

In the female, the principal organs of reproduction are the ovaries, the uterus, the Fallopian tubes, the vagina, and the vulva.

For information about these organs and their proper care, see **REPRODUCTIVE ORGANS, MALE,** and **REPRODUCTIVE ORGANS, FEMALE;** also **SEX GLANDS.**

SEXUAL DEVIATION

An emotional illness that is expressed in a form of sexual behavior of an abnormal sort; also known as sexual perversion. The sexual deviate is compelled by his inner drives to seek satisfaction through specific forms of abnormal behavior—sadism, homosexuality, masochism, exhibitionism, nymphomania, and many other variations. Sexual deviation is considered an illness with roots in deep emotional conflicts.

There are many complex factors which can lead to a sexual attitude not acceptable to society as a whole; not all of these are fully understood. In general, however, children who have a full and happy family life and whose parents are an example of a normal and healthy relationship are far less likely to develop emotional conflicts of the sort that can lead to sexual deviation. (For a series of discussions on family life, and of ways of achieving healthy family relationships, see the articles on **ADOLESCENCE, MARRIAGE,** and **SEX EDUCATION.**)

Sexual deviation may cause legal as well as personal difficulties. Most types of deviant activity are illegal and punishable by imprisonment. However, an increasing number of judges recognize that deviation is more an illness than a crime and they refer offenders to psychiatrists for treatment of the condition. Pronounced sexual deviation is treated by **PSYCHOTHERAPY,** which attempts to uncover and resolve the unconscious sources of the deviation.

SEXUAL REPRODUCTION

The fertilization of the female egg, or *ovum,* by male sperm, accomplished by the act of sexual intercourse. The fertilized egg goes through a series of cell divisions from which the baby develops. For a description of this process, see **REPRODUCTION.**

SHAMPOO

Cleansing the hair; or the substance used for doing so. Shampoos should be taken regularly, as often as necessary to keep the scalp and hair clean. For some people, this may be every two weeks or once a week. For someone who has oily hair, shampooing more frequently may be desirable and is not harmful to the hair.

Today plain soap has generally been replaced in shampooing by a variety of commercial preparations. These shampoos contain ingredients that make the shampoo easier to rinse out. Selection should be based on the quality of the local water supply, whether one's hair tends to be dry or oily, and whether one has noticed any special sensitivity to detergents.

Two soapings of the hair are usually needed, and it is a good idea to massage the scalp with the fingertips to spread the lather thoroughly over the scalp and through the hair. The shampoo or soap should be rinsed out completely; special cream rinses may then be used for dry or bleached hair.

For general information on care of the **HAIR,** see the article under that heading.

SHINGLES

An inflammation of a sensory nerve, usually accompanied by a series of small blisters on the skin along the path of the nerve, and involving one side of the body; also called *herpes zoster,* Latin for "girdle of blisters." The area which is blistered is usually painful. Shingles is apparently caused by the same virus that causes CHICKEN POX. It may appear among those who have been exposed to chicken pox and sometimes also accompanies other diseases such as pneumonia and tuberculosis.

Shingles may affect either a sensory nerve of the trunk, in which case the blisters usually appear on the chest or abdomen, or one of the *cranial nerves*. If the cranial nerves are involved, there may be some facial paralysis, which usually disappears. If the nerve which leads to the eye is affected, there may be some danger to the vision; this condition should be given prompt medical attention.

The first symptom of shingles is severe pain and NEURITIS in the area of the affected nerve. At first, this pain may be accompanied by fever. In most cases, the line of small blisters appears later. These blisters generally dry up in two to four weeks, with no aftereffects. In older people, however, the neuralgic pain may continue for months or years after the blisters heal.

There is no specific treatment for shingles, but the symptoms, including pain, can be relieved in various ways. Many people believe that this disease is not worth bothering the doctor about; however, there is much he can do, both in relieving discomfort and in preventing complications. In elderly people an attack of shingles should always have medical care because of the possibility of complications.

SHOCK

Disruption of the circulation, which can upset all bodily functions; sometimes referred to as *circulatory shock*. It occurs when blood pressure is inadequate to force blood through the vital tissues.

FIRST AID FOR SHOCK

DO	Call a doctor.
DO	Place patient on his back with head slightly lower than feet.
DO	Make sure that patient is breathing. If he is not, pull his tongue and jaw forward; remove any foreign material from mouth or throat.
DO	Begin artificial respiration immediately (if patient is still not breathing), preferably by mouth-to-mouth method.
DO	Control any active bleeding with pressure or a bandage directly on wound.
DO	Keep patient comfortably warm but avoid excessive heat.
DO NOT	Apply tourniquets to control bleeding unless absolutely necessary.
DO NOT	Move patient if severe injury is suspected.
DO NOT	Give unconscious person anything by mouth.

Shock is a dangerous condition which, when severe enough, may be fatal.

The term "shock" is often confusing, for it is used to refer to a variety of situations which may have no relationship to the circulatory system. People speak of receiving an *emotional shock*. Soldiers are said to suffer from *shell shock*, a special form of mental breakdown which is quite unrelated to the circulatory system or the blood pressure. People may receive an ELECTRIC SHOCK from faulty wiring. In certain cases of mental illness, physicians may prescribe SHOCK THERAPY, which produces transient unconsciousness but not circulatory collapse. Persons suffering from diabetes may occasionally experience INSULIN SHOCK from an overdose of insulin. In some parts of the country, a STROKE is called shock. None of these situations, however, directly affects the circulatory system as described in this article.

Mechanisms of Circulatory Shock

The essentials of circulatory shock are easier to understand if the heart and circulatory system are thought to act as a four-part mechanical device made up of a pump (the heart), a complex system of flexible tubes (the blood vessels), a circulating fluid (the blood), and a fine regulating system or "computer" (the nervous system) designed to control fluid flow and pressure. The diameter of the blood vessels is controlled by impulses from the nervous system which cause the muscular walls to contract. The rapidity and strength of the heartbeat are also affected by the nervous system, thereby also influencing blood pressure.

Consequently, the blood pressure is controlled by three main factors in the body: the pumping system of the heart, which should have sufficient strength and rate of contraction; an adequate quantity of blood to fill the circulatory system to capacity; and precise regulation of the heartbeat and the caliber of the blood vessels by the nervous system. Therefore, it is easy to understand that shock, which is associated with a dangerously low blood pressure, can be produced by factors which attack the strength of the heart as a pump, decrease the volume of the blood in the system, or permit the blood vessels to increase in diameter.

Types of Circulatory Shock

There are five main types of circulatory shock. *Low-volume* shock occurs whenever there is insufficient blood to fill the circulatory system. *Neurogenic* shock is due to disorders of the nervous system. Two types of shock, *allergic* shock and *septic* shock, are due to reactions which impair the muscular functioning of the blood vessels themselves. Finally there is *cardiac* shock which is caused by certain diseases of the heart.

Low-volume Shock. This is a common form of shock. Blood or blood fluids (plasma) may be lost in such quantities that the remaining blood cannot fill the circulatory system despite constriction of the blood vessels. The blood may be lost outside of the body, as when a vessel is severed by an injury. However, the blood may be also "lost" into spaces inside the body where it is no longer accessible to the circulatory system. Examples include blood loss caused by severe gastrointestinal bleeding from ulcers, by fractures of large bones with hemorrhage into surrounding tissues, and by major burns which attract large quantities of blood fluids to the burn site outside of blood vessels and capillaries. The treatment of low-volume shock requires replacement of the lost blood.

Neurogenic Shock. This form of shock, often called fainting, may be brought on by severe pain, fright, unpleasant sights, or other strong stimuli. The nervous system's usual regulatory capacity is overwhelmed. The diameter of the blood vessels increases, the heart slows, and the pressure falls to the point where the brain is not supplied with sufficient oxygen carried by the blood. The patient then faints. Helping the person to lie down with the head lower than the body is usually sufficient to relieve this form of shock.

Allergic shock, commonly called *anaphylactic* shock, is caused in rare circumstances when an individual receives an injection of a foreign protein to which he is highly sensitive. The blood vessels and other tissues are affected directly by the allergic reaction. Within a few minutes, the blood pressure falls and the individual has great difficulty in catching his breath. The sudden deaths which in rare cases follow bee

SHOCK

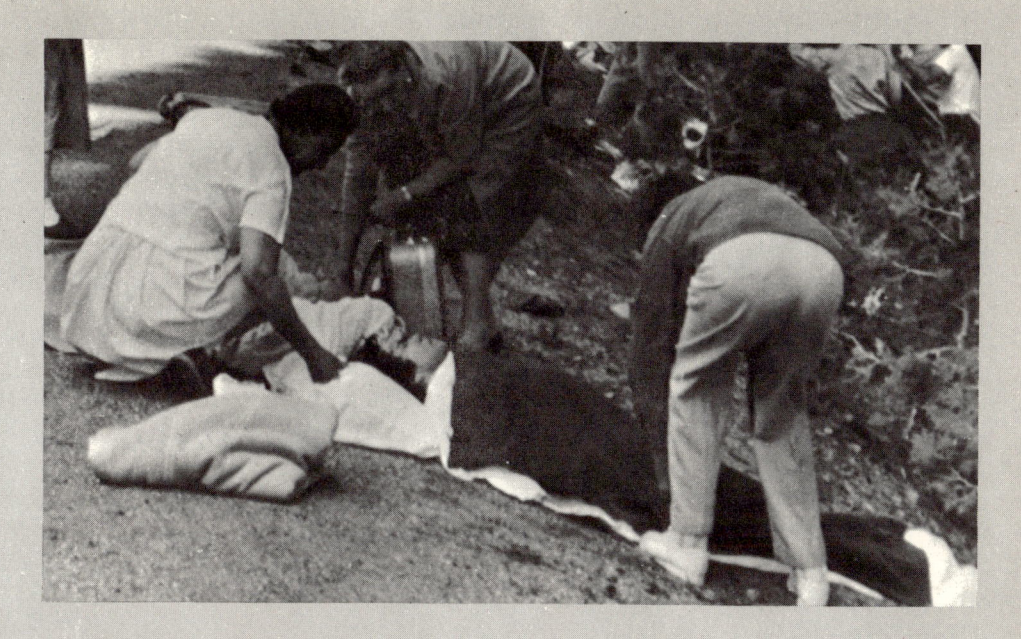

An injured person should never be moved unless absolutely necessary. Above, the patient has been covered and made comfortable, but has not been disturbed, although the feet are lower than the head.

stings or injections of certain medicines are due to anaphylactic reactions. People who know they are extremely allergic to such stings, and who are likely to be exposed to them, should ask their doctors for medications helpful in such emergencies. In some cases, a precautionary series of injections may be given by the doctor. (For a general discussion of allergies, see ALLERGY.)

Septic shock, resulting from infection by certain bacteria, is being recognized with increasing frequency. These organisms contain a toxin which seems to act on the blood vessels when released into the blood stream. The blood eventually pools within parts of the circulatory system which expand easily, causing the blood pressure to drop sharply.

Cardiac shock may be caused by conditions which interfere with the function of the heart as a pump. A severe myocardial infarction ("heart attack"), severe heart failure, and certain disorders of rate and rhythm cause cardiac shock.

The Patient in Shock

The precise progression of a normal person to a state of shock depends upon the cause of the disorder and the speed of onset. In hemorrhagic shock, for example, as blood is lost an individual with gradually progressing shock feels very restless at first. He becomes thirsty. As he goes into shock, his skin takes on a pallor and feels cold. Often he perspires profusely. The pulse speeds up but is weak and indistinct. He gradually feels lethargic and faint, and may show signs of "air hunger" (labored and difficult breathing). The nailbeds and lips take on a bluish hue. As shock deep-

SHOCK

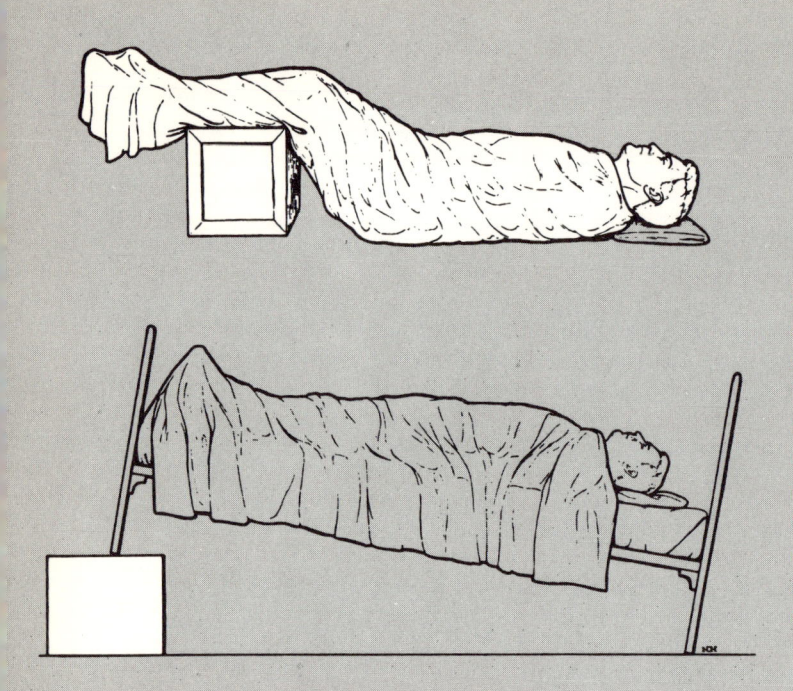

These are two methods of treating shock victims. After covering the person warmly, raise the feet higher than the head. If the victim is on the ground, raise his feet with a box, pillows, or a rolled-up blanket. If he is in bed, raise the foot of the bed 12 to 16 inches with blocks.

ens and the blood pressure falls, the patient becomes comatose and eventually dies if untreated.

Treatment

Shock is an emergency which requires immediate treatment. The diagnosis of shock in an unconscious patient may be sometimes difficult for the untrained, but the presence of the signs and symptoms described previously, or a severe injury with suspected bleeding, are sufficient evidence to indicate shock without a blood pressure reading. In all such cases, first aid should be given immediately.

The patient should be placed on his back with his head low to insure that the brain gets as much blood as possible. (If the patient has a severe head, neck, or back injury, however, he should not be moved unless someone experienced in such matters is present.) Infliction of pain should be avoided, since severe pain itself causes neurogenic shock. Make sure the patient is able to breathe and that his tongue or foreign material are not obstructing his airway. The tongue and jaw should be pulled forward if there is doubt about the airway. If the person is still not breathing, as in anaphylactic shock, inflate his lungs with your own breath in mouth-to-mouth respiration (see ARTIFICIAL RESPIRATION).

Active bleeding in an injured person should be controlled with pressure or a bandage directly on the site of bleeding. Tourniquets should not be used unless absolutely necessary. They may release a flood of dangerous toxins to the body when they are loosened later. The patient should be kept comfortably warm, but excessive heat should not be used. Heat dilates blood vessels and worsens shock. Do not give fluids to an unconscious person. They may flow into the lungs instead of the stomach.

A doctor carries out these same procedures. What he does in addition depends upon the condition of the patient and the cause of the shock. He may inject medicines which increase the blood pressure. He may administer blood or other fluids by vein to replace the losses. He will usually relieve pain with strong analgesics such as morphine (see PAIN RELIEVERS), or take measures to insure the strength of the heart if a weak heart is contributing to shock. The doctor may give oxygen therapy.

SHOCK THERAPY

A technique used in treating certain severe forms of MENTAL ILLNESS. The patient is rendered temporarily unconscious, usually by means of an electric current. This form of psychiatric treatment is now frequently referred to as *somatic therapy*, rather than shock therapy, because it does not necessarily produce a state of shock in the medical sense. Shock therapy has been a method of treatment since the 1930's, but more recently the development of medicines such as TRANQUILIZERS and "mood elevators" has reduced its use.

Uses and Effects. Shock therapy is used in treating severe mental illness. The different types of shock have somewhat different effects. *Electric shock* is most useful in cases of severe depression. For example it is sometimes used on patients with *involutional melancholia*, a condition which appears after the "change of life" in middle age. It is also employed in patients who are in the depressive stage of *manic-depressive* PSYCHOSIS.

Inhalant shock, which makes use of an ether compound, has much the same effect on the patient as electric shock therapy. Alleviation of even severe symptoms is rapid with these treatments.

Insulin shock, better called *insulin coma*, is a more prolonged form of treatment and is primarily helpful in treating cases of severe SCHIZOPHRENIA.

Methods of Administration. In electric shock therapy, electrodes are placed on either side of the patient's forehead and a brief current is applied. The patient immediately becomes unconscious and retains no memory of a shock. Care is taken to prevent injury during the convulsions that follow treatment.

Inhalant therapy, in which the patient breathes in the substance used, has the same effects, but is often accepted more readily by patients than electric shock therapy. Both treatments may be preceded by the administration of an anesthetic so that the patient is asleep during the entire procedure. Medication to relax the muscles so that the convulsion is very mild may also be employed.

In insulin therapy, a carefully measured quantity of insulin is injected into the patient, with coma and occasionally convulsions following. Sometimes insulin therapy is combined with electric shock for patients unresponsive to either treatment alone.

Objective. The objective of shock therapy is to enable patients who have withdrawn into fantasies or severe depression to re-establish contact with the world. It may then be possible to treat the causes of their mental illness with PSYCHOTHERAPY.

SHOULDER

The large JOINT where the bone of the upper arm, or *humerus*, joins the shoulder blade. The shoulder is a shallow *ball-and-socket* joint, similar to the hip joint. Of the five types of joints in the body, the ball-and-socket allows the greatest freedom of movement.

SHOULDER

At the shoulder, the smooth, rounded head of the humerus rests against the socket in the shoulder blade. The joint is covered by a tough, flexible protective *capsule* and is heavily reinforced by *ligaments* that stretch across the joint. The ends of the bones where they meet at the joint are covered with a layer of *cartilage,* tissue similar to bone but smoother and softer, which reduces friction and absorbs shock. A thin membrane, the *synovial membrane,* lines the socket and lubricates the joint with *synovial fluid.* Further cushioning and lubrication are provided by fluid-filled sacs or *bursas.*

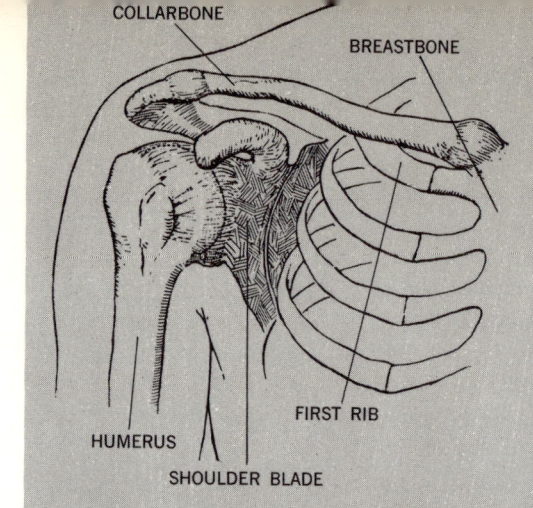

Location of the shoulder, which is a shallow ball-and-socket joint. The smooth, round head of the humerus, the long bone of the upper arm, fits into the cavity of the scapula, or shoulder blade.

Disorders

One of the most common disorders of the shoulder is *bursitis,* or inflammation of the bursa. This may occur after excessive use of the joint—for example, in painting a room or scrubbing a floor, or in athletics. The joint becomes painful and difficult to move. Treatment may take various forms (see BURSITIS).

The shoulder is one of the most common sites for a DISLOCATION, in which the ball of the humerus is dislodged from its socket in the shoulder blade. This injures the ligaments and the capsule, and may cause temporary paralysis of the arm as well as pain and swelling. A dislocated shoulder is usually caused by a blow or fall, but sometimes an unusual physical effort may pull the arm from the shoulder socket. A first dislocation often makes the joint more susceptible to future dislocations. Only a doctor should set a dislocated shoulder; inexpert efforts may do far more damage than the original injury.

It is important to know the correct way to lift and carry heavy objects without straining the shoulder or other parts of the body (see LIFTING AND CARRYING). If the shoulder muscles are strained and sore, the best treatment is resting the arm (if necessary, in a sling), massage, and application of moist or dry heat.

SIAMESE TWINS

An extremely rare condition in which identical twins are joined together at birth. The connection may be slight or extensive. It involves skin and usually muscles or cartilage of a limited region, such as the head, chest, hip, or buttock. The twins may share a single organ, such as an intestine, or occasionally may have parts of the spine in common. The twins are always of the same sex.

Siamese twins are the result of an abnormality in the development of identical twins. When a single egg, or ovum, is fertilized by a sperm and divides in such a way that each division develops separately, the result is identical twins (see TWINS). But in rare cases the identical twins either fail to separate completely or become fused.

If joined superficially, the twins are easily separated by surgery soon after birth. If more deeply united, they may have to go through life, if they survive, with their handicap. New techniques in surgery, however, are making it possible to separate some Siamese twins whose physical links are highly complex.

The term Siamese twins comes from a celebrated pair, Chang and Eng, who were born in 1811 in Siam (now Thailand). Identical in almost every way, Chang and Eng were joined at the chest. They were brought to the United States in 1829 and were exhibited throughout the country. Becoming American citizens, they later settled down on a farm in North Carolina.

Despite their handicap and the sideshow aspect of their lives, Chang and Eng were able to live normally in many ways. They could walk, run, swim, and engage in almost any activity. They married two sisters and had normal children. They lived to the age of 63, dying within three hours of each other.

SIGHT

The ability to see. The act of vision involves the **EYE**, the *visual center* in the brain, and the *optic nerve* and nerve fibers in the brain which connect the two.

For a description of the mechanism of sight, see **VISION**; see also the color foldout in volume 5.

SILICOSIS

A lung disease caused by the prolonged inhalation of silica dust. In the past it has been called such colorful names as potter's asthma, stonecutter's cough, miner's mold, and grinder's rot, according to the occupation in which it was acquired. Besides silicosis, various other lung diseases (see below) result from inhaling industrial substances; together, these "dust diseases" are called *pneumoconioses*.

Today silicosis is most likely to be contracted in such industrial jobs as sandblasting in tunnels and hardrock mining. But anyone can get it who is habitually exposed to the dust of silica, one of the commonest minerals. All types of miners, for example, may be subject to it, from gold miners to coal miners.

Silicosis usually takes about ten years of fairly constant exposure to develop. It may give few warning symptoms. As time goes on, an affected person experiences progressive shortness of breath, along with steady coughing which in the early stages is dry and unproductive of mucus. Later there may be mucus tinged with blood. Next comes loss of appetite, pain in the chest, and general weakness. By this time, the person has contracted a fully developed case of silicosis. The silica has produced a reaction that has scarred the lungs and made them receptive to the further complications of **BRONCHITIS** and **EMPHYSEMA**; it has also made them liable to develop **TUBERCULOSIS**.

Since silicosis is a serious disease, those who must work near silica should take precautions to breathe as little of it as possible. This can usually be effected by the use of face masks, proper ventilation, and other safety devices. The co-operation of industry, labor, and government in developing protective measures has made silicosis much less common today than it used to be.

Regular chest X-rays are recommended for all workers exposed to silica as the quickest and easiest way to detect silicosis. If discovered in its early stages, the disease can usually be arrested by a change of occupation and appropriate therapy. Once fully developed, the disease rarely yields to treatment.

Other Industrial Lung Diseases

The other pneumoconioses are all also occupational diseases in the sense

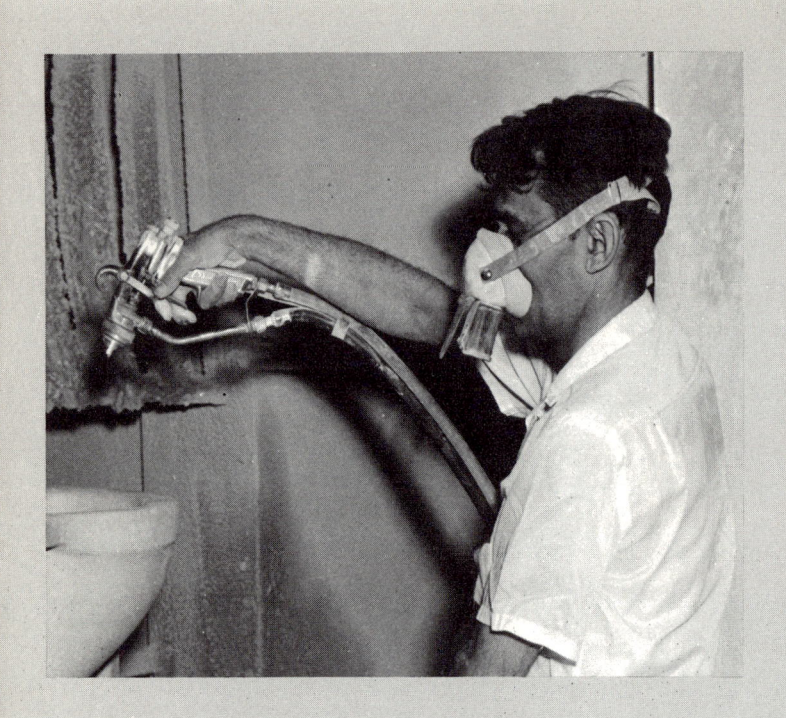

SILICOSIS

Silicosis is one of a number of diseases of the lungs, caused by inhaled dust or noxious fumes, that are called pneumoconioses. People, such as this spray painter, who are exposed to industrial dusts, fumes, or potentially dangerous chemical particles, should wear breathing masks to protect themselves.

that they are acquired by workers in the course of their jobs. Along with other industrial diseases, the pneumoconioses are included for benefit payments under Workmen's Compensation.

Asbestosis is perhaps the second most serious of the industrial lung disorders. It is caused by the inhalation of asbestos fibers, and produces a fibrotic thickening of the lung tissue similar to silicosis. Again, prevention or early diagnosis is important, for no effective treatment is available. Symptoms are a chronic cough, shortness of breath, and the expectoration of a brownish mucus in which asbestos fibers can be seen under a microscope.

Anthracosilicosis is caused by the inhalation of coal dust and silica. It is common among coal miners, especially those who mine anthracite coal. It is similar in its development and its effects to silicosis.

Beryllium lung disease is found in workers exposed to beryllium in the manufacture of fluorescent lamps, and in members of their families who are contaminated by the chemicals on the workers' clothing. Most known cases have been in women. If the worker leaves the job, the symptoms frequently continue to develop for varying periods. Like silicosis, this is a serious disease that can threaten life. Preventive measures can be taken, and regular chest X-rays are important.

Aluminum pneumoconiosis was first found in people working around bauxite smelters. This disease takes years to develop, but is serious enough to endanger life. The most significant symptom is painful, labored breathing. Experimentally, it has been shown that the aluminum particles from the smelters are deposited in the lungs in long, needlelike crystals, which show up in chest X-rays. Regular chest X-rays, as well as the use of masks and other preventive measures, are recommended.

Cadmium worker's disease is caused by the inhalation of the fumes of cadmium oxide at high temperature. Workers who inhale the fumes in any significant concentration suffer almost immediately from a dry throat, followed by chest constriction, coughing, extreme weakness, and a purplish discoloration of the skin. This is a serious disease that can damage the lungs, cause pneumonia, and endanger life. Reliable masks are needed as protection against this lung condition.

Baritosis and *stannosis* are among the much less dangerous lung disorders. They are caused by inhalation of the dust of barite or barium (baritosis) or of tin (stannosis). Usually there are no discomforting symptoms, no lung damage, and no complications.

Siderosis is a mild lung condition. It is caused by inhaling the dust of iron ore or the fumes of iron oxide. Workers engaged in electric arc welding or acetylene welding sometimes contract the disease. It produces no discomfort, causes no lung impairment or complications, and requires no treatment. Seldom aware of his condition, the worker continues his job with complete safety.

Bagassosis or *bagasse disease* is the result of inhaling bagasse dust (the pulverized and dried stalks of sugar cane). It is present only in areas where sugar is manufactured and in plants where bagasse is manufactured into insulating board. The disease lasts for two or three months, causing persistent fever and weakness. Then the symptoms disappear. No treatment has any effect on the course of the disease.

Byssinosis was originally ascribed to the inhalation of cotton fibers and was familiar to workers under the name "gin fever." This disease is now thought to be due to the inhalation of bacteria found frequently in old, stained cotton. A few hours' exposure is enough to bring on infection, with an abrupt attack of fever, chilliness, cough, chest pain, and a feeling of sickness. The condition runs its course within a few days.

SIMMONDS' DISEASE

A rare glandular disorder, marked by extreme weight loss; also called *hypopituitary cachexia*. It follows the destruction of the pituitary gland by surgery, infection, injury, or tumors; it may also occur after difficult labor in childbirth.

Simmonds' disease was first described by Dr. Morris Simmonds of Hamburg, Germany, in 1914. Symptoms, which vary in intensity, are general debility, pallor, dry and yellowish skin, a slow pulse, low blood pressure, atrophy of the genitalia and breasts, progressing to premature senility and apathy. Treatment is by regular administration of various hormones.

SINUS

A cavity, or hollow space, in a bone or other tissue. In common usage, the word sinus refers to any of the eight cavities in the skull that are connected with the nasal cavity. These are the *paranasal sinuses*.

The paranasal sinuses are arranged in four pairs, with members of each pair on the left and right sides of the head. The pairs are the *maxillary* (or *antrum*) *sinuses*, located in the cheekbones; the *frontal sinuses*, in the frontal bone of the forehead; the *sphenoid sinuses*, behind the nasal cavity; and the *ethmoid sinuses*, behind and below the frontal sinuses.

The functions of the sinuses are not certain. They are believed to help the

SINUS

nose in circulating, warming, and moistening the air as it is inhaled, thereby lessening the shock of cold, dry air to the lungs. They also are thought to have minor value in acting as resonating chambers for the voice.

Sinus trouble is a common ailment. The mucous membrane that lines the sinuses is an extension of the nasal membrane; a nasal infection can spread to one sinus, and then may spread to the rest. The mucous membrane becomes inflamed and swollen, blocking the drainage and ventilation of the sinuses. Such an infection, called *sinusitis*, can cause painful throbbing of the head and a nasal discharge. Steam inhalation and aspirin help to relieve the discomfort (see also SINUSITIS).

It is wise to consult a doctor in case of any prolonged sinus trouble because there can be unpleasant complications involving the eyes, ears, or the respiratory system.

Benign growths known as *polyps* or *cysts* sometimes develop in the sinuses, usually in the maxillary pair. They are believed to be caused by irritation. Harmless in themselves, they obstruct the sinuses, and doctors usually prefer to remove them by surgery.

SINUSITIS

Inflammation of one or more of the sinuses opening into the nose. Known as *paranasal sinuses*, these cavities consist of four pairs of sinuses, one of each being located on either side of the head (see SINUS). The inflammation is the result of an infection of the sinus membranes. Such an infection often occurs during a cold, when an infection in the nose spreads to the sinuses (sometimes encouraged by excessively strong blowing of the nose).

Sinusitis also may be a complication of tooth infection, of an allergy (such as *hay fever*), or of certain infectious diseases (such as *pneumonia* and *measles*). Many other causes of sinusitis include air pollution in cities, diving and underwater swimming, sudden extremes of temperature, and structural defects of the nose (such as DEVIATED SEPTUM) that interfere with breathing.

As the infected sinus membranes become inflamed and swell, the tiny openings that lead from each sinus into the nasal passages become partially or wholly blocked. At first only one or two sinus openings may be affected, but occasionally all can become obstructed at once. The mucus that accumulates

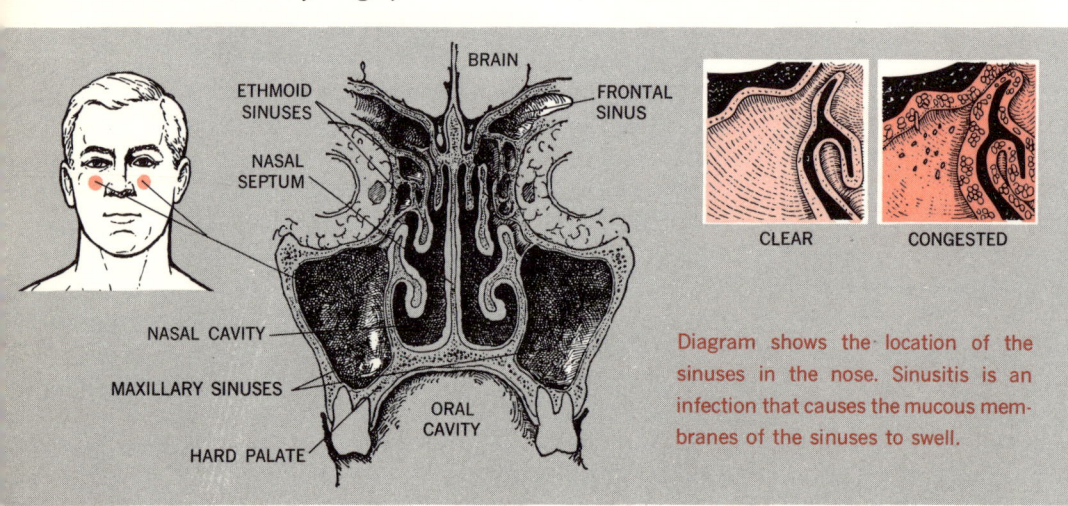

Diagram shows the location of the sinuses in the nose. Sinusitis is an infection that causes the mucous membranes of the sinuses to swell.

in the sealed-off sinus puts pressure on the sinus walls. This may cause discomfort, fever, pain, and difficult breathing.

Symptoms

A common symptom of sinusitis is a headache, usually located near the sinuses most involved. A headache above the eyes and on the forehead, for example, is probably caused by an infection of the frontal sinuses.

Another common symptom of sinusitis is a mucus discharge from the nose. This may be accompanied by a slight rise in temperature, dizziness, and a general feeling of weakness and discomfort. To a certain extent, symptoms of sinusitis resemble those of the common cold. The differences are that the characteristic early stages of a cold are either very mild or absent altogether, and that the later sinusitis symptoms are usually more severe.

If a sinus infection develops rapidly, shows marked symptoms, and is followed by complete recovery, it is *acute sinusitis*. If it comes on slowly, has milder symptoms, and lasts on and off for years, it is *chronic sinusitis*. Mild chronic sinusitis sometimes flares up at intervals into an acute attack.

Treatment

For temporary relief, it may help to inhale the steamy vapor rising from a basin of hot water (boiling water should be avoided since the steam can scald). A doctor can recommend nose drops that will shrink the membranes and help to clear the sinuses. An electric heating pad or a hot-water bottle, protected by a cloth cover to prevent burns, may ease pain if applied for 10 minutes every two hours over the painful area on the face or forehead. Aspirin, one tablet every two or three hours, will also give some relief. In certain cases, doctors may use diathermy or ultrasonic waves to reduce pain.

Since sinusitis, both acute and chronic, can lead to complications of the middle ear or of adjacent bones, it is important to consult a doctor when symptoms persist. He may prescribe sedatives to increase comfort and antibiotics to fight the infection. He may wash out or irrigate the sinuses and suggest suitable techniques for clearing them.

Plenty of rest and sleep is recommended in acute attacks of sinusitis. Smoke, dust, and other irritants to the nasal passages should be avoided, and smoking should be stopped entirely.

When other methods fail to correct troublesome chronic sinusitis of long standing, surgery is sometimes required. The opening to the sinus may be made larger to ensure drainage and ventilation. But such measures cannot always guarantee complete cure. If surgery is undertaken, it is customarily done from the inside of the nose or through the mouth so that no outward scars will be visible.

Though a change of climate can sometimes help cases of chronic sinusitis, it rarely is a necessity. Creating a better indoor climate with such devices as air conditioners and humidifiers often is equally beneficial in reducing the number and severity of sinus attacks. The gradual evaporation from pans of water placed on radiators will help to combat the excessive drying effect of steam heat and perhaps help to prevent sinus problems. However, significant improvement in indoor humidity can only be achieved with a humidifier (see CLIMATE AND HEALTH).

Psychotherapy may be of help to some patients with disabling, chronic sinusitis because continual emotional strain is one of the factors which can intensify the symptoms of sinusitis.

SKELETAL SYSTEM

The body's framework of bones; also called the skeleton.

The skeleton of an average adult consists of 206 distinct bones. Some adults have an extra bone or two.

Functions

The bones of the skeleton give support and shape to the body and protect delicate internal organs. Muscles attached to the skeleton make the body's motion possible.

In addition to supporting the body as part of the skeleton, the bones store calcium and help maintain the correct level of this vital chemical. The bone marrow also has the important task of making blood cells. The structure, composition, types, growth, and disorders of BONE are discussed in the article of that title.

Main Parts

For convenience, scientists refer to two main parts of the skeleton: an *axial skeleton*, including the bones of the head and trunk, and an *appendicular skeleton*, including the bones of the limbs. The axial skeleton has 80 bones; the appendicular skeleton, 126 bones.

Axial Skeleton. The axial skeleton includes the skull, the spine, and the ribs and the breastbone. The most important of these is the SPINE, also called the backbone, the vertebral column, and the spinal column. The spine consists of 26 separate bones. The twenty-four vertebrae have holes through them, and the holes are lined up vertically, forming a hollow tube. The spinal cord runs through this bony tube and is protected by it.

The seven topmost spinal bones, the *cervical* vertebrae, are the neck bones. These support the SKULL. The skull encloses and protects the brain; it also provides protection for the eyes, the inner ears, and the nose passages. The skull includes the cranium, the face bones, and the ear ossicles. Of the skull's 28 bones, only one—the lower jawbone—is movable.

Below the seven cervical vertebrae of the spine are 12 *thoracic* vertebrae. Attached to these are 12 pairs of ribs, one pair to a vertebra. The ribs curve around to the front of the body, where most of them attach directly to the breastbone, or sternum, or are indirectly attached to it by means of cartilage. The two bottom pairs of ribs remain unattached in front and so are called "floating ribs." Together, the thoracic vertebrae, the ribs, and the breastbone form a bony basket, called the rib (or thoracic) cage, that prevents the chest wall from collapsing and protects the heart and the lungs.

The remaining bones of the spine include five *lumbar* vertebrae, which support the small of the back, and two other bones, the *sacrum* and *coccyx*.

The axial skeleton also includes a single bone in the neck, the *hyoid* bone, to which muscles of the mouth are attached. This is the only bone of the body that does not join with another bone.

Appendicular Skeleton. The appendicular skeleton includes the shoulder girdle, arm bones, hip girdle, and leg bones. The shoulder (or pectoral) girdle, from which the arms hang, consists of the two collarbones (*clavicles*) and two shoulder blades (*scapulae*). The collarbones are joined to the breastbone.

The arm has three long bones. One end of the upper arm bone, the *humerus*, fits into a socket in the shoulder girdle; the other end is connected at the elbow to the *ulna* and the *radius*, the two long bones of the lower arm. Eight small bones, the *carpals*, comprise the

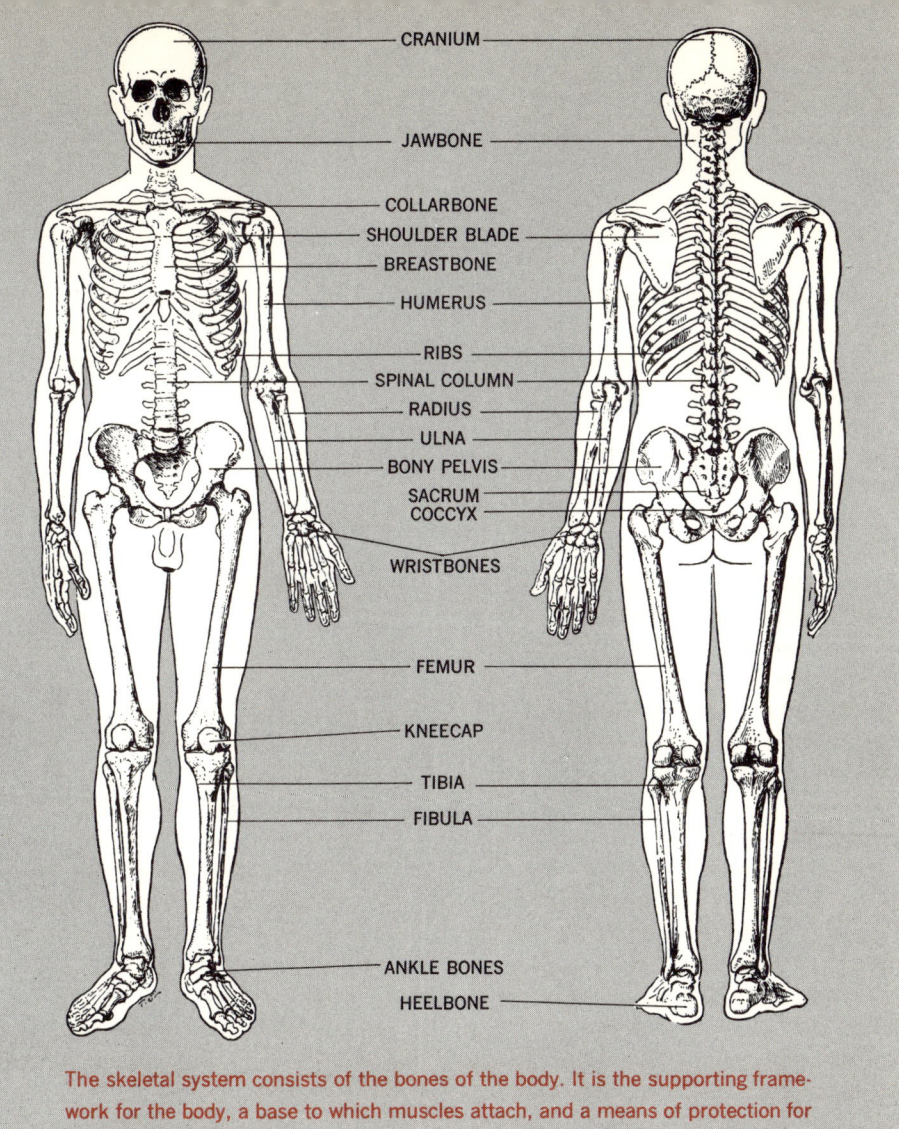

The skeletal system consists of the bones of the body. It is the supporting framework for the body, a base to which muscles attach, and a means of protection for delicate structures. It supplies calcium to the blood and houses marrow, which produces red blood cells. There are about 206 bones in the human body.

wrist. Five *metacarpals* form the palm of the hand, and the finger bones are made up of 14 *phalanges* in each hand.

At the lower end of the spine is the hip (or pelvic) girdle. The hip girdle and the last two bones of the spine, the sacrum and the coccyx, form the **PELVIS**. This part of the skeleton encircles and protects the internal organs of the urogenital tract. In each side of the pelvis is a socket into which a leg bone fits.

Leg bones are similar in construction to arm bones, but are heavier and stronger. The thighbone, or *femur*, which is the longest bone in the body, extends from the pelvis to the knee, and the *tibia* and *fibula* go from knee to ankle. The kneecap is a single bone, the *patella*. In each leg there are 7 ankle bones, or *tarsals;* 5 foot bones, or *metatarsals;* and 14 toe bones, or phalanges, in each foot.

Joints and Movement

Any place in the skeleton where two or more bones come together is known as a joint. The way these bones are joined determines whether they can move and how they move. The elbow, for example, has a hinge joint, which allows bending in only one direction. In contrast, both bending and rotary movements are possible in the hip joint, a ball-and-socket joint. Many joints, such as most of those in the skull, are rigid and permit no movement whatsoever.

Bones are bound together at joints by tough fibers called ligaments. These keep movements within desirable limits and help prevent the joints from being dislocated. Where the ends of bones meet at joints, they are cushioned by the rubbery tissue known as cartilage. The smooth, polished surface of cartilage permits the ends of bones that are joined to move with a minimum of friction.

For additional details about the structure and function of joints, as well as the diseases and disorders to which they are subject, see JOINT, ANKLE, ELBOW, KNEE, SHOULDER, and WRIST.

The force needed to move the bones is provided by muscles, which are attached to the bones by tendons. A muscle typically spans a joint so that one end is attached by a tendon to one bone, and the other end to a second bone. Usually one bone serves as an anchor for the muscle, and the second bone is free to move. When the muscle contracts, it pulls the second bone. Actually, two sets of muscles that pull in opposite directions take part in any movement. When one set contracts, the opposing set relaxes. See also MUSCLE.

The skeletal system is presented pictorially in the color foldout section inside the front cover of Volume 3.

SKIN

The skin is one of the important organs of the body. It performs a number of vital functions and serves as a protective barrier against germs. It helps shield the delicate, sensitive tissues underneath from mechanical and other injuries. It acts as an insulator against heat and cold, and helps eliminate body wastes in the form of perspiration. It guards against excessive exposure to the ultraviolet rays of the sun by producing a protective pigmentation, and it helps produce the body's supply of vitamin D. Its sense receptors enable the body to feel pain, cold, heat, touch, and pressure.

Composition of the Skin

The skin consists of two main parts: the *epidermis,* or outer layer, and the *dermis (corium),* or inner layer.

Epidermis. The epidermis is thinner than the dermis, and is made up of several layers of different kinds of cells. The number of cells varies in different parts of the body; the greatest number is in the palms of the hands and soles of the feet, where the skin is thickest.

The cells in the outer or horny layer of the epidermis are constantly being shed and replaced by new cells from its bottom layers in the lower epidermis. The cells of the protective, horny layer are nonliving and require no supply of blood for nourishment. As long as the horny outer layer remains intact, germs cannot enter.

Dermis. Underneath the epidermis is the thicker part of the skin, the dermis. This is made up of connective tissue which contains blood vessels and nerves. The dermis projects into the epidermis and forms ridges called *papillae.*

The nerves which extend through the dermis end in the papillae. The various skin sensations, such as touch, pain, pressure, heat, and cold, are felt through these nerves. The reaction to heat and cold causes the expansion and contraction of the blood capillaries of the dermis. This in turn causes more or less blood to flow through the skin, resulting in greater or smaller loss of body heat (see TEMPERATURE).

The *sweat glands* are situated deep in the dermis, where they collect fluid containing water, salt, and waste products from the blood and carry it away in tiny canals that end in *pores* on the skin surface, where it is deposited as perspiration.

The SEBACEOUS GLANDS, or *oil glands,* are also in the dermis. They secrete the oil which keeps the skin surface lubricated. Most oil glands are associated with hair follicles. There are no oil glands on the palms and soles.

Beneath the dermis is a layer of *fatty tissue,* also called the *subcutaneous tissue.* This tissue helps insulate the body against heat and cold, and cushions it against shock.

The *hair* and *nails* are outgrowths of the skin. The roots of the hair lie in *follicles,* or pockets of epidermal cells situated in the dermis. Hair grows from the roots, but the hair cells die while still in the follicles, and the closely packed remains that are pushed upward form the *hair shaft* that is seen on the surface of the skin (see HAIR).

The nails grow in much the same way as the hair. The nail bed, like the hair root, is situated in the dermis. The pink color of the nails is due to their translucent quality which allows the blood capillaries of the dermis to show through. (See FINGERNAILS and TOENAILS.)

Care of the Skin

Since the condition of the skin reflects the general health of the body, a nourishing diet, adequate exercise, and sufficient rest are essential for healthy skin. In addition, the skin should be kept clean. Cleanliness for the body as a whole entails bathing or showering regularly with soap and warm water in order to remove accumulated dirt, grease, and perspiration. After washing, the skin should be rinsed thoroughly and dried with a clean towel. If the skin is dry, it may be helpful to use a bath oil or apply a lubricating lotion after bathing. Germicidal soaps and antiseptics are not necessary for either men or women, and may be irritating. Hands should be washed several times a day and the fingernails should be given special attention (see HAND CARE).

The skin of the face is often delicate, and is continually exposed to sun, wind, and temperature changes. Because its condition is important to an attractive appearance, facial skin deserves special care. In general, the face should be cleaned at least twice a day—in the morning and at night. Men usually find it satisfactory to wash with soap and warm water. Some women may prefer to use one of the special gentle facial soaps or a cleansing cream or lotion that is less drying to the skin than soap. If soap is used, it should not be massaged into the skin; this may cause drying. Some persons like to use a complexion brush in washing the face, while others find it has a drying effect. (For suggestions on special techniques of skin care for invalids or bedridden persons, see HOME NURSING.)

Dry Skin and Oily Skin. The amounts of oils and perspiration secreted by the glands determine whether skin is dry, normal, or oily. Skin types vary widely and may be affected by hereditary tendencies, by general health, and by skin care. Some persons may have skin that is dry in some areas and oily in others, such as the regions around the nose and chin. Skin tends to become dryer in middle and old age, encouraging wrinkling.

Dry skin should not be washed too often with soap and water; instead, use a cleansing cream or oil or a soap substitute. Before going to bed, apply an emollient, or lubricating cream; these usually contain lanolin or cholesterol, blended with vegetable fats and oils. Plain lanolin should not be used. It may be helpful to use an emollient also during the day, especially in winter weather. The CHAPPED SKIN that sometimes occurs in winter should be treated in the same manner as dry skin.

Oily skin can also be a problem. To help correct it, wash at least three times a day, using soap and water or a detergent-based cleansing lotion. Avoid oily creams and lotions. Use of one of the special deep cleansers, perhaps once a day, may be helpful in removing oils and dirt from clogged pores. Make-up should not be used too heavily and should be removed completely at night, as it should be no matter what the skin type. The diet should also be watched, since eating fatty foods can aggravate oily skin.

If oily or dry skin is especially troublesome, a dermatologist may be able to recommend special care.

Perspiration. In an average day the body may lose more than a pint of perspiration, or sweat; heat, exertion, or strong emotion may raise this amount to several quarts. Contrary to popular belief, this sweat has very little odor. Unpleasant smells that seem to be caused by sweat occur because of the action of bacteria on perspiration that has remained on the skin or on clothing over a period of time. A person in good health can control this odor by bathing often and by using an antiperspirant or deodorant and talcum powder on the areas that perspire profusely, particularly under the arms. For a fuller discussion of this aspect of personal hygiene, see DEODORANT and BODY ODOR.

Excessive perspiration is uncommon and when it does occur it is usually not a cause for worry. In some cases it may be an inherited tendency or a symptom of other conditions affecting the body. For further information, see PERSPIRATION, *Abnormal Perspiration.*

Shaving. Men generally shave about once a day; those with heavy, dark beards may find it necessary to shave twice a day. The argument for an electric razor is that it is speedy and cannot scrape or cut the face. The safety razor, with changeable blades, may be preferred because it gives a closer shave. Some men with tough beards or sensitive skin combine the methods: they remove most of the growth with an electric razor, then complete the shave with lather and a safety razor, using an extra-sharp blade.

Before shaving, make sure the hands and nails are clean. Next wash the face briskly with warm soapy water and rinse. If a safety razor is being used, apply either a lather or a shaving cream. Use a good mirror and proceed carefully, using the free hand to pull taut the area that is being shaved.

After shaving wash the face again with warm water and apply generous amounts of aftershave lotion or plain 70% alcohol, which can be obtained at any drugstore. For cuts, if any, dab on cold water, then apply a piece of dry tissue paper. Usually the bleeding will be stanched in a few minutes, and the paper can be removed with cold water. If necessary, a styptic pencil may be used to stop bleeding.

Women often remove the hair from

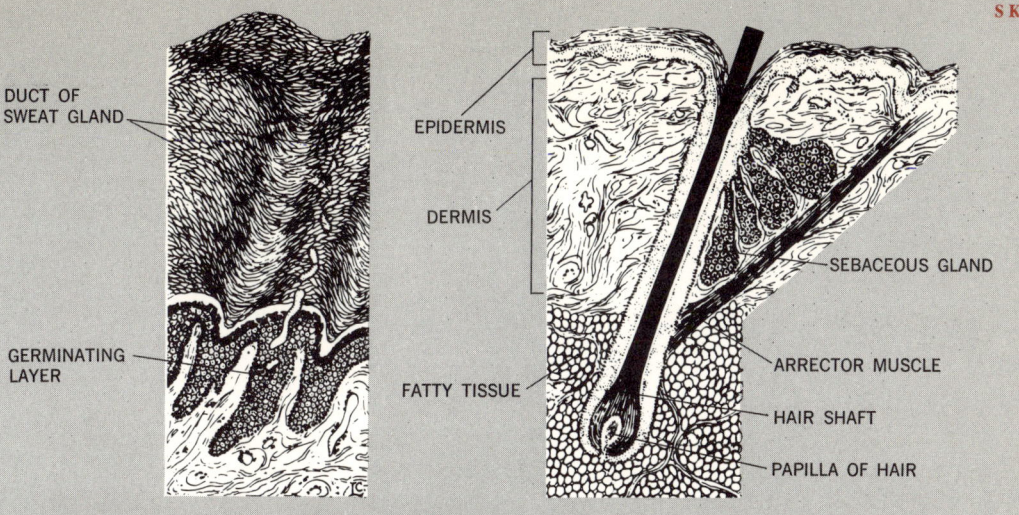

The epidermal structure is clearly seen in the diagram of skin at the soles of the feet, left, where it adapts to the function of the feet and thickens to give necessary additional strength. Diagram, right, shows the usual structure of the skin. There are three layers: the protective epidermis; the dermis, which contains blood vessels, nerves, glands, and hair roots; and the fatty cushion of subcutaneous tissue.

their underarm areas and legs by shaving. This can be done by using a safety razor, first applying plenty of warm soapy lather to soften the hair. Electric razors especially designed for women are also available. For a discussion of other methods of removing or lightening unattractive hair, including excess facial hair, see HAIR, *Excess Hair.*

Protection Against Sun's Rays. Prolonged exposure to the sun's rays leads to the development of a protective layer of brown pigment. This is what is referred to as a tan. Excessive exposure, however, causes a burn just like any other kind of burn (see SUNBURN AND SUNTAN).

All persons, no matter what their skin color, should avoid excessive exposure. It can aggravate existing skin problems, promote premature drying and wrinkling, and, over a period of time, be a cause of skin cancer. The danger is especially great for persons with very light skin. Light-skinned persons also tend to develop freckles, small scattered spots of the same brown pigment that develops in a tan.

In tanning, one should be especially careful to condition the skin by gradual exposure. The use of a good protective suntan cream or lotion is advisable. It also helps to lubricate the skin.

Some Skin Problems of Women

Men and women have many of the same skin problems. However, because of the more delicate nature of the average woman's skin and the great stress placed upon its appearance and beauty, women have a greater number of skin problems than men.

Cosmetics. Most regularly used cosmetics on the market today will not harm the skin. Occasionally, however, certain ingredients in cosmetics may cause an allergic reaction, such as itching or a rash. If such a reaction occurs, another brand should be tried; it may not contain the offending substance.

There are also special *hypoallergenic* cosmetics that may contain fewer irritants than the usual brands. Some lipsticks are more drying to the lips than others; experimenting with several brands will help most women to find a satisfactory one.

Because make-up may clog the pores, it is important to remove all of it completely every night by using soap and water, a cleansing cream, or some other type of skin cleanser.

Wrinkles. As skin grows older and drier, wrinkles and sagging areas develop, especially in the areas of the face around the mouth and eyes, where we may acquire smile or frown wrinkles. Women are especially sensitive to wrinkles. It is possible to reduce wrinkling somewhat by using lubricating creams and by avoiding too much exposure to the sun. Massaging the skin will not remove wrinkles, though it may feel pleasant and stimulating. So-called skin foods may lubricate the skin but will not really feed it, because the skin is nourished by the body, not by lotions or creams applied on the surface. Wearing cosmetic preparations or night masks will not help either. The creams that are advertised as skin rejuvenators and wrinkle removers do not appear to be effective. (See WRINKLES.)

For the average woman it is probably best to simply not waste time worrying about wrinkles. Avoid frowning and smile instead, so that when lines do appear they will enhance rather than detract from the appearance.

Cosmetic Surgery. For women who are unduly troubled by scars, by moles or certain other birthmarks, or by disfiguring blemishes, PLASTIC SURGERY can be a great boon. Wrinkles, too, can be minimized by this method. A qualified plastic surgeon can give frank advice about the probable benefits of treatment; perfect results are not always possible, but great improvement may be made. Not all such conditions, however, are suitable for this treatment. A woman considering plastic surgery should first talk the matter over with her doctor, who will recommend a reputable plastic surgeon if he thinks the operation advisable.

Disorders of the Skin

The skin reflects the general physical and emotional health. A skin disorder, for instance, may indicate disease within the body. For this reason, it is important that a particular skin condition be diagnosed and treated by a doctor rather than by home treatments that may be unnecessary or actually harmful.

It is important to remember that the skin, given the opportunity, tends to heal itself. Overtreatment may be worse than no treatment at all. For common skin ailments, bland treatments, such as cool or warm compresses, lotions, and ointments, are usually recommended. Under no circumstances should one scratch, pick, or rub an incipient skin irritation or inflammation.

The medical name for an inflammation of the skin is DERMATITIS, and any itching of the skin is called *pruritus*. Dermatitis may occur without pruritus, and vice versa, but often they occur together. A common example of dermatitis is CONTACT DERMATITIS, a rash that results from direct contact with a substance to which a person is allergic or sensitive. The most familiar contact dermatitis is that of POISON IVY, but there are many other substances that may cause an allergic skin condition (see ALLERGY). Other allergic skin conditions include HIVES, or itchy, burning swellings that suddenly appear and may disappear just as rapidly. Hives are often caused by an allergy to certain foods.

ECZEMA is an allergic skin rash that may result from sensitivity to foods or to irritating substances in the air.

Mechanical irritation, or heat or cold, may affect the skin. CHAFING is irritation caused by friction, usually from clothing or from the rubbing together of body surfaces that are damp with perspiration (see INTERTRIGO). Pressure and friction also cause the toughened, thickened skin seen in CALLUSES and CORNS. Heat rash, or PRICKLY HEAT, is an inflammation that may result when the pores become clogged, trapping perspiration inside the skin. CHILBLAINS are inflammations caused by exposure to cold, while FROSTBITE is the condition that occurs when areas of the skin have actually been frozen.

ACNE is a skin disorder that occurs most often in young people, and stems from an inflammation of the sebaceous glands. Its symptoms include the familiar pimples, blackheads, and whiteheads. A quite different disorder with a similar name is ACNE ROSACEA, a condition marked by reddening of the face and sometimes by enlargement of the nose.

RINGWORM is a fungus infection of the skin, caused by tiny parasitic organisms, and includes ATHLETE'S FOOT. SCABIES is caused by tiny parasitic mites that burrow into the skin of the hands, genitals, and other parts of the body. Among the other parasites that may invade the skin are lice, including the crab lice that may infest the pubic area.

A condition in which patches of reddened scaly skin appear, especially on knees, elbows, and scalp, is PSORIASIS. It may become chronic and may be aggravated by emotional stress.

CYSTS, or cavities filled with a soft or fluid substance, may develop in or beneath the skin. Familiar examples include the sebaceous cysts that may develop from whiteheads or blackheads.

BOILS and CARBUNCLES occur when bacteria gain entrance into the skin and cause the formation of pus. A related condition on the eyelid is a STY.

Streptoccoccal or staphylococcal bacteria cause IMPETIGO, which is marked by blisters and yellowish crusts and occurs most often in children.

A similar infection that affects the hair follicles at the pore openings of the skin is FOLLICULITIS. When such infection affects the follicles of the beard, it is called BARBER'S ITCH.

ERYSIPELAS, or *St. Anthony's fire*, is a streptoccocal infection of the skin and underlying tissues that can be very serious if not treated. This condition is one of several forms of CELLULITIS that may affect the skin.

COLLAGEN DISEASES, which cause deterioration of the connective tissues, may affect the skin. They include the relatively uncommon *lupus erythematosus* and *scleroderma*. PEMPHIGUS is a rare and serious disease that usually begins as a cluster of blisters on the nose or mouth and gradually involves the whole body.

Fever blisters, or COLD SORES, are caused by a virus. Another virus disease affecting the skin is SHINGLES, in which an infected nerve causes a skin eruption. WARTS are also caused by a virus.

The skin is subject to a number of *pigmentary disorders*. Some are congenital; others occur as the result of exposure to sunlight, heat, heavy metals, and other products, or as a result of local injury, or in association with various diseases.

Some persons lack pigmentation partially or completely. This condition, which is hereditary, is known as *albinism*. *Vitiligo* and *leukoderma* appear as white spots that occur because of decreased pigmentation. Vitiligo is congenital. Leukoderma may accompany certain infections, or may result from injury or exposure to rubber products. It occurs most often in Negroes. A skin specialist can suggest the best method of treating or minimizing these two conditions.

Excessive pigmentation includes the FRECKLES that light-skinned persons tend to develop from overexposure to sunlight. LIVER SPOTS are brownish patches, somewhat larger and darker than freckles, that sometimes appear on the skin of an older person. Both conditions are harmless.

MOLES are dark patches, varying in color from gray to brown to black. On the average, every person has at least 20. Some moles occasionally can become malignant and any change in their appearance should be brought to the attention of a doctor.

BIRTHMARKS, or *hemangiomas,* are areas in which the blood vessels form abnormally excessive networks in the skin. Some disappear with age; others can be treated surgically, with medications, or with X-rays.

Bronzing of the skin sometimes is associated with ADDISON'S DISEASE and *hemochromatosis* ("bronze diabetes").

Various kinds of tumors, or growths may be found on the skin. KELOIDS are benign tumors that usually originate in scar tissue. In many cases they can be removed with radium and X-ray therapy. Yellow tumors, or XANTHOMAS, are harmless growths caused by deposits of fat in the skin. They can be eliminated by a physician if they are unsightly. *Keratoses* are wartlike growths, often brown in color, that appear most frequently in older persons. Because they can develop into cancers, they should receive medical attention. Generally a physician will recommend that they be removed.

CANCER of the skin is the most common of all cancers. Fortunately it is comparatively easy to treat successfully, especially if it is diagnosed early. As protection against skin cancer, sores that persist for more than two or three weeks and suspicious lumps or growths that suddenly begin to enlarge or change color should be brought to a physician's attention.

Dermatology is the medical specialty concerned with the diagnosis and treatment of skin diseases. Today most skin disorders can be treated successfully if brought promptly to the attention of the family doctor or a DERMATOLOGIST.

SKIN TEST

Application of a substance to the skin, or injection of such a substance, to permit observation of the body's reaction to it. Such a test can show whether a person is sensitive to certain substances (see ALLERGY), and can detect certain allergic and infectious diseases.

Skin tests may be used in the diagnosis of MUMPS, TUBERCULOSIS, FUNGUS DISEASES, and infections resulting from animal parasites.

Types of Skin Tests

There are several types of skin tests, including the *patch* test, the *scratch*, or *scarification,* test, the *multiple puncture* test, and the *intradermal* test, made by injection. All of these techniques are used in the many tests for tuberculosis and allergies.

Patch Test. This is the simplest type of skin test. A small piece of linen or blotting paper is impregnated with a minute quantity of the substance to be tested and is applied to the skin, usually on the forearm. After a certain length of time the patch is removed and the reaction observed. If there is no reaction, the test result is said to be nega-

1. "CONTROL" USING ONLY DILUENT
2. PASTE FORM, NO DILUENT REQUIRED
3. POWDER FORM, APPLIED WITH A DROP OF DILUENT FROM END OF TOOTHPICK

APPLICATION OF ALLERGEN

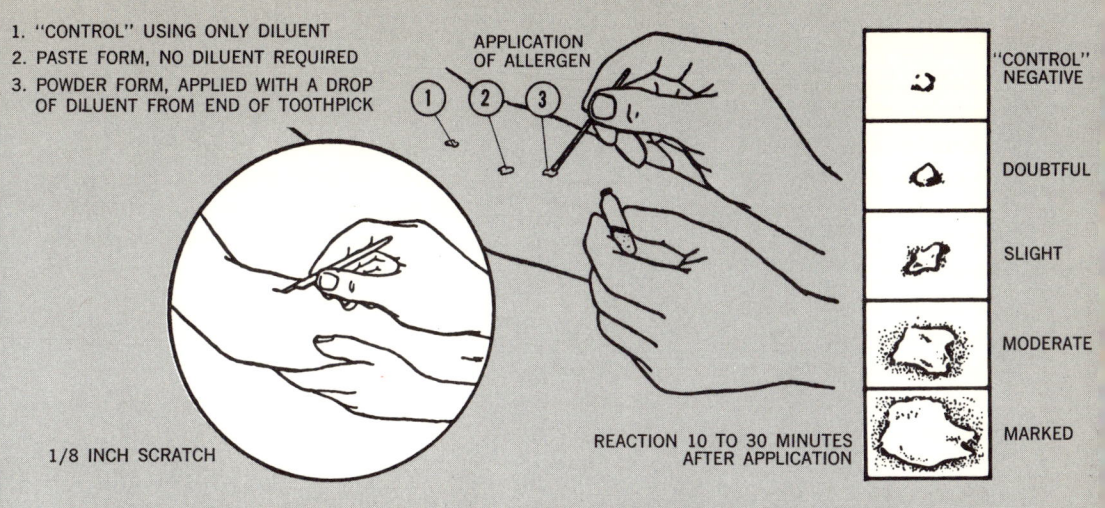

1/8 INCH SCRATCH

REACTION 10 TO 30 MINUTES AFTER APPLICATION

"CONTROL" NEGATIVE
DOUBTFUL
SLIGHT
MODERATE
MARKED

Diagram shows procedures and reactions of a scratch test for allergy. A minute quantity of a substance is put over a scratch on the skin. Reaction indicates the body's sensitivity to the substance.

tive; if the skin is reddened or swollen, the result is positive.

The patch test is one of those for *tuberculosis,* used especially in children. In the tuberculin patch test called *Vollmer's test,* a prepared adhesive strip is used on which there are two test squares, one saturated with concentrated old tuberculin and one with a liquid free of tuberculin. The tuberculin test material cannot cause the disease. When the strip is removed, usually within 48 hours, a reddened area under the test squares might indicate a positive reaction. This test is not always reliable, but it is a useful preliminary test.

In skin allergies, the patch test is mostly used in testing for **CONTACT DERMATITIS,** a skin rash caused by contact with a substance to which the person is allergically sensitive.

Scratch Test. In this test, one or more small scratches or superficial cuts are made in the skin, and a minute amount of the substance to be tested is inserted in the scratches and allowed to remain there for a short time. If no reaction has occurred after 30 minutes, the substance is removed and the test is considered negative. If there is some redness or swelling at the scratch sites, the test is considered positive.

ADHESIVE PATCH
CELLOPHANE
LINEN OR BLOTTING PAPER PATCH

NEGATIVE REACTION
POSITIVE REACTION

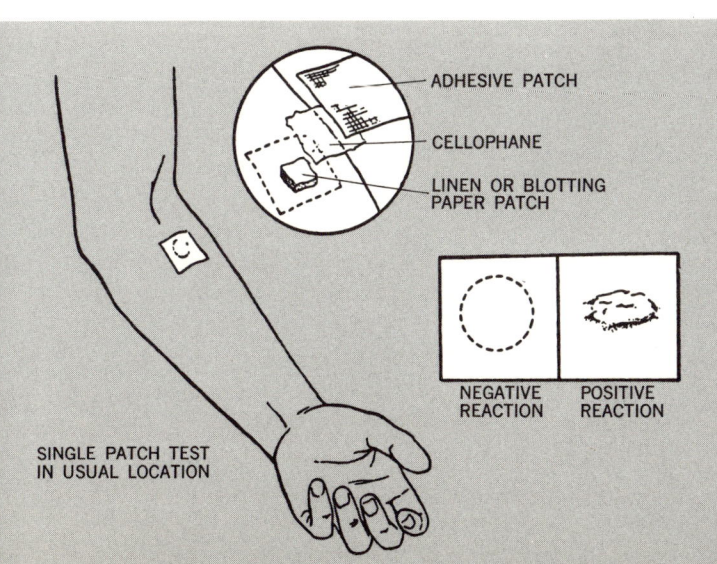

SINGLE PATCH TEST IN USUAL LOCATION

Diagram shows procedures and reaction to a patch test. This form of test is used to learn if the body is sensitive to certain allergens. It is also used to learn if an individual has been exposed to tuberculosis.

The scratch test is often used in testing for allergies. A complete screening for allergic sensitivity may require numerous skin tests. Only an extremely minute quantity of the substance can be used in each test since severe allergic reactions can occur. Because some people have an unusually sensitive skin, a *diluent,* or less irritating agent, is also applied to the skin in an adjacent area to make sure that if a reaction occurs in the area being tested, it is actually due to the allergen, and not to a general skin sensitivity.

The scratch test is also used for tuberculosis. *Pirquet's reaction,* for example, is a scratch test which makes use of tuberculin. (Many of the skin tests are named after the individual who developed the particular test.)

Multiple Puncture Test. The test substance, such as tuberculin, may also be administered by the multiple puncture method. Either the *Tine test* or the *Heaf test* may be used to determine a past or present tuberculous infection.

Intradermal Test. In this test, the substance, or allergen, is injected between the layers of skin. This type of test is widely used for allergies and for infectious and allergic diseases.

The intradermal test for tuberculosis, the *Mantoux test,* is considered more reliable than the patch test. The substance injected is a purified protein derivative, often referred to by its initials as PPD. In a positive result, the area becomes reddened or inflamed within 72 hours. This indicates past or present infection. An infection that has been present for at least two to eight weeks will usually show up on the test.

The *Schick test,* used to determine susceptibility or immunity to DIPHTHERIA, is one of the best known intradermal skin tests. A very small dose of diphtheria toxin is injected into the forearm. In a positive reaction the area becomes red and remains so for about a week. If no reaction occurs, the person is immune to the disease.

The *trichophytin test* is an intradermal skin test that is sometimes used for suspected cases of superficial fungus infections of the skin, such as RINGWORM. When a person has a fungus infection, an injection of trichophytin will produce a reaction similar to the tuberculin reaction. Skin tests, of course, are always made in an area separated from the infected area.

Intradermal tests may also be used in diagnosing HIVES caused by a parisitic infection such as SCHISTOSOMIASIS.

An intradermal test is performed before tetanus, diphtheria, or other antitoxin is administered to determine the sensitivity to the horse serum from which the antitoxin is made.

SKINNED KNEE

An abrasion of the knee in which the outer skin is scraped off. A typical kind of skinned knee is the so-called "floor burn" suffered by a child at play who scrapes his knee while sliding on the floor. Usually these abrasions can be treated at home by running lukewarm water over the wound, removing foreign particles with soap and water, then protecting the wound with a simple bandage to which a plain nonmedicated ointment has been applied. A mild antiseptic, such as hydrogen peroxide, may be used after washing the wound. See also ABRASION; SCRAPE.

SKULL

The bony structure of the head, enclosing and protecting the brain. The skull consists of two parts, the *cranium* and the facial section.

The cranium is the domed top, back, and sides of the skull. It is formed by comparatively large, smooth, and gently curved bones. These are connected to each other by dovetailed joints, making the mature skull rigid. At birth, however, the skull joints are flexible, allowing the infant's head to be compressed while emerging from the birth canal. The joints remain flexible to allow expansion until the cranial bones are fully formed.

A baby's skull contains several small areas, or *fontanels*, where the bones of the cranium do not meet. The two largest are on top of the skull. The forward fontanel is the largest. It closes about a year after birth as the skull bones expand. The smaller fontanel in back closes a few months after birth. When a child has reached the age of six, his skull is almost fully grown.

The facial section of the skull has smaller, more complex bones. These also become fixed to one another, except for the lower jaw, which is hinged to the rest of the skull.

The skull protects the **BRAIN** and special sense organs. The curve of the cranium serves to deflect blows, and together with the hair, scalp, and *dura mater*, the tough, outermost covering of the brain, protects the brain from direct blows. The skull also protects the eyes, ears, and nose. The openings to these organs are surrounded by bone and the organs are recessed in the skull.

The skull is carried by the highest vertebra, called the *atlas*. This joint permits a back and forth, nodding motion. The atlas turns on the vertebra below it, the *axis*, and this allows the skull to turn from side to side.

Skull Disorders

The skull is rarely affected by disease. Uncommon ones like **PAGET'S DISEASE** and **ACROMEGALY** cause the bones to increase in size. The skull may be fractured, like other bones, by blows, falls, or other accidents. In its effects, however, a skull fracture can be far more dangerous because of its proximity to the brain. Concussion is almost always present with such fractures. If the fracture is simple, it will usually heal itself. There may be complications, however. If the fracture is across an artery, surgery may be necessary.

Another danger is that a bone or fragment of bone may be pushed in and exert pressure on the brain, possibly

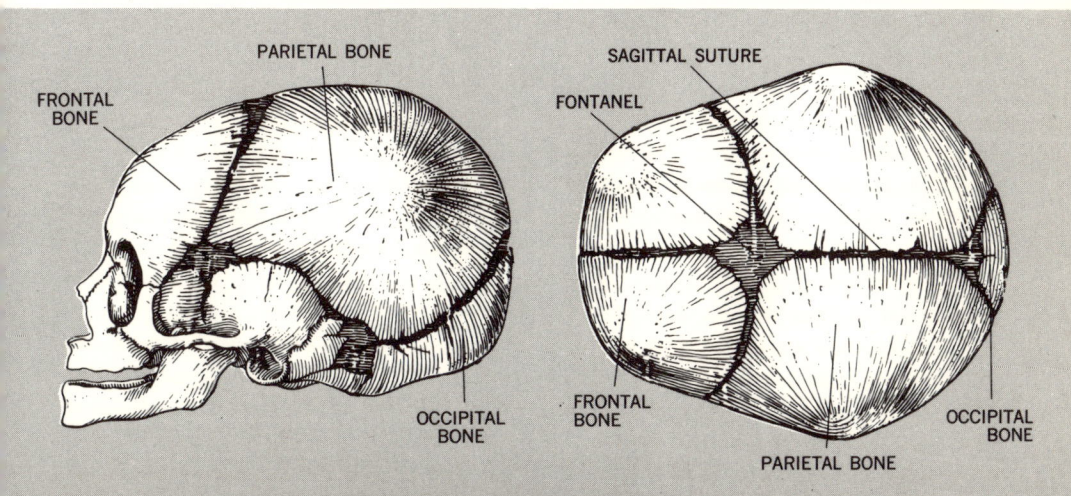

Profile, left, and a view of the top of the skull at birth. The heavily lined areas are the fontanels, where the bones of the cranium do not meet, which gives the immature skull flexibility. The fontanels close as the skull bones expand in growth and join each other by dovetailing, which makes the mature skull rigid.

SKULL

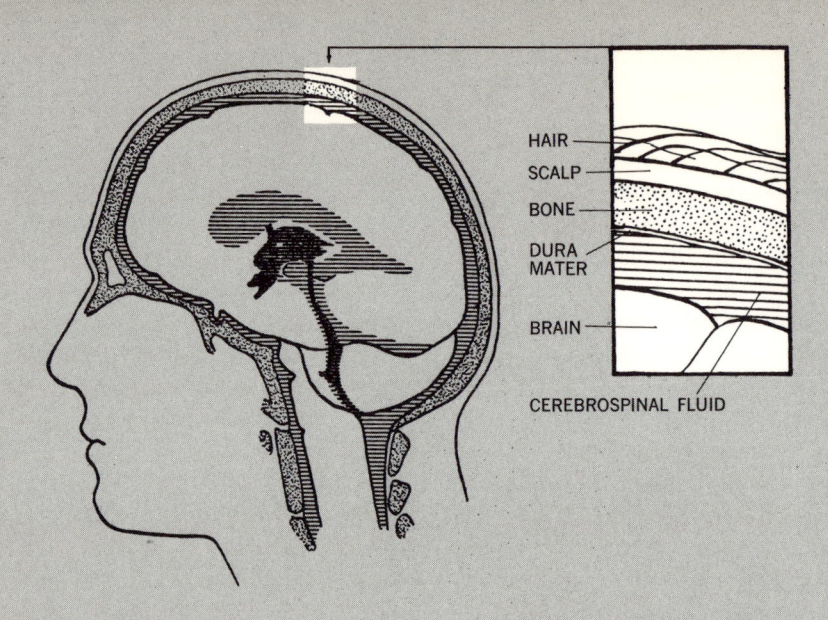

In addition to hair, skin, and the skull, which houses the brain and protects it with bone, the brain is protected within the skull by the meninges, which also cover the spinal cord. The meninges are three membranes, the dura mater, arachnoid, and pia mater. In the subarachnoid space between the arachnoid and pia mater membranes, a layer of cerebrospinal fluid forms a watery cushion.

causing convulsions. Such a bone intrusion must be corrected by surgery. Compound fractures of the skull present the additional danger of infection to the brain. At one time MENINGITIS was a common and serious result of compound fractures; it can now usually be controlled by antibiotics. (For more information on bone fractures, see FRACTURE.)

Safeguarding Against Skull Fractures. Skull fractures are most often caused by traffic accidents. Pedestrians should not jaywalk. Accidents in automobiles are not always avoidable, but skull fractures are less common and less severe when seat belts are used. It is foolhardy not to wear a crash helmet on a motor scooter or motorcycle, since any accident is likely to lead to head injury. In sports and in certain occupations such as building construction, injury may be avoided by protective equipment. In all ball games where injury to the skull is possible, any protective equipment available should be used. It is also wise to approach new sports, such as skiing, with caution until a certain amount of control has been developed.

In the home, simple falls can often be avoided by elementary precautions (see HOUSING AND HEALTH).

SLEEP

Sleep is essential to life. During sleep the body processes slow down, allowing tissues and organs to recuperate from previous activity. For the brain, sleep is even more vital. Experiments have shown that lack of sleep, which actually has little physical effect on the body if there has been adequate rest, seriously disturbs the mental processes. After 30 to 60 hours of continuous sleeplessness, such reactions as irritability, loss of memory, hallucinations, and even symptoms of schizophrenia may begin to appear.

Sleep Requirements

The amount of sleep necessary for good health varies greatly from one person to the next. Sleep requirements are greatest at birth, and a newborn infant will sleep close to 20 hours a day. Children between the ages of 1 and 4 require about twelve hours daily; those between 4 and 12 should have ten hours or so of sleep. Adolescents usually need from 8 to 10 hours of sleep, and adults from 6 to 9, although 8 hours seems to be the average. People who are ill or tire easily or engage in strenuous activities may need more than the average amount of sleep.

It has long been thought that the need for sleep diminishes with aging and that many elderly people need only 5 to 7 hours of sleep. Recent research suggests that this is not true. Most older people need 8 hours or more of sleep and are in noticeably better health if they get it.

At some time in their lives, most people suffer from INSOMNIA, or inability to sleep. The causes, physical and mental, vary widely. Often sleeplessness results from worry over problems that may be very real. However, persistent insomnia may also be a symptom of an emotional disturbance or a physical illness, and should be discussed with a doctor, who can diagnose the possible causes and suggest means of relief.

The Nature of Sleep

The nature of sleep is not as yet understood, though scientists have investigated it, experimented, and offered many theories in an effort to solve the mystery. Bodily changes characterize sleep: Blood pressure and body temperature drop, as do the level of adrenaline in the blood and the volume of urine; the skeletal muscles relax; the heartbeat and respiration slow down. But these changes also take place during rest, and it is the changes in the brain that, if fully understood, would probably explain the true nature of sleep.

Scientists have charted the minute electrical currents of the brain, called brain waves, with electroencephalographs, which are sensitive detecting devices. The graphs show steady wave patterns when a person is awake; then slow flat waves during the deep sleep that comes in the first hour or two of sleeping; and varying patterns as sleep grows less deep toward morning and near the time of awakening. But the graphs of brain waves do not explain the mechanical, chemical, or psychological processes by which the brain, like the rest of the body, slows down its activity, ignores many outside stimuli such as noise and light, and transmits fewer signals that cause action or conscious thought.

Inactivity itself is not the key to sleep. The body moves during sleep, and the average person changes position 30 to 40 times a night, the movement helping to keep his blood in circulation. The brain too, is active, with subconscious thought and dreams.

Theories About Sleep. Doctors can induce the physical and mental processes of sleep with SEDATIVES that depress, or slow down, the higher centers of the brain or the nervous system. But no one is certain how these processes are induced naturally. Though many theories have been suggested, none has yet been proved conclusively. They range from the ancient theory, dating from the Greeks, that sleep occurs when the blood supply to the brain has been reduced, to a modern concept, based on the research of the famous Russian scientist Ivan Pavlov, that sleep is a form of CONDITIONED REFLEX. According to the Pavlovian theory, the brain, which has learned or been "conditioned" to react to certain stimuli by becoming more active, has also acquired the habit of reacting to other stimuli by slowing down activity.

Thus the familiar sights of bedroom and bed, and the routine associated with getting ready for bed, are signals to the brain to begin the slowing-down process that leads to sleep. Supporters of this theory point out that persons who frequently have used sleeping pills and feel that they cannot get to sleep without them, often go to sleep readily when given pills that look like their usual sedative but actually contain only inactive ingredients.

Other theorists have suggested that chemical wastes accumulating in the body during waking hours tend to drug the higher centers of the brain, ultimately causing the slowing down of the brain and therefore sleep. Sleep can be attributed to the activity of the *hypothalamus*, a part of the **BRAIN** which apparently produces some of the characteristics of sleep. Some scientists base their theories on the action of outside stimuli such as lights and noise; when these are reduced, the brain receives fewer impulses or signals from the sensory organs, and, with fewer impulses to note or act upon, consciousness is dulled and sleep supposedly follows. However, reducing outside stimuli can only be an encouragement to, not a cause of, sleep; for darkness and quiet do not always assure sleep and there are times when a person falls asleep despite bright lights and noise.

Dreams

Disturbances that could wake a sleeper are often absorbed and incorporated into **DREAMS**, which can serve as a buffer between the sleeping brain and the stimuli of the outside world.

According to psychoanalytic theory, dreams express the dreamer's unconscious wishes and fears, many of which are unacceptable to his conscious mind. During sleep, when conscious controls are relaxed, the wishes come to the surface, cloaked in symbolism so that they are not too disturbing. If the emotions and experiences released by the unconscious are too powerful or too recognizable for comfort, the dream becomes a **NIGHTMARE** and usually the sleeper awakens with a start and at times in fright.

All people dream, though many people forget their dreams on awakening. Remembered dreams, interpreted and related to conscious experience, are important in **PSYCHOANALYSIS,** and they are significant tools in dealing with mental and emotional problems. The psychoanalyst, trained in interpreting the meaning of dreams, can help the patient understand the subconscious content and its relation to his emotional conflicts and tensions.

For further information about sleep, see **BABY CARE; CHILD CARE; SLEEPWALKING; SNORING.**

SLEEPING SICKNESS

The popular name for *encephalitis*, an inflammation of the tissues and the *meninges*, or coverings, of the brain. There are several different forms of the disease, none of which is common in the United States, although a few forms are occasionally epidemic in limited areas of the country. The name sleeping sickness comes from the drowsiness that is often characteristic of the disease. Encephalitis has no relationship to *African sleeping sickness* or its Latin American counterpart, *Chagas' disease*, both of which are discussed later in this article under the heading, *Trypanosomiasis.*

Encephalitis

The various forms of encephalitis can be divided roughly into three groups: those in which the brain tissues are directly infected with a virus; those in which the condition occurs as a complication, usually of some virus disease, such as influenza; and those in which the inflammation is produced by contact with a toxic substance, such as lead.

Domestic fowl, wild birds, and rodents are the principal hosts of the viruses believed responsible for encephalitis. They are transmitted from the host to man by the bites of mosquitoes and possibly ticks and other insects. It is thought that encephalitis is not directly transmissible from man to man, and **PUBLIC HEALTH** measures, including eradication of the hosts and carriers, are thus the chief method of controlling and preventing the disease.

The symptoms of encephalitis vary considerably, depending on the type and severity of the attack and the area of the brain affected. The first signs are usually fever and headache, pain and stiffness in the neck and back, nausea, and vomiting. In more severe cases these are followed by symptoms of mental disorder, such as persistent drowsiness and listlessness, delirium, and, rarely, coma. Sometimes an attack is so mild that the patient need hardly be put to bed; however, the disease usually takes an acute form, and occasionally becomes chronic.

Direct-infection Encephalitis. The forms of encephalitis caused by direct viral infection of the brain are potentially more serious than the postinfection forms. Since a number of different viruses can cause encephalitis and it is not always possible to identify the virus responsible, the danger of an epidemic is usually present. A separate virus is probably responsible for each epidemic form.

Two epidemic forms are *St. Louis encephalitis,* named after the epidemic which struck St. Louis, Mo., in 1933, and *Japanese encephalitis,* which took a toll among American troops in the Korean War. Both may attack the spine as well as the brain, in which case the disease is known as *encephalomyelitis.*

Another form of the disease is known as *lethargic* or, after its discoverer, *von Economo's encephalitis.* This form, which is characterized by extreme drowsiness and lassitude, occurred in epidemic form from 1916 to 1926, but recently only rare and isolated cases have been reported. It is not yet certain what causes this form, although, like the other, it is probably due to a virus.

Another form, *equine encephalomyelitis,* primarily affects horses, but can also occur in human beings, particularly children. It was first recorded in 1931, in California, and there have since been outbreaks in the east and west of the United States, the eastern form being the more serious.

Prevention and Treatment. People living in the vicinity of an encephalitis epidemic should get rid of any stagnant water that has accumulated in gutters and other places near the house. They should screen their windows and doors against mosquitoes, use mosquito bednets, and make liberal use of insecticides and insect repellents. Rodents should be exterminated with traps and rodenticides. The local health officers should be notified of signs of illness among domestic or farm animals.

Medical scientists are working to develop an encephalitis vaccine as well as a completely effective treatment for the disease. At present, the greatest hope of recovery lies in prompt diagnosis, hospitalization, and rest. The fever, pain, and headache can be relieved with medication. It is usually possible to relieve the severity of the aftereffects of an attack of encephalitis, which can sometime lead to the condition of muscular rigidity, tremor, and facial paralysis known as PARKINSON'S DISEASE.

Other Forms of Encephalitis. When the symptoms of encephalitis follow or occur during the course of an infectious disease, such as measles, whooping cough, chicken pox, poliomyelitis, or influenza, it is classified as *postinfection encephalitis*, and there is a good chance that the condition is not due to the presence of the virus in the brain tissues. This means that, providing the symptoms are promptly recognized and the physician's advice closely followed, the prospects of complete recovery are excellent. The same is true for encephalitis that occurs as a result of a disease, such as syphilis or meningitis, that has affected the brain tissues.

In a few extremely rare cases, encephalitis has occurred as an aftereffect of an injection with a virus vaccine, such as for smallpox.

Toxic encephalitis, in which the inflammation of the brain is produced by contact with poisonous substances, is now a very rare condition. It used to be an occupational hazard in certain industries, particularly those using lead.

Trypanosomiasis

Both African sleeping sickness and Chagas' disease are caused by minute parasites, called *trypanosomes*, that attack the blood and tissues.

African Sleeping Sickness. In Africa, the parasites are transmitted to man from cattle or other animals by the bite of the tsetse fly. Two main types of the disease have been identified: the Rhodesian, or East African, type, which is the most acute form, and the Gambian, or mid-African, type.

Usually the first symptom of sleeping sickness is the inflammation that appears within 48 hours at the site of the bite, although some people do not report such a reaction. Within several weeks, the parasites invade the blood stream and the lymph nodes; eventually they attack the central nervous system. Characteristic symptoms, which may appear within several weeks in the Rhodesian type and after six months or several years in the Gambian type, include intermittent fever, rapid heartbeat, and enlargement of the lymph nodes and spleen. In the advanced stage of the disease, there are personality changes, apathy, sleepiness, disturbance of speech and gait, and severe emaciation.

Suramin, pentamidine, and other medicines are used in treatment. Prevention includes injections of pentamidine or suramin as a temporary measure, but the most effective measure is eradication of the tsetse fly.

Chagas' Disease. Chagas' disease, which is found in Mexico and Central and South America, is transmitted from wild animals by means of the feces of a blood-sucking bug. The parasites multiply around the point of entry before entering the blood stream and eventually attacking the heart, brain, and other tissues.

The acute form of the disease often attacks children. Early symptoms include swelling of the eyelids and the development of a hard, red, painful nodule on the skin. Enlargement of the lymph nodes, liver, and spleen occur, along with inflammation of the heart muscles, psychic changes, and general debility. In adults the chronic form often resembles heart disease.

Preventive measures, such as the wearing of protective clothing and the use of insecticides, are of prime importance since there are no effective medicines for treatment.

SLEEPWALKING

Walking while asleep; also called *somnambulism.* Much mystery has been attached to sleepwalking, although it is actually no more mysterious than dreaming. The principal difference between the two is that the sleepwalker, besides dreaming, is also using a part of his brain that stimulates walking.

The sleepwalker usually seems to be sound asleep; he gets out of bed, walks about, and returns to bed without waking; in the morning he has no recollection of having left his bed. The walker often seems to have a purpose, and it is believed that he tends to act according to his subconscious wishes. In some cases the sleepwalker may also speak, or may even see, hear, and feel.

People have been known to perform complicated acts while sleepwalking. They may get dressed, open doors and windows, browse around the kitchen, or go out of doors. In certain cases sleepwalkers may even perform dangerous acts, yet they rarely harm themselves. For example, sleepwalkers have been known to walk along a high edge of a tall building without falling.

Frequently a sleepwalker will obey a definite, simple command to go back to bed, and will return to bed without waking up. Contrary to popular belief, however, it will not harm him to awaken him; but if he is awakened he may be confused and not know where he is. He should not be scolded or spoken to harshly, but should be led gently back to bed.

Sleepwalking is most likely to happen during periods of emotional stress. Usually it ceases when the source of anxiety is removed. Often it occurs only once or twice and does not happen again. If sleepwalking recurs frequently it may stem from serious emotional distress. A doctor should be consulted. He may suggest some form of PSYCHOTHERAPY to locate and eliminate the cause of the problem (see also PSYCHIATRY).

See also DREAMS; SLEEP.

SLIPPED DISK

The popular name for a ruptured disk, or pad of cartilage, between vertebrae. The condition occurs most commonly in the lower back, occasionally in the neck, and rarely in the upper back portion of the SPINE.

Pads of cartilage and fiber enclosing a rubbery tissue known as the *nucleus pulposus* lie between the vertebrae, or bones of the spine. The pads are the *intervertebral disks.* They act as cushions between the vertebrae, absorbing ordinary shocks and strains and shifting their positions to accommodate the various movements of the spine. But an excessive strain may weaken the cartilage to the extent that the nucleus pulposus protrudes through it and forms a bulge. This bulge may push against the nerve roots in the spinal canal, causing pain.

Causes and Symptoms

Rupture, or herniation, of the disks may be caused by injury or by a sudden straining with the spine in an unnatural position. The condition may also come on gradually as a result of a progressive deterioration of the disks.

Symptoms depend upon the location and the extent to which the disk material has been pushed out. Most cases involve the disks of the lower back between the fourth and fifth lumbar vertebrae or between the fifth lumbar vertebrae and the sacrum of the pelvis. The person affected feels severe pain in the lower back and has difficulty in walking. The sciatic nerve, which originates in the lower part of the spinal cord, is affected, with resulting pain

SLIPPED DISK

at the back of the thigh and lower legs, a condition known as SCIATICA. A cough, sneeze, or strain will send the pain along the course of the sciatic nerve to the calf or ankle.

When the disks of the neck, the cervical disks, are affected, severe pain in the back of the neck radiates down the arms to the fingers. Neck movements are restricted. Any neck motion, coughing, sneezing, or straining will accentuate the pain.

Diagnosis and Treatment

Treatment for slipped disk varies according to the seriousness of the condition. If the condition persists, a specialist in ORTHOPEDICS or neurosurgery should be consulted at the suggestion of the family doctor. Careful examination, including laboratory tests and X-ray photographs, are necessary to distinguish the condition from other disturbances of the spine. The X-rays may reveal various changes in the spine and a narrowing of the space between the vertebrae.

Conservative treatment for a ruptured disk of the lower back consists of bed rest on a firm mattress over a bedboard, local application of heat, and the use of aspirin or other analgesics to relieve pain. Traction may be applied to the legs. In chronic cases the wearing of a surgical support may be helpful. Care must be taken to avoid aggravating the condition by excessive physical effort.

Cases of ruptured disks of the neck are treated in a similar manner with bed rest, heat, analgesics, and traction. A collar may be worn to immobilize the neck when the patient is out of bed.

If the response to these measures is poor or if the condition becomes disabling, surgery may be necessary to relieve the pressure on the injured disk. Such operations are usually successful.

Precautions. The intervertebral disks deteriorate somewhat with the passage of time. Nevertheless, proper methods

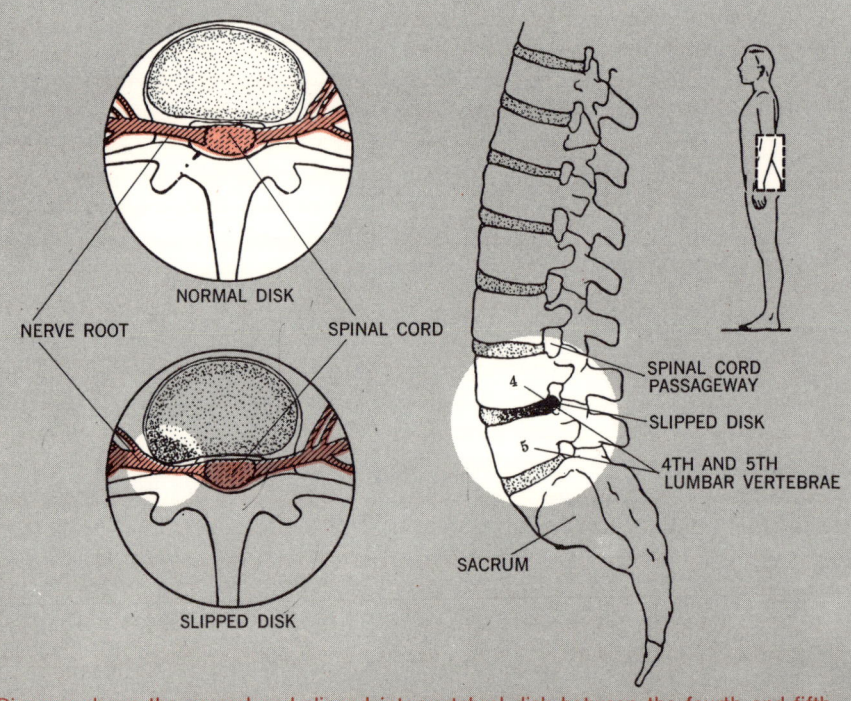

Diagram shows the normal and slipped intervertebral disk between the fourth and fifth lumbar vertebrae. When the disk slips, it presses on the part of the spine from which the sciatic nerve originates.

of bending, of lifting, and of carrying heavy objects will help a person avoid a slipped disk. For information on these methods, see **LIFTING AND CARRYING**.

SMALLPOX

A highly contagious, often fatal virus disease. Its most noticeable symptom is the appearance of severe blisters on the skin. Smallpox has become rare in most parts of the world because of widespread vaccination against the disease. Today there are fewer than one hundred cases a year in the United States. This is the result both of vaccination and of strict public health measures when a case does occur.

Smallpox is one of the most contagious diseases known. In the past, epidemics occurred regularly. The virus which causes the disease is present in the nose and throat of the infected person, in the blisters on his skin, and in his excretions. Any object which the patient has touched may carry the virus. The patient remains contagious throughout the course of the disease, from the first appearance of symptoms until the last scab has fallen off.

The *incubation period* of the disease, from exposure to the first appearance of symptoms, is generally 12 days, although it may vary from 8 to 21 days.

Symptoms

The first symptoms of smallpox are severe headache, chills, and high fever. Children may suffer from vomiting and convulsions. Within three or four days, a rash of small, reddened pimples appears, first on the face, then on the arms, wrists, hands, and legs. A small number of spots appear on the trunk. In a day or two, the spots become blisters and fill with clear fluid. Over the next week, the fluid turns into a yellowish, puslike substance and begins to dry up, leaving a crust or scab on the skin. These scabs fall off after three or four weeks, leaving disfiguring pits or pocks in the skin, particularly on the face.

Diagnosis

Early diagnosis and immediate treatment of smallpox may save the life of the patient and lower the chances of disfigurement, as well as help prevent the spread of the disease. However, in its early stage smallpox may be difficult to diagnose since the symptoms are similar to those of **CHICKEN POX**, a much less serious disease. One important difference is that the blisters of chicken pox occur in "crops" at the rate of about one crop a day; the blisters thus can be seen in different stages at the same time, while in smallpox they are all at about the same stage. Specific laboratory tests will aid in the diagnosis.

Isolation and Quarantine

A smallpox patient must be treated in a hospital where he can be rigorously isolated. No one is permitted to visit him, and great care is taken to prevent the spread of the disease. All those known to have been in contact with the patient are quarantined for 16 days, unless they have just been revaccinated, in which case they may be released from quarantine as soon as the vaccination has "taken." Those in quarantine are kept under careful observation, so that if they develop the disease they can be isolated and treated immediately. All contaminated objects are destroyed by burning or sterilized with high-pressure steam or boiling water. The patient's home is thoroughly cleaned and disinfected.

Treatment

There is at present no cure for smallpox. One important consideration in treating the disease is the possibility of skin infection through the blisters or pocks. To avoid this, the doctor may give the patient medicines to prevent or soothe itching, and may apply antibiotics to the skin to counteract secondary infection. The patient's fingernails will be cut short and his hands kept clean to further reduce the danger of infection.

Other than these measures, treatment consists largely of rest and good nourishment. Medicines may be given to lower the patient's fever, and he may be given sedatives to help him rest.

Prevention

It has been known for centuries that a person who has once been attacked by smallpox is immune to the disease thereafter. During epidemics, people would often deliberately expose themselves to the disease in the hope of contracting a mild case and becoming immune. Late in the 18th century, this knowledge was used to discover a safe way of establishing immunity to smallpox. The patient is infected with *cowpox*, a close relative of smallpox, which has a mild effect on humans. At the end of the cowpox illness, the patient is immune to smallpox. This process of *vaccination* has been responsible for bringing smallpox under control and almost eliminating it throughout much of the world.

The vaccination process takes about ten days to two weeks. A drop of vaccinia virus vaccine is placed on the skin, usually on the upper arm, and the surface of the skin is lightly scratched with a needle. In a day or two the area becomes reddened and a blister forms. After several days this hardens and turns brown. The patient may have a slight fever during this period and may feel slightly ill on the eighth or ninth day.

It is recommended that children first be vaccinated against smallpox at the age of 6 to 12 months. A booster is given every five years, and again if the child is exposed to the disease. Vaccination is to be deferred if the child is suffering from eczema. The United States requires that those entering the country have proof of successful vaccination within the previous three years. This requirement includes American tourists returning from abroad.

More information on how vaccination and similar measures protect against disease can be found in IMMUNIZATION.

SMELL

The sense that enables a person to be aware of odors. The sense of smell depends on the stimulation of sense organs in the nose by tiny particles carried in inhaled air. It is important not only for the detection of odors, but also for the enjoyment of food.

Flavor is a blend of TASTE and smell. Actually, taste registers only four qualities: salt, sour, bitter, and sweet. Other qualities of flavor depend on smell. That explains why food often tastes flat during a head cold: The blocking of the nasal passages prevents the organs of smell from registering the food's odor.

The organs of smell are small patches of special cells in the mucous membrane that lines the interior of the nose. One patch is located in each of the two main compartments of the back of the nose. Air currents do not flow directly over the patches as we breathe, which is why we have to sniff to detect a faint odor or to enjoy a fragrance to the fullest.

When we sniff, air currents carrying molecules of odorous chemicals enter special compartments, called *olfactory chambers*, where the chemicals are dissolved in mucous fluid. There they can act on the organs of smell in much the same way that solutions act on the taste buds of the tongue. The endings of the sensory nerves that detect odors, the *olfactory receptors,* quickly adapt to an odor and cease to be stimulated by it after a few minutes of full exposure. This is not a deadening of the senses; it is just a case of the receptors getting used to the smell. You may notice a strong odor when entering a room. After a while, you no longer smell it.

The sense of smell may be diminished or lost entirely, usually temporarily, as a result of an obstruction of the nose, a nasal infection, injury or deterioration of the nasal tissue, brain tumor, or mental illness. In rare instances, injury or disease damages the olfactory nerve to the point where loss of the sense of smell is permanent. The complete absence of the sense of smell is known as *anosmia.*

During pregnancy, women usually have a sharpened sense of smell. Some persons who suffer hallucinations imagine that they can smell certain odors when none are present.

Many animals depend on their sense of smell for their survival more than on their sight. Prehistoric humans may have, too. But for the modern man the sense of smell provides primarily taste and odor experiences, though people still save their lives by detecting the odor of leaking gas, gasoline, or other dangerous chemicals.

SMOKING

For centuries, smoking has been suspected of being a health hazard. In recent years a close relationship between smoking and diseases as serious as lung cancer and heart disease has definitely been established. While smoking is not the only cause of these diseases, its relationship to them and also to other diseases has been so strongly established that no smoker can afford to ignore the evidence. Parents especially owe it to their children to educate them in order that the cigarette habit will never begin.

In 1962 the Surgeon General of the United States organized a committee of experts to review some 8,000 statistical studies on the effects of smoking. The report of this committee, issued in January 1964, stated:

"In view of the continuing and mounting evidence from many sources, it is the judgment of the Committee that cigarette smoking contributes substantially to mortality from certain specific diseases and to the overall death rate.

"Cigarette smoking is a health hazard of sufficient importance in the United States to warrant appropriate remedial action."

General Effects on Health

Tobacco smoke contains a number of harmful substances, including poisons such as nicotine, various irritants, and cancer-producing compounds. Because cigarette smokers usually inhale this smoke, they are much more subject to its harmful effects than pipe and cigar smokers, who generally do not inhale. In smoking pipes and cigars, however, there is some danger to the heart because of the nicotine that is absorbed by the mouth. There is also the possibility of cancer of the lips, tongue, and mouth. Statistically, there is no question of the fact that nonsmokers are far less subject to the diseases which affect smokers.

Anyone who smokes regularly notices some physical effects. The smoker may be short of breath and hoarse and may have a persistent cough. He often complains of feeling tired, and he notices that his appetite is not up to par.

These complaints may not be serious; on the other hand, they can be symp-

FROM CEREMONY TO CONTROVERSY
Highlights in the History of Smoking

INDIANS OF NORTH AND SOUTH AMERICA were the first people to cultivate tobacco. They used it ceremonially in the ratification of treaties, and believed it to have medicinal value. The Mayans of ancient Mexico made the first cigars. They wrapped cured and fermented tobacco in its own leaves and smoked it during religious ceremonies.

JEAN NICOT, French ambassador to Portugal, is believed to have introduced tobacco to France about 1555, with a gift of seeds he sent to Queen Catherine de Medici. The plant genus, *Nicotiana,* to which tobacco belongs, is named after him.

POPULARIZATION OF SMOKING is credited to Sir Walter Raleigh who learned the practice from the Indians. In Europe, men and women of all classes began to use tobacco in its various forms. James I, of England, strongly opposed its use and tried in vain to stop it.

INHALING SNUFF, or finely ground tobacco, became widespread throughout Europe during the 18th century. At first, people carried small tobacco grinders in their pockets. Later, ground tobacco was sold and snuffboxes to hold it were made by jewelers in richly ornamented gold, silver, and ivory.

THE TOBACCO INDUSTRY, in 1963, rated annual world production of tobacco at about eight billion pounds. In the United States, in 1963, about 70 million Americans spent eight billion dollars for more than 523 billion cigarettes and more than 7 billion cigars.

CONTROVERSY over the health hazards of cigarette smoking began in 1895, when an obscure French doctor noted the coincidence of the use of tobacco with cancer of the mouth, tongue, and lips. In January 1964, a committee appointed by the Surgeon General of the United States reported to the Public Health Service, after 14 months of study, that it believed cigarette smoking was associated with cancer of the lungs and the esophagus. It also related chronic diseases of the lungs and of the heart to smoking.

toms of serious conditions associated with smoking. If they persist a doctor should be consulted.

Among the respiratory diseases closely related to cigarette smoking are LUNG CANCER, cancer of the larynx (upper throat or voicebox), chronic BRONCHITIS, and EMPHYSEMA, a serious and disabling lung disease. Coronary artery insufficiency and hypertensive HEART DISEASE are also closely related to smoking, as are PEPTIC ULCER, BUERGER'S DISEASE, and cancer of the bladder. Other diseases have been linked with smoking. The risk of incurring any of these diseases increases with the number of cigarettes smoked daily, the length of each cigarette consumed, and the length of time the smoking habit has persisted. And in general, heavy smokers as a group die younger than do nonsmokers.

Smoking and Lung Cancer

While deaths caused by other diseases have been diminishing in the last few decades, deaths from lung cancer have risen sharply. It is thought that this increase is partly a result of the rise in cigarette smoking that has occurred in the same period. Today the death rate from lung cancer for cigarette smokers is more than ten times greater than the rate for nonsmokers. While AIR POLLUTION is also thought to be a significant factor in lung cancer and other respiratory disorders, authorities agree that smoking is the more important factor.

When inhaled, tobacco smoke travels down the trachea, or windpipe, to the bronchial tubes (air tubes) of the lungs. It is in the lining of these tubes, as they divide at their entry into the lungs, that most lung cancer is found. This lining ordinarily secretes a fluid that traps small bits of dirt and smoke, and the hairlike *cilia* on the lining move the trapped substances out of the lungs. But tobacco smoke slows down or stops these processes, leaving the bronchi and lungs vulnerable to tobacco smoke and to other irritating substances that may be in the air. Some of these substances apparently can help induce cancer. It is also thought that the irritation from the smoke causes changes in the cell formation of the lining, giving rise to new kinds of cells that may be the forerunners of cancer.

Smoking and Heart Disease

Heart disease is the most common cause of death in the United States. Approximately one American male out of five between the ages of 35 and 65 has a heart attack. Many other factors besides smoking are associated with heart disease, but a significant association has been established between cigarette smoking and serious coronary artery disease. Male smokers have an appreciably higher death rate from coronary heart disease than do nonsmokers.

Fairly early in life, many American men start to develop a condition called *atherosclerosis,* in which the lining of the arteries develops coatings of fatty substances (see HARDENING OF THE ARTERIES). These coatings may thicken in time until they interfere with the normal flow of blood. If the coronary arteries, which lead to the heart muscle itself, cannot supply enough blood, other forms of heart disease, such as ANGINA PECTORIS, may develop. Experiments have shown that cigarette smoking can increase the amounts of fatty acids in the blood, and it is thought that this may be a factor in the relationship of coronary artery disease and smoking. It has also been pointed out that smoking, by diminishing the efficiency of the lungs and stimulating the nervous system, puts a strain on the heart.

Stopping Smoking

Persons who stop smoking are less likely to contract the diseases associated with smoking than persons who continue the habit. Stopping smoking can, however, be difficult. Smoking can be a strong physical habit, and it can also come to satisfy strong emotional needs.

Proof of the tremendous hold that tobacco has over mind and body lies in the difficulty most smokers have in giving it up. The fact that tobacco sales in the United States and other countries remain high, despite extensive publicity about the probable effects of smoking on health, indicates the difficulty of persuading the public to stop smoking or even to slow down.

The medical profession is trying to steer patients away from heavy cigarette smoking. In addition, county, city, state, and Federal government agencies have organized antismoking clinics. While there are many variations in antismoking programs, a typical routine might include the following:

1. The smoker is advised to keep an accurate record of his smoking, and to monitor his own progress in slowing down. Of course, each smoker must be guided by his own needs and ability to withdraw from the habit without turning to another form of self-satisfaction, like overeating.

2. A program of intermittent smoking is introduced. A smoker has all he wants for an hour, then abstains for increasing periods, from an hour to a full day. This weaning process can fairly soon get a heavy smoker down to half a pack a day, or less, thus reducing the health hazards.

3. Cigarette smokers are urged to switch to a pipe, to tide them over to the time they can stop altogether.

4. Medicines have been used in several ways, especially to make smoking unpleasant or to reduce the anxiety and irritability smokers often feel when they are cutting down. Smokers should consult their doctors rather than experiment with these medicines themselves.

5. In group therapy, smokers have the support and example of others who share their predicament. Lectures, discussions of mutual problems, and some use of medicines have resulted in a "cure" rate as high as 50 percent—that is, half the group stopped smoking and had not started again as long as a year later.

For persons who genuinely try but still cannot give up smoking, a reasonable compromise is possible, although it is not necessarily easy. The compromise is to switch from cigarettes to a pipe or cigars, realizing that cigarettes must remain on the forbidden list. Effecting this compromise is a way of moving from a high-risk to a lower-risk way of smoking.

Smoking and Adolescents

Because the confirmed adult smoker finds it so difficult to stop, it is doubly important to educate children so that they will not begin.

In response to the national concern over smoking, many schools have developed educational programs to try to convince students not to smoke.

The most effective method so far has been simply describing the long-term physical effects in detail, making clear the dangers of smoking and leaving the final choice up to the student. Obviously some teen-agers are able to accept the validity of long range established hazards and make the wise decision.

It is important that these educational programs be continued and expanded, in order to convince boys and girls that smoking is a real threat to their health and happiness.

WATER SAFETY GUIDE

By taking proper precautions and learning the basic principles of water rescue and first aid, you can protect your family against drowning accidents.

BASIC PRECAUTIONS

1. Choose a safe swimming place and be sure a good swimmer is present.
2. Supervise children in and near the water.
3. Before diving, make sure water is deep enough.
4. In surf, stay near shore if there is strong undertow or riptide.
5. Do not swim in strong currents, especially where there are rocks.
6. Following meals, wait 45 minutes to an hour before swimming.
7. Do not stay in water if you are cold or tired.
8. Learn what to do in case of cramps while swimming (see article on **WATER SAFETY**).
9. Do not overload a boat with passengers. Be sure all passengers of a small boat know how to swim; or at least have them wear life preservers.
10. If a small boat overturns and remains afloat, cling to it rather than striking out for shore; try to bring it to shallow water by kicking.

TO RESCUE A DROWNING PERSON

1. Call for help.
2. If possible, rescue person without going in water over your head. Try to reach him by extending arm, towel, rope, pole, or anything else handy. When he has grasped free end, pull him in.
3. If drowning person is farther out, rescue him by boat if one is available.
4. Attempt a swimming rescue only if other methods will not work and you are an experienced swimmer trained in lifesaving. For a review of lifesaving methods, see articles on **DROWNING** and **WATER SAFETY.**

FIRST AID IN DROWNING ACCIDENTS

Send someone for a doctor. Then proceed as follows:

IF PERSON HAS STOPPED BREATHING

Begin artificial respiration immediately, after removing any sand or mud visible in his mouth. When breathing is regular again, follow appropriate instructions below.

IF PERSON IS UNCONSCIOUS BUT STILL BREATHING

1. Place him in a reclining position, preferably on his right side.
2. Keep him warm with a blanket or coat.

IF PERSON IS FAINT, PALE, WEAK, AND HAS A RAPID PULSE

1. Keep him lying down with his head slightly lower than the rest of his body.
2. Turn his head to the side, if he is nauseated, so that he can vomit.
3. Keep him warm with a blanket or coat.
4. Give him fluids, such as plain water, tea, or coffee, if he is conscious and can swallow, and if medical help is not available shortly.
5. Do not give him any alcoholic beverages.

IF PERSON APPEARS TO BE ALL RIGHT

1. Have him lie down and rest.

SPECIAL DETACHABLE FIRST AID AND GENERAL HEALTH SECTIONS

The following sections appear at the end of each of the 12 volumes of THE MODERN MEDICAL ENCYCLOPEDIA. They are designed to be cut out and kept in a desk, medicine cabinet, car, or summer cottage for easy reference in case of need or emergency. The sections are:

VOLUME 1 **ARTIFICIAL RESPIRATION INSTRUCTIONS**
Illustrations and instructions for the three preferred methods of artificial respiration.

VOLUME 2 **MEDICINE CABINET CHECKLIST**
A complete list of medical supplies recommended for ordinary home use and for emergencies.

VOLUME 3 **WHAT TO DO IN CASE OF AUTOMOBILE ACCIDENT**
Instructions for helping injured persons, escaping from a submerged car, reporting accident to the proper authorities, protecting yourself against unfair insurance claims.

VOLUME 4 **CARE FOR CUTS, BRUISES, AND BURNS**
Illustrations showing how to clean and bandage cuts, how to help prevent bruises from swelling, how to soothe and protect burns.

VOLUME 5 **FAMILY IMMUNIZATION RECORD**
A chart to remind you when and how often your children need inoculations against common infectious diseases.

VOLUME 6 **ANTIDOTES FOR COMMON POISONS**
A table of common poisons and their antidotes that will tell you what you need to know in an emergency.

VOLUME 7 **EMERGENCY TELEPHONE NUMBERS**
A list of places you can call for help in case of emergencies requiring medical, fire, or police aid. (Space is provided to write in the numbers in your area.)

VOLUME 8 **HEIGHT-WEIGHT CHART**
A chart showing suggested weights according to your height, build, and age.

VOLUME 9 **CHECKLIST FOR THE NEW BABY**
A list of the equipment and clothes you will need when you return from the hospital with the new baby.

VOLUME 10 **WATER SAFETY GUIDE**
Instructions for guarding your family against accidents in the water, with illustrations of recommended lifesaving and first-aid methods.

VOLUME 11 **CALORIE CHART**
A table of calories for foods and beverages that will help you in planning diets for reducing or gaining weight.

VOLUME 12 **UNDERSTANDING MEDICAL TERMS**
Definitions of some basic medical terms with explanations and a guide to understanding their roots and variations.